ENGINEERING DRAWING

with an Introduction to AutoCAD

First-angle Projection

Dr. S.N. Lal
M.Tech., Ph.D.
Rtd Professor and Head of Mechanical Engineering
Bhagalpur College of Engineering, Bhagalpur
Guest Faculty, NIT Patna
Life member of ISTE

CENGAGE

Andover • Melbourne • Mexico City • Stamford, CT • Toronto • Hong Kong • New Delhi • Seoul • Singapore • Tokyo

CENGAGE

Engineering Drawing with an Introduction to AutoCAD First-angle Projection

S.N. Lal

Cover Image: Thinkstock

ISBN-13: 978-93-86858-34-4
ISBN-10: 93-86858-34-7

Cengage Learning India Pvt. Ltd.
418, F.I.E., Patparganj
Delhi 110092

Cengage Learning is a leading provider of customized learning solutions with office locations around the globe, including Australia, Brazil, India, Mexico, Singapore, United Kingdom, and United States. Locate your local office at:
www.cengage.com/global

Cengage Learning products are represented in Canada by Nelson Education, Ltd.

For product information, visit **www.cengage.co.in**

Preface

Engineering Drawing with AutoCAD is a core subject taught to the first-year engineering students of all branches of engineering in all engineering College and Universities. The book covers the complete syllabus of engineering drawing of all Engineering Colleges and will be quite useful for diploma and AMIE students as well.

Special attention has been given to the presentation of the book and to meet the basic requirements of the students. The primary feature of any engineering drawing book is its figures. Therefore, due care has been taken to make the figures clearer and, as far as possible, bigger in size to look prominent.

A large number of books on engineering drawing are available nowadays and many of them give only basic theory, examples, and final solution but none of them explains about how the solution is obtained. As a teacher of the subject, with a teaching experience of more than 50 years, I have personally observed that the present day average student feels difficulty in this subject due to complete lack of fundamental conception. The book gives the detailed step-by-step procedure for solving problems relating to projection of straight lines, projection of solids, section of solids, developments, isometric, etc. Here, even the examples are explained through small figures.

The book follows first-angle projection throughout as per BIS (Bureau of Indian Standards). However, the difference between first-angle and third-angle projections has been explained in detail.

A separate chapter has been included for pictorial drawing for the machine components to know the fundamentals of the object to understand the technique of orthographic projections.

A complete chapter on computer-aided drafting has been provided at the end. It is sub-divided into two parts: The first part is to know the details of the computer and the accessories and the second part is to know about the use of AutoCAD. A few examples are also presented, explaining how a command can be used to prepare drawings by AutoCAD.

Acknowledgements

The author expresses sincere thanks to the colleagues at the Department of Mechanical Engineering, NIT Patna, for encouragement and suggestions towards the completion of this book.

Special thanks are conveyed for Professors A.P. Verma and D.P. Singh for their invaluable suggestions for the improvement of this book.

The author is also grateful to the publishers, Cengage Learning India, for bringing out this book.

Any suggestions for improvement of the book will be acknowledged and highly appreciated.

Dr. S.N. Lal

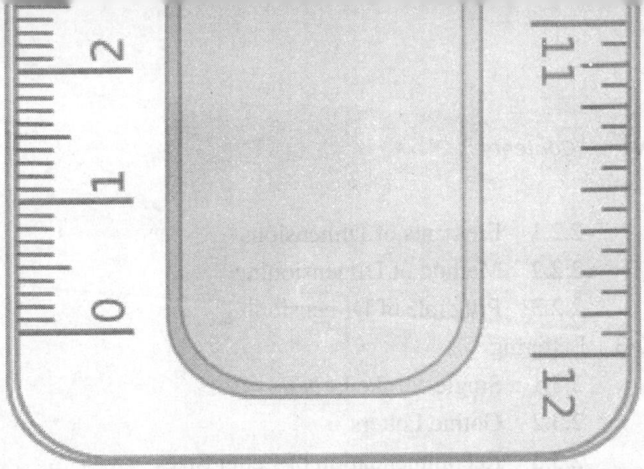

Contents

1

CHAPTER

Drawing Instruments and Kits

1.1 INTRODUCTION

It is usual practice to say that engineering drawing is the language for engineers. In true sense, it is a graphical representation and a language for communication.

To communicate, a drawing is prepared to understand the machine components easily and, hence, the drawing is made with standard conventions such that there should not be a communication gap between designers and workmen directly involved in manufacturing and fabrication jobs.

The drawing is prepared as per BIS (Bureau of Indian Standards).

Engineering drawings are made by means of different instruments and drawing kits. The quality of drawing depends entirely on the quality of instruments. It is, therefore, necessary that each student must keep good quality of drawing instruments to prepare a nice and appreciable drawing.

The following are the drawing instruments commonly used to prepare an appreciable and acceptable drawing, which will appeal to working engineers.

1.2 LIST OF DRAWING KITS

1. Drawing board
2. Drawing sheets
3. (a) T-square
   (b) Mini drafter

4. (a) Large-size compass
   (b) Small-size bow compass
5. (a) Large-size divider
   (b) Small-size bow divider
6. 45°– 45° set square
7. 30°– 60° set square
8. Engineer's scale
9. Protractor
10. French curves
11. Drawing pens or clips
12. Pencils of different grades H, 2H, HB, etc.
13. Erasers
14. Dusters
15. Miscellaneous items such as sand paper, sellotape, etc.

Some of these items have been explained in detail, as follows.

1.3 DRAWING BOARD

Engineering drawings are prepared on a drawing sheet of usual size fixed on a drawing board with the help of pins placed on each corner. The drawing board is usually made of seasoned softwood.

The size of the drawing board should be such as to provide enough space for a standard size of drawing sheets.

As regard the constructional details of drawing board, those are as shown in Fig. 1.1.

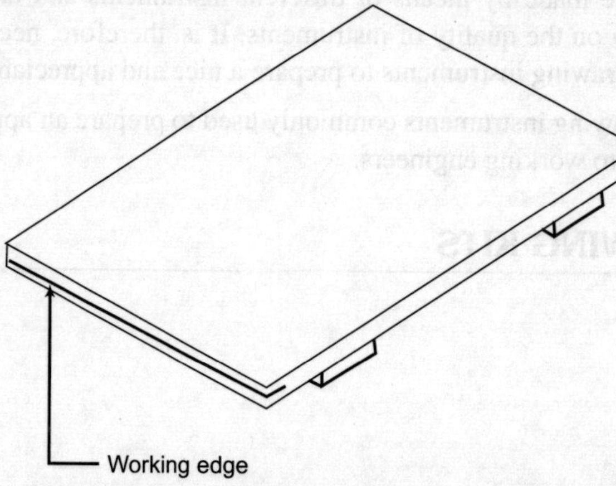

Fig. 1.1 Drawing board with details

Drawing boards are of different sizes as recommended by BIS (Bureau of Indian Standards), as presented in Table 1.1.

Table 1.1 Sizes of drawing boards

S. No.	Symbol	Size (mm)
1	D_0	1500 × 1000
2	D_1	1000 × 700
3	D_2	700 × 500
4	D_3	500 × 350

A groove is made in left edge of the board. A perfect straight strip of hardwood is fitted in the groove. This is used as the working edge of the board.

The T-square is moved along this edge.

1.4 DRAWING SHEETS

Drawings are prepared on drawing sheets, which are available in different standard sizes as shown in Table 1.2 and Fig. 1.2. They are preferred as specified by BIS (Bureau of Indian Standards).

Table 1.2 Size of drawing sheets as per BIS code

S. No.	Symbol	Size (mm)
1	A0	841 × 1189
2	A1	594 × 841
3	A2	420 × 594
4	A3	297 × 420
5	A4	210 × 297

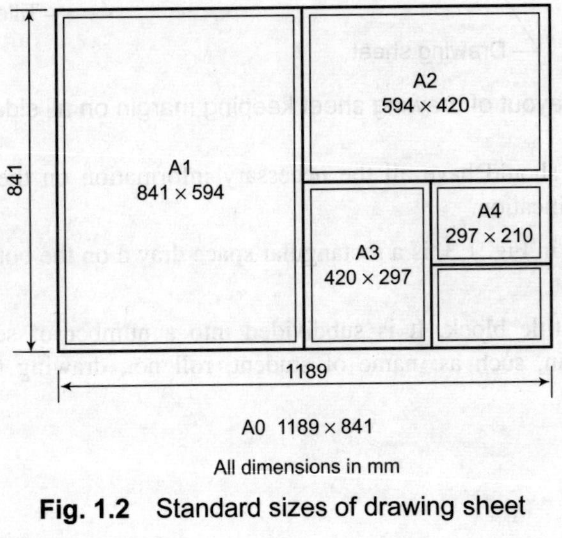

Fig. 1.2 Standard sizes of drawing sheet

Paper fixing on a drawing board is an important consideration. For ease in handling, it is better to fix drawing sheet on drawing board with the help of 4 drawing pins, one at each corner.

Presently, the draughtsmen use sellotape for fixing drawing sheets. Sellotape makes the surface of drawing sheets smooth, which permits the draughtsman to utilize the entire drawing sheet easily. The pins, placed at all four corners, do not permit smooth movement of drawing kits. Figure 1.3 shows a complete fixation of drawing sheets on a drawing board.

As per BIS, the border should have a minimum width of 30 mm for size A_0 from the left edge of the drawing sheet. All other edges should have at least 15 mm margin for convenience.

Some space, as shown in Fig. 1.3, should be left for title block for the specification of the drawing. The drawing should be prepared in the space left for drawing conveniently.

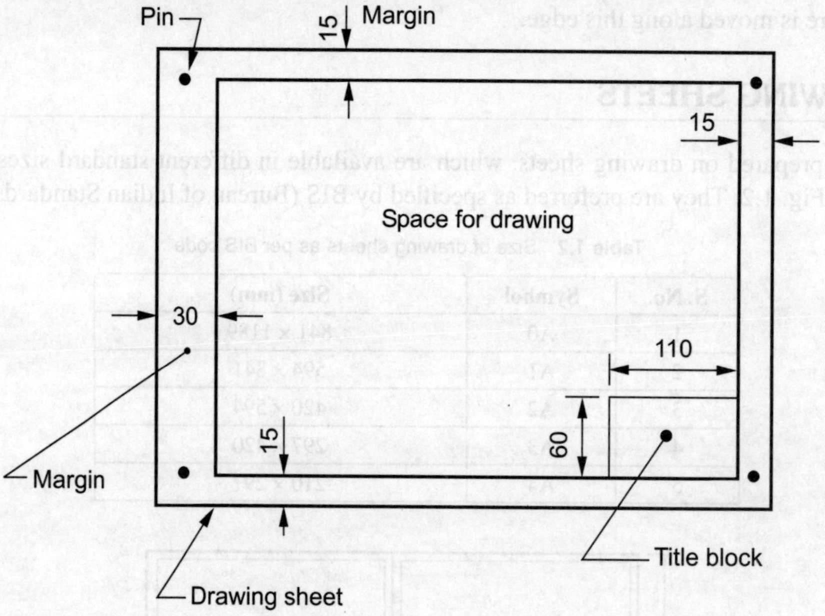

Fig. 1.3 Layout of drawing sheet keeping margin on all sides (in mm)

The drawing prepared should have all the necessary information on the sheet and any required information for easy identification.

A title block, as shown in Fig. 1.3, is a rectangular space drawn on the bottom right hand corner of the sheet.

Figure 1.4 shows the title block. It is subdivided into a number of segments for the specific information written therein, such as: name of student, roll no., drawing title, start date, drawing convention, scale, etc.

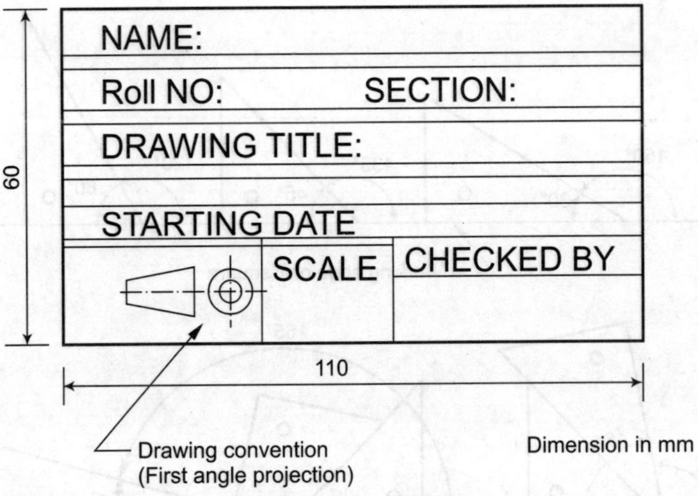

Fig. 1.4 Title block

1.5 T-SQUARE

The T-square is shown in Fig. 1.5.

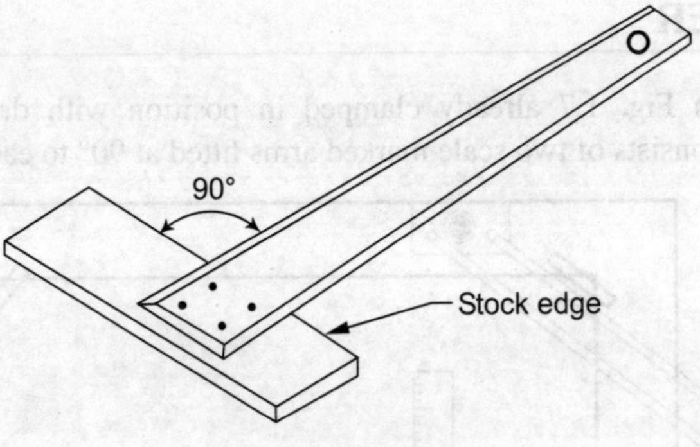

Fig. 1.5 T-square

The stock edge of the T-square is kept in touch with the working edge of drawing board slided over it. The working edge of T-square is used to draw horizontal lines and the inclined lines with the help of set-squares as shown in Fig. 1.6, keeping in touch with the set square edge. With the help of set square and T-square, parallel and perpendicular lines can be also drawn.

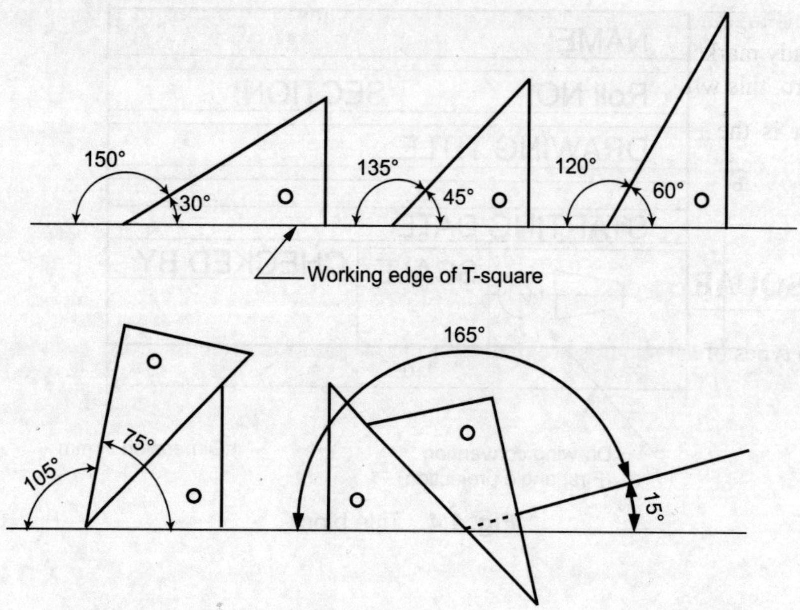

Fig. 1.6 Different angles drawn with the help of set-square

1.6 MINI DRAFTER

Mini drafter is shown in Fig. 1.7 already clamped in position with drawing board. As regards constructional details, it consists of two scale marked arms fitted at 90° to each other.

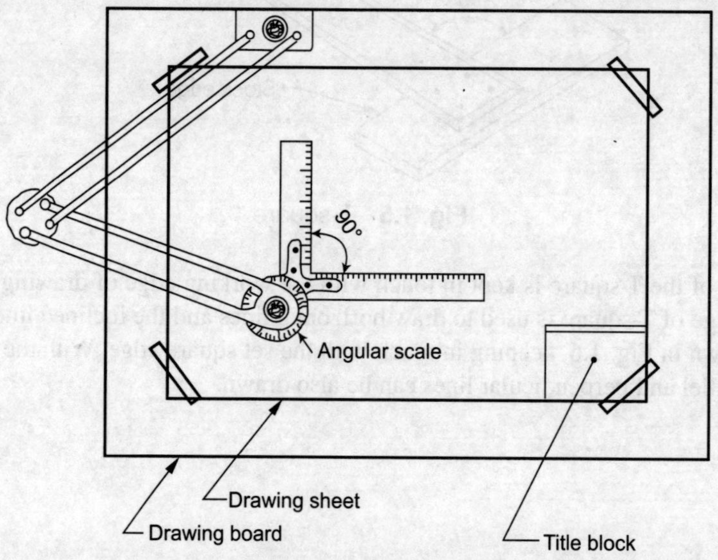

Fig. 1.7 Fixing mini drafter and drawing sheet

The two arms together can be set to any position and angle by means of a knob holding a circular protractor already marked with different angle. The protractor has a pointer to indicate angle. If pointer is moved to zero, this will set one arm horizontal and the other arm vertical.

Mini drafter is the replacement of T-square. It serves all purposes of T-square, set square, and protractor. In this case, the working edge of the drawing board has no use.

The students must know the usual method of clamping a mini drafter on drawing board.

1.7 SET SQUARES

Generally, two types of set squares are in use for the preparation of engineering drawing: 45°– 45° and 30°– 60° as shown in Fig. 1.8.

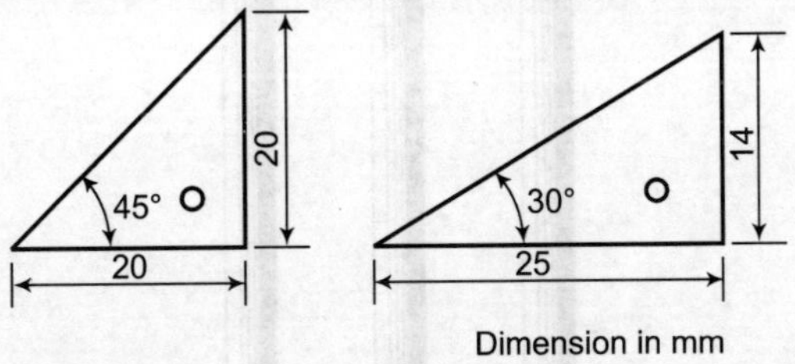

Fig. 1.8 45°– 45° and 30°– 60° set square

Set squares are made of transparent celluloid or plastic material. The edges are perfect without having abrasion. With the help of these two set squares and T-squares many horizontal, vertical, and inclined lines can be drawn as shown in Fig. 1.6.

Before starting the job, edges of the set square must be examined for accuracy of angles and lines. The edges of set square are assumed to be perfect and smooth.

In combination with these set squares, keeping them in different positions, different angles can be set as already shown in Fig. 1.6. The lines inclined at 15°, 30°, 45°, 60° to horizontal can be drawn.

1.8 DRAWING PENCILS

The quality of drawing and drafting depends mainly on the quality of pencil—accuracy and appearance varies with the quality of it. It is always preferable that good quality of pencil much be used.

In the market, pencils with different hardness are available. The type of pencils must be used depending upon the quality of drawing sheets and the line work.

Wood pencils are available in different grades as given below:

6B, 4B, 2B, B, HB → Soft category

(6B is the softest among all)

H, 2H, 4H, 6H → Hard category

(6H is the hardest among all)

HB and H lead pencil is medium hardness. They are generally preferred for lettering and dimensioning.

After drawing a few lines, the lead of a pencil becomes blunt. The lead of a pencil requires frequent cutting and sharpening.

Sometimes, draftsmen use lead holder pencil known a clutch pencil. This type of pencil is more convenient to use. The clutch pencil uses 0.2 to 0.3 mm diameter lead.

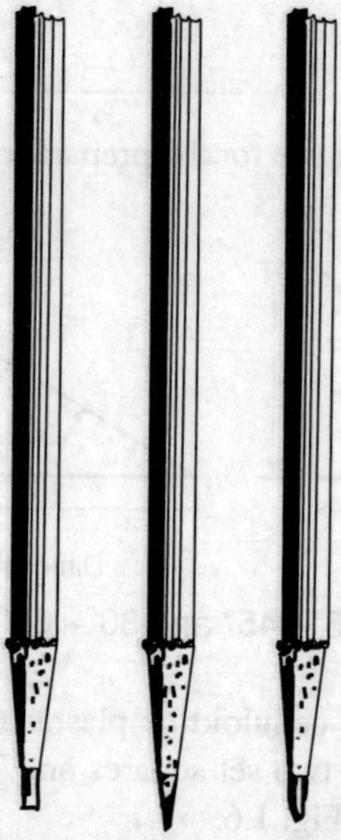

Fig. 1.9 Forms of lead cut

The lead of a pencil may be cut in three different forms as shown in Fig. 1.9(a), (b), and (c).

(a) Chisel point pencil

(b) Sharp point lead pencil

(c) Blunt lead pencil

The chisel point pencil is used for drawing straight lines as it needs less sharpening. Line intensity becomes sharp with this pencil. The chisel point can be prepared by rubbing the lead on a sand paper to make one side flat and from other side it is made to be straight as shown in Fig. 1.9(a).

Figure 1.9 (b) and (c) show sharp-point lead pencil and blunt lead pencil, respectively.

In making a drawing, letters and dimensions are finished with soft lead pencils. For writing thick letters, blunt conical lead pencils are used.

For writing small-size letters and figures, well-sharpened point lead pencil must be used as shown in Fig. 1.9(c).

1.9 INSTRUMENT BOX

For making a good drawing, a complete instrument box is needed. A complete instrument box has the following kits like big compass, bow compass, divider, ink liner, etc.

An instrument box is a little bit costly and, as such, the students may not be very willing to purchase it. At least, they should have good quality of compass, bow compass, and divider as shown in Fig. 1.10(a), (b), (c), and (d).

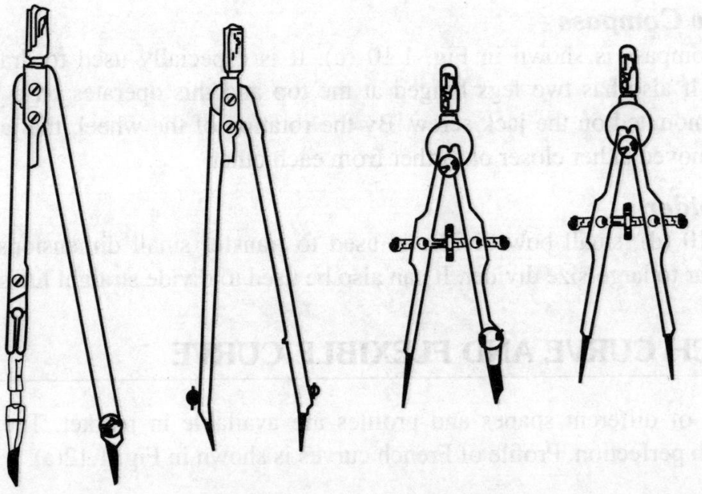

(a) Large size compass (b) Large size divider (c) Bow compass (d) Bow divider

Fig. 1.10 Set of instruments

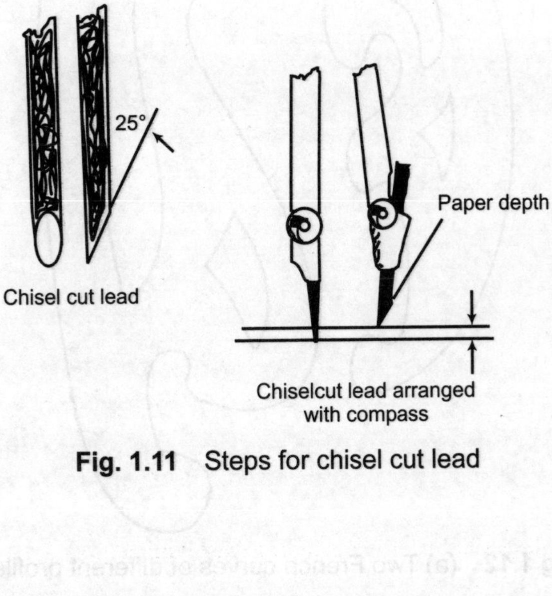

Fig. 1.11 Steps for chisel cut lead

Large-size Compass

A large-size compass is shown in Fig. 1.10(a). It is used for drawing circles and arc of diameter about 150 mm conveniently. It has two legs hinged at the top end. One leg has s needle that penetrates into the drawing sheet and the other leg will hold chisel-cut lead as in Fig. 1.11.

Large-size Divider

Large size divider, as shown in Fig. 1.10(b), is used to transform measurements from one place to another place. Sometimes, it can also be used to divide straight lines into any number of equal parts.

Small-size Bow Compass

Small-size bow compass is shown in Fig. 1.10 (c). It is especially used to draw a small circle of diameter 20 mm. It also has two legs hinged at the top and this operates on a jack screw. A small knurled wheel is mounted on the jack screw. By the rotation of the wheel, the jack screw moves the legs and they are moved either closer or farther from each other.

Small Bow Divider

Shown in Fig. 1.10 (d), small bow divider is used to transfer small dimensions from one place to another. It is similar to large-size divider. It can also be used to divide straight lines in equal parts.

1.10 FRENCH CURVE AND FLEXIBLE CURVE

French curves set of different shapes and profiles are available in market. They are used to draw smooth curves with perfection. Profile of French curves is shown in Fig. 1.12(a).

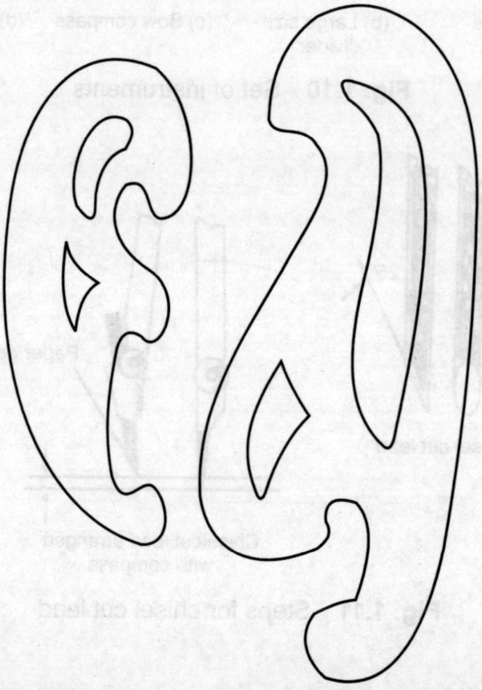

Fig 1.12 (a) Two French curves of different profiles

Students are advised to keep at least two French curves of different profiles.

The edge of a French curve must be examined properly so that the curve drawn will be smooth and the curve drawn must match with the curvature.

Flexible curve is as shown in Fig. 1.12 (b). It is the substitute of French curve. It is also used to draw smooth curves.

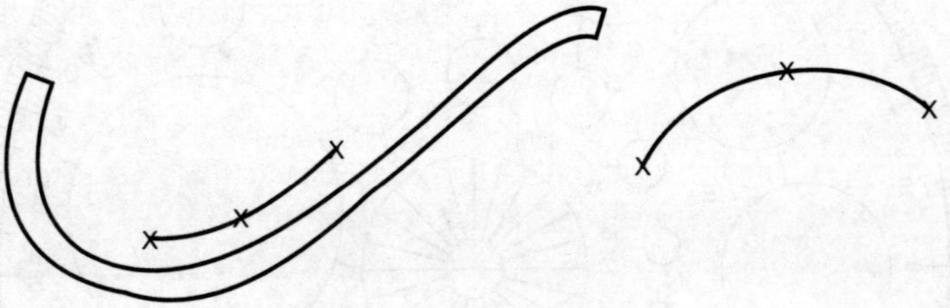

Fig. 1.12 (b) Flexible curve

A flexible curve can also be used in drawing in place of French curve. As regards constructional details, it is made up of lead metal bar enclosed in rubber. It is very flexible in nature and is found very useful in drawing any curvature. It is so flexible that it can be made to match with any profile. If three points are available, a curve can be matched with this curvature.

1.11 PROTRACTOR

Protractors of different shapes are available in market. They are either semi-circular on circular as shown in Fig. 1.13(a) and (b). They are made of either wood or transparent material. At the centre of it, two perpendicular lines are indicated. It is used to draw angles and also for the measurement of any angle.

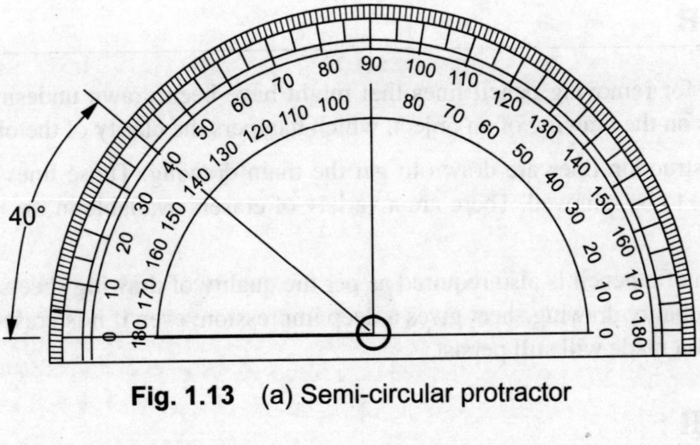

Fig. 1.13 (a) Semi-circular protractor

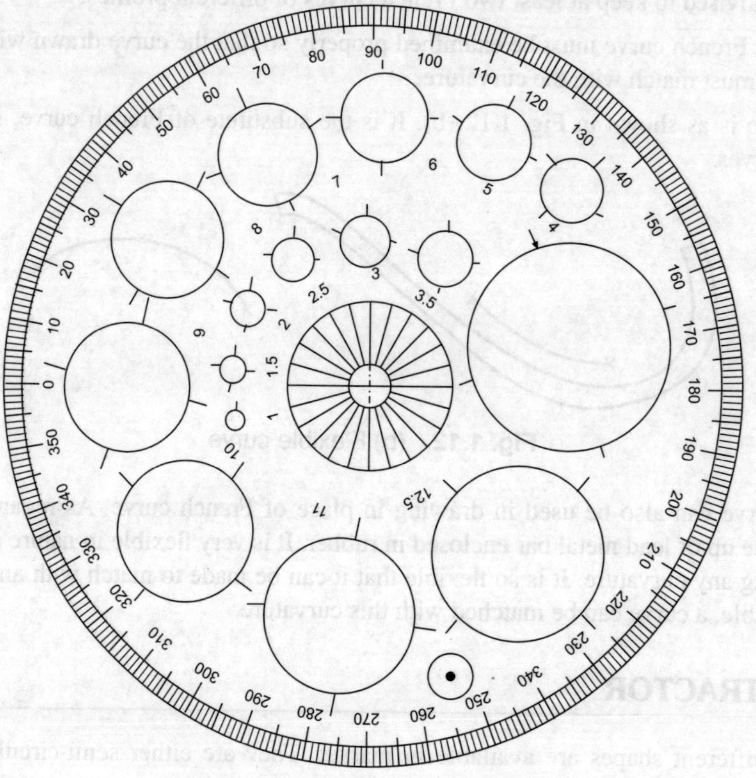

Fig. 1.13 (b) Circular protractor

1.12 ERASER

Soft eraser is used for removing pencil lines that might have been drawn undesirably with the main constructional lines on the drawing of an object, which hampers the clarity of the object.

Sometimes, construction lines are drawn to get the main drawing. Those lines are unwanted lines and, hence, they are to be removed. There are a variety of erasers available in the market and they are sold by tradenames.

Correct selection of a pencil is also required as per the quality of drawing sheets. A line drawn with hard lead on a low-quality drawing sheet gives a deep impression; even if it is erased with good quality eraser, the impression made will still persist.

1.13 DUSTER

The duster is also an important item. It should be of towel cloth or clean cloth. Before starting with the drawing, all drawing kits should be cleaned with duster to remove dust particles.

1.14 SELECTION OF SCALES

Set of scales are available in the market. They are made of wood, steel, and transparent material. A scale would have two edges already marked with divisions in cm or mm [Fig. 1.14(a)]. It is used to transfer the true dimensions of an object. A scale is essential to take the true dimensions of an object.

Depending on the size of the object, the drawing is to be made on a drawing sheet by selecting a suitable scale either full-size drawing (1 : 1), half of full size (1 : 2), or one-fourth of full size (1 : 4) reduced or enlarged size scale. These have been shown in Fig. 1.14(b).

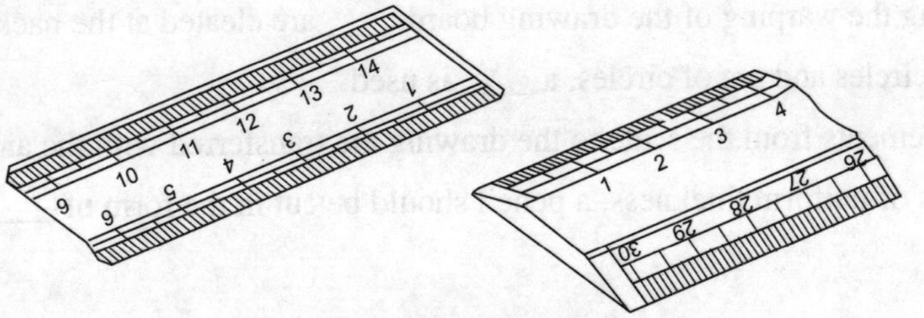

Fig. 1.14 (a) Set of scales

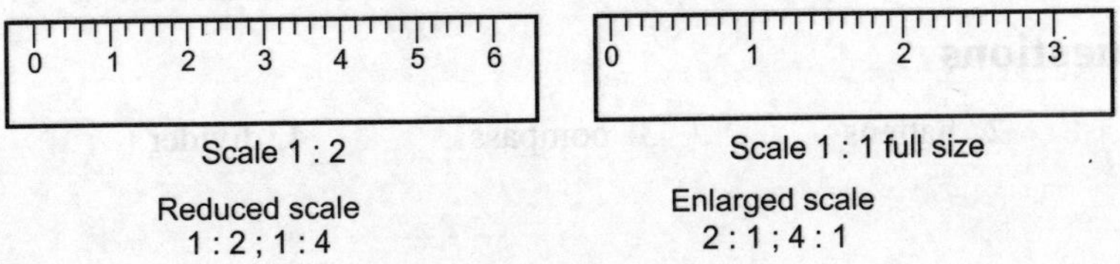

Fig. 1.14 (b) Scale

EXERCISE

Review Questions

1. Enlist the main components of a mini drafter.
2. Why is sellotape preferred as compared with drawing pins for fixing drawing sheets?
3. Why should a pencil be slightly rotated in fingers while drawing a line?
4. Where are conical pencils used?
5. With the help of a mini drafter, set 10°, 15°, 30°, 45°, 60°, 75°, and 90° angles with a horizontal angle.
6. Draw a horizontal line 100 mm long and divide it into 10 equal parts.
7. Draw a circle of 60 mm diameter and divide it into 4, 6, 8, and 12 equal parts.
8. Using protractor, draw the following angles: 17°, 44°, 156°, 92°.

9. What are the main parts of T-square?
10. Why are T-squares not used for drawing vertical lines?
11. With the help of T-square and set squares, draw 4 vertical lines and 4 lines at 30° angle and also at 60° angle.

Objective Questions

1. The working edge of the drawing board should be on the ____ side of the draftsman.
2. For preventing the warping of the drawing board ____ are cleated at the back.
3. For drawing circles and arc of circles, a ____ is used.
4. Scale measurements from the scale to the drawing are transferred with the aid of a ____.
5. To draw lines of uniform thickness, a pencil should be cut in the form of ____.

ANSWERS

Objective Questions

1. left 2. battens 3. compass 4. divider 5. chisel edge

2

CHAPTER

Line Conventions, Lettering, and Method of Dimensioning

2.1 LINE CONVENTIONS

There can be a large number of lines used for making a good drawing, such as boundary line, construction line, hidden line, centre line, dimension line, extension line, dotted line, etc.

The Bureau of Indian Standards (BIS) has recommended the types of lines to be used for different purposes of drawing. They are shown as given below special publication SP: 46; 1988 (Reaffirmed in 1993)

Table 2.1 Types of lines and their appropriate use

S. No.	Type of line	Line representation	Uses
1.	Continuous thick line		Visible outline and boundary line
2.	Continuous thin line		Dimension line, Extension line, Construction line, Leader line, Hatching line
3.	Continuous thin wavy		Short-break lines or irregular boundaries
4.	Continuous thin with zig-zag		Long-break lines
5.	Short-dashed line		Hidden line
6.	Long-chain lines		Centre line, Pitch circle
7.	Long-chain thin but thick at the end		Cutting plane lines
8.	Long-chain thick		Line or surface incidental for special treatment application
9.	Chain thin thick at the end and change of direction		Cutting plane

Application of different types of lines is shown in Fig. 2.1. A sectional view of machine components with all line conventions has been shown.

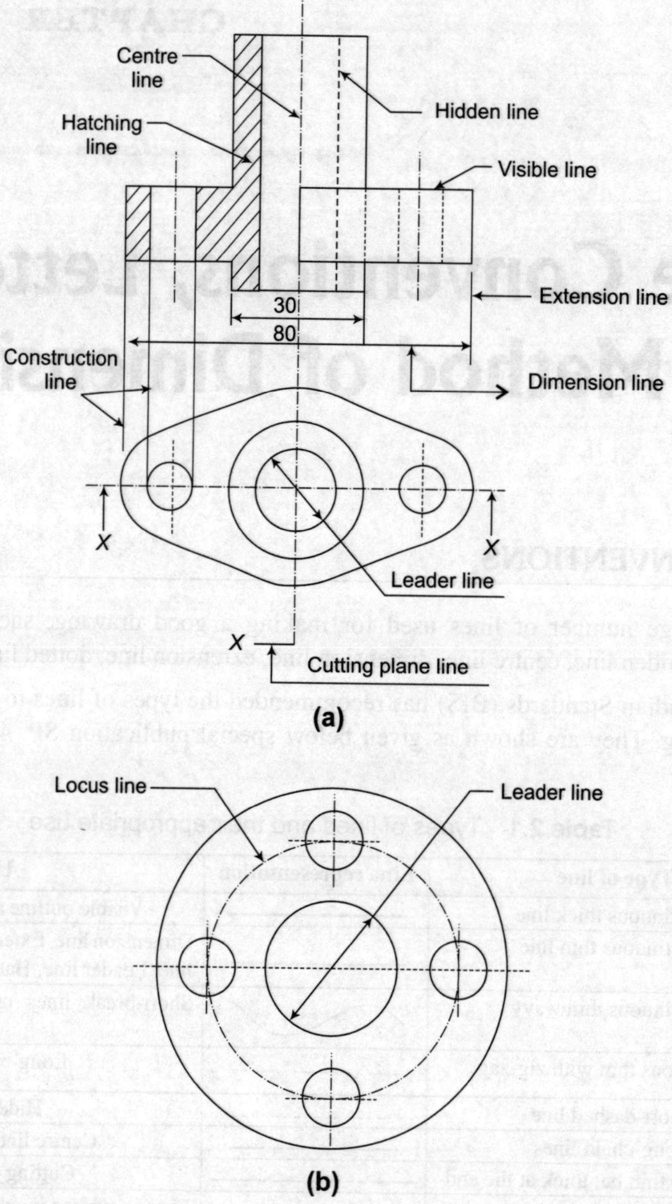

Fig. 2.1

2.2 DIMENSIONING METHODS

A drawing prepared will have all the dimensions of the machine components to visualize the shape and size of the object. Unless a shape is properly dimensioned, it cannot be manufactured accurately. Therefore, the drawing must be dimensioned with all conventional lines as in Table 2.1.

Without dimension, the drawing has no meaning. As far as possible, all dimensions are mentioned in mm. For example, a dimension 25 means 25 mm. 'mm' should not be tagged with 50 as shown in Fig. 2.2. However, in the lower part of the drawing, it should be written "All dimensions in mm".

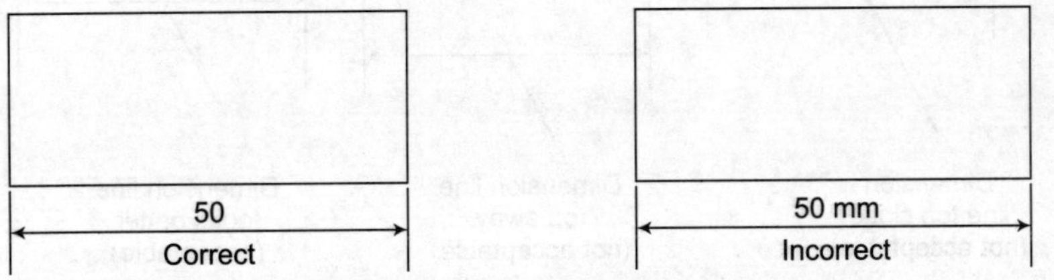

Fig. 2.2 All dimensions in mm

2.2.1 Elements of Dimensions

The dimensioning of an object includes the extension line, dimension line, leader line arrow heads, and dimension of the main object.

Extension Line: A short line (drawn with thin and less-intensity line) drawn perpendicular to an object to be dimensioned. It may be drawn continuously from the object end or a little gap of 1 or 2 mm from the end of the object to be dimensioned as shown in Fig. 2.3 (a) and (b).

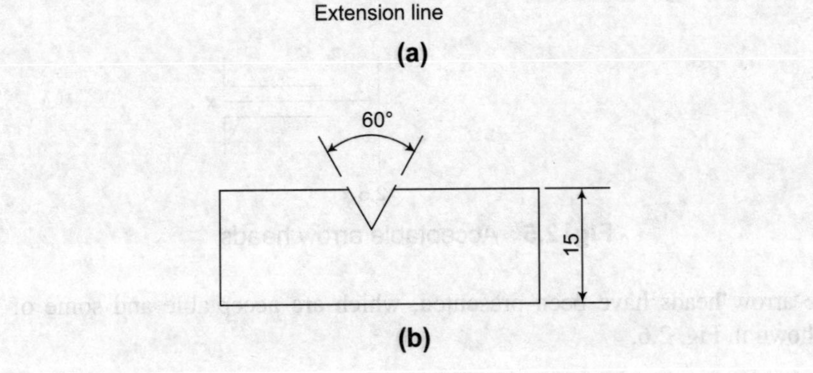

Fig. 2.3 (a) Extension line; (b) Extension line to show angles

Dimension Line (Fig. 2.4)

Dimension line is drawn between the two extension lines already drawn.

It should be drawn parallel to the object line to be dimensioned. As per convention, there shall be only one dimension line between any two extension lines.

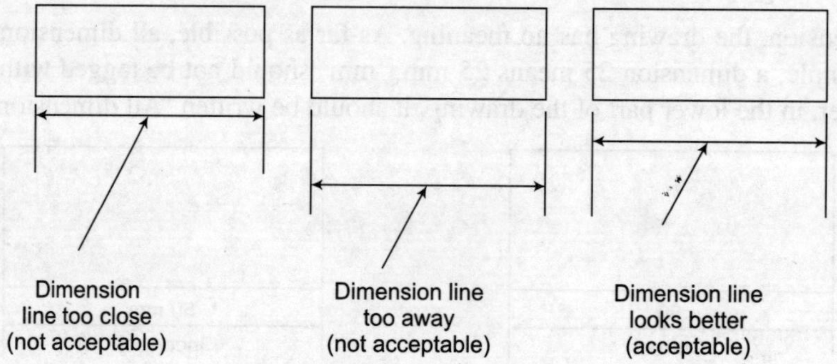

Fig. 2.4 Dimension technique

Arrow Head

Arrow heads are used to finish dimension line. Dimension lines should have two arrows, one at each end. The length of the arrow head is 2.5 times the width and it should also be in proportion with the length to be dimensioned.

The arrow head may be open, closed, or closed filled, and sometimes even an oblique stroke as shown in Fig. 2.5. Closed and filled arrow heads are more acceptable.

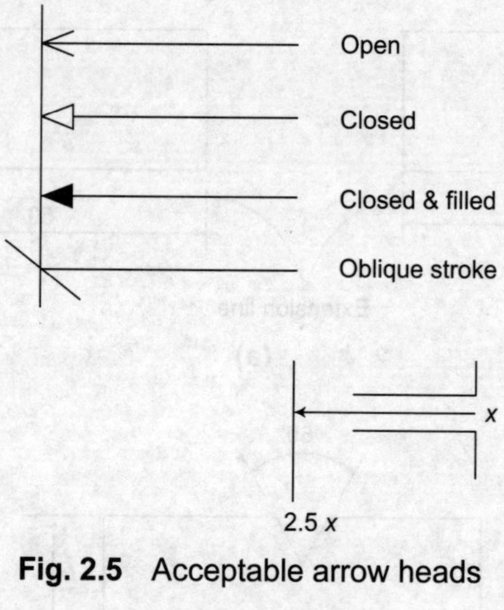

Fig. 2.5 Acceptable arrow heads

Some of the arrow heads have been presented, which are acceptable and some of them are not acceptable as shown in Fig. 2.6.

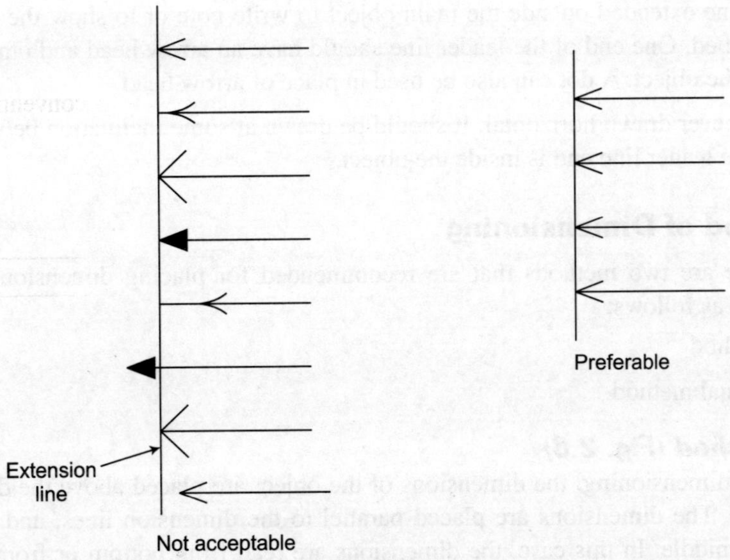

Fig. 2.6

Leader Line (Fig. 2.7)

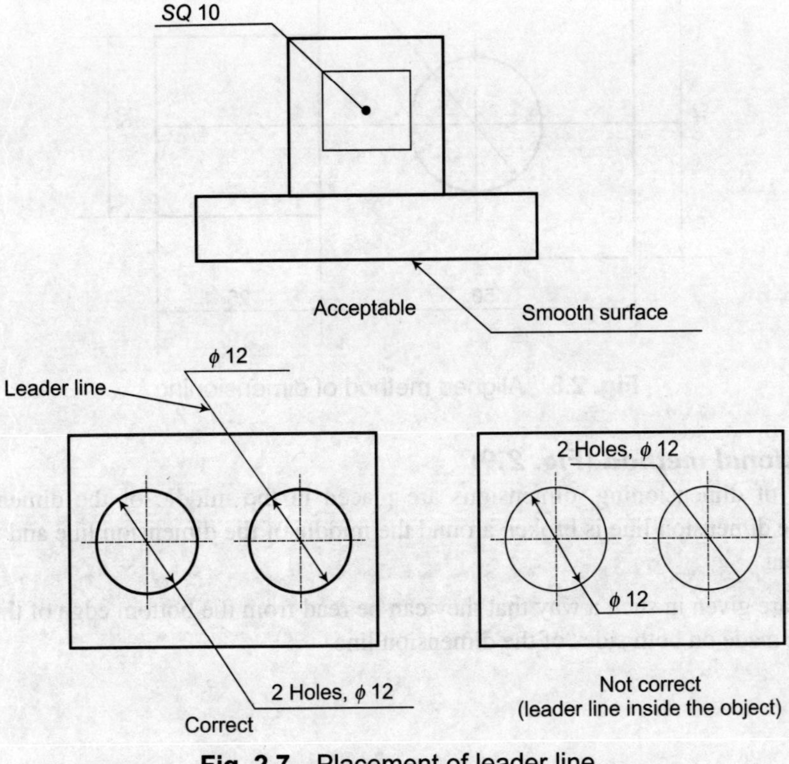

Fig. 2.7 Placement of leader line

Leader line is a line extended outside the main object to write note or to show the dimensions of the shape to be identified. One end of the leader line should have an arrow head and other end outside the boundary line of the object. A dot can also be used in place of arrow head.

Leader line is never drawn horizontal. It should be drawn at some inclination between 30° and 45°. A dot is used if the leader line end is inside the object.

2.2.2 Method of Dimensioning

As per BIS, there are two methods that are recommended for placing dimension of the object on drawing. They are as follows:

1. Aligned method
2. Uni-directional method

1. Aligned method (Fig. 2.8)

In this method of dimensioning, the dimensions of the object are placed above the dimension lines as shown in Fig. 2.8. The dimensions are placed parallel to the dimension lines, and should be placed preferably in the middle. In this case, the dimensions are read from bottom or from right side of the drawing. This method is more preferable.

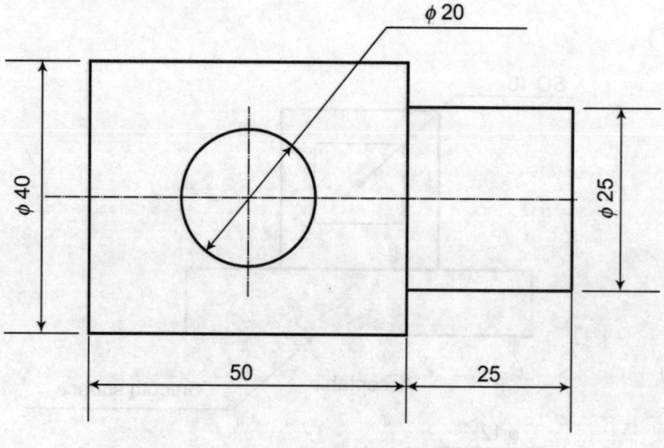

Fig. 2.8 Aligned method of dimensioning

2. Uni-directional method (Fig. 2.9)

In this method of dimensioning, dimensions are placed in the middle of the dimension line. The continuity of the dimension line is broken around the middle of the dimension line and the dimensions are placed therein.

Dimensions are given in such a way that they can be read from the bottom edge of the drawing. The arrow heads are made on both sides of the dimension line.

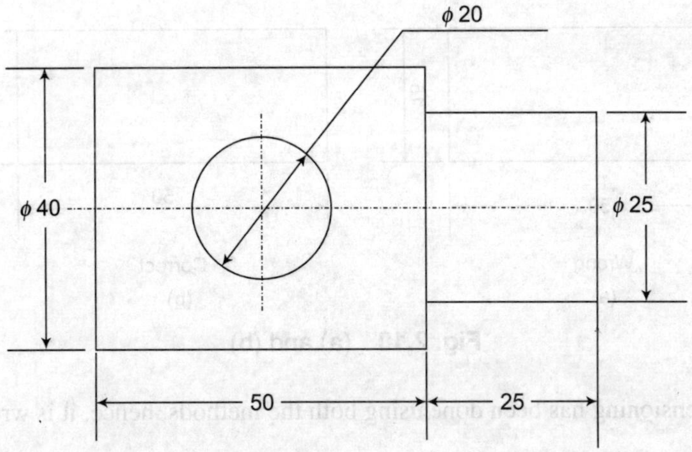

Fig. 2.9 Uni-directional method of dimensioning

2.2.3 Principle of Dimensioning

Before taking the job of dimensioning, certain points are to be remembered.

1. Alignment method is more appropriate and convenient; hence, the entire drawing will be dimensioned by this method.
2. Extension line should be drawn, extending slightly more than the dimension line.
3. Placement of leader line remains the same in both the methods.
4. Between any two extension lines, there should be only one dimension line.
5. Dimensions should be in mm in the entire drawing and 'mm' should not be combined with the dimension. A note, as below, is given under:

   'All dimensions in mm.'
6. Dimension lines should not cross each other.
7. Centre line should not be used as dimension line.
8. Hidden line should not be used as dimension line.
9. When the dimension is to be placed in hatched area, some gap may be provided therein.
10. The dimension line should be drawn about 8 mm away from the object. It should not be nearer to the object.
11. All notes should be placed horizontally.

(1)

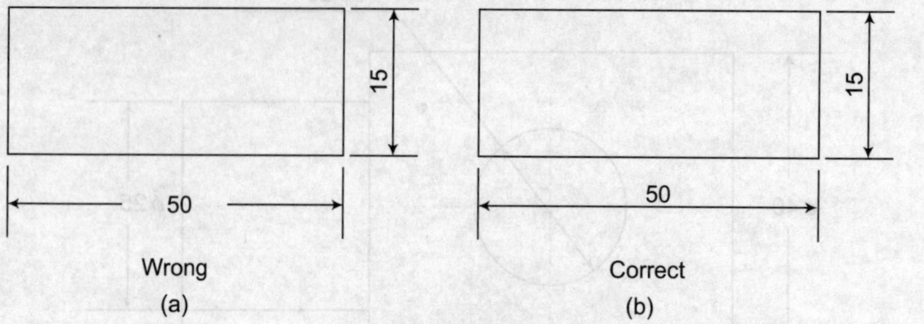

Fig. 2.10 (a) and (b)

In Fig. 2.10 (a), dimensioning has been done using both the methods, hence, it is wrong.

(2)

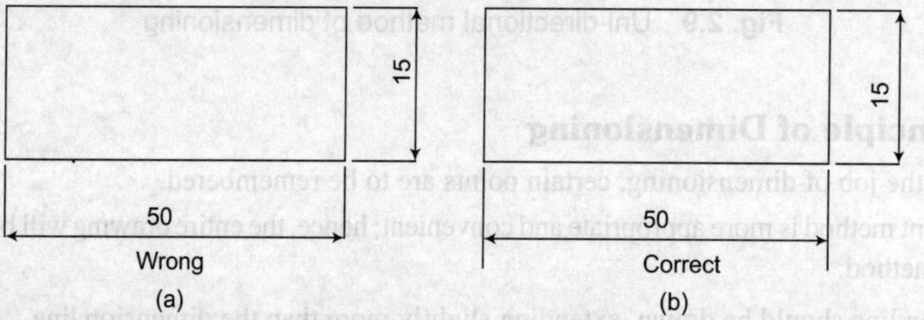

Fig. 2.11 (a) and (b)

Figure 2.11 (a) is wrong since the extension line has not been drawn, extending it slightly more than dimension line.

(3)

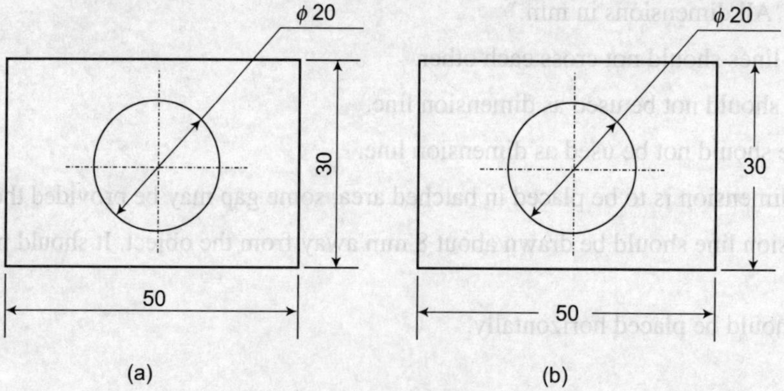

Fig. 2.12 (a) and (b)

In Fig. 2.12 (a) and (b), both, two different methods of dimensioning have been used, but the leader line in both drawings is same.

(4)

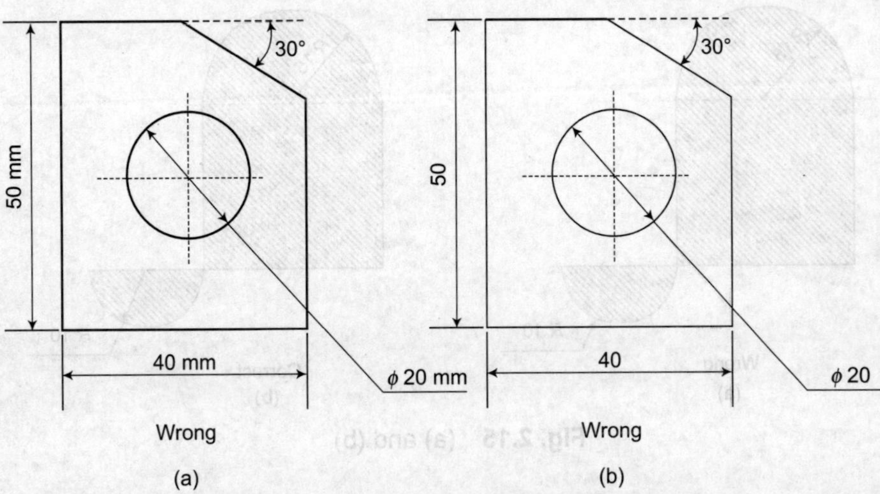

Fig. 2.13 (a) and (b) All dimensions in mm

Figure 2.13 (a) is wrong because the unit of dimension mm has been written after each dimension.

(5)

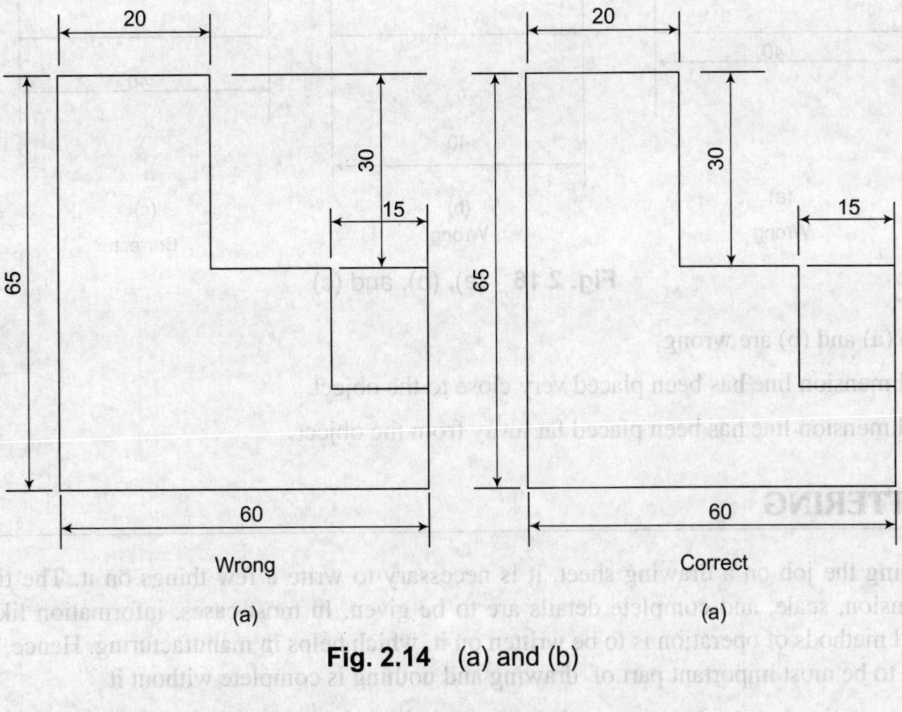

Fig. 2.14 (a) and (b)

In Fig. 2.14 (a), two dimension lines are crossing each other.

(6)

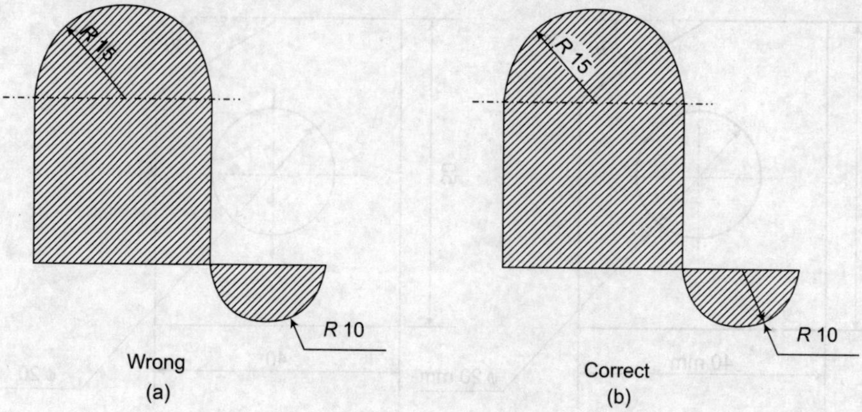

Fig. 2.15 (a) and (b)

Figure 2.15 (a) is wrong because blank space has not been left for spacing dimensions.

(7)

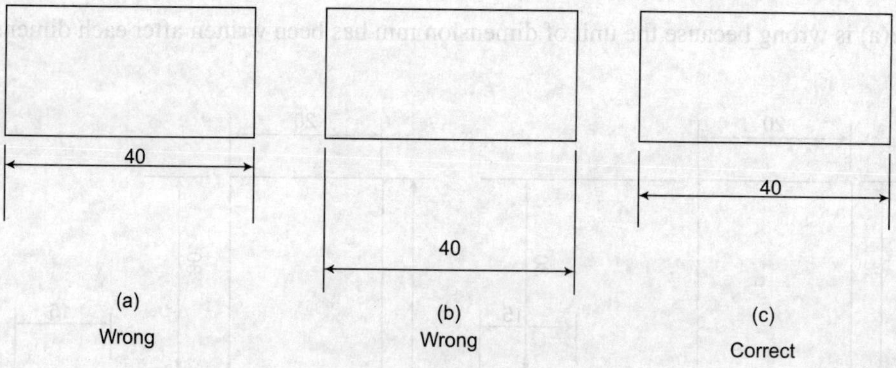

Fig. 2.16 (a), (b), and (c)

Figure 2.16 (a) and (b) are wrong

In (a), the dimension line has been placed very close to the object.

In (b), the dimension line has been placed far away from the object.

2.3 LETTERING

After finishing the job on a drawing sheet, it is necessary to write a few things on it. The title, subtitles, dimension, scale, and complete details are to be given. In most cases, information like bill of material and methods of operation is to be written on it, which helps in manufacturing. Hence, lettering is supposed to be most important part of drawing and nothing is complete without it.

The main requirement of lettering is the type and size of letters and the important technique of lettering that are presented in IS 9609-1983 and ISO 3098/1-1974(E).

One important fact to be remembered is that the lettering should not be time consuming and so it should be plain and in simple style.

As per BIS, single-stroke letters, as shown in Fig. 2.17, and Gothic letters, as shown in Fig. 2.18, are recommended.

2.3.1 Single-stroke Letters

These letters are the simplest forms of letters generally used in engineering drawing. Single-stroke letter means that the letter is written in one stroke of pencil only. Single stroke letters have categories as shown below.

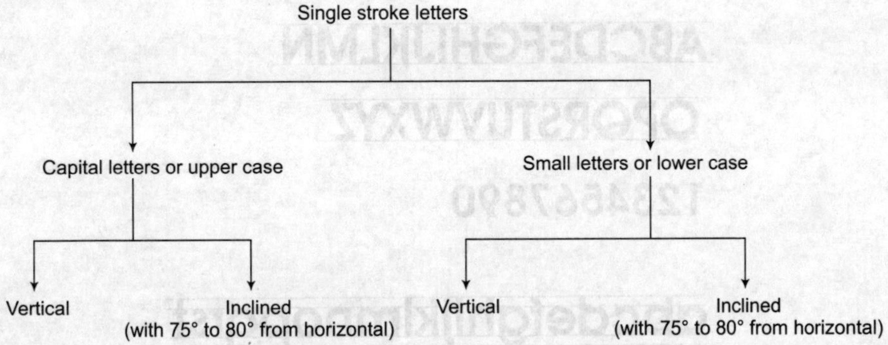

Lettering is generally done in capital letters and the sizes of letters are used as per the purpose.

Figure 2.17 (a) and Fig. 2.17 (b) show single-stroke vertical and inclined letters, respectively.

Fig. 2.17 (a) Single-stroke vertical letters (free hand); (b) Single-stroke inclined letters (free hand)

2.3.2 Gothic Letters

Gothic letters are also the simplest forms of letters like single-stroke letters. The only difference is that in case of Gothic letters, the stroke of letters are drawn with more thickness. The thickness of the stroke of the letters may vary from 1/5 to 1/8 of the height of letters. The size of letters (capital or small) is represented by its height.

The standard sizes of letters are 4, 5, 7, and 10 mm in both single stroke as well as Gothic. The ratio of height to width is 5/3 or 5/4.

The ratio becomes exceptional for letter 'I' and 'T'. Gothic letters have been represented in Fig. 2.18(a) and (b).

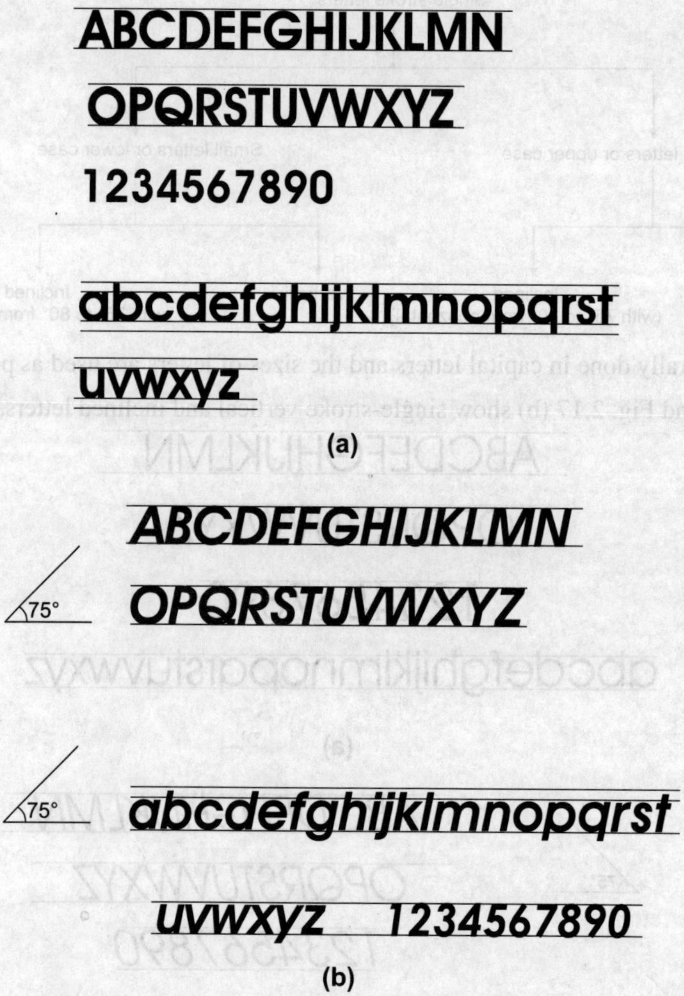

Fig. 2.18 (a) Gothic vertical letters (free hand); (b) Gothic inclined letters (free hand)

2.3.3 Recommendation of Letter Sizes

The following are the letter sizes used for different purposes:

Main title, plate number:	7 to 10 mm
Sub-title:	5 to 6 mm
Dimensions, notes etc.:	4 to 5 mm
Bill of materials:	4 to 5 mm

For the presentation of good letters, the students are advised to draw two horizontal lines (guide lines) with H or 2H lead pencil with faint impression as shown in Fig. 2.17(a), (b) and Fig, 2.18(a), (b) and then writing may be done.

In case of small case letters, four horizontal lines are to be drawn with H or 2H lead pencil with faint impression as shown in Fig. 2.17 (b) and Fig. 2.18 (b). For example, these have been shown in Fig. 2.19.

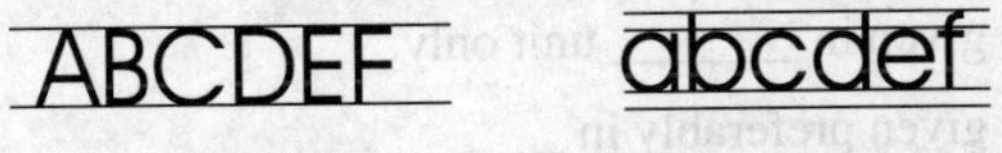

(a) Capital vertical (b) Small case vertical

Fig. 2.19 (a) capital vertical letters; (b) small vertical letters

However, good presentation and lettering is on personal ability and practices. There is a lot of hope for good lettering with personal efforts.

EXERCISE

Review Questions

1. Mention the two systems of dimensions with suitable examples.

2. While dimensioning a drawing, write the various principles to be followed.

3. Show with sketches the methods of dimensioning of circle and radii.

4. Explain the size and location dimensions with suitable sketches.

5. Show by sketches the aligned and uni-directional methods of dimensioning.

6. What should be the true nature of an arrow head? What is the proportion of an arrow head?

7. Draw hidden line, short-break line, centre line, long-break line, and cutting plane line.

8. Define single-stroke letter.

9. Define Gothic letter.

10. Why is a layout of sheet necessary?

11. With free hand, write the following words of 10 mm vertical:

(i) Indian Institute of Technology

(ii) Mahabharat

(iii) Drawing is a Language

12. Write the same words free hand, of 10 mm inclined at 75° from horizontal.

13. Write free hand in vertical and inclined lower case letters, taking height 10 mm.

14. Print free hand in vertical and inclined numbers, height 8 mm and 5 mm.

15. Draw the various conventional representations of lines in practice.

16. Prepare a title block.

17. Write the following in single-stroke letters: 'MANAGEMENT'.

18. Write the following in Gothic letter: 'MANAGEMENT'.

Objective Questions

1. Dimensioning methods on a drawing are ______ and ______.
2. Dimensions should be given in ______ unit only.
3. Dimensions should be given preferably in ______.
4. Extension line should be extended about 2 to 3 mm beyond the ______.
5. The dimension of circle should be shown by symbol ______.
6. In ______ system, the dimension is placed perpendicular.
7. In uni-directional system, all dimensions are placed such that they should be readable from ______ edge.
8. Two dimension lines should not ______ each other.
9. Dimension lines should be drawn about 8 mm away from the ______.
10. A line connecting a view to the note is called a ______.
11. Dimensions should be from hidden lines. (True/False)
12. The size of a letter is described by its ______.
13. For maintaining uniformity of the letters, two very thin parallel lines are drawn, called ______.
14. Good letters are achieved by ______.
15. Suitable location for total block on a drawing sheet is ______.

Answers

Objective Questions

1. aligned, unidirectional	**2.** one	**3.** mm
4. dimension line	**5.** say 50 ϕ	**6.** aligned
7. bottom	**8.** cross	**9.** outer lines
10. leader line	**11.** False	**12.** height
13. guide lines	**14.** continuous practice	**15.** right-hand bottom corner

3

CHAPTER

Sections and Section Conventions

3.1 INTRODUCTION

The orthographic view of complex machine components, if drawn looking from outside, gives a number of dotted lines for the hidden parts which are invisible from outside.

Too many dotted lines does not justify the actual shape of the internal structure of the object. Hence, the object is imagined to be sectioned by cutting plane and the object is projected to visualize the internal parts. Thus, the sections of machine components are always drawn to show the internal mechanism and the real shape of the object. The part of the object between the cutting plane and the observer is assumed to be removed. The cut surface is identified by hatching lines and the views are called *sectional views*. Sectional views of machine components are necessary to help in manufacturing operation.

There is an object whose pictorial drawing is shown in Fig. 3.1(a) and orthographic projections (top view and front view) are shown in Fig. 3.1(b). The object is symmetrical about the vertical plane. The hidden line of the view, shown in Fig. 3.1(b) by dotted line, makes the view difficult to read.

To avoid these difficulties, a complex body is assumed to be cut as shown in Fig. 3.2(a). The cutting plane cuts the object from top to bottom and it is viewed in the direction of A–A.

It is the sectional view of the object in full in section. A sectional view obtained by assuming that the object is completely cut by the plane is called a *full in section*.

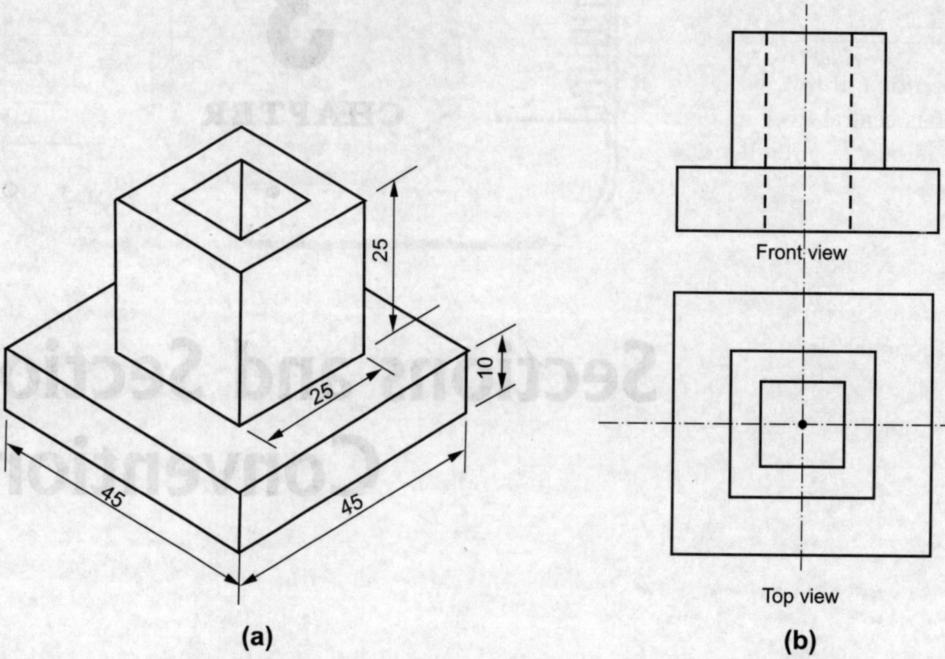

Fig. 3.1 (a) Pictorial drawing of an object; (b) Orthographic views

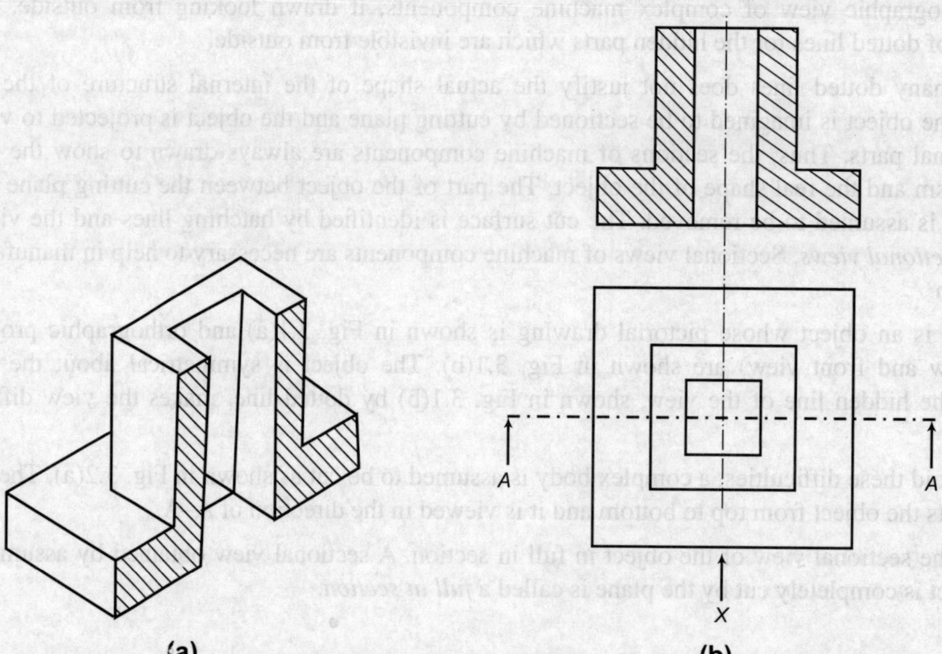

Fig. 3.2 (a) Portion of object left; (b) Sectional view (full in section)

3.2 TYPES OF SECTIONS

(i) Full in Section If the object is symmetrical about the vertical axis and the sectional plane passes through its axis central from its middle dividing the object into the equal parts and the portion of the object lying in between cutting plane and the observer is assumed to be removed, the section of the object is termed as sectional view full in section as shown in Fig. 3.2(a) and 3.2(b). For obtaining full in section, half portion of the object is imagined to be removed.

In this Fig. 3.2, cutting plane is A–A which divides the object into two equal parts.

(ii) Right half in section A half in section of the object is drawn for a symmetrical object. For half section, the sectional plane removes only one quarter of the object.

If two planes are considered perpendicular to each other and they cut the object and one quarter portion of the object is completely removed and the right lower corner is viewed at the sectional plane, the view in section is known as Right half in section as shown in Fig. 3.3(a).

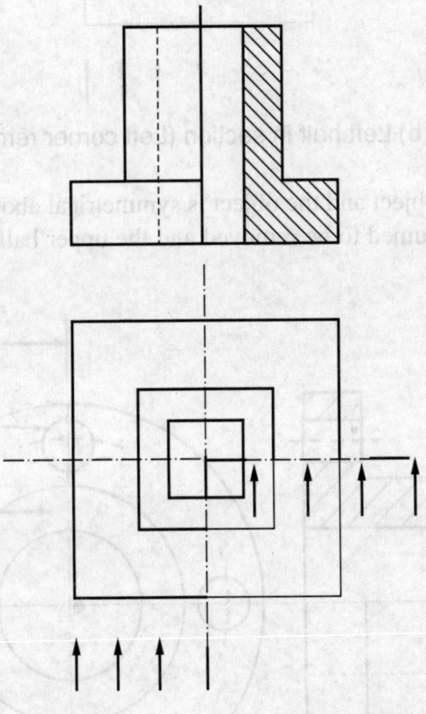

AR App

Fig. 3.3 (a) Right half in section (Right corner removed)

(iii) Left half in section Left half in section of the object means, the object is imagined to be sectioned by two planes perpendicular to each other and one of its left lower corner of the object is assumed to be removed to get the sectional left half in section in Fig. 3.3(b).

(iv) Upper half in section: Upper half in section of the object is preferred for symmetrical objects.

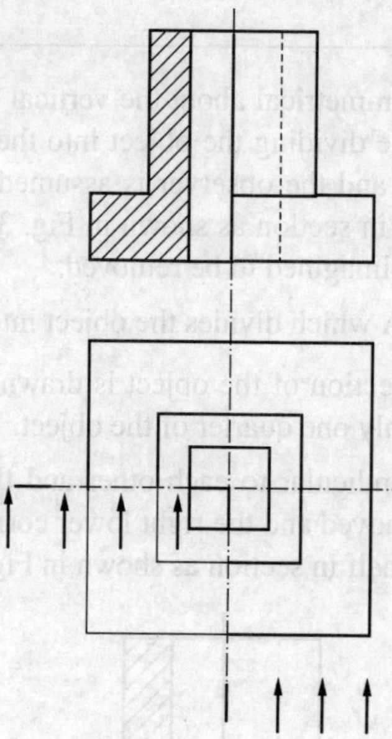

AR App

Fig. 3.3 (b) Left half in section (Left corner removed)

Two planes are cutting the object and the object is symmetrical about the horizontal axis. The upper one quarter of the object is assumed to be removed and the upper half in section is obtained as shown in Fig. 3.4(a).

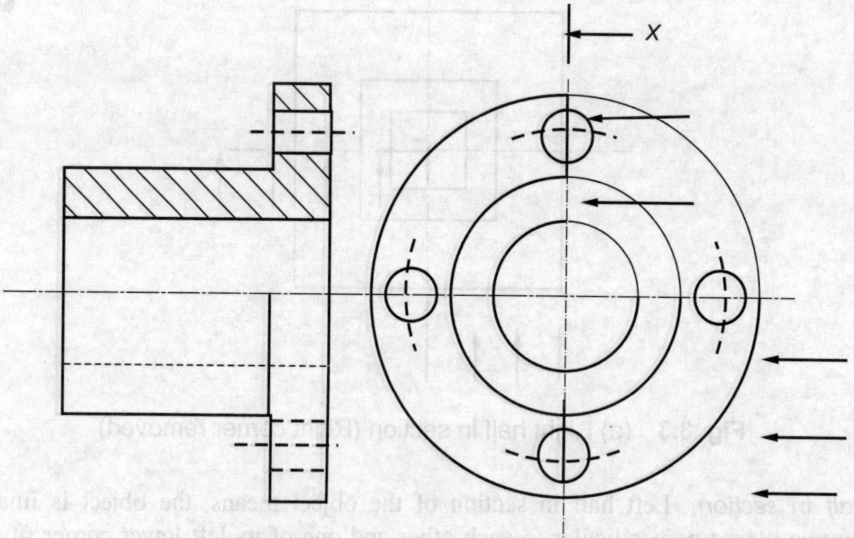

Fig. 3.4 (a) Upper half in section

(v) Lower half in section Lower half in section of the object is also preferred for symmetrical objects.

Two planes are cutting the object and the object is symmetrical about the horizontal axis. The lower one quarter of the object is assumed to be removed and the lower half in section in obtained by projecting the object as shown in Fig. 3.4(b).

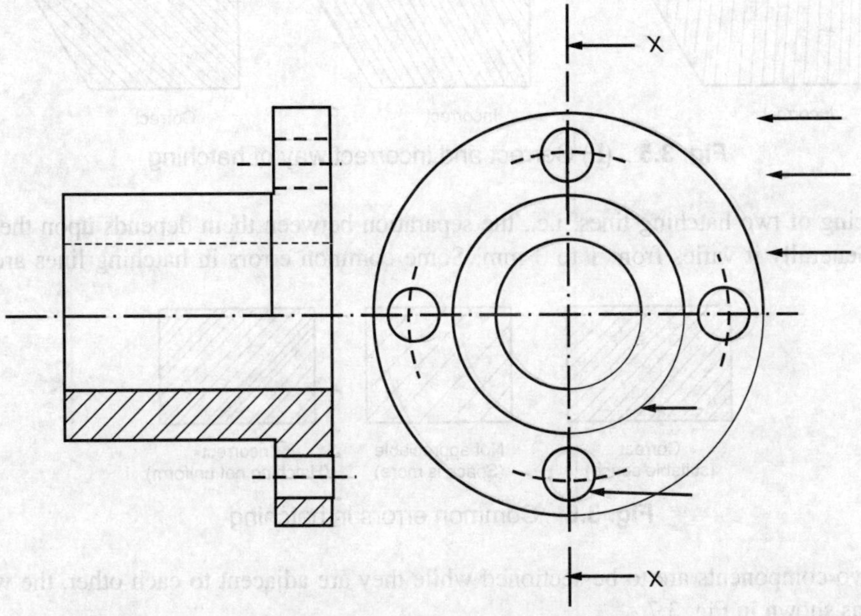

Fig. 3.4 (b) Lower half in section

3.3 HATCHING LINES

(i) The machine component is cut by a cutting plane, and the surface that is cut by the plane is responded by lines called *sectional lines* or *hatching lines*.

Hatching lines are faint lines, equally spaced, parallel to each other, and inclined at 45° on either sides.

These lines should be drawn as per suitability of the object as shown in Fig. 3.5 (a) and (b).

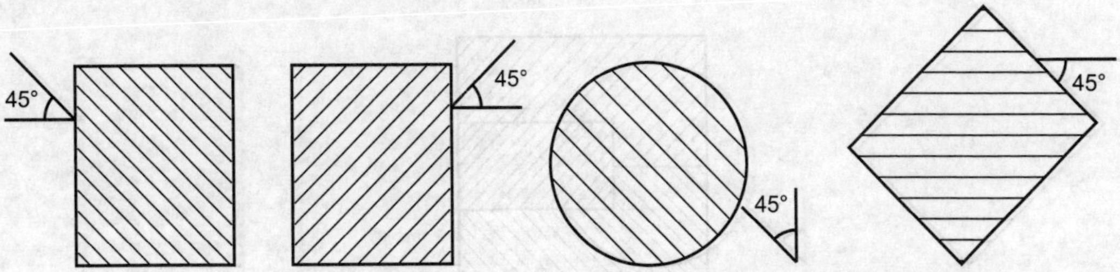

Fig. 3.5 (a) Correcting of hatching lines

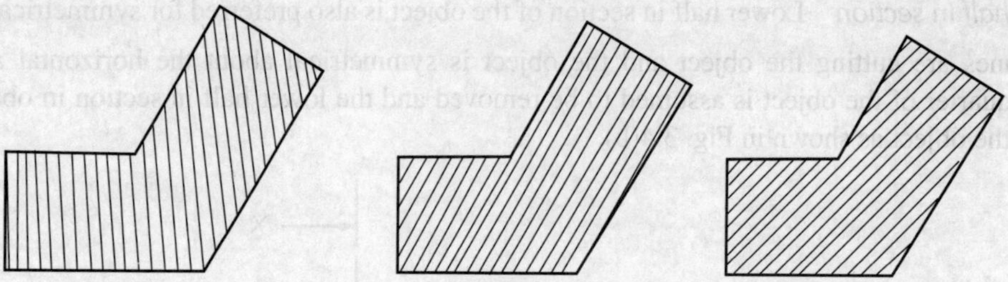

Fig. 3.5 (b) Correct and incorrect way of hatching

(ii) The spacing of two hatching lines, i.e., the separation between them depends upon the area to be sectioned. Generally it varies from 1 to 3 mm. Some common errors in hatching lines are shown in Fig. 3.6.

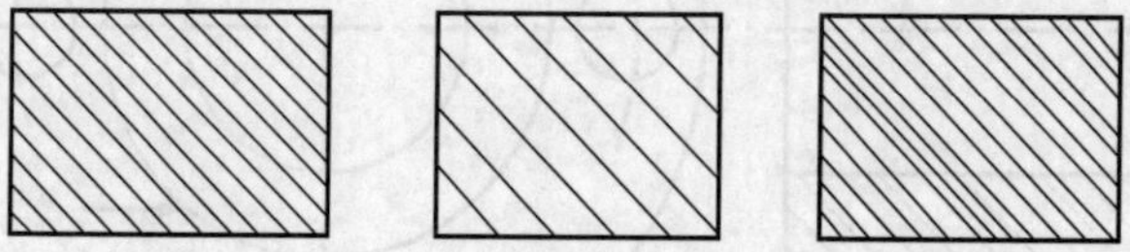

Fig. 3.6 Common errors in hatching

(iii) When two components are to be sectioned while they are adjacent to each other, the ways are to be followed as shown in Fig. 3.7.

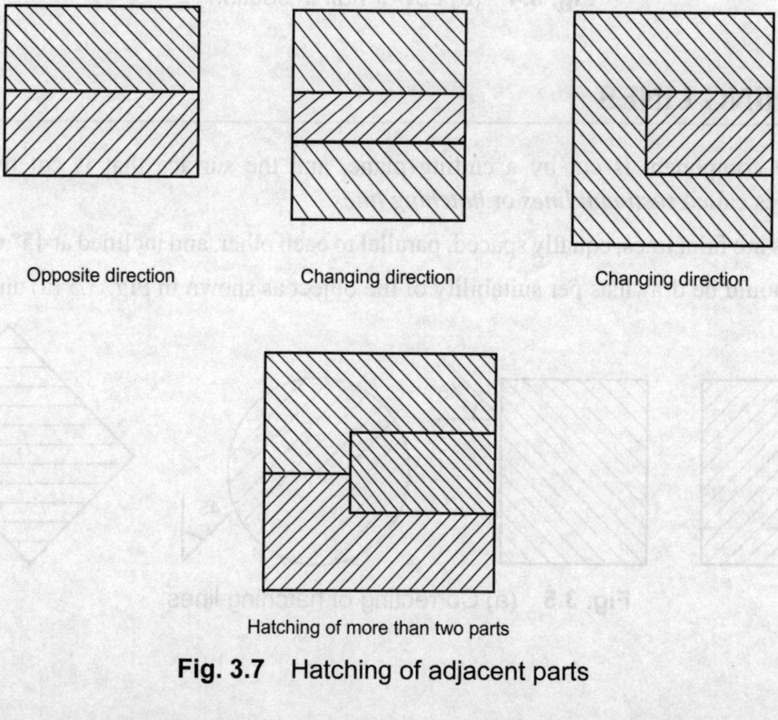

Fig. 3.7 Hatching of adjacent parts

(iv) If the area to be hatched is less and it is required to be dimensioned, the hatching line should be left blank for placing dimensions as shown in Fig. 3.8.

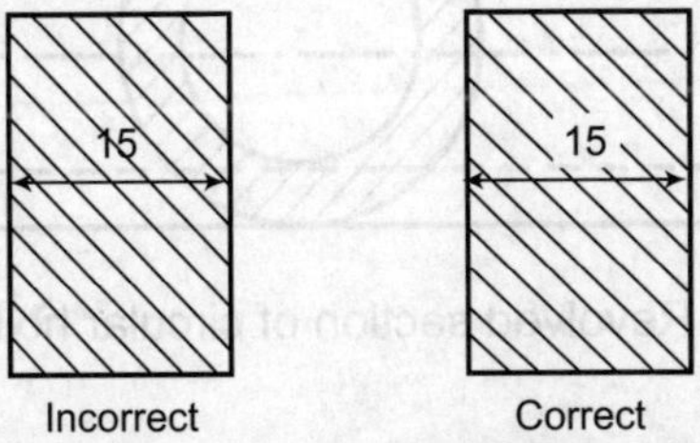

Fig. 3.8 Dimension is sectional area

3.4 SECTION OF SPECIAL CATEGORIES

(i) Revolved section An imaginary cutting plane is passed perpendicular to the centre line of the object, the section just obtained is revolved through 90°. The cross-section of the object is shown therein. The revolved sections for I-section and hollow circular cylinder are shown in Fig. 3.9(a), (b), and (c).

Fig. 3.9 (a) I-section pictorial drawing

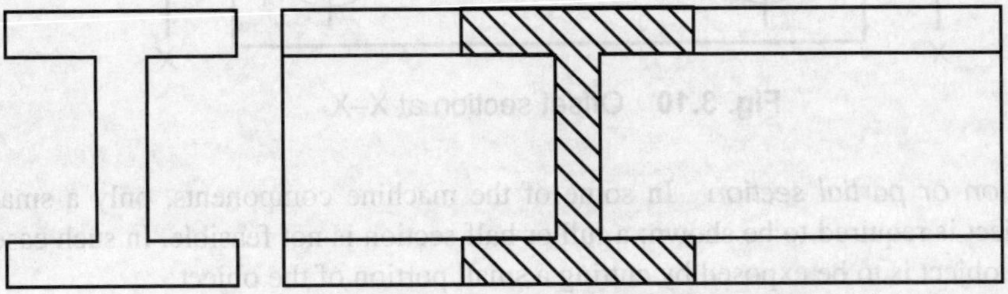

AR App

Fig. 3.9 (b) Revolved section shown in section

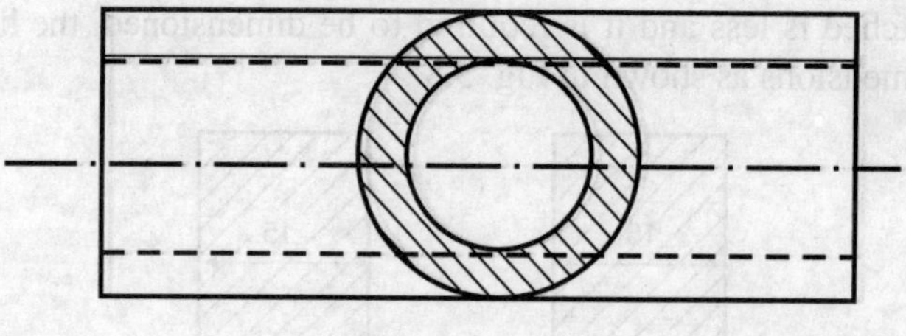

Fig. 3.9 (c) Revolved section of circular hollow cylinder

(ii) Offset section When the cutting plane does not pass through the main axis, it is offset by changing the direction and is made to pass through the required details.

The sectional view thus obtained is known as offset section as shown in Fig. 3.10.

In some cases, full in section and half in section do not fulfil the requirement for the details.

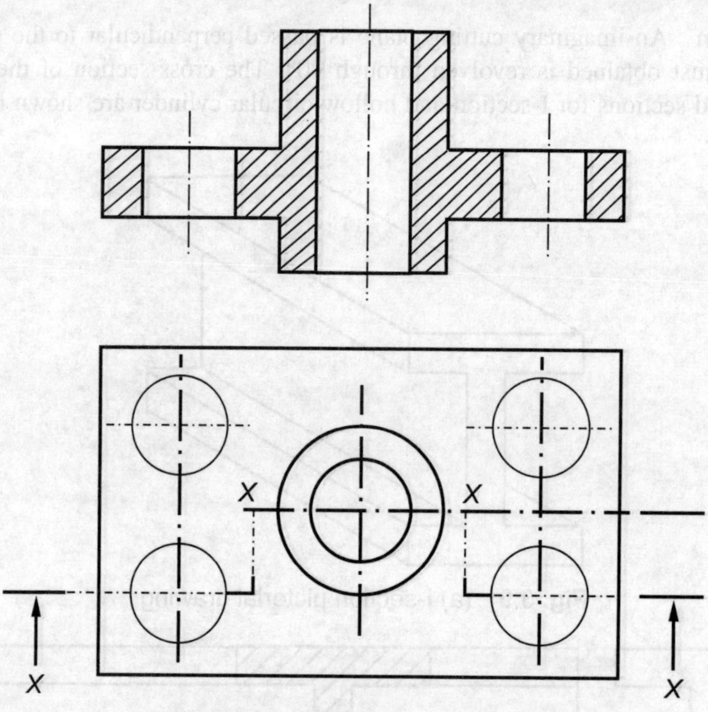

Fig. 3.10 Offset section at X–X

(iii) Broken section or partial section In some of the machine components, only a small hidden portion of the object is required to be shown; a full or half section is not feasible. In such cases, only a small detail of an object is to be exposed by cutting a small portion of the object.

Such a small sectional part is known as partial section, as shown in Fig. 3.11.

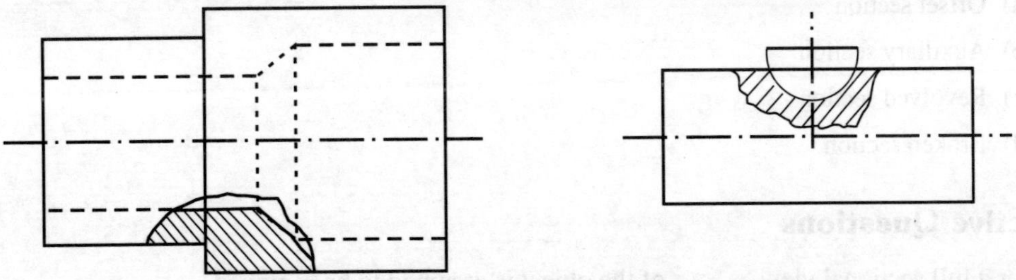

Fig. 3.11 Broken section or partial section

(iv) Auxiliary section It is obtained when the sectional plane is not parallel to either of the principal planes.

These sections are necessary to know the other details of the inclined portion of the components as shown in Fig. 3.12.

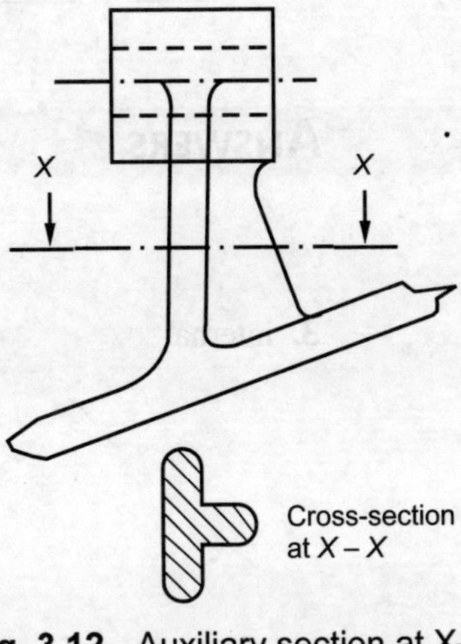

Fig. 3.12 Auxiliary section at X–X

EXERCISE

Review Questions

1. What is a section?
2. What do you mean by sectional view?
3. What do you mean by revolved section? Show by giving suitable figures.

4. What do you mean by the following terms? Explain with suitable diagrams.
   (a) Offset section
   (b) Auxiliary section
   (c) Revolved section
   (d) Broken section

Objective Questions

1. For a full sectional view, _____ of the object is assumed to be removed.
2. For a half sectional view, a _____ of the object is assumed to be removed.
3. The purpose of sectional view is to show the _____ shape of the object.
4. In sectional view, the part of the object between the cutting plane and _____ is to be removed.
5. Hatching lines are drawn at _____ to the axis of the section.
6. Space between two hatching lines varies from _____ to _____.

Answers

Objective Questions

1. half **2.** quarter **3.** internal **4.** observer **5.** 45°
6. 1, 3 mm

CHAPTER 4

Geometrical Constructions

4.1 INTRODUCTION

In engineering drawing, there are a number of geometrical constructions that are required to be made in the preparation of the actual drawing, such as constructional method for polygons in different positions for solving problem on solid projection.

4.2 TO BISECT A LINE *PQ* (FIG. 4.1)

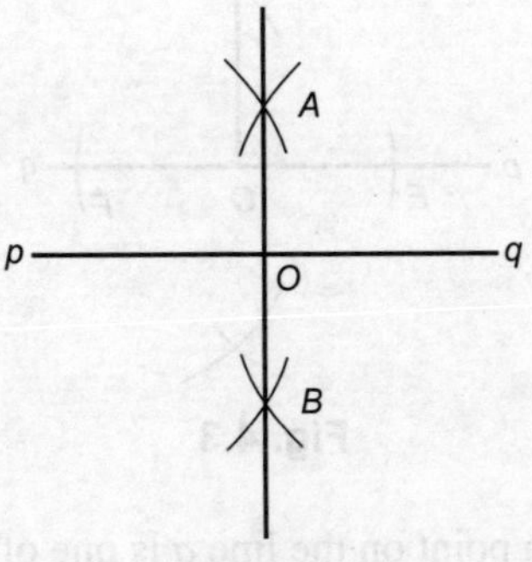

Fig. 4.1

(i) *pq* is a straight line.

(ii) With *p* and *q* as centre and radius greater than half of the length *pq*, draw an arc intersecting each other at A and B.

(iii) Join AB. This will bisect *pq* at the point O.

4.3 TO BISECT AN ARC *PQ* (FIG. 4.2)

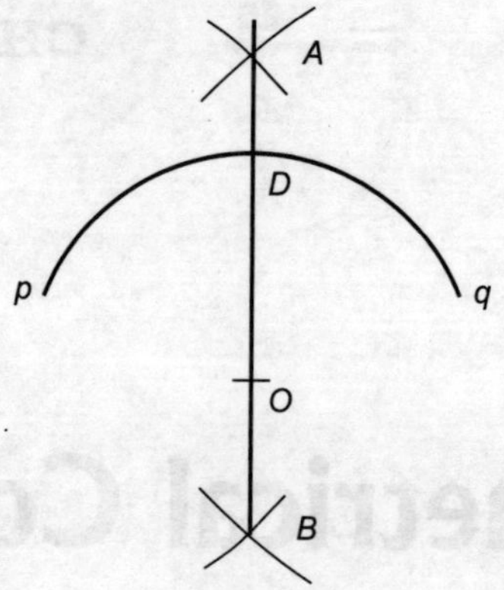

Fig. 4.2

(i) *pq* is a circular arc whose centre is at O.

(ii) With *p* and *q* as centres, draw arcs intersecting each other at A and B, respectively.

(iii) Join AB. This will bisect the arc at O.

(iv) Line AB cuts the arc at D.

4.4 TO DRAW A LINE PERPENDICULAR TO LINE *PQ* AT A POINT *O* (FIG. 4.3)

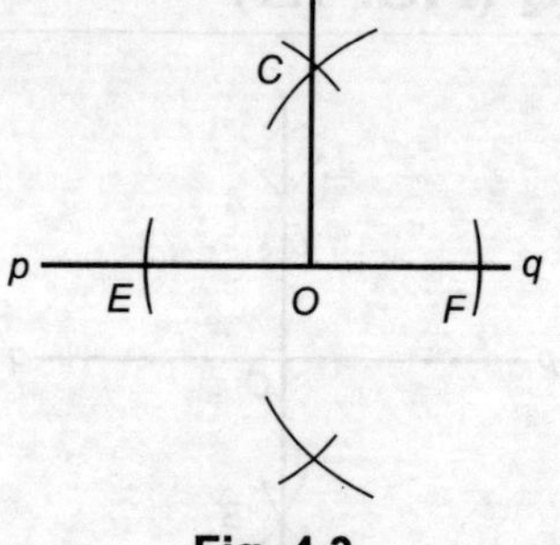

Fig. 4.3

(i) *pq* is a straight line and O, a point on the line *q* is one of the ends of the line.

(ii) With O as centre and any radius OE, draw two arcs to intersect *pq* at E and F.

(iii) With E and F as centres and radius greater than half EF, draw an arc to intersect at C.

(iv) Join CO, which is perpendicular to *pq*.

4.5 TO DRAW PERPENDICULAR TO A LINE *PQ* AT A POINT *O* ON IT WHEN *O* IS NEARER TO *Q* (FIG. 4.4)

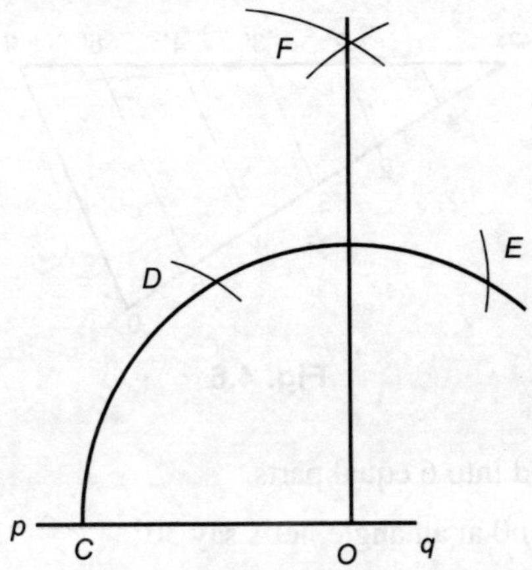

Fig. 4.4

(i) *pq* is a line and O is a point on it. O is nearer to *q*.

(ii) With O as centre and radius less than OP, draw an arc to intersect *pq* at C.

(iii) With the same radius equal to OC, draw an arc from C to D and from D to E.

(iv) With D and E as centres, draw an arc that intersects at F.

(v) Join OF, the required perpendicular to *pq*.

4.6 TO DRAW A PERPENDICULAR TO A LINE *PQ* THROUGH A POINT *O* WHICH IS NOT ON THE LINE (FIG. 4.5)

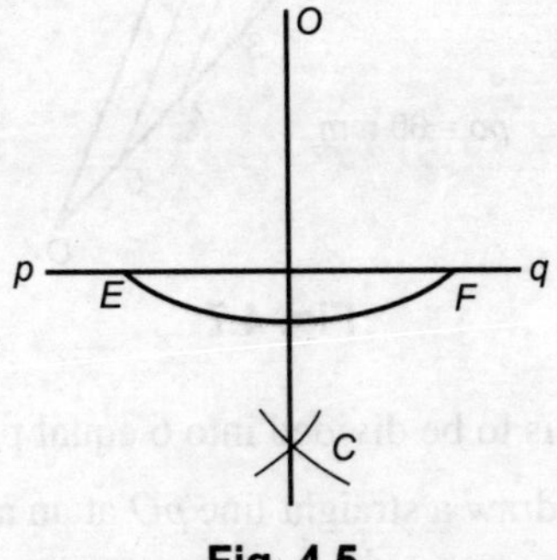

Fig. 4.5

(i) *pq* is a straight line and O is the point away from it.

(ii) With O as centre, draw an arc which cuts the line *pq* on E and F.

(iii) From centres E and F, draw arcs which intersect at C.

(iv) Join OC, the required perpendicular to *pq*.

4.7 TO DIVIDE A LINE *PQ* INTO EQUAL NUMBER OF PARTS (FIG. 4.6)

AR App

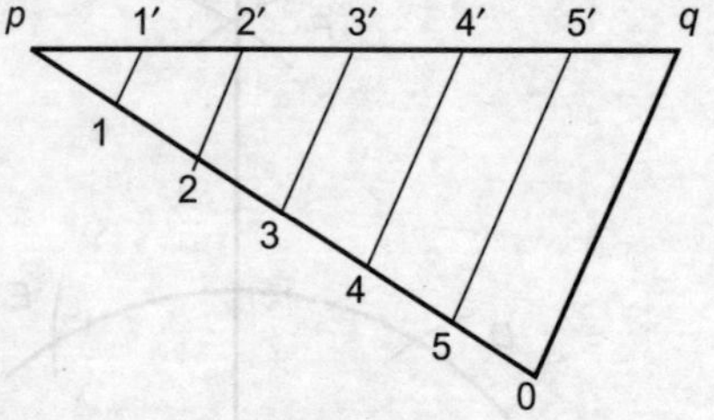

Fig. 4.6

(i) *pq* is a line to be divided into 6 equal parts.

(ii) Through *p*, draw a line *p*0 at an angle, let's say 30°

(iii) From *p* along *pO*, cut 6 equal parts of known convenient length (measurable distance) as *p*1, 12, 23, 34, 45, and 5*O*.

(iv) Join *qO*.

(v) Through 1, 2, 3, 4, and 5, draw a line parallel to 0*q* intersecting *pq* at 1′, 2′, 3′, 4′, 5′.

4.8 TO DIVIDE A SMALL LINE *PQ* (FIG. 4.7)

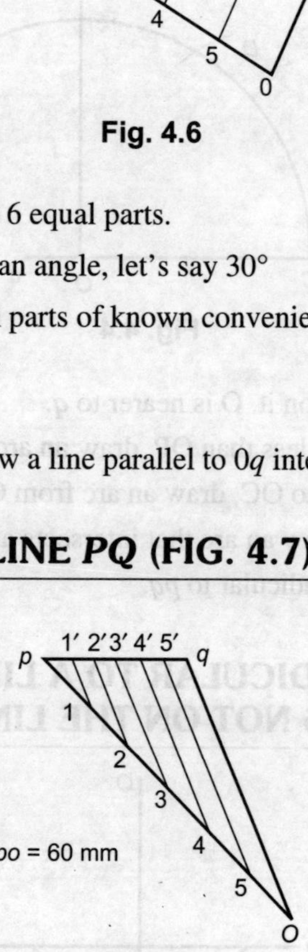

Fig. 4.7

(i) *pq* is a small length which is to be divided into 6 equal parts.

(ii) Through end *q* of the line, draw a straight line *pO* at an angle, say 45°.

(iii) From *p* along *pO*, cut 6 equal parts of known convenient length (measurable distance) as *p*1, 12, 23, 34, 45, and 5*O*

(iv) Joint *qO*.

(v) Through 1, 2, 3, 4, 5 draw a line parallel to *Oq* intersecting *pq* at 1′, 2′, 3′, 4′, 5′.

4.9 TO BISECT AN ANGLE [FIG. 4.8(A) & (B)]

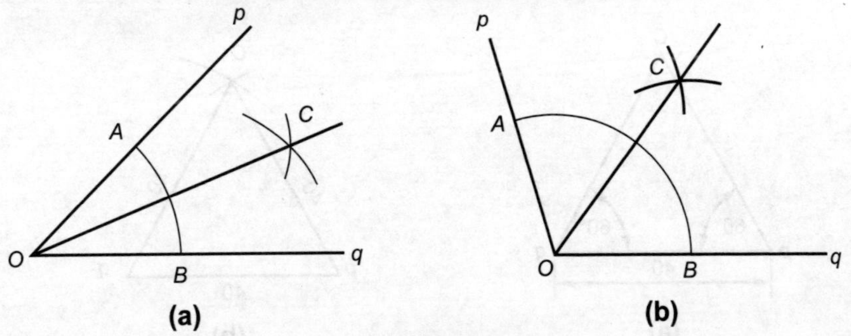

Fig. 4.8

(i) *poq* is an acute angle to be divided into equal angles.

(ii) With *O* as centre, draw an arc which cuts *Op* and *Oq* at A and B, respectively.

(iii) With centres at A and B, draw arcs with some convenient radii which intersect at C.

(iv) Join OC.

(v) OC is the bisector of ∠POq and ∠POC = ∠COq.

The same procedure can be applied with the obtuse angle given in Fig. 4.8(b).

4.10 TO DRAW AN ARC THROUGH THREE POINTS (FIG. 4.9)

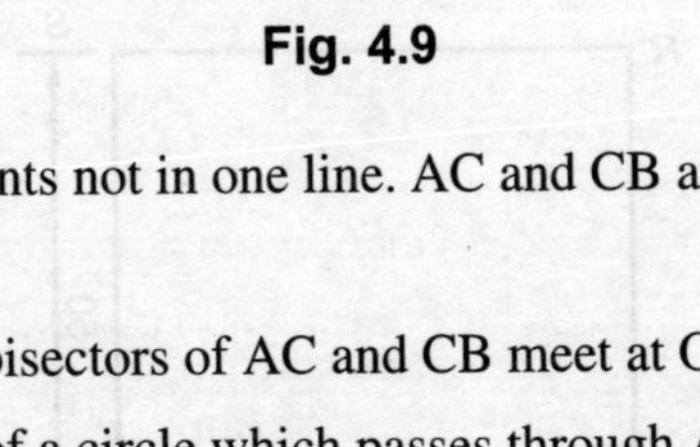

Fig. 4.9

(i) A, C, and B are three points not in one line. AC and CB are intersecting at point C.

(ii) Join AC and CB.

(iii) Divide AC and CB, the bisectors of AC and CB meet at O.

(iv) O is the required centre of a circle which passes through A, C, and B.

4.11 TO CONSTRUCT AN EQUILATERAL TRIANGLE OF SIDE 40 MM [FIG. 4.10(A) AND (B)]

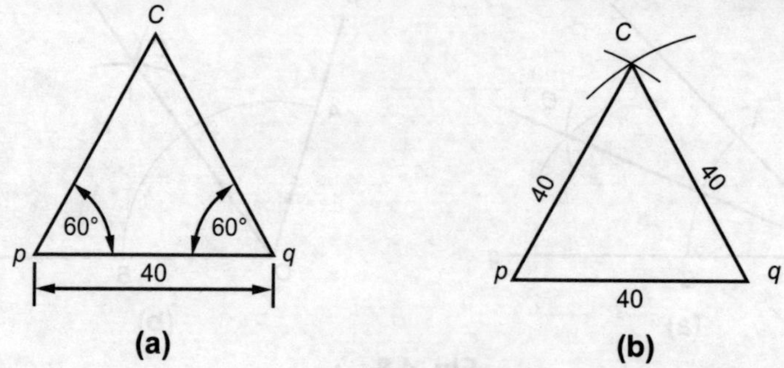

Fig. 4.10

(i) Equilateral triangle will have three equal sides and three equal angles, each of 60°.

Method I Fig. 4.10 (a)

(ii) With the help of T-square or mini drafter, draw a line *pq* = 40 mm.

(iii) With 30°–60° set square and T-square, draw a line through *p* making an angle of 60° with *pq*.

(iv) Similarly, through *q*, draw a line making the same angle 60°. They are intersecting at C.

(v) *pqc* is the required equilateral triangle.

Method II

(i) Draw a line *pq* = 40 mm.

(ii) With centres at *p* and *q*, an arc of radius equal to *pq* length is drawn. They are intersecting at C. *pqc* is the triangle.

4.12 TO CONSTRUCT A SQUARE OF LENGTH EQUAL TO 50 MM (FIG. 4.11)

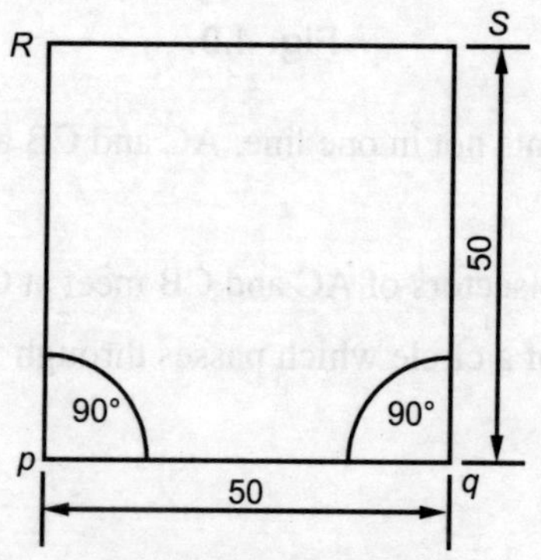

Fig. 4.11 Square

(i) Draw a line pq = 50 mm.

(ii) At p and q, draw a line perpendicular to pq. Draw an arc cutting at R and equal to 50 mm.

(iii) With centre at R and radius equal to pR, draw an arc intersecting at S.

(iv) $pqRs$ is the required square of each side equal to 50 mm.

4.13 TO CONSTRUCT A REGULAR PENTAGON OF EACH SIDE EQUAL TO 30 MM (FIG. 4.12)

Method I Figure 4.12 (a), (b), and (c).

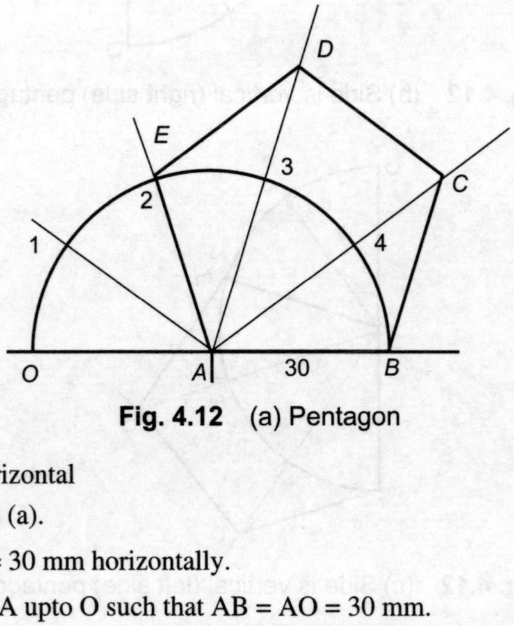

Fig. 4.12 (a) Pentagon

When one of its sides is horizontal

(i) Refer to Fig. 4.12 (a).

(ii) Draw a line AB = 30 mm horizontally.

(iii) Extend the line BA upto O such that AB = AO = 30 mm.

(iv) With A as centre and AB as radius, draw a semicircle.

(v) Divide the semicircle in 5 equal parts by trial and error (approximately) as 1, 2, 3, and 4.

(vi) Join A2, A3, and A4 and extend it.

(vii) Join A2 as one of its side.

(viii) With centre at 2 and radius equal to AB, draw an arc to cut the extension of A3 at D. Similarly, from D, cut it on A4 extension line at C.

Thus, *ABCDE* is the required pentagon 4.12(b) and (c).

When one of its side is vertical, the procedure for the construction remains the same as explained in Fig. 4.12(a).

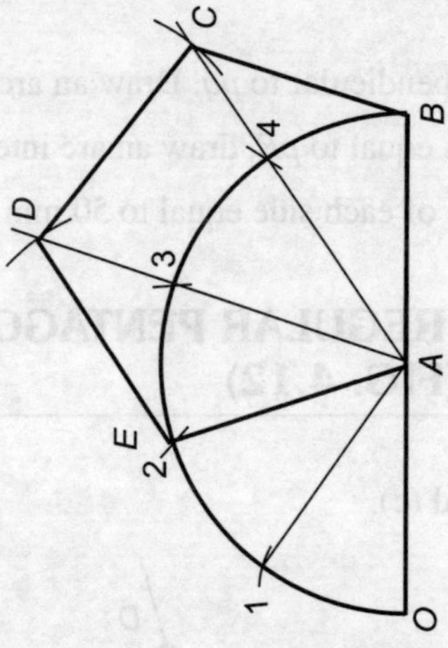

Fig. 4.12 (b) Side is vertical (right side) pentagon

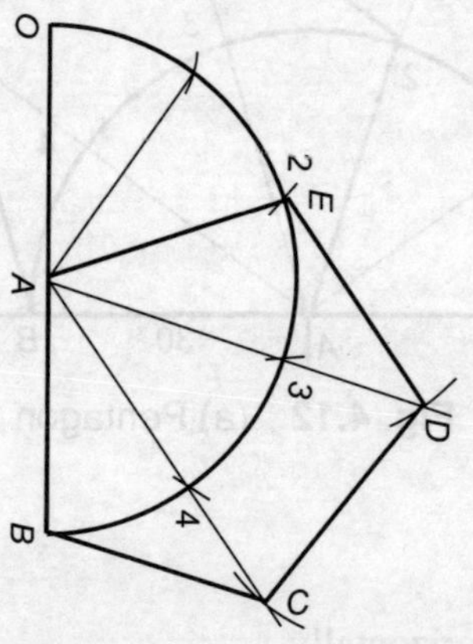

Fig. 4.12 (c) Side is vertical (left side) pentagon

Method II Fig. 4.12(d)

(i) Draw AB = 30 mm as one of the sides of the pentagon.

(ii) Extend BA upto O.

(iii) With A as centre and BA as radius, draw a semicircle.

(iv) Divide the semicircle in 5 equal parts as 1, 2, 3, and 4 starting from O.

(v) Join A2, E is also at 2. Now AB = AE.

(vi) Divide AB and AE. They intersect at *p*.

(vii) With *p* as centre, draw a circle.

(viii) With A as centre and AB as radius, cut the circle at E and from E to D on the extension line of A3.

(ix) Again from D, cut C on the extension of A4.

(x) Join BC, ED, and DC. They form the pentagon ABCDE, the required pentagon.

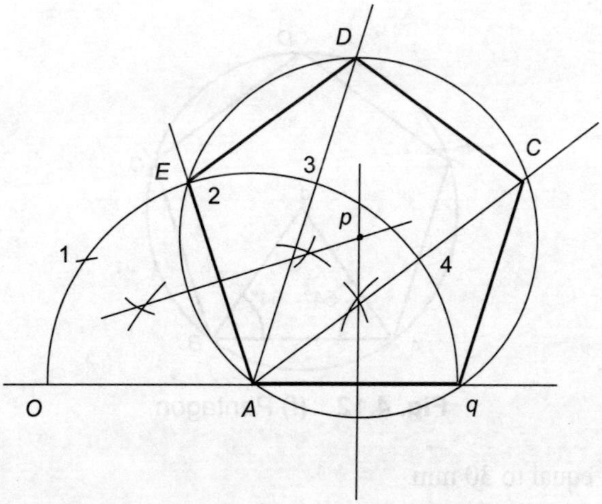

Fig. 4.12 (d) Pentagon

Method III Fig. 4.12(e)

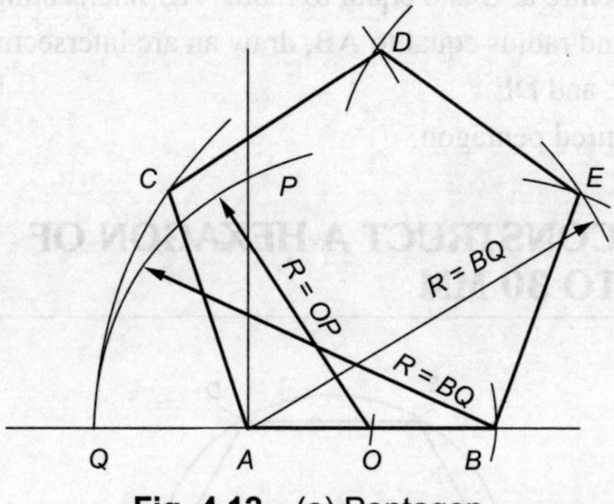

Fig. 4.12 (e) Pentagon

(i) Draw a line AB = 30 mm.

(ii) Bisect AB at O.

(iii) Draw a line AP perpendicular and equal to AB at A (AB = AP).

(iv) With centre O and radius OP, draw an arc intersecting AB produced at Q.

(v) BQ is the diagonal of pentagon.

(vi) With B as centre and BQ as radius, draw an arc. With A as centre and AB as radius, intersect this arc at C.

(vii) With A as centre and BQ as radius, draw an arc. With B as centre and AB as radius, intersect this arc at E.

(viii) With C and E as centre and radius AB, draw an arc to get point D.

(ix) Join CD and DE. This forms ABCDE, the required pentagon.

Method IV

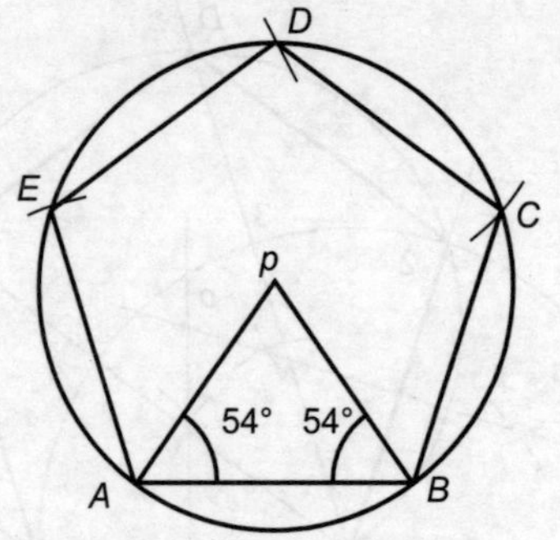

Fig. 4.12 (f) Pentagon

(i) Draw a line AB equal to 30 mm.
(ii) Draw an angle of 54° at A and B, meeting them at *p*.
(iii) With *p* as centre and radius equal to AP and BP, draw a circle.
(iv) Draw an arc intersecting the circle at C and radius equal to AB.
(v) Draw an arc with centre at C and equal to radius AB intersecting at D.
(vi) From D as centre and radius equal to AB, draw an arc intersecting the circle at E.
(vii) Draw AB, BC, CD, and DE.
(viii) ABCDE is the required pentagon.

4.14 METHOD TO CONSTRUCT A HEXAGON OF SIDE EQUAL TO 30 MM

AR App

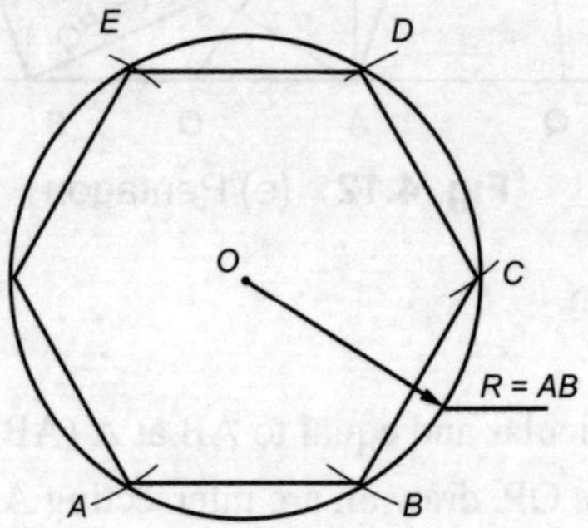

Fig. 4.13 (a) Hexagon

(i) Draw a circle with the length of the side AB = 30 mm as radius.
(ii) Intersect the circle with radius AB at C, D, E, and F.
(iii) Join all the intersection points A, B, C, D, E, and F.
(iv) ABCDE is the required hexagon.

4.13 (b)

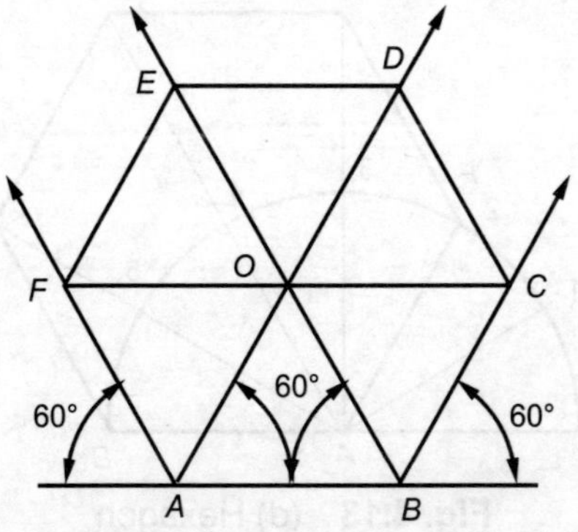

Fig. 4.13 (b) Hexagon

(i) Draw a line AB = 30 m horizontally.

(ii) At A, draw AF and AD at an angle of 60° using 30°-60° set square and T-square.

(iii) At B, draw BE and BC at an angle of 60° using set square angle of 60° using set square.

(iv) AD and BE intersect each other at O.

(v) Draw FC parallel to AB and it will pass through O.

(vi) At F and C draw line FE and CD at an angle of 60°.

(vii) Draw ED parallel to AB.

(viii) ABCDEF is the hexagon.

4.13(c)

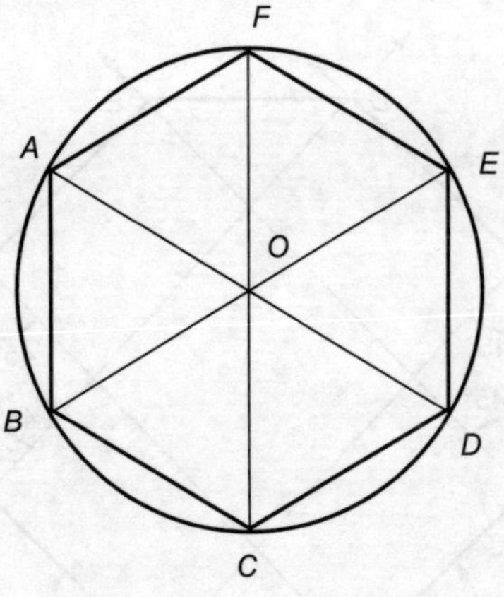

Fig. 4.13 (c) Hexagon

(i) Same as in Fig. 4.13. Only difference is one side AB is kept vertical instead of keeping it horizontal. The procedure remains the same as mentioned in Fig. 4.13.

4.13(d)

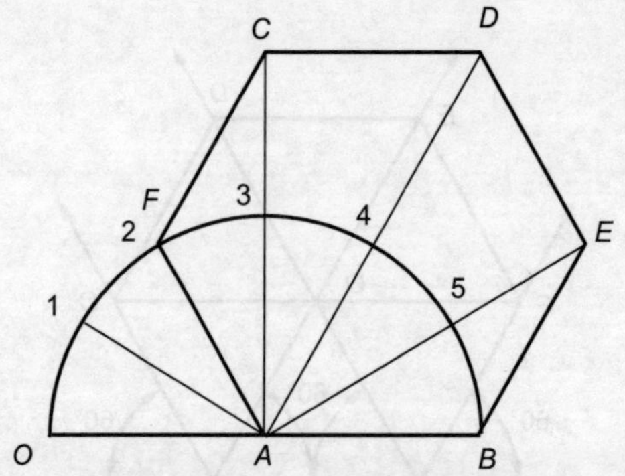

Fig. 4.13 (d) Hexagon

(i) Draw a line AB = 30 mm horizontally.

(ii) Extend the line BA upto O such that AB = AO = 30 mm.

(iii) With A as centre and AB as radius, draw a semicircle.

(iv) Divide the semicircle into 6 equal parts as 1, 2, 3, 4, and 5.

(v) Join A2, as one of its side.

(vi) With centre at 2 and radius equal to AB, draw an arc to cut the extension of A3 at C. Similarly, from C, cut it on the extension of A4 at D.

(vii) Join A5 and extend it. With B as centre and radius equal to AB, cut at E.

(viii) ABEDCF is the hexagon.

4.15 TO CONSTRUCT AN OCTAGON OF EACH SIDE EQUAL TO 30 MM

AR App

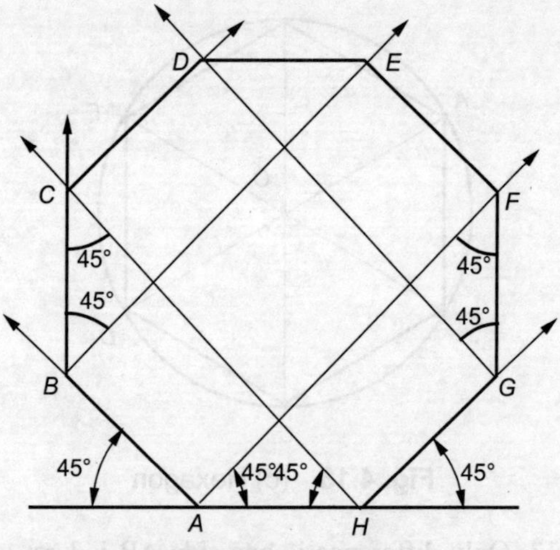

Fig. 4.14 Octagon

(i) Draw a line AH = 30 mm.

(ii) Draw AB and HC at 45° angle at A and H. AB = AH.

(iii) Draw AF and HG at 45° angle at A and H. AH = HG.

(iv) The line BC and GF drawn perpendicular to AH meet BC at C and AF at F.

(v) From G, draw a line GD parallel to AB and from B draw a line BF parallel to HG.

(vi) Join AB, BC, CD, DE, HG, GF, and FE.

(viii) ABCDEFGH is the required octagon.

4.16 TO INSCRIBE A REGULAR OCTAGON IN A SQUARE OF SIDE 80 MM

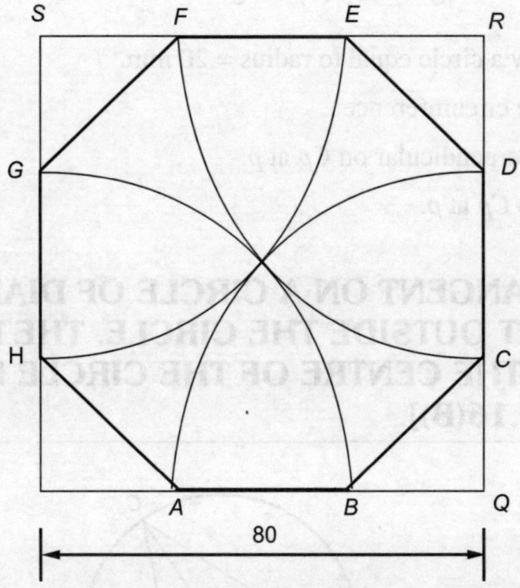

Fig. 4.15 Octagon

(i) Draw a square PQRS with each side equal to 80 mm.

(ii) Join the diagonal PR and QS, intersecting at O.

(iii) With P, Q, R, and S as centres and radius PO, draw arc t intersect the side of the square at A, B, C, D, E, F, G, and H.

(iv) Join ABCDEFGHA, the regular octagon.

4.17 TO DRAW A TANGENT ON A CIRCLE OF DIAMETER OF 40 MM AT ANY POINT ON IT (FIG. 4.16)

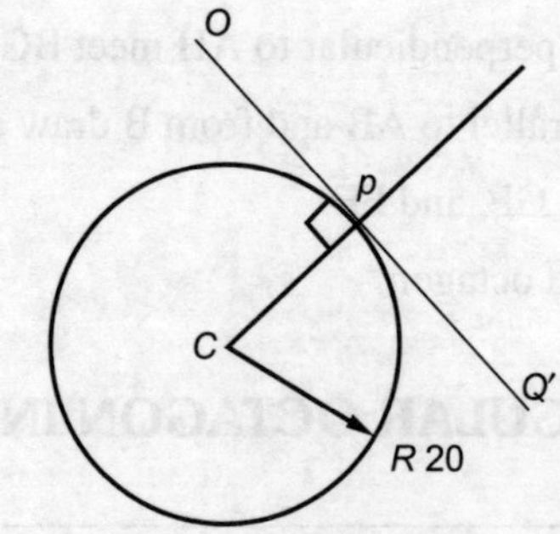

Fig. 4.16 (a) Tangent on a circle

(i) With centre C, draw a circle equal to radius = 20 mm.

(ii) *p* is the point on the circumference.

(iii) Join *Cp* and draw perpendicular on *Cp* at *p*.

(iv) 00′ is the tangent to *Cp* at *p*.

4.18 TO DRAW A TANGENT ON A CIRCLE OF DIAMETER 40 MM FROM A POINT OUTSIDE THE CIRCLE. THE DISTANCE OF POINT FROM THE CENTRE OF THE CIRCLE IS EQUAL TO 50 MM [FIG. 4.16(B)].

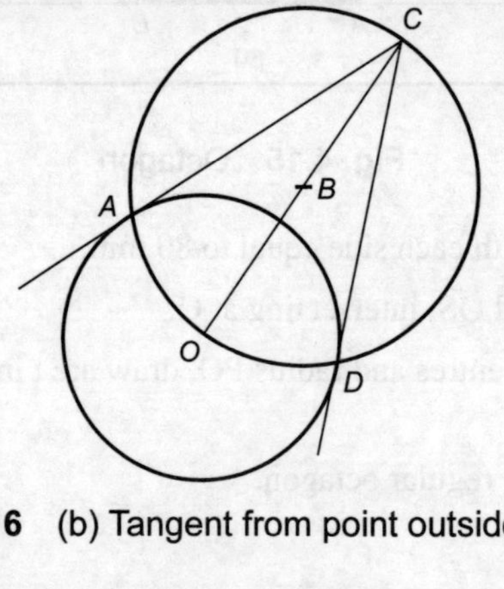

Fig. 4.16 (b) Tangent from point outside circle

(i) With centre at O, draw a circle of radius = 20 mm.

(ii) Locate point C at a distance of 50 mm from the centre O of the circle drawn.

(iii) Join OC and locate the middle point of this at B.

(iv) With centre B and radius equal to BO, draw a circle to intersect the given circle at A and D.

(v) Join C to A and C to D and extend them.

(vi) The line CA and CD are the two tangents.

4.19 TO INSCRIBE A CIRCLE IN A GIVEN TRIANGLE (FIG. 4.17)

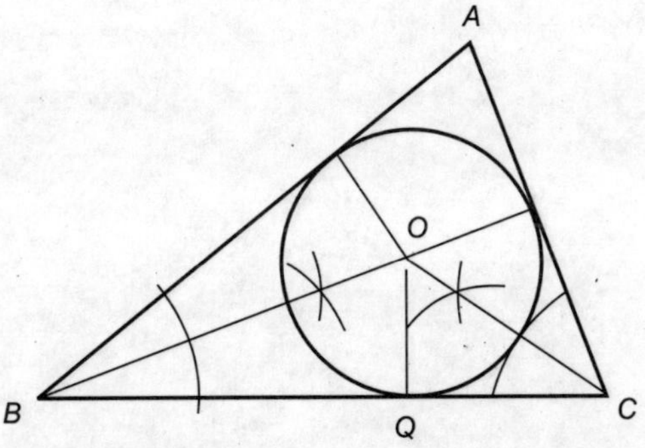

Fig. 4.17 Circle inside a triangle

(i) ABC is a triangle given.

(ii) Bisect angles ABC and BCA. The bisector intersecting at point O.

(iii) Draw a perpendicular from O on BC, meeting at Q.

(iv) With centre at O and radius OQ, draw the required circle.

4.20 TO INSCRIBE A CIRCLE IN A HEXAGONAL POLYGON (FIG. 4.18)

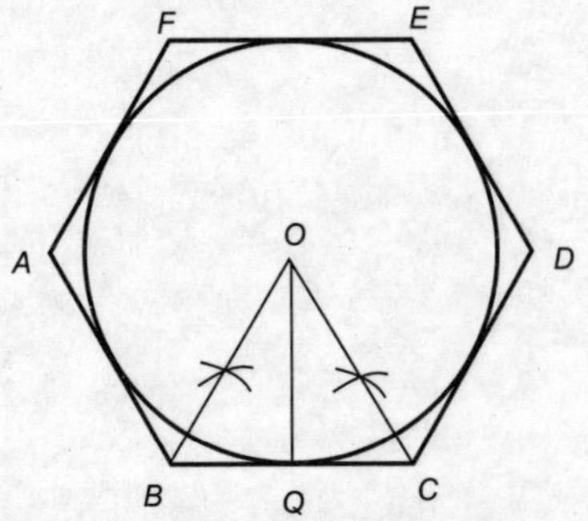

Fig. 4.18 Circle inside a hexagon

(i) ABCDEF is a hexagon.

(ii) Bisect any two angles, the bisector meet at O.

(iii) From O, draw perpendicular on BC at Q.

(iv) With centre at O and radius equal to OQ, draw the required circle which touches all the sides of the hexagon.

5

CHAPTER

Conic Sections/Geometrical Curves

5.1 INTRODUCTION

In engineering applications, a variety of curves are used. It is sometimes preferred that designers provide profiles in their structures, and, as such, it is important for the designers to study various curves and their uses.

A variety of curves such as conic section (circle, ellipse, parabola, hyperbola), cycloid spirals, involute, and other forms of curves are in use. The knowledge of these curves is important for the students so that these curves can be drawn correctly. This chapter deals with the geometrical construction of conic section and a few special curves.

5.2 DEFINITION OF A CONE

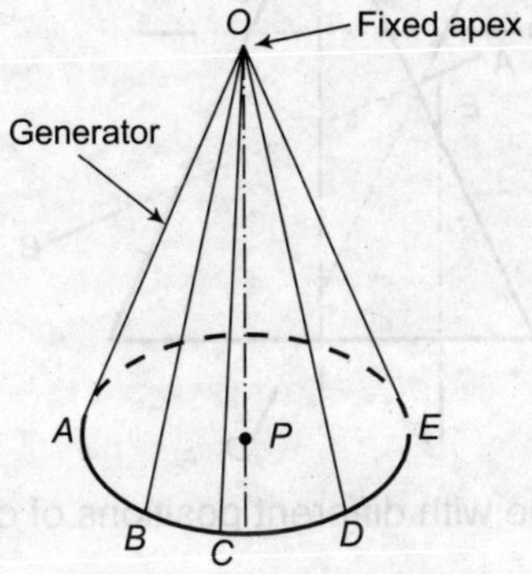

Fig. 5.1 Generated cone

Let OA be a straight line which moves in such a manner that the end 'A' always lies along the circumference of a base circle and 'O' remains fixed at a point on a line to the base circle at its centre. This is known as *right circular cone*. A line perpendicular to the base circle is called *axis of the cone*; OA, OB, OC, and OD are called *generators*. If the axis OP of the cone is perpendicular to the base, it is called right circular cone. In fact, a surface generated by the line is called *cone* as shown in Fig. 5.1.

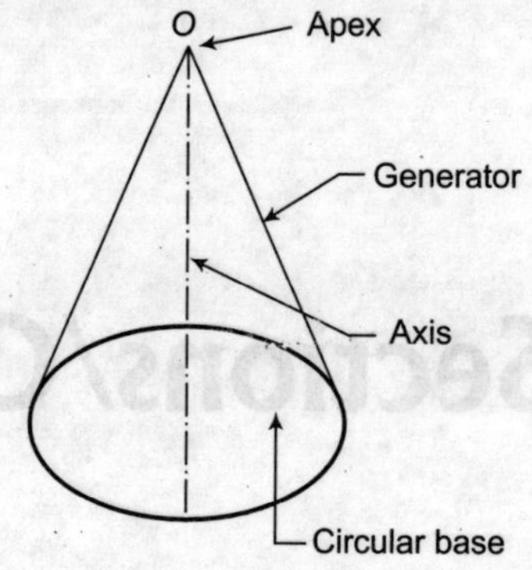

Fig. 5.2 Cone showing important terms

A 'right circular cone' has its axis perpendicular to its base. Figure 5.2 shows a right circular cone, its axis, apex, generator, and circular base. Top point, O, is called apex. The line joining the apex and the centre of the base circle is known as *axis*. The line joining the apex and the circumference of the base circle is known as *generator*.

5.3 CONIC SECTIONS

Conic sections are the sections of a right circular cone obtained by cutting different sectional planes. Depending on the position of the sectional plane with respect to the axis of the cone, it is called 'conic section'.

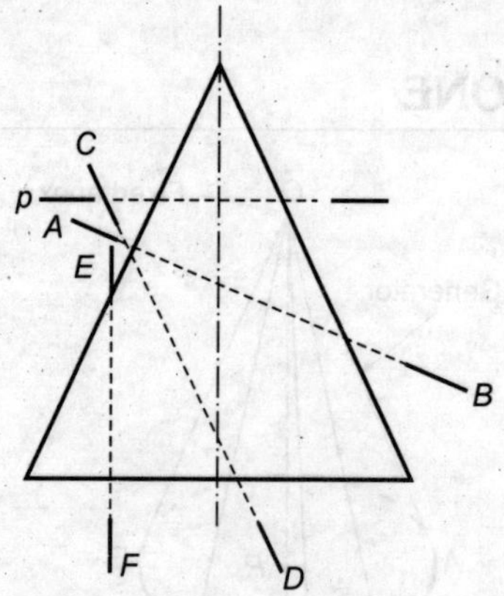

Fig. 5.3 Cone with different positions of cutting plane

Circle, ellipse, parabola, and hyperbola are called conic sections as they all are obtained by cutting planes in different positions in a right circular cone. The positions of the cutting plane are shown in Fig. 5.3.

pq: is the cutting plane perpendicular to the axis; it gives a circle.

AB: is inclined to the axis; it gives an ellipse.

CD: is the cutting plane parallel to end generator; it gives a parabola.

EF: is the cutting plane parallel to the axis of the cone; it gives a hyperbola

pq, AB, CD, and EF are the cutting planes.

Figure 5.3 shows how a right circular cone is cut in different cutting planes, in different positions. A curve is obtained and the projection of this cut curve is the true shape. The curve is known as conic section and could be circle, ellipse, parabola, and hyperbola.

5.4 CIRCLE

A circle is obtained by cutting a right circular cone by a cutting plane perpendicular to the axis and parallel to the base circle as shown in Fig. 5.4.

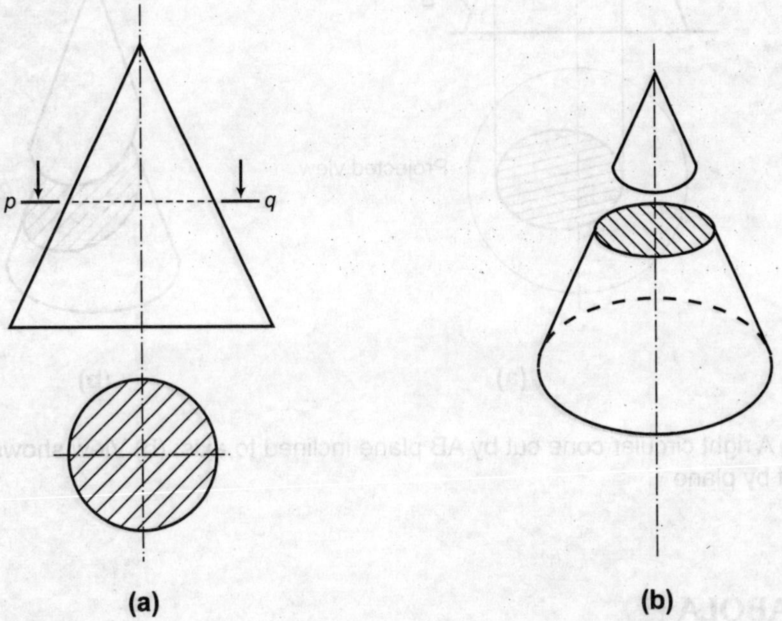

Fig. 5.4 (a) Cutting plane *pq* gives a circle; (b) View shows the top portion and bottom portion

5.5 ELLIPSE

An ellipse is obtained by cutting a right circular cone by a plane AB inclined to the axis and the base circle. The plane cuts all the generators as shown in Fig. 5.5. Mathematically, a cone can be defined as a straight line called generator passing through a fixed point called apex or vertex and makes a constant angle (semi-vertical angle) with the axis through the fixed point, generating a surface which is called right circular cone.

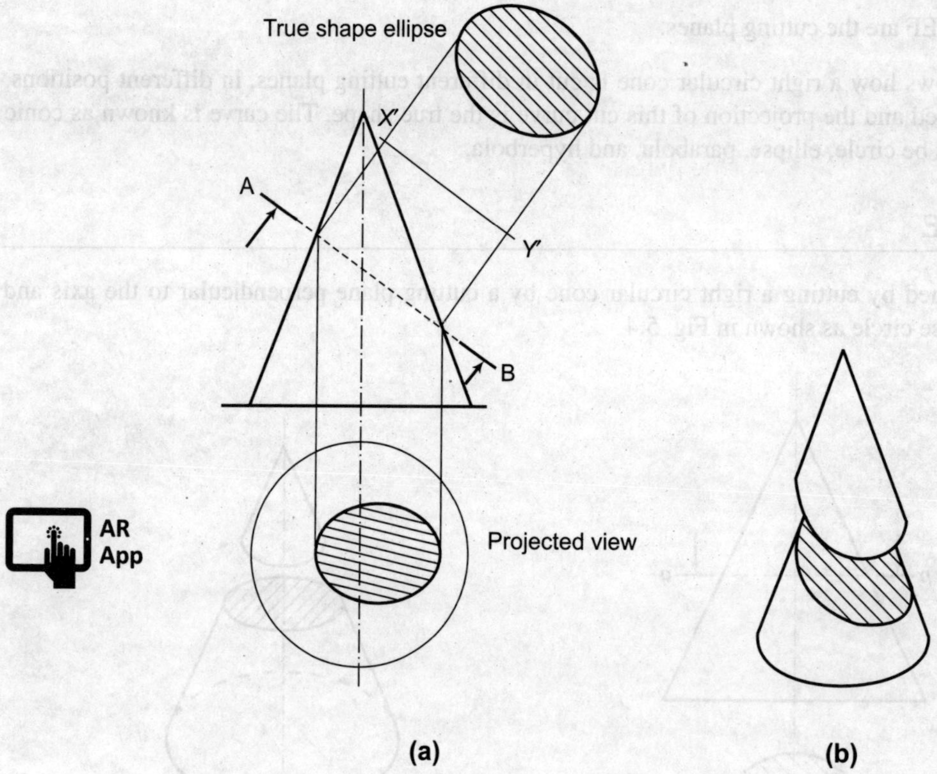

Fig. 5.5 (a) A right circular cone cut by AB plane inclined to axis; (b) View shows the top portion cut by plane

5.6 PARABOLA

Parabola is obtained by cutting a plane parallel to one of the generators of a right circular cone. A cone is cut by a plane CD parallel to its generator, as shown in Fig. 5.6.

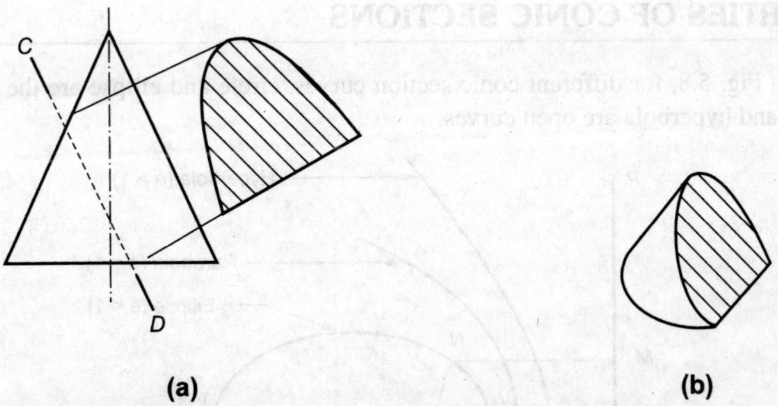

Fig. 5.6 (a) Cone is cut by CD plane parallel to generator cut is a parabola; (b) View shows the top portion removed

5.7 Hyperbola (Rectangular)

When a double cone is cut by a cutting plane 'EF' parallel to the axis on one side of the axis, the section is called *hyperbola*.

As the plane cuts two cones, two curves are obtained in opposite directions as shown in Fig. 5.7.

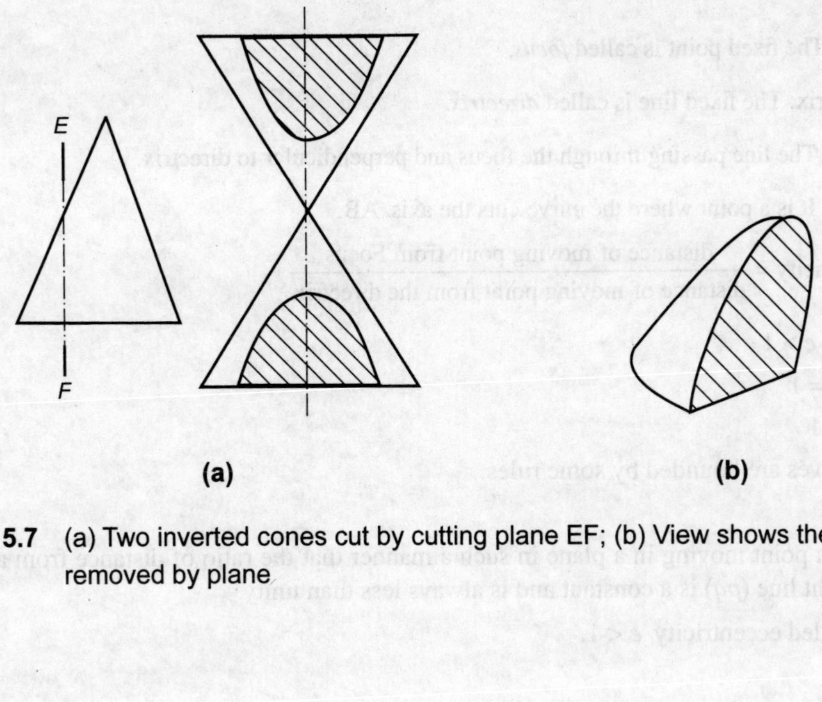

Fig. 5.7 (a) Two inverted cones cut by cutting plane EF; (b) View shows the portion removed by plane

5.8 PROPERTIES OF CONIC SECTIONS

As it is clear from Fig. 5.8, for different conic section curves, circle and ellipse are the closed curves whereas parabola and hyperbola are open curves.

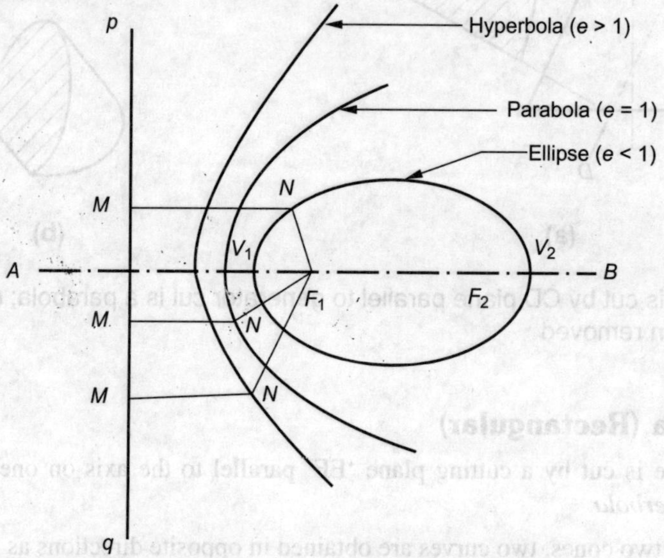

Fig. 5.8 Ellipse, parabola, and hyperbola

F = Focus: The fixed point is called *focus.*

pq = Directrix: The fixed line is called *directrix.*

AB = Axis: The line passing through the focus and perpendicular to directrix.

V = Vertex: It is a point where the curve cuts the axis, AB.

$$e = \text{Eccentricity} = \frac{\text{distance of moving point from Focus}}{\text{distance of moving point from the directrix}}$$

For Hyperbola, $e > 1$

Parabola, $e = 1$

Ellipse, $e < 1$

Conic section curves are bounded by some rules.

Ellipse

It is the locus of a point moving in a plane in such a manner that the ratio of distance from a point (F) to the fixed straight line (*pq*) is a constant and is always less than unity.

The ratio is called eccentricity, $e < 1$.

Parabola

It is the locus of a point moving in a plane in such a way that the ratio of the distance from a fixed point (F) to the fixed straight line (*pq*) is equal to unity.

The ratio is called eccentricity, $e = 1$.

Hyperbola

It is the locus of a point moving in a plane in such a way that the ratio of the distance from a fixed point (F) to the fixed straight line (*pq*) is a constant and is always greater than unity.

The ratio is called eccentricity, $e > 1$.

5.8.1 Construction of Ellipse (e < 1)

(a) Rectangular method/oblong method (Fig. 5.9)

PROBLEM 5.1

Consider a rectangular field of length 100 m and width 50 m. Inscribe an elliptical tile floor in it. A suitable scale may be chosen to accommodate on drawing sheets (Fig. 5.9).

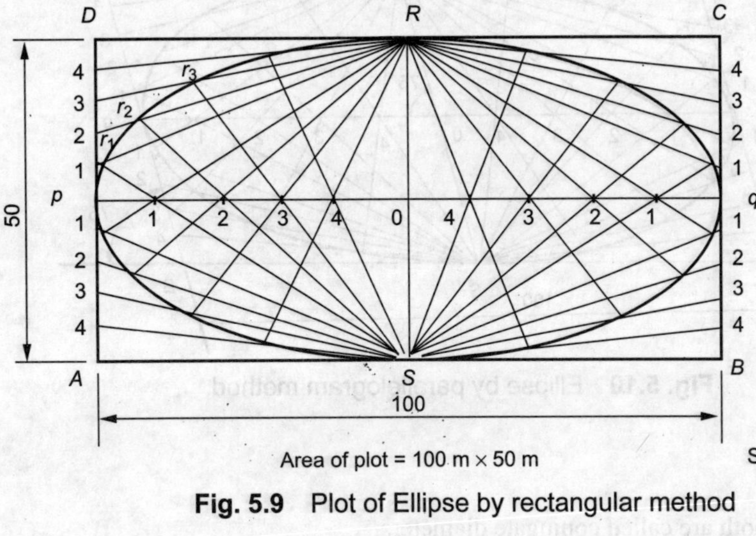

Fig. 5.9 Plot of Ellipse by rectangular method

Solution:

(i) Draw major axis pq = 100 m and minor axis RS = 50 m bisecting each other at O at 90° to each other on a suitable scale (1 cm = 10 cm).

(ii) Construct a rectangle ABCD as shown in Fig. 5.9.

AB = CD and AD = BC

(iii) Divide AP and Bq into 5 equal parts and numbered as 1, 2, 3, 4.

(iv) Divide p0 also into 5 equal parts.

(v) Join 1, 2, 3, and 4 with R as shown in the figure

(vi) Join 1, 2, 3, and 4 with S as shown in the figure.

Meeting them at r_1, r_2, r_3, and so on.

(vii) Join all the points and draw an ellipse of quarter portion.

Similarly, other parts can also be drawn to get a complete ellipse.

(b) Parallelogram method

PROBLEM 5.2

Construct an ellipse to be inscribed in a parallelogram of dimension 100 m × 50 m by choosing a suitable scale (1 m = 10 m).

The angle between conjugate diameter is 75°.

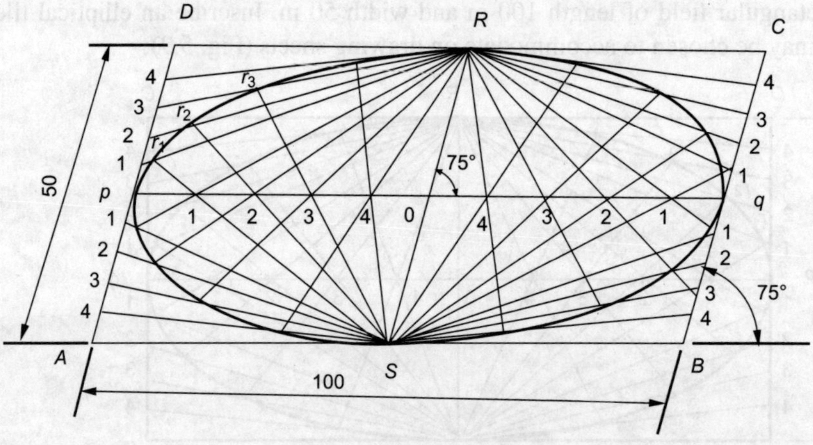

Fig. 5.10 Ellipse by parallelogram method

Solution:

In Fig. 5.10, *pq* and *RS* both are called conjugate diameters.

(i) Draw a parallelogram with conjugate diameter *pq* = 100 m and RS = 50 m on scale. Taking angle of 75° between two conjugate diameters.

(ii) Complete parallelogram as ABCD.

(iii) The process of construction should be followed as in Problem 5.1 (Fig. 5.9).

PROBLEM 5.3

Find the major and minor and the centre of a given ellipse shown in Fig. 5.11.

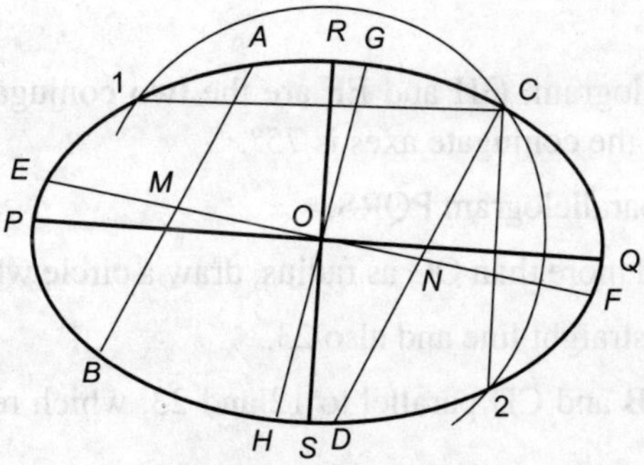

Fig. 5.11 Ellipse

Solution:

(i) EF and GH are the two conjugate axes drawn.

(ii) Draw two parallel chords AB and CD.

(iii) Locate the middle point as M and N.

(iv) Join MN and extend it to meet ellipse at E and F. The middle point of EF is the centre.

(v) With O as a centre and any suitable radius, draw an arc which cuts the ellipse at three points 1, C, and 2.

(vi) Join 1C and C2.

(vii) From centre O, draw two lines PQ and RS parallel to 1C and C2, respectively.

PQ and RS measure the major and minor axes.

PROBLEM 5.4

Find the major and minor axes of an ellipse when conjugate axes are given (Fig. 5.12).

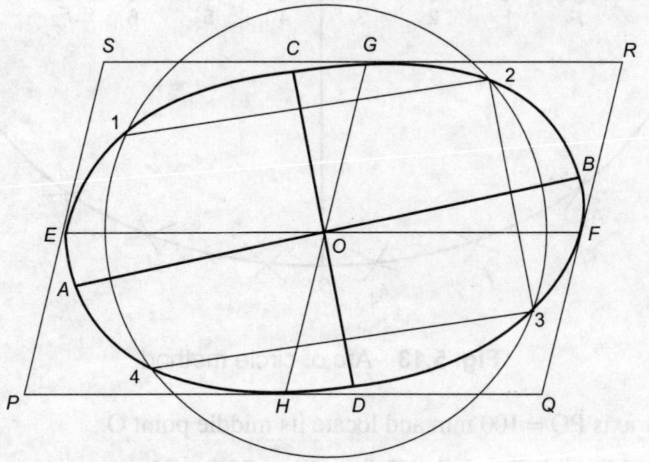

Fig. 5.12 Ellipse

Solution:

(i) PQRS is the parallelogram. GH and EF are the two conjugate diameters intersecting at O. Angle between both the conjugate axes is 75°.

(ii) Ellipse is drawn in parallelogram PQRS.

(iii) With O as centre and more than OG as radius, draw a circle which cuts the ellipse at 1, 2, 3, 4.

(iv) Join 12 and 43 by a straight line and also 23.

(v) Through O, draw AB and CD parallel to 12 and 23, which represent major and minor axes, respectively.

5.8.2 Arc of Circle Method

PROBLEM 5.5

The major axis of an ellipse is 100 mm and the distance between its foci is 70 mm. Draw an ellipse.

Solution:

See Fig. 5.13.

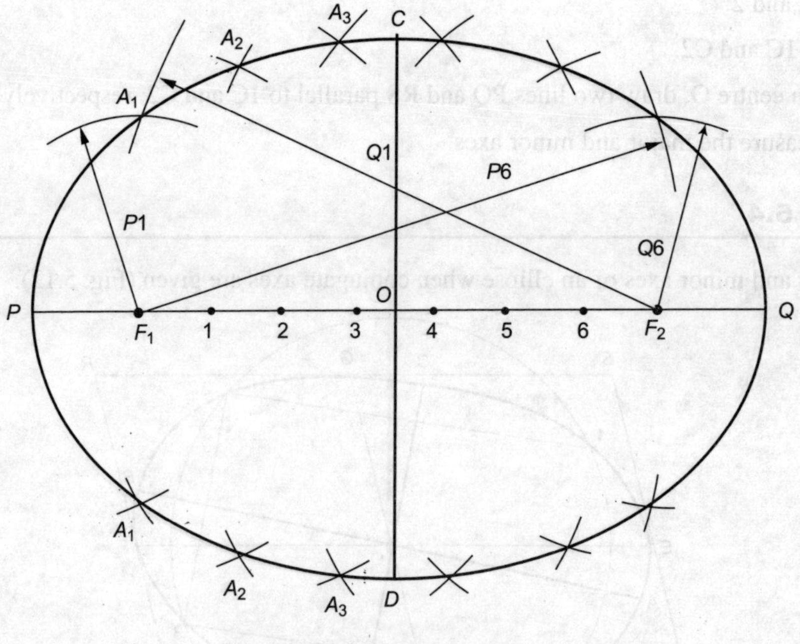

Fig. 5.13 Arc of circle method

(i) Draw major axis PQ = 100 mm and locate its middle point O.

(ii) Locate F_1 and F_2 on PQ such that $F_1O = OF_2 = 70/2 = 35$ mm.

(iii) Divide F_1F_2 into 7 equal parts, each part of 10 mm.

(iv) Mark the point as 1, 2, 3, … in between F_1 and F_2.

(v) With F as centre and radius = P – 1, draw arcs on both the sides of PQ.

Again, with F_2 as centre and radius = Q_1, draw arcs on both the sides. Both are cutting at A_1

(P 1 + Q – 1 = AB = major axis)

(vi) With F_1 as centre and radius = P–2, draw an arc. Again, with F_2 as centre and radius = Q – 2, draw an arc, both arcs cutting A_2.

(vii) This can be repeated with the other points 3, 4, 5, and 6 with radius as (P – 3, Q – 3), (P – 4, Q – 4), and so on.

(viii) A_1, A_2, A_3, … are the points on a curve.

Join all the points with smooth curve.

PROBLEM 5.6

Draw an ellipse, when the minor axis is 50 mm and distance between the foci is 60 mm (Fig. 5.14).

Solution:

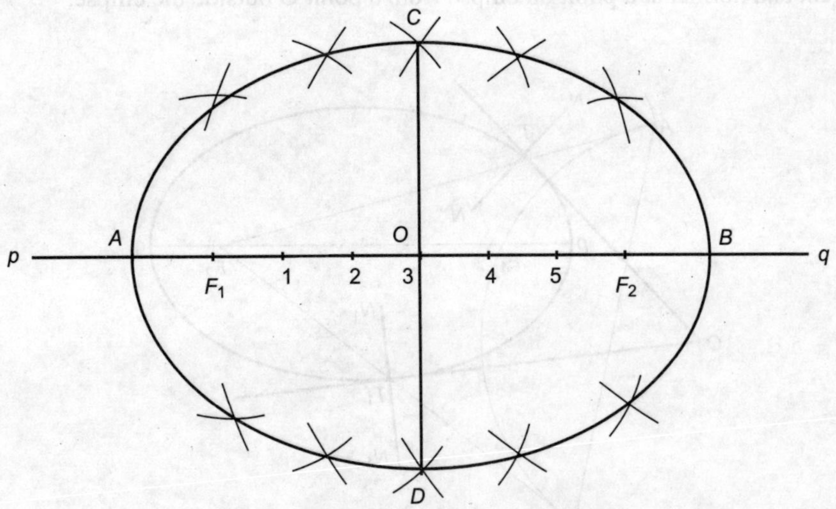

Fig. 5.14 Intersecting arc method

See Fig 5.14.

(i) Draw a line pq and CD perpendicular to each other at O.

CD = minor axis = 60 mm (given)

OC = OD = 60/2 = 30 mm

$F_1F_2 = 60$ mm (given)

Find major axis to be known.

$CF_1 = CF_2 = \frac{1}{2}AB$ (AB = Major axis)

$AB = CF_1 + CF_2$

$$CF_1 = CF_2 = \sqrt{F_1O^2 + OC^2} = \sqrt{30^2 + 30^2} = \sqrt{1800} = 42.42$$

Major axis = AB = $2CF_1 = 2 \times 42.42 = 84.84$ mm.

(ii) Major axis, AB = 84.84 mm

Minor axis, CD = 50 mm

(iii) Any suitable method like rectangular method.

Concentric circle method and intersecting are methods that can be used to find the ellipse.

(iv) Using the method as explained in Problem 5.5 (Fig. 5.13), it can be drawn.

PROBLEM 5.7

Draw the tangent and normal at a point on ellipse from a point O outside the ellipse.

Solution:

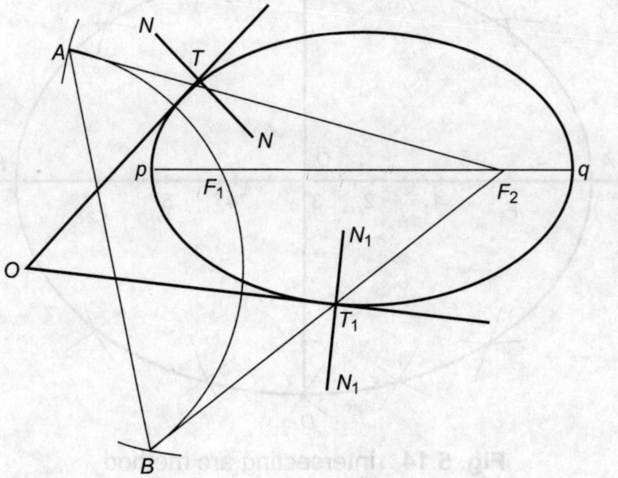

Fig. 5.15 Tangent and normal on an ellipse

See Fig. 5.15.

(i) With O as centre and radius = OF_1, draw an arc. F_1 and F_2 are the foci of the ellipse.

(ii) With F_1 as a centre and radius equal to major axis, draw an arc cutting the previous arc at A and B.

(iii) Join AF_2 and BF_2 which cuts the ellipse at T and T_1, respectively.

(iv) Join OT and OT_1 to represent the required tangent. Draw N–N and N_1–N_1 perpendicular to OT and OT_1 at T and T_1, respectively. They are the required normal.

PROBLEM 5.8

Draw the tangent and normal at any point S on an ellipse. Major axis of 100 and minor axis of 70 mm.

Solution:

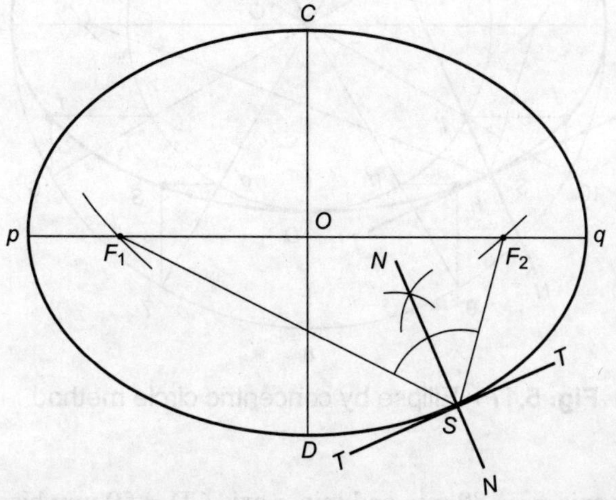

Fig. 5.16 Tangent and normal at any point on ellipse

(i) *pq* is the major axis = 100 mm and CD is the minor axis = 70 mm.

Draw the major axis and minor axis, bisecting each other at O.

(ii) Obtain F_1 and F_2 by cutting the arc on major axis *pq* with C as the centre and radius = Op.

(iii) Join F_1S and F_2S.

(iv) Bisecting angle F_1SF_2, NN is the required normal at a point S on the ellipse.

(v) Draw T–T perpendicular to NN at S. TT is the tangent to point S.

5.8.3 Concentric Circle Method

PROBLEM 5.9

Draw an ellipse having major axis = 80 mm and minor axis = 50 mm. Draw tangent and normal at a point S on it.

Solution:

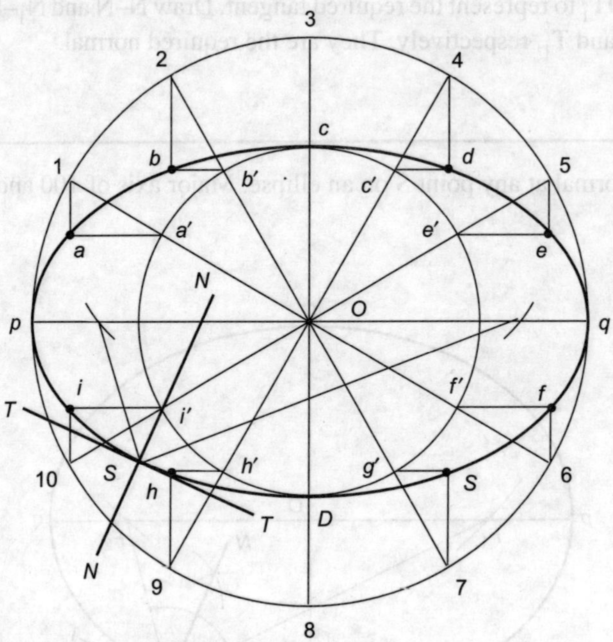

Fig. 5.17 Ellipse by concentric circle method

See Fig. 5.17.

(i) Draw the major axis pq = 80 mm and minor axis CD = 50 mm bisecting each other at right angle at O.

(ii) Draw two circles with pq and CD as diameters. Divide both circles in 12 equal parts, numbering of divisions as A, 1, 2, 3, … 10 and a^1, b^1, c^1, e^1, … i^1.

(iii) Through 1, draw a line parallel to CD.
Through a′, draw a line parallel to q.
Both the lines meet at a.

(iv) By similar procedure, obtain b, c, d, …, etc.

(v) Draw a smooth curve joining all points
p, a, b, c, d, e, … i, and p.

5.8.4 Eccentricity/Focus—Directrix Method

PROBLEM 5.10

Draw an ellipse, if distance of focus from the directrix is 35 mm and the eccentricity, e = 2/3

Solution:

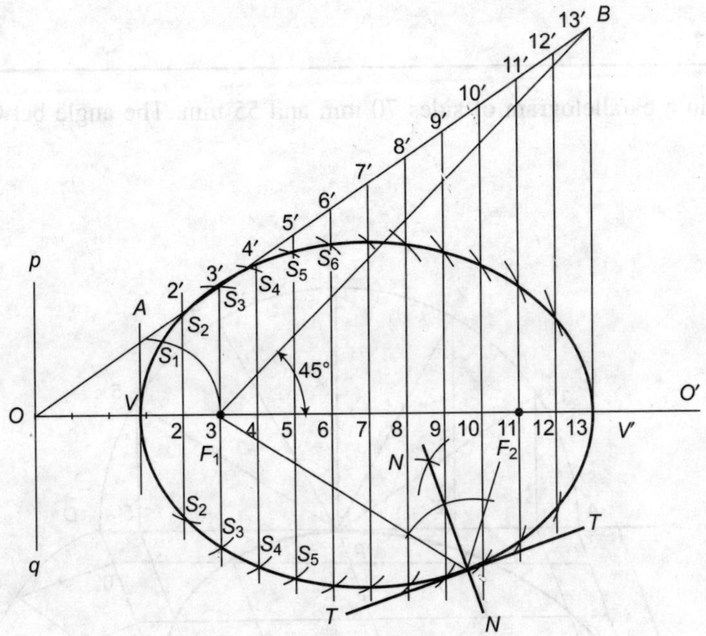

Fig. 5.18

See Fig. 5.18.

(i) Draw a directrix *pq* and axis 00′.

(ii) Mark OF_1 = 35 mm.

(iii) Divide OF_1 into 5 equal parts as 2 + 3 = 5 equal parts and mark V at the 3rd division from O.

Now $e = \frac{VF_1}{OV} = \frac{2}{3}$.

(iv) At V, draw perpendicular VF_1 = VA.

(v) Join OA and proceed ahead.

Through F_1, draw a line at 45° to meet OA at B.

(vi) Draw perpendicular BV′ on OO′.

(vii) Mark the points 1, 2, 3, … 13 on VV′ and erect perpendicular through them meeting DB at 1′, 2′, 3′, …

(viii) With F_1 as centre and radius = 11′, cut an arc on the perpendicular through 1, to locate S_1, on both sides.

Similarly, with F_1 as centre and radius 22′ to get S_1, S_2, S_3 with all points.

(ix) Draw a smooth curve for the requirement ellipse.

5.8.5 Circumscribing Parallelogram Method

PROBLEM 5.11

Inscribe on ellipse in a parallelogram of sides 70 mm and 55 mm. The angle between these sides is 70°.

Solution:

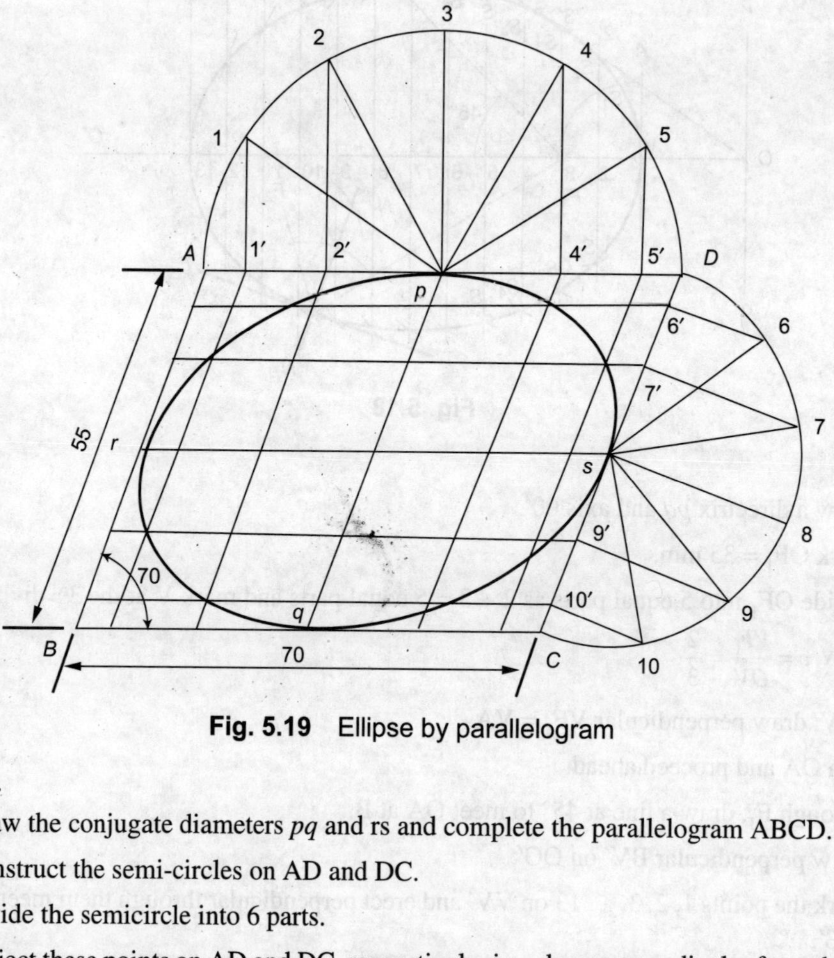

Fig. 5.19 Ellipse by parallelogram

See Fig. 5.19.

(i) Draw the conjugate diameters *pq* and rs and complete the parallelogram ABCD.

(ii) Construct the semi-circles on AD and DC.

(iii) Divide the semicircle into 6 parts.

(iv) Project these points on AD and DC, respectively, i.e., draw perpendicular from these points to AD and DC to intersect them at 1′, 2′, …, etc.

(v) These parallel lines intersect at points on the ellipse. Join them to get a smooth curve.

5.9 PARABOLA

Parabola is also a conic section. The eccentricity of parabola is equal to 1. Parabola is an open-end curve with a focus F and directrix *pq*, and a line perpendicular to the directrix is called the axis (OO′). When a cone is cut by a plane parallel to one of the side generator, the section obtained is called parabola.

Mathematically, parabola is a curve generated by a point moving in such a manner that at any point, its distance from the focus is always equal to the distance from the directrix.

For this case, $e = 1$.

PROBLEM 5.12

Draw a parabola, when focus is 30 mm from directrix.

Solution:

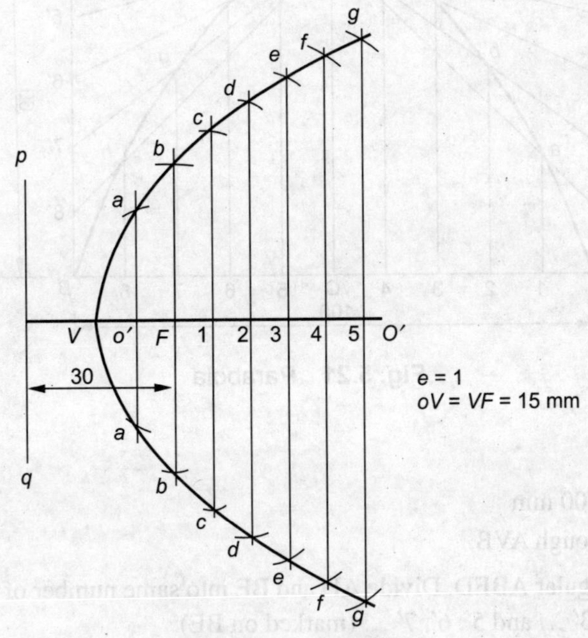

AR App

Fig. 5.20 Parabola

See Fig. 5.20.

(i) Draw *pq* and OO′ perpendicular to each other.

Locate F. OF = 30 mm.

V can be located; OV = VF = 15 mm ($e = 1$).

(ii) Divide line VO′ into a number of small divisions and erect lines from O′, F, 1, 2, 3,…, 5.

(iii) Taking radius = OO′ and centre at F, draw an arc on erected line of O′, which cuts at both the sides.

Similarly, taking centre as *F* and radius equal to 01, cut on the erected line from 1, it will cut on C on both the sides.

When all points are obtained as *a*, *b*, *c*, *d*, …, they can be joined with a smooth curve.

PROBLEM 5.13

Draw a parabola, when the axis is given as 60 mm and ordinate is given as 50 mm.

Solution:

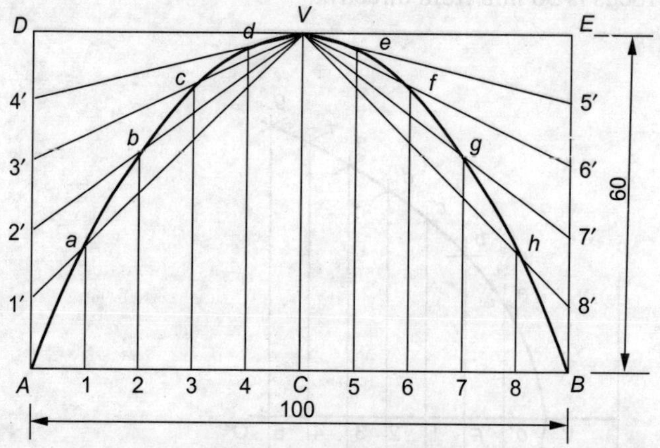

Fig. 5.21 Parabola

See Fig. 5.21.

axis = *VC* = 60 mm

Double ordinate = AB = 100 mm

The parabola will pass through AVB.

(i) Draw the rectangular ABED. Divide AD and BE into same number of equal parts, mark these points as 1′, 2′, 3′ … and 5′, 6′, 7′ … (marked on BE).

(ii) Join all marked points from V on both the sides.

(iii) Divide AB also in equal number of parts and mark as 1, 2, 3 …

Draw vertical lines from 1, 2, 3 …

(iv) Line drawn V1′ will meet at erected line from 1 and similarly V2′ will meet at vertical line drawn at 2, and so on.

(v) Joining all points a, b, c, d …, a smooth circle can be drawn.

This will represent a parabola.

PROBLEM 5.14

Draw a parabola if the base is 80 mm (double the ordinate) and the axis (or abscissa) = 35 mm, and at the base end makes 60° to the base.

Solution:

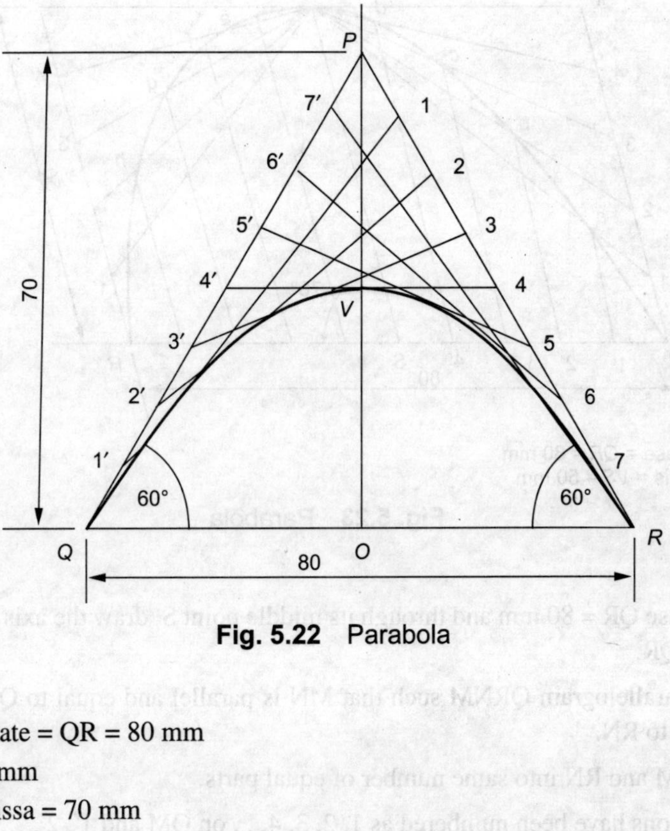

Fig. 5.22 Parabola

See Fig. 5.22.

Base or double ordinate = QR = 80 mm

Abscissa = *VO* = 35 mm

PO = double of abscissa = 70 mm

(i) Draw the base QR = 80 mm. Through Q and R, draw line at 60° to the base meeting them at P.

(ii) Divide QP and RP into the same number of equal parts, say 8 equal parts.

They have been numbered as shown in Fig. 5.21, i.e., 1′, 2′, 3′ in ascending order on QP,

and 1, 2, 3, … in descending order on PR.

(iii) Join 1–1′, 2–2′, 3–3′, and so on.

(iv) Draw a smooth curve starting from Q and ending at R. The parabola is represented in Fig. 5.22.

PROBLEM 5.15

Draw a parabola of base 80 mm and axis = 50 mm, inclined at 70° from the base.

Solution:

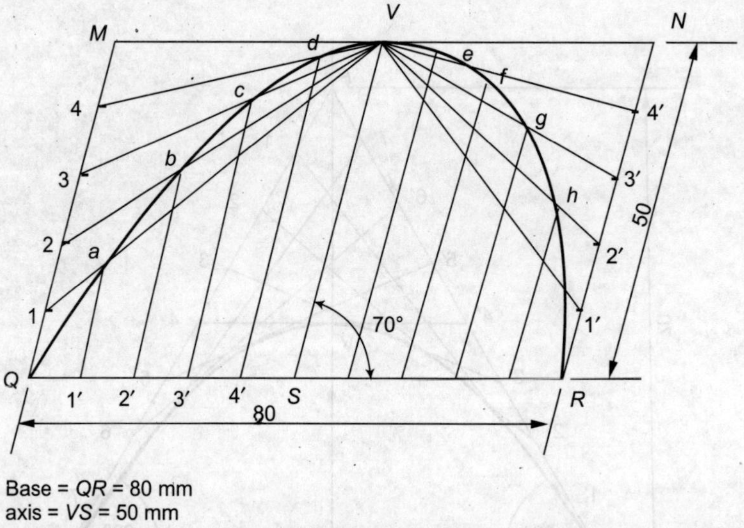

Fig. 5.23 Parabola

See Fig. 5.23.

(i) Draw a base QR = 80 mm and through its middle point S, draw the axis SV = 50 mm inclined at 70° to QR.

(ii) Draw a parallelogram QRNM such that MN is parallel and equal to QR and MQ is parallel and equal to RN.

(iii) Divide QM and RN into same number of equal parts.

The divisions have been numbered as 1, 2, 3, 4, .., on QM and 1′, 2′, … on RN.

(iv) Join *V*1, *V*2, *V*3, … and also V1′, V2′, V3′ …

(v) Draw QS in same equal divisions and also SR.

(vi) Draw vertical line from 1′, 2′, 3′ …

They are cutting at *a*, *b*, *c*, *d*, and so on.

(vii) Join all the points *a*, *b*, *c* ... by a smooth curve.

This will complete the parabola.

PROBLEM 5.16

Draw a parabola if the distance of the focus from the directrix is 30 mm.

Solution:

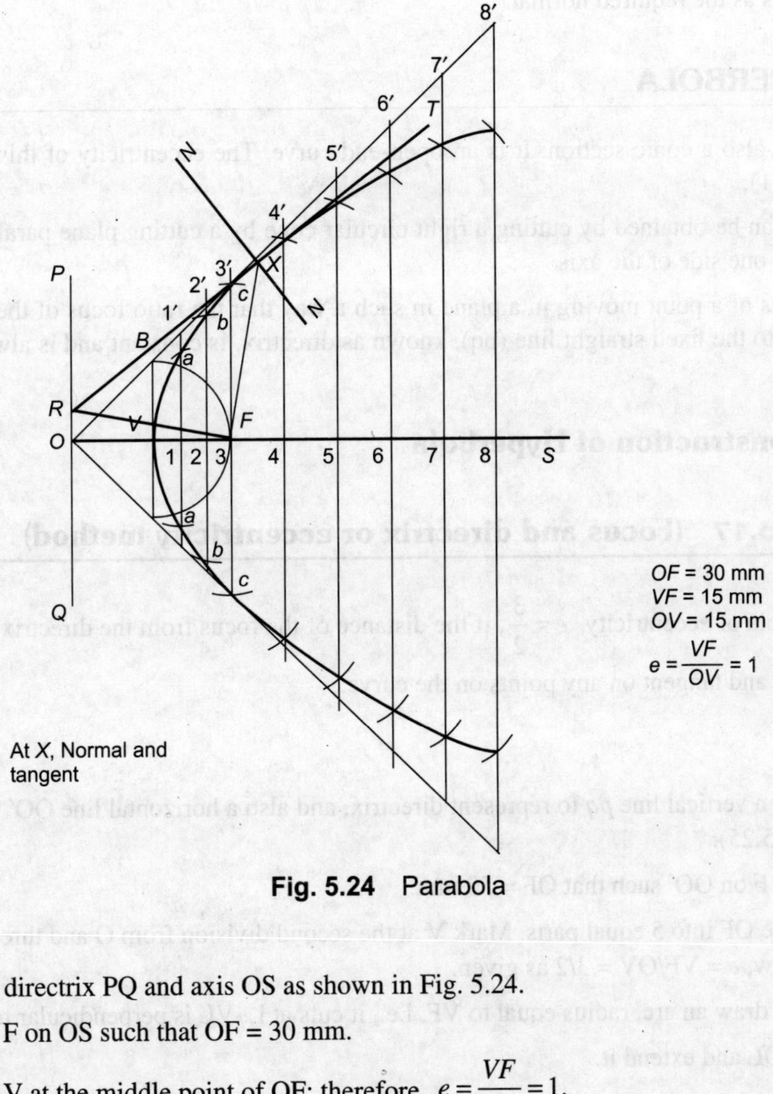

Fig. 5.24 Parabola

See Fig. 5.24.

(i) Draw directrix PQ and axis OS as shown in Fig. 5.24.

(ii) Mark F on OS such that OF = 30 mm.

(iii) Mark V at the middle point of OF; therefore, $e = \frac{VF}{OV} = 1$.

(iv) At V, erect a perpendicular VB = VF, join OB.

(v) Mark a few points, 1, 2, 3 … on VS. Draw perpendicular from 1, 2, 3 … meeting OB produced at 1′, 2′, 3′ … 8′.

(vi) With F as the centre and radius 11′, similarly with F as centre and radius 2–2′, 3–3′, etc., cut arcs on corresponding perpendicular located as *a, b, c* ..., and so on.

(vii) Draw smooth curve passing through V, *a, b, c* ...

(viii) Join FX. Draw line FR perpendicular to FX. Join RX as the required tangent. Draw perpendicular to this as the required normal.

5.10 HYPERBOLA

A hyperbola is also a conic section. It is an open-end curve. The eccentricity of this curve is greater than unity ($e > 1$).

Hyperbola can be obtained by cutting a right circular cone by a cutting plane parallel to the axis of the cone and in one side of the axis.

It is the locus of a point moving in a plane in such a way that the ratio focus of the distance from a fixed point (F) to the fixed straight line (pq), known as directrix, is constant and is always greater than unity.

5.10.1 Construction of Hyperbola

PROBLEM 5.17 (Focus and directrix or eccentricity method)

Draw a hyperbola of eccentricity, $e = \frac{3}{2}$, if the distance of the focus from the directrix = 50 mm. Draw also the normal and tangent on any points on the curve.

Solution:

(i) Draw a vertical line *pq* to represent directrix, and also a horizontal line OO′ to represent axis (Fig. 5.25).

(ii) Mark F on OO′ such that OF = 50 mm.

(iii) Divide OF into 5 equal parts. Mark V at the second division from O and three divisions from F. Now, e = VF/OV = 3/2 as given.

(iv) At V, draw an arc, radius equal to VF, i.e., it cuts at L. VL is perpendicular to OO′.

(v) Join OL and extend it.

(vi) Mark a few points 1, 2, 3, ... on VO′ and draw perpendicular through all points, meeting on the erected line at 1′, 2′, 3′, 5′ ...

(vii) With F as a centre and radius, 11′ cut two lines on the perpendicular through 1 to cut at both the sides as in Fig. 5.25.

Similarly, with F as centre and radii 22′ and 33′, cut them at *b, c,* and other points.

(viii) Draw a smooth curve passing through V, *a*, *b*, *c*, … This is the required hyperbola.

(ix) Let S be a point on the curve. Join S with F by a line. Draw FT perpendicular to SF. The line cuts the directrix at T.

(x) Join TS. It will represent the tangent at S.

Draw NN perpendicular to TT. It will represent normal to S on the curve.

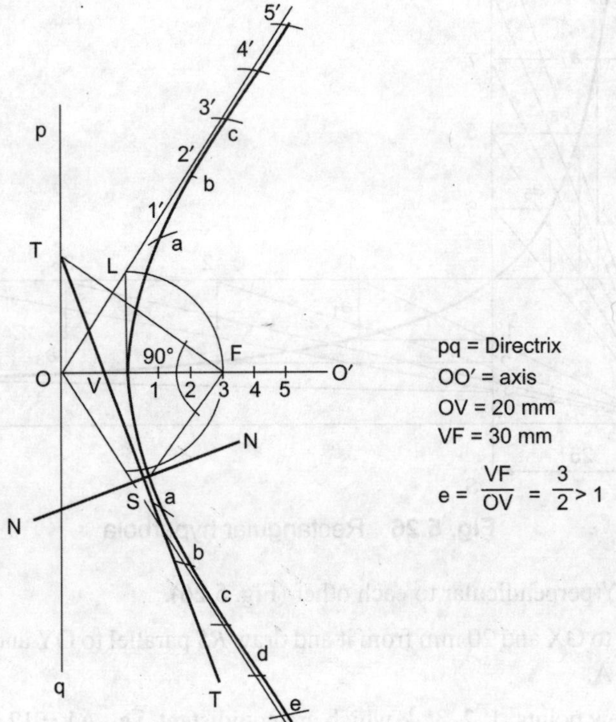

Fig. 5.25 Hyperbola, *e* = 3/2 given

AR App

5.10.2 Rectangular Hyperbola

A curve obtained by the movement of a point on its path in such a way that the product of its distance from two fixed line at right angle to each other is a constant.

PROBLEM 5.18

Draw a rectangular hyperbola if a point on it is at a distance of 20 mm and 25 mm, respectively, from two asymptotes.

Solution:

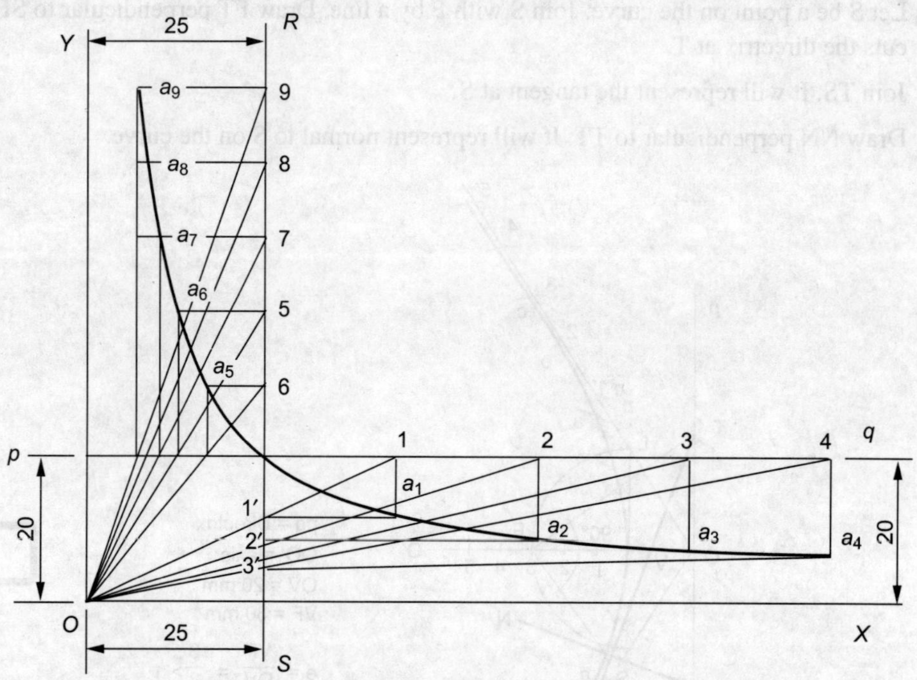

Fig. 5.26 Rectangular hyperbola

(i) Draw OX and OY perpendicular to each other (Fig. 5.26).

(ii) Draw *pq* parallel to OX and 20 mm from it and draw *RS* parallel to OY and 25 mm from OY. They cut each other at A.

(iii) On Aq, mark a few points, 1, 2, 3, 4, which are equidistant, i.e., A1 = 12 = 23 = 34.

(iv) On AR, mark a few points, 5, 6, 7, 8, …, at equal intervals.

(v) Join O1, O2, O3, …, and also O5, O6, O7, …, and so on. Mark 1′, 2′ at the intersection of these lines with *RS* and pq.

(vi) Draw a line perpendicular to 1; extend it to meet 1′ horizontally. They cut each other at a′.

The same procedure can be adopted with all the points.

It can be followed with the drawing.

5.11 SPECIAL CURVES

There are some special curves that come in the category of plane and space curves. Although conic sections have great importance in engineering field, number of special curves such as cycloid, involute, spiral, etc., are also used and they have wide applications. The methods of construction of these curves are presented as follows.

5.11.1 Cycloid

A curve that is generated by a fixed print on the circumference of a circle rolling along a fixed straight line without slipping is known as *cycloid*.

PROBLEM 5.19

A circular wheel of diameter 35 mm rolls on a straight line on the ground without slipping. A point A lies on the rim of the wheel. Draw the locus of point A for one revolution of the wheel. Draw the tangent and normal at point P on the curve.

Solution:

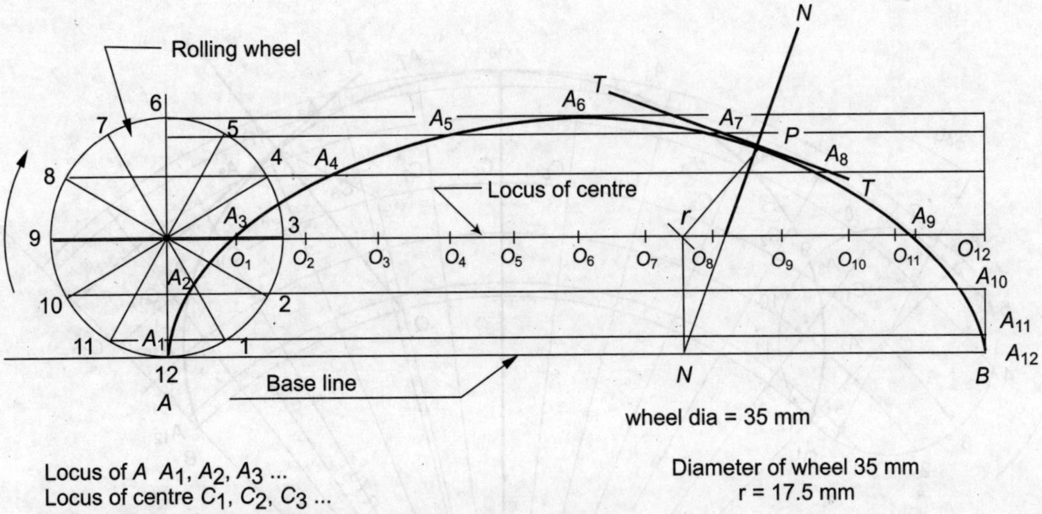

Fig. 5.27 Cycloid

(i) Draw the wheel circle of diameter 35 mm. Draw the base line AB equal to the circumference of the rolling wheel. A is the point on the wheel (Fig. 5.27).

(ii) Divide the rolling circle into 12 equal parts and it is numbered as 1, 2, 3, …, etc.

(iii) Draw a line passing from the centre and divide this into 12 equal parts, 0_1, 0_2, 0_3, … representing the locus of the centre.

(iv) Through 1, 2, 3, 4, … draw horizontal lines.

(v) With 0_1, 0_2, 0_3, …, etc., as the centres and radius equal to OA = 17.5 mm, cut the line through 1, 2, 3, …, etc., to find A_1, A_2, A_3 … etc.

(vi) Join A, A_1, A_2, A_3, …, etc., by a smooth curve. The curve represents the required cycloid.

(vii) With P as a centre and radius = 17.5 mm, cut an arc on the centre line.

Draw perpendicular to base line. Join NP, it will represent normal and perpendicular to it as TT tangent.

5.11.2 Epicycloid

A curve, generated by a point on the circumference of a circle which rolls outside the circumference of a directing circle without slipping, is called epicycloid.

PROBLEM 5.20

Draw an epicycloid of rolling circle of diameter 35 mm, which rolls another circle outside of it. The diameter of base circle is 70 mm. The curve is drawn for one complete revolution.

Solution:

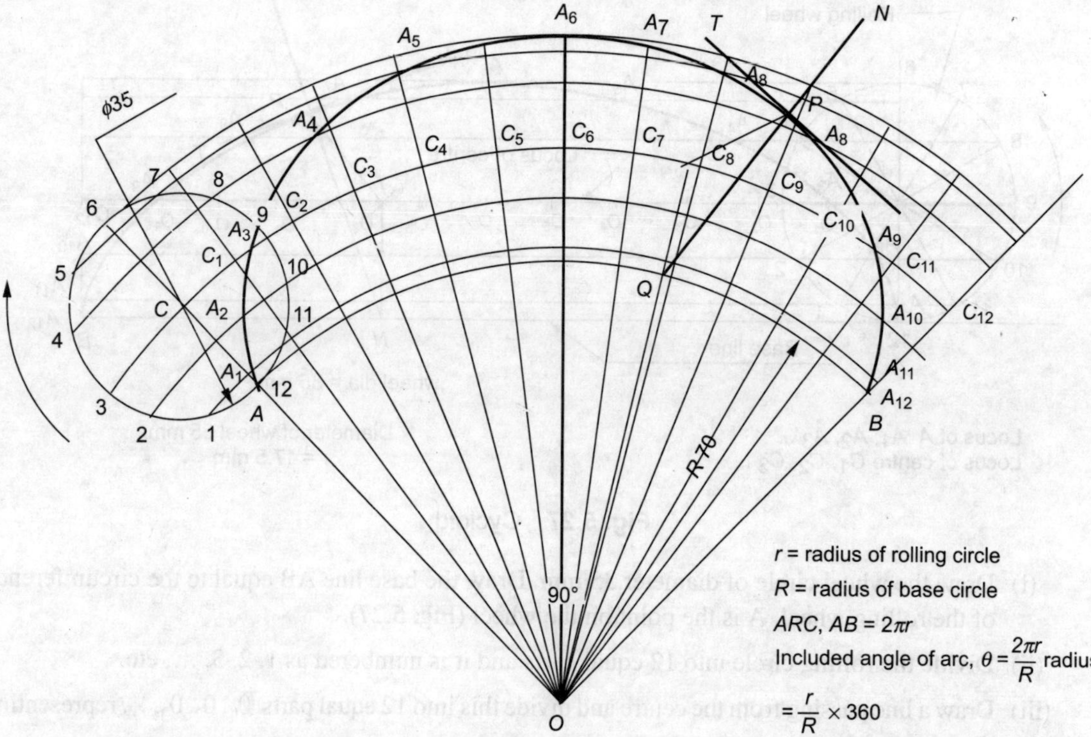

r = radius of rolling circle

R = radius of base circle

$ARC, AB = 2\pi r$

Included angle of arc, $\theta = \frac{2\pi r}{R}$ radius

$= \frac{r}{R} \times 360$

$= \frac{35/2}{70} \times 360 = 90°$

Fig. 5.28 Epicycloid

See Fig. 5.28.

(i) In one complete revolution, the rolling circle will move from A to B, which will be equal to $2\pi r$ distance. The angle subtended by the arc AB at O be θ.

$$\theta = \frac{2\pi r}{R} \text{ Radians} = \frac{35/2}{70} \times 360 = 90°$$

(ii) Take any point O as a centre and radius = 70 mm, draw an arc for the base circle as AB which has included angle $\theta = 90°$.

(iii) Extend OA and locate C on it. Taking C as the centre draw a circle of diameter = 35 mm.

(iv) With O as a centre and radius = OC, draw an arc C_{12}.

(v) Divide the rolling circle into 12 equal parts shown as 1, 2, 3, … 12.

(vi) With O as centre and radii = 0–1, 0–2, 0–3, etc.,

draw arcs through 1, 2, 3, …, etc., which are parallel to AB.

(vii) Divide θ in 12 equal parts; each part will be = 75°. The divisions cut at centre as C_1, C_2, C_3, …

(viii) With C as centre and radius = CA, draw an arc which cuts the arc passing through 1. With C as centre and radius = CA, draw an arc passing through 2, and so on, from C_3, C_4, C_5, …

The cutting points are represented as A_1, A_2, A_3, … A_{12}.

(ix) Join A_1, A_2, A_3, ..., etc., by a smooth curve which represents the required epicycloids.

5.11.3 Hypocycloid

A curve obtained by a point on the circumference of a circle which rolls inside another circle without slipping is called hypocycloid.

PROBLEM 5.21

A rolling circle of diameter 25 mm rolls inside another base circle of radius 100 mm. Draw the hypocycloid traced by a point on the rolling circle for one complete revolution.

r = rolling circle radius = 25 mm

R = Radius of directing (base) circle = 100 mm

Included angle of arc, $\theta = \frac{2\pi r}{R}$ radians

$$= \frac{r}{R} \times 360° = \frac{25}{100} \times 360 = 90°$$

The method of construction for hypocycloid remains the same as for epicycloids. The centre C of rolling circle is inside the base circle.

Solution:

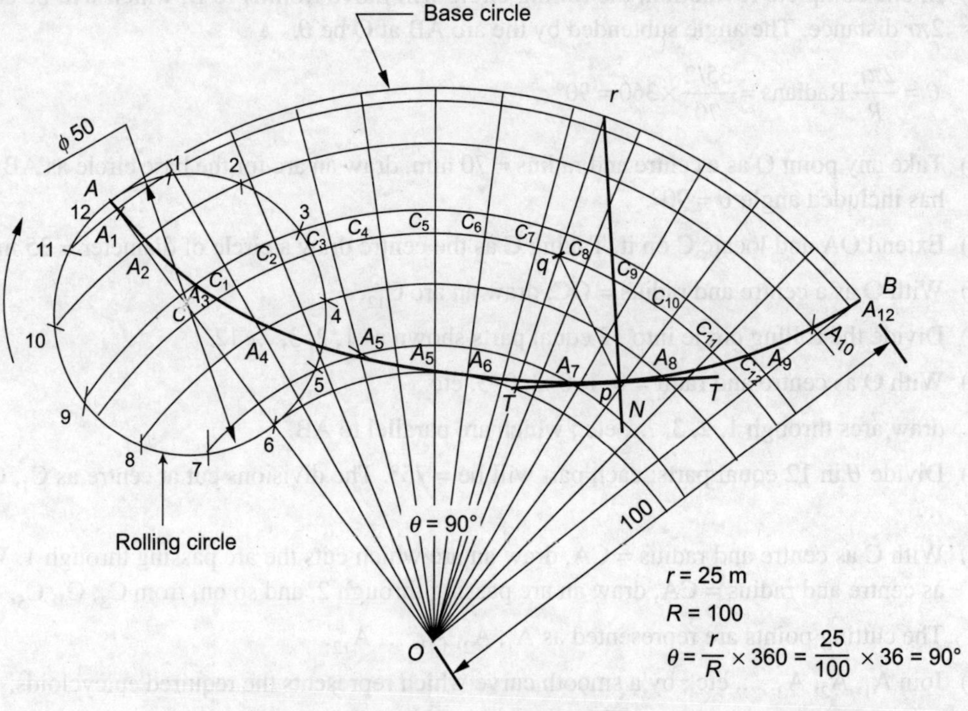

Fig. 5.29 Hypocycloid

(i) With O as the centre and radius = 100 mm, draw a base circle arc AB with included angle 90°.

(ii) Draw a rolling circle of diameter = 50 mm inside the base circle.

(iii) Divide the rolling circle into 12 equal parts as 1 2, 3, …, etc., in clockwise direction as in Fig. 5.29.

(iv) Taking O as centre, draw an arc passing from 1, 2, 3, … etc.

(v) Taking O as centre and OC as radius, draw an arc which represents the locus of centre.

(vi) Divide 90° into 12 equal parts and division lines are drawn.

(vii) Taking centre at C_1 and radius equal to rolling circle, draw an arc to cut the arc through 1 at A_1.

Similarly, get the other points.

(viii) Draw a smooth curve joining all points A_1, A_2, A_3, …, etc.

(ix) P is the point on a curve where normal and tangent are to be drawn with P as a centre and radius equal to $r = 25$ cm. Cut the locus of the centre at q. Join qr. rN becomes normal to the curve and perpendicular to this is TT which represents the tangent.

5.11.4 Involute

A curve generated by a point on the end of a thread when unwound from a circle or polygon is called involute. The curve is applicable with any polygon or a circle.

PROBLEM 5.22

Draw the involute of a square of side 15 mm.

Solution:

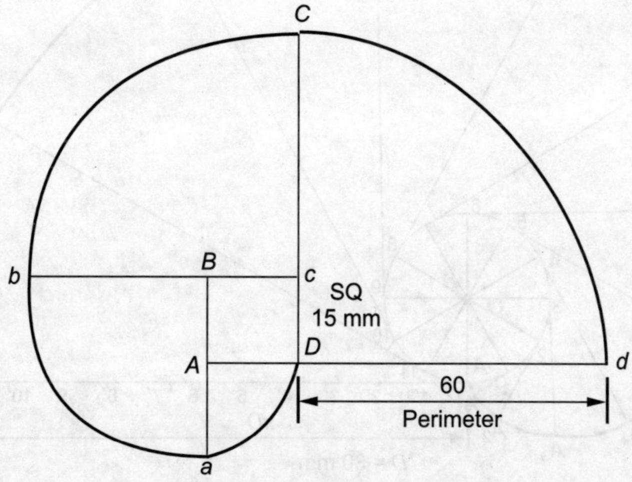

Fig. 5.30 Involute of a square

(i) Draw a square ABCD of side equal to 15 mm.

(ii) With A as a centre and radius equal to AD, draw an arc to cut BA produced at *a*.

(iii) Next with B as a centre and B*a* as radius, draw an arc to intersect CB produced at *b*.

Then, with C as a centre and radius equal to cb, draw an arc to intersects DC produced to C.

(iv) Lastly, with D as centre and DC as radius, draw an arc to intersect AD produced at d.

(v) Draw a smooth curve joining Dabcd, which represents the involute of a square.

5.11.5 Involute of Circle

Involute of a circle is used as the profile of gear teeth. Cams are manufactured to involute shape to have proper rolling contact between roller and follower to maintain constant speed.

PROBLEM 5.23

Draw the involute of a circle of diameter 30 mm.

Solution:

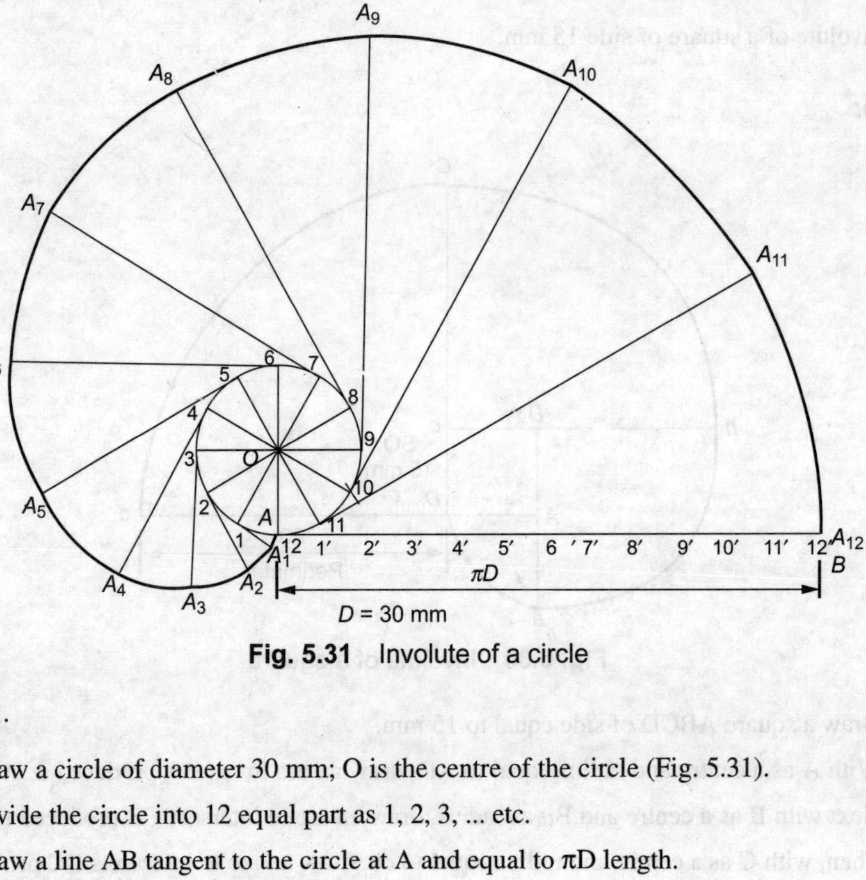

Fig. 5.31 Involute of a circle

See Fig. 5.31.

(i) Draw a circle of diameter 30 mm; O is the centre of the circle (Fig. 5.31).

(ii) Divide the circle into 12 equal part as 1, 2, 3, ... etc.

(iii) Draw a line AB tangent to the circle at A and equal to πD length.

(iv) Divide AB into 12 equal parts as 1′, 2′, 3′, … etc.

(v) Draw a tangent to 1, 2, 3, …, etc., and mark A_1, A_2, A_3,… A_{12}.

(vi) Draw tangent at 1; cut a distance equal to one part of πD; again, at line tangent drawn at 2, cut a distance equal to 2 part of πD.

This has to be repeated at all points. This has been marked as A_1, A_2, A_3 … A_{12}.

(vii) Draw a smooth curve joining all points A_1, A_2, … A_{12}.

This will represent an involute of a circle.

5.11.6 Archimedian Spiral

PROBLEM 5.24

Construct an archimedian spiral for $1\frac{1}{4}$ convolution when the minimum radius is zero and maximum radius is 60 mm.

Solution:

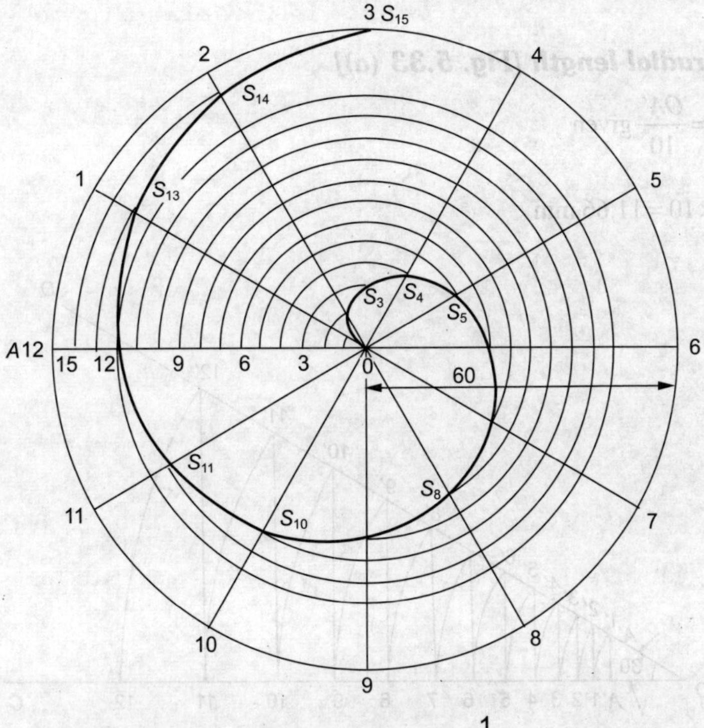

Fig. 5.32 Archimedian spiral for $1\frac{1}{4}$ convolution

See Fig. 5.32.

(i) Draw a line OA = 60 mm (maximum radius).

(ii) Divide this line OA into 15 equal parts (for one convolution, it should have been divided into 12 equal parts).

(iii) Division should be marked with 01, 02, 03, … 015.

(iv) With O as centre and radius 01, 02, 03, … etc., draw an arc to intersect the radius at points S, S_2, S_3, … S_{15}.

(v) Join all the points by a smooth curve. This is the required spiral.

5.11.7 Logarithmic Spiral

PROBLEM 5.25

Draw the logarithmic spiral for one convolution such that the initial vector radius is 10 mm and the ratio between adjacent radii vectors containing an angle of 30° is $\frac{7}{6}$. Also, draw a tangent and normal at any given point p on the curve.

Solution:

(a) To find the radial length [Fig. 5.33 (a)]

$$\frac{OA'}{OA}=\frac{7}{6}=\frac{OA'}{10} \text{ given}$$

$$OA'=\frac{7}{6}\times 10=11.66 \text{ mm}$$

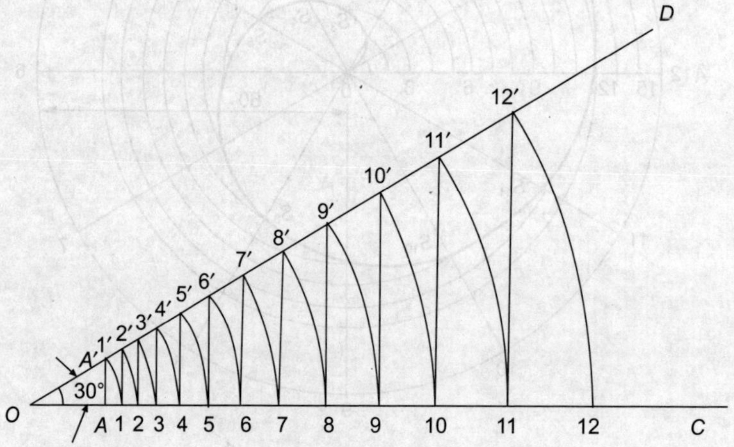

Fig. 5.33 (a) Radial length

(i) Draw two lines OC and OD at an angle of 30°.

(ii) On line OC, mark A such that OA = 10 mm.

(iii) Mark a point A′ on the line OD such that $OA'=\frac{7}{6}\times OA$ = 11.66 mm.

(iv) Join AA′.

(v) With centre O and radius OA′, draw an arc meeting the line OC at 1.

(vi) From 1, draw a line parallel to AA′ meeting the line OD at 2′.

(vii) With centre O and radius O2′, draw an arc meeting the line OC at 2.

(viii) The construction is repeated for all points. Obtain the points 3, 4, 5, … etc., on OC line.

(b) Construction of curve [Fig. 5.33 (b)]

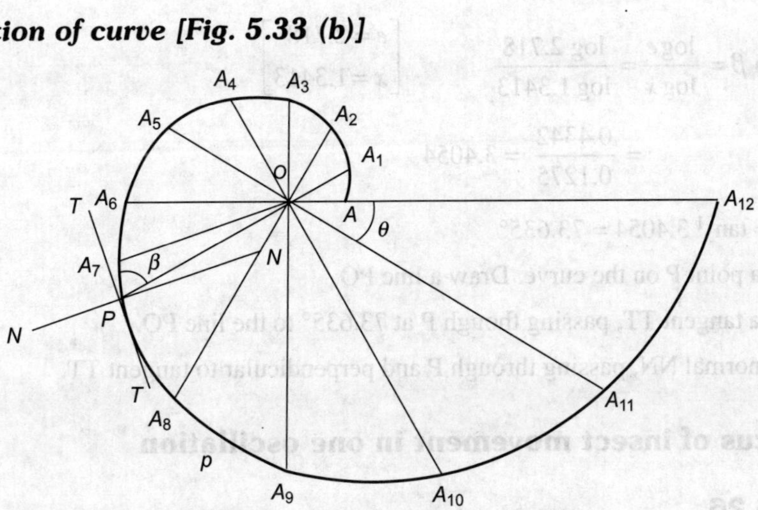

Fig. 5.33 (b) Construction of curve

(i) Draw a line OA = 10 mm.

(ii) Draw radial lines through O at 30° angle interval.

(iii) Mark points A_1, A_2, A_3, …, etc., on the radial lines such that $OA_1 = O1$, $OA_2 = 02$, $OA_3 = 03$, … and so on. These lengths be taken from Fig. 5.32 (a) earlier.

(iv) A smooth curve is obtained joining all points A_1, A_2, A_3, ..., and so on.
The curve represents the required curve.

(v) To draw a tangent and normal on the spiral:
The constant of logarithmic spiral is given as $r = x^{\theta}$.

Where r = radius vector
x = constant of spiral
θ = angle between radii vector

We have $r = x^{\theta}$

Taking log on both sides

$$\log r = \theta \log x$$

When $\theta = 0°$, $\log r = 0$

$$r = \log^{-1}(0) = 1$$

When $\theta = 30° = \frac{\pi}{6} = 0.523$ radian

$$r = \frac{7}{6} \times 1 = 1.166$$

$$\log 1.166 = 0.523 \log x$$

$$x = \log^{-1}(0.1275) = 1.3413$$

$$\tan\beta = \frac{\log e}{\log x} = \frac{\log 2.718}{\log 1.3413} \qquad \begin{bmatrix} e = 2.718 \\ x = 1.3413 \end{bmatrix}$$

$$= \frac{0.4342}{0.1275} = 3.4054$$

$$\beta = \tan^{-1} 3.4054 = 73.635°$$

(vi) Mark a point P on the curve. Draw a line PO.

(vii) Draw a tangent TT, passing though P at 73.635° to the line PO.

(viii) Draw normal NN, passing through P and perpendicular to tangent TT.

5.11.8 Locus of insect movement in one oscillation

PROBLEM 5.26

A 90 mm long pendulum moving from rest makes one complete oscillation and swings through 60° to the left. During this period, an insect moves from top to the bottom of the pendulum in one complete oscillation. Find the path traced by the insect.

Solution:

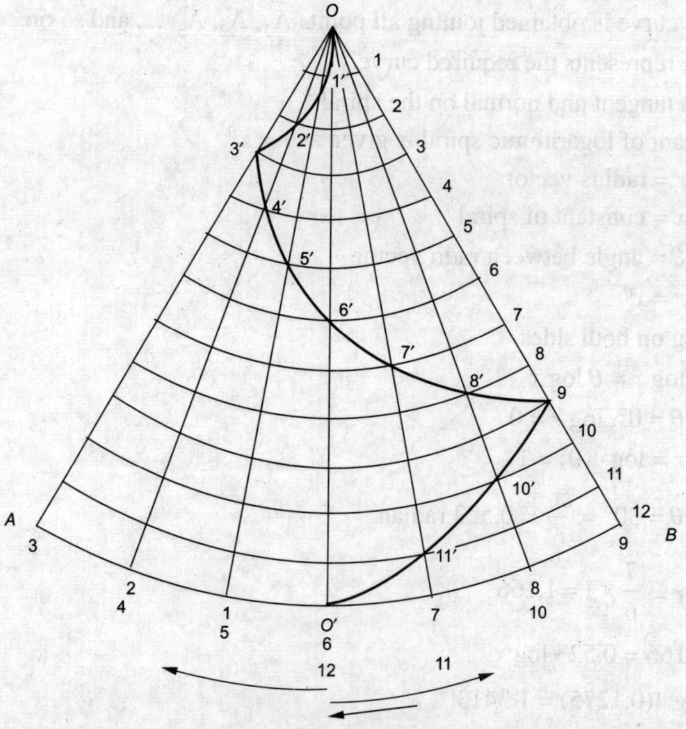

Fig. 5.34 Moving pendulum (Locus of moving insect)

Pendulum moves from rest. In one swing it covers an angle of 60°, ∠AOB = 60° (Fig. 5.34).

In one complete oscillation, the insect moves from 0 to 0′.

Divide the arc AB into 6 equal parts. They have been numbered as shown.

OB is divided into 12 equal parts.

The pendulum moves from OO′ to OA, from OA to OB, and from OB to OO′.

The position of the insect has been shown as 0, 1′, 2′, 3′, …, etc.

Join all points by a smooth curve.

5.11.9 Locus of a point on Sliding Ladder

PROBLEM 5.27

A ladder 9 m long is on the ground and the other end is resting on a vertical wall. The ladder slips slowly on the wall downward without leaving wall contact. Draw the locus of a point on the ladder which is 4 m away from the top end.

Solution:

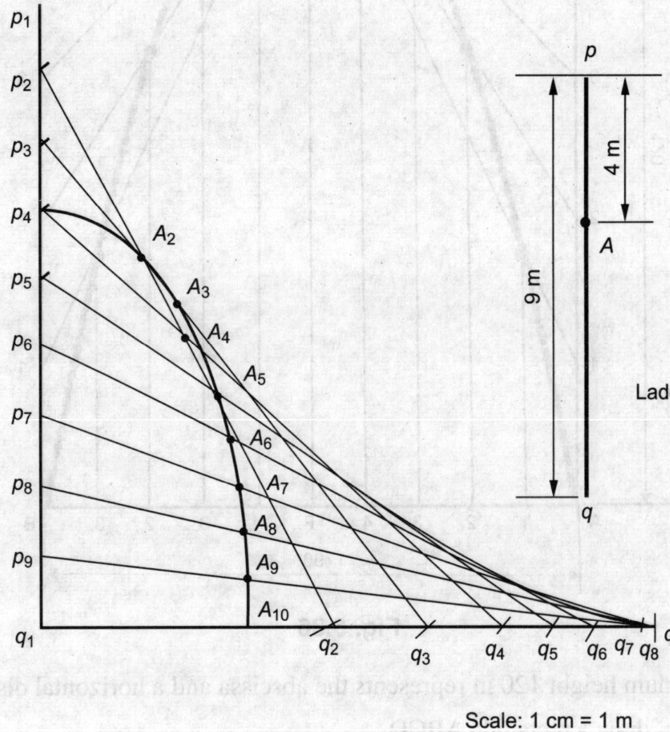

Fig. 5.35 Locus of point

(i) p_1q_1 is the first position of the ladder when it is just touching the wall vertical on this ladder, there is point A_1, 4 m below p_1 (Fig. 5.35).

(ii) When the ladder slips on the wall, $p_2q_2, p_3q_3, p_4q_4, \ldots$, etc., shows the different position of the ladder. In this position, $A_1, A_2, A_3, \ldots$, etc., are the respective positions of point 4 m from top always.

(iii) Joining all points A_1, A_2, A_3, etc., a smooth curve is obtained. This is the required locus of point A on the ladder.

PROBLEM 5.28

A ball is thrown up, reaches a maximum height of 120 m, and travels a horizontal distance of 90 m. Trace the path of the ball assuming it to be parabolic.

Take the suitable scale.

Solution:

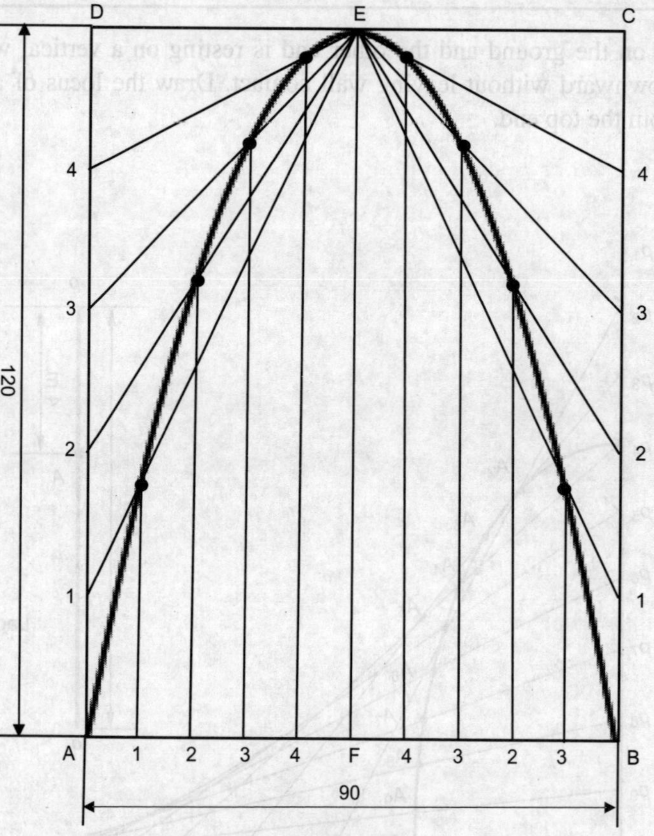

Fig. 5.36

In this case, the maximum height 120 m represents the abscissa and a horizontal distance of 90 m.

Taking a suitable scale, draw a rectangle ABCD.

A parabola can be drawn in a similar way by the previous method.

EXERCISE

Review Questions

1. What do you mean by right circular cone?
2. What is the meaning of a conic section?
3. Define eccentricity mathematically.
4. What are the different types of conic sections?
5. Define mathematically ellipse, parabola, and hyperbola.
6. What is rectangular hyperbola?
7. A circle of 30 mm diameter rolls on a straight line with no slipping. In the initial position, the diameter RS of the circle is parallel to the line on which it rolls. Draw the locus of the point R and S for one complete revolution of the circle.
8. A circle of 30 mm diameter rolls along a straight line with no slipping. Draw the curve traced out by a point 'R' on the circumference for $1\frac{1}{2}$ revolution of the circle. Name the curve. Draw the tangent and normal at a point on it 30 mm from the line.
9. A wheel of 40 mm diameter rolls on a straight path without slipping. Trace the path of a point on one of the spokes 15 mm from the rim towards the centre of the wheel for one complete revolution.
10. Draw the involute of a given equilateral triangle of side 20 mm.
11. Draw the involute of square of side 15 mm.
12. Define conic sections and also eccentricity.
13. The vertex of a hyperbola is 65 mm from its focus. Draw the hyperbola if the eccentricity is 5/2.
14. A fixed point 'f' is 8 cm from a fixed straight line. Draw locus of a point 'p' moving in such a way that its distance from the fixed straight line is:

    (i) 3/2 times its distance from 'f'

    (ii) equal to its distance from 'f'

    (iii) 2/3 times its distance from 'f'

    Plot at least 6 points. Name the curve.

    Also draw a normal tangent to each curve at a point on it 4 cm from 'f'.
15. Construct a hyperbola when the distance between the focus and the directrix is 40 mm and the eccentricity is 4/3. Draw a tangent and normal at any point on the hyperbola.
16. Construct an ellipse when the length of the major axis is 120 mm and the distance between the foci is 80 mm. Determine the length of its minor axis. Also draw the tangent and normal at any point on the curve.
17. The major axis of an ellipse is 100 mm and the minor axis is 50 mm. Find the foci and construct the ellipse by intersecting arc method.

    Draw a pair of tangents from point 'R' outside the ellipse.

18. A plot of ground is in the shape of a rectangle 100 m × 50 m. Inscribe an elliptical lawn with taking a scale 1:1000. Construct by oblong method.

19. A ball thrown from the ground level reaches a maximum height of 5 m and travels a horizontal distance of 10 m from the point of projection.

    Trace the path of the ball (parabola). This to be solved by rectangular method.

20. A cricket ball is thrown and reaches a maximum height of 20 m and falls on the ground at a distance of 70 m from the point of projection. Assume that the point of projection is from ground level. Draw the path of the ball.

21. A fountain jet discharges water from ground level at an inclination of 55° to the ground. The jet travels a horizontal distance of 9 m from the point of discharge and falls on ground. Trace the path of the jet. Hint: Apply tangent method for parabola.

Objective Questions

1. ________ is the section obtained, when a right circular cone is cut by a sectional plane parallel to the axis cutting the base
2. When a cone is cut by a cutting plane passing through the apex and the base, it is known as ______.
3. ______ is the section obtained when a right circular cone is cut by a cutting plane inclined to the axis.
4. ______ is the section obtained when a right circular cone is cut by a cutting plane parallel to a generation and which cuts the base.
5. Parabolic curve profile is used to construct arch and bridges by civil engineers. (True/false)

Answers

Objective Questions

1. Hyperbola 2. Triangle 3. Ellipse 4. Parabola 5. True

CHAPTER 6

Scales

6.1 INTRODUCTION

Engineering drawings of machine components are prepared on a limited area of drawing sheets. When the object and machine components are very large, such as cylinder block of an internal combustion engine, crank shaft, buildings, ships, etc., the drawings of these items cannot be prepared on a limited area on the drawing sheets and, hence, a suitable scale is chosen. In such cases, the size of drawing prepared will be smaller than the size of the object. This is only possible by using 'REDUCING SCALE'.

Similarly, the drawing of very small machine components such as pinion of watch and electronic chips cannot be made on actual size because this will be too small to visualize and also to prepare the drawing would be difficult. In such cases, a suitable scale is chosen to prepare the drawing. This can be done by choosing "ENLARGING SCALE". The prepared drawing would be bigger in size.

If the drawing is made on full-size scale, the actual size of an object is shown on drawing. It will be on "FULL SIZE SCALE".

"As per BIS, *scale* is defined as the ratio of linear dimension of an element of an object as represented in the original drawing to the real linear dimension of the same element of the object itself".

For making any drawing on drawing sheets, a suitable scale is to be chosen, as follows:

SCALE 1:1 — represents full-size scale

SCALE 1:S — For reducing scale, S < 1

SCALE S:1 — For enlarging scale, S > 1

'S' may be 2, 4, 10, 20, etc.

Table 6.1 Recommended Scale

S. No.	Items	Recommended Scales
1.	Full-size scale	1:1
2.	Enlarging scale	50:1, 5:1, 20:1, 2:1, 10:1
3.	Reducing scale	1:2, 1:20, 1:200, 1:2000, 1:5, 1:50, 1:500, 1:5000, 1:10, 1:100, 1:1000, 1:10000

6.2 REPRESENTATIVE FRACTION/ SCALE FACTOR

Ratio of the drawing size of an object to its actual size is called *representative fraction* (R.F.)

$$\text{R.F.} = \frac{\text{Size of an object on drawing}}{\text{Actual size of the object}}$$

For finding out the value of R.F., the unit of numerator and denominator will be the same.

(i) For example, if 50 mm length of an object is represented by 10 mm length on drawing

$$\text{R.F.} = \frac{10 \text{ mm}}{50 \text{ mm}} = \frac{1}{5}$$

This means that the scale of the drawing is one-fifth of the full size.

For this case, scale will be a *reducing scale*.

(ii) If 50 mm length is represented by 50 mm length on drawing,

$\text{R.F.} = \frac{50}{50} = 1/1$ For this, it is *full- size scale.*

(iii) If 50 mm length of an object is represented by 200 mm length on drawing,

$$\text{R.F.} = \frac{200}{50} = 4 = \frac{4}{1}$$

For this case, a drawing is drawn on 4 times the full-size scale.

So, it is drawn on *enlarged scale*.

(i) A scale with the ratio 1:1 is called full-size scale.

(ii) If the ratio is 1:100, it is called reducing scale.

(iii) If the ratio is 10:1, it is called enlarged scale.

Sometimes, the conversion of units is necessary.

10 mm (millimetre) = 1 cm (centimetre)

10 cm (centrimetre) = 1 dm (decimetre)

10 dm (decimetre) = 1 m (metre)

10 m (metre) = 1 decametre (dam)

10 decametre = 1 hectometre (hm)

10 hectometre = 1 kilometre

1 hectare = 10,000 m^2

6.3 CONSTRUCTION OF SCALE

The BIS has recommended and standardized the plain scales that are available in the market. If the proper scale is not readily available, it is made on the drawing sheet. The following items must be known for the construction of a scale:

(i) Representative fraction (R.F.)

(ii) The units in which measurements are required

(iii) Maximum length to be measured by scale

Length of scale = R.F. × Maximum length to be measured

6.4 TYPES OF SCALES

(a) Plain scale

(b) Diagonal scale

(c) Vernier scale

(d) Scale of chords

6.5 PLAIN SCALES

A plain scale is constructed by a line divided into a number of equal parts, the first of which is further sub-divided into fractional part to measure up to first decimal places only.

Such as 2.3 cm, 10.5 km, etc.

Before constructing a plain scale, the following information is necessary:

(i) The total length of the scale is divided into a suitable number of equal divisions.

(ii) The first main division is sub-divided into its fractional parts.

(iii) The zero is placed at end of the first main division.

(iv) The unit should be numbered to the right of the zero marked.

(v) Representative fraction (R.F.) calculated is placed and written below the constructed *scale*.

Example of plain scale

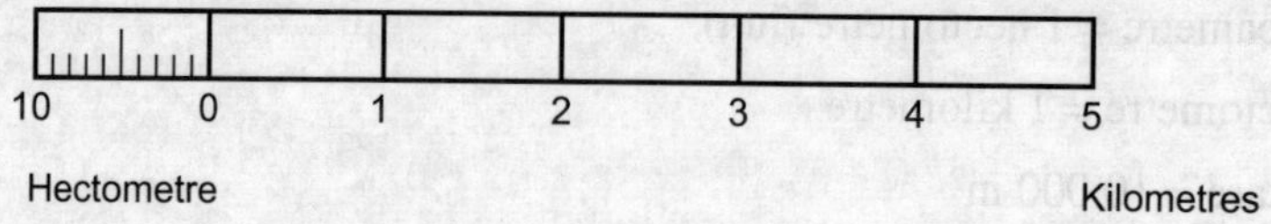

Fig. 6.1

PROBLEM 6.1 (FIG. 6.2)

Construct a plain scale of 1 cm = 0.9 m to show a single metre and single decimeter and long enough to measure up to 10 m. On this scale, show the measurement of 8 m 6 dm.

Solution:

The following steps are to be taken:

(i) Calculate R.F.

$$\text{R.F.} = \frac{\text{Length on drawing}}{\text{Actual length of object}} = \frac{1\text{ cm}}{0.9\text{ m}} = \frac{1}{90}$$

(ii) Length of scale = R.F. × Maximum distance to be measured

$$= \frac{1}{90} \times 9 \times 100 = 10\text{ cm}$$

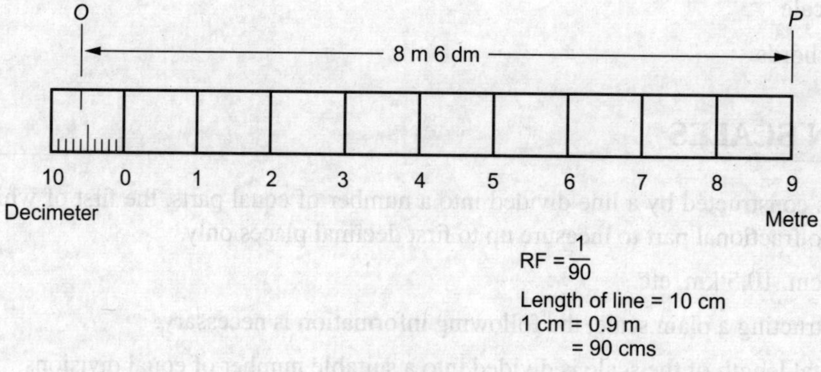

Fig. 6.2

$$\text{R.F.} = \frac{1}{90}$$

Length of line = 10 cm

1 cm = 0.9 m

= 90 cm

Steps:

(i) Calculate R.F. as 1/90.

(ii) Calculate the length of scale = 10 cm.

(iii) Draw a line 10 cm in length and divide it into 10 equal parts.

(iv) Divide the first division into 10 equal parts; each part will represent one decimeter.

(v) Mark the division from right to left.

(vi) Mark zero after the first division and place 1, 2, 3, etc., to the right.

(vii) Mark the distance 8 m 6 dm as OP from right end of scale.

(viii) Complete the scale and write R.F. at the bottom of constructed scale.

PROBLEM 6.2 (FIG. 6.3)

Construct a plain scale of $\frac{1}{80}$ to read metres and decimetres and long enough to measure up to 8 m. Mark a distance of 7.3 m on it.

Solution:

(i) R.F. is given, R.F. = $\frac{1}{80}$

(ii) Length of scale = R.F. × maximum length to measure

$$= \frac{1}{80} \times 8\text{ m} = \frac{1}{80} \times 800 = 10\text{ cm}$$

(iii) Draw a line of 10 cm and divide into 8 equal parts.

(iv) Repeat next step as in Problem 6.1.

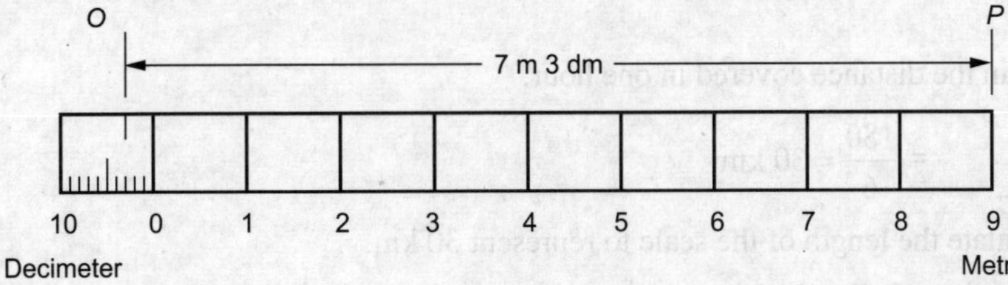

Fig. 6.3

PROBLEM 6.3 (FIG. 6.4)

A rectangular plot of 64 km^2 is represented on a certain map by a rectangle of small area 1 cm^2. Draw a plain scale to read 20 km and single km on it, and long enough to measure 5.4 km.

Solution:

(i) Calculate R.F.

$$1\text{ cm}^2 = 64\text{ km}^2$$

$$1\text{ cm} = \sqrt{64} = 8\text{ km}$$

$$1\text{ cm} = 8 \times 1000 \times 100\text{ cm}$$

$$\text{R.F.} = \frac{1}{800000}$$

(ii) Calculate the length of scale.

$$= \frac{1}{800000} \times 80 \times 1000 \times 100 = 10\text{ cm}$$

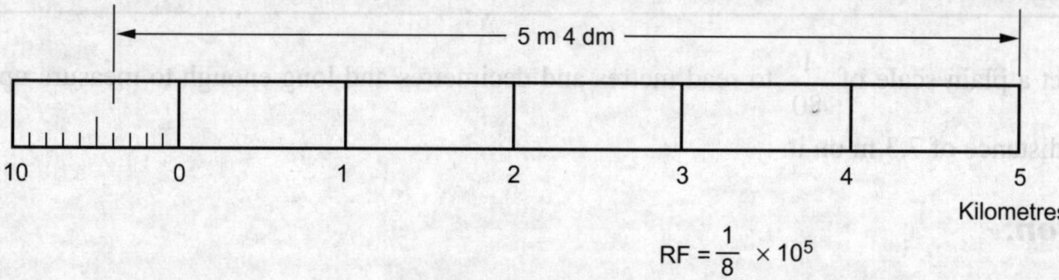

Fig. 6.4

PROBLEM 6.4 (FIG. 6.5)

The distance between station A and station B is 180 km. A train covers the distance in 6 hr. Calculate and prepare a scale to measure the distance covered by the train in a single minute and up to 1 hr. The scale is $\frac{1}{20,0000}$. Show on it a distance covered in 28 minutes.

Steps:

(i) Obtain the distance covered in one hour.

$$= \frac{180}{6} = 30\text{ km}$$

(ii) Calculate the length of the scale to represent 30 km.

$$= \text{R.F.} \times 30\text{ km}$$

$$= \frac{1}{20000} \times 30 \times 1000 \times 100 = 15\text{ cm}$$

Therefore, 30 km is represented by 15 cm length of scale and is covered in 1 hr or 60 minutes

(iii) Draw a line of 15 cm and divide it into 3 equal parts.

(iv) Divide one line into 3 equal parts. Each part represents 10 km.

(v) Divide the other line placed over the previous line into 6 equal parts each part will represent 10 minutes.

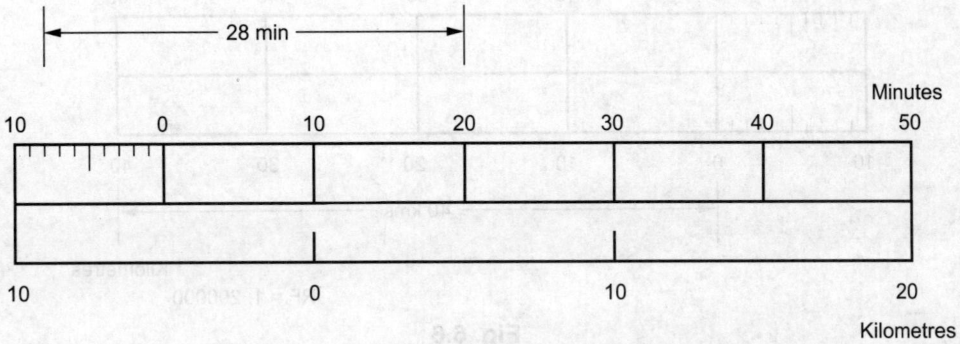

Fig. 6.5

PROBLEM 6.5 (FIG. 6.6)

A bus is moving at a speed of 30 km/hr. Construct a plain scale to read up to a km and a minute. The scale should measure up to 40 km. The R.F. of the scale is 1 : 200000. Represent on this scale the distance which is covered by the bus in 32 minutes.

Steps:

(i) $$\text{R.F.} = \frac{1}{200000} = \frac{\text{Total length of scale}}{\text{Total distance to be measured}}$$

$$\text{Total length of scale} = \frac{\text{Total distance to be measured}}{20000}$$

$$= \frac{40 \times 1000 \times 100}{200000} = 20 \text{ cm}$$

Therefore, 40 km distance is represented by 20 cm length of scale and is covered in 60 minutes time.

(ii) Draw a line of 20 cm length and divide it into 5 equal parts. Each part represents 10 km. Divide also the first part in 10 equal parts.

(iii) Speed of the train = 30 km/hr

$$= \frac{30}{60} = \frac{1}{2} \text{ km/min}$$

$$\text{Total time represented on scale} = 40 \times \frac{1}{2} = 20 \text{ min}$$

(iv) Divide this also into 5 equal parts. Each part will represent 20/5 = 4 min

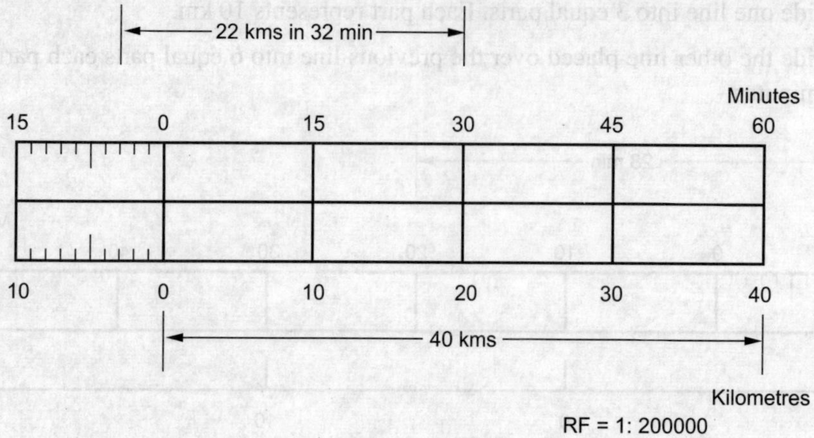

Fig. 6.6

PROBLEM 6.6 (FIG. 6.7)

A square plot of 16 sq km is represented on a certain map by a similar square of 1 cm^2. Draw a plain scale to show 10 km and single km on it, and long enough to measure up to 60 km.

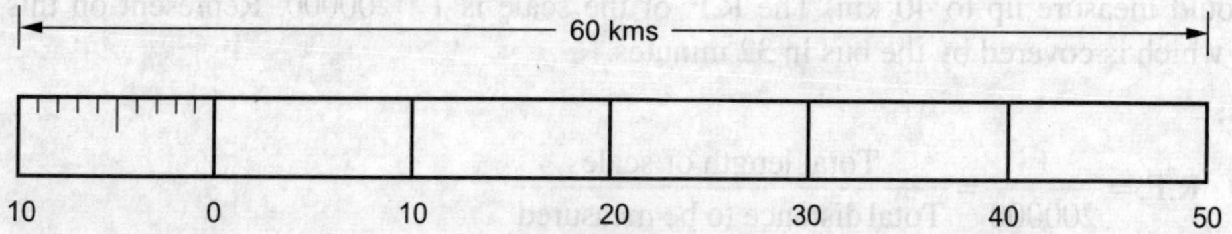

Fig. 6.7

Steps:

(i) Calculate R.F. as

$1\ cm^2 = 16\ km^2$

$1\ cm = \sqrt{16} = 4 km$

$1\ cm = 4 \times 1000 \times 100\ cm$

$$R.F. = \frac{1}{400000} = \frac{1}{400000}$$

(ii) Calculate the length of scale.

$$= \frac{1}{400000} \times 60 \times 1000 \times 100 = 15\ cm$$

(iii) Draw a line of 15 cm and divide it into 6 equal parts.

Each part will be of 10 km.

(iv) Mark 0 after the first division and continue 10, 20, 30, etc., to the right of the scale.

(v) Divide the I[st] division into 10 equal parts to represent 1 km each.

6.6 DIAGONAL SCALES

Plain scales are used to read length in two units such as km and m.

It is used to read up to correct first decimal place, such as 0.1, 10.2, etc.

Diagonal scales are used to represent any of the three units of measurements such as km, m, and cm. or 10.12, 10.15, etc.

With the help of diagonal scale, very minute distances can be accurately measured.

When the measurements are to be measured in three units m, dm, and cm or dm, cm, mm, etc.

6.6.1 Principle of Diagonal Scale

To obtain diversions of a given short line *pq* in multiplies of 1/10 of its length 0.1 *pq*. 0.2 *pq* as shown Fig. 6.8.

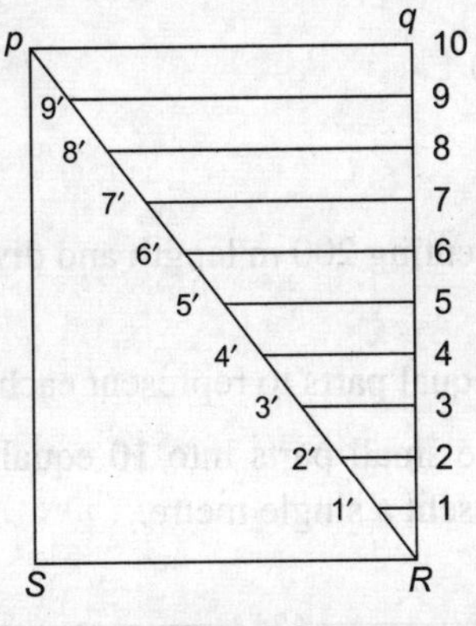

Fig. 6.8

(i) At one end *q*, draw a line perpendicular *qR* perpendicular to pq and divide it into 10 equal parts.

(ii) Draw a rectangle *pqRS*.

(iii) Now 11′ = 0.1 *SR*, 22′ = 0.2 *SR*, etc.

So, $\frac{11'}{pq} = \frac{R1}{qR} = \frac{0.1\,qR}{qR} = 0.1$

$11' = 0.1\,pq = 0.1\,SR$

Their principle is used in the construction of the diagonal scale.

PROBLEMS ON DIAGONAL SCALE

PROBLEM 6.7 (FIG. 6.9)

On a drawing, a line 11 cm long represents a distance of 220 m.

Draw a diagonal scale for the line to read up to a single metre. On the scale, mark a distance of 134 m on the scale.

Steps:

(i) Calculate R.F.

$$\text{R.F.} = \frac{\text{Drawing size}}{\text{Actual size}}$$

$$= \frac{11}{220 \times 100} = \frac{1}{2000}$$

(ii) As 134 m is required to be measured, consider 200 m.

Therefore, drawing size = R.F. × actual size

$$= \frac{1}{2000} \times 200 \times 100$$

$$= 10 \text{ cm}$$

(iii) Draw a line of 10 cm representing 200 m length and divide it into 5 equal parts, each part will represent 40 m.

(iv) Divide the first part into 4 equal parts to represent each part equal to 10 m.

(v) Further divide each of these small parts into 10 equal parts using the principle of diagonal scale. Such a part will represent a single metre.

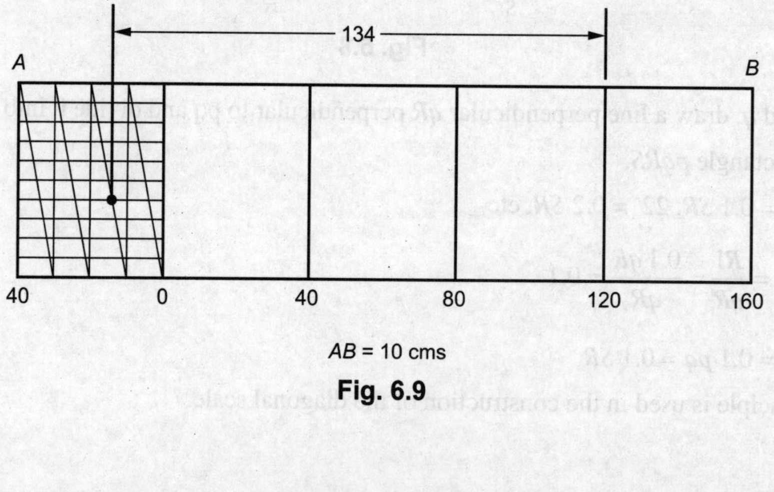

AB = 10 cms

Fig. 6.9

PROBLEM 6.8 (FIG. 6.10)

An area of 25 sq km is represented by 121 sq cm on a map. Determine R.F. of scale and also construct a diagonal scale to show km, hectometer, and decimeter, and also to measure up to 10 km. On this diagonal scale, show the distance of 8 km, 6 hectometre, and 5 decametre (1 hectometre = 100 metres).

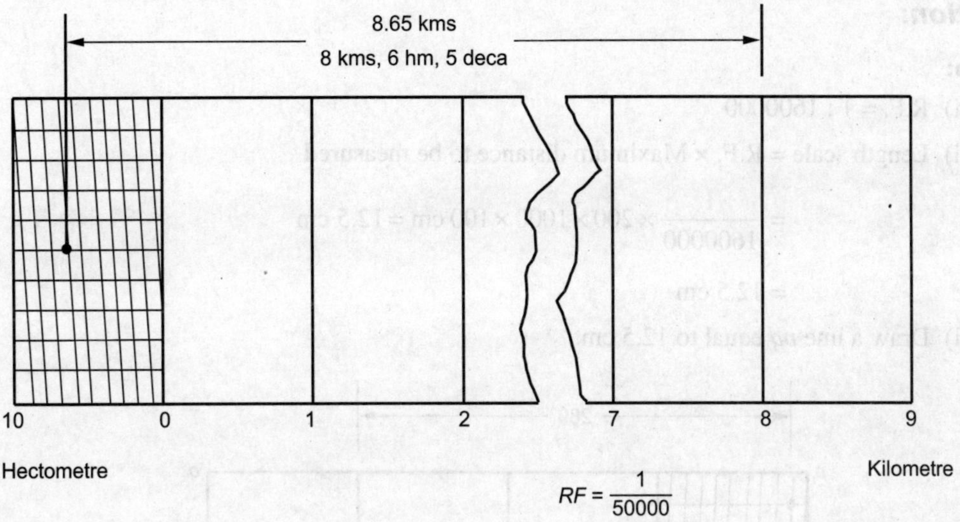

Fig. 6.10

Solution:

Step:

(i) Calculate R.F.

$$\text{R.F.} = \frac{\text{Diagram scale}}{\text{Actual scale}}$$

Now (11 × 11) sq cm represents (5 × 5) sq km.

11 cm is representing 5 km.

$$\text{R.F.} = \frac{11}{5 \times 1000 \times 100} = \frac{1}{50000}$$

$$\text{Actual length of scale} = \frac{1}{50000} \times 5 \times 1000 \times 100 = 10 \text{ cm}$$

(ii) Draw a line of 10 cm and divide it into 10 equal parts. Each part will represent 1 km.

(iii) Divide the first part into 6 equal parts, each representing one hectometre.

PROBLEM 6.9 (FIG. 6.11)

Construct a diagonal scale of R.F. = 1 : 1600000 to show kilometres and should be able to measure up to 400 km. On this scale, show the distance of 165 km and 289 km.

Solution:

Step:

(i) R.F. = 1 : 1600000

(ii) Length scale = R.F. × Maximum distance to be measured

$$= \frac{1}{1600000} \times 200 \times 1000 \times 100 \text{ cm} = 12.5 \text{ cm}$$

$$= 12.5 \text{ cm}$$

(iii) Draw a line *pq* equal to 12.5 cm.

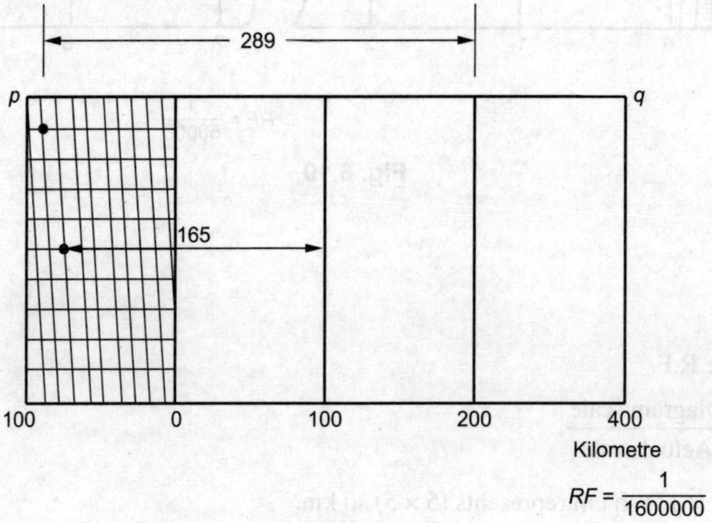

Fig. 6.11

PROBLEM 6.10 (FIG. 6.12)

A cube of 3 cm side represents a tank of 3375 m^3 volume. Find the R.F. of the scale and prepare a diagonal scale to measure a distance up to 50 m. Also show a distance 25.6 m and 43.3 m on it.

Solution:

Step:

(i) $3 \times 3 \times 3\ cm^3 = 3375\ m^3$

$$3\ cm = \sqrt[3]{3375} = 15\ m$$

$$= 1500\ cm$$

$$R.F. = \frac{3}{1500} = \frac{1}{500}$$

(ii) Calculate the length of scale = R.F. × Maximum distance to be measured

$$= \frac{1}{500} \times 60 \times 100$$

$$= 12\ cm$$

(iii) Draw a line *pq* of 12 cm

(iv) Divide it into 5 equal parts to represent 10 m.

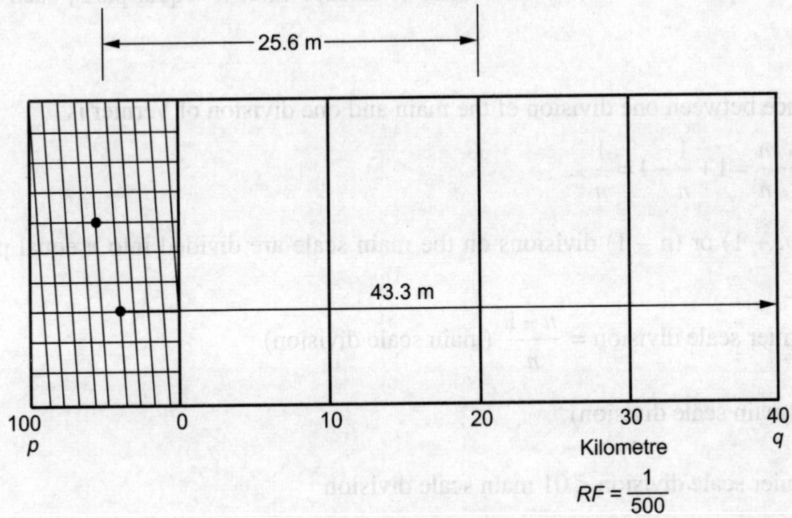

Fig. 6.12

6.7 VERNIER SCALE

Vernier scale is constructed to measure with greater accuracy and to account for the fractional divisions.

The scale is being used extensively in slide calipers, screw gauges, and precision measuring instruments.

A Vernier scale will have a main scale divided into smaller divisions and a Vernier scale.

There are two types of Vernier scales:

1. *Direct/Forward Vernier scale* $n - 1$ divisions on primary are divided into n equal divisions.
2. *Retrograde/Backward Vernier scale* $n + 1$ divisions on primary are divided into n equal divisions.

In both the cases, the difference between the main scale division and one Vernier scale division equals to $1/n$ and is known as least count of the Vernier.

The difference between two main scale divisions and two Vernier scale divisions is $2/n$.

Least count: It can be the smallest distance that can be measured accurately by the Vernier scale and is the difference between a main scale division and a Vernier scale divisions.

The theory of construction of a Vernier scale is as follows:

If a length 'n' unity is divided into 'n' equal parts, each part equals to unity.

Now, if a line equal to $(n + 1)$ of these units is divided into 'n' equal parts, each part is equal to $\frac{n+1}{n}$ units.

The difference between one division of the main and one division of Vernier is

$$\frac{n+1}{n} - \frac{n}{n} = 1 + \frac{1}{n} - 1 = \frac{1}{n}$$

Generally, $(n + 1)$ or $(n - 1)$ divisions on the main scale are divided into n equal parts on Vernier scale.

Then 01 Vernier scale division = $\frac{n-1}{n}$ (main scale division)

or $\left(1 - \frac{1}{n}\right)$ (main scale division)

Here 01 Vernier scale division < 01 main scale division

01 Vernier scale division can also be = $\frac{n+1}{n}$ (main scale division)

or $\left(1 + \frac{1}{n}\right)$ (main scale division)

Here, 01 Vernier scale division > 01 main scale division. The least count (LC) is the smallest dimension. Correct to which a measurement can be made with a Vernier.

For forward LC = (01 main Div – 01 Vernier Div)

For backward LC = (01 Vernier Div – 01 main Div)

PROBLEM 6.11 (FIG. 6.13)

Construct a Vernier scale to take the measurement of m, decimeter and centimeter to measure up to 4 m. The RF of the scale is $\frac{1}{25}$ and mark the measurement 2.15 m.

Solution:

Steps:

1. Least count is to measure metre, decimetre, and centimetre

   Smallest measurement is cm

   Small distance to be measured

   = 1 cm = 0.01 m

2. Length of scale = R.F. × maximum distance to be measured

   $= \frac{1}{25} \times 4 \times 100 = 16 \text{ cm}$

3. Draw a line of 16 cms length and divide it into 4 equal parts

   Each part represent 01 m

   Each sub-division on main scale is divided into 10 equal parts.

   $01 \text{ main scale division} = \frac{01 \text{ m}}{10} = 01 \text{ dm}$

   Construction of Vernier scale to read (cm).

4. Take 11 divisions of main scale and divide this into 10 equal parts on Vernier scale, so 01

   $\text{Vernier scale division} = \frac{11 \text{ main division}}{10}$

   $= \frac{11 \times 1 \text{ dm}}{10} = 1.1 \text{ dm} = 11 \text{ cm}$

5. Mark 0, 55, and 110 towards the left from 0 on the Vernier scale.

6. Write the units of main division (METRES)

   Sub-division (DECIMETRES) and Vernier division (CENTIMETRES) as shown in Fig.

7. 2.15 m = (Vernier scale division × 5) (main div × 16)

   = 0.11 × 5 + (0.1 m × 16)

   = 0.55 + 1.6 = 2.15

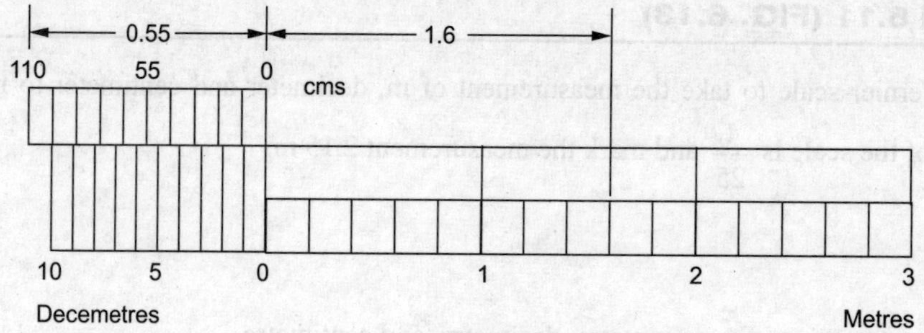

Fig. 6.13

PROBLEM 6.12 (FIG. 6.14)

Construct a Vernier scale whose R.F. = 3 to show cm, one tenth of cm, and 1/100th of cm, to read up to 5 cm. Indicate on the scale the measurement for 4.22 cm and 2.36 cm.

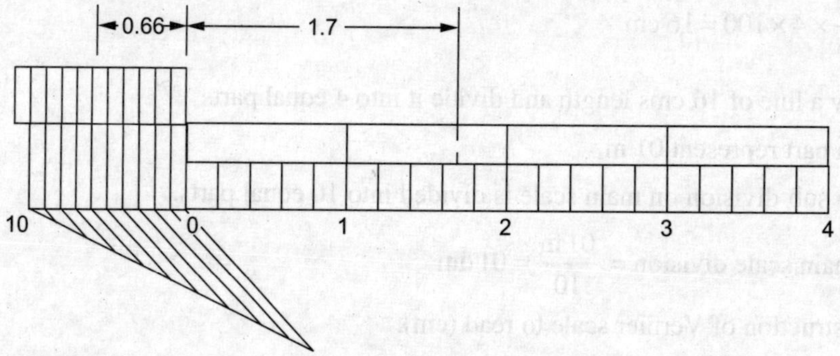

Fig. 6.14

Solution:

Steps:

1. Least count = smallest distance to be measured

   = 01 cm/100 = 0.01 cm

2. Length of the scale = 3 × 5 = 15 cm
3. Draw the main scale of 15 cm length and divide it into 5 equal parts.
4. Each subdivision is divided into 10 equal parts, so 01 main scale division = $\frac{1 \text{ cm}}{10} = 0.1$ cm
5. To construct the Vernier scale, take 11 divisions on main scale and divide into 10 equal parts on the Vernier.

$$01 \text{ Vernier scale division} = \frac{11 \times 0.1 \text{ cm}}{10}$$

$$= 0.11 \text{ cm}$$

$$\text{Measurement of } 2.26 \text{ cm} = 1.7 + 0.11 \times 6$$

$$= 1.7 + 0.66$$

$$4.22 \text{ cm} = 4 + 0.11 \times 2$$

$$= 4 + 0.22$$

PROBLEM 6.13 (FIG. 6.15)

Construct a *forward* reading Vernier scale to read distance correctly to a decametre on a map in which the actual distance is reduced in the ratio of 1 : 50000. The scale should be long enough to measure up to 8 km. Mark on the scale, a length of 4.34 km.

Solution:

1. $\text{R.F.} = \frac{\text{drawing scale}}{\text{actual scale}} = \frac{1}{5000}$

$$\text{Length of scale} = \frac{1}{50000} \times 8 \times 1000 \times 100 = 16 \text{ cm}$$

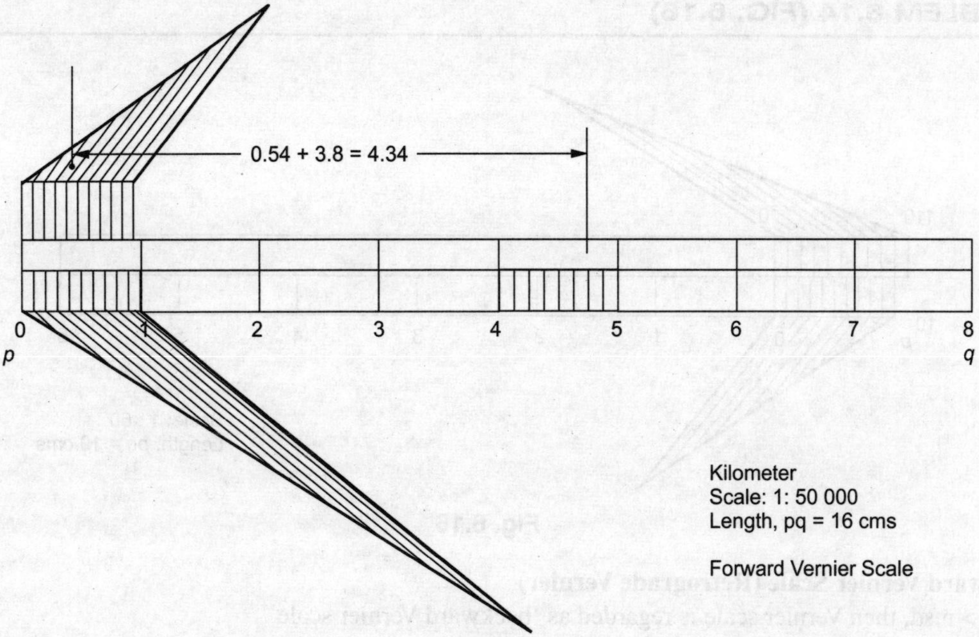

Fig. 6.15

2. 16 cm is divided into 8 equal parts, each part is 1 km.
3. This is further divided into 10 divisions;

   Each division = 0.1 km = 1 hectometer

   1 main scale division (msd) = 0.1 km = 1 hectometer

   $$\text{LC (least count)} = \left(\frac{1}{10}\right) \text{msd}$$

   LC = 1 msd – 1 Vernier scale division (vsd)

   $$\left(\frac{1}{10}\right) \text{msd} = 1 \text{ msd} - 1 \text{ vsd}$$

   $$\text{or} \qquad 1 \text{ vsd} = 1 \text{ msd} - \left(\frac{1}{10}\right) \text{msd}$$

   $$= \frac{9}{10} \text{ msd} = 0.09 \text{ km}$$

   To represent 4.34 km on the scale

   $$6 \text{ vsd} = 6 \times 0.09 = 0.54 \text{ km}$$

   The balance of 3.8 km can be represented on the main scale.

PROBLEM 6.14 (FIG. 6.16)

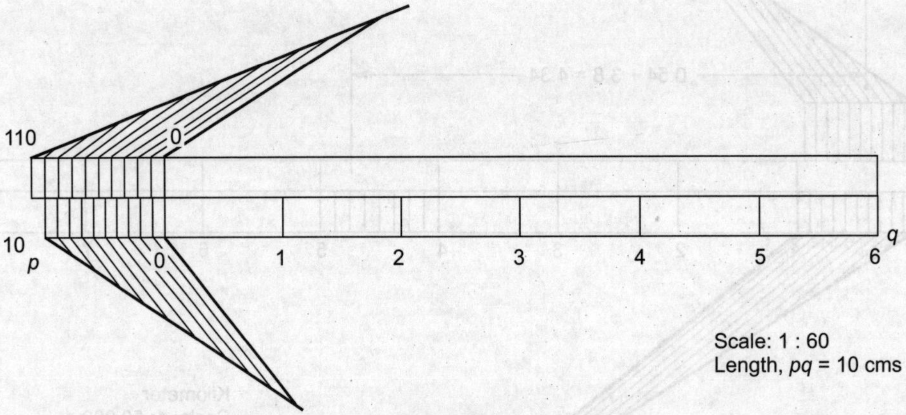

Fig. 6.16

Backward Vernier Scale (Retrograde Vernier)

If vsd > msd, then Vernier scale is regarded as 'backward Vernier scale'

LC = vsd – msd

In backward Vernier scale, vsd and msd are numbered in direction opposite to main division.

Construct a backward Vernier scale for R.F. = $\frac{1}{60}$ to read centimetres and suitable to measure up to 6 m.

Mainscale

Length of scale = $\frac{1}{60} \times 6 \times 100 = 10$ cm

Forward Vernier (Direct Vernier)

PROBLEM 6.15 (FIG. 6.17)

Construct a forward Vernier scale of R.F. = $\frac{1}{60}$ to read centimeter and suitable to measure up to 6 m.

Solution:

If msd > vsd, then Vernier scale is called forward Vernier scale.

For this case, LC = msd – vsd

vsd and msd are numbered in the same direction as that of main division on the main scale.

Solution:

Length of scale = $\frac{1}{60} \times 6 \times 100 = 10$ cm

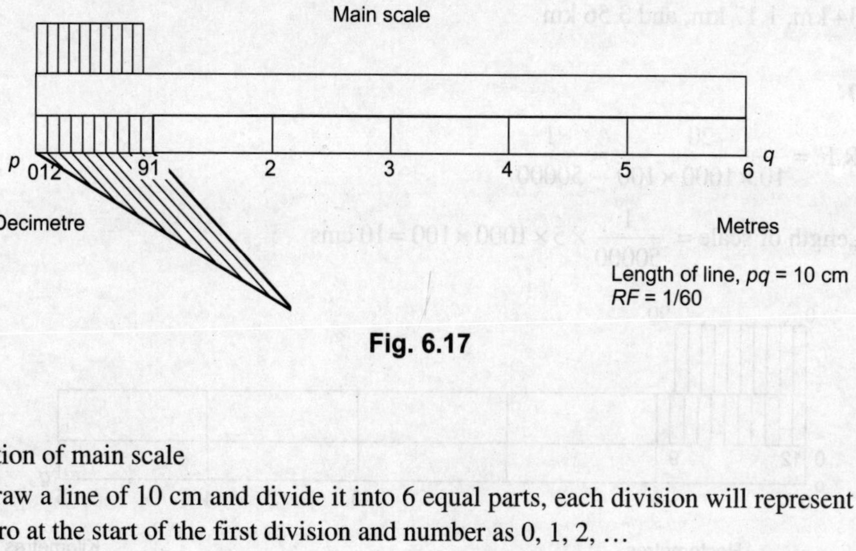

Fig. 6.17

Steps:

Construction of main scale

(i) Draw a line of 10 cm and divide it into 6 equal parts, each division will represent 1 m. Mark zero at the start of the first division and number as 0, 1, 2, …

Divide all into 10 equal parts, each will represent decimetre.

Construction of forward Vernier

LC = 1 cm and msd represents 1 dm

$$LC = 1\text{ cm} = \frac{1}{100}\text{ msd}$$

LC = msd – vsd

$$\left(\frac{1}{10}\right)\text{msd} = \text{msd} - \text{vsd}$$

10 vsd = 9 msd

Length of Vernier = 9 msd

Draw a Vernier of length equal to 9 msd above the first msd.

The length of Vernier will represent

9×1 dm = 9 dm

Divide this also in 10 equal parts, so that each vsd will represent 9/10 = 0.9 dm

Note that LC = 1 dm – 0.9 dm

= 0.1 dm = 1 cm

PROBLEM 6.16 (FIG. 6.18)

On a drawing, the distance of 10 km is shown by 20 cm long line. Find R.F.. Construct the forward Vernier scale to read decametres and measure up to 5 km. Show the following distances:

0.34 km, 1.17 km, and 3.56 km

Solution:

(i) $$\text{R.F.} = \frac{20}{10 \times 1000 \times 100} = \frac{1}{50000}$$

$$\text{Length of scale} = \frac{1}{50000} \times 5 \times 1000 \times 100 = 10\text{ cms}$$

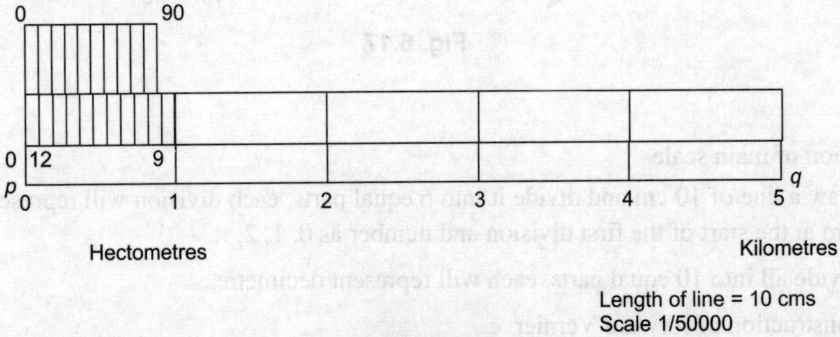

Fig. 6.18

Constructional details

Main scale

Divide line in 5 equal parts, one division will represent 1 km.

First part is subdivided into 10 equal parts, each part will represent 1 hectometre.

msd = 1 hm

$$LC = 1 \text{ dam} = \frac{1}{10} \text{ msd}$$

$$LC = \text{msd} - \text{vsd}$$

$$\frac{1}{10}\text{msd} = \text{msd} - \text{vsd} \quad \text{or } 10 \text{ vsd} = 9 \text{ msd}$$

Construct a Vernier of length = 9 msd above the scale

Divide the Vernier into 10 equal divisions, each vsd will represent 0.9 hm = 9 dam

PROBLEM 6.17 (FIG. 6.19)

On a drawing, the distance of 10 km is shown by a 20 cm long line.

Find R.F. Construct a backward Vernier scale of this R.F. to read decametre and measure up to 5 km.

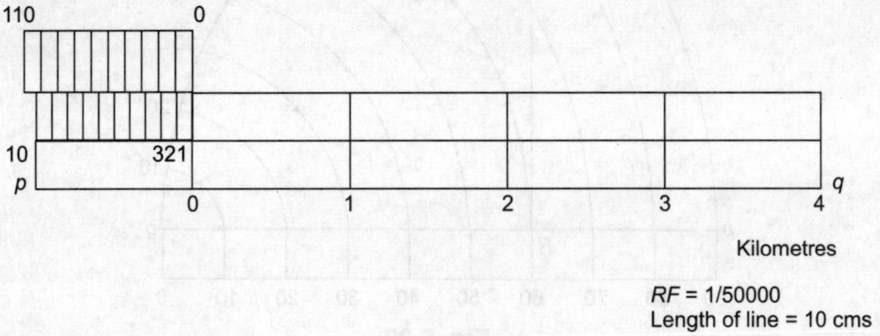

Fig. 6.19

Solution:

$$\text{R.F.} = \frac{20}{10 \times 1000 \times 100} = \frac{1}{50000}$$

$$\text{Length of scale} = \frac{1}{50000} \times 5 \times 1000 \times 100 = 10 \text{ cm}$$

Least count = vsd – msd

$$\frac{1}{10}\text{ msd} = \text{vsd} - \text{msd}$$

or 10 vsd = 11 msd

or Vernier length = 11 msd

(i) *Main scale:* Divide line into 5 equal parts; one division will represent 1 km. First part be sub-divided into 10 equal parts, each part will represent 1 hectometre.

(ii) *Vernier scale:* Draw a Vernier of length = 11 msd and divide it into 10 equal parts so that vsd = 1.1 hm = 11 dam

6.8 SCALE OF CHORDS

The scale of chords is constructed to draw angles without the use of a protractor. The constructional methods will be as follows (presented in Fig. 6.20).

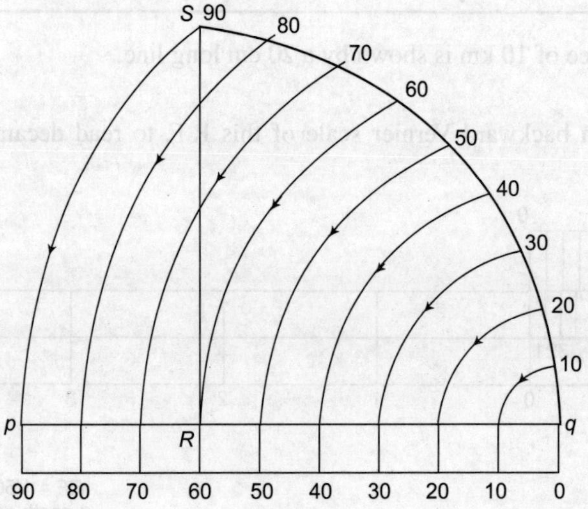

Fig. 6.20

Constructional details:

1. Draw a straight line Rq to any suitable length.
2. Draw RS perpendicular to Rq at R.
3. Draw an arc of a circle with R as centre and Rq as radius to intersect the line Rq and RS at q and s, respectively.
4. By trial and error, divide the arc into 9 equal parts and sub-divide each part into two equal parts.
5. With q as centre and through all the division points, draw arcs to intersect qR produced at 10, 20, 30, 40, … etc.

EXERCISE

Review Questions

1. What is the purpose of a scale?
2. What are the different types of scales?
3. What is the difference between plain scale and diagonal scale?
4. What is the principle of a diagonal scale?
5. What is representative fraction?
6. Give the difference between reducing and increasing scales.
7. What is scale factor? Is it the same as R.F.?
8. Construct a plain scale of 10 cm = 10 cm to show a single metre and single decimetre, and long enough to measure up to 15 m. Show on this scale a distance of 11.3 m.
9. Construct a plain scale to show metres and decimetres. 4 cm on the scale is equal to 1 m distance. The scale should be long enough to measure up to 2 m. Show on this scale a distance of 1 m 4 dm.
10. A rectangular plot 8 sq. km in area is represented on a certain map by a similar rectangular area of 1 sq. cm. Draw a plain scale to show 6 km and single km, and long enough to measure up to 40 km. Find R.F. of the scale. Also show the distance of 20 km on it.
11. Construct a diagonal scale of 1 : 50 to measure a tape up to the length 8 m.
12. Construct a diagonal scale of 1 : 50 to show metres, decimetres, and centimetres, and long enough to measure up to 6 m.

    Also indicate on the scale a distance of 6 m 4 dm and 3 cm.
13. Construct a diagonal scale of R.F. = 1/400.

    If should be long enough to measure 6 m. Show a distance of 55.7 m on it.
14. Draw a version scale of R.F. = 4 to show centimetres, $1/10^{th}$ of cm, and $1/100^{th}$ of cm to read up to 8 cm. Mark on the scale the length 5.03 cm and 2.35 cm.
15. The actual length of 200 m is represented by a line of 10 cm on a drawing. Draw a Vernier scale to read up to 300 m. Mark on the scale a length of 242 m.

Objective Questions

1. _______ = representative fraction × maximum distance to be measured
2. Ratio of length of the drawing of object to the actual length of the object is called _______.
3. When a drawing is made to the same size of the object, the name of the scale is _______.
4. Drawing of a building, maps are drawn using _______.
5. Drawing of a part of watch, maps are drawn using ___________.
6. When the measurements are desired in two units, _______ scale is used.
7. The relative value of R.F. of enlarging, reducing, and full-size scales are ______, _______ and _______, respectively.

ANSWERS

Objective Questions

1. Length of scale
2. representative fraction
3. full size
4. reducing scale
5. enlarging scale
6. plain
7. >1, <1, 1

CHAPTER 7

Projection and Orthographic Projection

7.1 INTRODUCTION

Any machine component has three dimensions. In engineering drawing, the shape of a component is visualized by taking the projection on a picture plane. The projection of an object is the image of that object taken by the rays of light from the observer which is placed at an infinite distance from the object.

While drawing a projection, the following elements are considered:

1. Object/machine components
2. Projection plane (plane on which projection is desired)
3. Rays of light/Projector
4. Observer

If the observer is placed at an infinite distance from the object to be visualized, the rays used to visualize will be all parallel to each other and also perpendicular to the projection plane. The projection of an object on the projection plane will be of the same size as the object as shown in Fig. 7.1 (a) and (b).

A rectangular plate ABCD is kept in front of the vertical plane (VP) in between the observer and the picture plane. It is visualized by the observer at infinite distance from the object. The rays are passing through the end points of ABCD which are all parallel to each other and perpendicular to the picture plane.

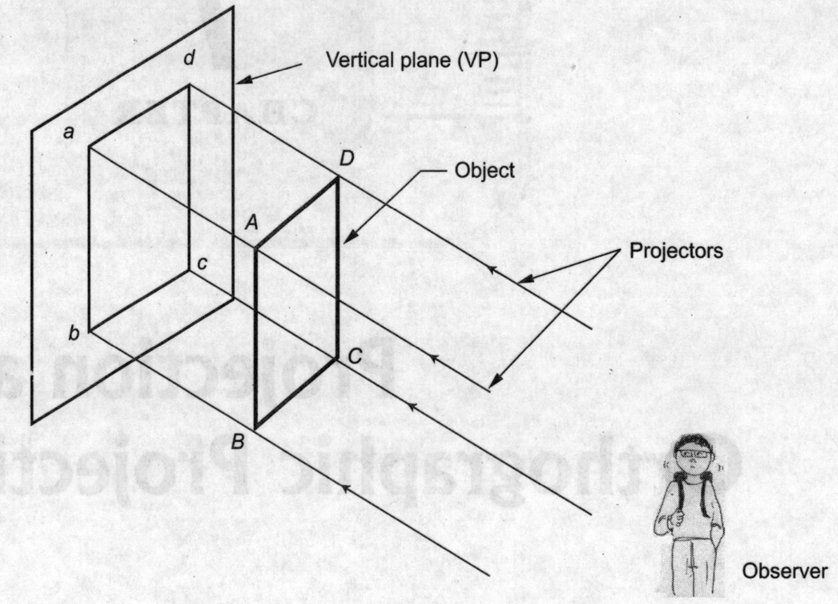

Fig. 7.1 (a) Projection on vertical plane

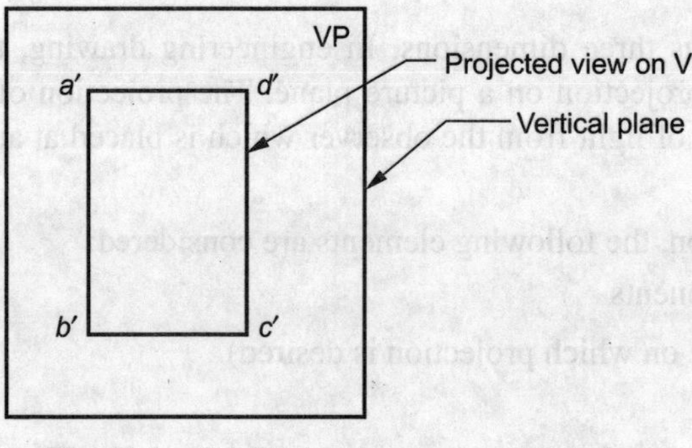

Fig. 7.1 (b) Projection on vertical plane

The front surface of the object gives the true shape. *a′b′c′d′* is the projected view of plate ABCD on vertical plane.

The resulting view is the projection on VP called *front view* or *elevation*.

Similarly, the projection of plate ABCD on a horizontal plane (HP) also gives the true shape, and the projected view is *abcd*. The resulting view on HP called *top view* or *plan* as shown in Fig. 7.2 (a) and (b).

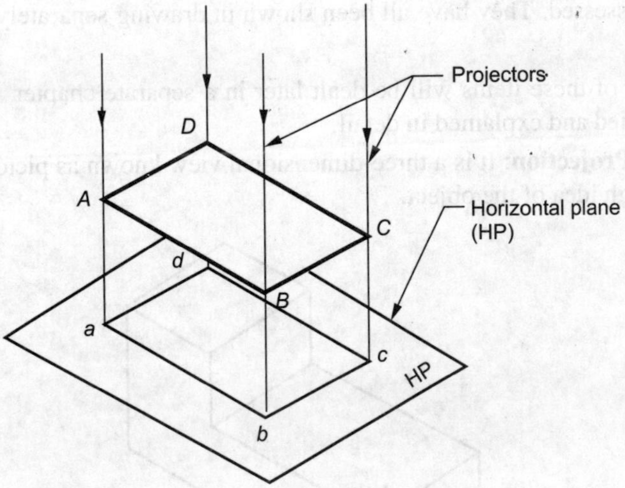

Fig. 7.2 (a) Projection on HP

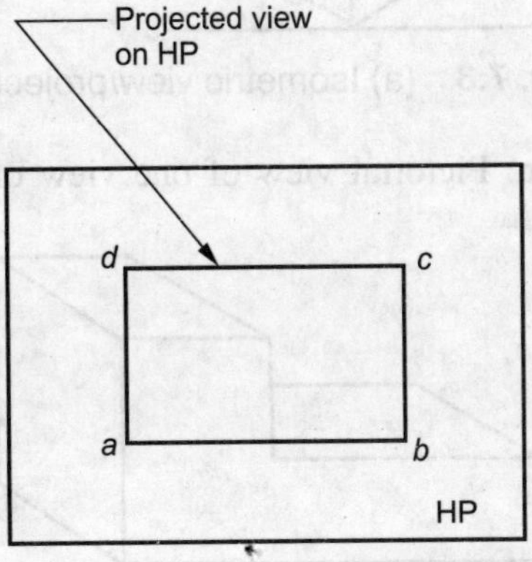

Fig. 7.2 (b) Projection on HP

7.2 METHODS OF PROJECTION

There are four types of projections that are very commonly used in engineering drawing:

(i) Isometric view/Isometric projection

(ii) Oblique parallel projection

(iii) Perspective view

(iv) Orthographic projection

Isometric view/projection, oblique parallel projection, and perspective view projection are the pictorial view/drawing. The shape of the object is completely presented in *one view* only, which is a three-dimensional picture. Rough estimation of the object shape can be done. The exact details of the object cannot be assessed. They have all been shown in drawing separately in Fig. 7.3(a), (b), (c), and (d).

However, the study of these items will be dealt later in a separate chapter. Presently, orthographic projection will be studied and explained in detail.

(i) **Isometric view/Projection**: It is a three-dimensional view known as pictorial drawing. Only one view gives a rough idea of the object.

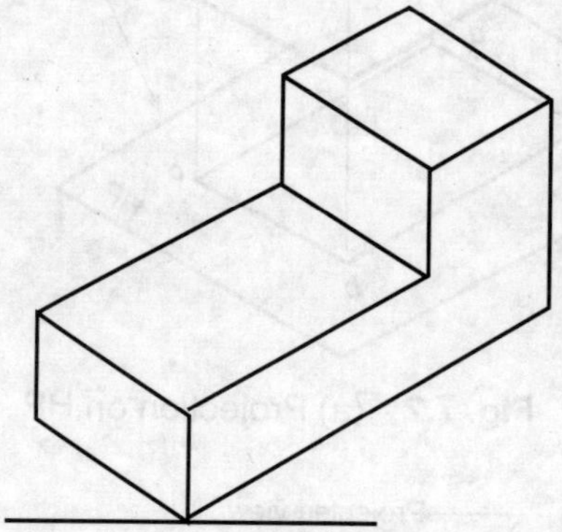

Fig. 7.3 (a) Isometric view/projection

(ii) **Oblique parallel projection**: Pictorial view of one view only gives rough estimation of the object.

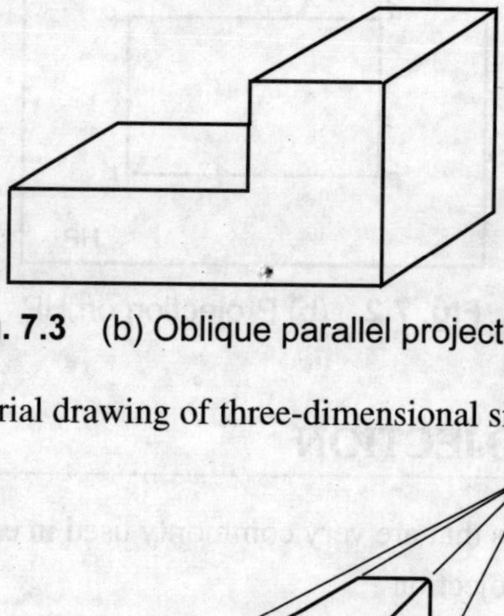

Fig. 7.3 (b) Oblique parallel projection

(iii) **Perspective drawing**: Pictorial drawing of three-dimensional single view only.

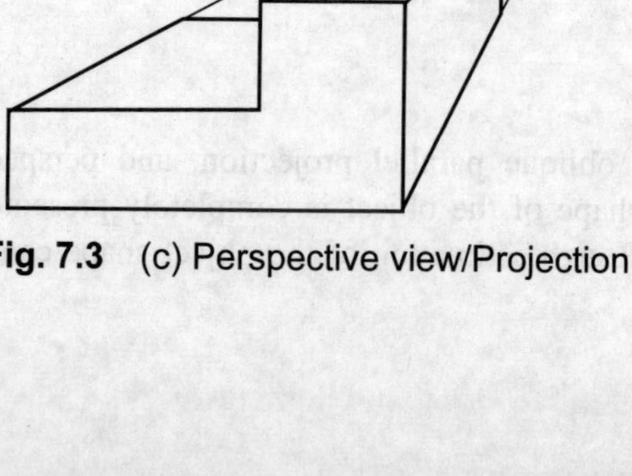

Fig. 7.3 (c) Perspective view/Projection

(iv) **Orthographic projection**: Orthographic view/projection is the universally used drawing. In order to define the entire shape and dimensions of the object, all the three views are necessary. The methods for drawing all the three views will be dealt in detail. The three views have been drawn and shown in Fig. 7.3(d) of the object shown in isometric projection in Fig. 7.3(a).

All three views give the complete dimensions of the object.

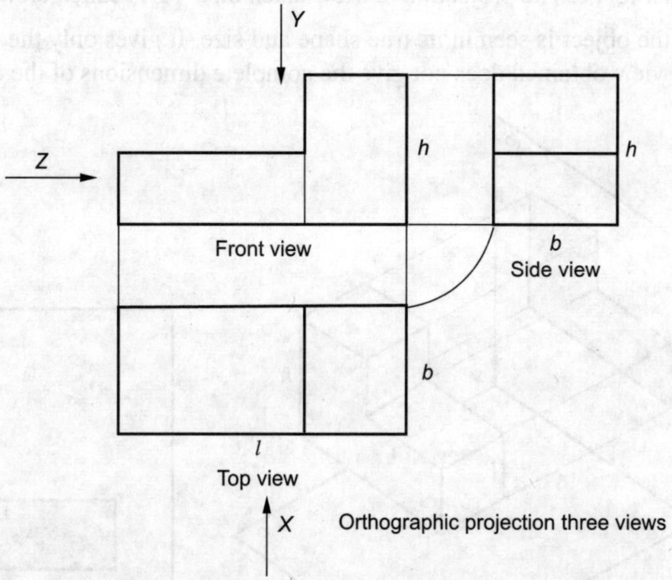

Fig. 7.3 (d) Orthographic view (not on scale)

l length of the object

b width of the object

h height of the object

Front view $l \times h$ (projection on front VP)

Top view $l \times b$ (projection of HP)

Side view $h \times b$ (projection on side VP)

7.3 ORTHOGRAPHIC PROJECTION

This is a method of engineering drawing of different views of an object on a plane by projectors taken all parallel to each other and perpendicular to the plane on which projections are obtained, which are known as *orthographic projections*, i.e., all projectors used to visualize the objects are orthogonal. Orthographic projections are also said to be *right-angled projections*.

7.4 ORTHOGRAPHIC VIEW ON VP

The VP is called *principal plane* or *reference plane*.

Consider an object in Fig. 7.4 placed between picture plane and the observer standing at infinite distance from the object. The object is projected on a VP. Here, the projectors are all parallel to each other and perpendicular to VP. The projection or view taken on a VP is called elevation or front view.

The front view of the object is seen in its true shape and size. It gives only the length (*l*) and height (*h*) of the object. The view obtained does not give the complete dimensions of the object like width (b).

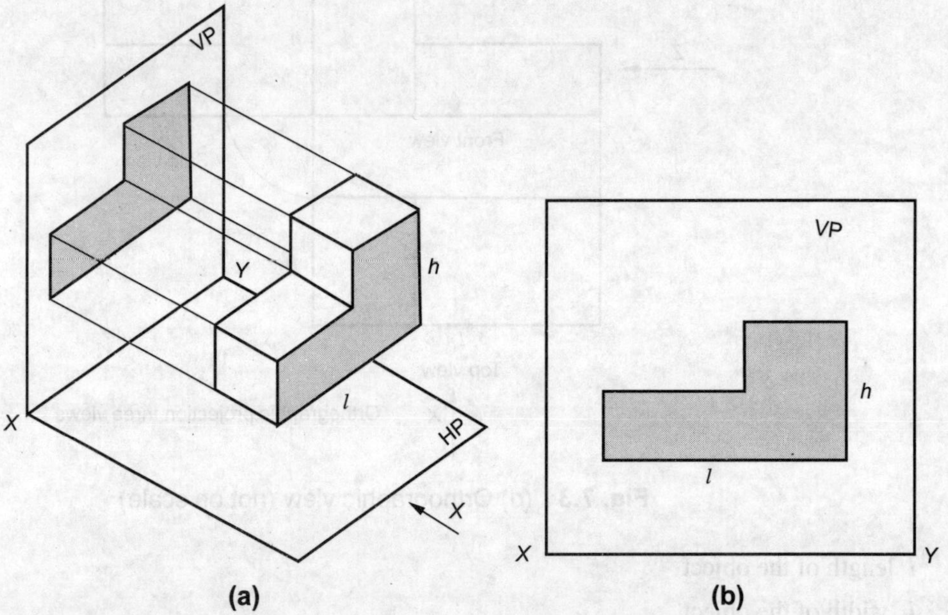

AR App

Fig. 7.4 (a) Projection on VP; (b) Front view (shaded area)

7.5 ORTHOGRAPHIC VIEW ON HP

The HP is also called *reference plane*. As the projection taken on VP cannot give the complete dimensions of the object, the object is projected on another plane which is perpendicular to VP, known as *horizontal plane*. The object is placed above HP as shown in Fig. 7.5(a) and (b) and is visualized by projectors in a similar manner. The projected view on HP is called *plan* or *top view*.

Both planes intersect at *XY* and are perpendicular to each other. The projected view gives the dimensions—length and width—and it is the true shape and size. The projection of the object on HP is shown in Fig. 7.5(a) and (b). The projection is taken in the direction of Y.

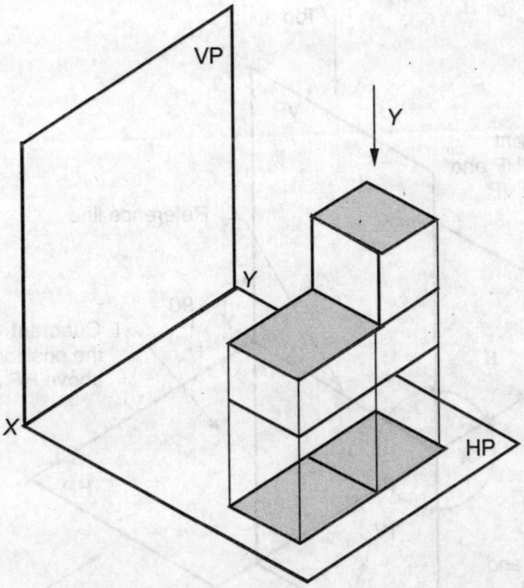

Fig. 7.5 (a) Projection on HP XY line intersection of HP and VP

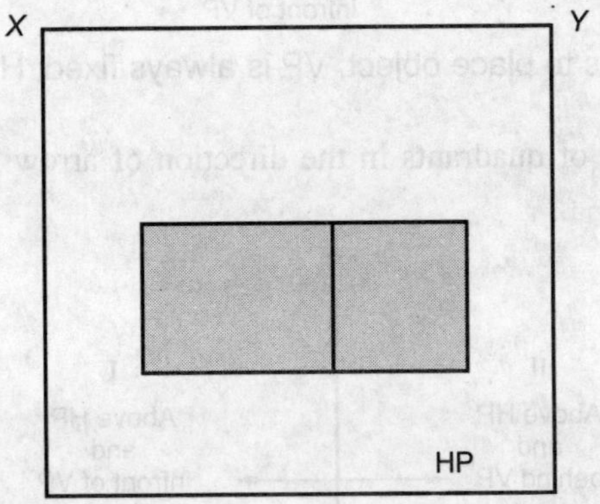

Fig. 7.5 (b) Top view (shaded area)

AR App

7.6 FOUR QUADRANTS

When two reference planes (HP and VP) are intersecting at XY, they form four quadrants in space. These quadrants are counted as I, II, III, and IV in anticlockwise direction as shown in Fig. 7.6(a).

The object is imagined to be placed in any of the quadrants and are visualized in either direction. The projections are taken on HP and VP.

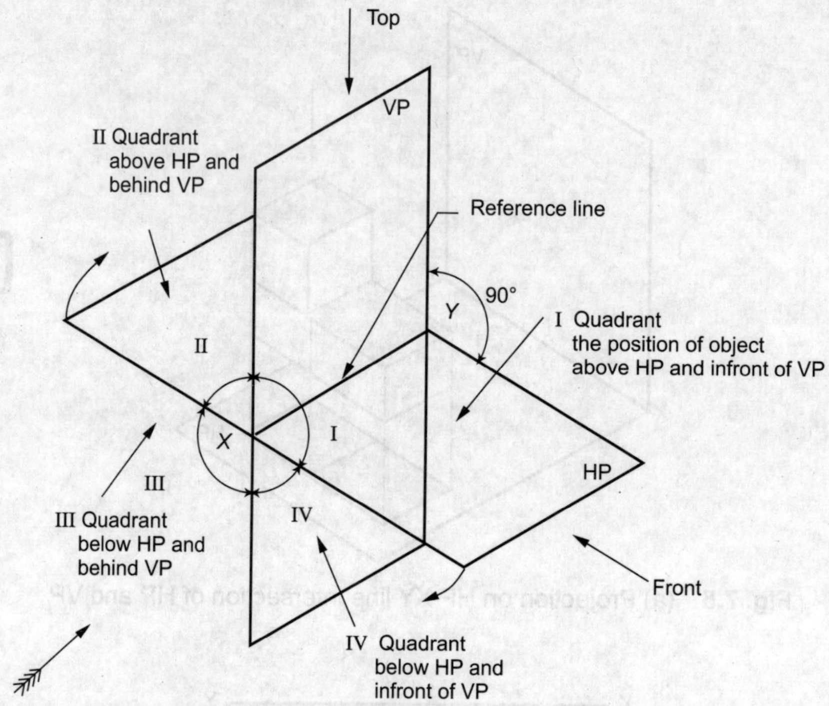

Fig. 7.6 (a) Four quadrants to place object; VP is always fixed, HP is to be rotated clockwise

If side view, i.e., projection of quadrants in the direction of arrow is to be taken, it looks like as shown in Fig. 7.6(b).

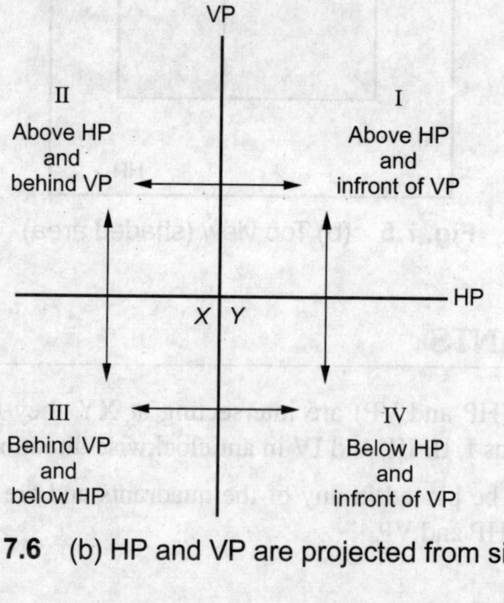

Fig. 7.6 (b) HP and VP are projected from side

7.7 METHODS OF PROJECTION

It is known that drawing sheets are flat surfaces and drawing is to be prepared on a flat sheet.

HP and VP, both reference planes, are intersecting at XY. It is the drawing conversion that VP is kept fixed and HP is rotated through 90° *clockwise* about XY axis such that VP and HP both become flat as shown in Fig. 7.7(a). Thus, above XY becomes the existence of VP and below XY will represent HP. Now the two projections are drawn on two-dimensional flat drawing sheets.

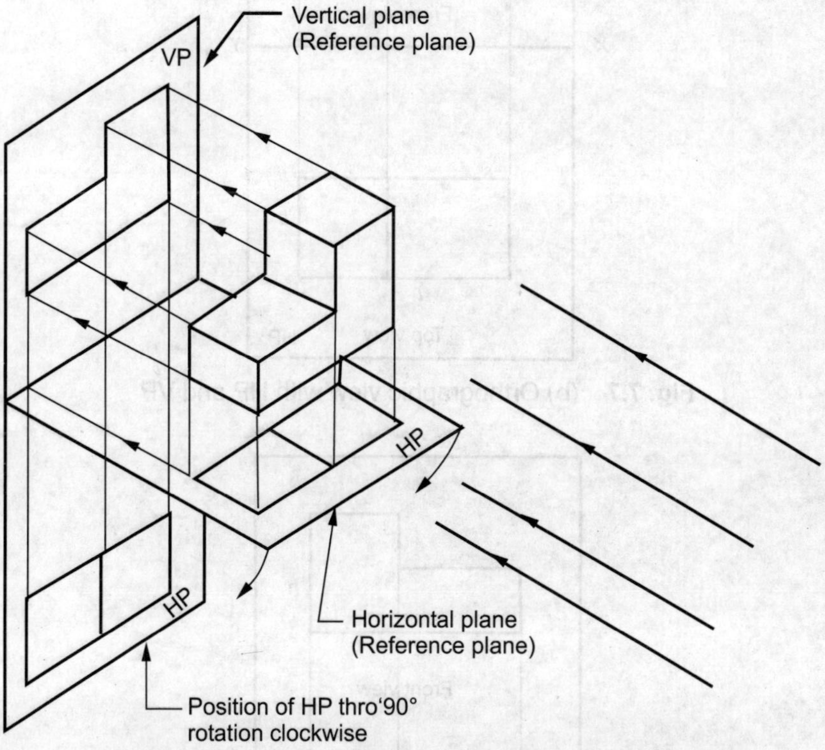

Fig. 7.7 (a) Placement of object in front of HP and VP

By doing so, HP coincides with VP and thus existence of quadrants II and IV vanishes completely. Only, quadrants I and III exist.

Figures 7.7(b) and (c) show the projected views on HP and VP. The object has been placed between HP and VP in I quadrant. The projection of object on VP is called *front view*. The projection of object on HP is called *plan* or *top view*.

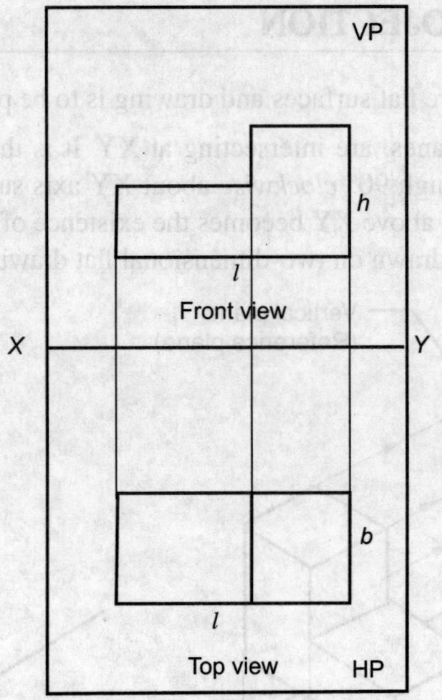

Fig. 7.7 (b) Orthographic view with HP and VP

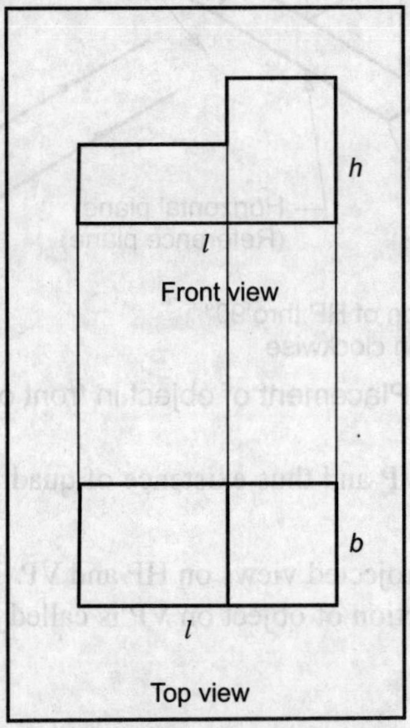

Fig. 7.7 (c) Orthographic view, HP and VP removed

7.8 FIRST ANGLE PROJECTION

When the object is placed in first quadrant, the projections drawn on HP and VP are called *first angle projections*.

Figure 7.7(a) gives the impression of first angle projection. In this projection, the object is placed between the observer and the plane. The front view is drawn above XY (reference line) and the top view is draw below XY (reference line) as presented in Fig. 7.7(b) and (c).

Both planes, HP and VP, are intersecting at XY and form the quadrants as explained earlier. When the projections are taken, HP is projected on VP; the projection of HP lies on XY. Similarly, when VP is projected on HP, the projection of VP lies on XY.

BIS (Bureau of Indian standards) has given recommendation that *first angle projection* is to be adopted in all engineering drawings. Hence, all drawing problems will be dealt in first angle projection. However, some problems may be solved following the III angle projection.

7.9 THIRD ANGLE PROJECTION

The object is placed in third quadrant. The plane of projection lies between the object and the observer.

In this case, HP and VP both planes are considered to be transparent. The front view is drawn below XY line and the top view is drawn above it. The viewer are shown in Fig. 7.8(a) and (b).

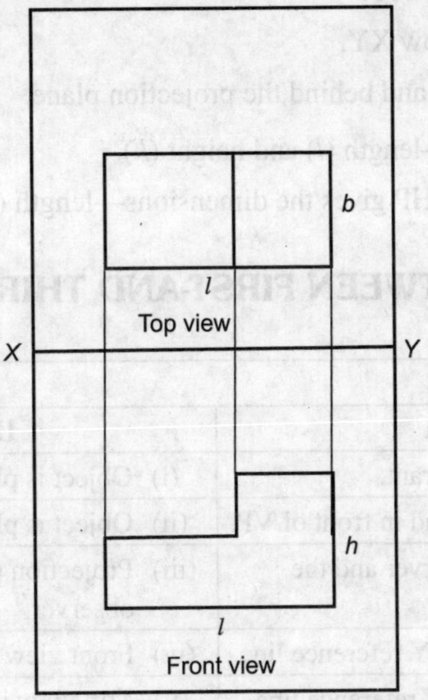

Fig. 7.8 (a) Front view and top view in III angle projection with HP and VP

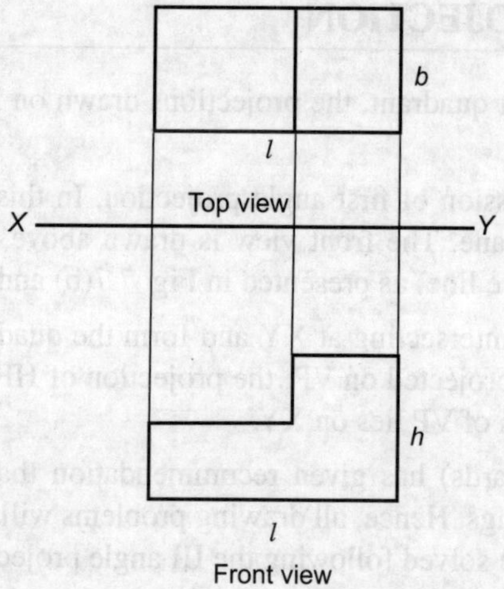

Fig. 7.8 (b) Projections without planes

The following points are to be remembered in III angle projections:

(i) The object is placed in third quadrant.

(ii) The projection plane lies between the object and the observer.

(iii) The projection planes are considered transparent.

(iv) The top view is drawn above XY.

(v) The front view is drawn below XY.

(vi) The object is situated below and behind the projection plane.

Front view gives the dimensions—length (*l*) and height (*h*).

The top view in the projection on HP gives the dimensions—length (*l*) and width (*b*).

7.10 DIFFERENCE BETWEEN FIRST-AND THIRD-ANGLE PROJECTION

I angle projection	III angle projection
(i) Object is placed in first quadrant.	(i) Object is placed in third quadrant.
(ii) Object is placed above HP and in front of VP.	(ii) Object is placed below HP and behind VP.
(iii) The object lies between observer and the projection plane.	(iii) Projection plane lies between the object and observer.
(iv) Front view is drawn above XY reference line.	(iv) Front view is drawn below XY reference line.
(v) Top view is drawn below XY reference line.	(v) Top view is drawn above XY reference line. Both the reference frames are considered to be transparent.

Symbol used	Symbol used
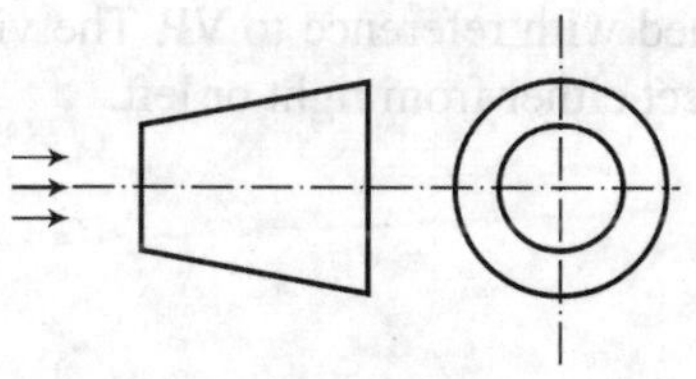 Frustum of cone (First angle projection)	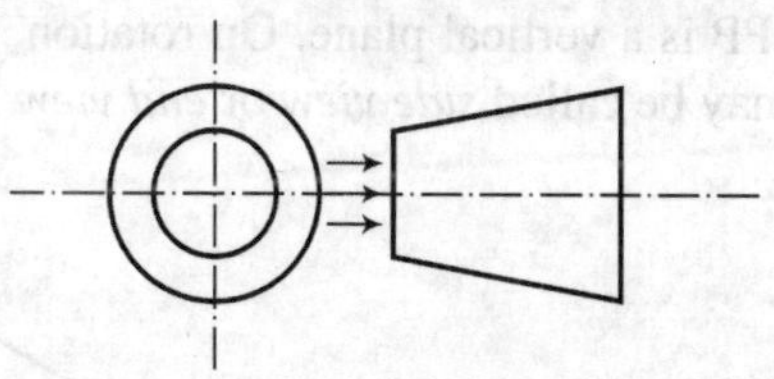 Frustum of cone (Third angle projection)

7.11 SECOND ANGLE PROJECTION

The object is placed in quadrant II. The object lies above HP and behind VP. VP is considered transparent to visualize the object.

When HP is turned clockwise conventionally, both the projected views will coincide with each other. Some of the dimensions may be identical and, hence, identification of the views will be difficult. Overlapping of the views is possible and, so, II angle projection is not acceptable.

7.12 FOURTH ANGLE PROJECTION

The object is placed in quadrant IV. The object is kept in front of VP and below HP.

When HP is turned clockwise, conventionally through 90°, both the projected views will coincide with each other. Both the views fall below XY line. There is no existence of quadrant IV. Identification of the views will be difficult.

Overlapping of the views is possible and, hence, fourth angle projection is not acceptable and conventionally, it is not considered.

7.13 MAIN VIEWS

Any object or machine component has three dimensions. The projection on VP and HP gives only two dimensions. The projection of VP will give length (*l*) and height (*h*). The projection on HP will give length (*l*) and width (*b*). In addition, there are many dimensions which may be common and also the size of the object in terms of height (*h*) and width (*b*) is missing.

Under these conditions, the true picture of the object cannot be assessed with single view. The complete visualization of the object cannot be made and, hence, one more view which will have height (*h*) and width (*b*) is needed to assess the complete details of the object. In most of the cases, an additional view, i.e., view at the object from left or from right on a side vertical plane, which is perpendicular to HP and VP reference plane, can be used. The side plane is known as *profile plane* (PP).

The projections of object on HP, VP, and PP are known as the main views of the object.

The PP is a vertical plane. On rotation, this must be aligned with reference to VP. The view drawn on PP may be called *side view* or *end view* looking at the object either from right or left.

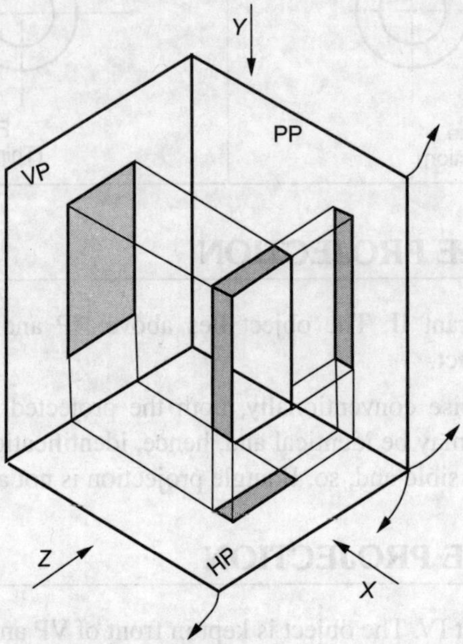

Fig. 7.9 Object placed in first quadrant in front of HP, VP, and PP

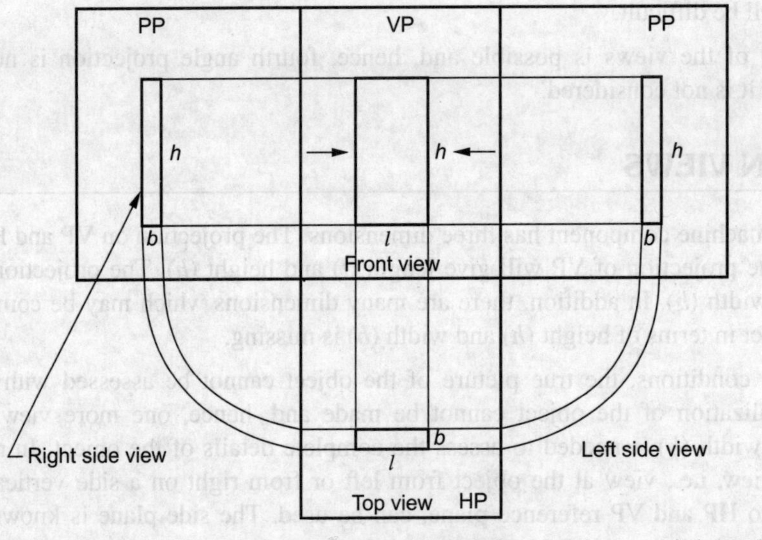

Fig. 7.10 Orthographic views (front view, top view, left side view, and right side view)

Figure 7.9 shows that an object is placed in the first quadrant in first angle projection in front of VP, HP, and PP, for getting front view, top view, and left side views. The projected views have been shown on different planes with shaded area.

Figure 7.10 represents the corresponding projections. Projection of the object on VP is front view. Top view is drawn by projecting the object on HP. The projection on PP, as seen from left and is drawn in right, and also the projection is drawn by projecting the object from right and view is placed left to the front view.

The placement of side view, seen from right has been drawn in left, is known as right side view. The placement of side view, seen from left has been drawn in right, is known as left side view.

7.14 METHODS OF PROJECTION IN I AND III ANGLE PROJECTION

With regard to drawing projection of object on PP, there is a difference of process to be adopted in first and third angle projections.

(i) In first angle projection, PP is placed on the right side of VP to get the left side view and PP is placed on left side of VP to get the right side view.

(ii) In third angle projection, PP is placed on the left side of VP to get the right side views and PP is placed on the right side of VP to get left side view.

The method can be seen from the conventional symbol drawing and the drawing presented in

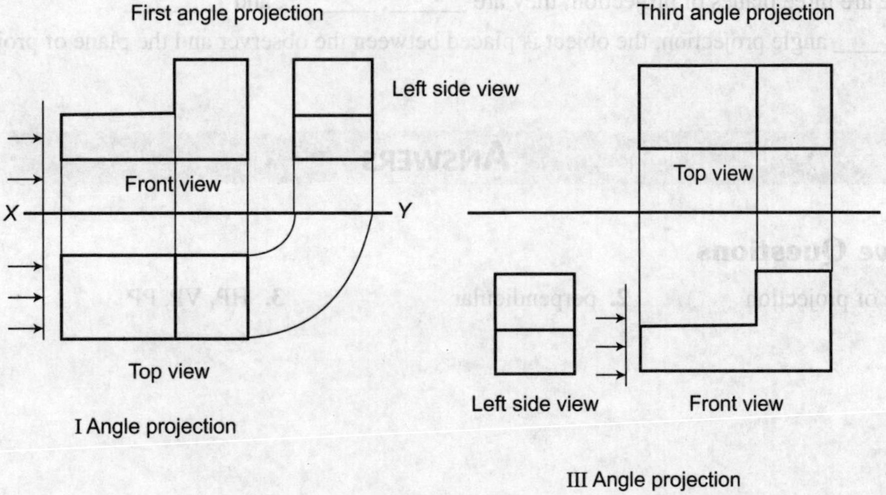

Fig. 7.11 Projection difference in I and III angle

EXERCISE

Review Questions

1. Explain orthographic projection.
2. Describe the methods of obtaining orthographic projection.
3. Explain in detail, the difference between first angle and third angle projections.
4. Why are the projections of an object not drawn in second and fourth quadrants?
5. What is a profile plane? State its use.
6. What is the symbol of first angle projection?
7. What is the symbol of third angle projection?
8. What is a principal plane?
9. What do HP and VP stand for?

Objective Questions

1. In third angle projection, the ______ is positioned between the observer and the object.
2. In orthographic projection, the line of sight are ______ to the plane of projection.
3. There are three planes of projection; they are ______, ______, and ______
4. In ______ angle projection, the object is placed between the observer and the plane of projection.

ANSWERS

Objective Questions

1. plane of projection
2. perpendicular
3. HP, VP, PP
4. first

CHAPTER 8

Projection of Points

8.1 INTRODUCTION

A point is dimensionless and, hence, the existence of a point can be represented by a black 'dot' encircled with a small circle. When a point is in space, it can be in either of the quadrants formed by HP and VP.

8.2 PROJECTION OF A POINT IN FIRST QUADRANT

When a point lies in first quadrant, it will be above HP and in front of VP.

PROBLEM 8.1

A point A is 40 mm in front of VP and 30 mm above HP. Draw its projections. [Fig. 8.1(a), (b), and (c)]

***Solution*:**

1. Fig. 8.1(a) shows the pictorial view showing the first quadrant. Point A lies between two planes HP and VP.
2. Point A is 30 mm above HP. Point A is projected on VP by Aa′ by a projector perpendicular to VP. Hence, a′ is the front view of A.

   O is just perpendicular to XY from a′.

   Oa′ is also 30 mm from XY.

AR App

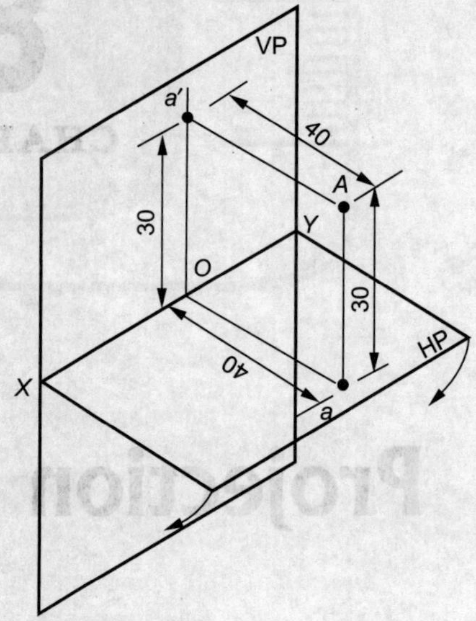

Fig. 8.1 (a) Point A in first quadrant

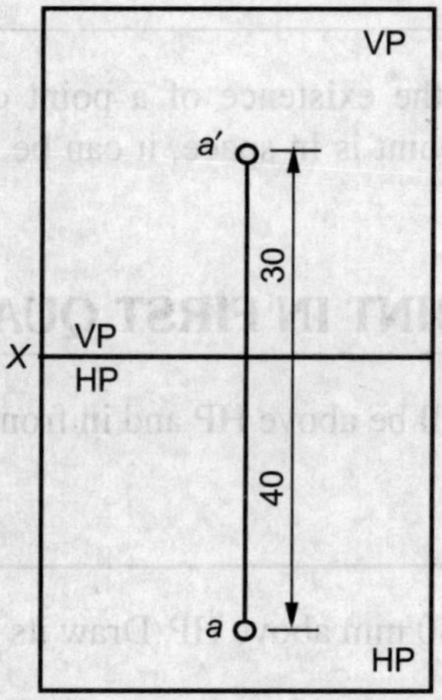

Fig. 8.1 (b) HP after rotation

3. Point A is 40 mm in front of VP.

   Point A is projected on HP by a projector perpendicular to HP.
   Hence, Aa is perpendicular to HP.

   ‘a’ is the top view.

   Oa is also equal to 40 mm.

   We see that Aa′oa is a rectangular plane, which is perpendicular to both HP and VP.

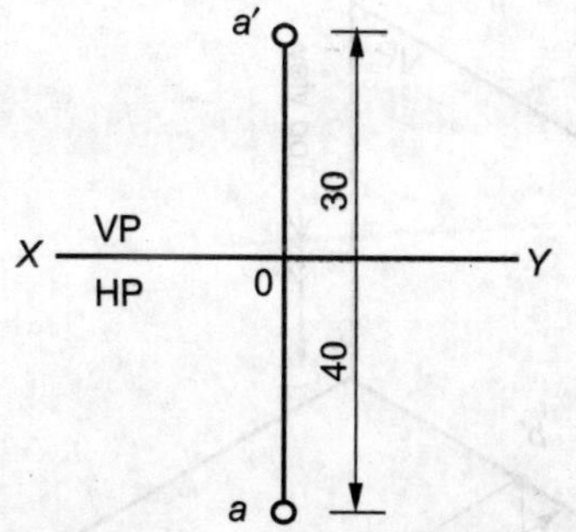

Fig. 8.1 (c) Projections of point A

4. Now, HP is rotated through 90° clockwise as shown in Fig. 8.1(a).

   After rotation, VP and HP become one plane flat surface.

   The plane aoa′A becomes a line perpendicular to XY, which has been shown in Fig. 8.1(b).

   Here, plane is converted to line joining Aa′ called projector, which is perpendicular to XY.
5. Draw XY and draw a projector at any point on XY. Mark a′ 30 mm above XY on the projection as shown in Fig. 8.1(c).
6. On the same projector, mark a, 40 mm below XY. a is the top view.

   a′ is the front view of the point A in first quadrant in first angle.

PROBLEM 8.2

Draw the projection of a point B lying on HP and 40 mm in front of VP. [Fig. 8.2(a) and (b)]

***Solution*:**

1. Project B on VP.
2. Point B is 40 mm in front of VP.

   Therefore, its top view will exist at b on HP itself.
3. Draw a line XY and draw a line representing projector at any point on XY. [Fig. 8.2(b)].

   Mark b′ on XY. On the same projector, mark b, 40 mm away from XY.

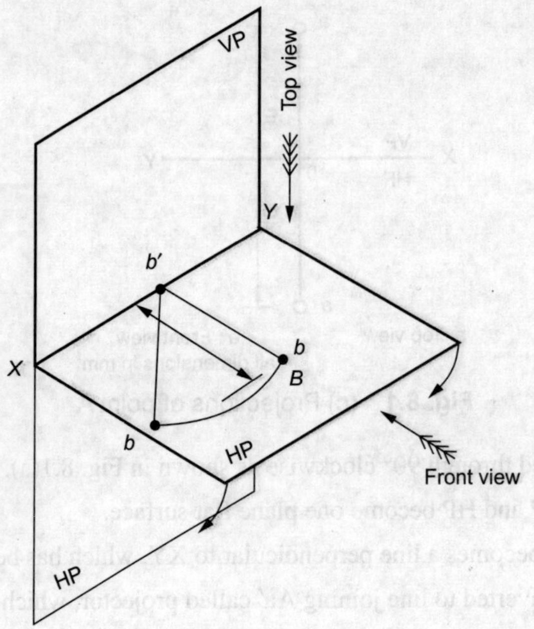

Fig. 8.2 (a) Pictorial view showing position of B

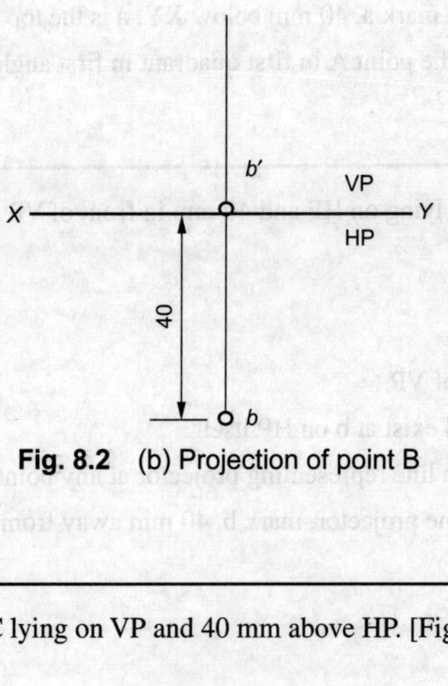

Fig. 8.2 (b) Projection of point B

PROBLEM 8.3

Draw the projection of a point C lying on VP and 40 mm above HP. [Fig. 8.3(a) and (b)].

Solution:

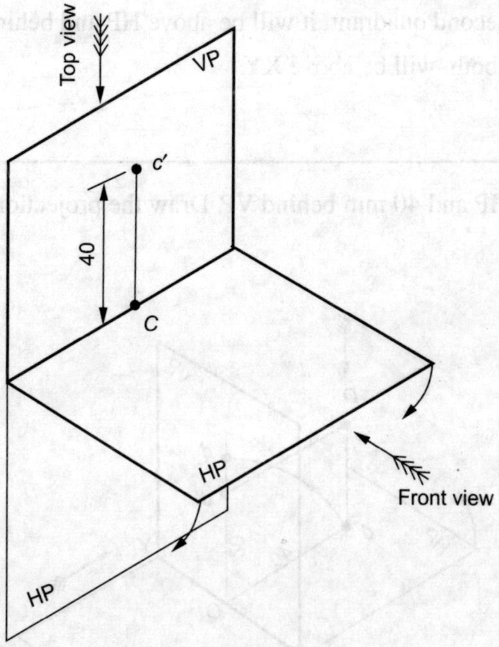

Fig. 8.3 (a) Pictorial view showing position of C

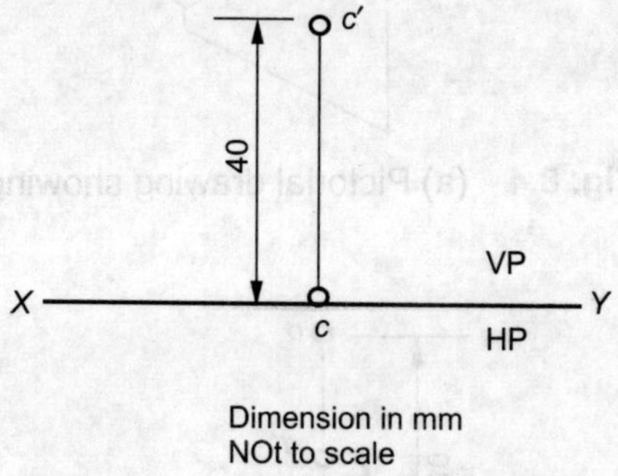

Fig. 8.3 (b) Projection of point C

1. Fig. 8.3(a) shows the pictorial view of HP and VP in quadrant I showing the position of C.
2. Point C is 40 mm above HP and in VP. Hence, the front view of point c lies at a height of 40 mm above XY represented by c′ and the top view lies on XY represented by c.
3. In this problem, HP will not be rotated and there is no need.
4. Draw a line XY and draw a projector at any point on XY.
   On the same projector, mark c′ 40 mm above XY and also c on XY.

   c is the top view of c and falls on XY. c′ is the front view at 40 mm above XY.

8.3 PROJECTION OF A POINT IN SECOND QUADRANT

When a point is situated in second quadrant, it will be above HP and behind VP.

Top view and front view, both, will be above XY.

PROBLEM 8.4

A point O is 20 mm above HP and 40 mm behind VP. Draw the projection of the point D. [Fig. 8.4 (a) and (b)]

***Solution*:**

AR App

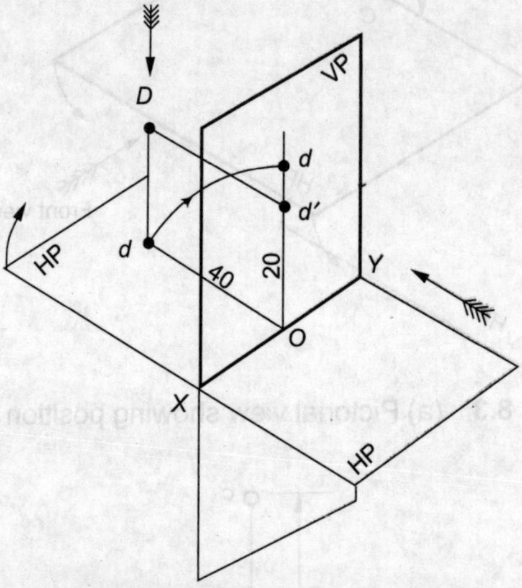

Fig. 8.4 (a) Pictorial drawing showing

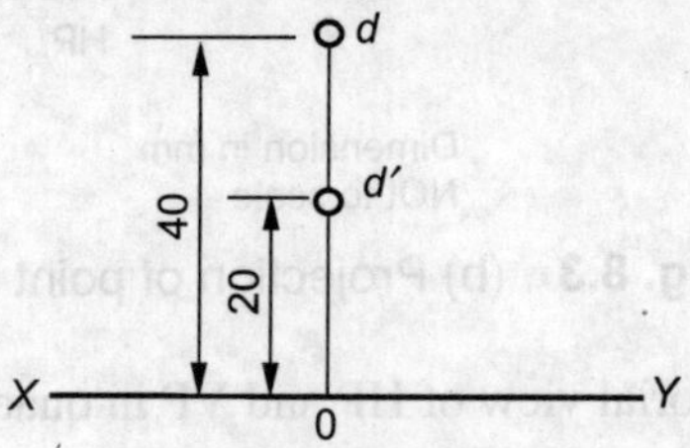

All dimension in mm
Not on scale

Fig. 8.4 (b) Projection of point D

1. Point D lies in quadrant II, 20 mm above HP. Taking the projection of D on VP, d′ is the front view of D and is 20 mm above XY.

2. Project D on horizontal plane. Point D is 40 mm behind VP. d is the top view of point D and 40 mm behind XY as in Fig. 8.4(a).
3. Rotate HP about XY through 90° in clockwise direction.

   HP coincides with VP.

   The projection taken on HP will come in contact with VP.
4. Dd′od is forming a rectangle which will converge to a line as a projector. The top view d of point D gets rotated through point o that lies on XY which falls on the same generator above d′.
5. Draw a line representing XY and a projector is drawn perpendicular to XY. Mark d′ as front view at 20 mm above XY and d as top view at 40 mm above XY. They are the orthographic projections in the same line. Both the projections are above XY.

8.4 PROJECTION OF A POINT IN III QUADRANT

When a point lies in third quadrant, it will be behind VP and below HP.

In this case, top view and front view both will be reverse of quadrant I projection. Top view will be drawn above XY and front view will be drawn below XY.

PROBLEM 8.5

A point E is 30 mm below HP and 20 mm behind VP. drawing projection of point.

Solution:

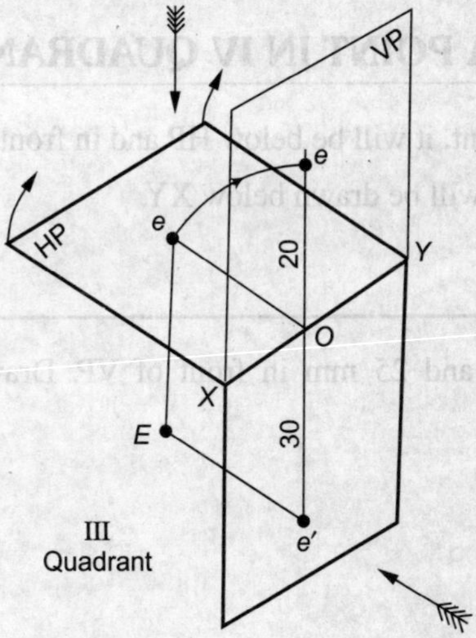

AR App

Fig. 8.5 (a) Pictorial drawing showing II quadrants and the position of points

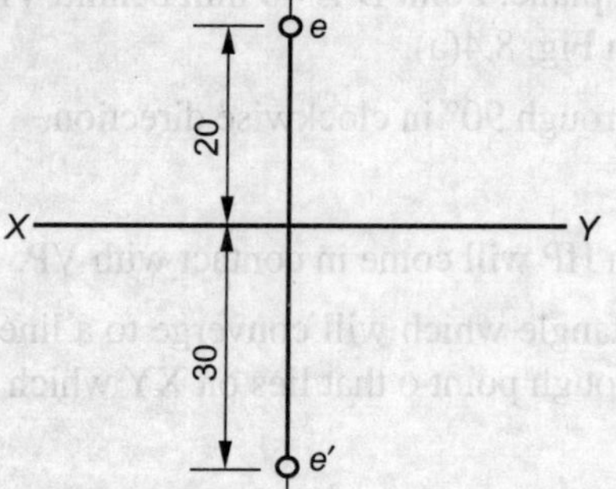

Fig. 8.5 (b) Projection of point in III angle

Figure 8.5(a) shows the pictorial drawing showing quadrant III and the placement of point E below HP and behind VP.

1. Point E is placed in quadrant III. The point is 30 mm below HP and 20 mm behind VP.
2. Front view of E is e′ and is projected on VP; and the top view of E is projected on HP.
3. Point E is visualized taking HP and VP as transparent planes.
4. Now HP is rotated clockwise through 90°. HP coincides with VP. The projection on HP also gets rotated and comes on the same projector line perpendicular to XY.
5. Projection will look like as shown in Fig. 8.5(b). On XY, draw a projector. On this projector, mark e and e′ as the projections.

   Top view is above XY and front view is below XY.

8.5 PROJECTION OF A POINT IN IV QUADRANT

When a point lies in fourth quadrant, it will be below HP and in front of VP.

Top view and front view, both, will be drawn below XY.

PROBLEM 8.6

A point F is 30 mm below HP and 25 mm in front of VP. Draw the projection of the point F. [Fig. 8.6(a) and (b)]

Solution:

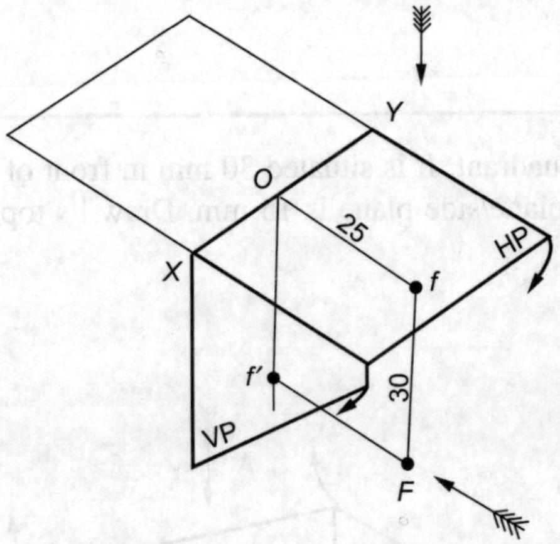

Fig. 8.6 (a) Pictorial drawing of IV quadrant with location of point F

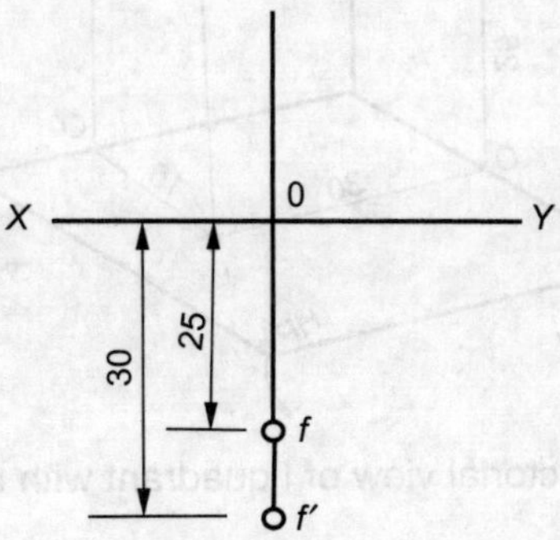

Fig. 8.6 (b) Projection of point F (not to scale)

1. Point F is in quadrant IV. It is 30 mm below HP and 25 mm in front of VP.
2. Look at point F in the direction of arrow. Take the projection on VP and transparent HP.

   Projection of F on VP is f′. Projection of F on HP is f.
3. Rotate HP conventionally. HP after rotation coincides with VP. look at Fig. 8.6(a) of projector will also coincides with of projector.
4. Fig. 8.6(b) is the projection. Draw a line XY. At any point on XY, draw a projector line perpendicular to XY. The projections f and f′ both will be marked on the projector. They are on the same side.

8.6 PROJECTION OF A POINT ON PROFILE PLANE

PROBLEM 8.7

A point P is lying in the first quadrant. It is situated 30 mm in front of VP and 25 mm above HP. The distance of point from profile plane/side plane is 15 mm. Draw its top view, front view, and left side view.

Solution:

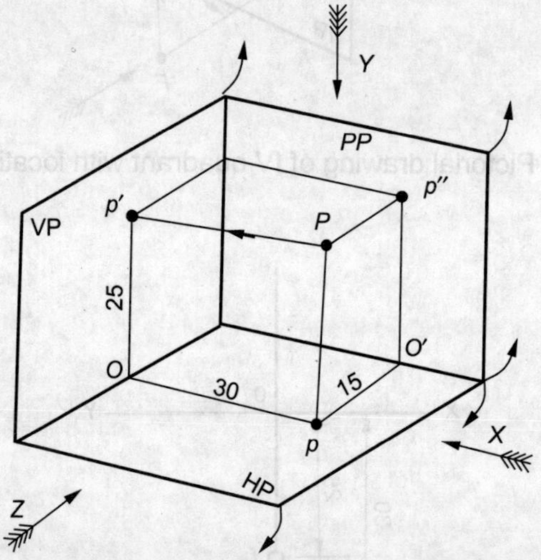

Fig. 8.7 (a) Pictorial view of I quadrant with right end plane

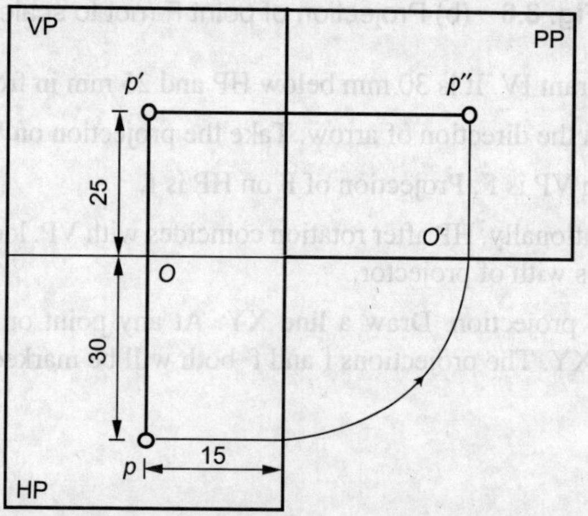

Fig. 8.7 (b) Opening of planes conventionally with projections with right end plane

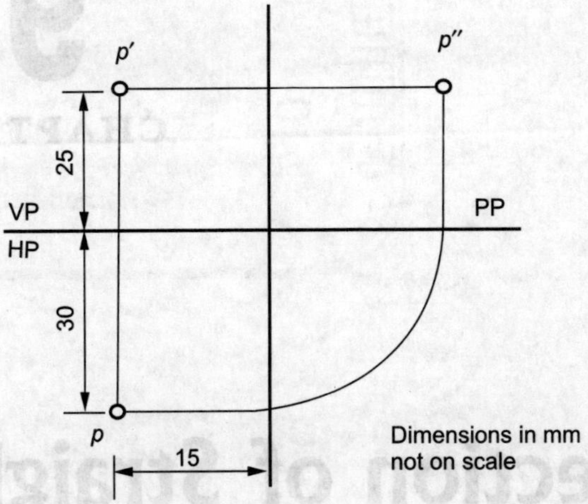

Fig. 8.7 (c) Orthographic view of point with projection on PP

1. Figure 8.7(a) shows the pictorial view showing quadrant I with right side PP or right end plane.

   The point P lies between the planes HP, VP, and PP.

2. Because left side view is needed in the problem, it means we need to look at the point P from left and PP will be towards right.

3. Mark the projection on VP as p′, projection on HP as p, and projection on PP as p″ as per convention.

4. Figure 8.7(b) shows the expanded view of three planes together and location of projected view therein.

   The rotation of PP has been done and will be placed towards right side of the reference VP.

5. Figure 8.7(c) represents the projection of point P on VP, HP, and PP.

9

CHAPTER

Projection of Straight Lines

9.1 INTRODUCTION

Infinite number of points are joined together and are adjusted in a straight path, collectively forming a straight line with two end points. A straight line is identified by its two end points. The shortest distance between any two end points is called a straight line. In the previous chapter, we have already seen the technique of the projection of points.

The projection of a straight line is obtained by joining the respective projections of two end points of straight lines in positions. A straight line may have different positions in space. It may occupy different positions in any one of the quadrants.

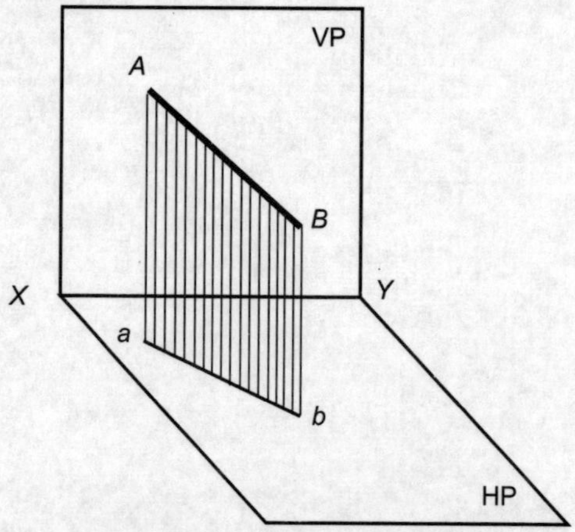

Fig. 9.1 Projection of line HP

Figure 9.1 is the representation of projection of a line AB on HP. A line AB is constituted by infinite number of points. A and B are the two end points of the straight line.

It is placed between HP and VP in the first quadrant. If each point is projected, the projected points will also be on path ab. So, *ab* is the projection of the straight line on HP.

PROBLEM 9.1

A line AB is 20 mm long, is perpendicular to VP, and is parallel to HP. The end A is nearer to VP is 20 mm in front of it and the line is placed 40 mm above HP. Draw the projections.

Solution:

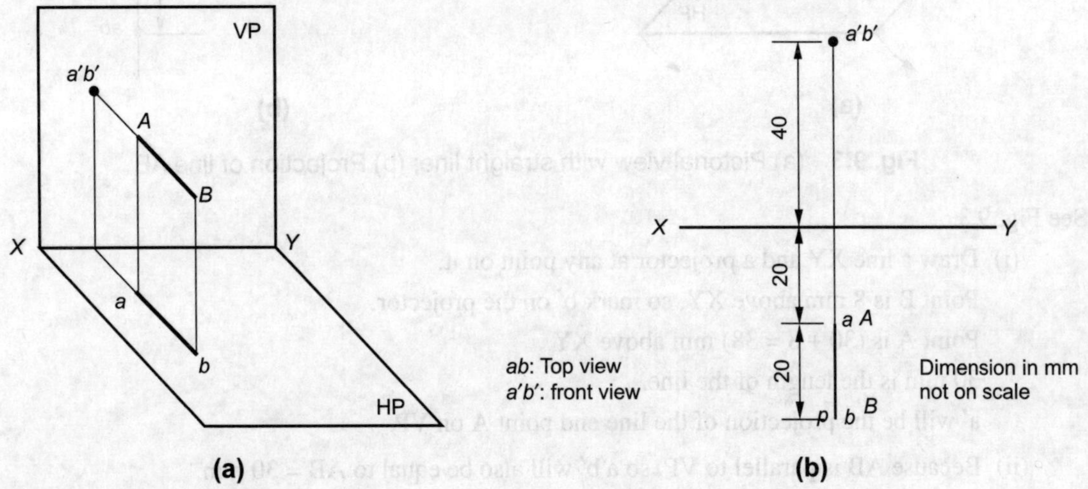

Fig. 9.2 (a) Pictorial drawing showing position of straight line; (b) Projection of straight line

See Fig. 9.2.

(i) The position of line is identified by being above and in front, so the line is in the first quadrant.

(ii) Line AB is parallel to HP and so projection on HP will be *ab* and it is also the true length of the line.

(iii) Line AB is perpendicular to VP, so the projection of AB will be a point on VP. *a′b′* both will lie on a single point 40 mm above XY.

PROBLEM 9.2

A line AB is 30 mm long and parallel to VP and perpendicular to HP. End B is nearer to HP and it is 8 mm above HP. The line is 20 mm in front of VP.

Solution:

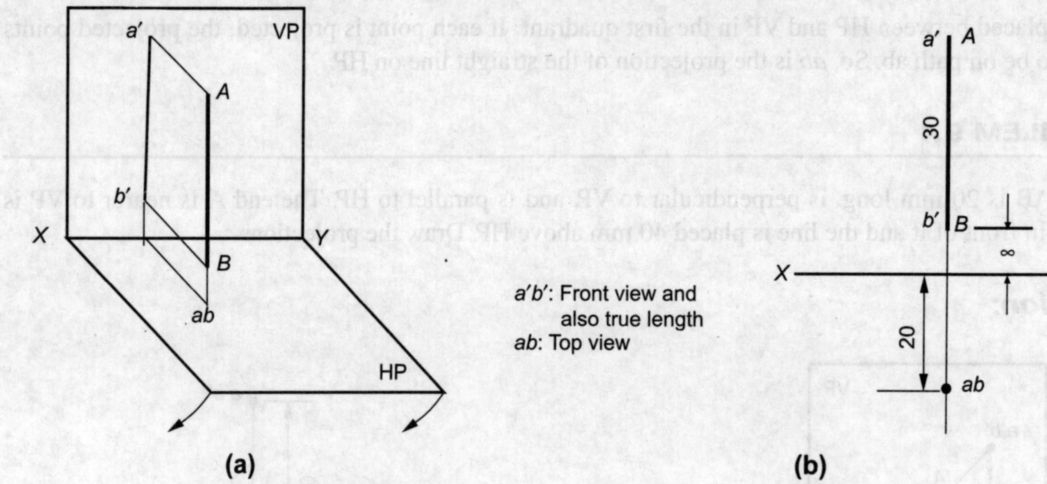

Fig. 9.3 (a) Pictorial view with straight line; (b) Projection of line AB

See Fig. 9.3.

(i) Draw a line XY and a projector at any point on it.
Point B is 8 mm above XY, so mark b′ on the projector.
Point A is (30 + 8 = 38) mm above XY.
30 mm is the length of the line.
a′ will be the projection of the line end point A on VP.

(ii) Because AB is parallel to VP, so a′b′ will also be equal to AB = 30 mm.

(iii) Looking from the top to get top view.
Because AB is perpendicular to HP, the projection of AB will lie on the same point ab.
ab is the projection of line AB on HP.
ab is 20 mm in front of XY.

PROBLEM 9.3

A straight line 50 mm long is parallel to both the reference plane HP and VP. The line is 20 mm in front of VP and 25 mm above HP. Draw the projection of the line. Also draw the left end view of the line in projection on PP.

Solution:

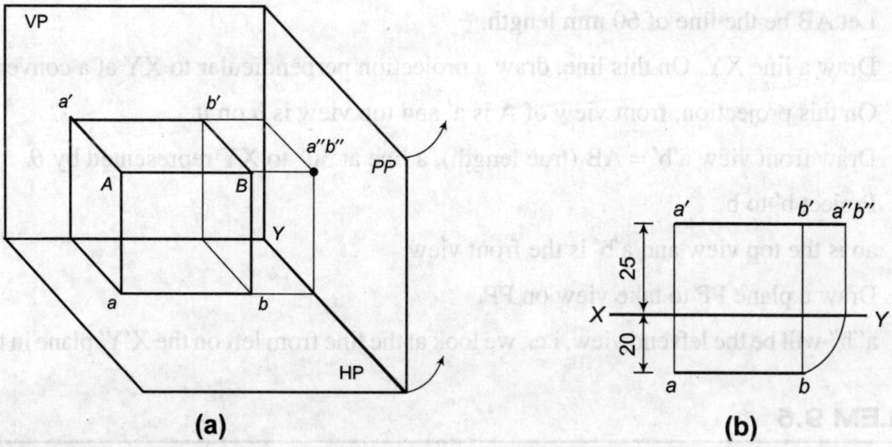

Fig. 9.4 (a) Pictorial view showing position of the line; (b) Projected view

See Fig. 9.4.

(i) Line AB is parallel to both the reference planes HP and VP. So, its view from the top and view from front both will be the true length of the line a′b′ = ab = AB = 50 mm.

(ii) Line is parallel to HP and VP both, so the end view of this line on PP will be a″b″, a point and it should be right side of elevation a′b′.

PROBLEM 9.4

A straight line 60 mm long is inclined 30° to HP and parallel to VP. The nearest end of the line is 20 mm above HP and 15 mm in front of VP. Draw its projections and draw left end view.

Solution:

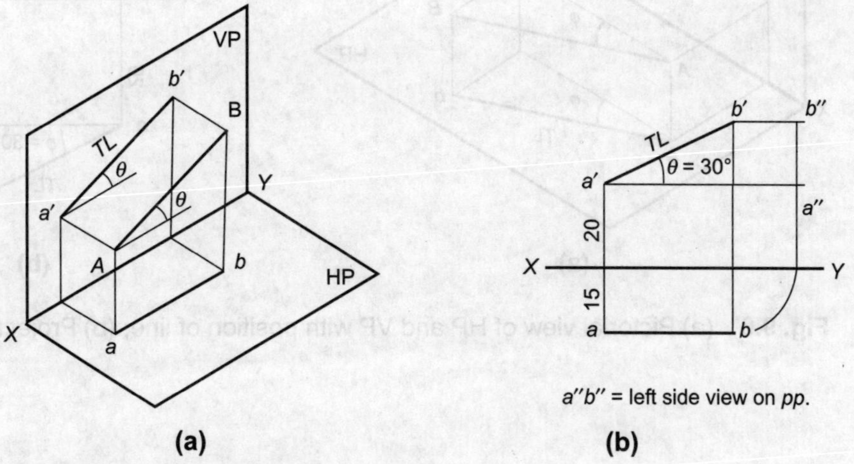

Fig. 9.5 (a) Pictorial of straight line with HP and VP; (b) Projection of straight line.(not on scale)

See Fig. 9.5.

(i) Let AB be the line of 60 mm length.

(ii) Draw a line XY. On this line, draw a projection perpendicular to XY at a convenient point.

(iii) On this projection, front view of A is a′ and top view is *a* on it.

(iv) Draw front view a′b′ = AB (true length), a line at 30° to XY represented by θ.

(v) Project b′ to b.

(vi) ab is the top view and a′b′ is the front view.

(vii) Draw a plane PP to take view on PP.

a″b″ will be the left end view, i.e., we look at the line from left on the X′Y′ plane in the right side.

PROBLEM 9.5

A line 60 mm long is inclined at 30° to VP and parallel to HP. The nearest end of the line is 20 mm in front of VP and 10 mm above HP. Draw projection [Fig. 9.6 (a)].

Solution:

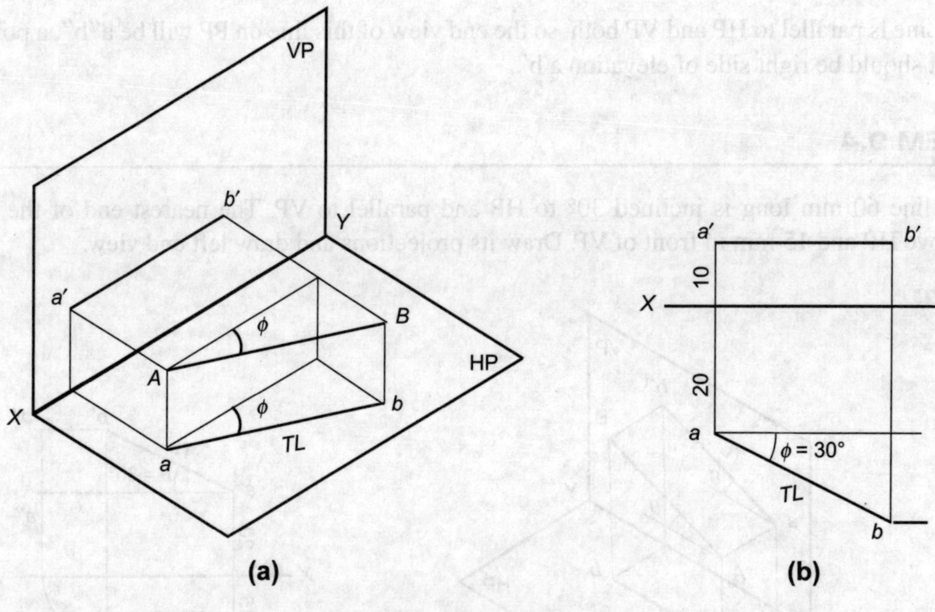

Fig. 9.6 (a) Pictorial view of HP and VP with position of line; (b) Projection of line

See Fig. 9.6 (b).

(i) Line is parallel to HP and so projection of the line on VP will be parallel to XY.

(ii) Draw a line XY and draw a projector line perpendicular to it.

(iii) On this projector, draw projection of A; a′ is the front view and a is the top view.

(iv) Draw top view ab = AB (true length), a line at 30° at a.

(v) Project b to b′.

(vi) a′b′ is the elevation and ab is the top view.

PROBLEM 9.6

A line AB 60 mm long is parallel to VP. End A is 30 mm in front of VP and 30 mm above HP. End B of the line touches HP. Draw the projections [Fig. 9.7 (a)].

Solution:

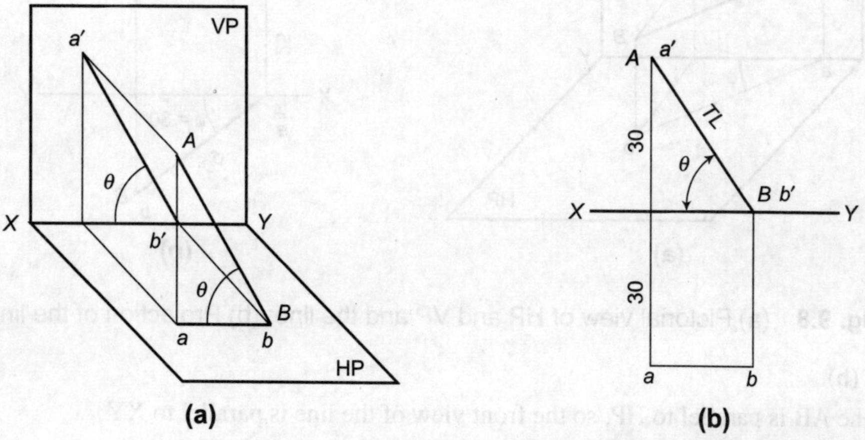

Fig 9.7 (a) Pictorial of HP and VP and position of the line; (b) Projection of the line

See Fig. 9.7 (b).

(i) Line AB is parallel to VP, so top view of line will be parallel to XY.

(ii) The end B of the line is on ground, the front view of B will lie on XY.

(iii) Draw XY and draw a projector at a convenient point perpendicular to XY.

(iv) End A is 30 mm above HP and 30 mm in front of VP.

(v) On this projector, take 30 mm on both the sides of XY to represent a′ as front view and a as top view.

(vi) From a′ as centre, draw an arc equal to the length of the line = 60 mm to cut XY at b′.

(vii) b′ is the front view of end B.

Draw a line downward from b′, it will cut at b.

ab is the top view and a′b′ is the top view which is also the true length = 60 mm.

θ angle can be measured.

PROBLEM 9.7

A line AB is 50 mm long, is parallel to HP, and is 25 mm above HP. End A of the line touches VP and the line is inclined 30° to VP [Fig. 9.8 (a)].

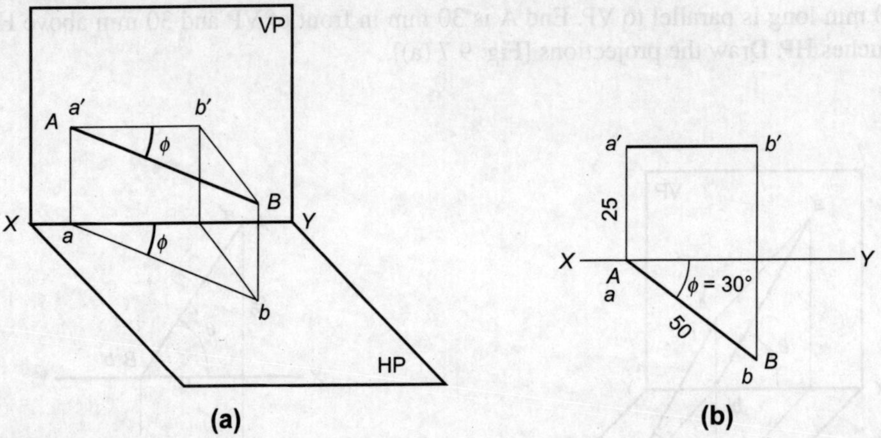

Fig. 9.8 (a) Pictorial view of HP and VP and the line; (b) Projection of the line

See Fig. 9.8 (b).

(i) Line AB is parallel to HP, so the front view of the line is parallel to XY.

(ii) The end A of the line touches VP, so the top view of end A lies on XY.

(iii) Draw XY and a projector at a convenient point perpendicular to XY.

(iv) Straight line is 25 mm above HP.

(v) Take point A touching XY and at A draw a perpendicular of 25 mm to a′.

(vi) At A, draw 30° angle as AB = 50 mm.

(vii) Cut AB = 50 mm

(viii) Draw a projector which meets a′b′

a′b′ = front view

ab = AB = top view = 50 mm

PROBLEM 9.8

The end *B* of a straight line is 55 mm above HP and 20 mm in front of VP. The other end A of this line is 10 mm above HP and the line makes an angle of 30° with HP. The distance between the end projections of the line is 55 mm. Draw the front view and top view of the line and inclination of line from VP. It is also required to find out the true shape of the line AB.

Solution:

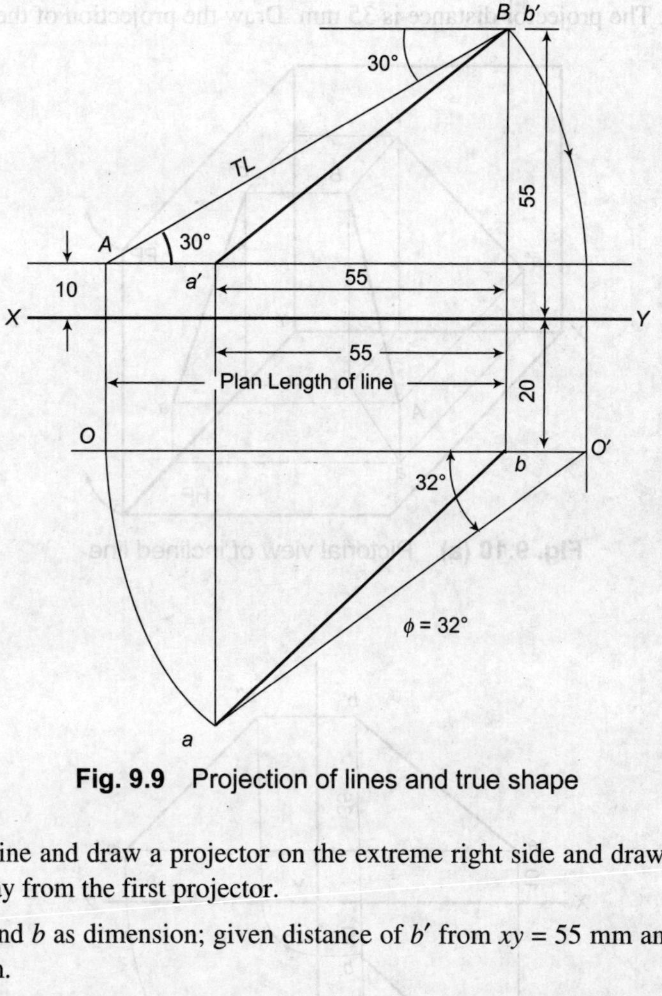

Fig. 9.9 Projection of lines and true shape

See Fig. 9.9.

(i) Draw XY line and draw a projector on the extreme right side and draw another projector at 55 mm away from the first projector.

(ii) Locate *b′* and *b* as dimension; given distance of *b′* from *xy* = 55 mm and distance of *b* from *xy* = 20 mm.

(iii) Point A is 10 mm above *xy*. The projector of end A will lie on another projector. Locus of end A lies on the height of 10 mm. Draw a horizontal line at 10 mm which cuts the projector at *a′*.

(iv) At B, draw angle $\theta = 30°$. The line cuts at A. *a′* has been located. AB represents the true length of the line.

(v) Project from A up to O. Take *b* as centre and *b*O as radius, draw an arc which cuts at a. Join *ab*. *ab* is the top view of the line.

(vi) To know ϕ, i.e., the inclination of line from VP, rotate $a'b'$ till it becomes horizontal and then project it up to 0′. Join $a0'$, which is also the true length of the line.

Measure angle $\phi = 32°$.

PROBLEM 9.9

End A of line is 40 mm in front of VP and 10 mm above HP. End B of the line is 35 mm above HP and 10 mm in front of VP. The projector distance is 35 mm. Draw the projection of the line AB and the end side view (Fig. 9.10).

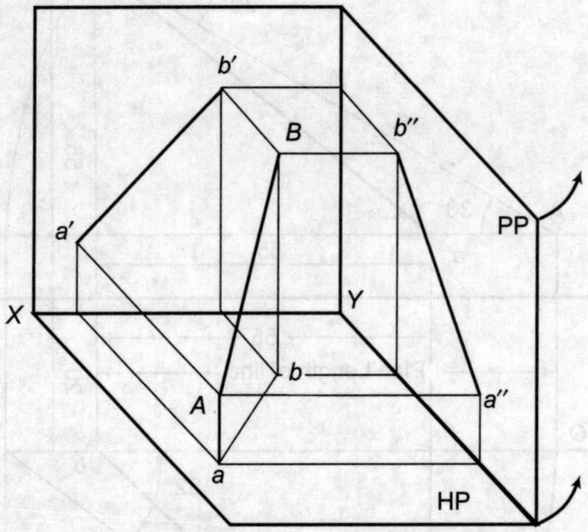

Fig. 9.10 (a) Pictorial view of inclined line

***Solution*:**

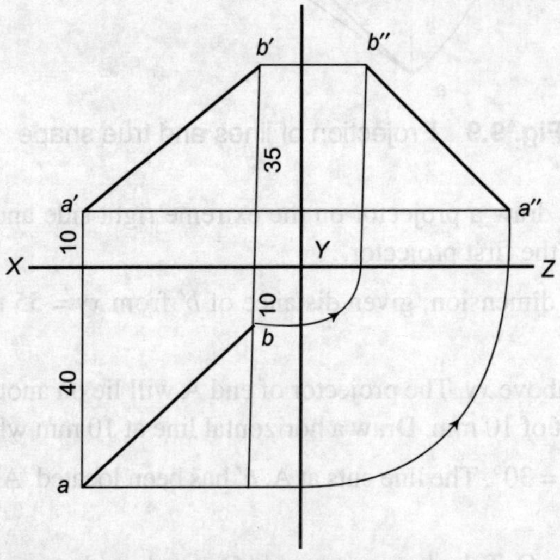

Fig. 9.10 (b) Orthographic projections and left side view

See Fig. 9.10 (b).

(i) Draw a line XY and also draw two projectors perpendicular to XY. Distance between two projectors is 35 mm.

(ii) Locate *a′* and *a* on left projector. *a′* and *a* are the front view and top view of end A, taking the dimensions given in the problem.

(iii) Locate *b* and *b′* as the top view and front view of end B of the straight line.

(iv) Join *a′b′*, and *ab* is the projection of line AB.

(v) Draw a side plane in the right side of the straight line to draw left side view.

PROBLEM 9.10

The end A is 10 mm above HP and 10 mm in front of VP. The end B is 40 mm above HP and 50 mm in front of VP.

The projections of A and B both fall on the same projection line. Draw plane and elevation of the line and also projection on PP.

Solution:

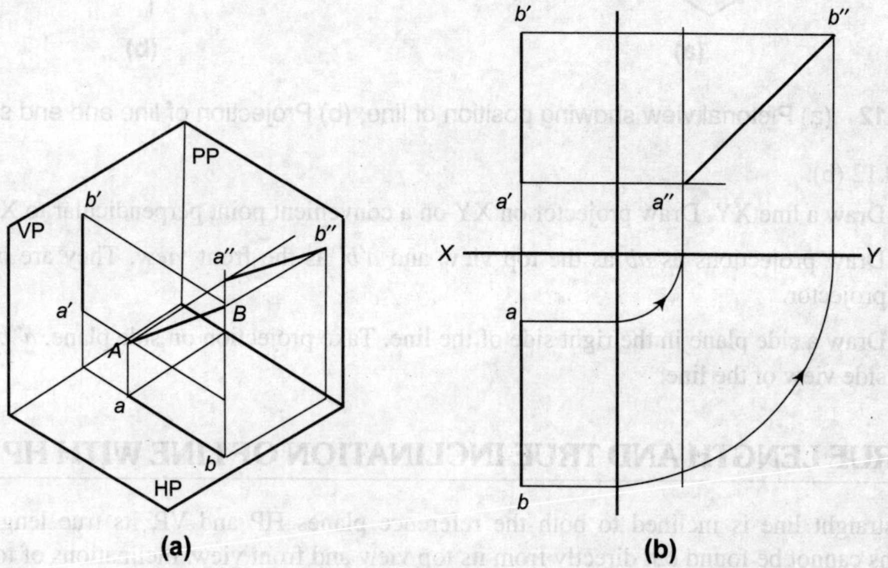

Fig. 9.11 (a) Pictorial view of straight line; (b) Projection of straight line

See Fig. 9.11.

(i) Draw a line XY and draw a projector on it.

(ii) Draw projection and locate *aa′ bb′*. They are same projectors.

(iii) Draw left side view as *a″b″*.

PROBLEM 9.11

The end A of line is 40 mm above HP and 10 mm in front of VP. Other end B of line is 10 mm above HP and 35 mm in front of VP. The projector of end A and B both fall on a single line [Fig. 9.12 (a)].

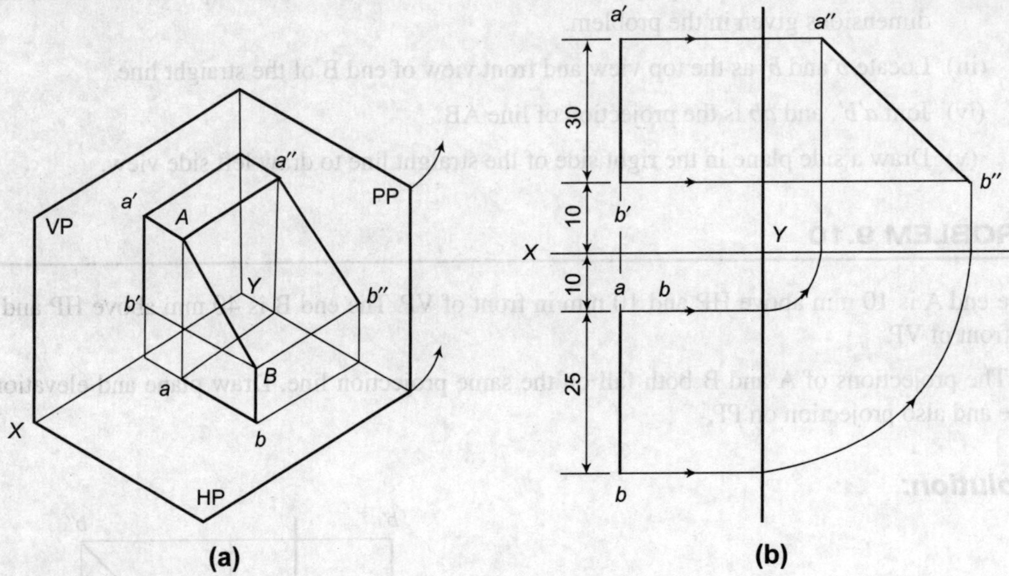

Fig. 9.12 (a) Pictorial view showing position of line; (b) Projection of line and end side view

See Fig. 9.12 (b).

(i) Draw a line XY. Draw projector on XY on a convenient point perpendicular to XY.

(ii) Draw projections as *ab* as the top view and *a′b′* as the front view. They are on the same projector.

(iii) Draw a side plane in the right side of the line. Take projection on side plane. *a″b″* is the left side view of the line.

9.2 TRUE LENGTH AND TRUE INCLINATION OF LINE WITH HP AND VP

When a straight line is inclined to both the reference planes HP and VP, its true length and true inclinations cannot be found out directly from its top view and front view. Inclinations of top view and front view always measure the apparent angle which is more than the true inclination of the line. The true length of the line will be greater than its top view and the front view.

There are three methods to find out the true length and the true inclinations of the line with HP and VP.

(i) Rotation of line methods

(ii) Trapezoidal methods

(iii) Auxiliary plane methods

The first two methods will be explained now. The auxiliary plane technique will be presented when the auxiliary plane portions will be dealt with.

9.2.1 Rotation of Line Method

Before taking up the actual cases to find the true length and true inclinations, a few simple cases will be dealt with to have a clear understanding of the problem.

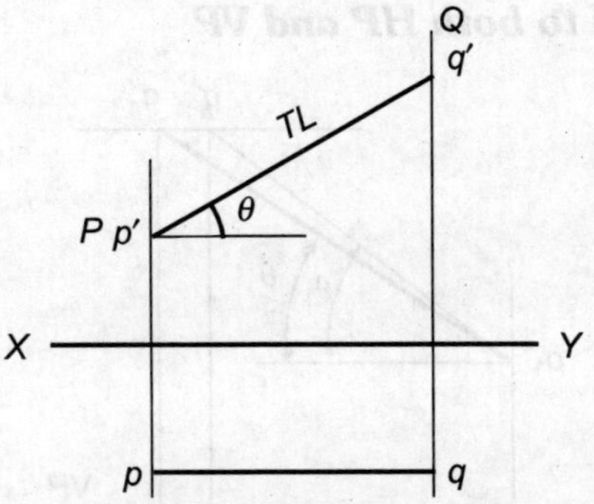

Fig. 9.13 Projection of line

(a) When a line is parallel to VP

Figure 9.13 represents the projection of line PQ in which the line is parallel to VP. $p'q'$ is the front view and pq is the top view which is parallel to XY.

Because the line is parallel to VP, hence, top view is parallel to XY. Front view $p'q'$ is the true length of the line and front view makes an angle θ, which is the true inclination with HP.

Line NB is parallel to VP, i.e., top view is parallel to XY. Then front view under this condition will be the true length and the front view makes an angle θ with HP, and it is the true angle with HP.

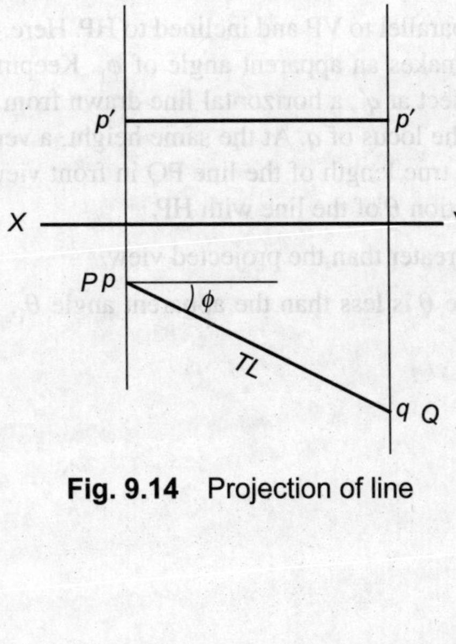

Fig. 9.14 Projection of line

(b) When a line is parallel to HP

Figure 9.14 represents the projection of line PQ in which the line is parallel to HP. *pq* is the top view and p′q′ is the front view which is parallel to XY. Because the line is parallel to HP, hence, front view is parallel to XY.

NB line is parallel to HP, i.e., front view is parallel to XY. Then top view under this condition will be the true length and top view makes an angle ϕ with VP and is the true angle with VP.

(c) When a line is inclined to both HP and VP

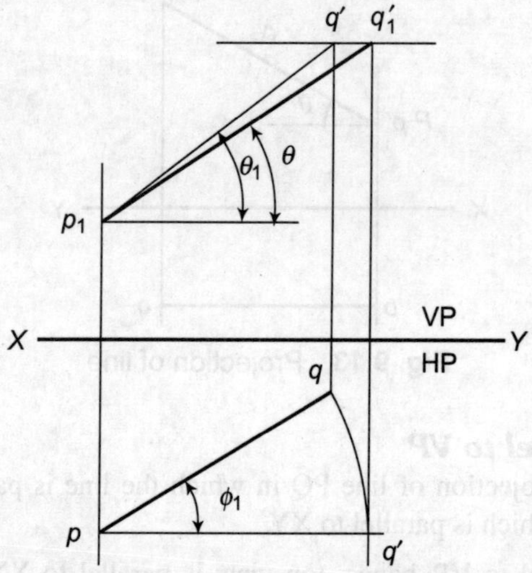

Fig. 9.15 Projection of line with inclination with HP and VP

Figure 9.15 shows the projection of line PQ. The projection of the line makes θ_1 apparent angle with HP and ϕ_1 apparent angle with VP.

Let the straight line be made parallel to VP and inclined to HP. Here, the top view *pq* is to be rotated and is made parallel to XY. *pq* makes an apparent angle of ϕ_1. Keeping end point *p* fixed and radius equal to *pq*, draw an arc to intersect at *q*′, a horizontal line drawn from *p*. From *q*′ draw a vertical line upward to meet at q'_1, which is the locus of *q*. At the same height, a vertical line has been drawn from *q* to meet at *q*′. Join *pq*′. It is the true length of the line PQ in front view and the angle made with this with horizontal is the true inclination θ of the line with HP.

The true length of the line is greater than the projected view.

The true inclination of the line θ is less than the apparent angle θ_1, when a line is inclined to both HP and VP.

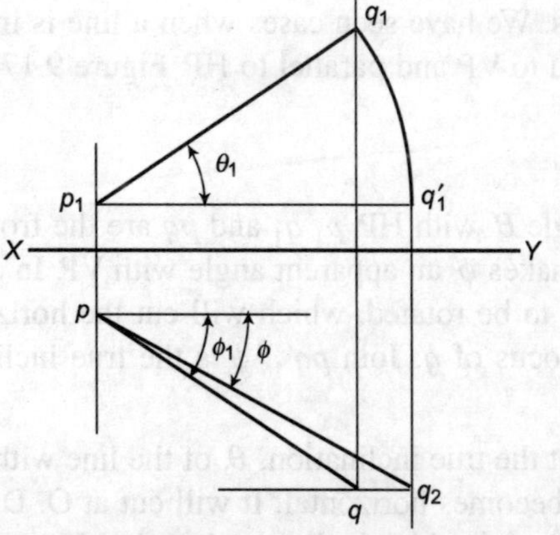

Fig. 9.16 Projection of line with inclination with HP and VP

Figure 9.16 shows the projection of line PQ. The projection of line makes θ_1 apparent angle with HP and ϕ_1 apparent angle with VP.

Let the straight line be parallel to HP and inclined to VP by rotating $p_1\, q_1$ front view. Here, the front view $p_1\, q_1$ is to be rotated and it is made parallel to XY. *pq* makes an apparent angle of ϕ'. Keeping end point *p* fixed and radius equal to $p_1\, q_1$, draw an arc to intersect at q'_1, a horizontal line drawn from p_1.

From q'_1, draw a vertical line downward to meet at q_2, which is the locus of *q* at the same horizontal line. Join pq_2. It is the true length of line PQ in top view and the angle made with the horizontal is the true inclination ϕ with VP. True length found in both the cases will be the same on measurement. θ and ϕ are true inclinations with HP and VP.

(d) Line inclined to both HP and VP

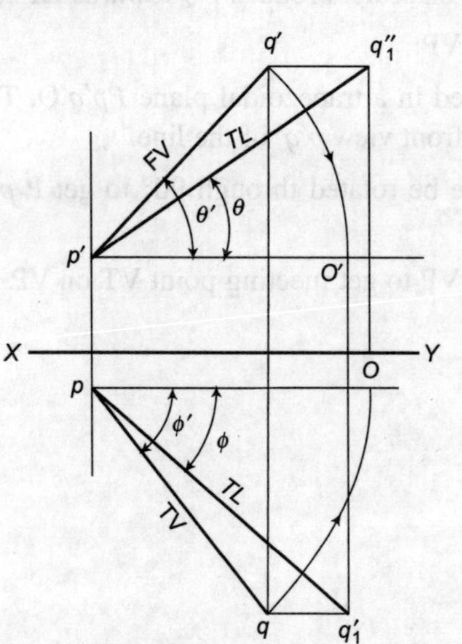

Fig. 9.17 Line inclined to HP and VP

We have a clear understanding of the method to solve a problem through different cases of the associated inclination problems. We have seen cases when a line is inclined to HP and parallel to VP and also when a line is inclined to VP and parallel to HP. Figure 9.17 represents a line inclined to HP and VP.

Here is the projection of PQ.

$p_1\, q_1$ makes an apparent angle θ' with HP. $p_1\, q_1$ and pq are the front view and top view of the line PQ. pq is the top view which makes ϕ' an apparent angle with VP. In order to find the true inclination, ϕ, of the line with VP, $p_1\, q_1$ is to be rotated, which will cut the horizontal line at O′. From O′, draw vertical line to cut at q'_1, the locus of q. Join pq'_1. ϕ is the true inclination with VP. pq'_1 is the true length of the line.

Similarly, in order to find out the true inclination, θ, of the line with HP, and the true length, pq, the top view is to be rotated till it becomes horizontal. It will cut at O. Draw perpendicular which cuts at q'', which is the locus of q'. Join $p'q''$ which is the true length. Measure θ, which is the true inclination with HP.

9.3 TRAPEZOIDAL PLANE METHOD

The trapezoidal plane method is also one of the simplest method to find the true inclination with HP and VP and also the true length of the line when the line is inclined to both the planes.

Let a line PQ makes an angle θ with HP and ϕ with VP. Draw its projection on HP and VP as per the statement in first quadrant (Fig. 9.18).

Let the straight line be contained in a trapezoidal plane PpqQ. This plane contains the true length of the line, which is at angle θ with HP, and top view pq of the line. Now, let the trapezoidal plane get rotated through an angle 90° to obtain P_1pqQ on HP. It looks like Fig. 9.18 (a). The projection will look like Fig. 9.18 (b) drawn not on scale. Produce PQ towards HP to get meeting point HT on HP.

As regards the projections on VP:

Let a straight line be contained in a trapezoidal plane $Pp'q'$Q. This plane contains the true length which is inclined at ϕ to VP and front view $p'q'$ of the line.

Now, let the trapezoidal plane be rotated through 90° to get $P_2p'q'Q_2$ on VP. It will look like Fig 9.19 (a) in front view.

Line PQ is produced towards VP to get meeting point VT on VP. The projection is drawn as shown in Fig. 9.19 (b).

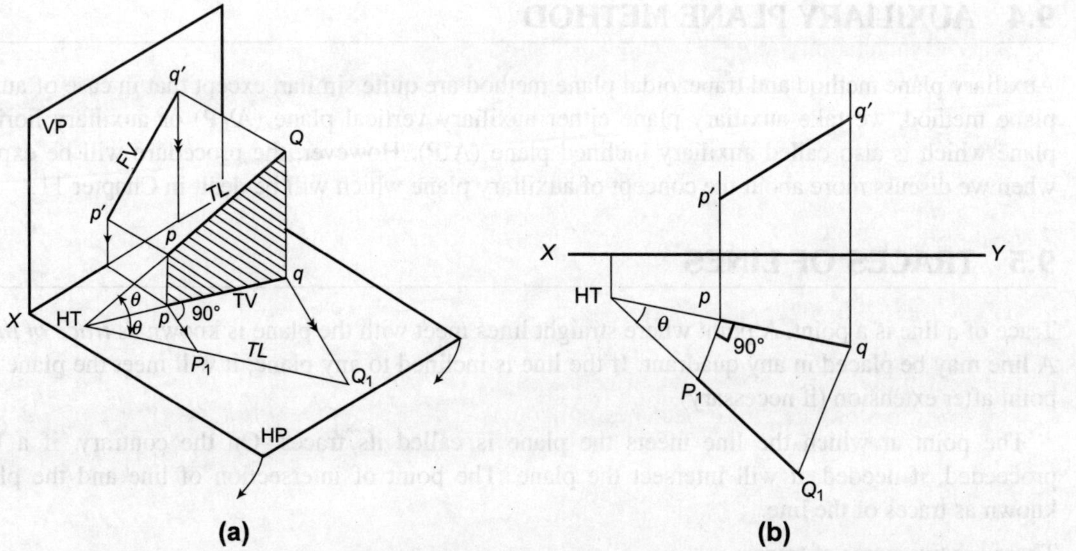

Fig. 9.18 (a) Pictorial view of the line; (b) Projection on HP with inclination θ

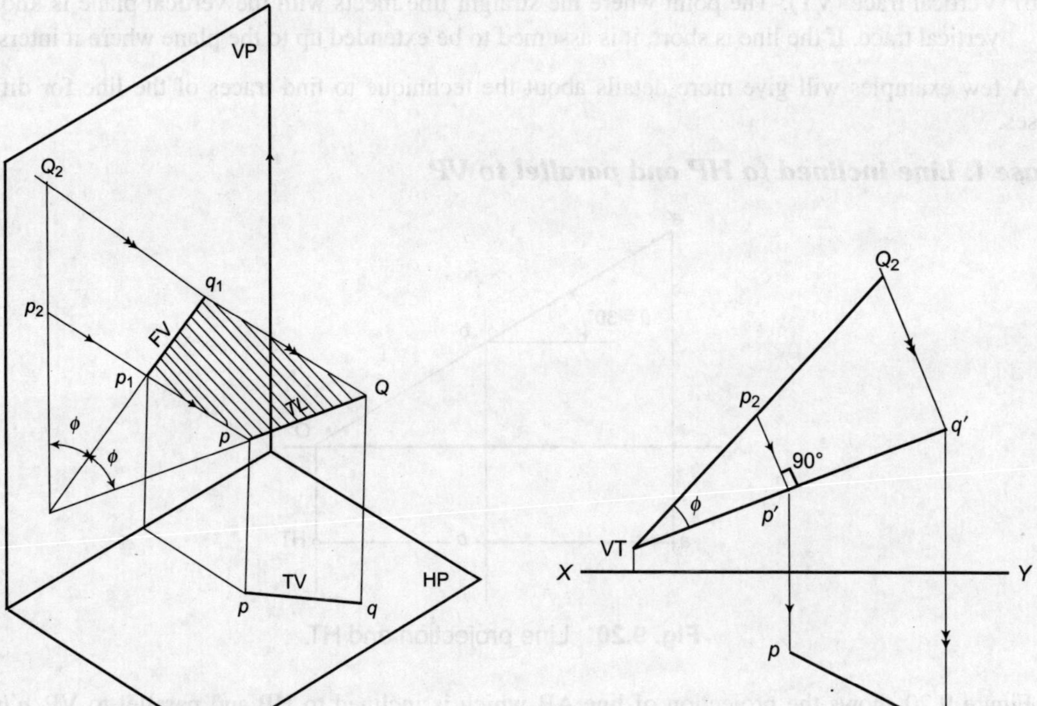

Fig. 9.19 (a) Pictorial view of line; (b) Projection on VP with inclination ϕ

9.4 AUXILIARY PLANE METHOD

Auxiliary plane method and trapezoidal plane method are quite similar, except that in case of auxiliary plane method, we take auxiliary plane either auxiliary vertical plane (AVP) or auxiliary horizontal plane which is also called auxiliary inclined plane (AIP). However, the procedure will be explained when we discuss more about the concept of auxiliary plane which will be dealt in Chapter 11.

9.5 TRACES OF LINES

Trace of a line is a point. A point where straight lines meet with the plane is known as *trace of the line*. A line may be placed in any quadrant. If the line is inclined to any plane, it will meet the plane at any point after extension (if necessary).

The point at which the line meets the plane is called its traces. On the contrary, if a line is proceeded, if needed, it will intersect the plane. The point of intersection of line and the plane is known as traces of the line.

There are two types of traces:

(a) Horizontal trace (HT): The point where the straight line meets the horizontal plane.

(b) Vertical trace (VT): The point where the straight line meets with the vertical plane is known as vertical trace. If the line is short, it is assumed to be extended up to the plane where it intersects.

A few examples will give more details about the technique to find traces of the line for different cases.

Case I: Line inclined to HP and parallel to VP

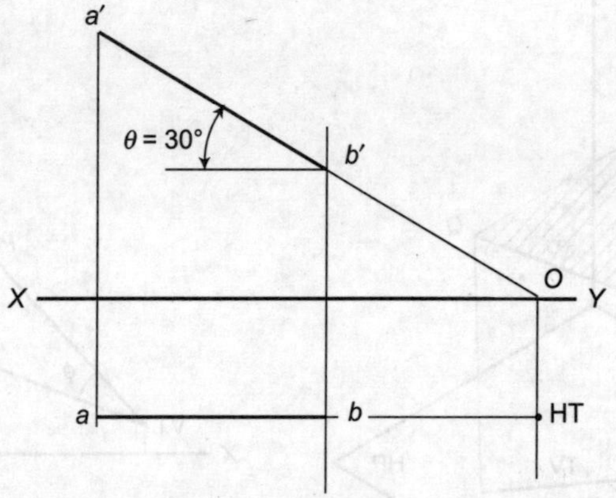

Fig. 9.20 Line projection and HT

Figure 9.20 shows the projection of line AB which is inclined to HP and parallel to VP. *a′b′* and *ab* are the front view and the top view of the line. The elevation/front view (*a′b′*) is extended to meet XY at O. From O, draw perpendicular to XY. The top view is also extended to meet at HP. It is quite obvious that elevation is extended, top view will also extend in the same manner. In this case, because the line is parallel to VP, there shall be no VT. The distance of HT can be measured from XY.

Case II: Line inclined to VP and parallel to HP

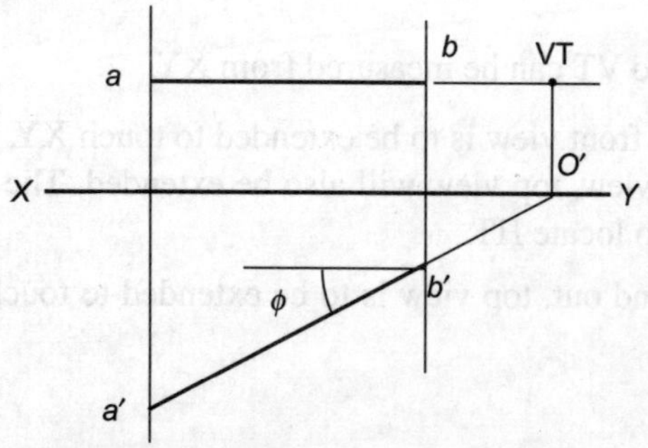

Fig. 9.21 Projection of line with VT

Figure 9.21 shows the projection of line AB which is inclined to VP and parallel to HP, *a′b′* is the Top view and ab is the front view. The top view, *a′b′*, is extended to meet XY at O′. From O′, draw perpendicular to meet the extension of ab at VT. In this case, there is no HT.

Case III: Line inclined to HP and VP both

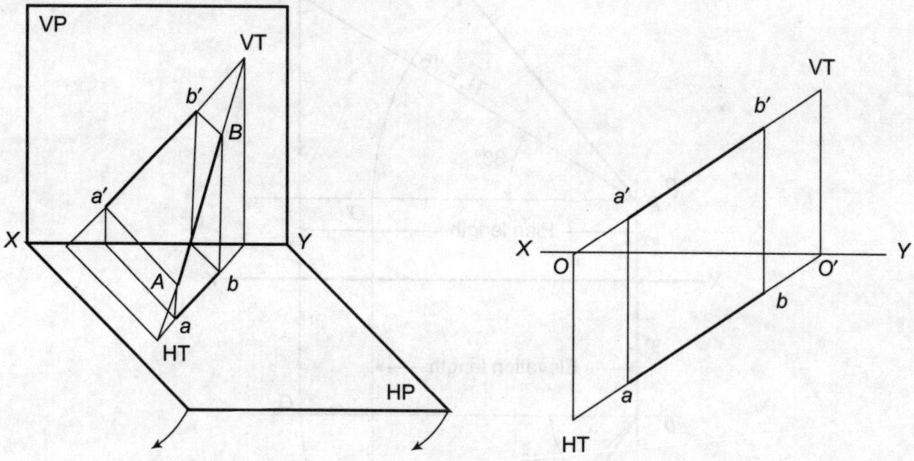

(a) (b)

Fig. 9.22 (a) Pictorial view of HP and VP with the line projection; (b) Projection of line with HT and VT

See Fig. 9.22.

(i) Draw a line XY and also two projectors.

(ii) Draw the projections of the line *a′b′* and *ab*.

(iii) To determine HT, produce *b′a′* to meet XY at O. Draw perpendicular on XY, locate HT on produced *ba*.

(iv) To obtain VT, produce *ab* (top view) to meet XY at O′. Draw perpendicular at O′ to meet VT on extension of *a′b′*.

The distance of HT and VT can be measured from XY.

Note: If HT is to be found out, front view is to be extended to touch XY, i.e., it has already touched the ground. On extension of front view, top view will also be extended. The point where front view meets ground, draw a perpendicular to locate HT.

Similarly, if VT is to be found out, top view is to be extended to touch XY. Take the corresponding point to get VT.

PROBLEM 9.12

A line PQ 75 mm long is inclined at an angle of 30° to HP and 45° to VP. The point P is 15 mm above HP and 25 mm in front of VP. Draw the projection of the straight line.

Solution:

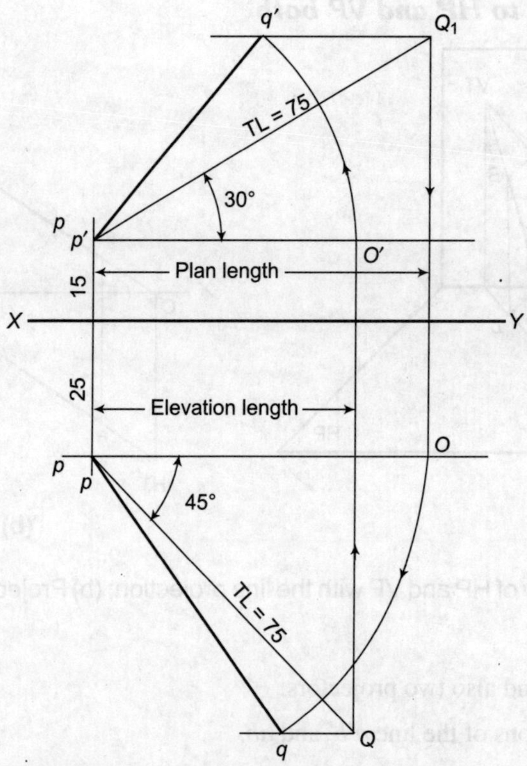

Fig. 9.23 Projections of straight lines

See Fig. 9.23.

(i) Draw a line XY. Select a point on XY to take projectors.
On this projector, mark p' and p at a distance of 15 mm above XY and 25 mm below XY.

(ii) At p' draw a horizontal line.
Taking point P as fixed, i.e., without changing the position of p and p', take a line equal to true length of the line (75 mm) at 30° inclination, it will be at Q_1.

(iii) Similarly, at p draw a horizontal line.
A line equal to 75 mm is drawn at 45° to horizontal line at p. It will meet at Q.

(iv) At Q and Q_1, draw horizontal lines to find the locus of the line.

(v) From Q_1 draw a vertical line to meet at O below XY.

(vi) Taking p as centre and pO as radius, draw an arc to cut at q locus of Q.
Join pq which is the required top view.

(vii) Again from Q, draw a vertical line to meet at O′.
Taking p' as centre and p′O′ as radius, draw an arc to cut at q' locus of Q_1.
Join $p'q'$ which is the required front view.

PROBLEM 9.13

A line PQ has its end P 10 mm above HP and 15 mm in front of VP. End Q is 45 mm above HP and 40 mm in front of VP. The distance between end projectors is 40 mm. Draw the projection of the line and find its true length and the true inclinations with HP and VP by using (a) rotation of line method (b) trapezoidal method.

Solution:

(a) Rotation of line method

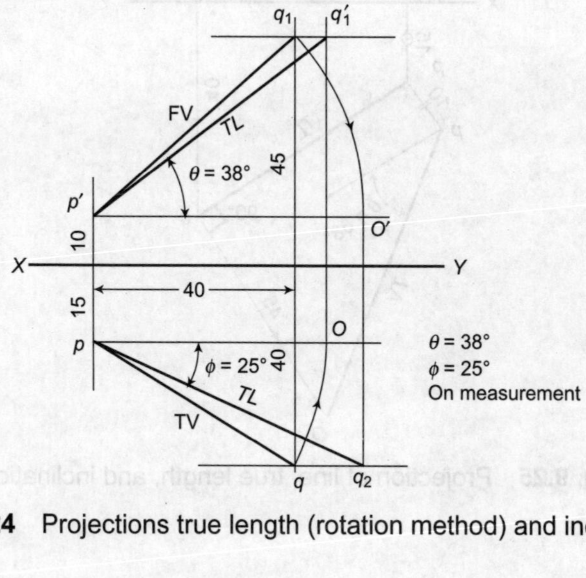

Fig. 9.24 Projections true length (rotation method) and inclination

(i) Draw line XY and draw two lines perpendicular to XY 40 mm apart.

(ii) Locate the projection of two ends of the line on the projector.

(iii) Mark pp' and also qq'.

(iv) Join pq as the top view and also $p'q'$ as the front view.

(v) Taking p' as centre and $p'q'$ as the radius, draw an arc up to O′ on a horizontal line drawn from p'. Draw perpendicular from O′ up to q_2.

(vi) Taking p as centre and pq as the radius, draw an arc up to O on a horizontal line from p. Draw perpendicular from O to q'_1.

(vii) Draw horizontal line from q_1 and also from q_2 to q, the locus of points.

(viii) Join $p'q_1$ and also pq. They are the projections of line PQ.

(b) Trapezoidal method

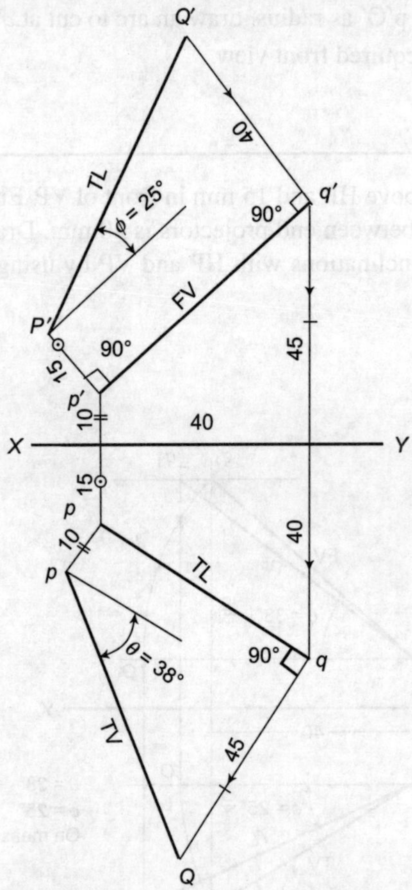

Fig. 9.25 Projection of line, true length, and inclination

See Fig. 9.25.

(i) Draw XY line and locate the projections of two ends of the line on two projectors drawn perpendicular to XY.

The distance between the projectors is 40 mm.

(ii) Join $p'q'$ and pq, they are projectors of the line.

(iii) Draw perpendicular to p_1q' and pq.

At p_1, take 15 mm and at q_1, take 40 mm.

Similarly, at p, take 10 mm and at q, take 45 mm.

(iv) Join P′Q′ and PQ. They are the true lengths.

θ and ϕ are the true angles with HP and VP.

PROBLEM 9.14

A line PQ 65 mm long has one of its end P 45 mm in front of VP and 10 mm above HP. The top view of the line measures 45 mm. The other end Q of the line is 20 mm in front of VP and above HP. Draw the front view of the line and measure the distance and also find θ.

Solution:

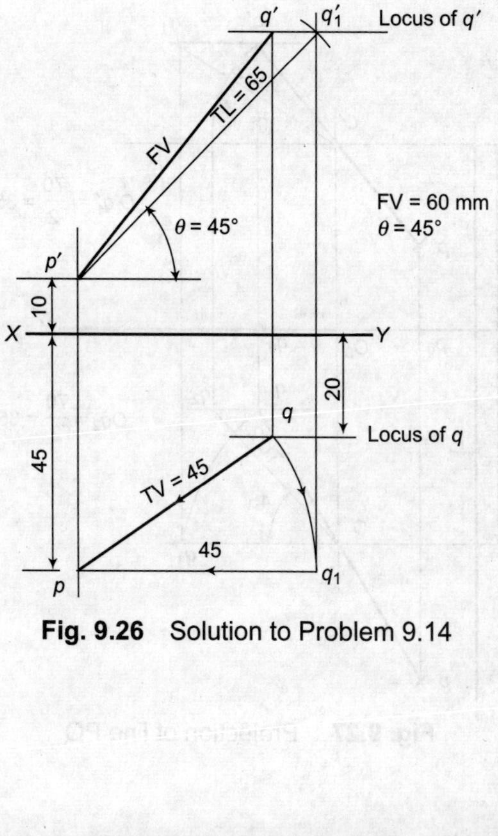

Fig. 9.26 Solution to Problem 9.14

See Fig. 9.26.

(i) Draw XY and a projector perpendicular to it. Mark p' and p at 10 mm above and 45 mm below XY.

(ii) Q is 20 mm in front of VP and, therefore, draw a horizontal line 20 mm below XY to represent locus of end q.

(iii) The top view of the line with p as a centre and 45 mm as radius, cut the locus of q at q.

Now join pq which is the top view of the line PQ.

(iv) With p as a centre and pq as radius, draw an arc to cut at q, a horizontal line from p.

(v) The true length of line is 65 mm, already given, taking p_1 as centre and radius equal to 65 mm. Draw an arc to intersect the projected line from q', which cuts at q'_1.

(vi) Draw a horizontal line from q'_1. From q, draw a vertical line to intersect at q'.

(vii) Join $p'q'$ which is a front view. $p'q'$ measures 60 mm and $\theta = 45°$.

PROBLEM 9.15

A line PQ, 70 mm long, is inclined at 30° to HP and 45° to VP. The middle point of the line is 35 mm above HP and 40 mm in front of VP. Draw the projection of the line.

Solution:

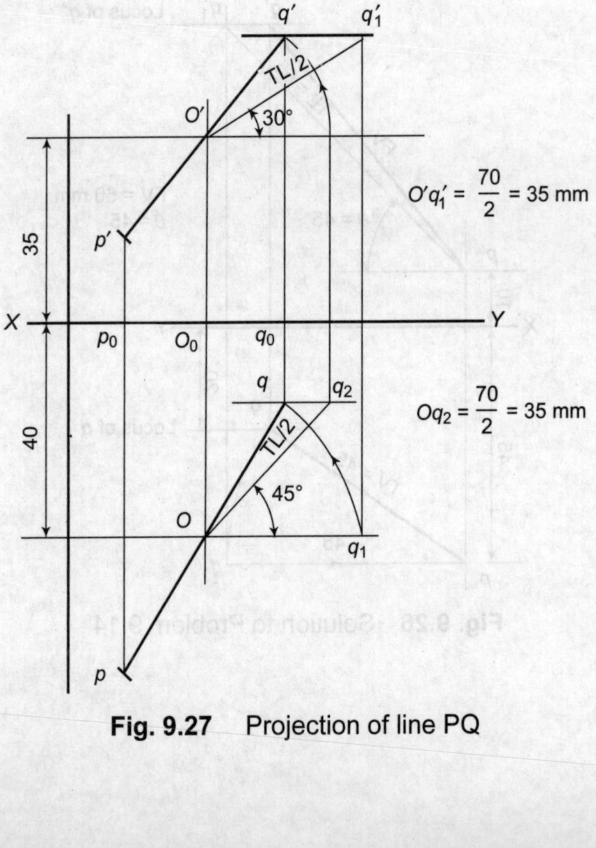

Fig. 9.27 Projection of line PQ

(i) Draw XY and a projector line at O_0 and locate O′ as front view at 35 mm above XY and O as top view 40 mm below XY.

(ii) Divide straight line in two equal parts considering upper part of the straight line taking O as centre of straight line which is 35 mm above XY and 40 mm below XY.

(iii) From O′, take $O'q'_1$ = 35 mm (half of straight line) at an angle of 30°.

Again from O draw Oq_2 = 35 mm at 45°.

Draw horizontal line at q'_1 and q_2 to get loci of q' and q.

(iv) From q'_1, draw vertical line which cuts at q_1.

Take O as centre and Oq_1 as radius, draw an arc to cut this at q.

(v) Draw a vertical line from q to cut at q', $O'q'$ is the front view of the half of straight line.

This may be extended up to p' ($O'q' = O'p'$) for full straight line.

Join Oq which is a top view of half of the straight line. Extend this up to p.

(vi) $p'q'$ is the front view for the complete straight line. pq is the top view.

PROBLEM 9.16

Draw the projection of a straight line PQ, 60 mm long, inclined at 45° to HP and 30° to VP. The end P is in HP and end Q is in VP. Find the shortest distance between PQ and the ground line.

Solution:

(1) Draw XY on this line. Draw a line equal to 60 mm at an angle of 45° to HP. Let this represent the top end of the line as q'.

(2) Project q from q' on XY line.

(3) Draw qq_2 line equal to true length of the line = 60 mm at an angle of 30° to VP.

(4) From q_2, draw the locus of the line parallel to XY.

(5) With q as the centre and qp as radius, draw an are cutting the line XY at p. Join pq which is the top view.

(6) Project p on XY to get p'. Join $p'q'$ which is the front view.

(7) Draw side view as $p''q''$. Draw a line perpendicular to this line $p''q''$ from the point where two planes are meeting. This is the shortest distance that can be measured.

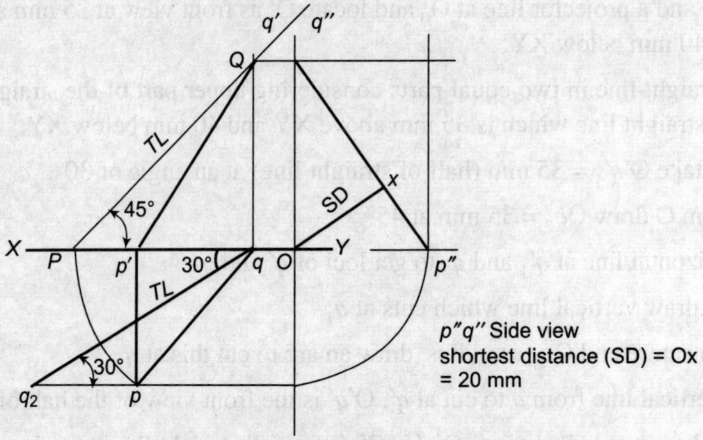

Fig. 9.28 Solution to Problem 9.16

PROBLEM 9.17

A straight line PQ is 70 mm long. The upper end of the line is on VP and the lower end is on the ground.

The top view and front view measure 40 mm and 50 mm, respectively. Find the projections and shortest distance between the line and XY.

Solution:

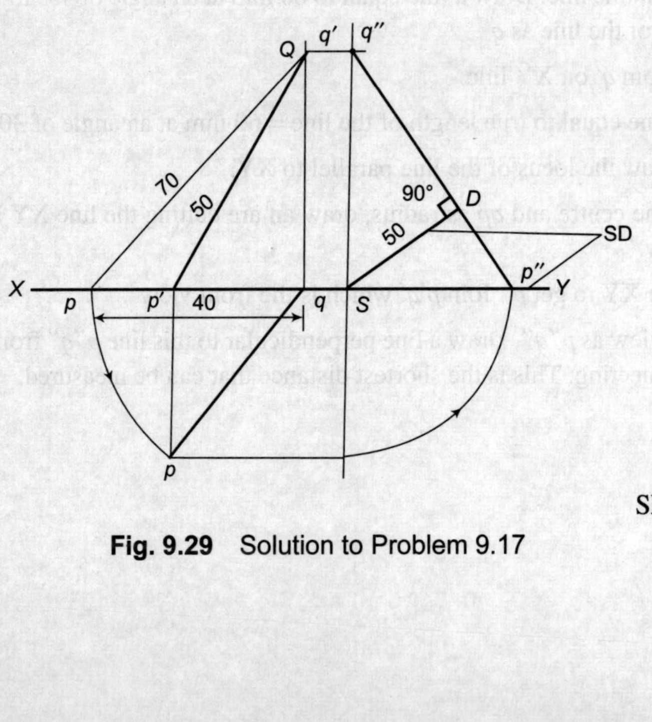

SD = shortest distance

Fig. 9.29 Solution to Problem 9.17

Solution:

(1) Draw a line $pq = 40$ mm on XY line.

From q, draw a vertical line on XY and cut $q'p = 70$ mm on it.

Taking q' as centre and radius equal to 50 mm join XY at p'. $q'p' = 50$ mm

(2) Draw a vertical line at p' below. Now, with q as centre and radius equal to qp, draw an are which cuts vertical line on p. Join pq which represents top view = 40 mm.

(3) Draw side view as $p''q''$. Draw perpendicular on the line from the point where two planes are meeting. The common perpendicular will represent SD = shortest distance.

PROBLEM 9.18

One end of line PQ is in the first quadrant, 15 mm above HP and 25 mm in front of VP. The other end of the line is in third quadrant 35 mm behind VP and 35 mm below HP. The distance between the two projectors is 55 mm. Draw the projections of the line and find its true length by rotation method and also by trapezoidal method. Compare the true length measured by them. Also find the true inclination of the line.

Solution:

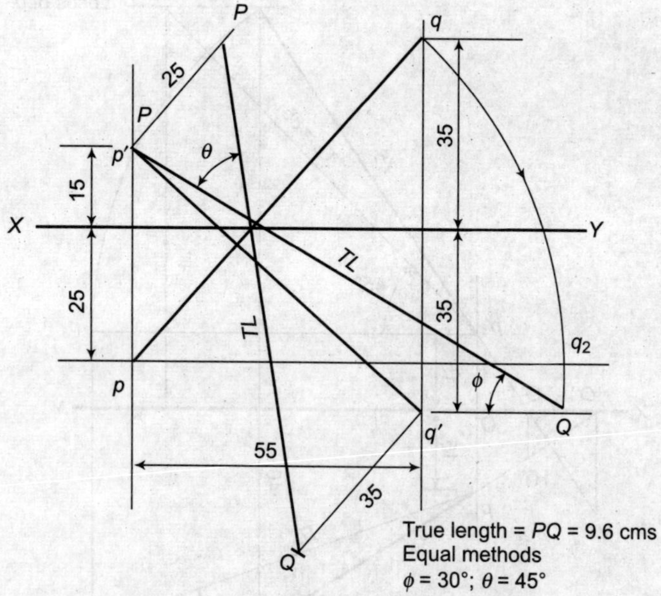

Fig. 9.30 Solution to Problem 9.18

See Fig. 9.30.

(i) Draw XY and also two projectors 55 mm apart.

(ii) Locate p' 15 mm above and p 25 mm below XY on left projector.

(iii) Locate q 35 mm above and q' 35 mm below XY on right projector.

(iv) Join p_1q' and pq as the front view and top view of the line.

(v) Taking p as centre and pq as radius, draw an arc up to q_2 and then drop perpendicular up to Q.

(vi) Join p'Q which is the true length of the line = 9.6 cm.

(vii) At p', draw perpendicular p'P = 25 mm.

(viii) At q_1' draw perpendicular q'Q = 35 mm.

(ix) Join PQ which is also the true length = 9.6 cm.

PROBLEM 9.19

A line PQ, 85 mm long, is inclined at 45° to HP. The end P is 15 mm above HP and 15 mm in front of VP and end B is 40 mm in front of VP. Draw the projection of the line if its front view measures 75 mm.

Locate traces of the line and the inclination of the line with VP.

Solution:

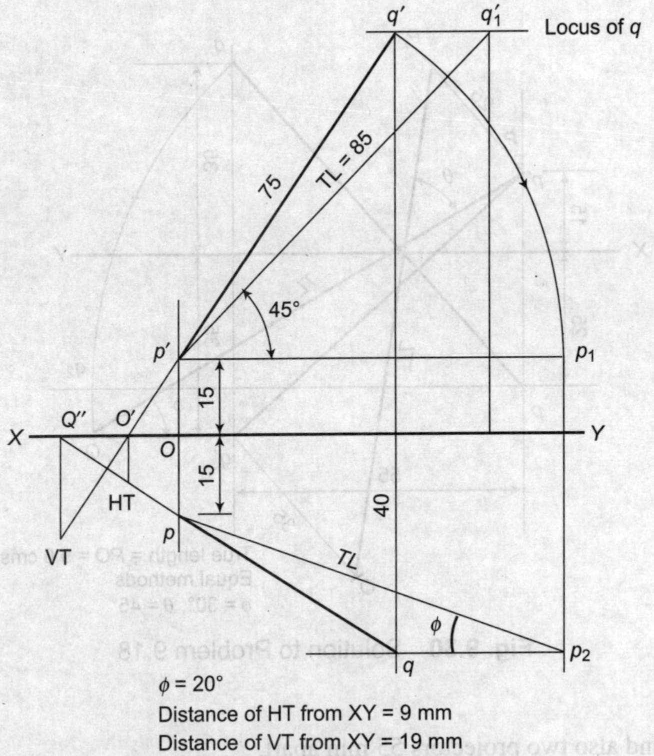

Fig. 9.31 Solution to Problem 9.19

See Fig. 9.31.

1. Draw XY and also a projector at O perpendicular to XY.
2. Locate p' and p at an equal distance of 15 mm from XY.
3. At p′ draw 45° and take $p'q_1'$ equal to 85 mm length.
4. Draw the locus of q horizontally.

   From p' take 75 mm to cut at q' (front view = 75 mm).
5. Draw a line perpendicular at q' to q. q is the view of Q, 40 mm below XY.
6. Join pq which is the top view of the line PQ.
7. Extend $q'p'$ to O′ on XY. Draw perpendicular which meets at HT on extension of qp.
8. Extend qp to O″ on XY. Draw vertical, which cuts at VT extension of $q'p'$.

   ϕ can be found by rotation method.

PROBLEM 9.20

One end of the line AB is in the third quadrant, 25 mm behind VP and 15 mm below HP. The other end is in the first quadrant 45 mm above HP and 12 mm in front of VP. The distance between the two projectors is 60 mm. Draw the projection of the line and find its true length, inclinations θ and ϕ, and also HT and VT.

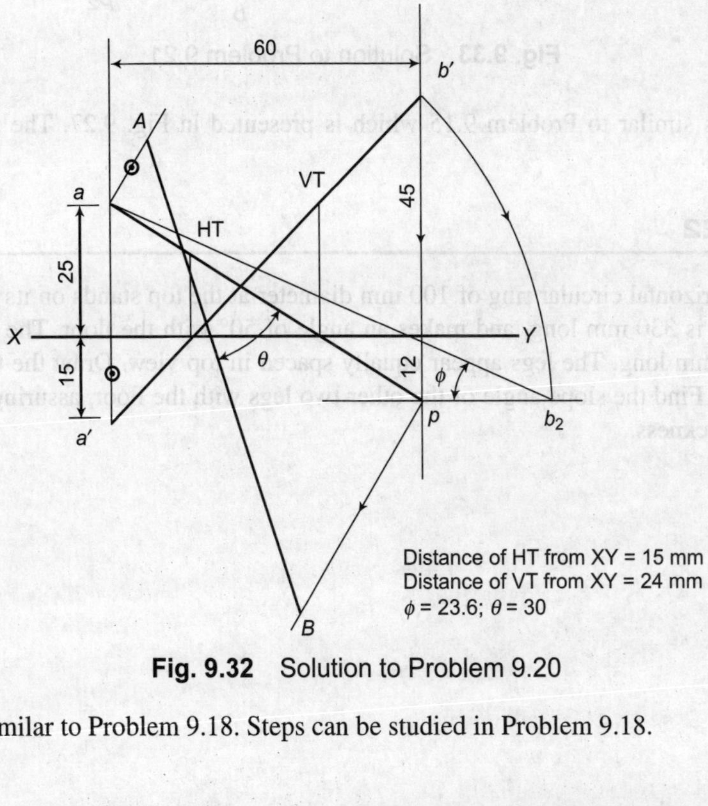

Fig. 9.32 Solution to Problem 9.20

Problem 9.20 is similar to Problem 9.18. Steps can be studied in Problem 9.18.

PROBLEM 9.21

A line PQ 80 mm long is inclined at 45° to HP and 30° to VP. Its mid-point is in VP and 15 mm above HP. The end P is in the third quadrant and end *Q* is in the first quadrant. Draw the projection of the line. Locate HT and VT of the line.

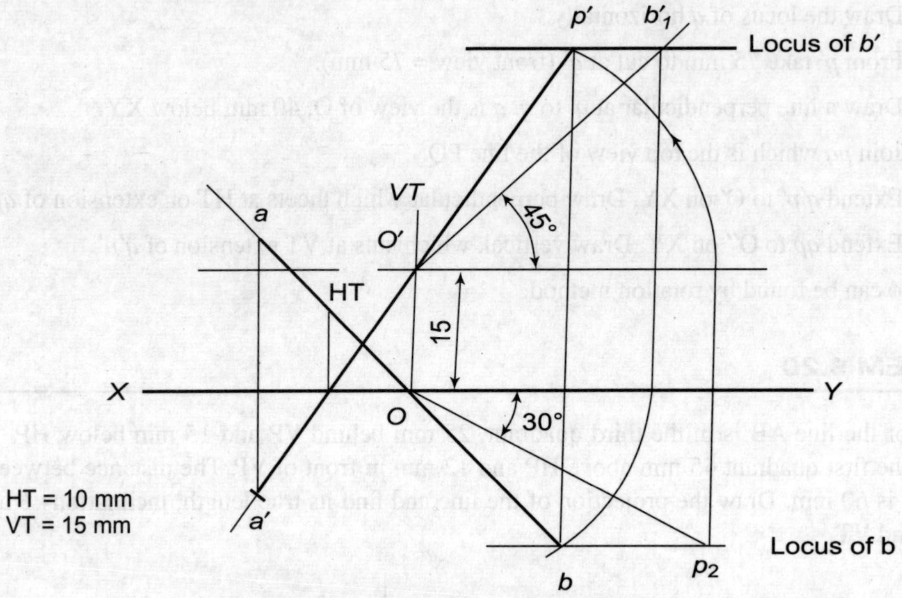

Fig. 9.33 Solution to Problem 9.21

Problem 9.21 is similar to Problem 9.15 which is presented in Fig. 9.27. The steps may be read from Problem 9.15.

PROBLEM 9.22

A tripod with a horizontal circular ring of 100 mm diameter at the top stands on its three unequal legs on a floor. one leg is 330 mm long, and makes an angle of 50° with the floor. The other two legs are 320 mm and 360 mm long. The legs appear equally spaced in top view. Draw the top view and front view of the tripod. Find the slope angle of the other two legs with the floor, assuring the ring and legs to be of the line thickness.

Solution:

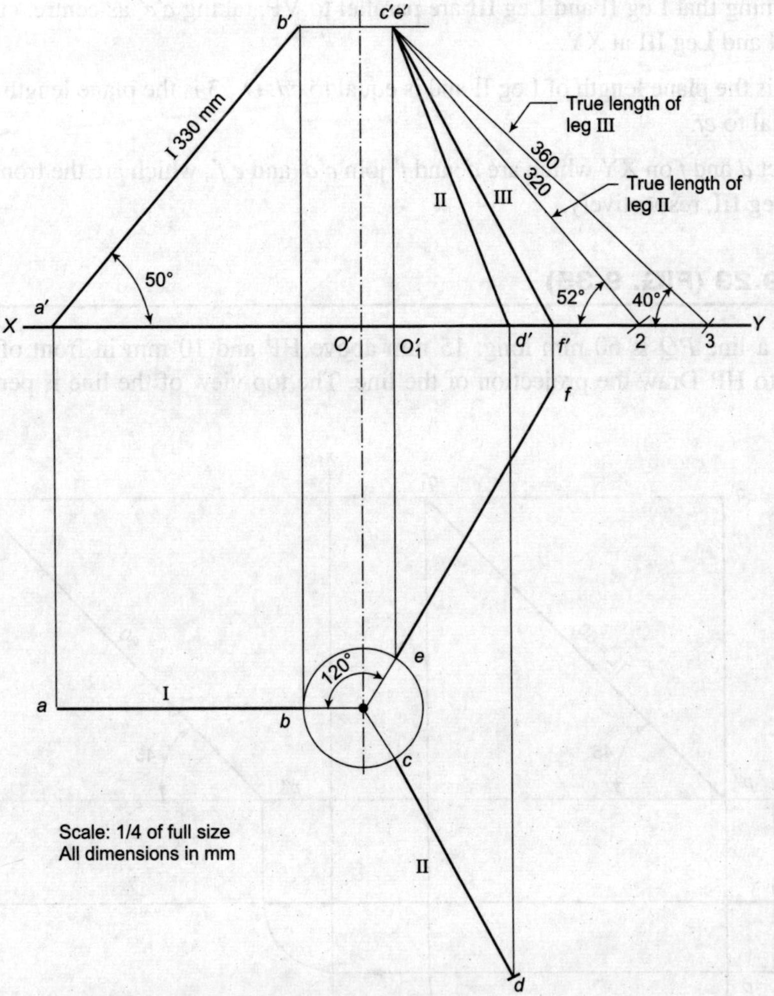

Fig. 9.34 Solution to Problem 9.22

(i) Scale has been chosen as 1/4th of full size.

(ii) Draw a horizontal line XY.

(iii) The lower end of Leg I (330 mm) is on ground so *a′* is the front view and a is the top view. Draw *a′b′* as the true length of Leg I at an angle of 50° with XY. *ab* represents top view (i.e., Leg I is parallel to VP).

(iv) In touch with b, draw a circle of diameter 100 mm. The circle has been projected at *a′* by a horizontal line.

(v) Other two legs are equally spaced. In top view they are attached at *c* and *e*. *c* and *e* have been projected at *c′e′* which are the connecting point of Leg II and Leg III.

(vi) Knowing that Leg II and Leg III are both attached with $c'e'$.

(vii) Assuming that Leg II and Leg III are parallel to VP, taking $c'e'$ as centre, cut the distance of Leg II and Leg III at XY.

(viii) O'_1 2 is the plane length of Leg II and is equal to *cd*. O'_1 3 is the plane length of Leg III which is equal to *ef*.

(ix) Project *d* and *f* on XY which are *d'* and *f'* join *c'd'* and *e'f'*, which are the front views of Leg II and Leg III, respectively.

PROBLEM 9.23 (FIG. 9.35)

The point *P* of a line *PQ* is 60 mm long, 15 mm above HP and 10 mm in front of VP. The line is inclined at 45° to HP. Draw the projection of the line. The top view of the line is perpendicular to *xy* line.

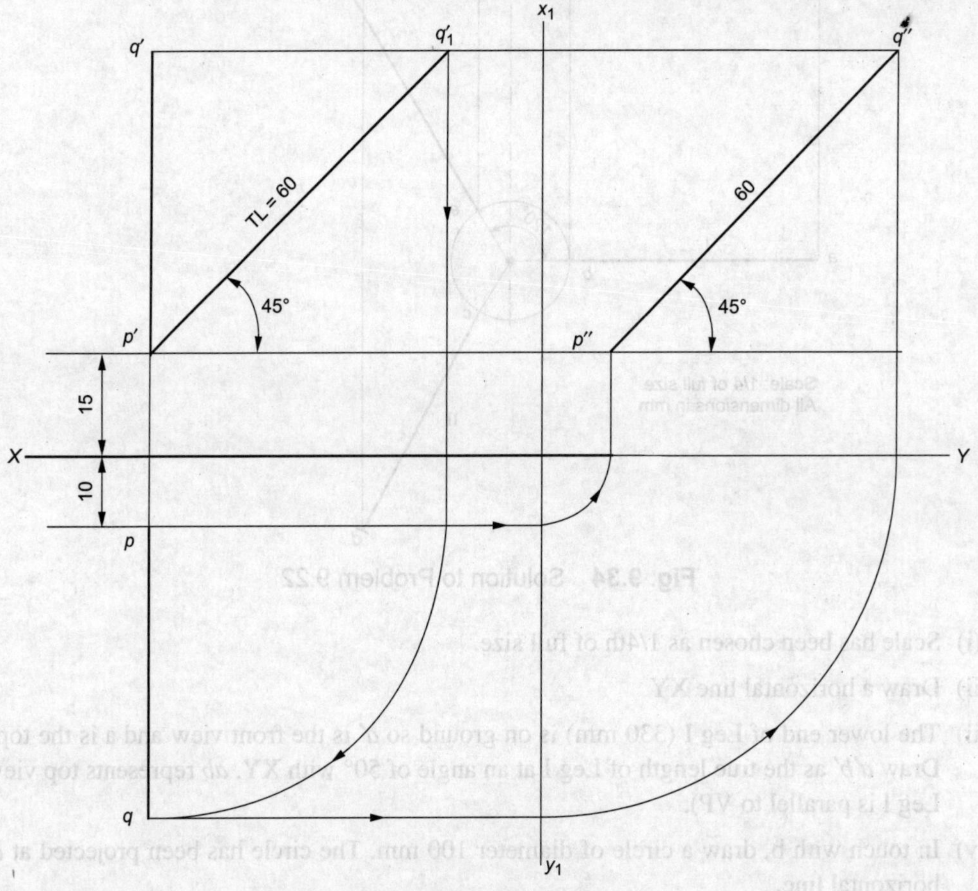

Fig. 9.35 Solution to Problem 9.23

Solution of the problem is self-explanatory.
See Fig. 9.35.

(1) Draw XY line and mark the position of *P* as p' and p, 15 mm above and 10 mm in front of VP.

(2) Draw $p'q'$ = 60 mm at the inclination of 45° to XY line.

(3) Draw a line perpendicular to XY from q'_1, and by rotation get the point q.

From q'_1, draw a horizontal line to get q'.

(4) $p'q'$ is the front view and pq is the top view.

(5) Draw side view $p''q''$ as explained earlier.

PROBLEM 9.24 (FIG. 9.36)

A hall is 8 m × 6 m × 4 m. By the principle of drawing, find out the true distance between the top corner and the bottom corner diagonally opposite to it.

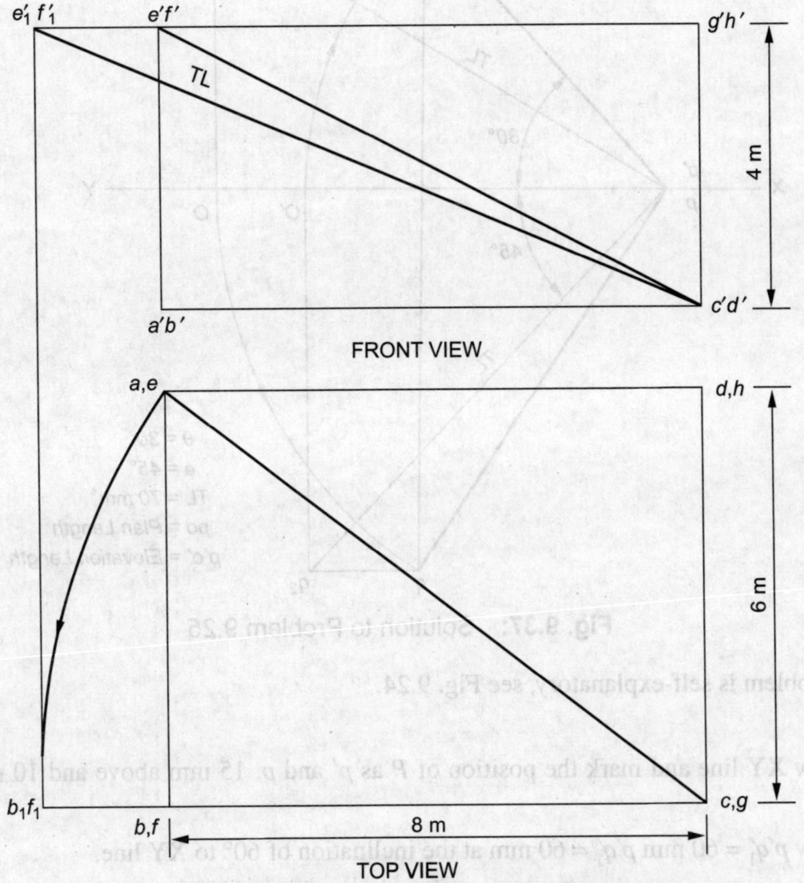

Fig. 9.36 Solution to Problem 9.24

Steps:

(1) Draw front view and top view of the hall taking suitable scale.

(2) Locate the opposite corner points in top view and front view. Top view and front view both are the projections of the distance between them. Assuming a straight line joining the two points.

(3) By rotation technique, the true shape is drawn.

PROBLEM 9.25 (FIG. 9.37)

A line *PQ* 70 mm long has its end *P* on HP and VP both. It is inclined at 45° to VP and 30° to HP. Draw the projection.

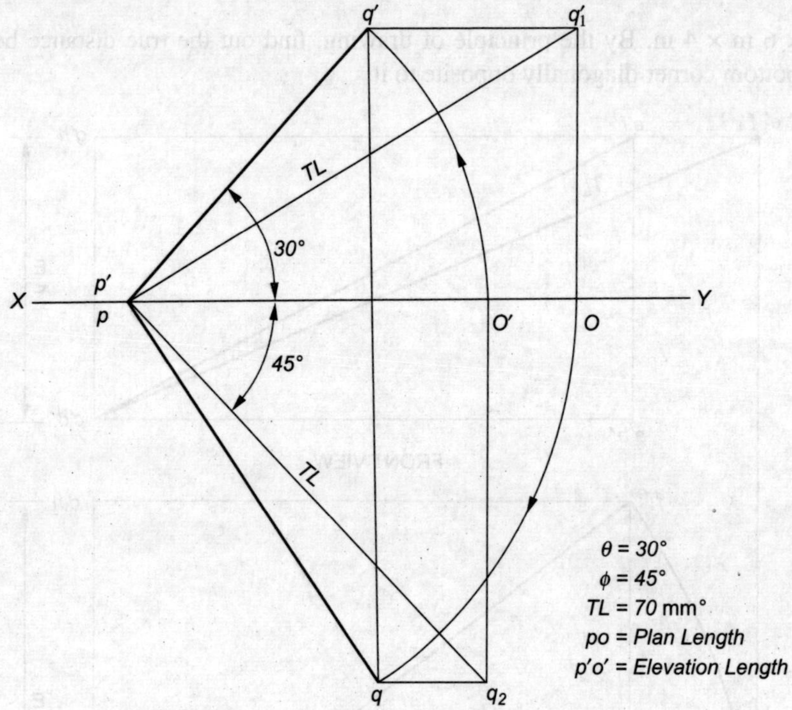

Fig. 9.37: Solution to Problem 9.25

Solution of problem is self-explanatory, see Fig. 9.24.

Steps:

(1) Draw XY line and mark the position of *P* as p' and *p*, 15 mm above and 10 mm in front of VP.

(2) Draw $p'q_1' = 60$ mm $p'q_1' = 60$ mm at the inclination of 60° to XY line.

(3) Draw a line ⊥ to *x y* from q_1' and by rotation get the point *q*. From q_1' draw horizontal line to get q'.

(4) $p'q'$ is the front view and pq in the top view.

(5) Draw a side view $p''q''$ as explained earlier.

PROBLEM 9.26 (FIG. 9.38)

A line *PQ* has its end *P* in HP and 55 mm in front of VP. Its front view is inclined at 50° to *xy*. The length of the line is 75 mm. The other end of the line is in VP. Draw the projection of the line and find out its true inclination with HP and VP.

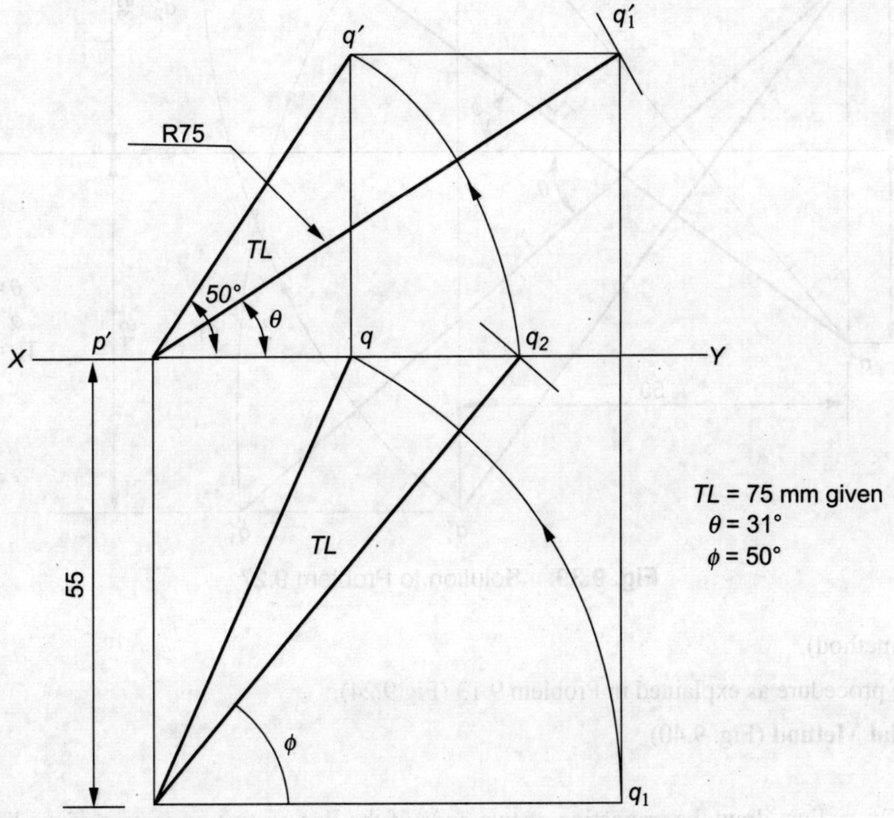

Fig. 9.38: Solution to Problem 9.26

The solution of the problem is self-explanatory.

PROBLEM 9.27 (FIG. 9.39)

A line *PQ* has its end *P* 20 mm above HP and 25 mm in front of VP, end *Q* 45 mm below HP and 35 mm behind VP. The distance between the end projectors is 50 mm. Draw the projections of the line and find out true length and the true inclinations with HP and VP by the following:

(i) Rotation method

(ii) Trapezoidal method

Rotation Method

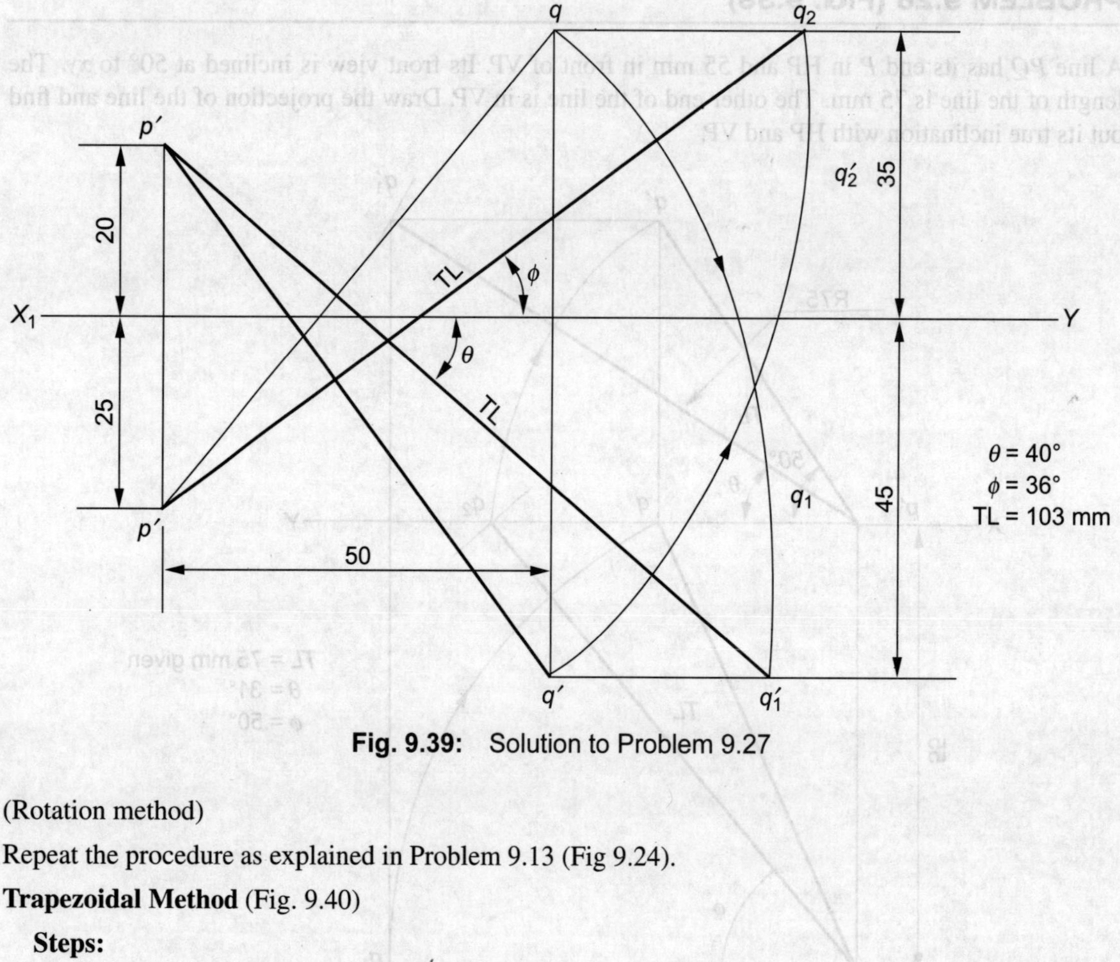

Fig. 9.39: Solution to Problem 9.27

(Rotation method)

Repeat the procedure as explained in Problem 9.13 (Fig 9.24).

Trapezoidal Method (Fig. 9.40)

Steps:

(1) On *xy* line, draw the projection of two ends of the line on two projectors of the line 50 mm apart.

(2) *P′q′* is the front view and *p q* is the top view.

(3) Since the projections of points *p′* and *q′* are on the opposite directions on the perpendicular drawn on *p′* and *q′*. Cut along the perpendicular drawn through *p′* as marked (✓), locate point *P*. Similarly, locate Q_1 marked (×). Join *P′* and Q_1 which gives true length, and measure the angle, ϕ.

(4) Repeating the procedure for end Q, locate P_1' and Q_1', join P_1' and Q_1', which is the true length, and measure θ.

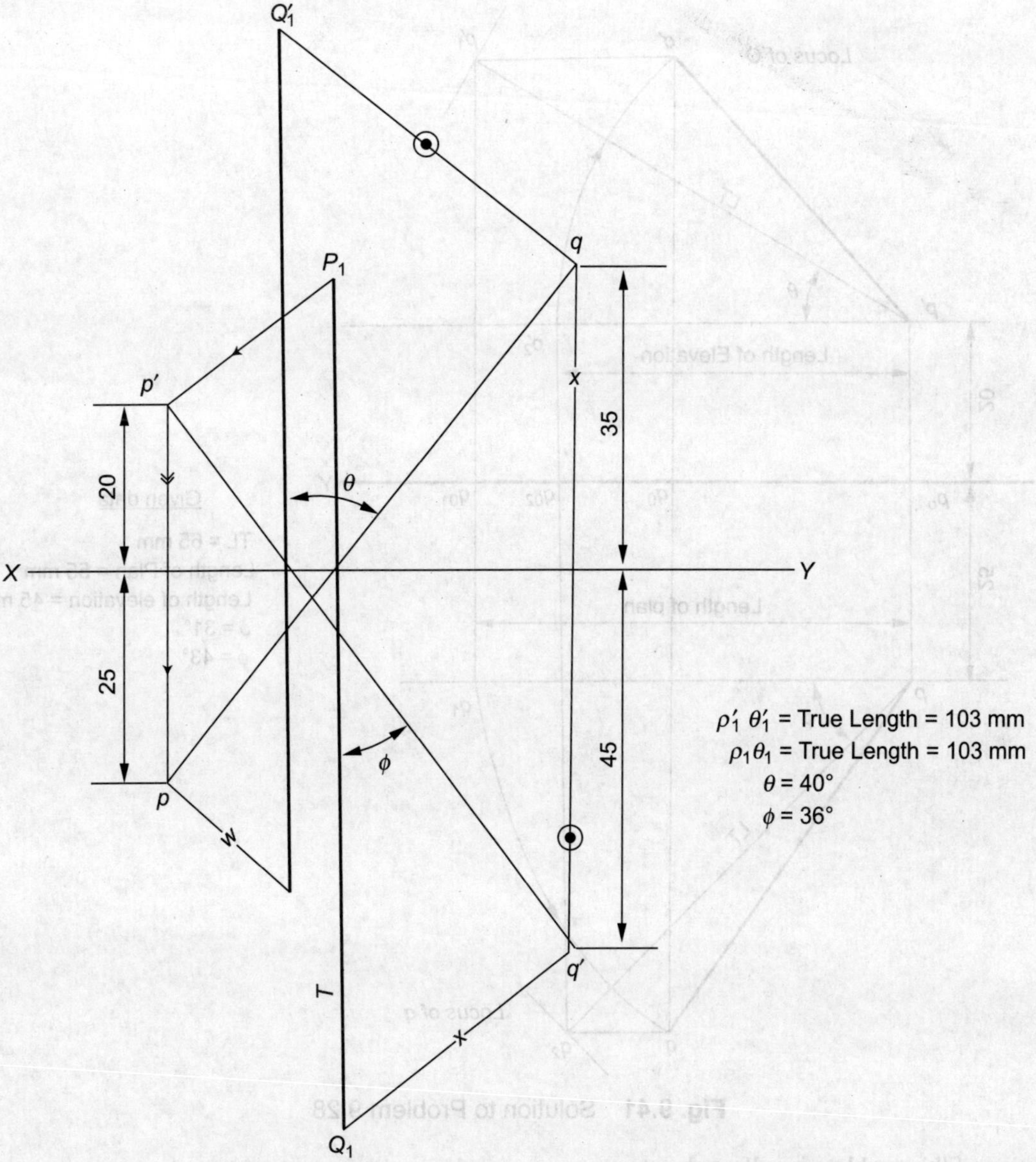

Fig. 9.40: Solution to problem (Trapezoidal method)

PROBLEM 9.28 (FIG. 9.41)

The length of the plane and elevation of a line *PQ* is 65 mm long, measures 55 mm and 45 mm, respectively. End *P* is 20 mm above HP and 25 mm in front of the VP. Draw its projections and determine the true inclination with HP and VP, respectively.

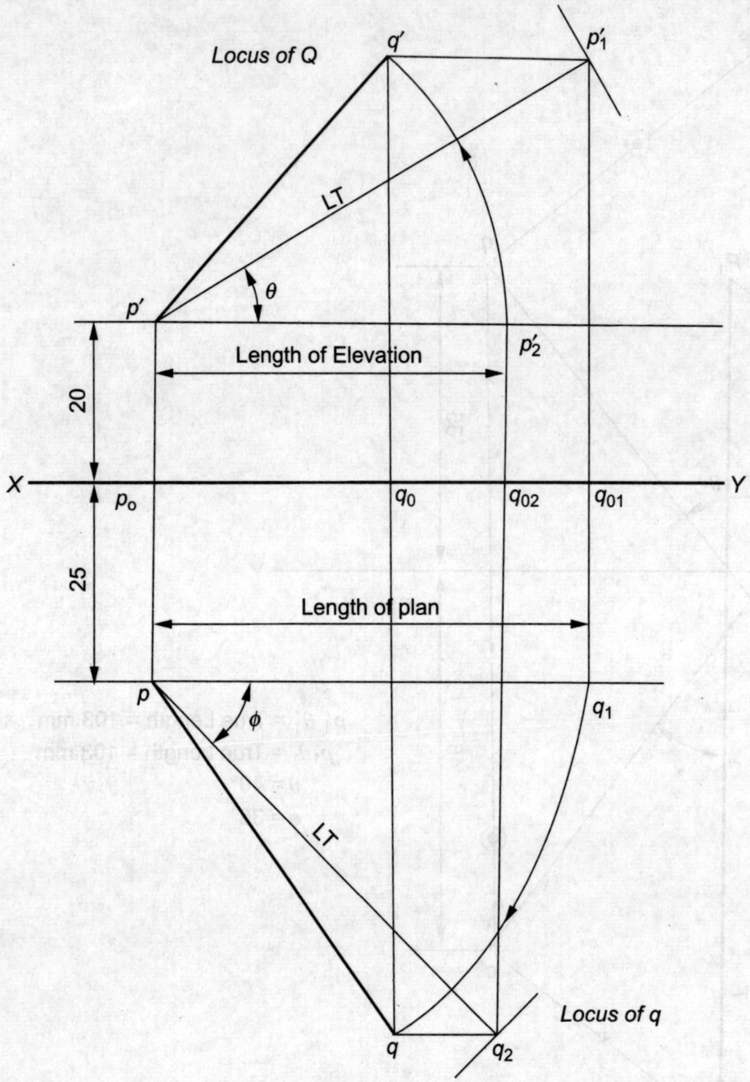

Given data

TL = 65 mm

Length of Plan = 55 mm

Length of elevation = 45 mm

$\phi = 31°$

$\phi = 43°$

Fig. 9.41 Solution to Problem 9.28

Solution of this problem is self-explanatory.

Steps:

(1) Solution of this problem is self explanatory.

PROBLEM 9.29 (FIG. 9.42)

The front view of a line *PQ* is 65 mm, the end *P* is 20 mm above HP and the end Q is 30 mm in front of VP. The line is inclined at 30° to HP and 45° to VP. Draw the projections of line and find its true length and the traces.

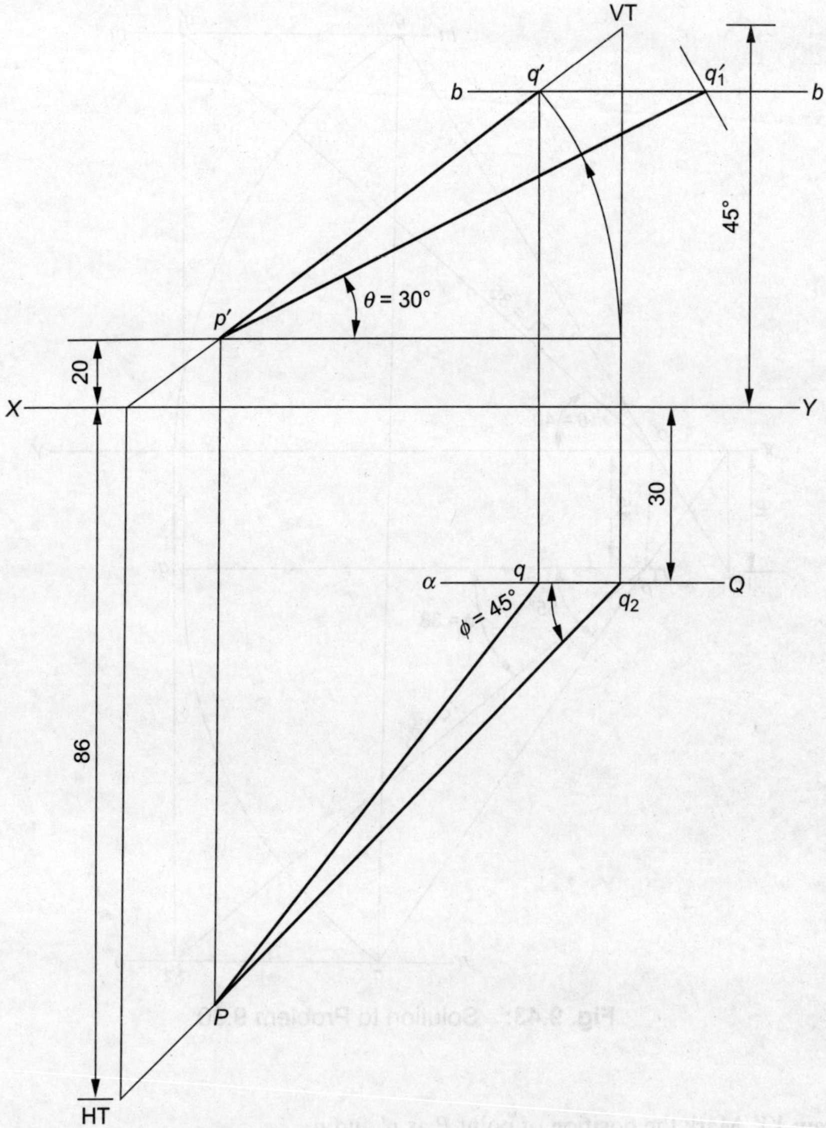

Fig. 9.42: Solution to Problem 9.29

Solution of this problem is self explanatory.

PROBLEM 9.30 (FIG. 9.43)

A line *PQ*, 85 mm long is inclined at 40° to HP and its top view makes an angle of 55° with VP. The end *P* of the line is in HP and 15 mm in front of VP. Draw its front view and find out the true inclination with VP. Locate HT and VT.

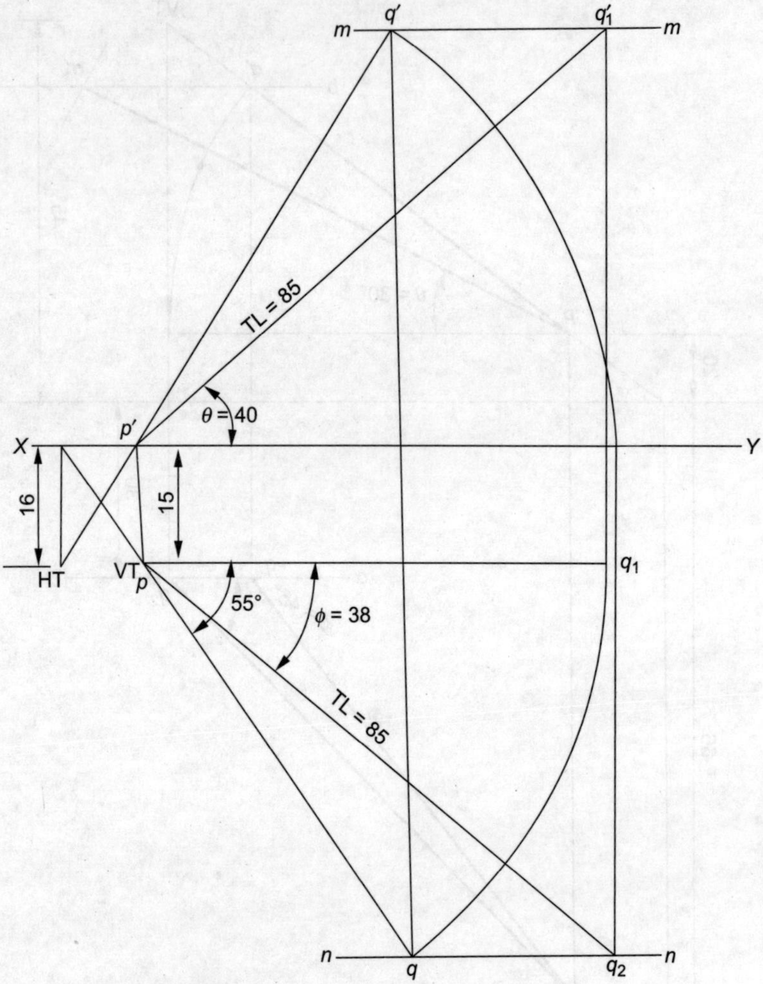

Fig. 9.43: Solution to Problem 9.30

Steps:

(1) Draw *XY*. Mark the position of point *P* as *p′* and *p*.

(2) Draw line *p*, *q′*, = 85 mm at 40° angle to *XY* line.

(3) Through q_1', draw a vertical line.

(4) With *p* as centre and radius equal to *pq*, draw an arc which meets on q_1 such that pq_1 makes an angle of 55° to *xy*. *pq* is the top view.

(5) From q, draw a vertical line to cut with the locus of q_1'.

(6) Join *p′q′* which is the front view of the line.

(7) Measure the angle ϕ and locate traces HT and VT.

PROBLEM 9.31 (FIG. 9.44)

The end *A* of a line *AB* is 15 mm above HP and its VT is 15 mm below HP. The front view of the line measures 45 mm and is inclined at 45° to *XY*. Draw the projection of the line if end *B* is in the first quadrant and the line is inclined at 30° to VP. Find the true length and inclination of the line with HP. Find HT also.

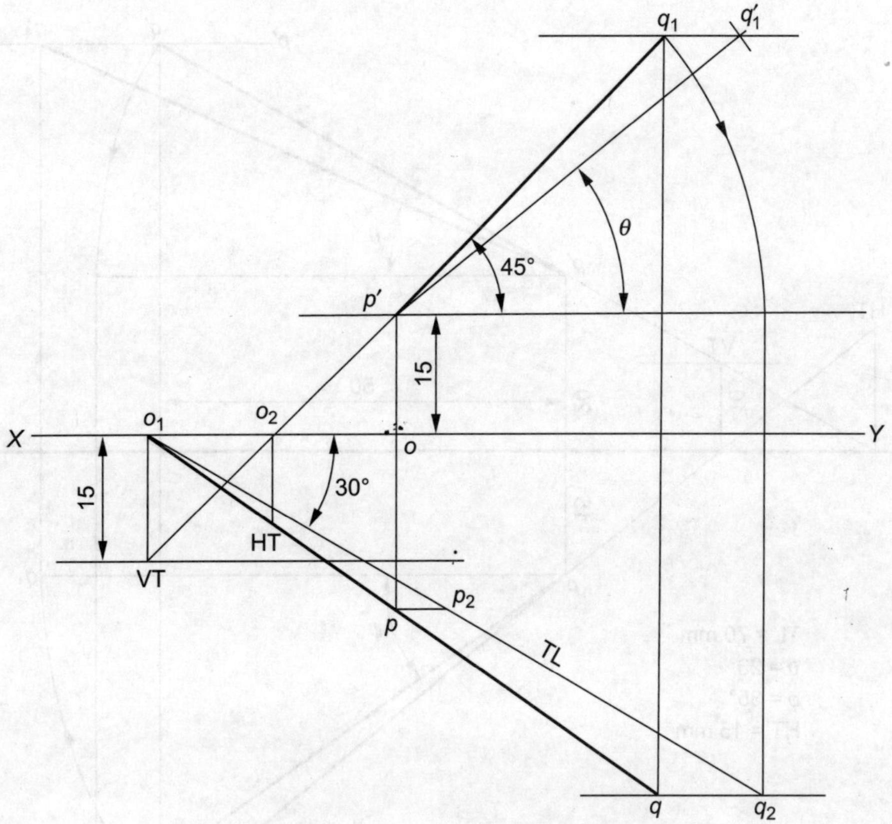

Fig. 9.44: Solution to Problem 9.31

Steps:

(1) Draw *XY*. At *O*, draw a vertical line. Locate *p*′. 15 mm above *XY*, draw a horizontal line at 15 mm below *XY*.

(2) At 45° angle, draw *p*′*q*′ equal to 45 mm. Extend *q*′*p*′ which cuts *XY* on O_2, and proceed below up to a line 15 mm below *XY*. From VT, draw O_1, ⊥ to *XY*.

(3) At *o*′ draw an angle of 30°.

(4) Take *p*′ as the centre and $p'q_1$ as the radius, project this line which meets at q_2. Draw horizontal line qq_2. Join *pq* which is the top view.

(5) Measure $pq_2 = 50$ mm, $\theta = 40°$.

PROBLEM 9.32 (FIG. 9.45)

A line PQ has its end P, 20 mm above HP and 15 mm in front of VP. End Q is 55 mm in front of VP. The vertical trace (VT) is 10 mm above HP.

Draw the projection of the line if the distance between the projectors is 50 mm. Find also the true length, θ, ϕ, and HT.

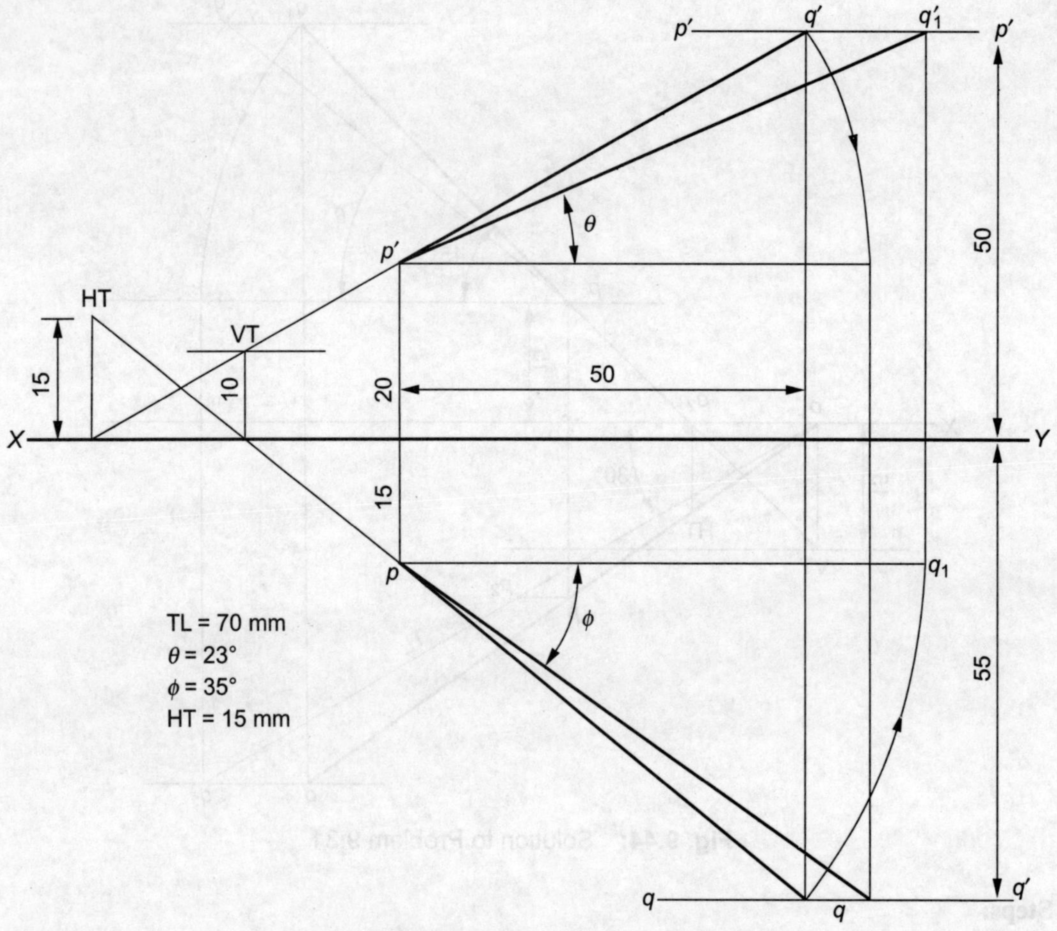

Fig. 9.45: Solution to Problem 9.32

The solution to the problem is self-explanatory.

Step:

The solution to the problem is self-explanatory.

PROBLEM 9.33 (FIG. 9.46)

A straight line *PQ* has its end *P* 20 mm in front of VP while the other end *Q* is 50 mm in front of VP. The length of the top view of the line is 55 mm and the HT of the line is 15 mm in front of VP. Draw the projections of the line if the line is inclined at 30° to HP. Also find VT of the line.

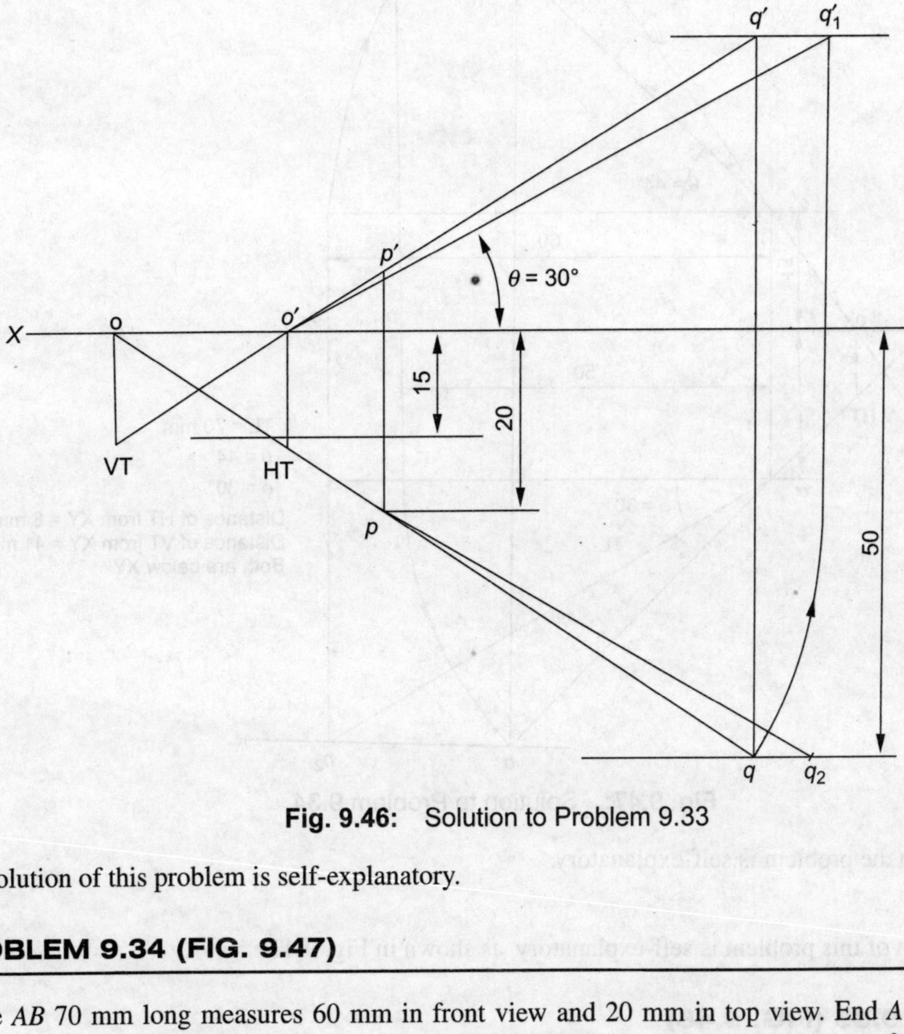

Fig. 9.46: Solution to Problem 9.33

The solution of this problem is self-explanatory.

PROBLEM 9.34 (FIG. 9.47)

A line *AB* 70 mm long measures 60 mm in front view and 20 mm in top view. End *A* of the line is 15 mm above HP and 50 mm in front of VP. Draw the projection of the line and traces, θ and ϕ.

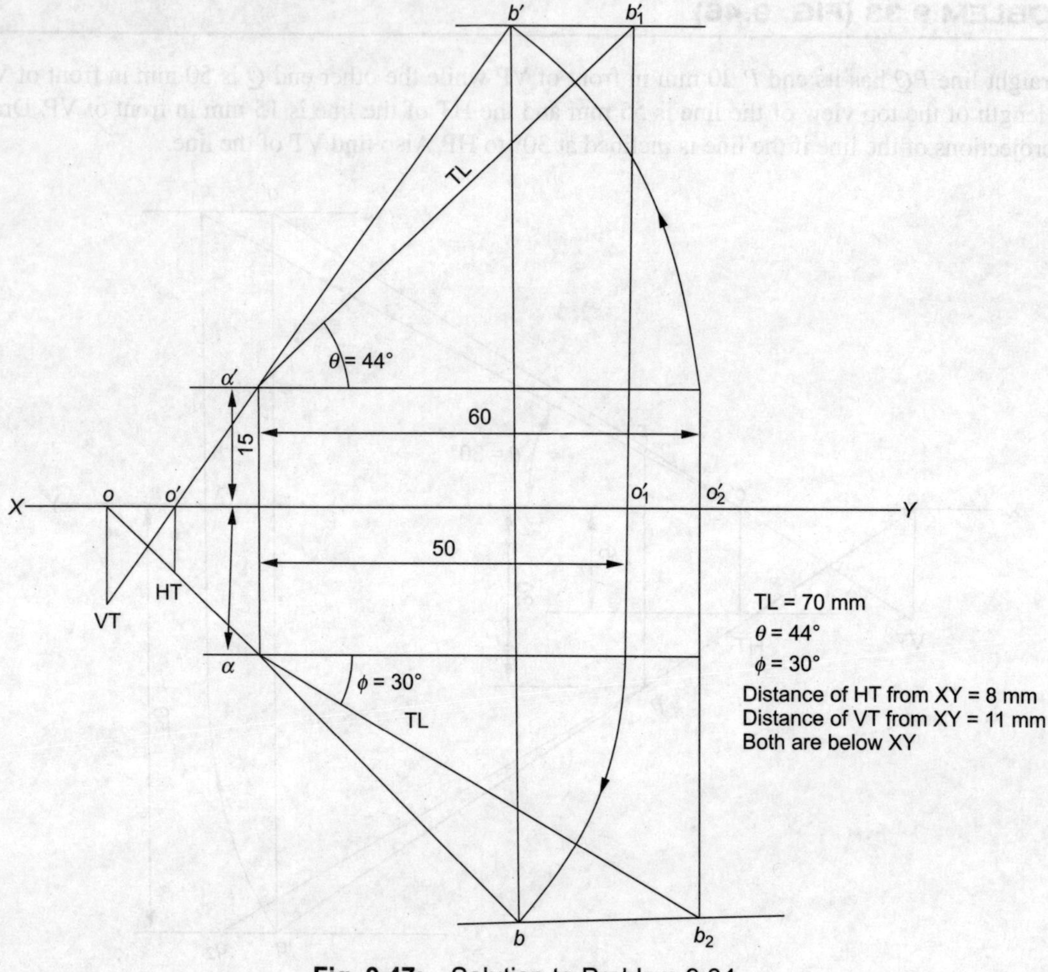

Fig. 9.47: Solution to Problem 9.34

The solution to the problem is self-explanatory.

Steps:

The solution of this problem is self-explanatory, as shown in Fig. 9.47.

PROBLEM 9.35 (FIG. 9.48)

The end '*P*' of *a* straight line *PQ* is 20 mm in front of VP. The end *Q* is 55 mm in front of VP. The HT of the line is 10 mm in front of VP. The length of its front view measures 60 mm and makes an angle of 45° to *xy*, the length of its top view is 55 mm. Draw the projection of the line and find *TL*, *θ*, *ϕ*, and VT of the line.

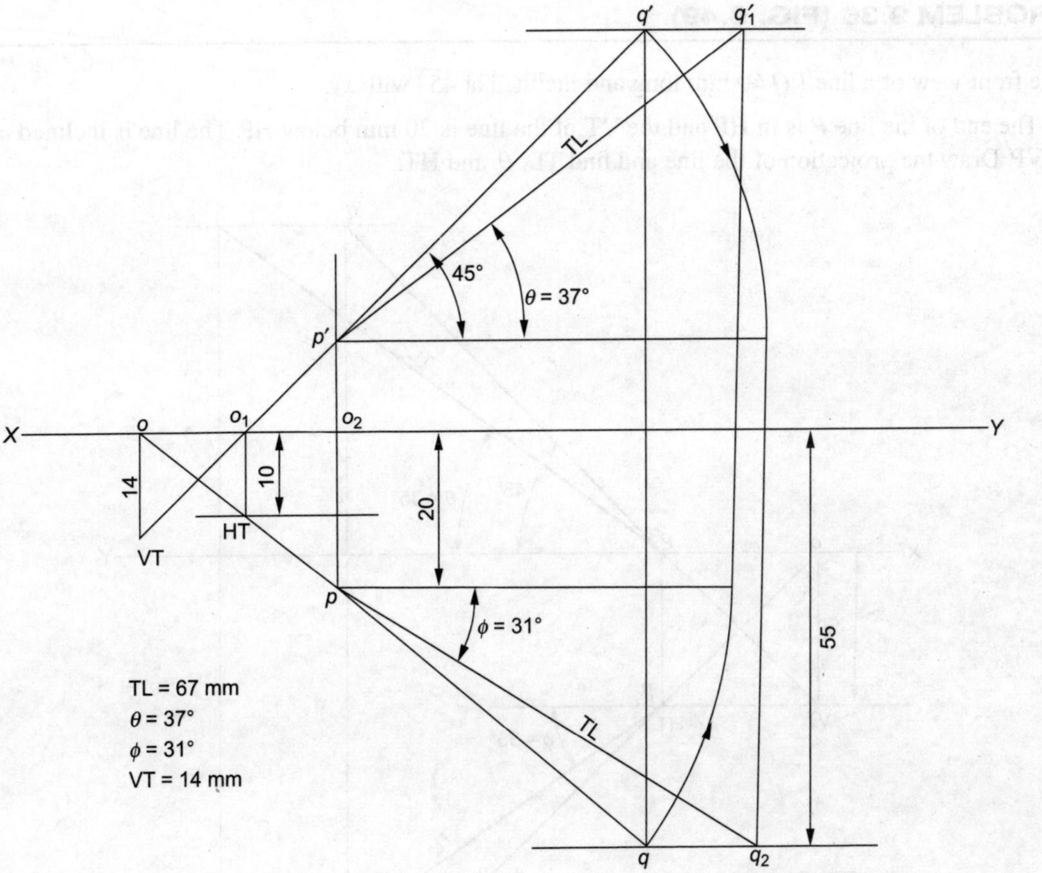

Fig. 9.48: Solution to Problem 9.35

Steps:

(1) Draw *XY* line. At any point O_2 on *XY*, draw *a* projection line. Locate *p*, top view of end point *p* at 20 mm in front of VP.

(2) Draw a line parallel to *XY* at a distance of 10 mm to locate HT on this line.

(3) Below *XY*, draw a horizontal line equal to 55 mm. From *P* take a distance *pq* = 55 mm.

(4) Draw a line *qp* and join with HT and extend it to *XY* line meeting at *O*. Draw a line at *O* perpendicular to *XY*. At O_1, make an angle of 45°. On this line, *p'q'* is the length of the front view equal to 60 mm

(5) Join *q'p'* and extend to meet with VT perpendicular to *O* at *XY*.

(6) *p' q'* is the front view and *pq* is the top view.

(7) Follow the procedure to find *TL*, θ, and ϕ.

PROBLEM 9.36 (FIG. 9.49)

The front view of a line *PQ* 60 mm long and inclined at 45° with *xy*.

The end of the line *P* is in HP and the VT of the line is 20 mm below HP. The line is inclined at 35° to VP. Draw the projection of the line and find TL, θ, and HT.

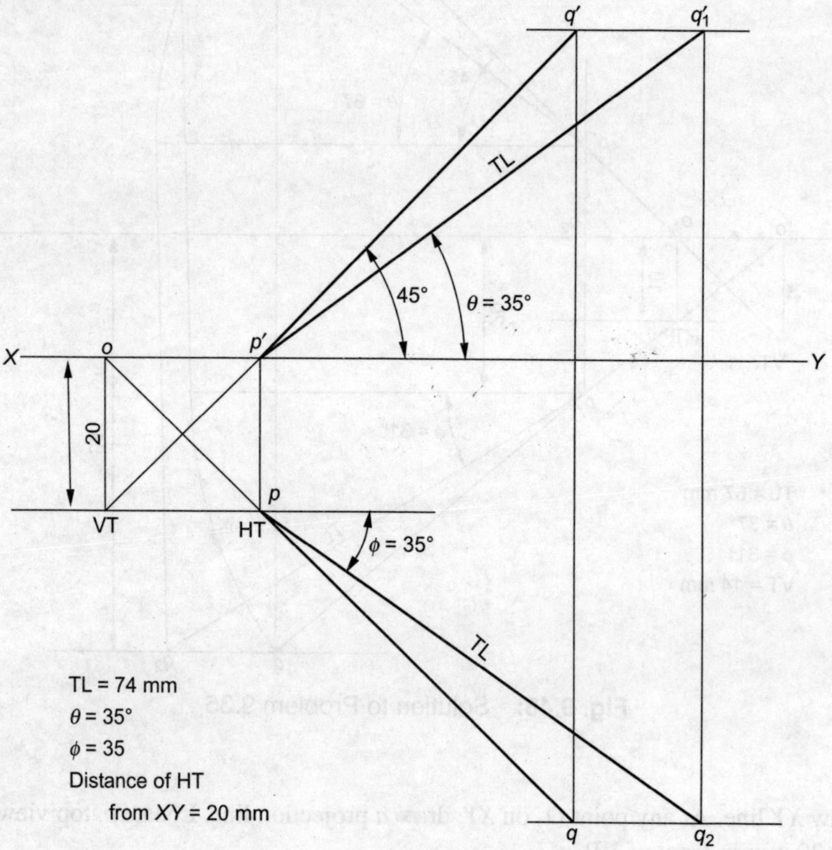

Fig. 9.49: Solution to Problem 9.36

Steps:

(1) Draw *XY* line and locate front view of *P* as *p*′ on *XY* below *p*′, *p*, top view of the line is located. This will be HT of the line.

(2) Draw *p*′*q*′ the front view at 45° inclination.

(3) Below *XY*, draw a line at 20 mm. Extend *p*′*q*′ line which cuts VT line at VT. Draw perpendicular at *O*.

(4) Join *op* and extend this line to meet at *q*, the projected from *q*′.

(5) At P, draw a line at 35° inclination to meet at q_2, the locus of q. pq_2 will be the *TL*.

(6) Draw a projector from q_2 to meet at q_1', the locus line of q′. Join $p'q_1'$, which is also the true length. Measure θ and ϕ both are 35°.

PROBLEM 9.37 (FIG. 9.50)

The front view of a line *PQ* makes an angles of 35° with the horizontal plane. The HT of the line is 35 mm in front of VP, while its VT is 25 mm below HP. End *P* of the line is 10 mm above HP and end *Q* is 90 mm in front of VP. Draw the projection of line, true length, and inclination with HP and VP.

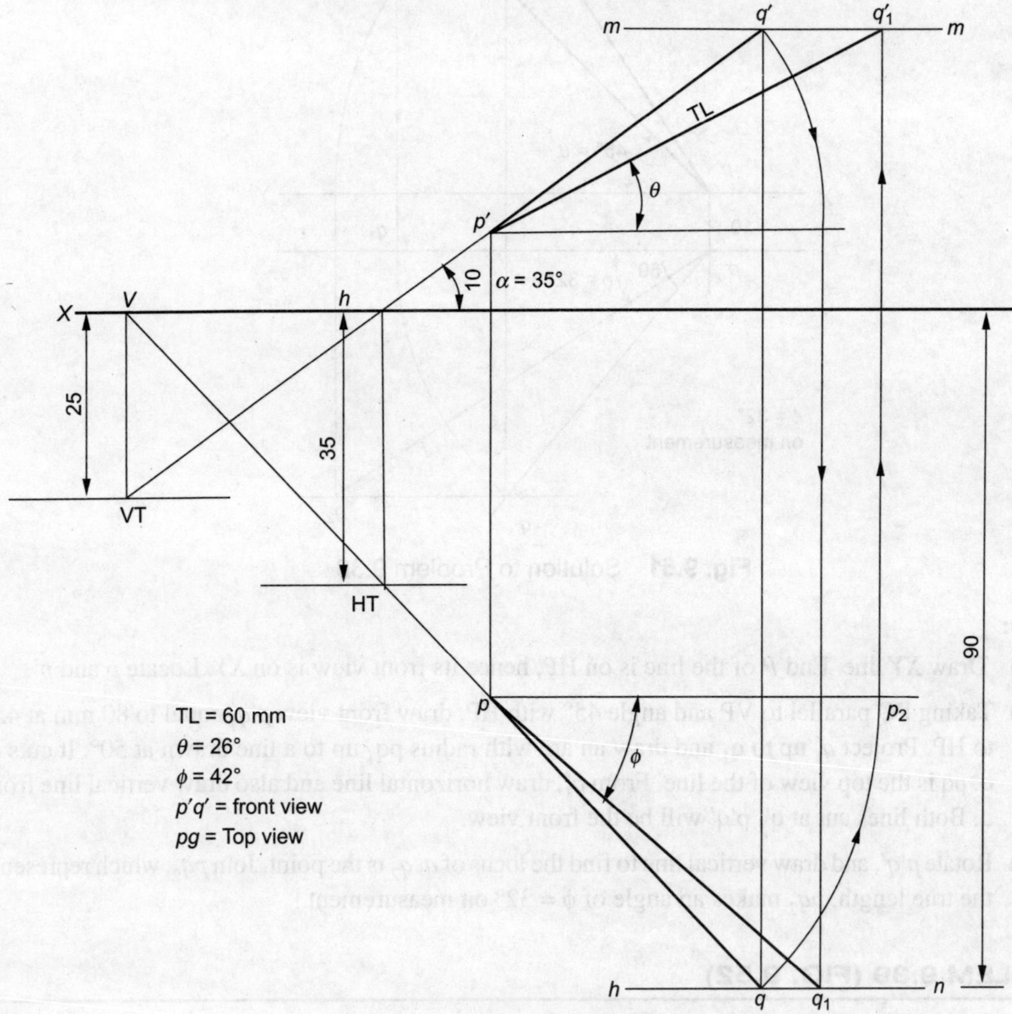

Fig. 9.50: Solution to Problem 9.37

PROBLEM 9.38 (FIG. 9.51)

A line *PQ* 80 mm long, is inclined at 45° to *HP* and its top view makes an angle of 50° with *VP*. The end *P* is in *HP* and 10 mm in front of *VP*, Draw its front view and find the true inclination with *VP*. Locate the traces.

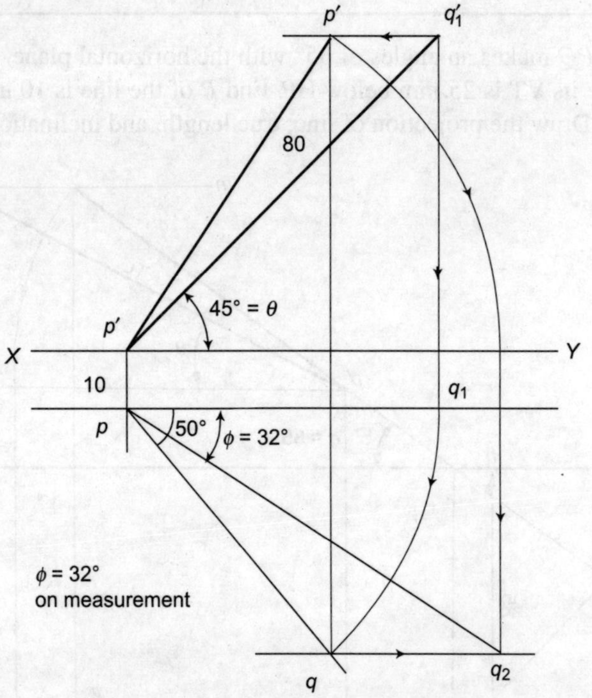

Fig. 9.51 Solution to Problem 9.38

Steps:

(1) Draw *XY* line. End *P* of the line is on HP, hence its front view is on *XY*. Locate *p* and *p′*.

(2) Taking PQ parallel to VP and angle 45° with HP, draw front view $p'q_1'$ equal to 80 mm at 45° to HP. Project q_1' up to q_1 and draw an arc with radius pq_1 up to a line drawn at 50°. It cuts at q. pq is the top view of the line. From q_1', draw horizontal line and also draw vertical line from q. Both lines cut at q′. p′q′ will be the front view.

(3) Rotate *p′q′*, and draw vertical line to find the locus of *q*. q_2 is the point. Join pq_2, which represents the true length. pq_2 makes an angle of ϕ = 32° on measurement.

PROBLEM 9.39 (FIG. 9.52)

A straight line *PQ*, 80 mm long, makes an angle of 30° with *HP*. The end *P* is 10 mm above *HP* and 15 mm in front of *VP*. The front view of the line is 60 mm. Draw the top view of the line and find inclination of the line with *VP*.

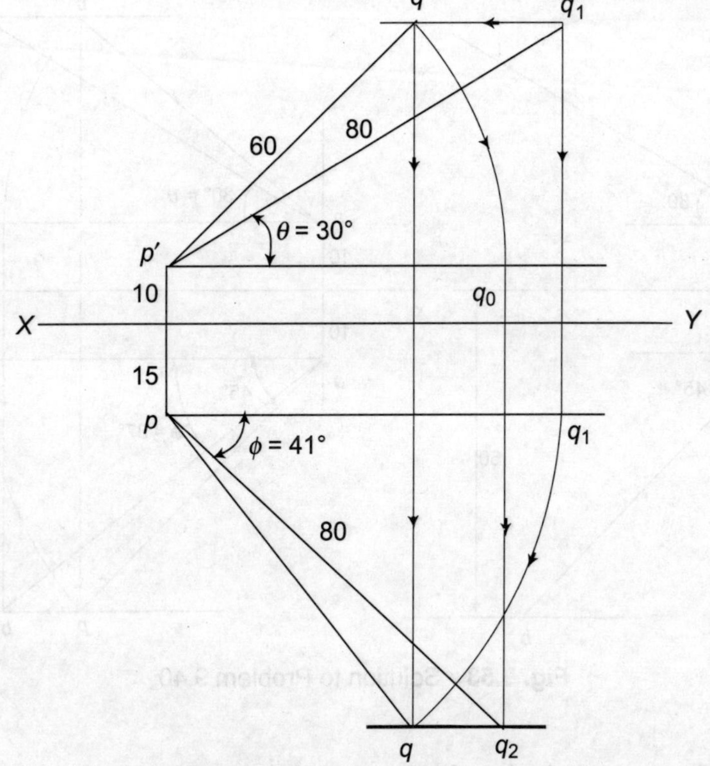

Fig. 9.52 Solution to Problem 9.39

Steps:

(1) Draw xy and mark p and q′ of end p of the line. At p′, draw a line $p'q_1' = 80$ mm and 30° with xy.

(2) Draw a horizontal line from q_1'. Take p′ as centre and radius equal to 60 mm, cut at q′.

(3) From q_1' draw perpendicular to q_1. Taking p as centre and radius equal to pq_1, drop q′ vertically to cut both at q. pq becomes top view.

(4) From p′, draw an arc at radius p′q′ to q_0 and draw a vertical line to q_2. Join pq_2 which is the true length and measure angle $\phi = 41°$.

PROBLEM 9.40 (FIG. 9.53)

The end *A* of the line *AB* is 10 mm above *HP* and 10 mm in front of *VP*. The end *B* of the line is 50 mm in front of *VP*. The top view makes an angle of 45°. Line *AB* makes an angle of 30° with *xy*. Determine its true length and true inclination with *VP*.

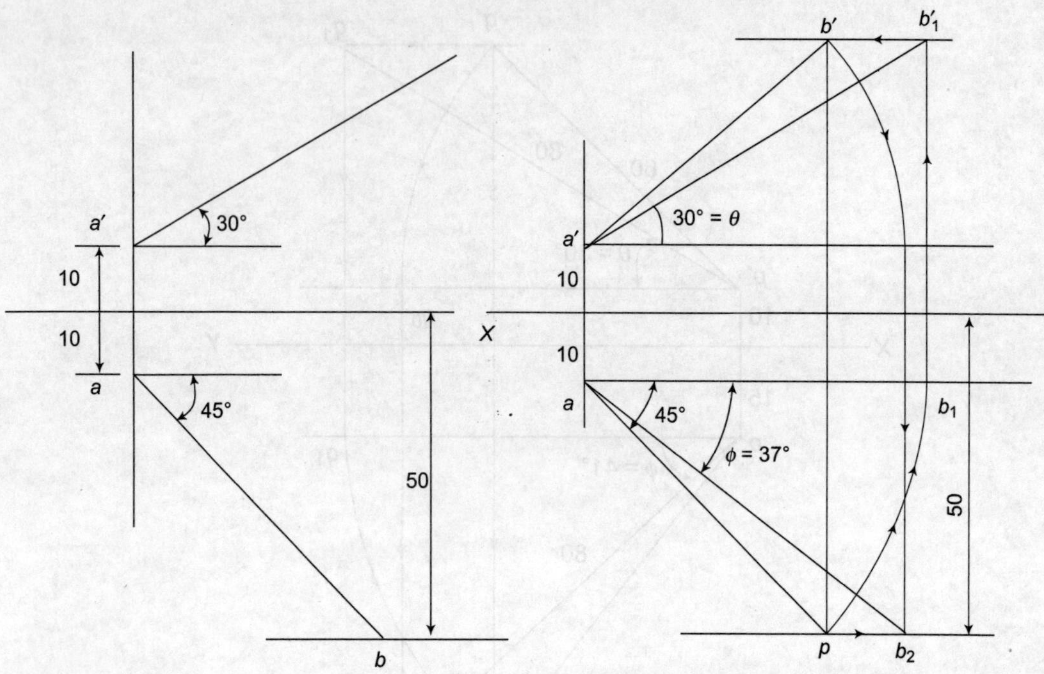

Fig. 9.53 Solution to Problem 9.40

Steps:

(1) Draw xy. Locate the projection of end A as a and a′ on xy. ab is the top view of the line making 45° to xy. Taking a as centre and ab as radius, draw an arc up to b_1. Draw a perpendicular to xy and extend up to b_1'. Draw a perpendicular to xy and extend up to b_1'. Draw a horizontal line to cut b′, a′b′ is the front view of the line and $a'b_1'$ is the true length.

(2) From b' draw an arc taking a' as centre and draw perpendicular to xy to cut b_2. Join a b_2 which gives the true length of the line and measure angle $\phi = 37°$.

True length of the line on measurement = 65 mm

PROBLEM 9.41 (FIG. 9.54)

A line PQ has its one end P 45 mm below HP and 15 mm behind VP.

The other end Q of the line is 12 mm above HP and 30 mm in front of VP. The distance between the end projector is 50 mm. Determine the traces of the line. Draw the projections and inclinations by the two methods.

Method II is by trapezoidal method.

Steps:

(1) At end p and q, draw perpendiculars as pP_2 and qQ_2 equal to O_1p' and pP_2 and O_2q' and qQ_2, respectively. Join P_2Q_2. Required true length, P_2Q_2 makes angle θ with pq.

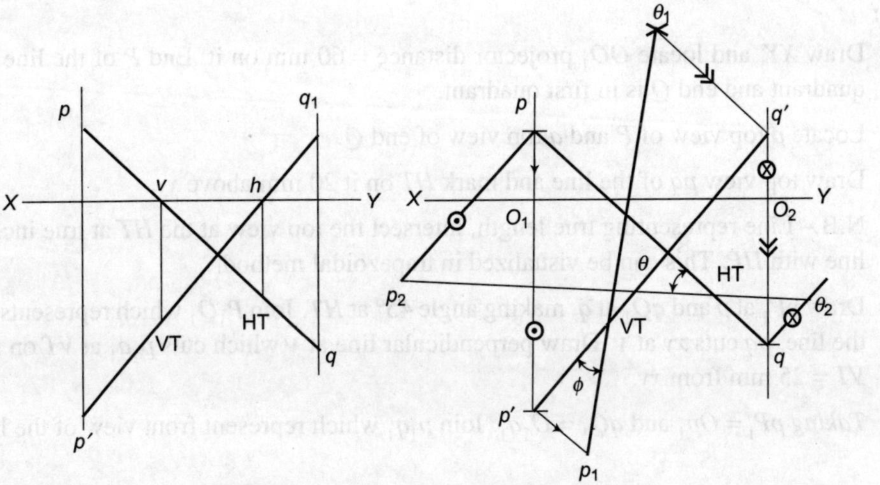

Fig. 9.54 Solution to Problem 9.41

(2) Similarly, End p′ and q′ draw perpendicular as $p'P_1'$ and $q'Q_1$ equal to $o_1p = p'P_1$ and $q'Q_1 = O_2q$. Join P_1Q_1, which is also the true length of the line. P_1Q_1 makes an angle ϕ with the p′q′. VT and HT are located as shown. On measurement, $P_2Q_2 = P_1Q_1 = 90$ mm; $\theta = 39°$, $\phi = 31°$.

PROBLEM 9.42 (FIG. 9.55)

A line *PQ* has it end *P* is 25 mm behind *VP* and below *HP*. The other end *Q* is 15 mm in front of *VP* and above *HP*.

The distance between the end projector is 60 mm. The line is inclined at 45° with *HP* and its *HT* is 20 mm behind *VP*.

Draw the projection of the line, the true length and the *VT* of the line.

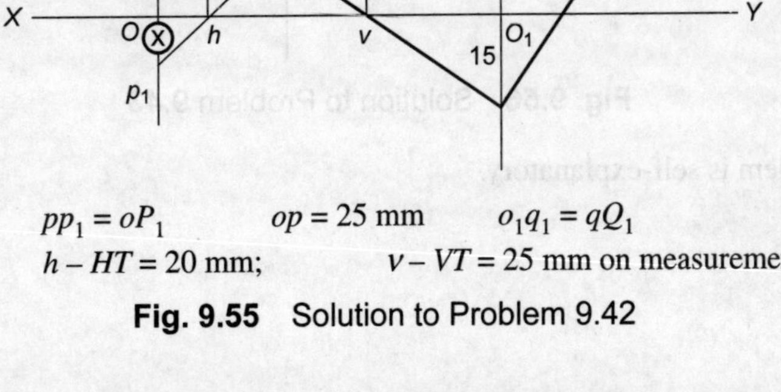

$oo_1 = 60$ mm $\quad pp_1 = oP_1 \quad op = 25$ mm $\quad o_1q_1 = qQ_1$

$o_1q = 15$ mm $\quad h - HT = 20$ mm; $\quad v - VT = 25$ mm on measurement

Fig. 9.55 Solution to Problem 9.42

Steps:

(1) Draw *XY*, and locate OO_1 projector distance = 60 mm on it. End *P* of the line is in the third quadrant and end *Q* is in first quadrant.

Locate *p* top view of *P* and *q* top view of end *Q*.

Draw top view *pq* of the line and mark *HT* on it 20 mm above *xy*.

N.B.– Line representing true length, intersect the top view at the *HT* at true inclination of the line with *HP*. This can be visualized in trapezoidal method.

(2) Draw pP_1 at *p* and qQ_1 at *q*, making angle 45° at *HT*. Join P_1Q_1 which represents true length of the line. *pq* cuts *xy* at *v*. Draw perpendicular line at *v* which cuts p_1q_1 at *VT* on measurement. *VT* = 25 mm from *xy*.

(3) *Taking* $pP_1 = Op_1$ and $qQ_1 = O_1q_1$. Join p_1q_1 which represent front view of the line

PROBLEM 9.43 (FIG. 9.56)

A line *PQ* has its end *P* in front of *VP* and 25 mm above *HP*. End Q is 45 mm below *HP* and behind *VP*. There is a point on straight line which is *VT* and 10 mm below *HP*. The line *PQ* had equal inclination with *HP* and *VP*. Draw the projection and find true length and inclination of the line with *HP*, if the distance between projectors of ends is 55 mm.

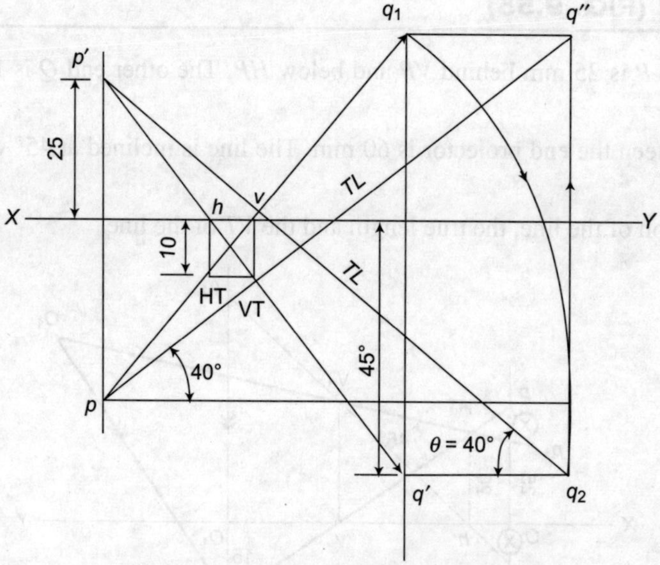

Fig. 9.56 Solution to Problem 9.43

Solution of this problem is self-explanatory.

PROBLEM 9.44 (FIG. 9.57)

A line *PQ*, 100 mm long is inclined at 45° to *HP* and 30° to *VP*, Its middle point *m* is in *VP* and 20 mm above *HP*.

The end *P* is in third quadrant and *Q* is in first quadrant. Draw the projection of line *PQ*.

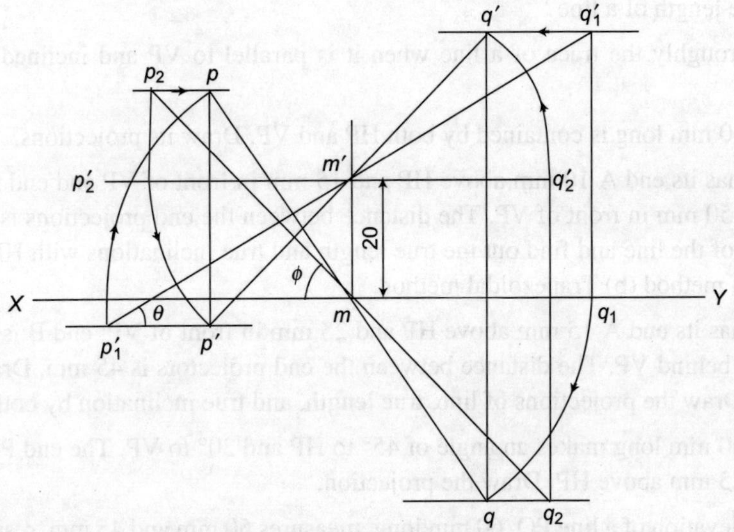

Fig. 9.57 Solution to Problem 9.44

Steps

(1) '*m*' is the middle point of the line.

Draw the projection of the middle point *m*.

(2) Through *m*′, draw a line at 30° to *xy* and mark as p_1'.

$p_1' q_1' = 100$ mm length of line, $p_1'm' = m' q_1' = 50$ mm.

(3) Through p_1' and q_1' draw locus line.
From q_1' draw a vertical line to cut *xy* at q_1.

Now mq_1 is the top view for half the length of the line.

(4) Through *m*, draw a line at 45° to *xy*.

Mark $p_2\, m\, q_2 = 100$ mm true length.

$p_2 m = q_2 m = 50$ mm
Draw locus line from q_2 and p_2.

With *m* as the centre and *mq* as radius, draw an arc to intersect the locus of q_1 and *q*.

(5) Draw a line perpendicular from q to intersect the locus q_1' at *q*′. Join *p*′*q*′; pmq is the top view.

EXERCISE

Review Questions

1. What do you mean by HT and VT?
2. What is true length of a line?
3. Show it is roughly the trace of a line when it is parallel to VP and inclined to HP. Name the trace.
4. A line PQ 50 mm long is contained by both HP and VP. Draw its projections.
5. A line AB has its end A 10 mm above HP and 15 mm in front of VP and end B is 45 mm above the HP and 50 mm in front of VP. The distance between the end projections is 45 mm. Draw the projections of the line and find out the true length and true inclinations with HP and VP by using (a) Rotation method (b) Trapezoidal method.
6. A line PQ has its end A 15 mm above HP and 25 mm in front of VP; end B is 45 mm below HP and 35 mm behind VP. The distance between the end projectors is 45 mm. Draw the projections of 45 mm. Draw the projections of line, true length, and true inclination by both the methods.
7. A line PQ 60 mm long makes an angle of 45° to HP and 30° to VP. The end P is 15 mm in front of VP and 25 mm above HP. Draw the projection.
8. Plane and elevation of a line PQ, 60 mm long, measures 50 mm and 45 mm, respectively. End P is 15 mm above HP and 20 mm in front of VP. Draw its projections. Determine the true inclination with HP and VP.
9. A line AB, 60 mm long, is inclined at 30° to HP and 45° to VP. Its middle point C is 30 mm above HP and 40 mm in front of VP. Draw its projection.
10. A line PQ has its end P 15 mm above HP and end Q is 60 mm in front of VP. The front view of the line is inclined at 45° to *xy* line. The HT of the line is 12 mm in front of the VP and its VT is 15 mm below HP. Draw its projections and true length and also the true inclination.
11. A line AB, 85 mm long, measures 70 mm in elevation and 60 mm in plane. Draw the projections of the line where point A is 20 mm above HP and 10 mm in front of VP. Find HT and VT of the line.
12. A line PQ appears as 60 mm in front view. The end P is 15 mm above HP while end B is 20 mm in front of VP. The line is inclined at 30° to HP and 45° to VP. Draw its projection and find traces and true length.
13. A line PQ has its end P in HP and 45 mm in front of VP. Its front view is inclined at 60° to *xy* and has a length of 65 mm. The other end Q is in VP. Draw the projection and find out its true inclination with HP and VP.
14. A wireless tower 25 m high is tied at the top by two guide ropes having an angle of depression of 30° and 45°. The other end of the ropes are connected to two poles at a height of 4 m and 3 m,

respectively. The two poles are 10 m apart. Draw projection of the whole arrangement and find out the length of the ropes.

15. An electric lamp hung by an electric wire in the centre of a hall 4.5 m × 3.5 m × 6 m at a distance of 2.5 m from the ceiling. Determine graphically its distance from one of the corners of the floor.

16. *ABC* is an equilateral triangle of 75 mm side. The end *A* is in HP and *B* is in V.P. Side *AB* is inclined at 30° to HP and 45° to VP. Side *BC* is inclined at 35° to HP. Draw the top view and front view of the triangle and find the inclination of side *AC* with HP.

17. A line *PQ*, 60 mm long, has its and *A* in both HP and VP. It is inclined at 45° to HP and 30° to VP. Draw the projection of the line *PQ* and determine its traces.

18. A line *AB*, 100 mm long, is 30° and 45° inclined to HP and VP, respectively. End *A* is 10 mm above HP and its VT is 20 mm below HP. Draw the projections of the line and its HT.

19. A point *A* is 45 mm below HP and 15 mm behind VP. Point *B* is 10 mm above HP and 25 mm in front of VP. The distance between the projection of *A* and *B* is 40 mm. Find the traces of the line joining *A* and *B*.

Objective Questions

1. A straight line is defined as the _______ distance between two end points.

2. When a line is perpendicular to one of the planes, it is _______ to the other plane.

3. When a line is inclined to _______ and parallel to _______, its top view represents true length.

4. When a line is inclined to ______ and parallel to _______, its front view represents the true length.

5. Trace of a line is a _______.

6. When a line is inclined to HP and parallel to VP, the inclination of the front view with XY represents its _______.

7. When a line is contained by a profile plane, the sum of the angle of inclination with HP and VP is equal to _______.

8. The side view of a line is a _____.

9. When a line is parallel to both the reference plane, it has _______ trace.

ANSWERS

Objective Questions

1. Shortest	**2.** Parallel	**3.** VP, HP	**4.** HP, VP	**5.** Point
6. True inclination	**7.** 90°	**8.** Point	**9.** No	

10

CHAPTER

Projection of Planes and Auxiliary Planes

10.1 INTRODUCTION

A plane is a two-dimensional surface. It has negligible thickness. A plane may be of any shape and figure as shown in Fig. 10.1.

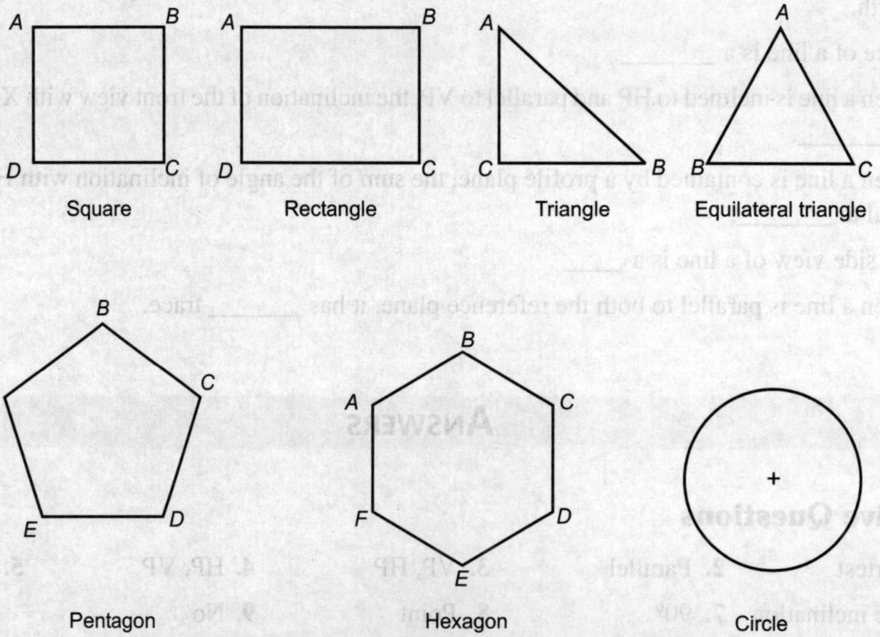

Fig. 10.1 Planes of various shapes and figures

10.2 TYPES OF PLANES

1. **Principal planes:** Horizontal plane (HP) and vertical plane (VP) are the reference planes on which projections are taken. They are also called principal planes.
2. **Secondary planes:** Any plane other than HP and VP reference planes is known as the secondary plane.

They are of different types depending on the orientation of the plane with reference to the other:

(i) Plane perpendicular to HP and VP both.

(ii) Plane perpendicular to HP and parallel to VP.

(iii) Plane perpendicular to VP and parallel to HP.

(iv) Plane perpendicular to HP and inclined to VP.

(v) Plane perpendicular to VP and inclined to HP.

(vi) Oblique plane, i.e., plane inclined to both HP and VP.

(i) Plane perpendicular to HP and VP both (Fig. 10.2)

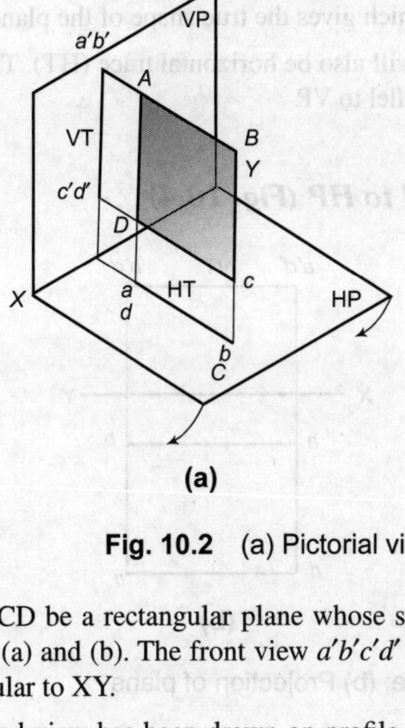

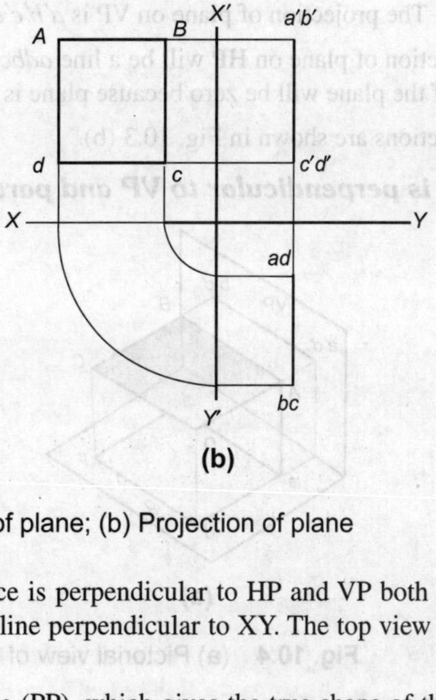

Fig. 10.2 (a) Pictorial view of plane; (b) Projection of plane

Let ABCD be a rectangular plane whose surface is perpendicular to HP and VP both as shown in Figs. 10.2 (a) and (b). The front view *a′b′c′d′* is a line perpendicular to XY. The top view *adbc* is also perpendicular to XY.

Right end view has been drawn on profile plane (PP), which gives the true shape of the rectangle. This is in left side of front view. End of plane has been extended to HP and VP, which gives the HT and VT as shown in Fig. 10.2 (a).

(ii) Plane perpendicular to HP and parallel to VP (Fig. 10.3)

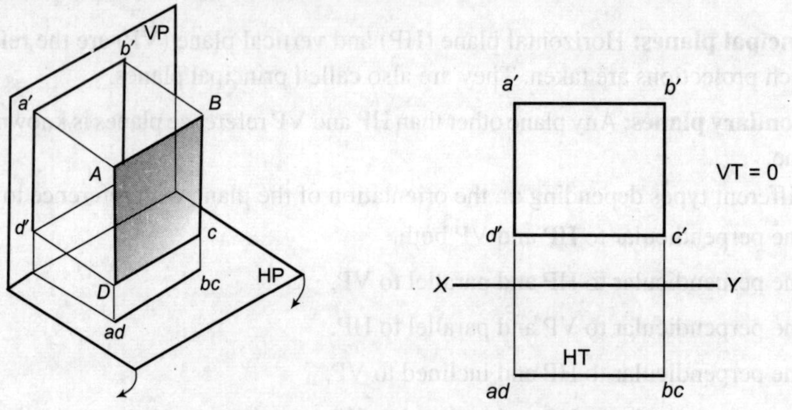

(a) (b)

Fig. 10.3 (a) Pictorial view of plane; (b) Projection of plane

Let ABCD be a rectangular plane which is parallel to VP and perpendicular to HP as shown in Fig. 10.3 (a). The projection of plane on VP is *a′b′c′d′* which gives the true shape of the plane.

The projection of plane on HP will be a line *adbc*. It will also be horizontal trace (HT). The vertical trace (VT) of the plane will be zero because plane is parallel to VP.

The projections are shown in Fig. 10.3 (b).

(iii) Plane is perpendicular to VP and parallel to HP (Fig. 10.4)

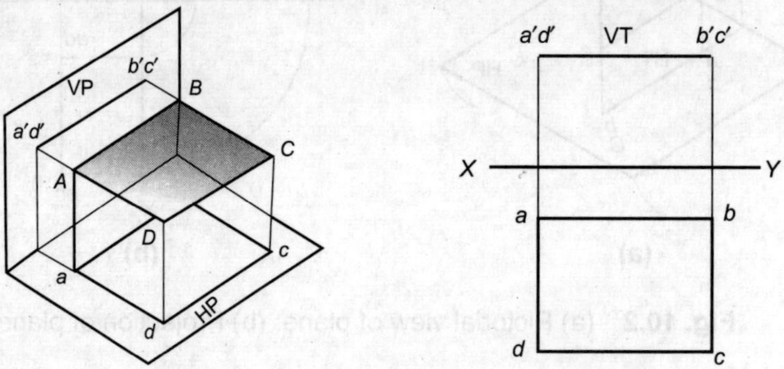

(a) (b)

Fig. 10.4 (a) Pictorial view of plane; (b) Projection of plane

Let ABCD be a rectangular plane which is perpendicular to VP and parallel to HP as shown in pictorial view Fig. 10.4 (a) and its projections on HP and VP are in Fig. 10.4 (b).

The projection of plane on HP is given as *abcd* which shows the true shape of the plane. The projection on VP is given as a line *a′b′c′d′* parallel to XY.

The plane surface is extended to meet VP to get VT. This plane will have no HT because it is parallel to HP. The projection of the plane is shown in Fig. 10.4 (b).

(iv) Plane is inclined to HP and perpendicular to VP (Fig. 10.5)

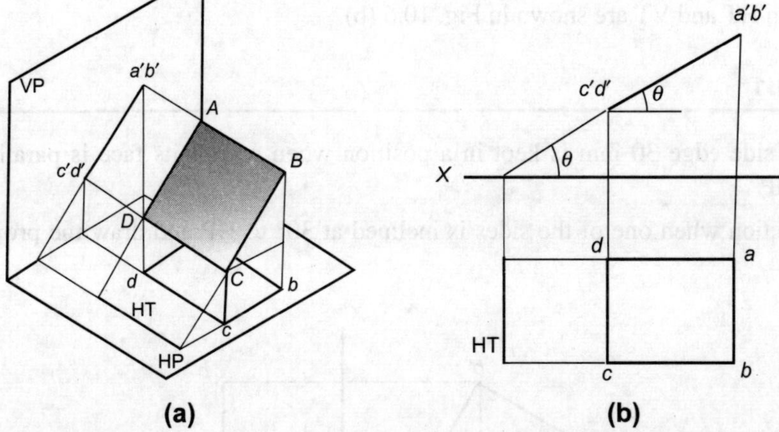

Fig. 10.5 (a) Pictorial view of plane; (b) Projection of plane

Let ABCD be a rectangular plane which is inclined at angle θ and perpendicular to VP as shown in Fig. 10.5 (a).

The projection of plane on HP is given as *abcd*. The projection of plane on VP is a straight line $c'd'a'b'$. The plane surface is extended to meet HP on a line which represents HT. The VT of this plane is not in existence because the plane is perpendicular to VP. The projection of the plane and horizontal traces are shown in Fig. 10.5 (b).

(v) Plane which is inclined to VP and perpendicular to HP (Fig. 10.6)

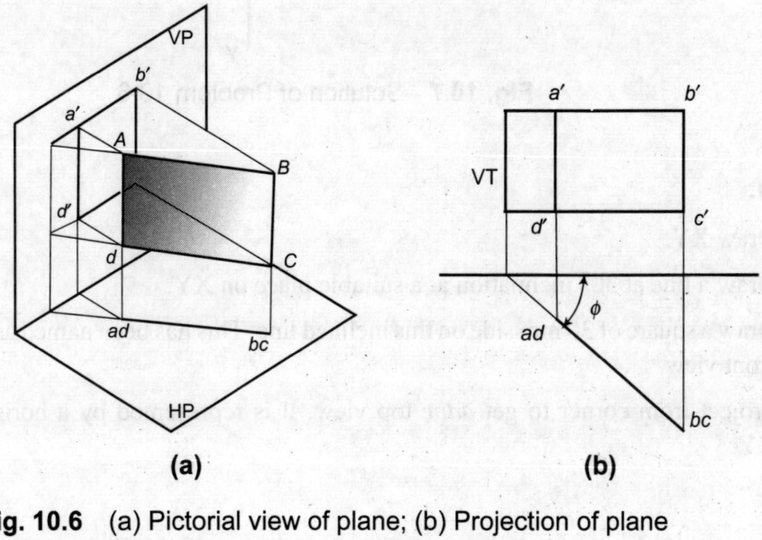

Fig. 10.6 (a) Pictorial view of plane; (b) Projection of plane

Let a rectangular plane ABCD be inclined at an angle ϕ to VP and perpendicular to HP as shown in Fig. 10.6 (a). The plane is projected on VP; the front view is represented as $a'b'c'd'$. It is smaller than the true shape of the plane. The projection of the plane on HP is a line inclined at ϕ angle and is represented as top view *adbc*. It is extended to meet VP to get VT, which is a line perpendicular to XY. The plane is also extended to meet HP, which is also a line inclined at angle ϕ represented as HT of the line. The projection HT and VT are shown in Fig. 10.6 (b).

PROBLEM 10.1

A square plate of side edge 30 mm is kept in a position when one of its face is parallel to VP and perpendicular to HP.

Draw the projection when one of the sides is inclined at 30° to HP and draw the projection on PP (Fig. 10.7).

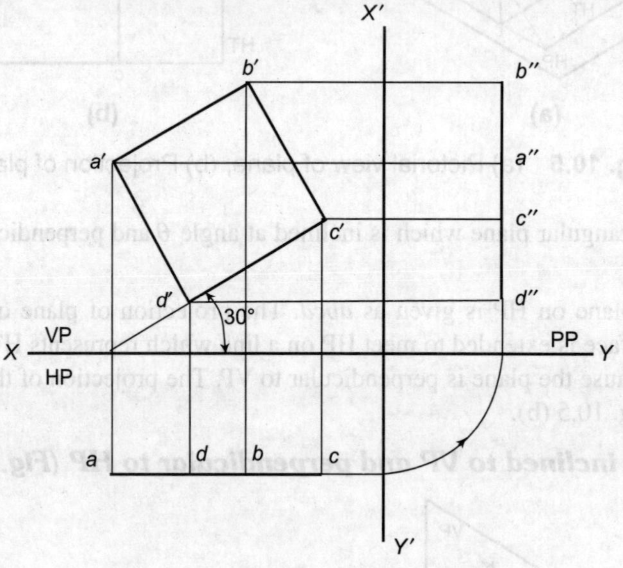

Fig. 10.7 Solution of Problem 10.6

Solution:

1. Draw XY.
2. Draw a line at 30° inclination at a suitable place on XY.
3. Draw a square of 30 mm side on this inclined line. This has been named as $a'b'c'd'$, representing front view.
4. Project from corner to get *adbc* top view. It is represented by a horizontal line parallel to XY.

5. Draw a line X′Y′ perpendicular to XY to represent PP.
6. Draw the left side view on PP as per the conventions.

PROBLEM 10.2

A pentagonal plate of side 25 mm is placed with one of its corner on HP and the surface of the plate is inclined to 55° to *a*. Draw its projection (Fig. 10.8).

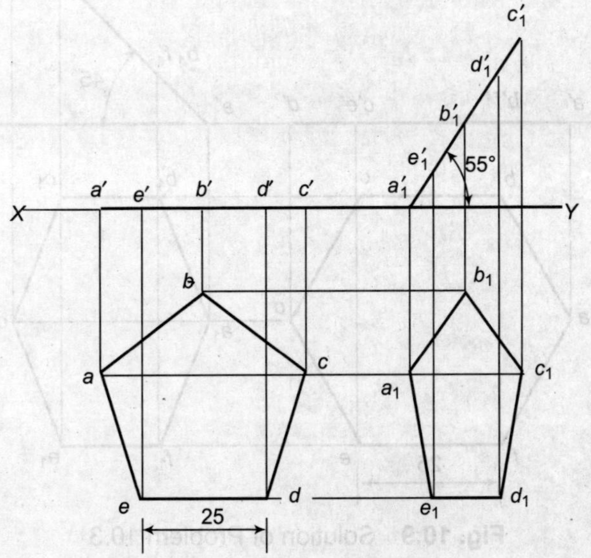

Fig. 10.8 Solution of Problem 10.2

Solution:

1. Draw XY.
2. Draw a pentagon front view as $a'e'b'd'c'$ and top view as *abcde*.

   The plate is kept parallel to HP.
3. Draw another line on the same line XY at an inclination of 55° to XY.
4. Reproduce the top view on this line.
5. Project the top view which becomes smaller as $a_1b_1c_1d_1e_1$.
6. Draw a horizontal line from each corner of the original pentagon.

   Take the corresponding points.

   The final top view is shown as $a_1b_1c_1d_1e_1$.

PROBLEM 10.3

A hexagonal shaped plate of side 25 mm is kept with a corner on HP and the surface is inclined at 45° to HP and perpendicular to VP. Draw the projection of the plate (Fig. 10.9).

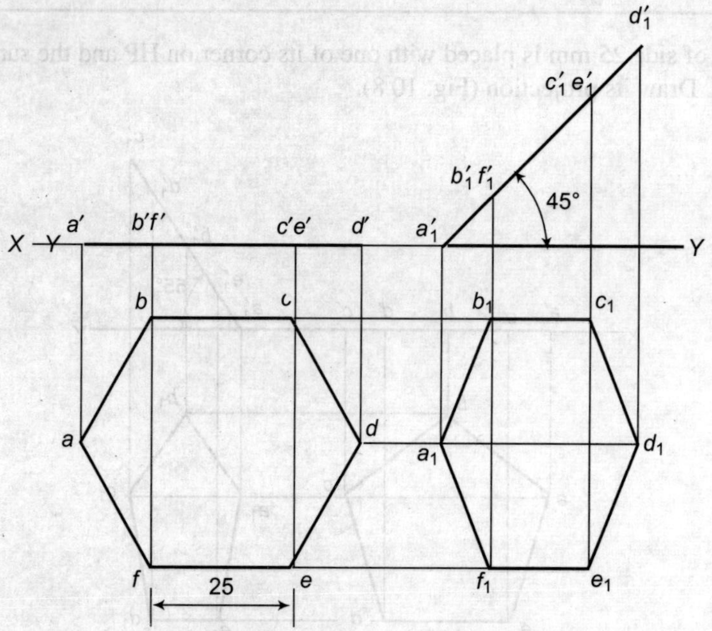

Fig. 10.9 Solution of Problem 10.3

Solution:

1. Draw XY.
2. Below XY, draw a plane of the hexagon as *abcdef*.
3. Project the top view on XY as $a'b'f'c'e'd'$.

   It will be a line because the plate is on HP and parallel to XY.
4. At some distance away, reproduce the top view at 45° inclined line at XY.
5. Project from each point downward and also project a horizontal line from each corner of the hexagon.
6. Take all the corresponding points.

   $a_1b_1c_1d_1e_1f_1$ is the final view of top view.

PROBLEM 10.4

A circular plate of diameter 40 mm is resting on HP. At one point on the circumference, the surface makes an angle of 45° to HP and perpendicular to VP. Draw its projection (Fig. 10.10).

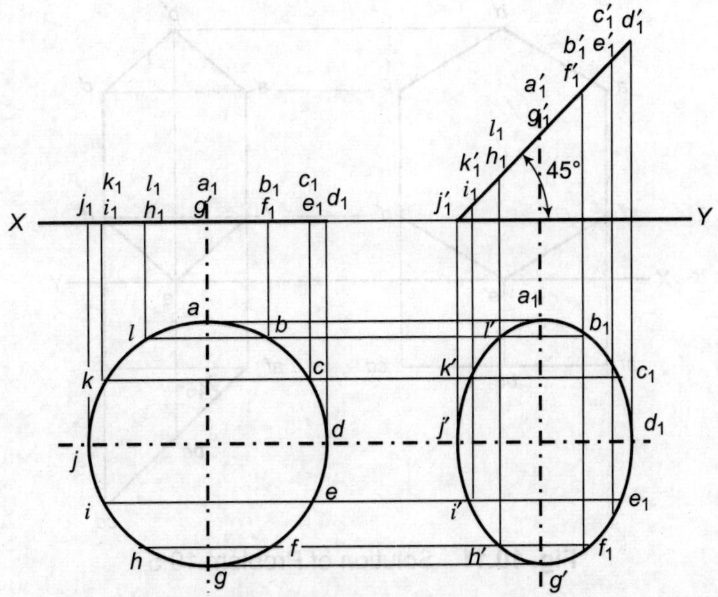

Fig. 10.10 Solution of Problem 10.4

Solution:

1. Draw a line XY.
2. Draw its top view, a circle of 25 mm diameter.
3. Project it from all points on a circle which is a line on XY.

   The circle has been divided into 12 equal parts.
4. Draw another line equal to the front view,originally drawn and reproduce it at 45° inclination line.
5. Project it vertically from all points on the line and also draw horizontal lines, meeting at $a_1b_1c_1d_1e_1f_1g_1h_1i_1j_1k_1l_1$.
6. Join all points by drawing a smooth curve to get an ellipse.

PROBLEM 10.5

A hexagonal plate of size 25 mm with a side on VP and surface inclined at 45° to VP and perpendicular to HP. Draw the projections by two separate techniques (Fig. 10.11).

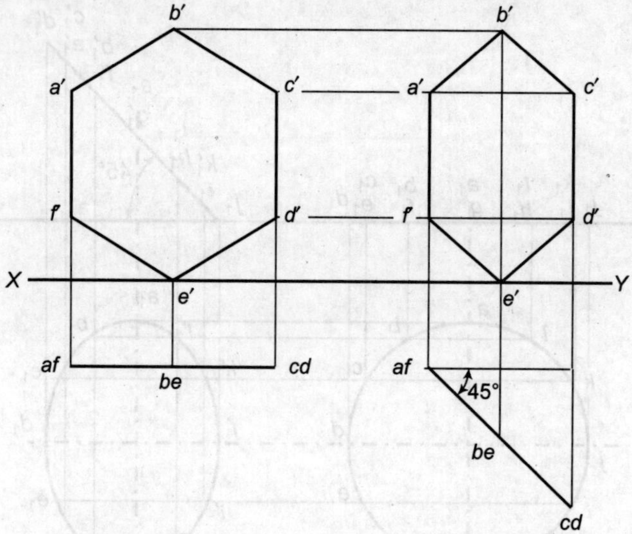

Fig. 10.11 Solution of Problem 10.5

Solution:

1. Draw a line XY horizontally.
2. Draw front view of hexagon, taking one side of it perpendicular to XY.
   a′b′ … *e′f′* is the initial front view and a horizontal line parallel to XY as top view.
3. At some other point, draw a line at 45° inclination from XY. Reproduce the top view on it.
4. Project from all points horizontally and vertically up from all points from top view.
   a′b′c′ … *f′a′* will be the required front view.
   The shape becomes smaller than the true shape.

PROBLEM 10.6 (CAN BE DRAWN BY ANOTHER METHOD AS WELL)

In this method, keeping the same initial position of the plate, only tilting of the plate is required (Fig. 10.12).

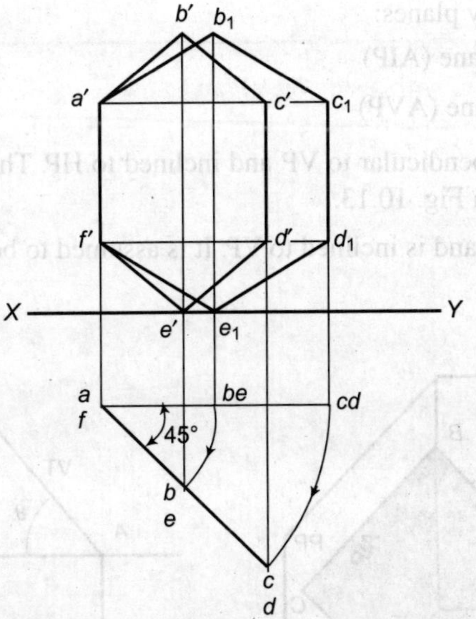

Fig. 10.12 Solution of Problem 10.6

Solution:

1. Draw the front view of the hexagonal plate with its true shape as shown in Fig. 10.12 ($a'b_1c_1d_1e_1f'$).
2. Draw the top view representing the true shape projection.
3. Draw a line at an inclination of 45° from the horizontal line.
4. From each point, draw vertical lines from the top view and also horizontal lines from each corner of the true shape of hexagon.

   $a'b'c'd'e'f'$ is the final shape after taking the final position. It has been shown by dark lines.

10.3 AUXILIARY PLANES AND THE PROJECTIONS

It is a common practice to take projections on two principal planes HP and VP, and sometimes the shape obtained on HP and VP becomes insufficient to describe the object of peculiar shape and complex nature. Hence, to know about the true shape of the object, it is required to be projected on some other planes other than reference plane, which will be called as auxiliary planes and views obtained by taking projections on those planes will be known as auxiliary views.

Auxiliary planes are supposed to be imaginary planes. Profile plane (PP) is also one of the auxiliary plane which is placed either right or left of the object.

Due to auxiliary planes, a lot of benefits are observed.

There are two types of auxiliary planes:

1. Auxiliary inclined plane (AIP)
2. Auxiliary vertical plane (AVP)

AIP is a plane which is perpendicular to VP and inclined to HP. The AIP is assumed to be inclined to an angle θ to HP as shown in Fig. 10.13.

AVP is perpendicular to HP and is inclined to VP. It is assumed to be inclined at an angle ϕ to VP as shown in Fig. 10.14.

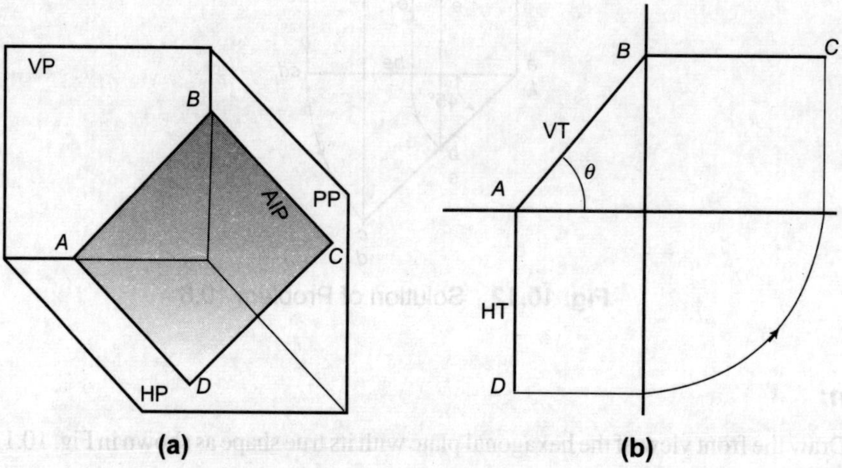

Fig. 10.13 (a) Pictorial view of AIP; (b) Projection of AIP

AIP is perpendicular to VP and inclined to HP

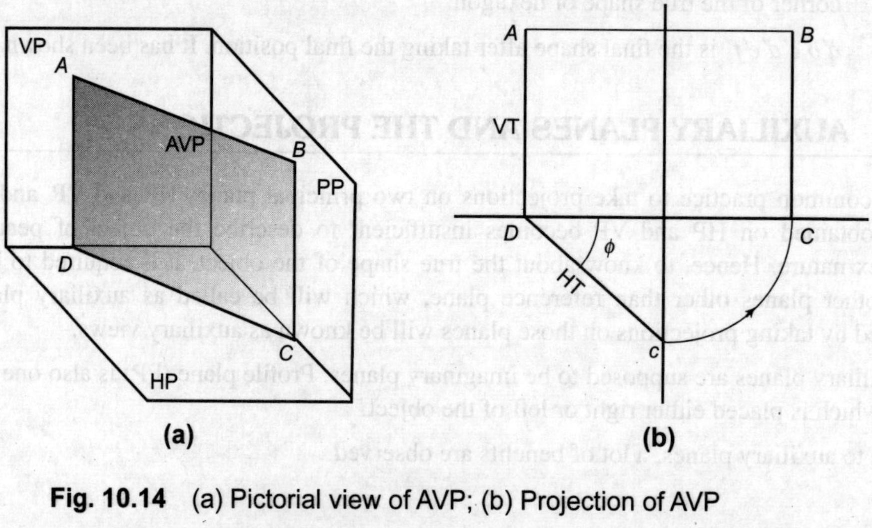

Fig. 10.14 (a) Pictorial view of AVP; (b) Projection of AVP

AVP is perpendicular to HP and inclined to VP

Auxiliary plane is inclined to HP and VP and is perpendicular to PP (Fig. 10.15).

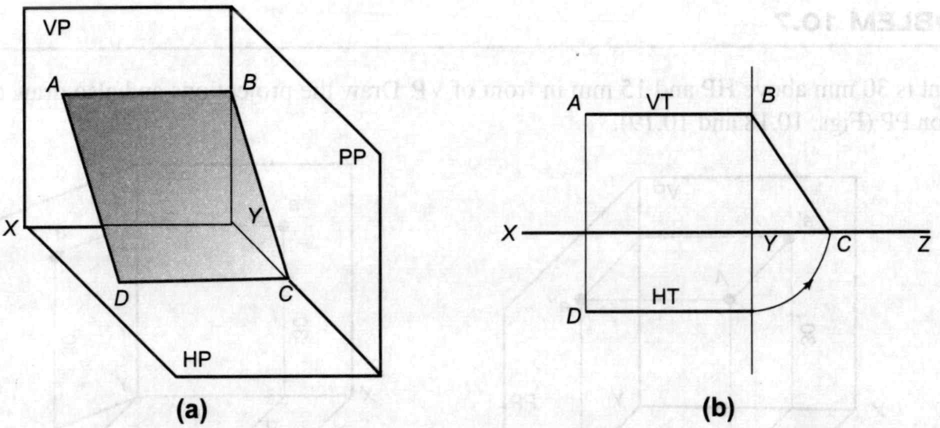

Fig. 10.15 (a) Pictorial view of plane inclined to HP and VP and perpendicular to PP; (b) Projection of plane

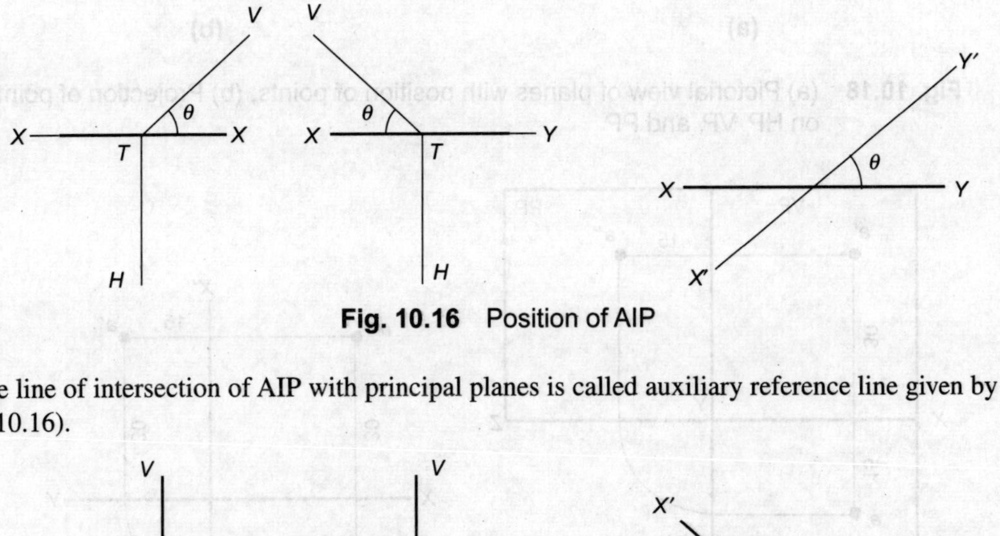

Fig. 10.16 Position of AIP

The line of intersection of AIP with principal planes is called auxiliary reference line given by X′Y′ (Fig. 10.16).

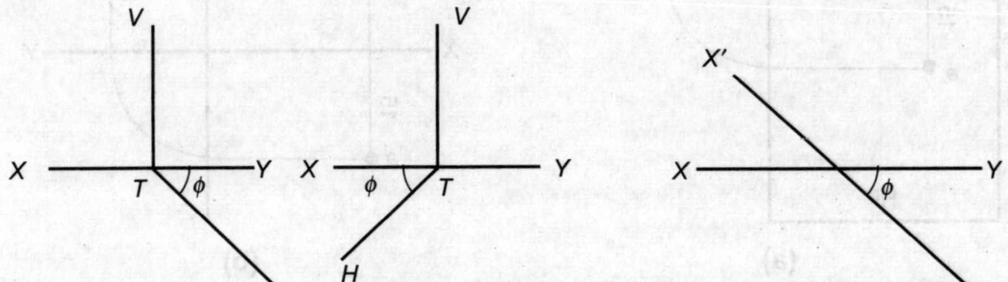

Fig. 10.17 Position of AVP

The line of intersection of AVP with principal plane is called auxiliary reference line given by $x'y'$ (Fig. 10.17).

PROBLEM 10.7

A point is 30 mm above HP and 15 mm in front of VP. Draw the projections and also draw the left side view on PP (Figs. 10.18 and 10.19).

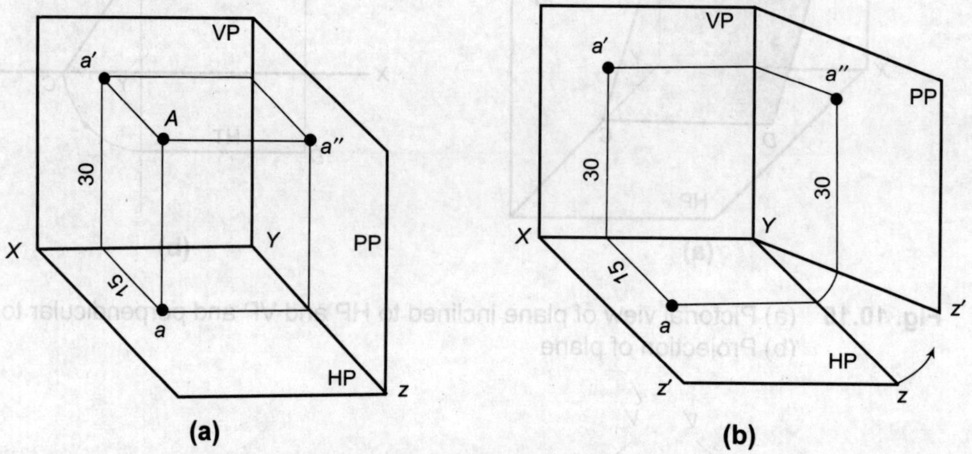

Fig. 10.18 (a) Pictorial view of planes with position of points; (b) Projection of points on HP, VP, and PP

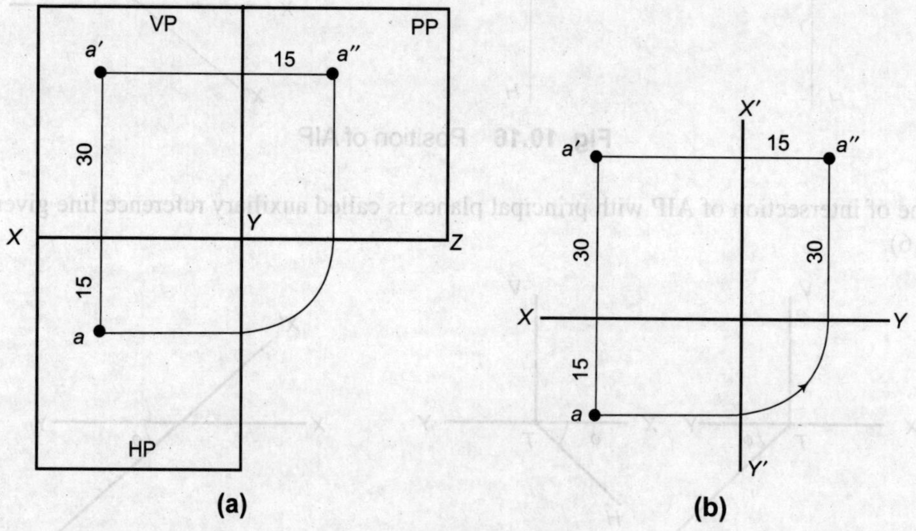

Fig. 10.19 (a) Projection of points with planes; (b) Projection of points

Solution:

1. Draw a line XY. Draw the projection of point A, the front view *a′* is 30 mm above XY and top view *a* is at a distance of 15 mm below XY.
2. Draw an auxiliary reference line X′Y′ perpendicular to XY.

   From front view *a′*, draw a line to project on X′Y′ line. Locate the distance *a* to XY (15 mm) from X′Y′ on that projector line.

   a″ is the projection of point A on PP. The PP plane is in the right side of VP and, hence, this is left side view of point A.

PROBLEM 10.8

A point P is 30 mm above HP and 40 mm in front of VP. Draw the projection and also draw the auxiliary top view of the point AIP inclined at 45° to HP (Fig. 10.20).

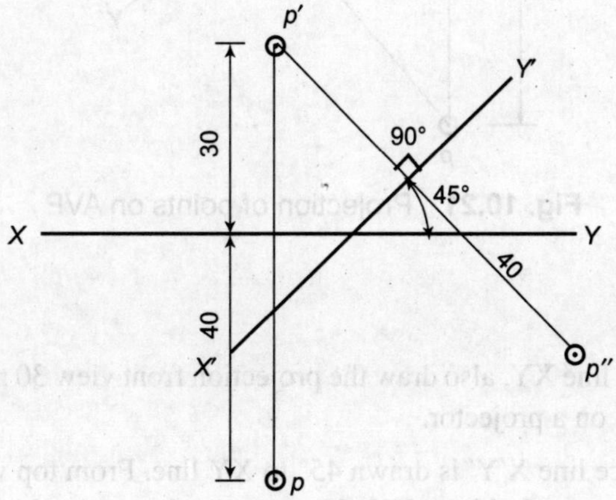

Fig. 10.20 X′Y′ is AIP

p″ is auxiliary top view, so projection from front view has been taken.

Solution:

1. Draw XY line. Draw the projections front view *p′* 30 mm above XY and top view *p* 40 mm below XY on a projector.
2. Auxiliary reference line X′Y′ is drawn at an angle of 45° to XY. From *p′*, draw projector line to X′Y′. Locate *p″* at a distance of 40 mm from X′Y′.

   p″ is the auxiliary top view.

PROBLEM 10.9

A point *P* is 30 mm above HP and 50 mm in front of VP. Draw its projections and also draw the auxiliary front view on AVP inclined at 45° to VP (Fig. 10.21).

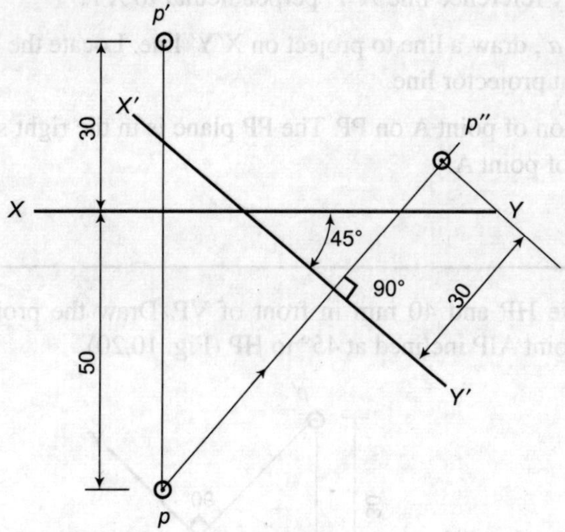

Fig. 10.21 Projection of points on AVP

Solution:

1. Draw a horizontal line XY, also draw the projection front view 30 mm above XY and top view 50 mm below XY on a projector.
2. Auxiliary reference line X′Y′ is drawn 45° to XY line. From top view of point *p* is projected on X′Y′. The distance of *p*′ from XY (30 mm) may be cut on this new projector line. Locate *p*″.

As we know X′Y′ is basically a VP, so projection is taken from top view and the height above horizontal is cut to get the required view on it; so *a*″ is the auxiliary front view.

PROBLEM 10.10

A straight line PQ has its end *P* 15 mm above HP and 50 mm in front of VP. The other end Q is 40 mm above HP and 10 mm in front of VP. The distance between the projectors is 50 mm. Draw its projections, true lengths, and also the inclination of line from HP and VP (Fig. 10.22).

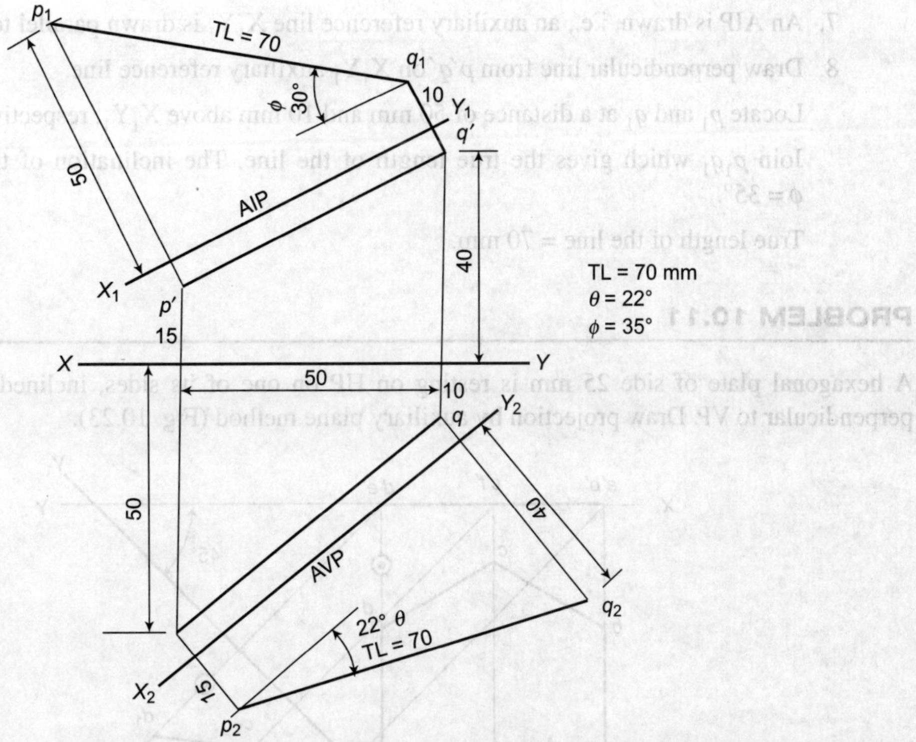

Fig. 10.22 Projections, TL, θ, and ϕ with the use of auxiliary reference plane

Solution:

1. Draw XY line and draw two projector lines perpendicular to XY 50 mm apart.
2. Locate the projection of P on projector as p', front view 15 mm above XY and 50 mm below XY to locate top view p.
3. On the other projector for end Q of *st* line, locate q' as front view 40 mm above XY and also q as top view 10 mm below XY.
4. Join $p'q'$ as front view and also join pq as top view.
5. An AVP is drawn, i.e., a reference line X_2Y_2 is drawn parallel to top view pq.
6. Draw perpendicular line from p and q on X_2Y_2 auxiliary reference line.

   Locate p_2 at a distance of 15 mm from X_2Y_2. Similarly, locate q_2 at a distance of 40 mm from X_2Y_2 and join p_2q_2, which gives the true length of the line. The inclination of the line with HP is $\theta = 22°$. True length = 70 mm.

7. An AIP is drawn, i.e., an auxiliary reference line X_1Y_1 is drawn parallel to front view $p'q'$.
8. Draw perpendicular line from $p'q'$ on X_1Y_1 auxiliary reference line.

   Locate p_1 and q_1 at a distance of 50 mm and 10 mm above X_1Y_1, respectively.

   Join p_1q_1 which gives the true length of the line. The inclination of the line with VP is $\phi = 35°$.

   True length of the line = 70 mm.

PROBLEM 10.11

A hexagonal plate of side 25 mm is resting on HP on one of its sides, inclined at 45° to HP and perpendicular to VP. Draw projection by auxiliary plane method (Fig. 10.23).

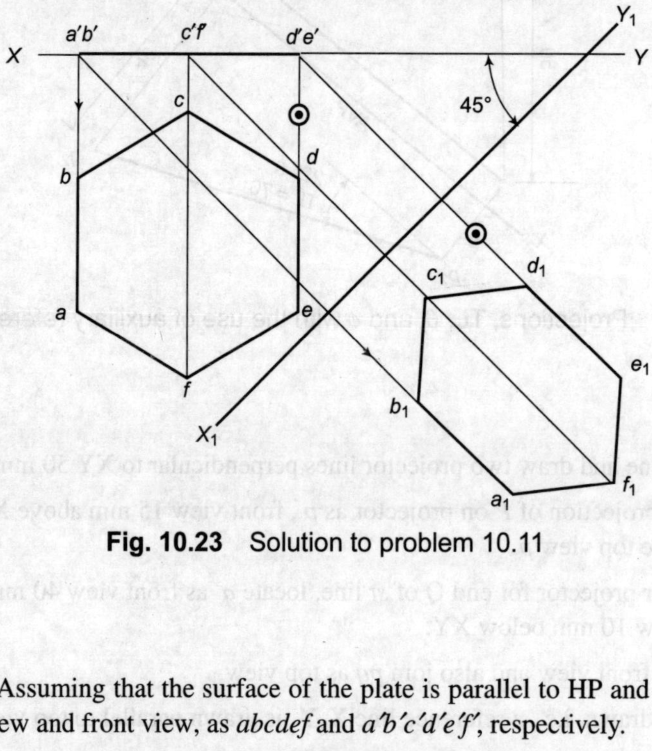

Fig. 10.23 Solution to problem 10.11

Solution:

1. Draw XY. Assuming that the surface of the plate is parallel to HP and perpendicular to VP, draw top view and front view, as *abcdef* and *a′b′c′d′e′f′*, respectively.
2. Draw an auxiliary reference line X_1Y_1 inclined at 45° to XY.
3. Draw projection from *a′b′c′d′e′f′* perpendicular to X_1Y_1 and mark the distance from the top view of all points. For point *a*, it has been shown a v mark.
4. Join $a_1b_1c_1$ … , etc., to get the top view of the hexagon. The shape becomes smaller.

PROBLEM 10.12

A rectangular plate of sides 30 mm × 20 mm is resting on HP with one of its side. The surface is inclined at 45° to HP and the resting side is inclined at 30° to VP. Draw the projections (Fig. 10.24).

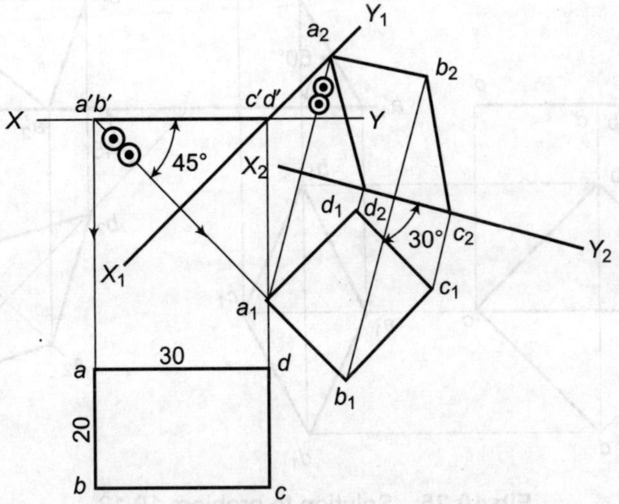

Fig. 10.24 Solution to problem 10.12

Solution:

1. May be taken similar to Problem 10.10.
2. May be taken similar to Problem 10.10.
3. Similar to Problem 10.10.
4. Similar to Problem 10.10
5. Draw second auxiliary reference X_2Y_2 inclined at 30° to side c_1d_1 of top view after projection on X_1Y_1.
6. Draw projectors from a_1, b_1, c_1, and d_1 perpendicular to X_2Y_2 line. Mark the distance a′ to X_1Y_1 from a_2 to X_2Y_2, the distance is shown by |⊙ ⊙| symbol and similarly for all corners, $a_2b_2c_2d_2$ is the required projection.

PROBLEM 10.13

A square lamina ABCD of 30 mm side rests on one of its corners on the ground. Its plane is inclined at an angle of 60° to HP and diagonal BD is inclined at 45° to VP and parallel to HP. Draw the projections (Fig. 10.25).

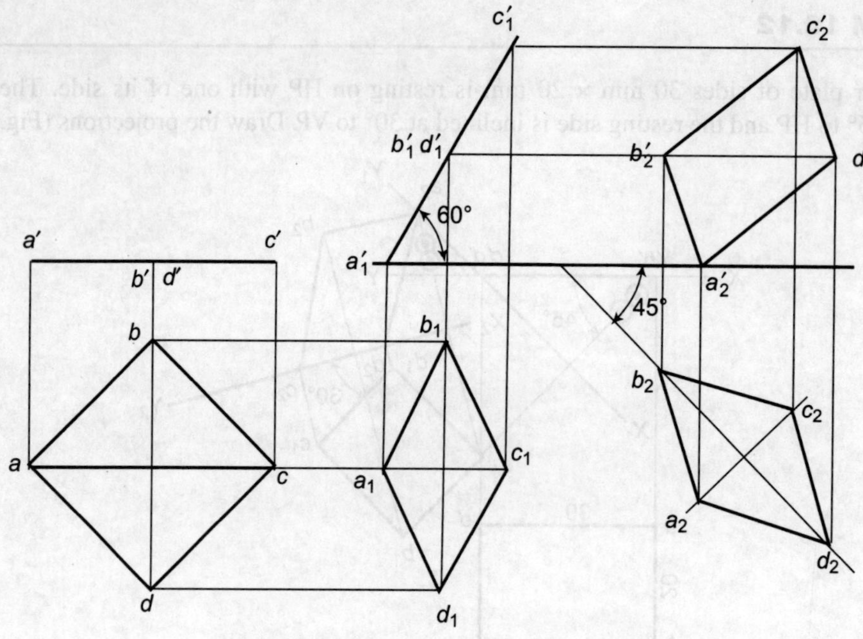

Fig.10.25 Solution to problem 10.13

Solution:

1. Draw a square lamina *abcd* of 30 mm side in top view, assuming the lamina to be lying in HP.
2. Project front view *a′b′c′d′* from top view, which will be a line on *xy*.
3. Tilt the front view above *a′* so that it makes an angle of 60° with *xy* and name the points on it by adding suffix.
4. Project the corresponding top view $a_1b_1c_1d_1$.
5. Reproduce top view $a_1b_1c_1d_1$ and $a_2b_2c_2d_2$ such that diagonal b_2d_2 makes an angle of 45° to *xy*.
6. Project the final front view upward from the top view and horizontally from the II stage front view as shown in Fig. 10.25.

PROBLEM 10.14 (FIG. 10.26)

A square thin plate of negligible thickness *PQRS* of 35 mm side has its one side *PQ* in HP and inclined at 45° to VP and the plane of the plate is inclined at 60° to HP. Draw the projections.

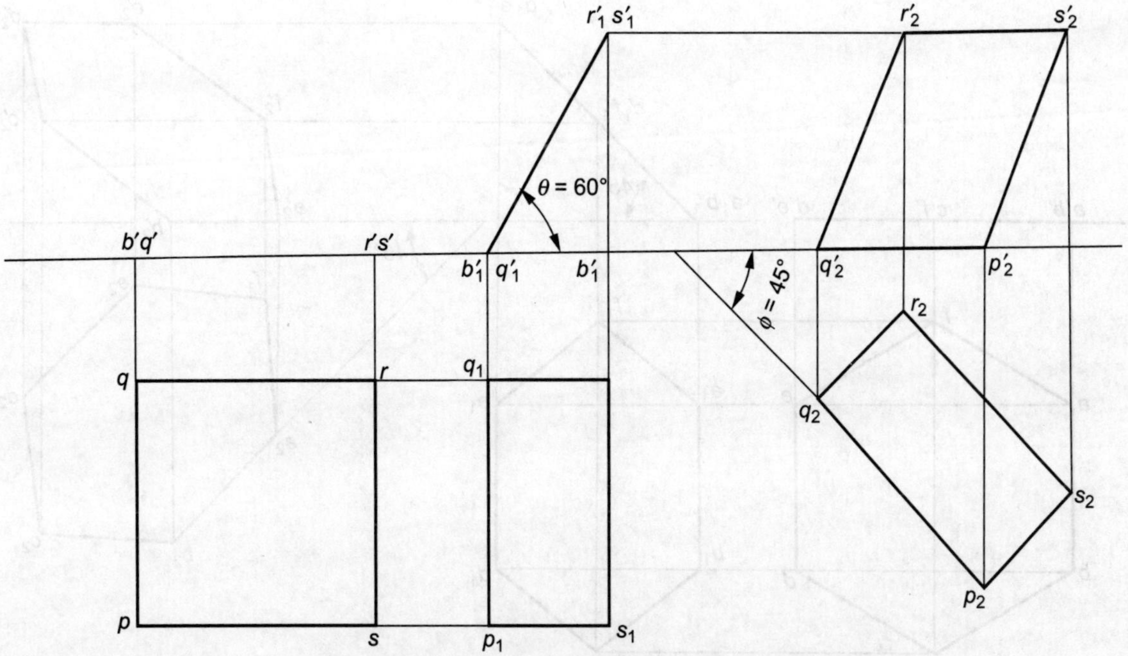

Fig. 10.26 Solution of Problem 10.14

Steps:

(1) Draw the projection of *PQRS* in the initial position *p q r s* is the top view and *p′ q′ r′ s′* is the front view.

(2) Front view is tilled about *p q* which will be line $p_1' \, q_1'$, at an angle of $\theta = 60°$.

(3) Project the top view as $p_1 q_1 r_1 s_1$.

(4) Draw the top view in 2 stage as $p_2\, q_2\, r_2\, s_2$ such that $p_2\, q_2$ makes an angle of 45° to *xy*.

(5) From $p_2\, q_2\, r_2\, s_2$, project the final front view as $p_2'\, q_2'\, r_2'\, s_2'$, as shown in Fig. 10.26.

PROBLEM 10.15 (FIG. 10.27)

A thin hexagonal plane *ABCDEF*, of side 25 mm side, rests on HP with one of the sides such that it makes an angle of 45° with HP and the resting side on which it rests, inclined at 45° with VP. Draw its projection.

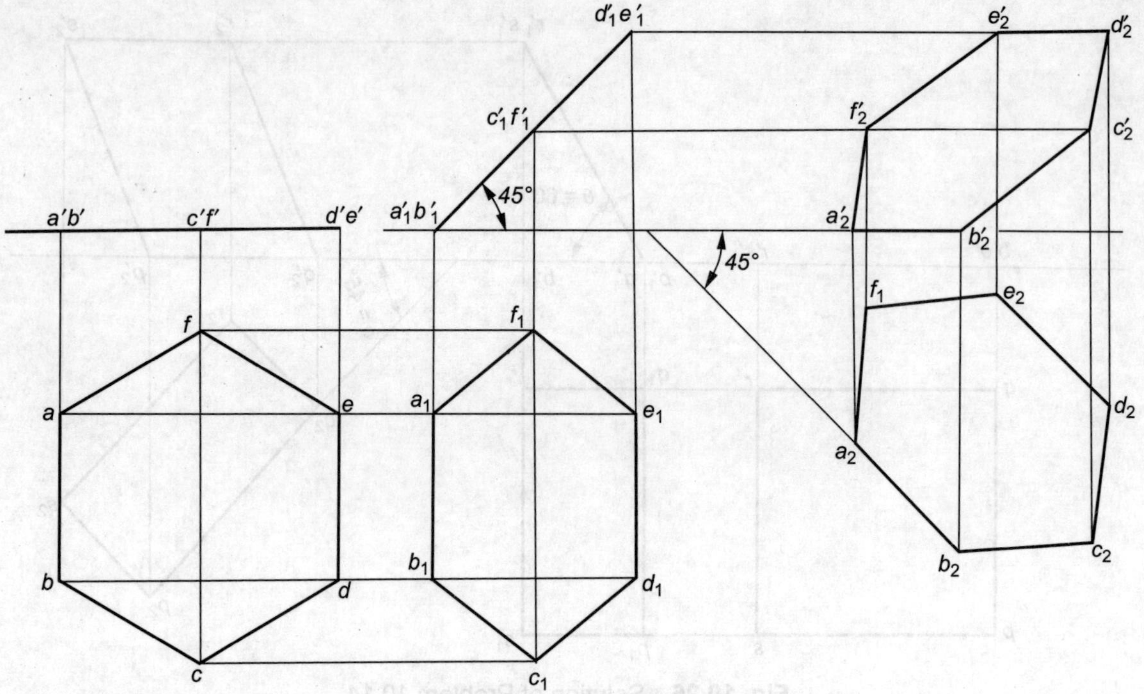

Fig. 10.27 Solution to Problem 10.15

Steps:

(1) Draw *a* hexagon *a b c d e f* of 25 mm side in top view lying on HP keeping side *ab* perpendicular to *xy*.

(2) Draw front view $a_1' \; b_1' \; c_1' \; d_1' \; e_1' \; f_1'$ at the inclination of 45° from *xy*.

(3) Projecting $a' \; b' \; c' \; d' \; e' \; f'$ draw top view as $a_1 \; b_1 \; c_1 \; d_1 \; e_1 \; f_1$.

(4) Reconstruct the top view at an angle of 45° at *xy*, coinciding $a_2 \; b_2$ from the line.

(5) Project the final front view from reconstructed top view $a_2 \; b_2 \; c_2 \; d_2 \; e_2 \; f_2$ as shown in Fig. 10.27.

(6) Find front view as $a_2' \; b_2' \; c_2' \; d_2' \; e_2' \; f_2'$.

PROBLEM 10.16 (FIG. 10.28)

A hexagonal lamina *ABCDEF* of 25 mm side has its plane inclined at 45° to the VP and its one side *BC* is parallel to HP and inclined to HP by 45°. Draw its projection when the top view of the hexagonal plane is 15 mm away from VP.

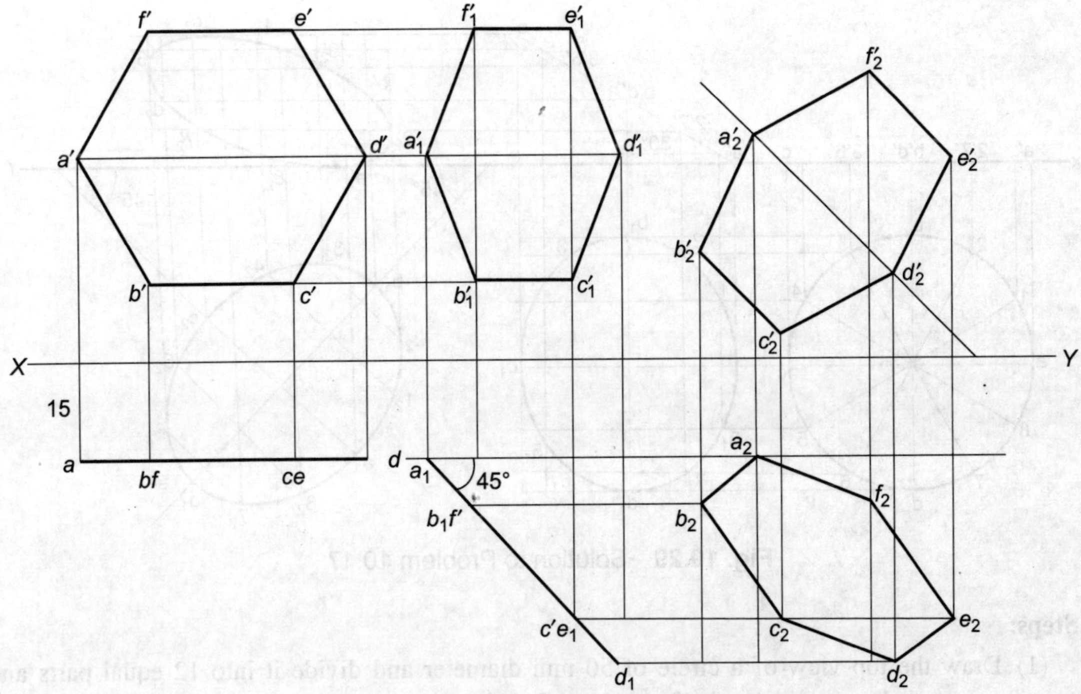

Fig. 10.28 Solution to Problem 10.16

Steps:

(1) Draw *a* hexagonal lamina $a'\ b'\ c'\ d'\ e'\ f'$ of 25 mm side in front view and keeping the side b' c' parallel to *xy*.

(2) Draw top view $a\ b\ c\ d\ e\ f$ projecting from front view, keeping $b'\ c'$ parallel to HP and the top view in 15 mm in front of vertical plane

(3) Tilting the top view at 45° with *xy* as in 2 stage project and the front view as $a_1'\ b_1'\ c_1'\ d_1'\ e_1'$ f_1'.

(4) Reproduction of the front view of 2 stage as $a_2'\ b_2'\ c_2'\ d_2'\ e_2'\ f_2'$, such that the $b_2'\ c_2'$ makes an angle of 45° to *xy*.

(5) Project the final top view as $a_2\ b_2\ c_2\ d_2\ e_2\ f_2$ shown in Fig. (10.28).

PROBLEM 10.17 (FIG. 10.29)

A circular thin plane of 50 mm diameter is resting on HP on one end *A* of its diameter *AC* when it is inclined to HP while it makes 45° inclination to VP.

Draw projections.

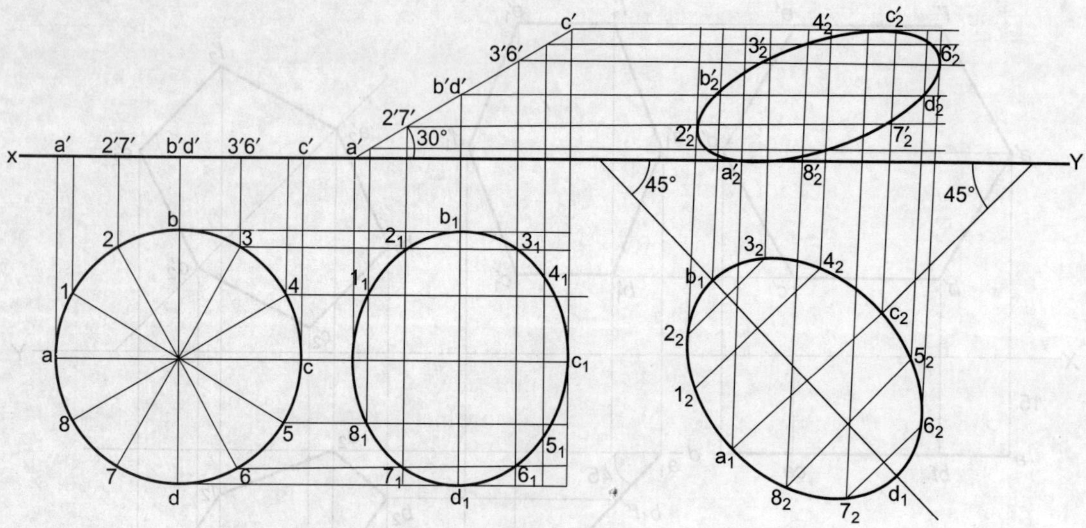

Fig. 10.29 Solution to Problem 10.17

Steps:

(1) Draw the top view of a circle of 50 mm diameter and divide it into 12 equal parts and corresponding it on *xy* as the front view of *a′ c′* on the line on *XY*.

(2) Tilt the front view about *a′* on *xy* making an angle of 30° with *XY*.

(3) Make the top view corresponding to *a′ b′ c′ d′*—

(4) Reproduce the top view $a_1\ b_1\ c_1$—as $a_2\ b_2\ c_3$—, such that $a_2\ c_2$ makes an angle of 45° to *xy*.

(5) Draw the final front view.

EXERCISE

Review Questions

1. Define plane.
2. What is an auxiliary plane?
3. What is principal plane?
4. What is AIP? Show by figure.
5. What is AVP? Show by figure.
6. What are the advantages of taking auxiliary views?
7. Define auxiliary inclined plane and name the view drawn on it.

8. Define auxiliary vertical plane and name the views drawn on it.

9. A regular lamina ABCD of 25 mm side has one side on HP. Its surface is inclined at 45° to HP and perpendicular to VP.
Draw the projections and show its traces.

10. A square lamina ABCD of 30 mm side rests on one of its corners on the ground. Its plane is inclined at an angle of 45° to the HP and diagonal BD inclined at 60° to VP and parallel to HP. Draw its projections.

11. A regular pentagonal lamina ABCDE of 30 mm side rests on HP on one of its sides such that it is inclined to HP at 45° and the side on which it rests is inclined at 30° to VP. Draw its projections.

12. A regular pentagonal lamina ABCDE of 30 mm side rests on the ground with one of its sides such that it is inclined to HP at 45° and the side on which it rests, inclined at 30° to VP. Draw its projections in the third angle.

13. A regular pentagonal lamina of side 30 mm has one of its corners in VP and the plane of lamina is inclined at 45° to VP. The side of the lamina opposite to that corner is parallel to VP and inclined at 45° to HP. Draw the projections.

14. A pentagonal lamina of side 25 mm has one of its corner in VP and the plane of lamina is inclined at 45° to VP. The side of the lamina opposite to that corner is parallel to VP and inclined at 40° to HP. Draw its projection.

15. A rectangular thin plane *ABCD* of 50 × 25 mm rests on its shorter side in the VP and the surface makes 35° angle with VP. The longer side of the plane is inclined at 45° to the HP. Draw its projection.

16. An equilateral triangular thin plate *PQR* of 25 mm side lies on one of its side in VP. Draw the projections of the plate when the plate surface is vertical and inclined at 45° to VP. One of the sides of the triangular plate is inclined at 30° to the HP.

17. An equilateral triangle *PQR* of 45 mm side is parallel to HP with one of its sides inclined at 30° to VP and the end of the side nearer to VP is 25 mm in front of VP and 30 mm above HP. Draw it projection and locate its traces too.

18. A square lamina *PQRS* of 30 mm side is parallel to HP and is 15 mm from it. Draw its projections in the first quadrant only and locate the traces.

19. A regular hexagonal lamina *PQRSTU* of 25 mm side has its corner *p* in HP. Its plane is inclined at 45° to HP and perpendicular to VP. Draw its projection and locate its traces.

20. A regular pentagonal lamina *PQRST* of 25 mm side has its side *QR* in HP. Its plane is perpendicular to HP and inclined at 45° to VP. Draw its projections and locate its traces too.

21. A circular lamina of 25 mm radius appears as an ellipse of 45 mm major axis and 25 mm minor axis in the view from above. Draw the projections.

Objective Questions

1. After taking views on auxiliary plane should be rotated about the plane to which it is ________.
2. There are __________ possible positions of the object at which auxiliary view may be drawn.
3. Two planes are parallel when their ________ views are parallel.
4. When a straight line is perpendicular to a reference plane, its projection on the plane will be a point which is called ______________.

Answers

Objective Questions

1. perpendicular 2. four 3. edge 4. point view

11

CHAPTER

Projection of Solids

11.1 INTRODUCTION

A solid is a three-dimensional object bounded by planes/faces associated with lines, corner, and curved surfaces. The object will have its length, breadth, and height.

To understand the real shape of the object, it is necessary to draw at least two orthographic views. Sometimes, two views are not enough to know the details and, hence, additional views are drawn on auxiliary planes, such as profile plane, auxiliary vertical plane and, auxiliary inclined plane.

11.2 CLASSIFICATION OF SOLIDS

Solids may be divided mainly into two groups. A detailed classification of solids is given as follows:

Solid

Polyhedra
(1) Tetrahedron
(2) Cube
(3) Octahedron
(4) Dodecahedron
(5) Icosahedron
(6) Prism
- (a) Triangular prism
- (b) Square prism
- (c) Pentagonal prism
- (d) Hexagonal prism

(7) Pyramid
- (a) Triangular pyramid
- (b) Square pyramid
- (c) Pentagonal pyramid
- (d) Hexagonal pyramid

Solid of revolution
(1) Right circular cylinder
(2) Oblique cylinder
(3) Right circular cone
(4) Oblique cone
(5) Sphere

11.3 POLYHEDRON

A regular polyhedron has flat surfaces, also termed as faces/sides, and also corners.

In this case, all faces are of the same size and shape.

11.3.1 Tetrahedron

It has four equal faces, each an equilateral triangle, as shown in Fig. 11.1.

AR App

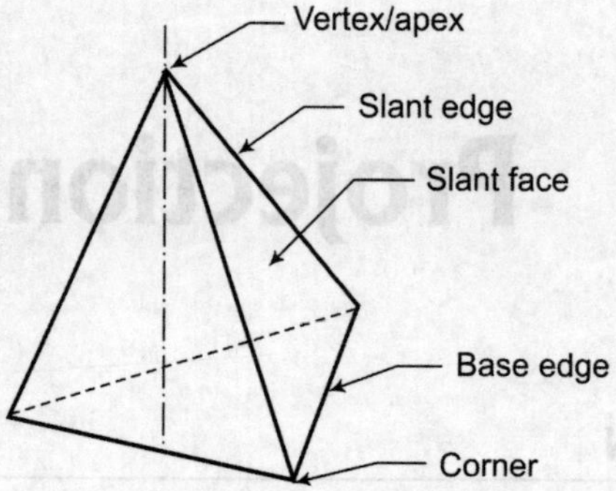

Fig. 11.1 Tetrahedron

11.3.2 Cube/Hexahedron

It has six equal faces. Each face is a square as shown in Fig. 11.2

AR App

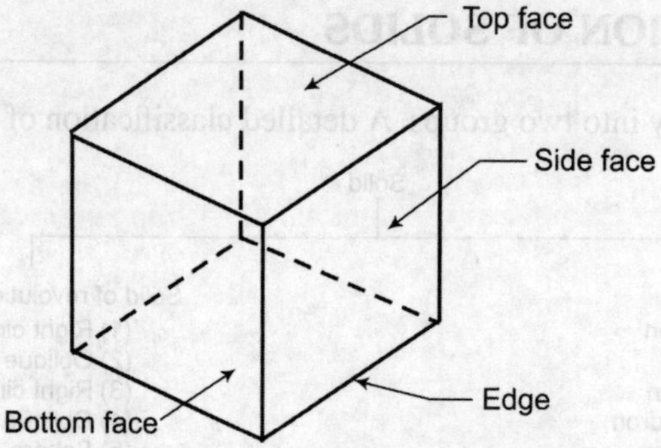

Fig. 11.2 Cube/hexahedron

Octahedron

It has eight equal faces. Each face is an equilateral triangle as shown in Fig. 11.3.

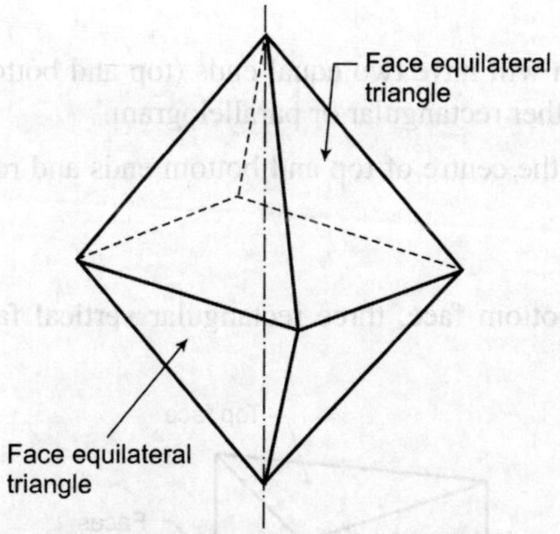

Fig. 11.3 Octahedron

Dodecahedron

It has 12 equal faces. Each face is a regular pentagon as shown in Fig. 11.4.

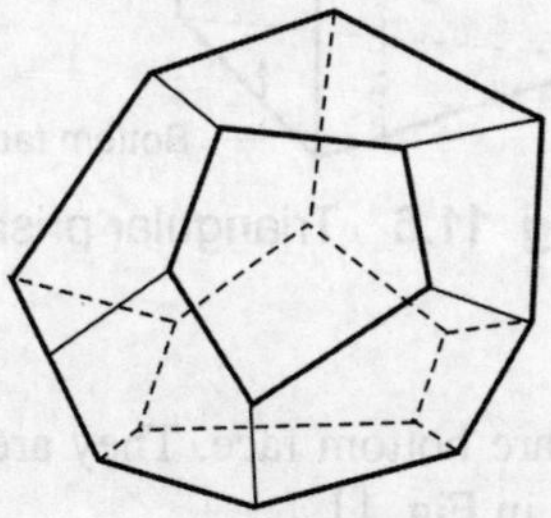

Fig. 11.4 Dodecahedron

Icosahedron

Icosahedron has 20 equal faces. Each face is an equilateral triangle as shown in Fig. 11.5.

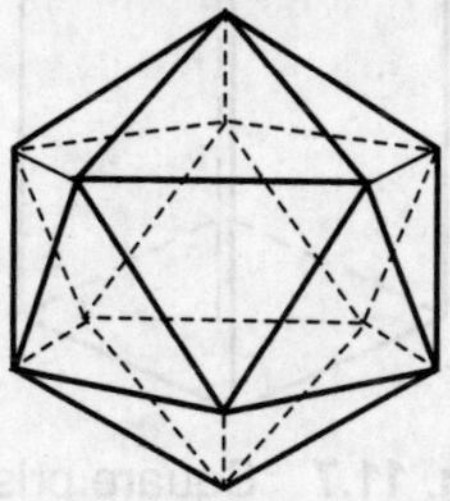

Fig. 11.5 Icosahedron

Prism

A prism is a polyhedron which will have two equal ends (top and bottom) parallel to each other. The two ends are joined by faces either rectangular or parallelogram.

A chain line is joined from the centre of top and bottom ends and represents the axis of the prism. All faces are equal rectangle.

Triangular Prism

It has one top face and one bottom face, three rectangular vertical faces, and three equal edges as shown in Fig. 11.6.

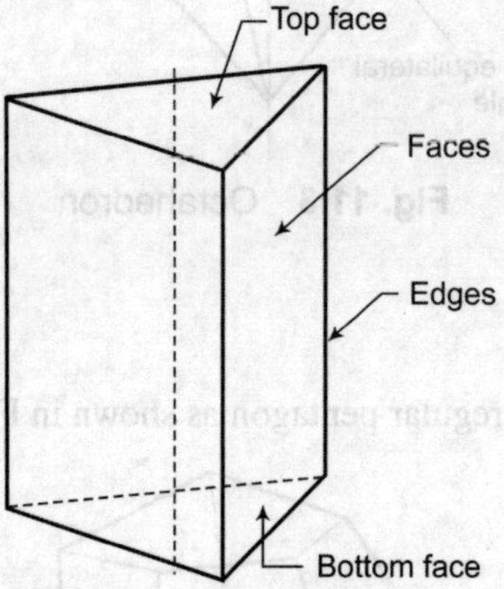

Fig. 11.6 Triangular prism

Square Prism

It has one square top face and one square bottom face. They are joined by four equal-size rectangular vertical faces with four edges as shown in Fig. 11.7.

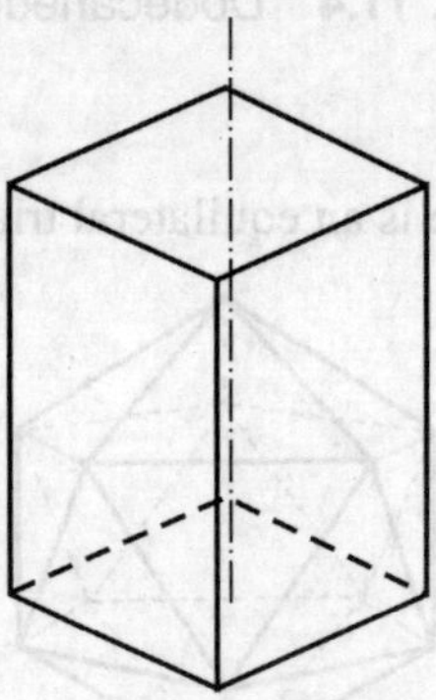

Fig. 11.7 Square prism

Pentagonal Prism

It has one pentagonal top face and one pentagonal bottom face of equal size.

Both the faces are joined by five equal-size rectangular faces with five edges.

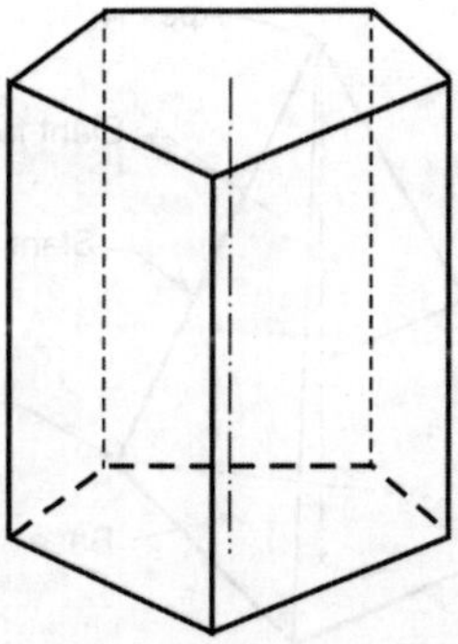

Fig. 11.8 Pentagonal prism

Hexagonal Prism

It has one hexagonal top face and one hexagonal bottom face of equal sizes. Both the faces are joined by six equal-size rectangular faces with six edges.

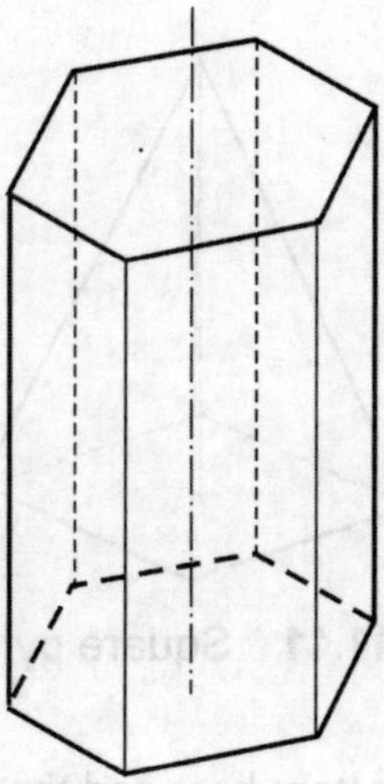

Fig. 11.9 Hexagonal prism

11.3.3 Pyramid

A pyramid is a polyhedron. A pyramid has only one bottom face of base. The bottom face edges are joined by triangular flat surfaces which are called slant faces. All slant faces are of equal size and same shape. Pyramids are associated with many corners and edges. All slant edges are meeting at one point called vertex or apex.

Triangular Pyramid

It has a triangular bottom base and three triangular slant faces associated with three equal-size slant edges. They are joining at a common point called apex or vertex. A chain line which joins from the centre of the base to the apex is called axis. The perpendicular distance from apex to the centre of base is called altitude or height of the pyramid.

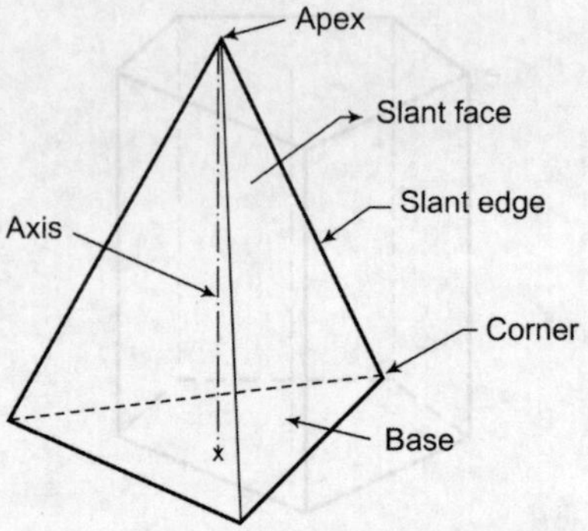

Fig. 11.10 Triangular pyramid

Square Pyramid

It has a square bottom base and there are four triangular slant faces associated with four slant edges. They are joining at a common point called apex or vertex. A line that joins the apex to the centre of the square base is known as axis of the pyramid. Distance between apex and the base centre is called altitude or height of the pyramid.

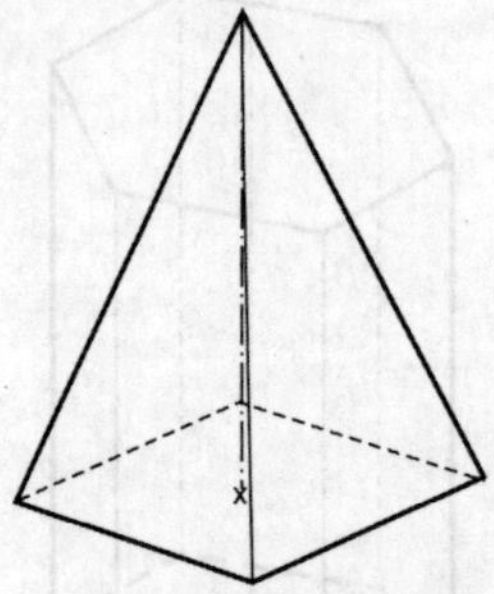

Fig. 11.11 Square pyramid

Pentagonal Pyramid

The base is a polygon. It has a pentagon bottom base and there are five triangular slant faces associated with five slant edges. They are joining at a common point called apex or vertex. A line from the centre of the pentagon and the apex is a vertical line perpendicular to the base and is known as the altitude or height of the pyramid.

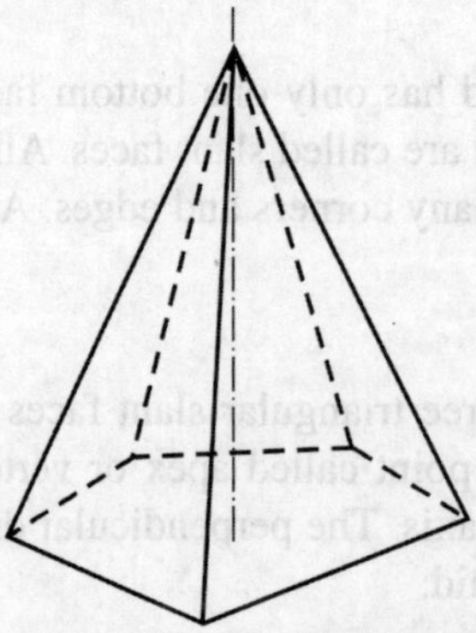

Fig. 11.12 Pentagonal pyramid

Hexagonal Pyramid

It has a hexagonal bottom base and there are six triangular slant faces associated with six slant edges. They are joining at a common point called apex.

A line from the centre of the base and the apex is a vertical line perpendicular to the base and termed as the altitude or the height of the pyramid.

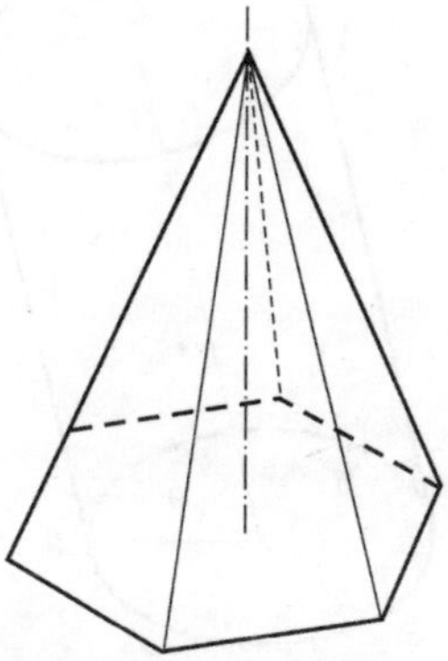

Fig. 11.13 Hexagonal pyramid

11.4 SOLID OF REVOLUTION

The solids like cylinder, cone, and sphere are known as solid of revolution. It is formed by the rotation of a plane about its axis which is fixed at one of its generator.

11.4.1 Cylinder

Right Circular Cylinder

A right circular cylinder is generated by rotating a rectangular plane about its axis and a generator at the circumference. It has two circular ends (top and bottom).

The bottom end is also called base of the cylinder as shown in Fig. 11.14(a).

It this case, all generators are of equal length.

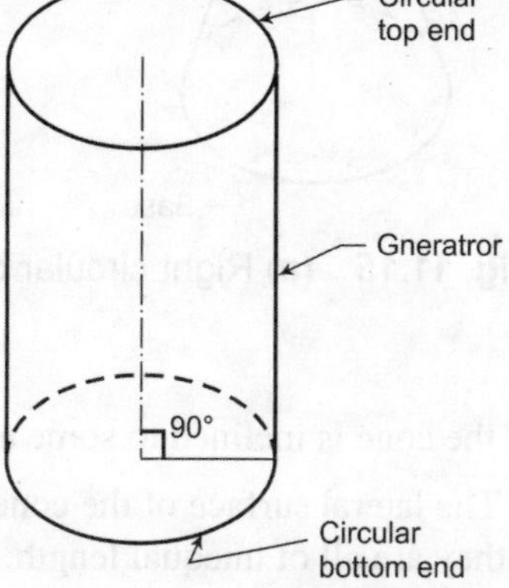

Fig. 11.14 (a) Right circular cylinder

Oblique Cylinder

An oblique cylinder is one whose axis is inclined to the base. The lateral surface is connected by two circular bases. The length of generator are not the same; they are of unequal lengths as shown in Fig. 11.14 (b). The axis makes an angle θ with the base.

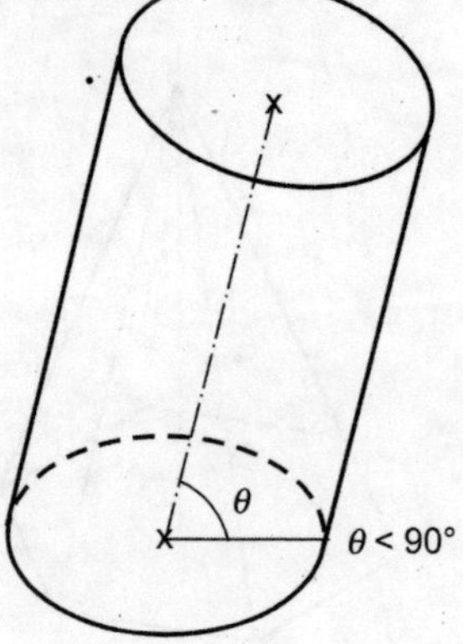

Fig. 11.14 (b) Oblique cylinder θ = angle with base

11.4.2 Cone

A right circular cone is a solid generated by rotating right-angle triangle plane about its axis and a generator connecting apex and the point on a circumference of the circle. The lateral surface of the cone is connected by a circular base. The base of the cone is circular.

In case of right circular cone, all the generators are of equal length as shown in Fig. 11.15(a).

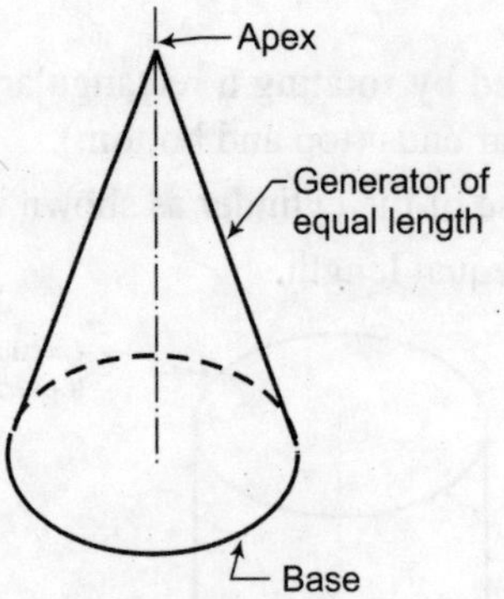

Fig. 11.15 (a) Right circular cone

Oblique Cone

In case of oblique cone, the axis of the cone is inclined to some angle θ to the base. $\theta < 90°$.

The base of the cone is circular. The lateral surface of the cone is connected between apex and point on circumference of the circle and they are all of unequal length.

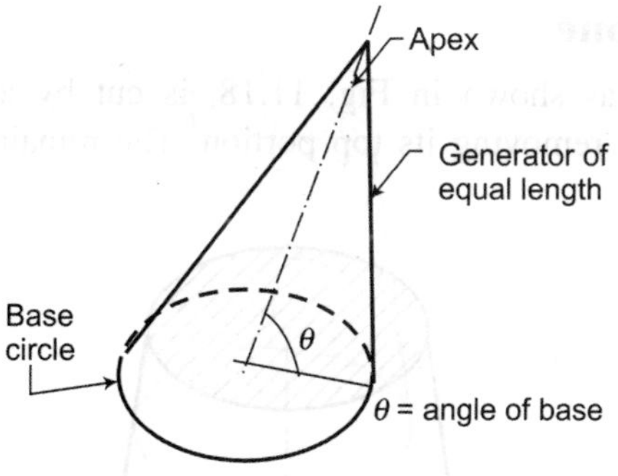

Fig. 11.15 (b) Oblique cone

11.4.3 Sphere

Sphere is formed by rotating a semicircle about its diameter as shown in Fig. 11.16. All points on the surface of the sphere are equidistant from the centre of the sphere.

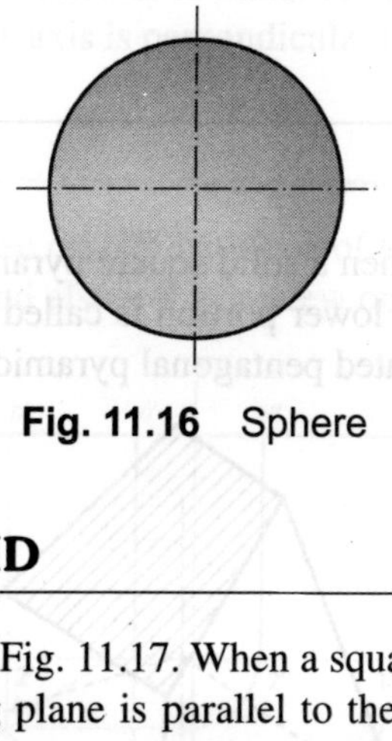

Fig. 11.16 Sphere

11.5 FRUSTUM OF A SOLID

Frustum of square pyramid is shown in Fig. 11.17. When a square pyramid is cut by a horizontal plane perpendicular to the axis or the cutting plane is parallel to the base, and the top portion is removed. The remaining portion is known as frustum of square pyramid. It may have the frustum of other pyramids also.

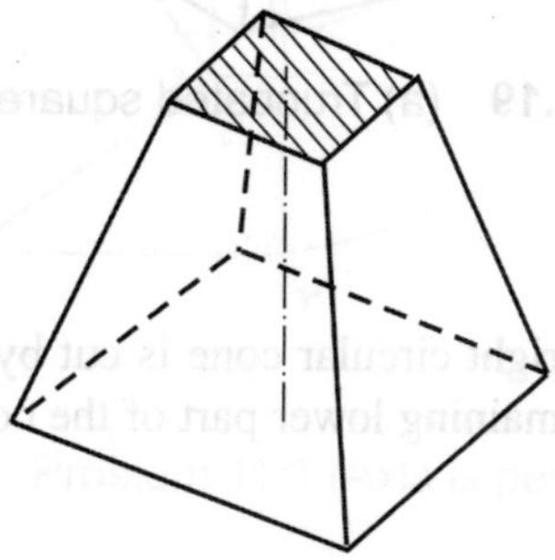

Fig. 11.17 Frustum of square pyramid

Steps:

(1) Draw XY and at any point on XY, draw a line at 35° to XY. Draw a square of 35 mm edge in top view.

(2) Project the front view and side view as shown in Fig. 11.20. The edge which is not visible has been shown in dotted lines.

PROBLEM 11.2 (FIG. 11.21)

A square prism of side base 35 mm and height of the prism 45 mm with one of its longer edge lies on HP such that the prism axis is perpendicular to VP and its one rectangular face makes an angle of 35° to HP.

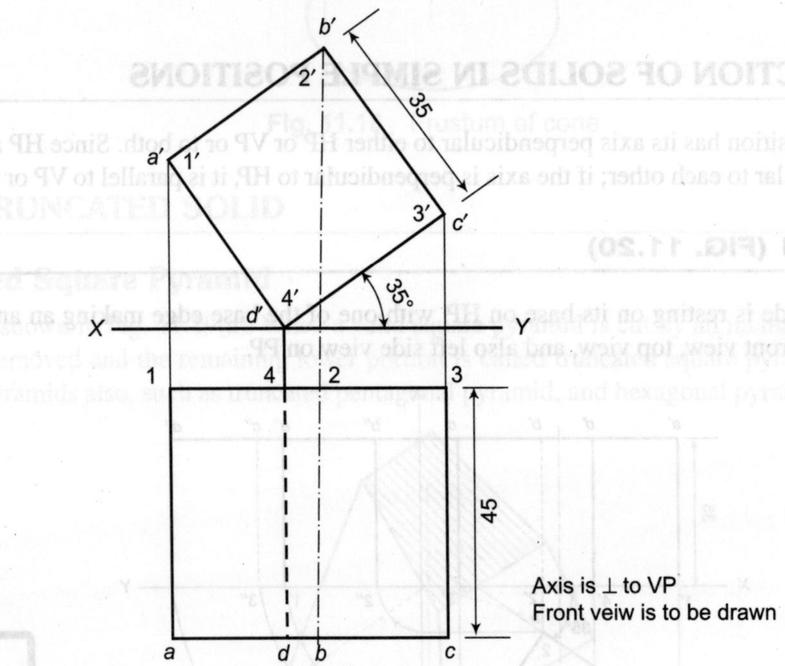

Fig. 11.21 Solution of Problem 11.2

Steps:

(1) Draw *XY* axis ⊥ to *VP*, the front view will be of true shape. Draw a square of size 35 mm at an inclination of 35° at a point on *XY*.

(2) One longer edge is on HP.

(3) Project from all points, draw the top view as shown in Fig. 11.21.

PROBLEM 11.3 (FIG. 11.22)

A right circular cylinder of base diameter 30 mm and height 40 mm is resting on HP. Draw the projections. A point p′ is marked on front view. Draw the top view of point *P*.

p′ is lying on one of the generator, 25 mm from *XY* and 5 mm from left end.

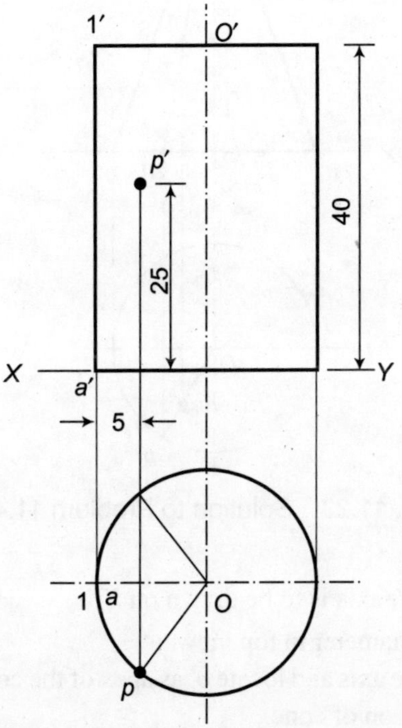

Fig. 11.22 Solution of Problem 11.3

Steps:

(1) Draw *XY* and at any point draw the axis of cylinder.

(2) On this axis, draw a circle of diameter 30 mm in top view.

(3) Project the front view which will be a rectangle. The axis is equal to 40 mm.

(4) Locate *p*′ as projection of point *p* on front view, one of its projector 5 mm from 1′*a*′ projector and height of *p*′ 25 mm from *XY*.

(5) Locate the top view of the projector as *op*. p of the top view will lie on the circumference.

PROBLEM 11.4 (FIG. 11.23)

A right circular cone, 30 mm base diameter and height 40 mm, is resting on its base on HP. Draw the projections.

In top view, there is top view of generator as *op*. On this top view, there is a point *S*. It is required to draw the front view of point *S*.

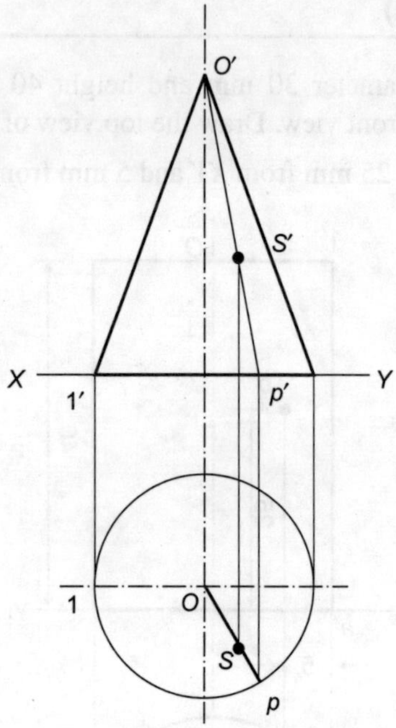

Fig. 11.23 Solution to Problem 11.4

Steps:

(1) Draw a horizontal line *XY*, axis is to be drawn on *XY*.

(2) Draw a circle of 30 mm diameter in top view.

(3) Through centre 0, draw the axis and locate *o′* as apex of the cone at a height of 40 mm from *XY*.

(4) Draw the complete elevation of cone.

(5) *op* is the top view of one of the projectors corresponding to *S*. There is front view as *o′p′*.

(6) *S* is the top view projection from *S*, it cuts the front view of projector *o′p′* on *S′*.

PROBLEM 11.5 (FIG. 11.24)

A hexagonal prism, of side of the base 20 mm and axis 40 mm long has one of its base edge parallel to VP. Draw the projection when it is resting on HP. *P* is any point whose top view and front view has been taken.

Steps:

(1) Draw *XY*.

(2) Draw a hexagon of 20 mm side in top view, keeping one side parallel to *XY*.

(3) Project the front view from the top view and take the height equal to 40 mm.

(4) Name the corner points as shown in Fig. 11.24.

(5) *P* is any point at any height, *p′* is the front view.

(6) Project from *p′* it cuts 45 side the corresponding top view till be *p*.

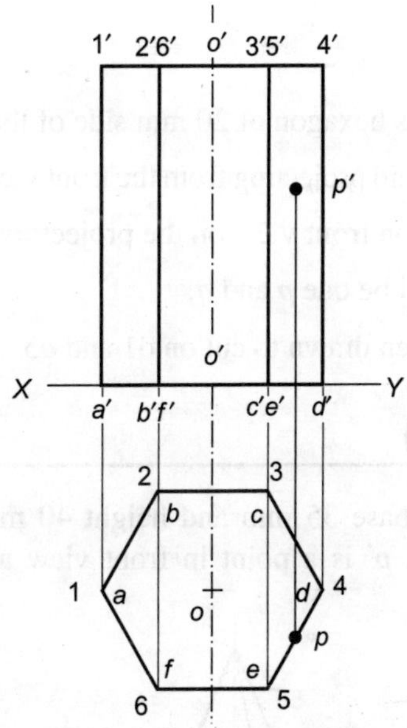

Fig. 11.24 Solution to Problem 11.5

PROBLEM 11.6 (FIG. 11.25)

A hexagonal pyramid has side of the base 20 mm and axis 40 mm long, having one of its base edge parallel to VP. Draw the projections. p' and q' are the two points on the two different generators on front view. Draw the corresponding top view locating the proper position of the points.

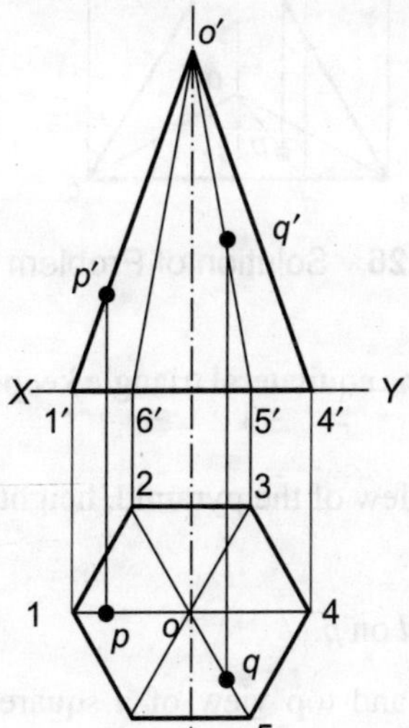

Fig. 11.25 Solution to Problem 11.6

Steps:

(1) Draw XY.

(2) Draw top view of the base as hexagon of 20 mm side of the base.

(3) Draw front view of the pyramid projecting from the front view. Height of the pyramid is 40 mm.

(4) p' and q' are the two points on front view on the projectors $o'1'$ and $o'4'$.

(5) Corresponding top view will be one p and q.

From p' and q', the projectors have been drawn to cut on o1 and $o5$.

PROBLEM 11.7 (FIG. 11.26)

A triangular pyramid of side of the base 35 mm and height 40 mm having one of its base edge is parallel to VP. Draw the projections. p' is a point in front view as shown in Fig. 11.26. Draw the corresponding position in top view.

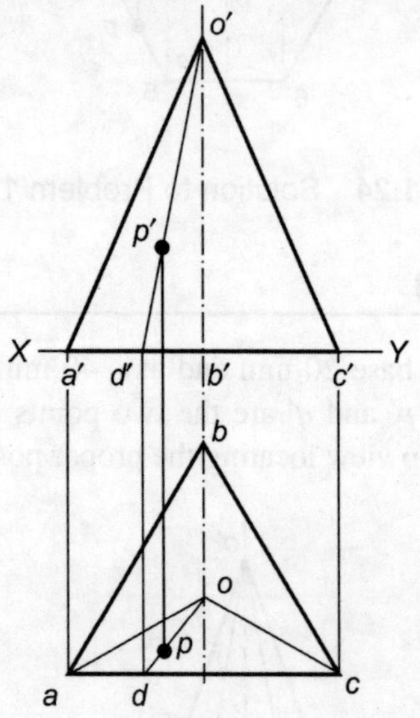

Fig. 11.26 Solution of Problem 11.7

Steps:

(1) Draw XY and the top view of the equilateral triangle keeping one of the side of the base parallel to XY.

(2) Draw the corresponding top view of the pyramid, height may be taken as 40 mm.

(3) p' is the point on $o'd'$.

(4) Project point p', which cuts od on p.

Figure 11.27 shows the front view and top view of a square pyramid having two adjacent base edges equally inclined to VP. p and q are the two points whose front view is shown as p' and q'. Drop perpendiculars from p' and q' and locate corresponding points p and q on top view.

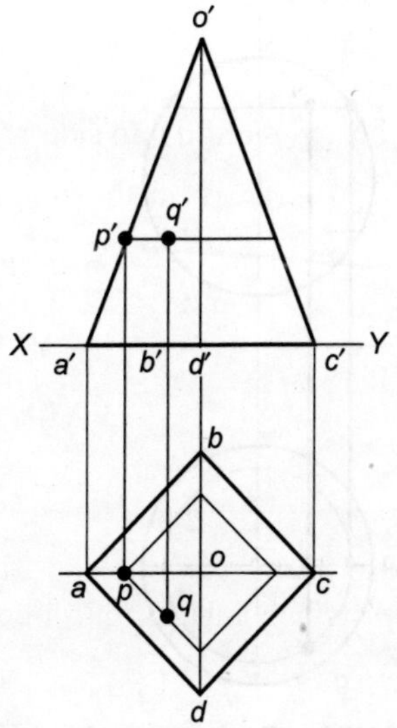

Fig. 11.27 Projection of square pyramid

Figure 11.28 is the projection of a cone p' and lies on a circle that has been drawn in top view. Draw the projection from p' and cut the circumference at p. p is the top view.

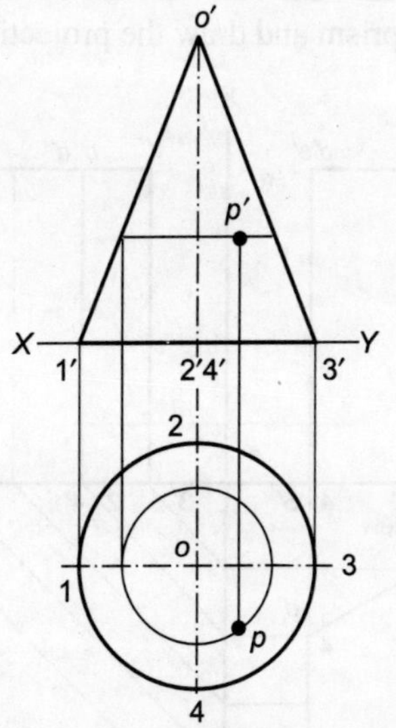

Fig. 11.28 Projection of a cone

Figure 11.29 shows the front view and top view of a sphere, $p'q'$ are the two points in front view. Draw the projectors from p' and q'. It cuts the circle at p and q. $p'q'$ lies on a circle which has been drawn in top view.

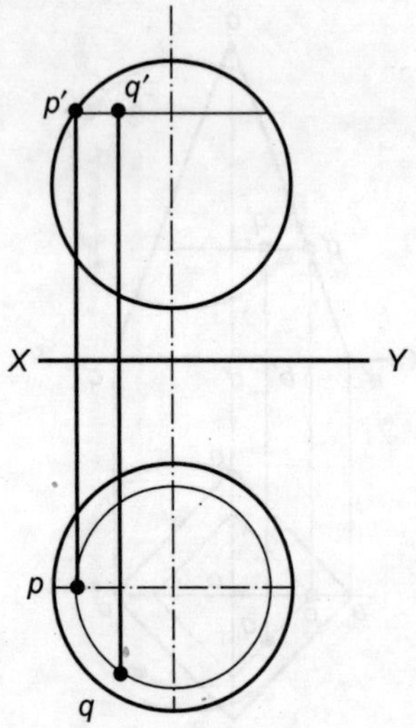

Fig. 11.29 Projection of sphere

PROBLEM 11.8 (FIG. 11.30)

A hexagonal prism, side of the base 20 mm and axis 45 mm, having one of its base edge perpendicular to VP. Draw front and top views of the prism and draw the projection on PP.

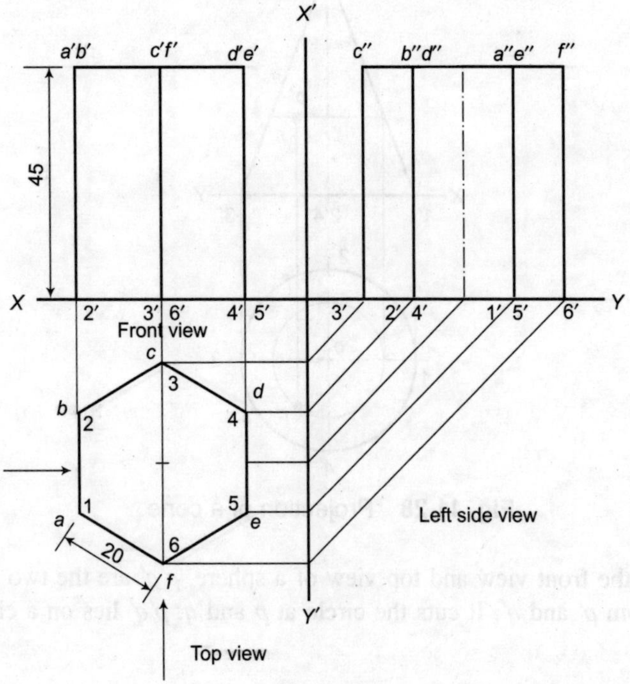

Fig. 11.30 Solution of Problem 11.8

Steps:

(1) Draw *XY* and draw a hexagon of 20 mm side of the base in the top view, keeping one of its sides perpendicular to *XY* as shown in Fig. 11.30.

(2) Project the front view from top view. Take height 45 mm. Naming of all the corners is as shown.

(3) A *PP* has been drawn ⊥ to *XY* as *X′Y′*. Take the projection. This is the left side view projection on *PP*.

PROBLEM 11.9 (FIG. 11.31)

A hexagonal pyramid, side of base 20 mm and axis 45 mm long, having one of the base edge parallel to VP with its axis perpendicular to HP. Draw its front view, top view, and left side view.

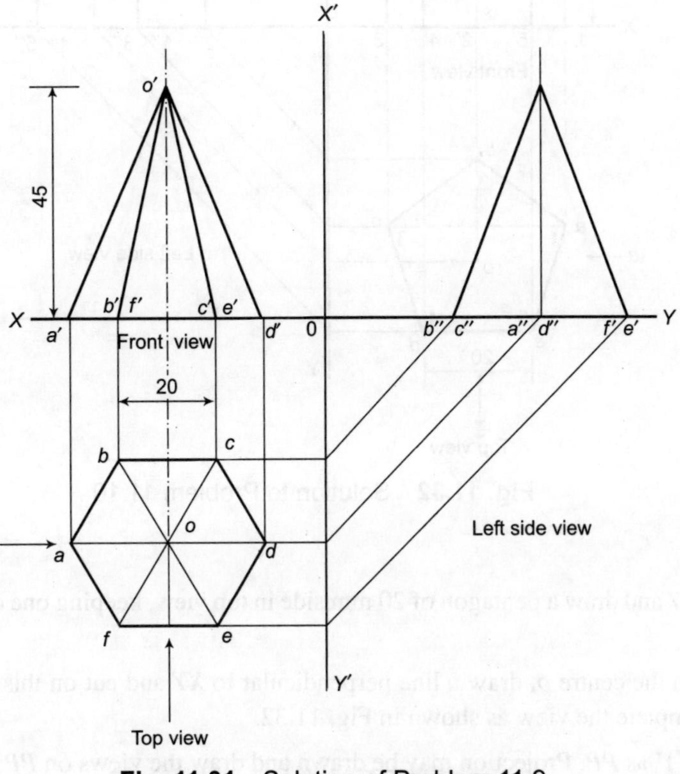

Fig. 11.31 Solution of Problem 11.9

Steps:

(1) Draw *XY* and draw a hexagon of 20 mm side base in top view, keeping one of the sides parallel to *XY*.

(2) Project the front view from top view and take height of pyramid as 45 mm. Name the corners as given.

(3) Draw a line *X′Y′* ⊥ *XY* which represents *PP*. Project the top view and keep it in front of front view. The view represents the left side view.

PROBLEM 11.10 (FIG. 11.32)

Draw projection of a pentagonal prism of 20 mm side base and height 45 mm, having one edge of its base parallel to *XY*. Draw left side view on *PP*.

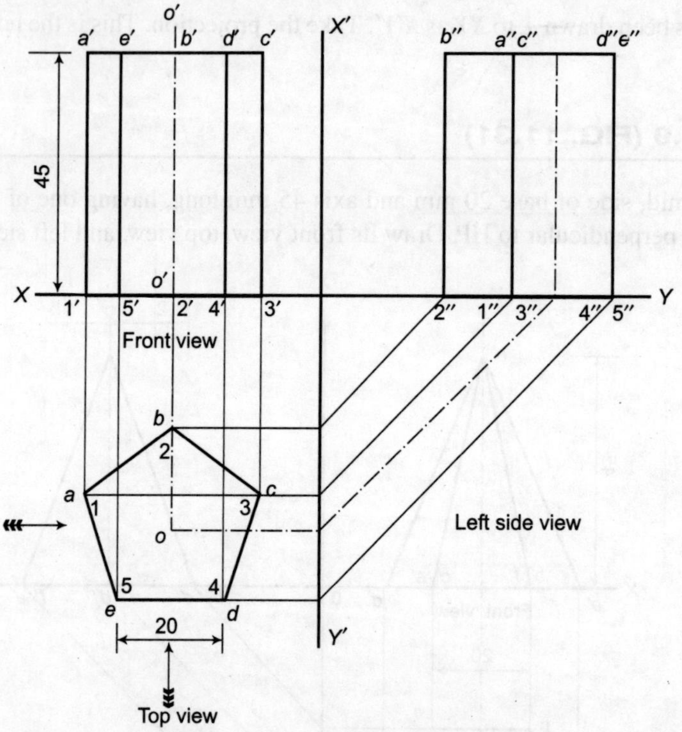

Fig. 11.32 Solution to Problem 11.10

Steps:

(1) Draw *XY* and draw a pentagon of 20 mm side in top view, keeping one of its base edge parallel to *XY*.

(2) Through the centre *o*, draw a line perpendicular to *XY* and cut on this line 45 mm long from *XY*. Complete the view as shown in Fig. 11.32.

(3) Draw *X′Y′* as *PP*. Projection may be drawn and draw the views on *PP*.

PROBLEM 11.11 [FIG. 11.33 (A) AND (B)]

(a) A hexagonal prism, side of the base 20 mm and axis 45 mm long, lies on one of its rectangular face on HP and the axis is perpendicular to VP. Draw the front view and top view.

(b) A pentagonal prism, side of the base 20 mm and axis 45 mm long, lies on one of its edge on HP with its axis perpendicular to VP.

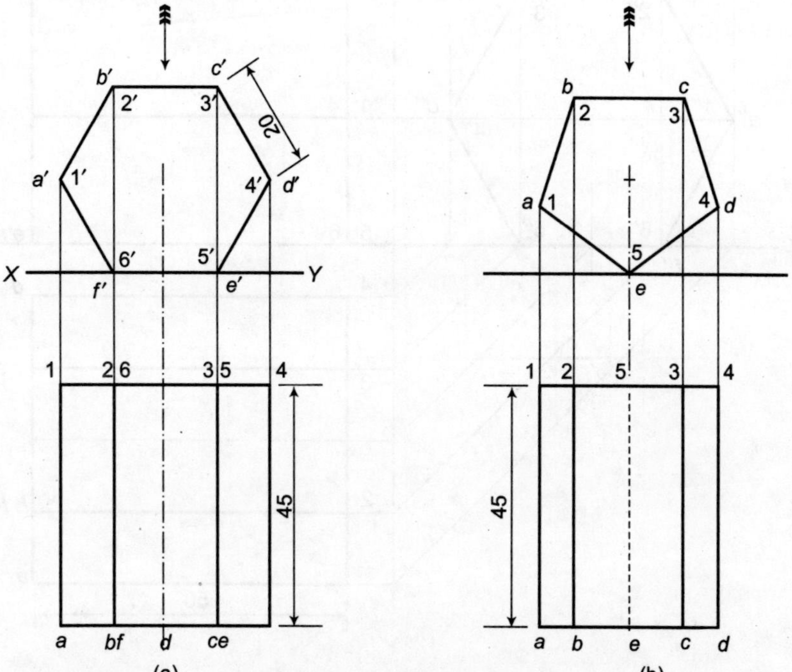

Fig. 11.33 (a) Solution to 11.11(a); (b) Solution to 11.11(b)

Steps for (a):

(1) Draw a hexagon of 20 mm side base in front view, keeping one of the rectangular faces on *XY*.

Project the top view from front view and cut equal to 45 mm as height.

Complete the views and name them as shown in Fig. 11.33 (a).

Steps for (b):

(1) Draw a pentagon of 20 mm side in front view, keeping one of the edges (vertical) on XY.

The same procedure should be adopted as in Fig. 11.33 (a).

PROBLEM 11.12 (FIG. 11.34)

A hexagonal prism, edge of base 25 mm and length 50 mm lies on one of its rectangular faces on HP such that its axis is parallel to both HP and VP. Draw its projection.

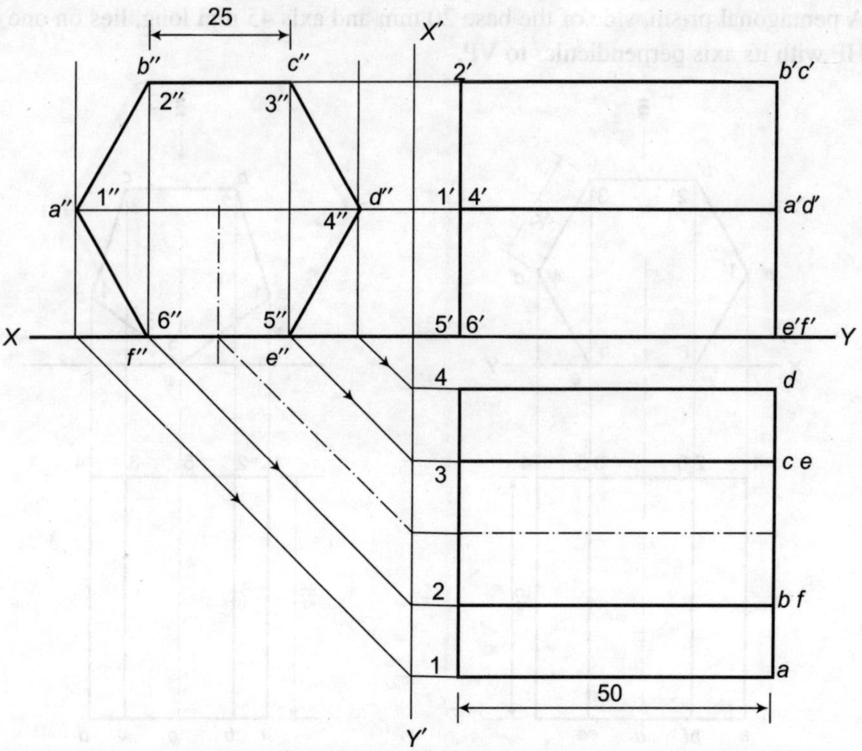

Fig. 11.34 Solution to Problem 11.12

Steps:

(1) In this problem, the axis of prism is parallel to both HP and VP. So, the problem is to be started with side view, because it gives the true shape of the hexagon.

(2) One of the rectangular faces is kept on HP on XY line.

(3) Project the front and top views as shown in Fig. 11.34. The length of the prism is taken as 50 mm.

PROBLEM 11.13 (FIG. 11.35)

Method I (by changing position)

A hexagonal pyramid, side of the base 25 mm and axis 50 mm long, rests with one of the edges of its base on HP and its axis is inclined at 35° to HP and parallel to VP. Draw its projection.

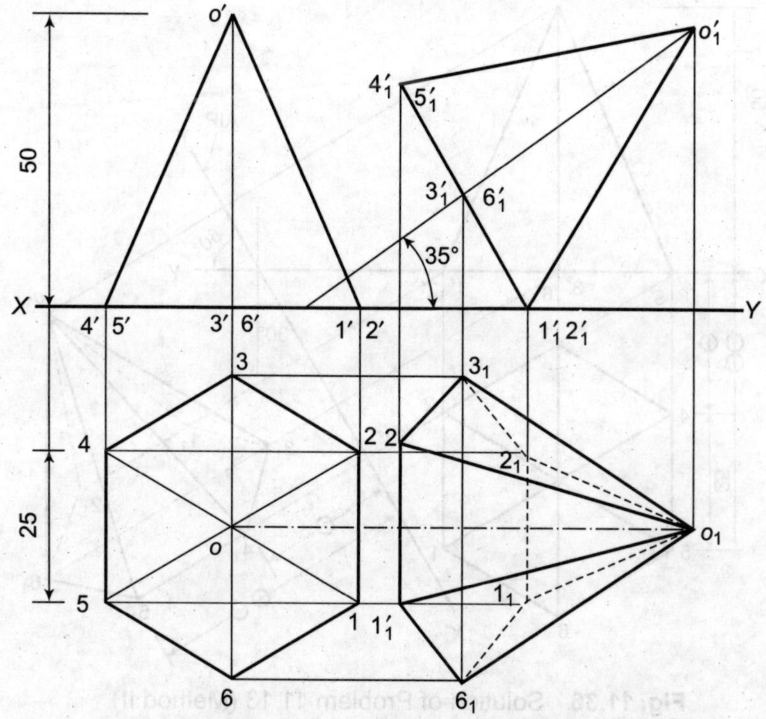

Fig. 11.35 Solution of Problem 11.13 (Method I)

Steps:

(1) In solid projection, initial position of object is very important.

Initially assume the axis is perpendicular to HP and one base edge is perpendicular to VP. Draw front view and top view.

(2) Reproduce the front view with axis 30° with *XY* and 1′2′ edge remaining on HP.

(3) Project all points vertically from the new front view and horizontally from the first top view. Complete the new top view as shown in Fig. 11.35.

Method II (By changing reference plane) Fig. 11.36.

Problem 11.13 can be also solved by taking another reference plane.

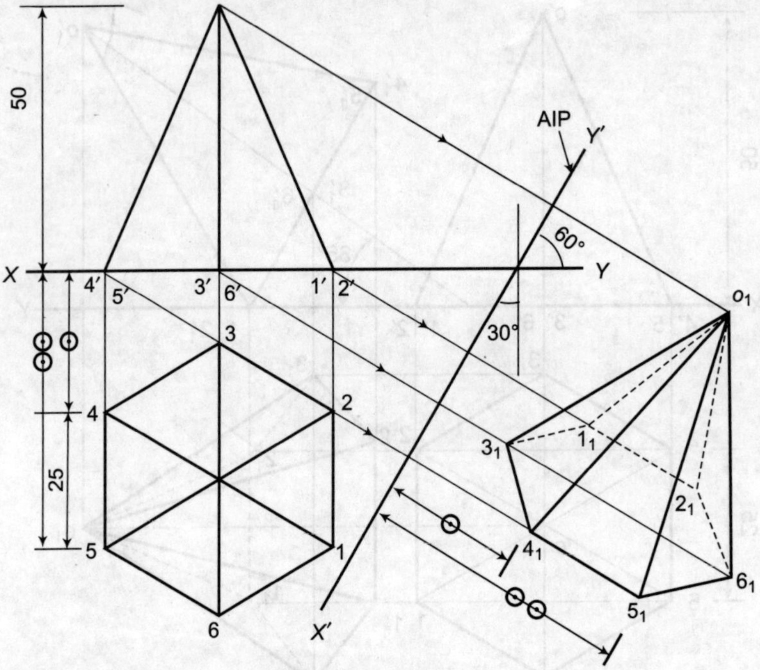

Fig. 11.36 Solution of Problem 11.13 (Method II)

Steps:

(1) Initial position of hexagonal projections remains the same as in Method I.

(2) A new reference line *X′Y′* has been taken at the inclination of 30° to the axis and is 60° from *XY*. The auxiliary inclined plane (AIP) is represented as *X′Y′*.

(3) From front view, project the required top view on *X′Y′* keeping the distance of each point from *X′Y′* equal to the distance of the first top view from *XY* as shown in Fig. 11.36.
For example, distance of 4 from *XY* = ⊙. The same distance is indicated for 4_1 from *X′Y′*.
Similarly, the distance of 5 from *XY* = ⊙⊙. The same distance is indicated for 5_1 from *X′Y′*.
Similarly, distances have been taken for other points. Complete the figures as shown.

PROBLEM 11.14 (FIG. 11.37)

A pentagonal prism, side of the base 30 mm and axis 50 mm long, rests with one of its base edge on HP, such that the vertical rectangular face containing same base edge makes an angle of 60° to HP and the axis is parallel to VP. Draw its projection.

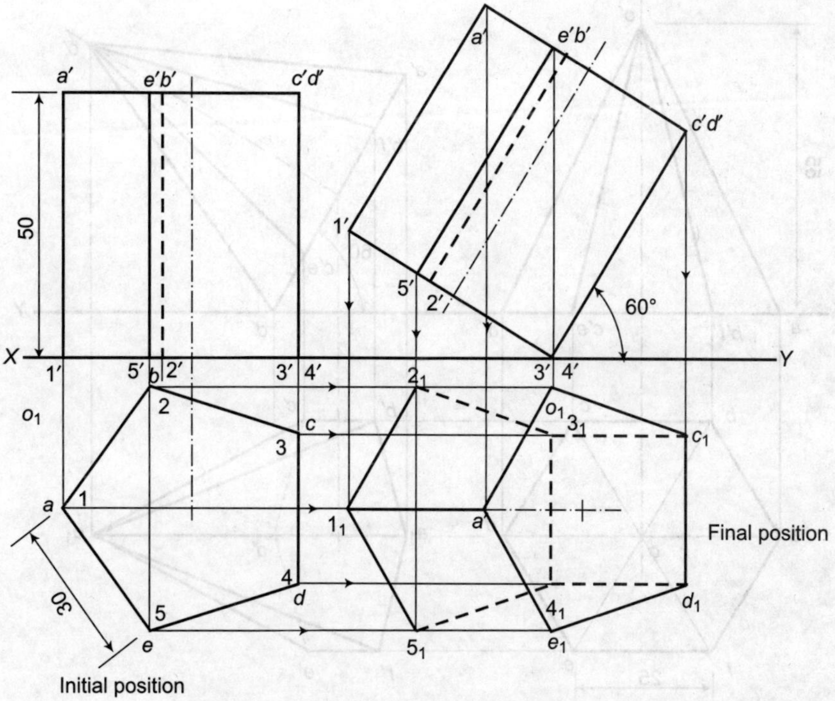

Fig. 11.37 Solution to Problem 11.14

Steps:

(1) Draw the initial position of pentagonal prism, keeping one of the base edge perpendicular to VP. The base edge 34 becomes a point on VP, hence rotation can be done with this point.

(2) Take a line at the inclination of 60° to HP and recast the front view from initial position keeping 3′4′ on *XY*. The final front view is drawn.

(3) Draw the projector lines from final front view below and also draw horizontal line from initial top view. Join the corresponding points as shown in Fig. 11.37.

(4) Draw all lines which fall in boundary with thick lines. If we look for top, most of the lines are invisible. Invisible lines should be joined by dotted lines.

PROBLEM 11.15 (FIG. 11.38)

A hexagonal pyramid, side of the base 25 mm and axis 55 mm long, rests with one of its corner on HP such that its base makes an angle of 60° to HP and its axis is parallel to VP. Draw the projections.

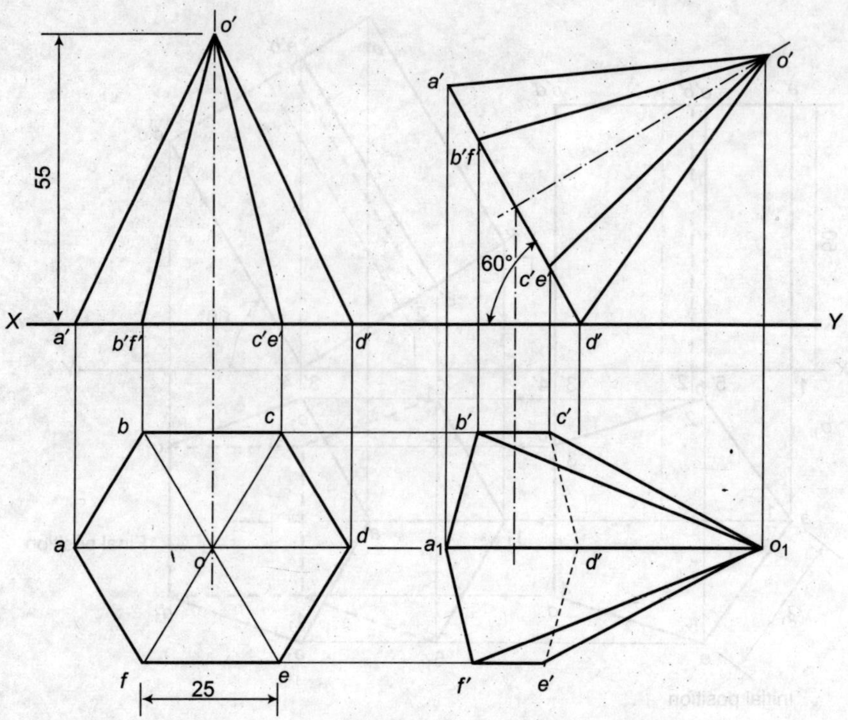

Fig. 11.38 Solution to Problem 11.15

Steps:

(1) Since the pyramid has to rest with one of its base corner on HP. Initially, the pyramid in its simple position, i.e., resting with its base on HP, such that top view *od* is parallel to VP.

Draw front view and top view in initial position.

(2) Tilt the front view such that *d1* will be on XY. The base of the pyramid makes 60° with XY. Draw the final front view.

(3) Project the final top view. If we look at the pyramid from the top, the base will not be visible. Except for the outer lines, hidden line should be drawn.

PROBLEM 11.16 (FIG. 11.39)

A hexagonal prism, side of the base 20 mm and axis 55 mm long, lies with one of its rectangular faces on HP, such that the axis is inclined at 45° to the VP. Draw its projection.

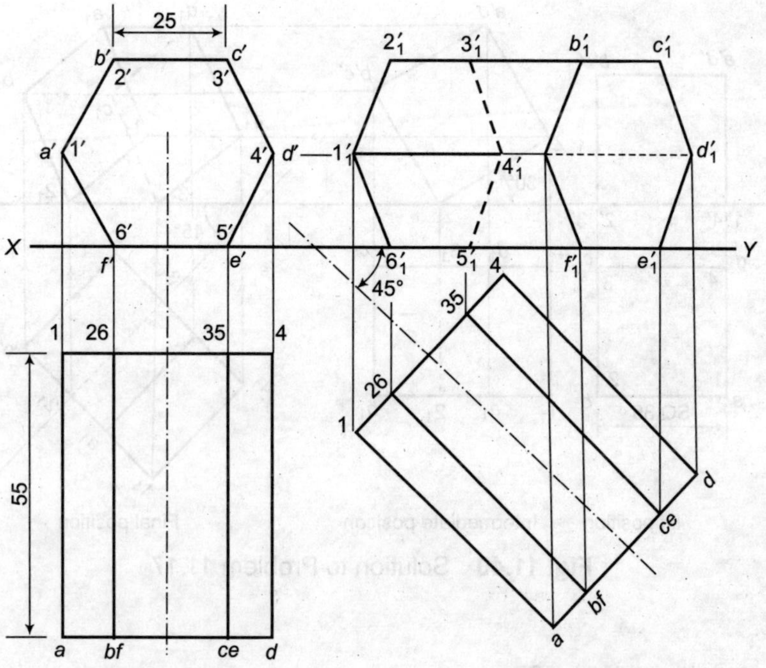

Fig. 11.39 Solution to Problem 11.16

Steps:

(1) Hexagonal prism is lying with its rectangular face on HP and axis perpendicular to VP. Draw initial position of the object's front view and top view as shown in Fig. 11.39.

(2) Next, draw the final position of the top view taking axis of the prism at 45° to *XY*.

(3) From all points of top view, project on *XY* and also horizontal line from initial front view and join the corresponding points.

(4) Draw the boundary line of final front view. The entire lower face is visible. They should be joined by thick lines.

(5) Point 4 is invisible, we can not visualize it. So it must be connected with a dotted line as shown.

PROBLEM 11.17 (FIG. 11.40)

A cube 35 mm side is resting on HP with one of its base edge. The face containing this edge makes an angle of 30° with HP. The bottom face with this edge makes an angle of 45° with VP. Draw the projection.

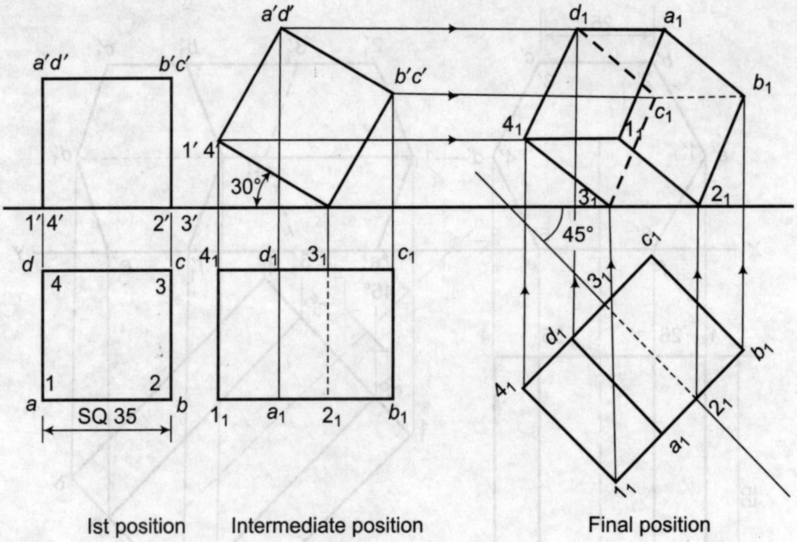

Fig. 11.40 Solution to Problem 11.17

Steps:

(1) Cube is resting with edge 23.

(2) Draw first position keeping 23 perpendicular to VP.

(3) Bottom face 1234 top view and front view becomes a line as 1′4′2′3′.

(4) Tilt the front view such that it makes 30° with HP.

(5) Project from II position of top view to get II front view.

(6) Now draw a line at 45° to *XY*. The shape of II top view remains the same. Keeping 3′2′ on the same line. Make the final top view with respect to 3′2′ line.

(7) Project from all points of final top view vertically and draw horizontal lines from all corners of II position of front view.

(8) Join all the corresponding points to get the final top view, as shown in Fig. 11.40.

PROBLEM 11.18 (FIG. 11.41)

A right circular cylinder, diameter of base 40 mm and height 50 mm, rests on HP on its point on base rim such that its axis is inclined at 45° to HP and the top view of the axis is inclined at 60° to VP. Draw the projection.

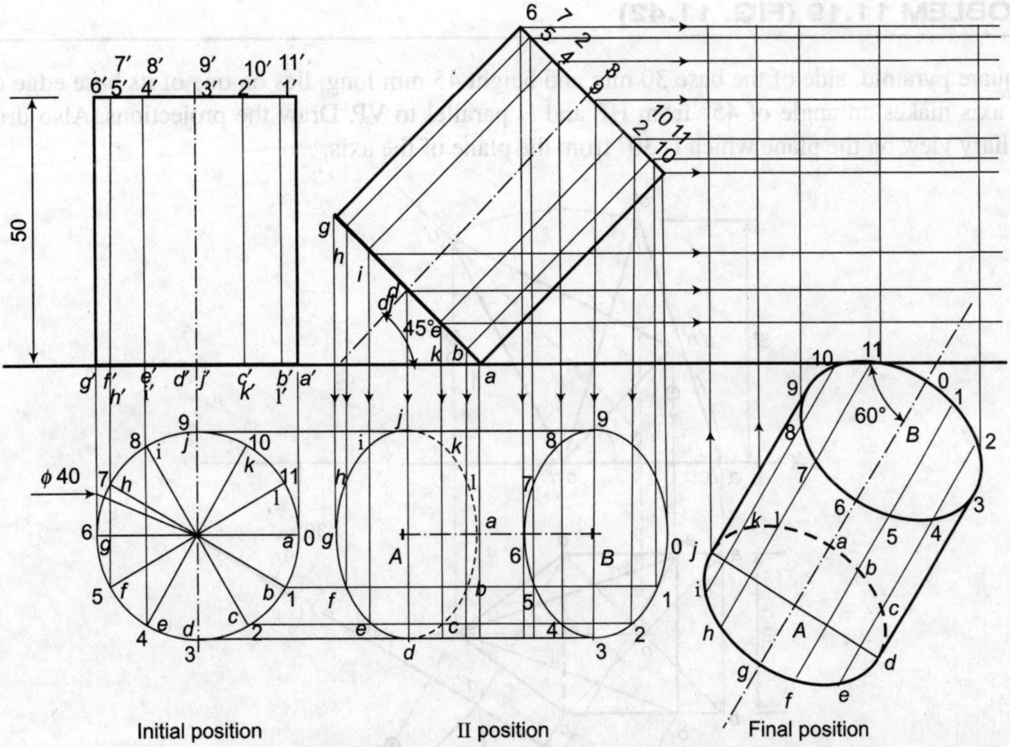

Fig. 11.41 Solution to Problem 11.18

(One auxiliary front view is still unfinished for the students to complete.)

Steps:

(1) In the initial stage, the axis is perpendicular to HP and parallel to VP. Draw front view and top view of cylinder keeping base on *XY*. Divide the base circle into 12 equal parts and project these points upward to get front view.

(2) Redraw the front view in II position keeping the axis at 45° to XY. Project from all points downward and also draw horizontal lines from the first top view to get the respective points. The lower circular base becomes ellipse. This is not visible from the top and, hence, it has been shown by dotted line. Upper end is fully under vision, So this complete ellipse can be visualized.

(3) In the final position, the axis is oriented at 60° from XY; redraw the ellipse on this line. Number the corresponding horizontal line from the II front line. Final front view can be drawn. This is left to the students.

PROBLEM 11.19 (FIG. 11.42)

A square pyramid, side of the base 30 mm and height 45 mm long, lies on one of its base edge on HP. The axis makes an angle of 45° from HP and is parallel to VP. Draw the projections. Also draw the auxiliary view on the plane which is 30° from the plane of the axis.

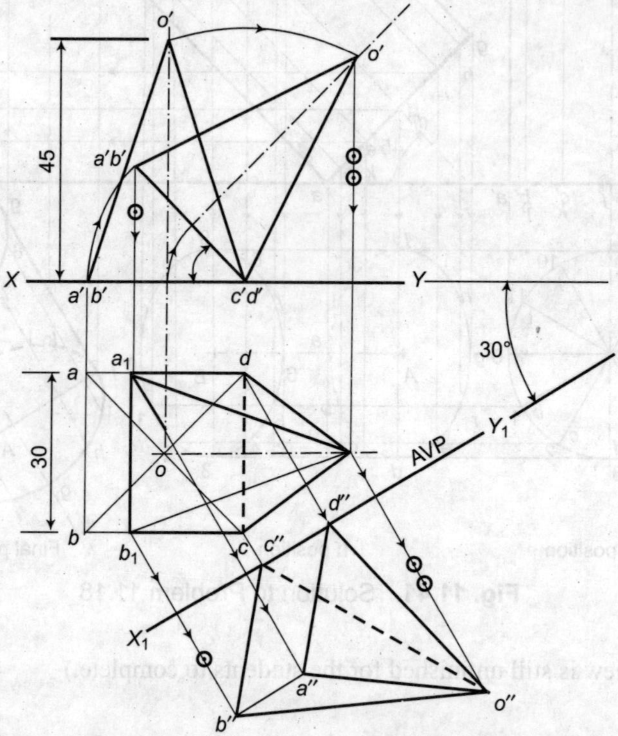

Fig. 11.42 Solution to Problem 11.19

Steps:

(1) Draw a square pyramid projection of base edge 30 mm and height 45 mm with slightly faint line, keeping base edge parallel to XY.

The top view of *CD* base edge becomes a point. The rotation can be made with this point without shifting the object on *XY*.

(2) Taking *cd'* as centre, the entire top view can be redrawn with the axis at 45° from *XY*. It takes the new position.

(3) Project all points to get the final top view. *CD* edge cannot be seen from the top, the projection of top view is shown by dotted lines.

(4) An AVP is taken at 30° with *XY* and projection taken from the final front view. Draw the auxiliary view.

PROBLEM 11.20 [FIG. 11.43 (A) & (B)]

A right circular cone, diameter of the base 40 mm and height 50 mm, rests on its base point on the rim at HP with its axis inclined at 45° to *XY* such that:

(a) Top view of the axis inclined at 30° to VP

(b) Axis inclined at 30° to VP

Draw the projection.

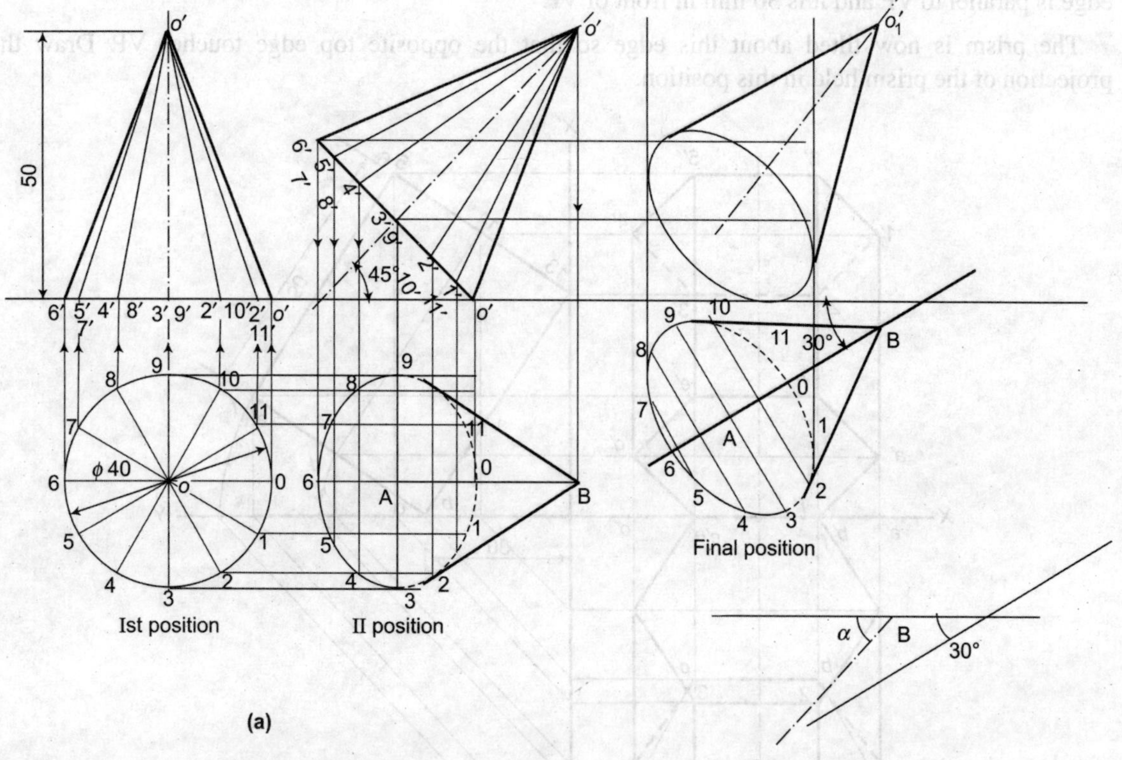

Fig. 11.43 (a) Solution to Problem 11.20

In part (a), the plane of axis makes an angle of 30°.

In part (b), the axis makes an angle of 30° to *XY* and, hence, apparent angle is to be found as shown in Fig. 11.43(b). α' is the angle which should be taken in place of 30° and it is more than 30° as shown in the figure for part (b). Part (b) to be solved by the students. Upto II position, it is common to (a).

PROBLEM 11.21 (FIG. 11.44)

A hexagonal prism, edge of the base 25 mm and height 50 mm, is held on HP such that one of its base edge is parallel to VP and it is 30 mm in front of VP.

The prism is now tilted about this edge so that the opposite top edge touches VP. Draw the projection of the prism held in this position.

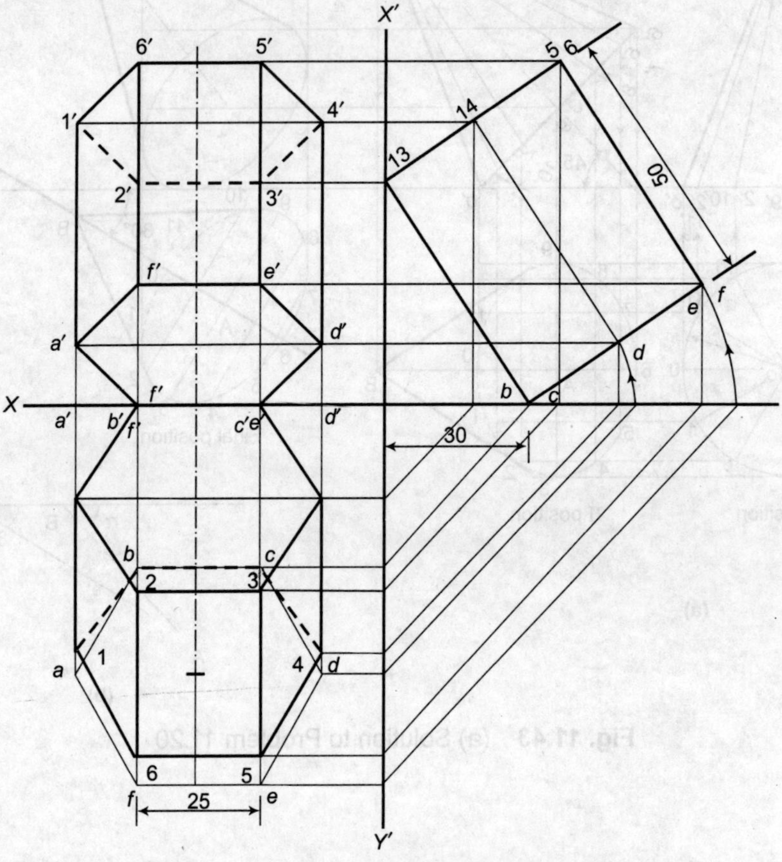

Fig. 11.44 Solution to Problem 11.21

PROBLEM 11.22 [FIG. 11.45(A) & (B)]

A hexagonal pyramid of base of side 25 mm long and altitude 50 mm is resting on one of its base edges on the ground. The edge makes an angle of 45° to VP and the face containing the edge makes 60° to HP. Draw the projection.

Method I

(By changing positions)

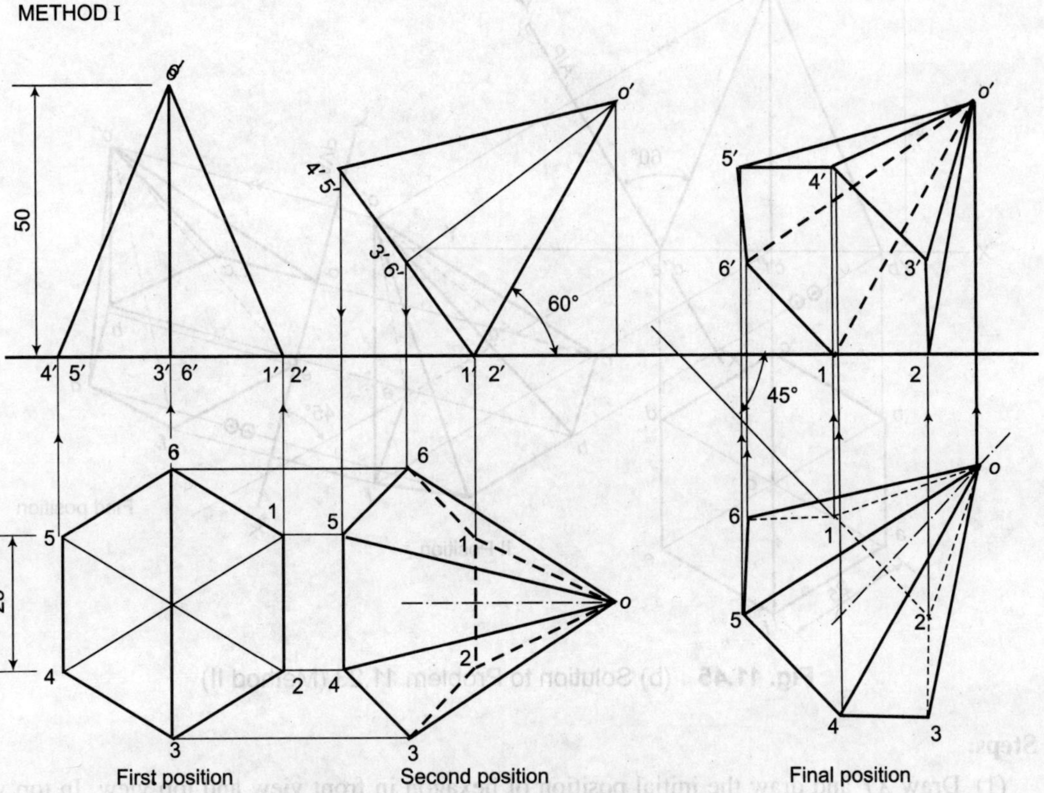

Fig. 11.45 (a) Solution to Problem 11.22

Method II

(By auxiliary plane methods)

PROBLEM 11.23 [FIG. 11.45 (B)]

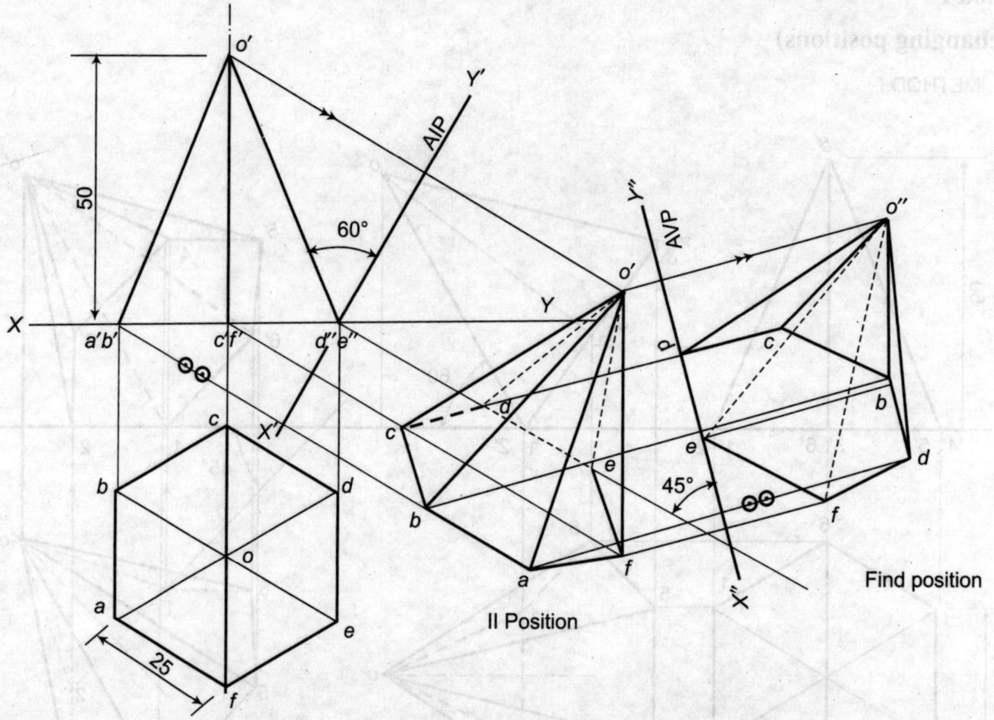

Fig. 11.45 (b) Solution to Problem 11.23 (Method II)

Steps:

(1) Draw *XY* and draw the initial position of hexagon in front view and top view. In top view, hexagon with edge '*de*' is perpendicular to *XY*.

(2) Draw *X″Y″* auxiliary plane (AIP) passing through *d″e″* at 60° with o′– *d″e″*.

(3) Draw the corresponding auxiliary view from above. It is the II position.

(4) Now draw *X″Y″* making 45° with *de* of the auxiliary view. *X″Y″* is the AIP with respect to auxiliary view in II position. Draw the corresponding view, projecting all points of auxiliary view in II positions.

(A) By Changing Position of Solid (Fig. 11.46)

PROBLEM 11.24 (FIG. 11.46)

A square prism of base edge 30 mm and height 50 mm has one of its rectangular faces make an angle of 45° with HP and a resting edge of the base make an angle of 30° with VP. Draw its projection.

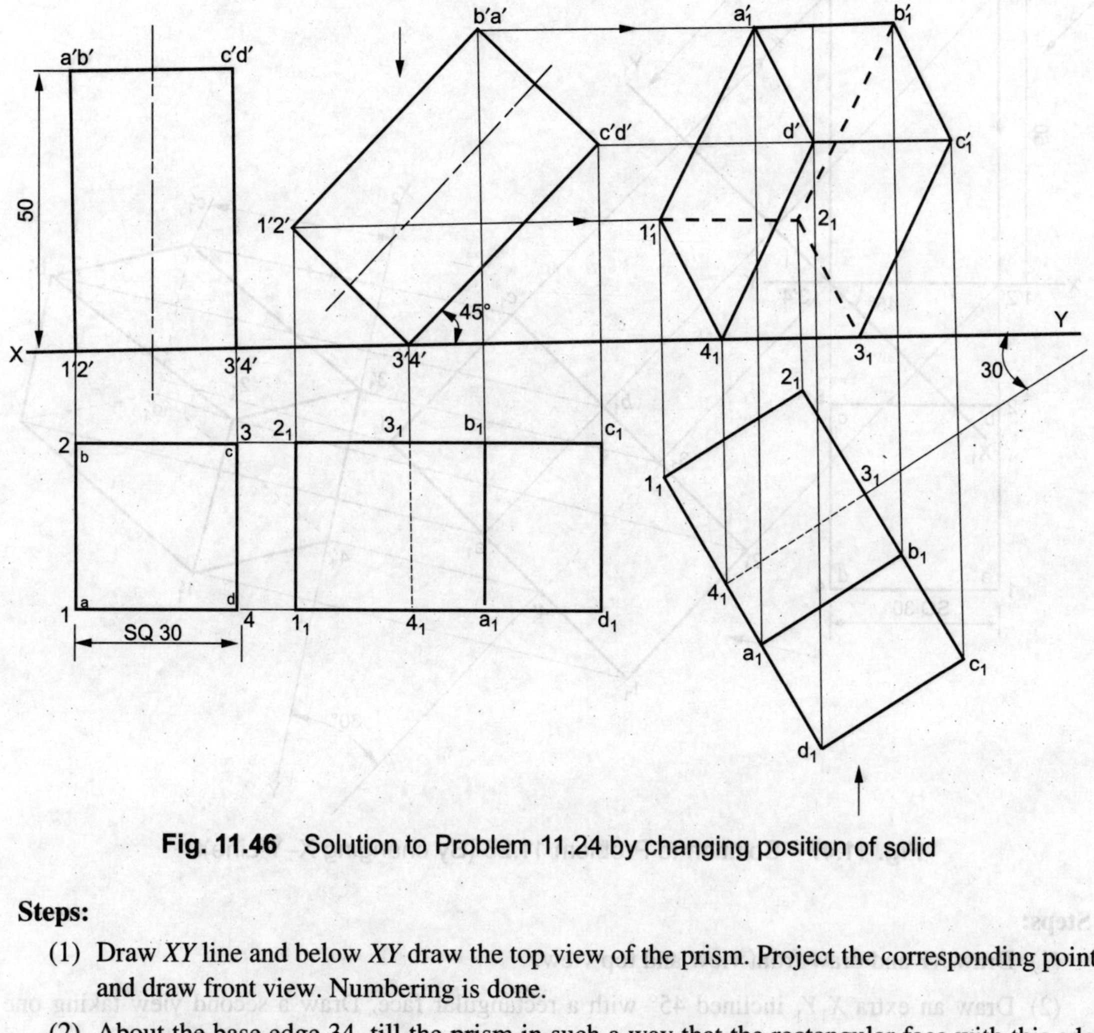

Fig. 11.46 Solution to Problem 11.24 by changing position of solid

Steps:

(1) Draw *XY* line and below *XY* draw the top view of the prism. Project the corresponding points and draw front view. Numbering is done.

(2) About the base edge 34, till the prism in such a way that the rectangular face with this edge makes an angle of 45° with *XY*.

(3) Reconstruct the top view with 34 edge making an angle of 30° with *XY*. Project this on VP to get the front view. The final view is shown in Fig. 11.46.

(B) By Changing X–Y Line (Fig. 11.47)

PROBLEM 11.25 (FIG. 11.47)

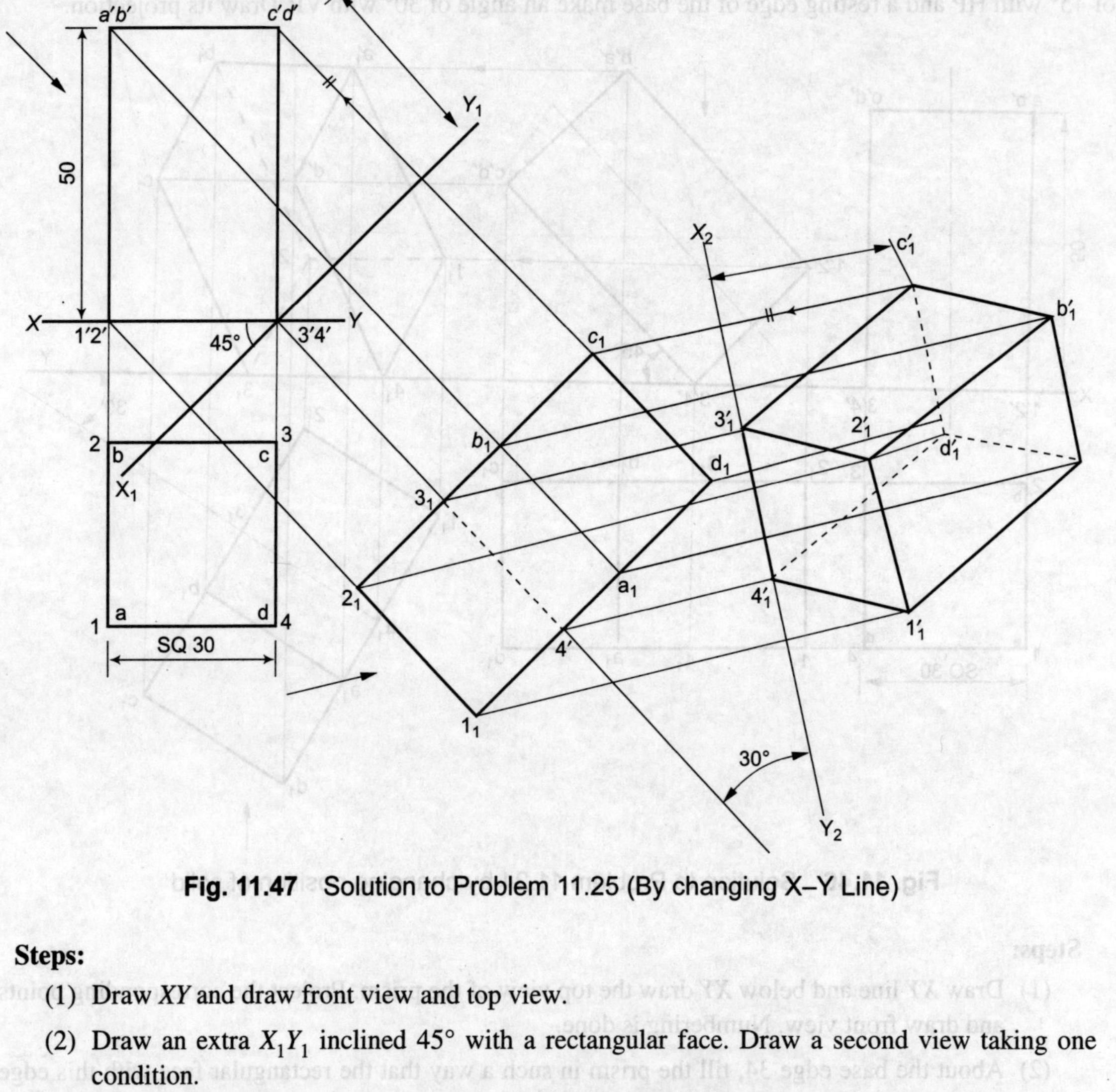

Fig. 11.47 Solution to Problem 11.25 (By changing X–Y Line)

Steps:

(1) Draw *XY* and draw front view and top view.

(2) Draw an extra X_1Y_1 inclined 45° with a rectangular face. Draw a second view taking one condition.

(3) Draw a third X_2Y_2 and project the 2 views over it and draw the view over it.

It in the final view taking both the condition as given in Fig. 11.47.

PROBLEM 11.26 (FIG. 11.48)

A tetrahedron of base edge 50 mm resting on one of its base edges on horizontal plane and inclined at 45° to VP. The triangular face containing the same base edge is on HP. Draw the projections.

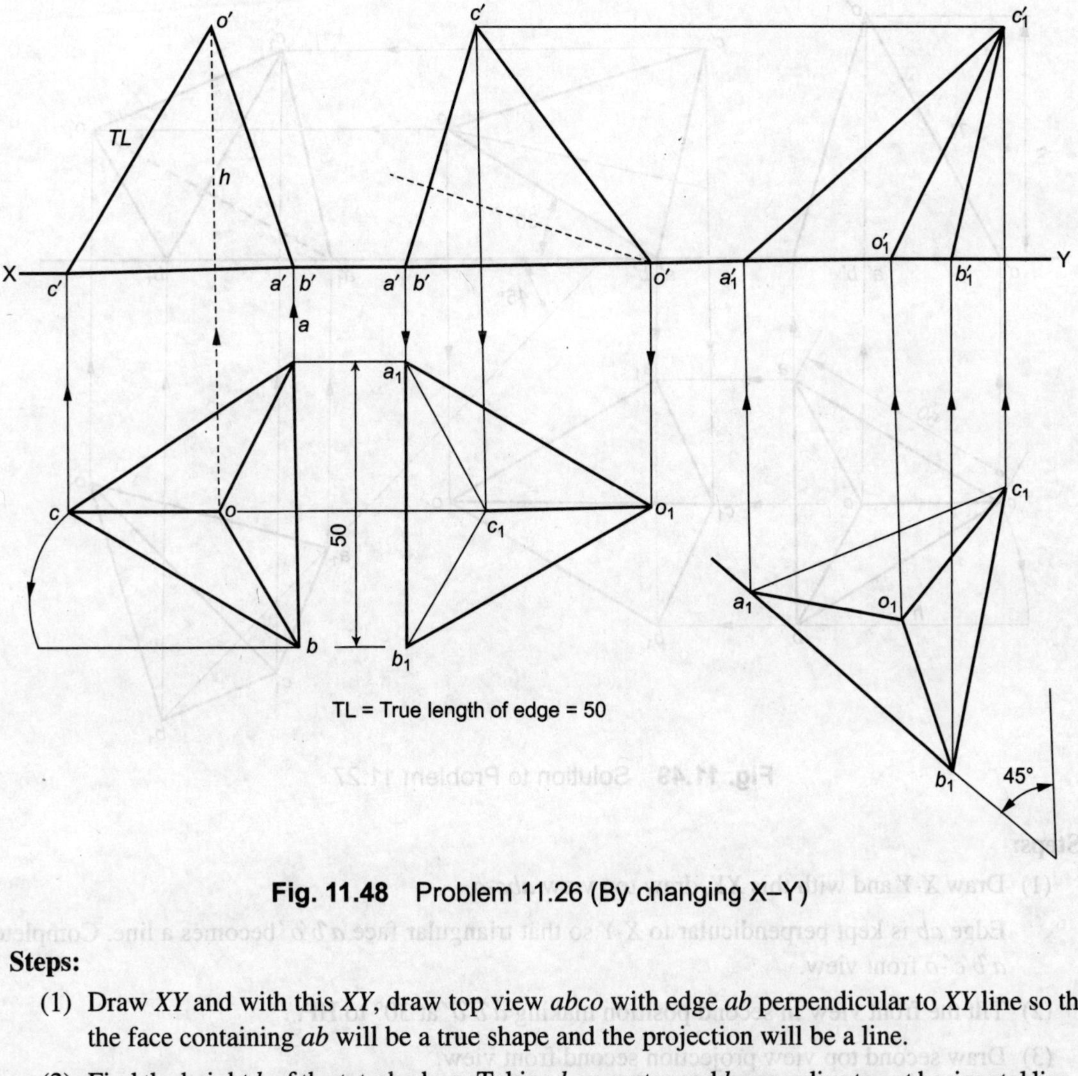

Fig. 11.48 Problem 11.26 (By changing X–Y)

Steps:

(1) Draw *XY* and with this *XY*, draw top view *abco* with edge *ab* perpendicular to *XY* line so that the face containing *ab* will be a true shape and the projection will be a line.

(2) Find the height *h* of the tetrahedron. Taking *b* as centre and *bc* as radius to cut horizontal line as in the figure. Height *h* is taken on the projection from *o*. Thus *a′b′c′o′* front view in drawn.

(3) Second front view is drawn such that *a′b′o′* will be on HP corresponding $a_1b_1c_1o_1$ top view is drawn.

(4) Reconstruct the second top view on the line 45° with the edge a_1b_1. Thus the final front view is drawn as in Fig. 11.48.

PROBLEM 11.27 (FIG. 11.49)

A tetrahedron of base edge 50 mm resting on one of its base edges on HP and inclined at 45° to VP. The face containing the same base edge makes an angle of 30° to HP. Draw the projection.

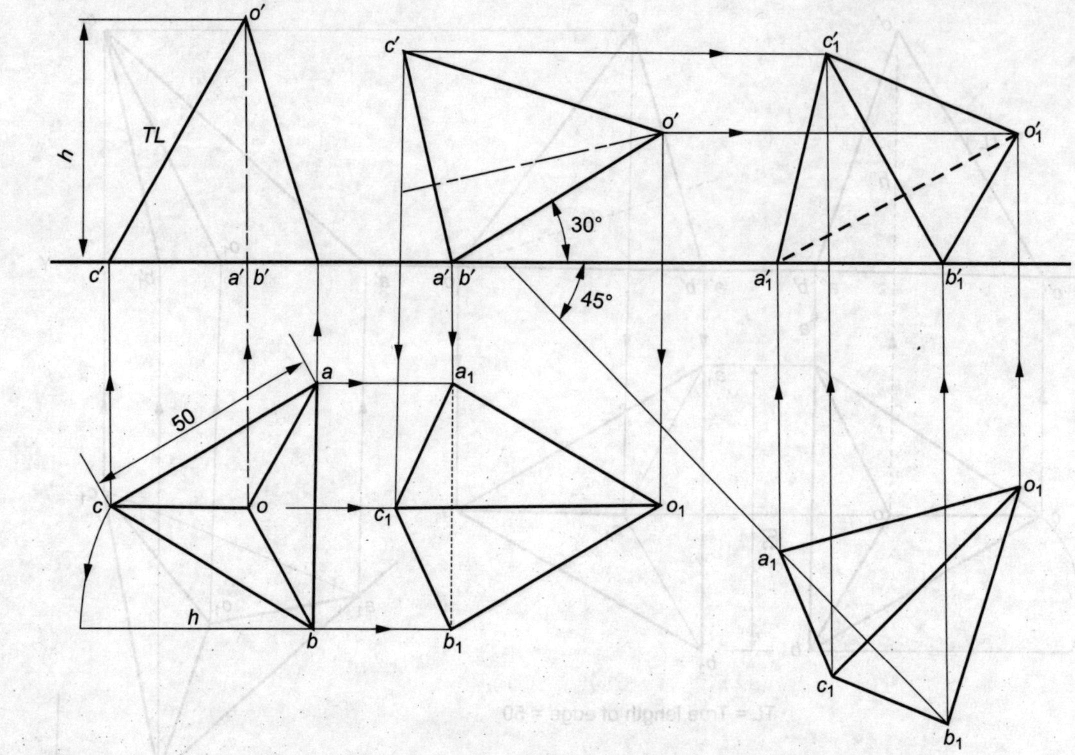

Fig. 11.49 Solution to Problem 11.27

Steps:

(1) Draw *X-Y* and with this *XY*, draw top view *abc-o*.

Edge *ab* is kept perpendicular to *X-Y* so that triangular face $a'b'o'$ becomes a line. Complete $a'b'c'$-o front view.

(2) Tilt the front view in second position making $a'b'o'$ at 30° to HP.

(3) Draw second top view projection second front view.

(4) Reconstruct the third top view so that the resting edge a_1b_1 makes an angle of 45° to VP. Projecting the third top view draw the final front view as shown in Fig. 11.49.

PROBLEM 11.28 (FIG. 11.50)

A pentagonal pyramid of base edge side 25 mm and height 55 mm has one of its slant faces on the horizontal plane and the edge of the base contained by that slant face makes an angle of 35° to VP. Draw its projections.

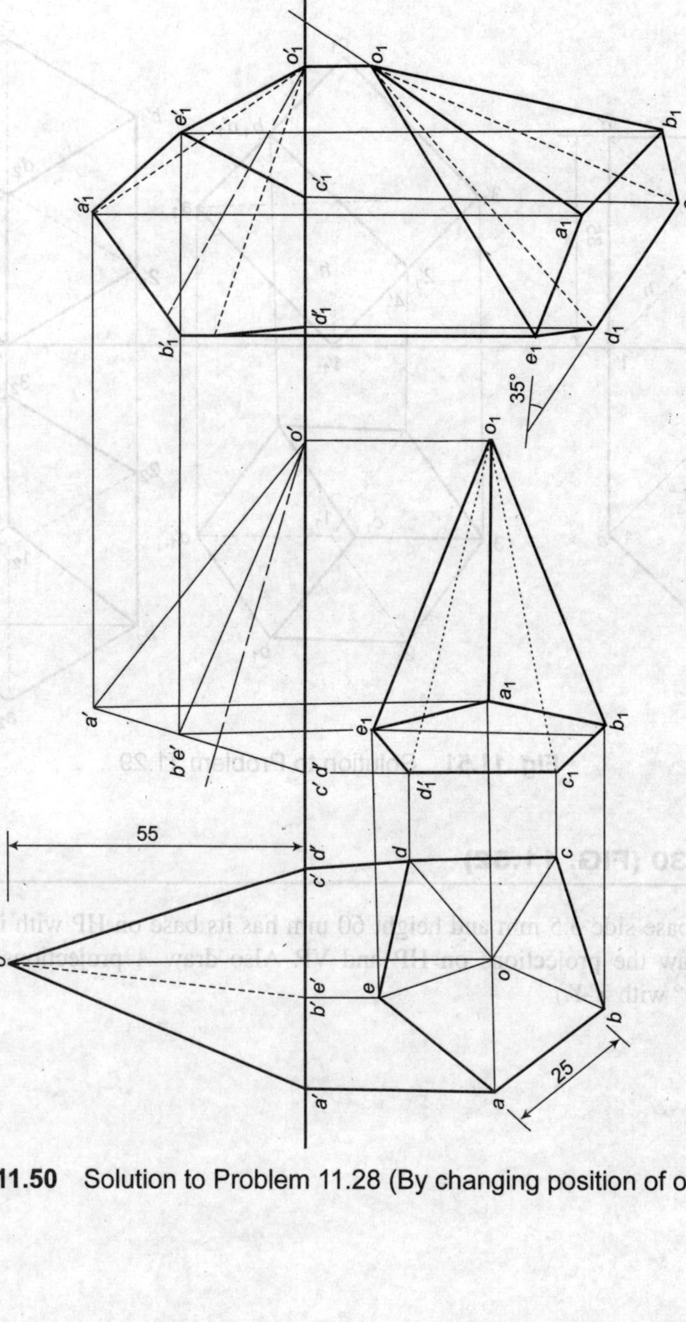

Fig. 11.50 Solution to Problem 11.28 (By changing position of object)

PROBLEM 11.29 (FIG. 11.51)

A cube of 35 mm long edge is resting on one of its corner on HP, with its solid diagonal parallel to HP and perpendicular to VP. Draw the projection of the cube.

Important note:

The front view of the cube is its isometric projection as shown in Fig. 11.51.

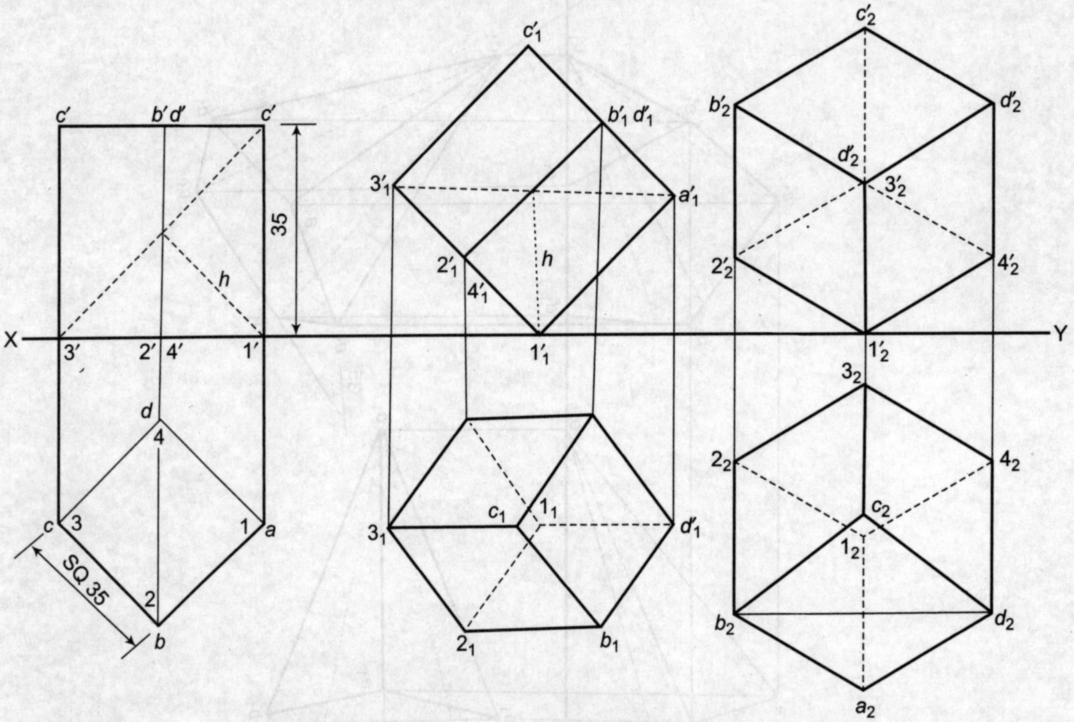

Fig. 11.51 Solution to Problem 11.29

PROBLEM 11.30 (FIG. 11.52)

A square prism of base side 3.5 mm and height 60 mm has its base on HP with its two faces equally inclined to VP. Draw the projections on HP and VP. Also draw *A* projections on AIP. (Auxiliary Inclined Plane at 45° with *X-Y*.)

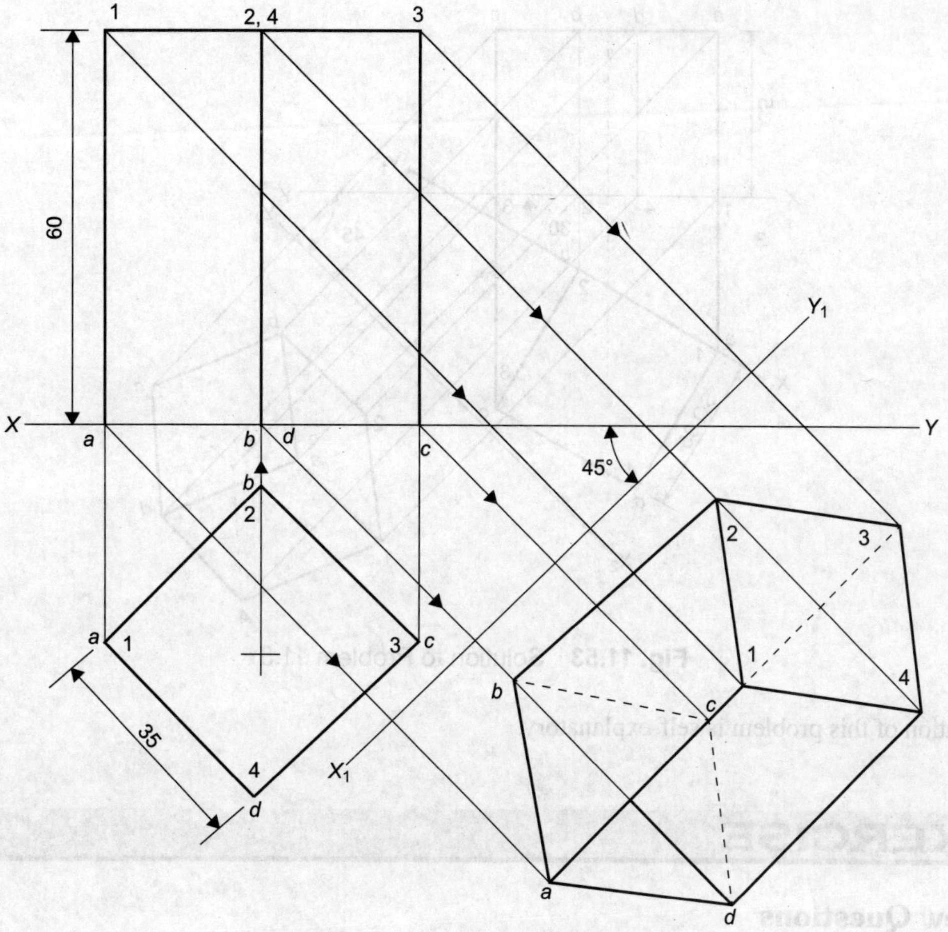

Fig. 11.52 Solution to Problem 11.30

Solution of this problem is self-explanatory.

PROBLEM 11.31 (FIG. 11.53)

A cube of 35 mm long edges is resting on HP and one of its vertical face is inclined at 30° to VP.

Draw the projection. Also draw an auxiliary view on a plane at the inclination to VP, i.e., projection on AIP.

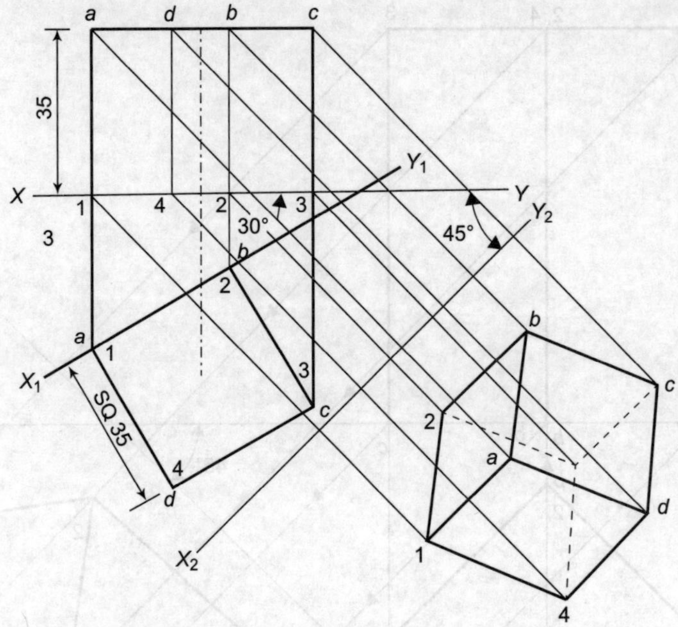

Fig. 11.53 Solution to Problem 11.31

Solution of this problem is self-explanatory.

EXERCISE

Review Questions

1. What is a solid?
2. What is the difference between right and oblique solids?
3. Differentiate between prism and pyramid.
4. What are the different types of solids?
5. A square pyramid, edge of the base 25 mm and height 45 mm, rests on its base on HP, with its base edge equally inclined to VP. Draw the three views of the square pyramid.
6. A right regular hexagonal pyramid, edge of the base 25 mm and axis 55 mm long, has an edge of the base in HP, such that its axis is inclined at 30° to HP and parallel to VP. Draw the projections by the two methods.
7. A hexagonal prism, edge of the base 25 mm and height 60 mm, rests on one of its base edges in HP such that its axis is inclined to HP at 45° and parallel to VP. Draw its projections by using both the methods.

8. A right circular cone, diameter of the base 55 mm and height 75 mm, lies on HP on one of its edges such that its axis is parallel to VP. Draw its projections.
9. A pentagonal pyramid, edge of base 25 mm and height 60 mm, lies on HP on one of its slant edge and has its axis parallel to VP. Draw its projections by using both the methods.
10. A pentagonal prism, side of base 25 mm and height 65 mm, rests on one of its base corners on HP such that its long edge containing the corner is inclined to the HP at 45° and the side of base opposite to the corner is inclined at 45° to VP. Draw the projections.
11. A right circular cone, diameter of base 45 and height 60 mm, lies on one of its generator in HP such that the generator is inclined to VP at 30°. Draw the projection.
12. A pentagonal pyramid, edge of the base 25 mm and height 60 mm, is held on ground plane on one of its base corner such that its axis is inclined at 30° to ground plane and 45° to VP. Draw the projections.
13. A right circular cylinder, diameter of base 45 mm and height 65 mm, rests on HP on its base rim such that its axis is inclined at 45° to HP and the top view of the axis is inclined at 60° to VP. Draw the projection.
14. A hexagonal pyramid, side of base 25 mm and 50 mm long, is resting on an edge of its base on the horizontal plane in such a way that it makes an angle of 45° to VP. The slant face containing the same edge makes an angle of 60° to HP.
15. A right hexagonal pyramid, side of base 30 mm and height of axis 45 mm, is resting on one of its triangular faces on the horizontal plane and the edge of the base contained by that triangular face make an angle of 30° to VP. Draw the projections taking apex nearest to VP.
16. Draw the top view and front view of a square pyramid, side of base 30 mm and axis 55 mm long, is freely suspended from one of the corners of its base with its axis in a vertical plane making an angle of 45° with VP.
17. A right pentagonal prism, 80 mm high with each side of the base 30 mm, is resting on one of the base edges on the horizontal plane and inclined at 30° to VP, and the face containing that edge is inclined at 45° to HP. Draw the projections of the pentagonal prism.
18. A circular cone of 60 mm base diameter and axis 75 mm long is resting on one of its generator on horizontal plane is such a way that its axis makes an angle of 30° with VP and apex towards VP. Draw its projection.
19. A right circular cone base diameter 50 mm and axis 75 mm ling is resting on the HP on a point of base circle with its axis making an angle of 45° with HP and its top view axis makes 30° angle with VP. Draw its projection.
20. Draw the front view and top view of right circular cylinder, base diameter 30 mm and axis 70 mm long, when it is resting on its circular rim in such a way that its axis makes an angles of 30° with HP and the top view of its axis is inclined at an angle of 45° to VP.

Objective Questions

1. An object having _____ dimensions is called a solid.
2. If a solid rests on its base on HP, its axis must be kept _____ to HP.
3. To represent a solid in orthographic projections, at least _____ views are required.
4. A solid having four equal equilateral triangle faces is called a _____.
5. An oblique solid is one which has its axis _____ to its base.
6. A solid with two identical ends is called a _____.
7. A cone is generated by the revolution of a _____ about its altitude.

Answers

Objective Questions

1. three
2. perpendicular
3. two
4. tetrahedron
5. inclined
6. prism
7. right angle triangle

12

CHAPTER

Section of Solids

12.1 INTRODUCTION

Section of solids means to cut the solid on imagination and visualize to know the interior details and the interior mechanism of an object, and to draw its sectional views and the true shape of the section.

In true sense, the solid is never cut by a sharp knife but on imagination, certain parts are assumed to be cut and removed, and the remaining part of the object is visualized. The projections are obtained on two reference planes.

So far, we have learnt the projection of solid. In orthographic projection of an object, the hidden part, and the interior details which are not under our vision, is represented by dotted lines. If the object or m/c components are complex in nature, there will be a large number of hidden lines and, as such, there will be a large number of hidden lines coinciding with each other; and in those cases, it becomes difficult to know the complete details internally and also the true shape of it.

Hence, an object is assumed to be cut by a plane, known as cutting plane or sectional plane, and the surface that we obtain is known as section. The projections of these sections are taken on either horizontal plane (HP) or vertical plane (VP); they will be called sections on HP or on VP.

The true shape of the section will be different from the sectional view of HP and VP.

True Shape: True shape of the portion of the object which is cut by section at plane is known as true shape of the section.

It is found when an auxiliary plane is taken parallel to the sectional plane and the projection is taken on the plane; the view obtained will give the true shape of the section.

12.2 SECTIONAL PLANES

The solids are assumed to be cut by the sectional plane, described as follows and shown in Fig. 12.1:

(i) Sectional plane parallel to HP and perpendicular to VP.

(ii) Sectional plane parallel to VP and perpendicular to HP.

(iii) Sectional plane perpendicular to both HP and VP plane.

(iv) Sectional plane perpendicular to HP and inclined to VP.

(v) Sectional plane perpendicular to VP and inclined to HP.

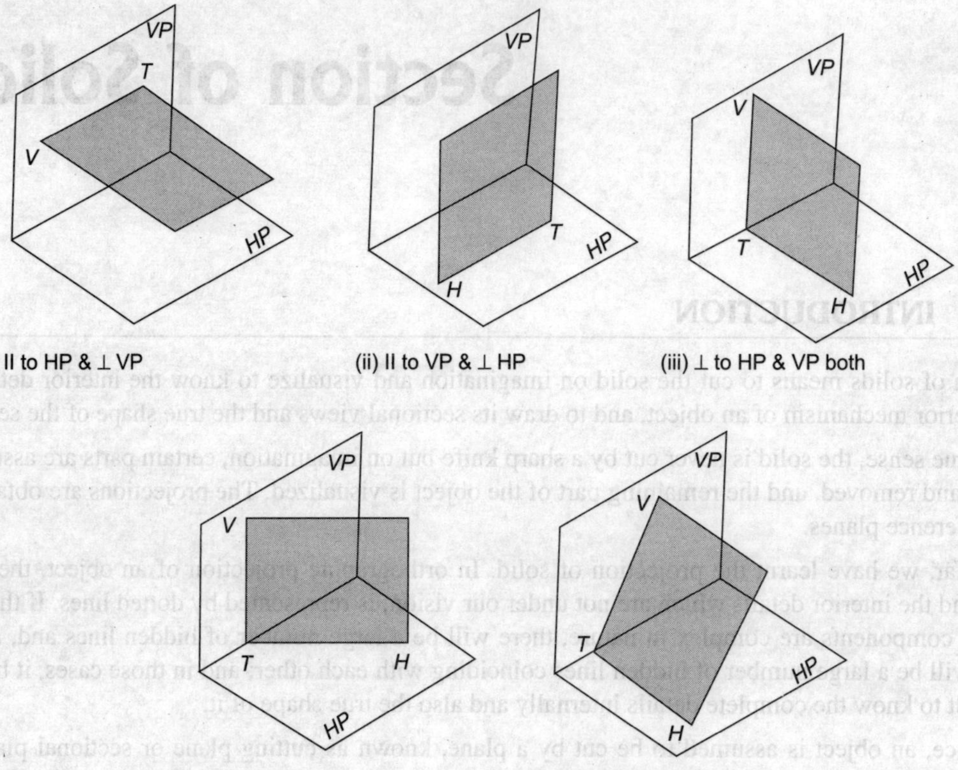

(i) II to HP & ⊥ VP

(ii) II to VP & ⊥ HP

(iii) ⊥ to HP & VP both

(iv) ⊥ to HP and *L* to VP
(AVP)
Auxiliary Vertical Plane

(v) ⊥ to VP & *L* to HP
(AIP)
Auxiliary Inclined Plane

Fig. 12.1 Pictorial view of cutting planes

12.3 SECTION LINES AND CONVENTIONS

The cut surface or cut section of the object is shown by a number of inclined and parallel lines called section lines. These are called *hatching*. Generally, these lines are drawn with faint lines with less intensity conventionally as compared to the boarder lines of the object.

The sectional lines are drawn at 45° to the horizontal, inclined either towards right or left, as per the requirement (Fig. 12.2).

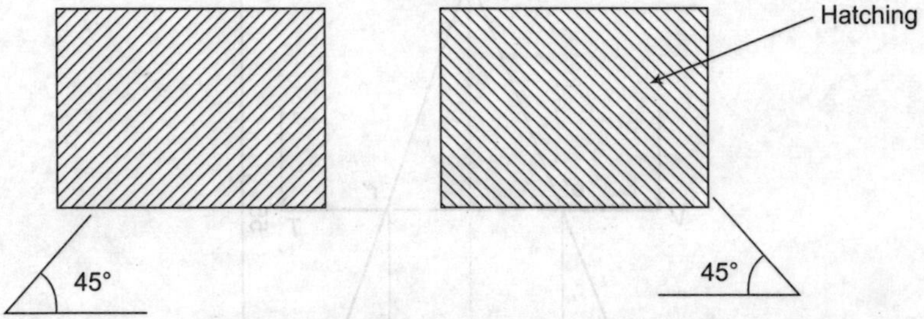

Fig. 12.2 Conventionally acceptable

These lines are drawn equidistant with each other. The shape between two lines depends upon the size or area of the section to be hatched.

If the sectional part to be hatched is small, the space between the two hatching lines should also be selected little less or vice versa. Spacing should vary from 1.5 mm to 4 mm (Fig. 12.3).

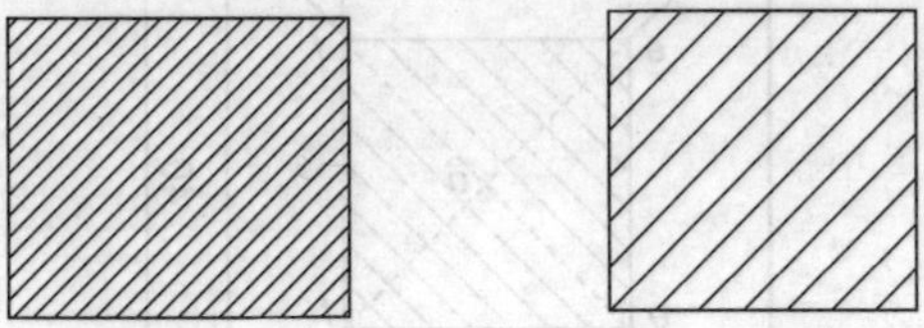

(a) Less Gap (b) More Gap

Fig. 12.3 Method of hatching, for less area (a) is better as compared to (b)

12.4 SECTIONAL PLANE PARALLEL TO HP AND PERPENDICULAR TO VP

Sectional plane is parallel to HP and perpendicular to VP; hence, it will have no HT but will have a vertical trace (VT) and will be parallel to XY. The sectional views on HP will be a true shape.

PROBLEM 12.1 (FIG. 12.4)

A square pyramid, edge of the base 40 mm and height 55 mm rests on its base on HP with one of its base parallel to XY. A section plane parallel to HP cuts the pyramid bisecting its axis. Draw its front view and sectional top view (Fig. 12.4).

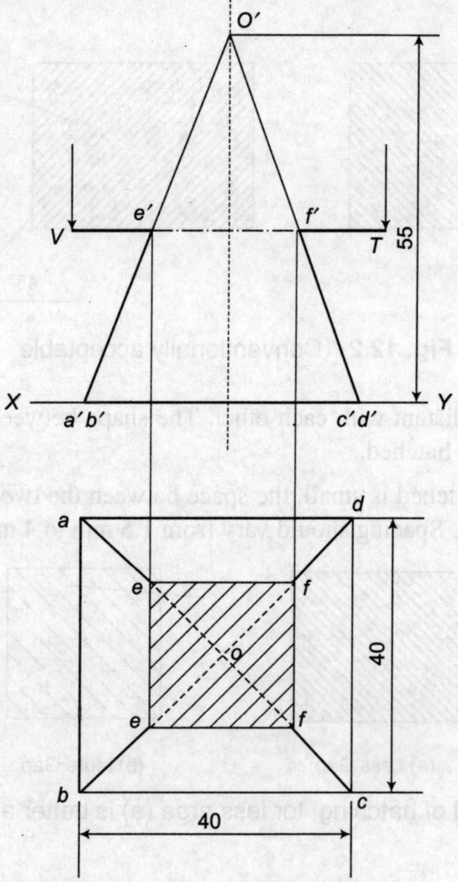

Fig. 12.4 Solution to Problem 12.1

Solution:

1. Draw the projections of the square pyramid in required position.
2. As the sectional plane is parallel to HP and perpendicular to VP, the projection of this plane on VP will be a line parallel to XY and perpendicular to the axis.

   The plane is bisecting the axis of the pyramid.

3. O′a′b′ and o′c′d′ are the front view of the two slant edges and a triangular face which is cut by the section plane.

   e′ is the front view of the point which is cut by the plane. The projection of e′ vertically will cut off the top view Oa and Ob at e. Similarly, f′ will give f. So, ee′f′f will be a square and required sectional top view. Front view will be a line as shown in Fig. 12.4.

PROBLEM 12.2 (FIG. 12.5)

A pentagonal pyramid, edge of the base 25 mm and height 50 mm, rests on its base on HP with one of the base perpendicular to XY. A sectional plane parallel to HP cuts the pyramid at 20 mm from XY (Fig. 12.5).

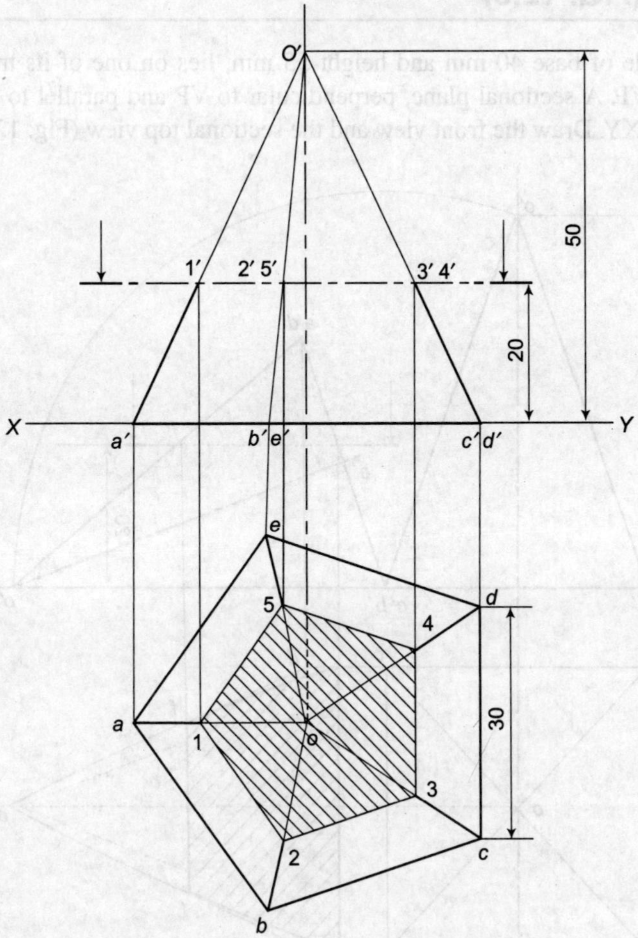

Fig. 12.5 Solution to Problem 12.2

Solution:

1. Draw the projections of the pentagonal pyramid keeping one of its base edges perpendicular to XY.
2. Draw sectional plane parallel to XY and passing through the axis at a point 20 mm above the XY in front view.
3. The sectional plane cuts O′a′, O′b′, O′e′, O′c′, and O′d′ at 1′, 2′5′, 3′4′. The projection of all points at 1, 2, 3, 4 and 5.

Join all points and the sectional top view is hatched.

PROBLEM 12.3 (FIG. 12.6)

A square pyramid, side of base 40 mm and height 55 mm, lies on one of its triangular faces in HP. Its axis is parallel to VP. A sectional plane, perpendicular to VP and parallel to HP, cuts the pyramid which is 20 mm from XY. Draw the front view and the sectional top view (Fig. 12.6).

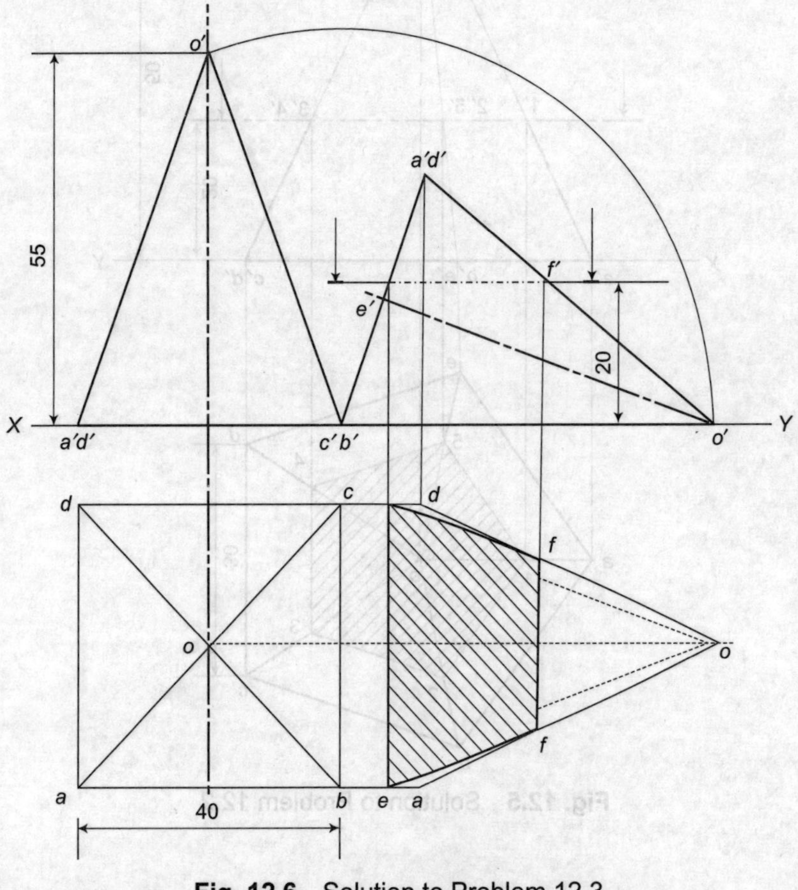

Fig. 12.6 Solution to Problem 12.3

Solution:

1. Draw the initial position of square pyramid. The plane Obc is the top view of a triangular face whose front view is represented by a line O′c′b′, i.e., this plane is perpendicular to VP, hence rotation can be done.
2. Have the rotation and get the final position of front view keeping O′b′c′ lying on XY. In final front view, take a sectional plane at a height of 20 mm from *XY*.
3. All intersection of the sectional plane have to be located. Project these points and get the final top view as shown in Fig. 12.6.

PROBLEM 12.4 (FIG. 12.7)

A right circular cone, base diameter 50 mm and height 55 mm, lies on one of its generator in HP such that the axis of the cone is parallel to XY. A sectional plane parallel to XY and perpendicular to VP cuts the cone at 20 mm above XY. Draw the sectional top view (Fig. 12.7).

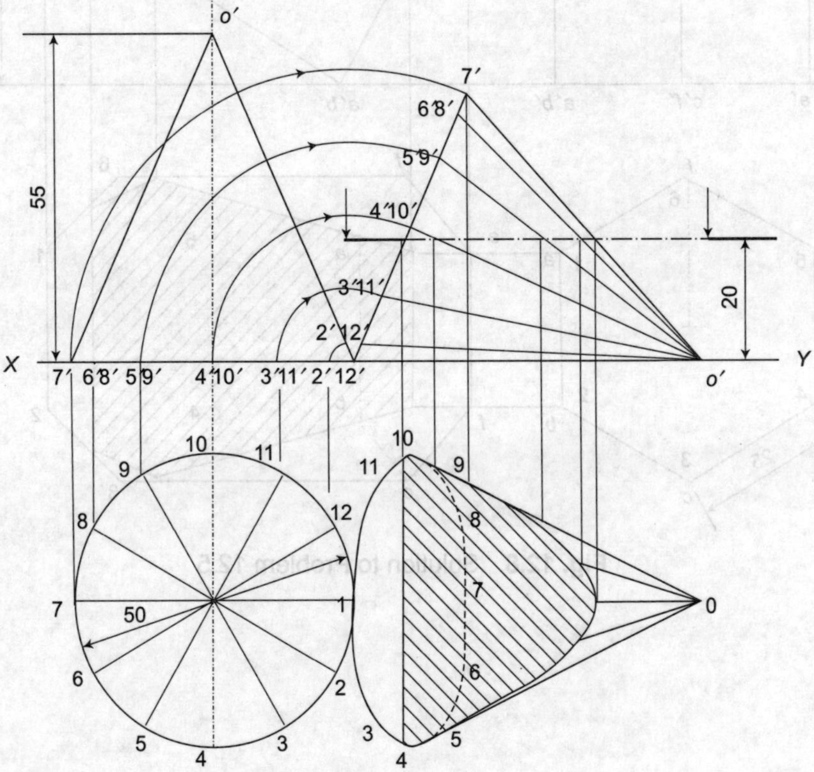

Fig. 12.7 Solution to Problem 12.4

PROBLEM 12.5 (FIG. 12.8)

A hexagonal prism, base edge 25 mm and height 60 mm is lying on HP on one of its base edge, such that its axis is parallel to VP and inclined at 30° to HP. A sectional plane cuts the prism. Draw the sectional plan of the section (Fig. 12.8).

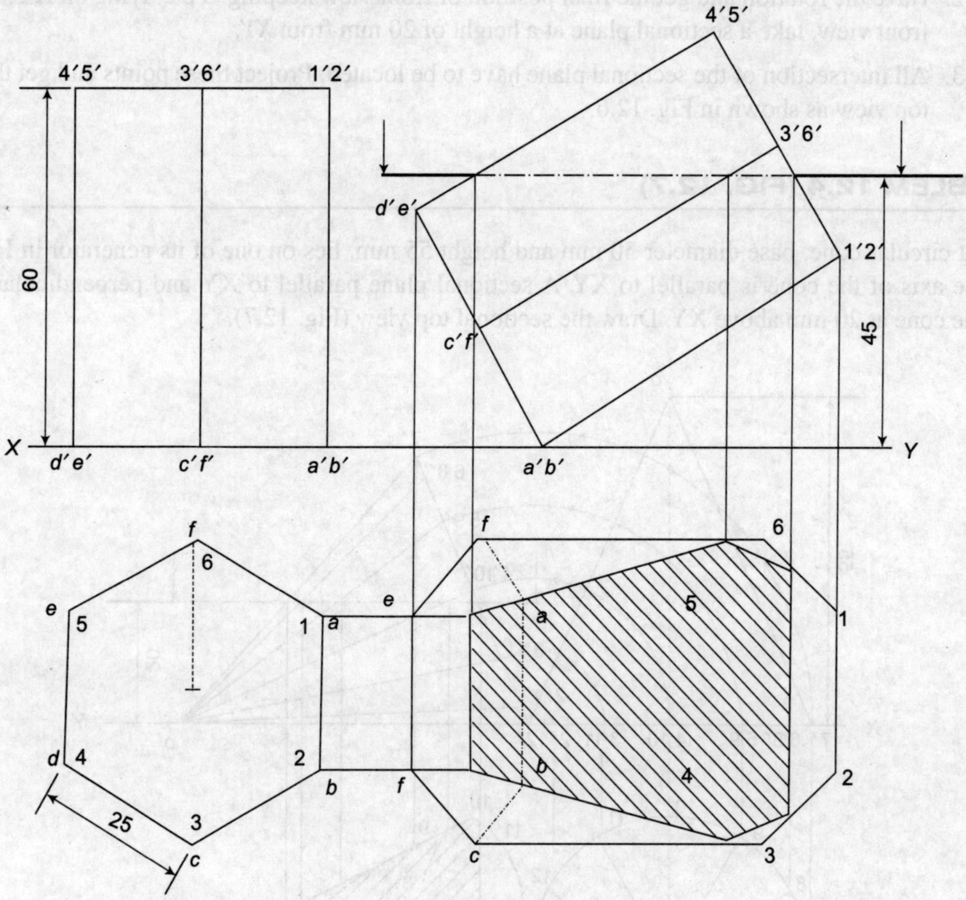

Fig. 12.8 Solution to Problem 12.5

12.5 SECTIONAL PLANE PERPENDICULAR TO VP AND INCLINED TO HP

PROBLEM 12.6 (FIG. 12.9)

A right circular cone of base 40 mm diameter and height 60 mm resting with its base on HP. It is cut by a sectional plane perpendicular to VP, inclined at 60° to HP and cuts the axis at 25 mm from the base. Draw the sectional top view, side view, and true shape (Fig. 12.9).

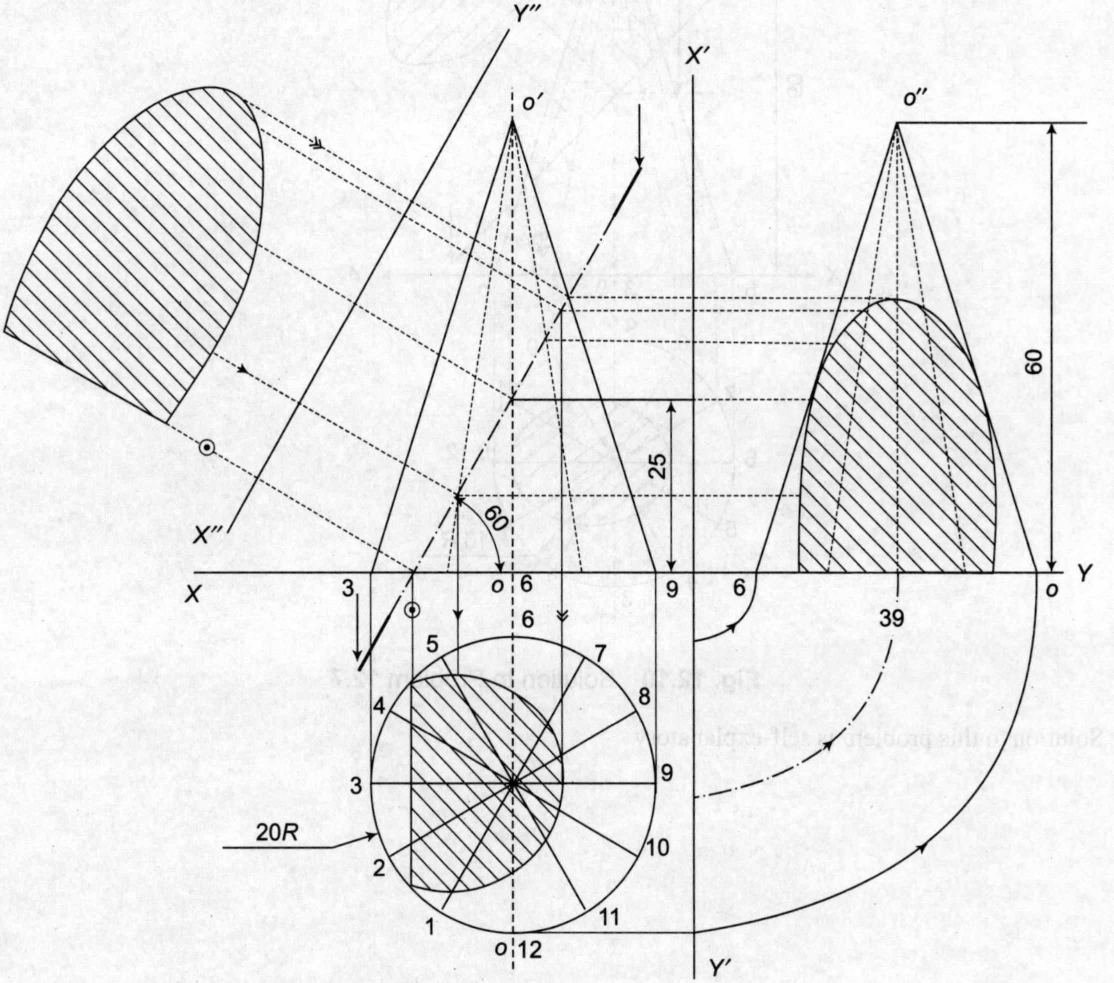

Fig. 12.9 Solution to Problem 12.6

PROBLEM 12.7 (FIG. 12.10)

A right circular cone of base 32 mm diameter and height 50 mm resting with its base on HP. It is cut by an auxiliary inclined plane (AIP) inclined at 45° to HP and cuts the axis at 25 mm from the top of the apex. Draw the sectional top view and true shape of the section (Fig. 12.10).

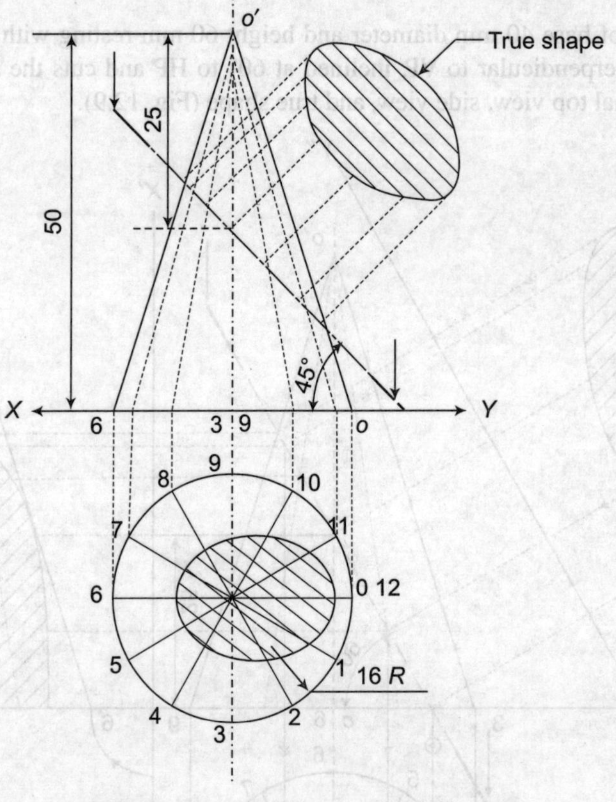

Fig. 12.10 Solution to Problem 12.7

Solution to this problem is self-explanatory.

PROBLEM 12.8 (FIG. 12.11)

A right circular cylinder of 40 mm diameter and 50 mm long is resting on one of its circular base on HP. It is cut by a sectional plane (AIP) inclined at 55° to HP and perpendicular to VP and the HT of the cutting plane is 6 mm from the end of the cylinder. Draw the sectional top view, side view, and true shape (Fig. 12.11).

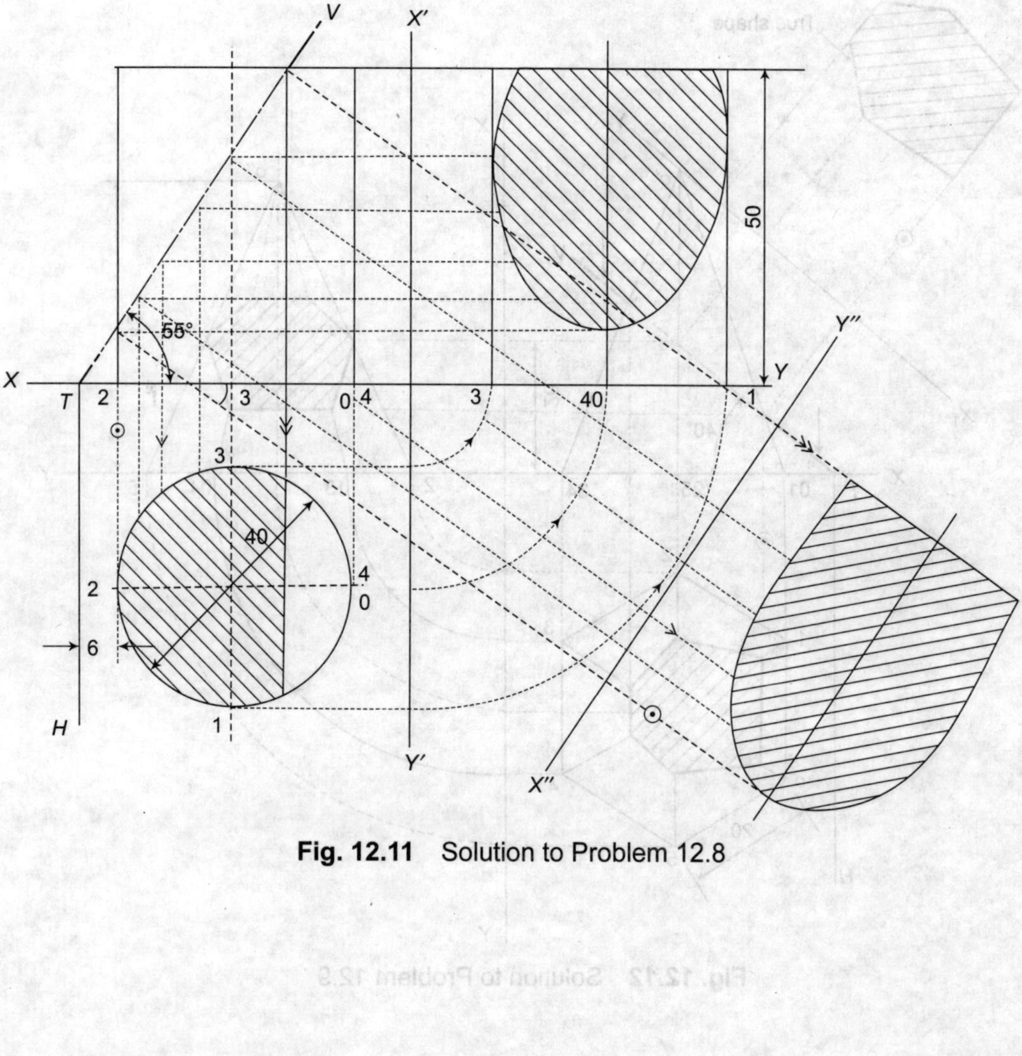

Fig. 12.11 Solution to Problem 12.8

PROBLEM 12.9 (FIG. 12.12)

A hexagonal pyramid, side of the base 20 mm and height 45 mm, rests with its base on HP and one of its base edge perpendicular to XY. It is cut by an AIP inclined at 40° to HP and passing through a point on the axis 20 mm above the base. Draw the sectional top view, true shape, and left side view (Fig. 12.12).

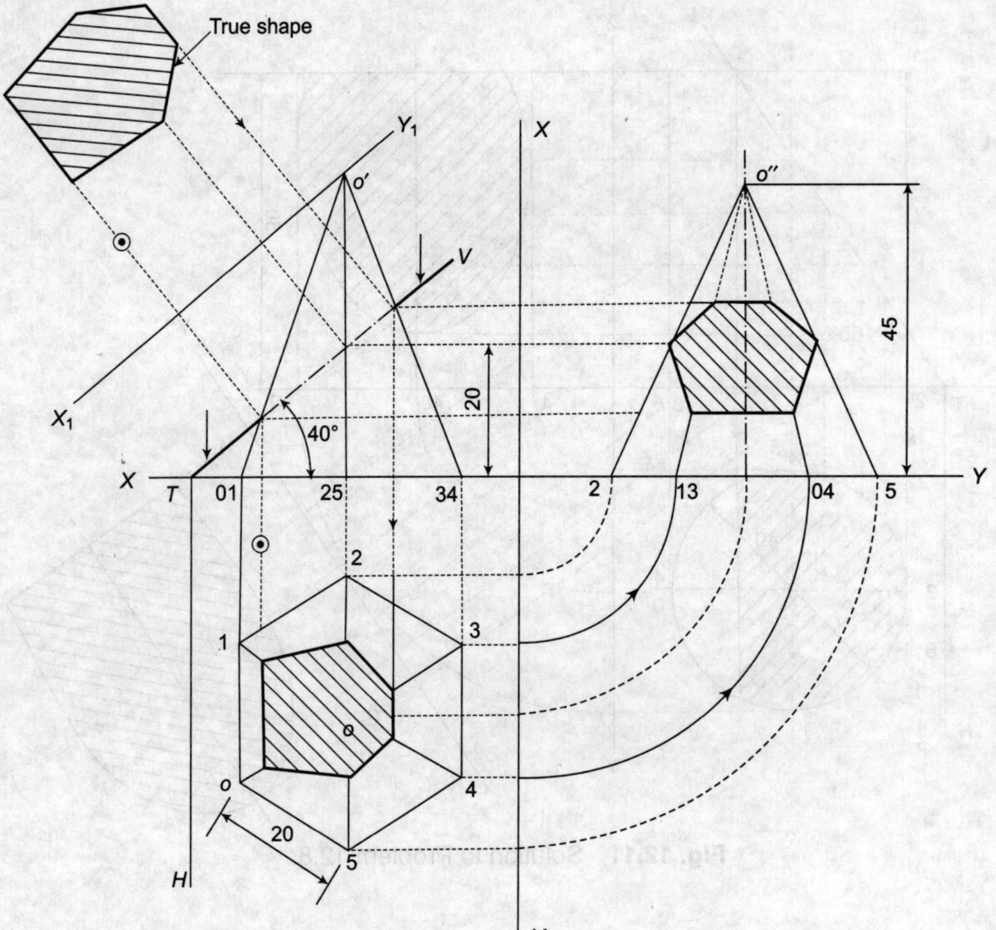

Fig. 12.12 Solution to Problem 12.9

PROBLEM 12.10 (FIG. 12.13)

A square pyramid of base edge 35 mm and height 50 mm rests on its base on HP with its two base edges equally inclined to VP. It is cut by an AIP inclined at 30° to XY, cutting the axis of pyramid at 20 mm from the base. Draw its front view, sectional top view, left side view, and the true shape (Fig. 12.13).

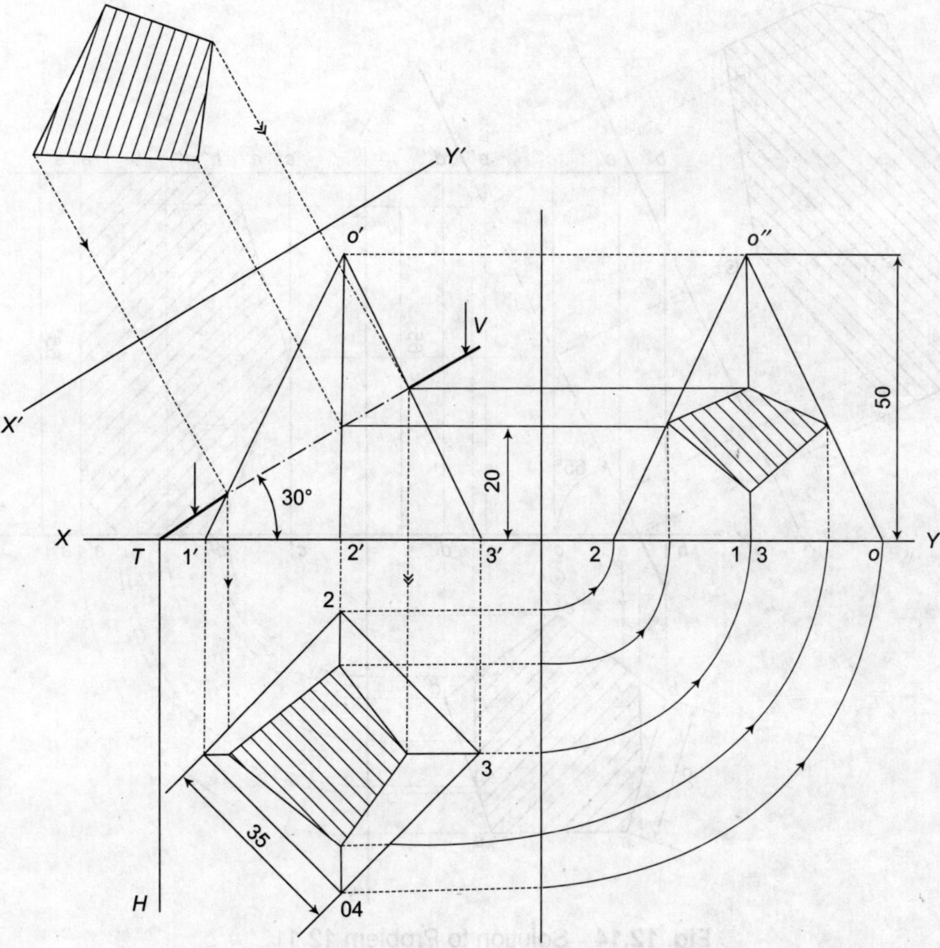

Fig. 12.13 Solution to Problem 12.10

PROBLEM 12.11 (FIG. 12.14)

A pentagonal prism, side of the base 25 mm and height 65 mm, rests with its base on HP and an edge of its base parallel to VP. It is cut by a sectional plane perpendicular to VP inclined at 65° to HP and passing through the middle point of the axis. Draw the sectional top view, true shape, and left side view of the section (Fig. 12.14).

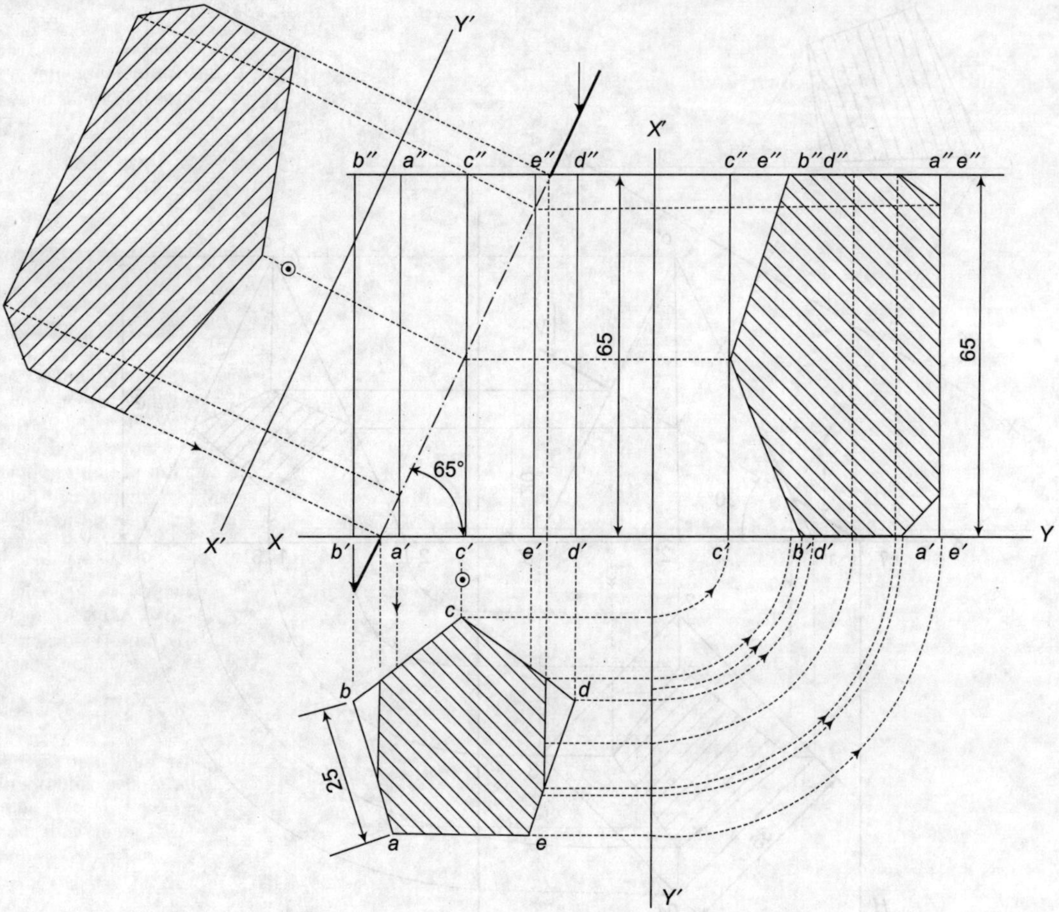

Fig. 12.14 Solution to Problem 12.11

PROBLEM 12.12 (FIG. 12.15)

A sphere of 50 mm diameter rests on HP. It is cut by an AIP perpendicular to VP and inclined 45° to HP towards the right side of the sphere. The HP of the plane is 15 mm from the end of the sphere. Draw the sectional top view and true shape of the section (Fig. 12.15).

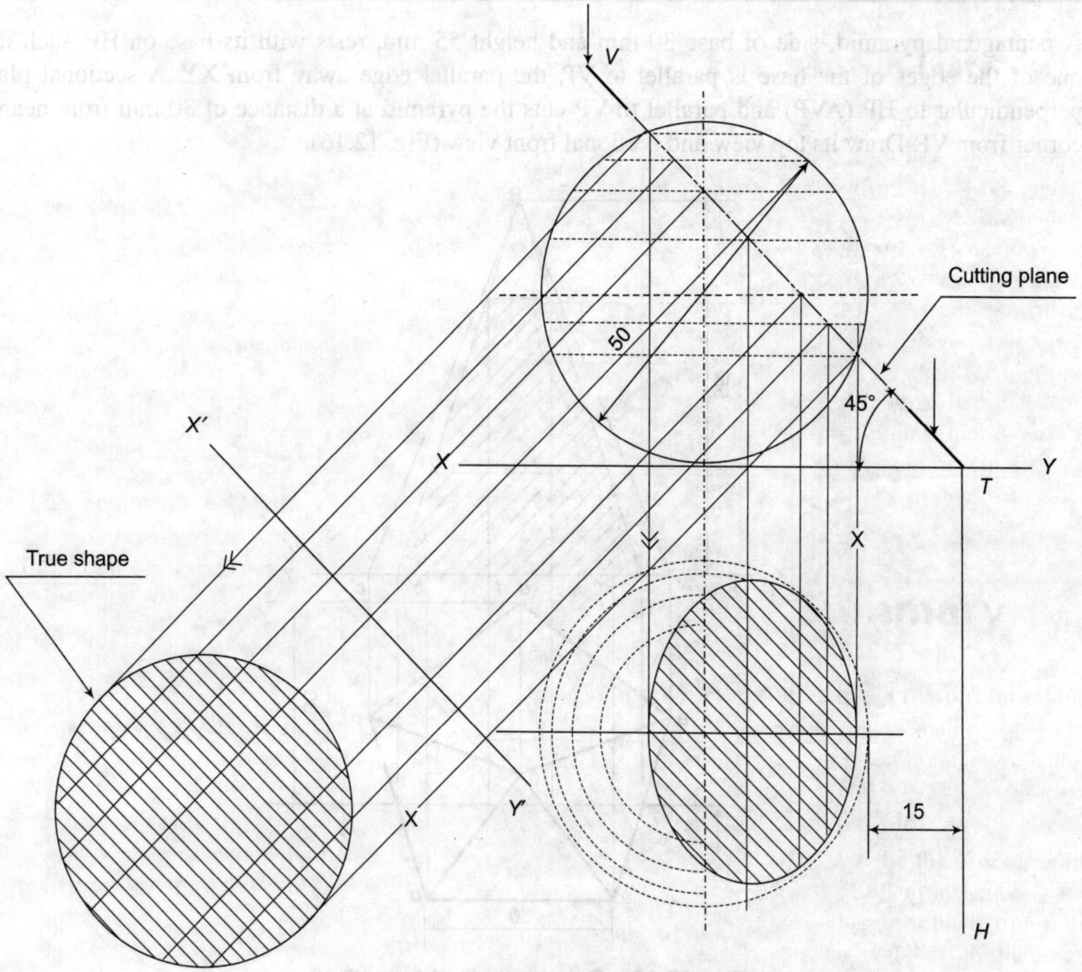

Fig. 12.15 Solution to Problem 12.12

12.6 SECTIONAL PLANE PARALLEL TO VP AND PERPENDICULAR TO HP

PROBLEM 12.13 (FIG. 12.16)

A pentagonal pyramid, side of base 30 mm and height 55 mm, rests with its base on HP, such that one of the edges of the base is parallel to VP, the parallel edge away from XY. A sectional plane perpendicular to HP (AVP) and parallel to VP cuts the pyramid at a distance of 30 mm from nearest corner from VP. Draw its top view and sectional front view (Fig. 12.16).

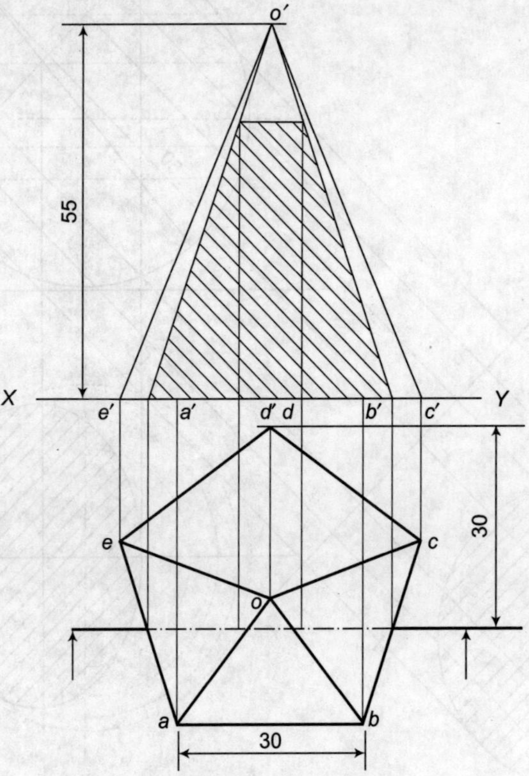

Fig. 12.16 Solution to Problem 12.13

PROBLEM 12.14 (FIG. 12.17)

A hexagonal prism, side of the base 30 mm and axis 60 mm, lies with one of its rectangular faces on HP and its axis is inclined at 45° to VP. A sectional plane perpendicular to HP (AVP) and parallel to VP cuts the prism. The cutting plane passes through a point P at the axis 38 mm from the end nearest to XY (Fig. 12.17).

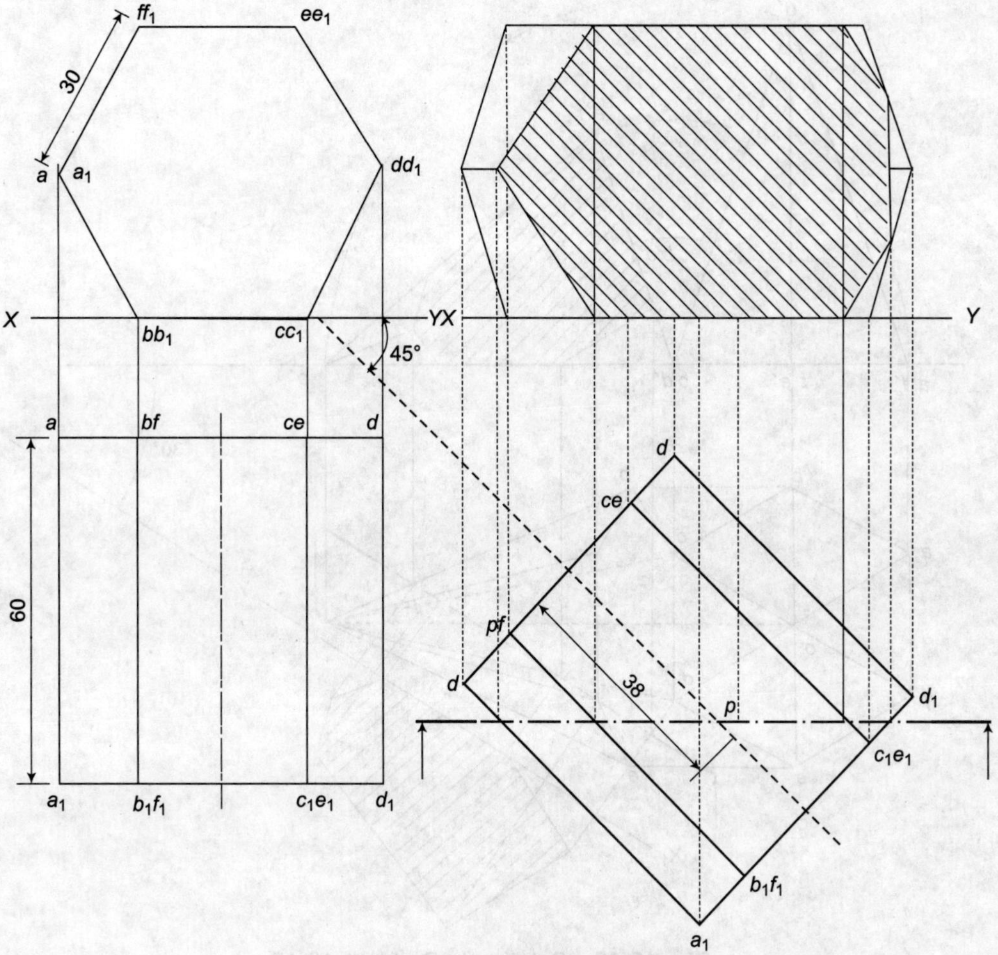

Fig. 12.17 Solution to Problem 12.14

Solution is self-explanatory.

PROBLEM 12.15 (FIG. 12.18)

A hexagonal pyramid, side of the base 25 mm and height 60 mm, is lying on HP with one of its triangular faces, and the axis is parallel to VP. It is cut by a plane inclined to VP by 30° and passing through the middle point of the axis. Draw its sectional front view and true shape of the section (Fig. 12.18).

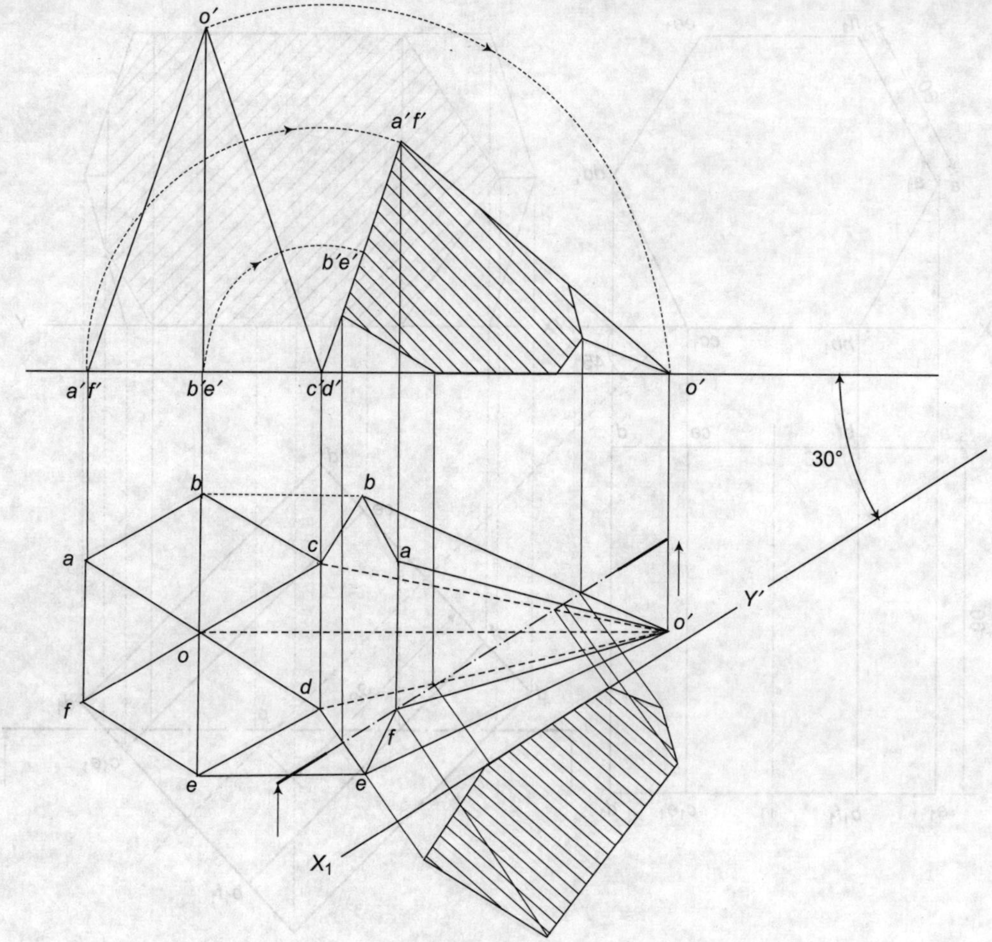

Fig. 12.18 Solution to Problem 12.15

PROBLEM 12.16 (FIG. 12.19)

A right circular cone of base 40 mm diameter and height 55 mm rests with its base on HP. It is cut by an AVP inclined at 40° to VP at a distance of 6 mm from its axis. Draw the sectional front view and the sectional right side view (Fig. 12.19).

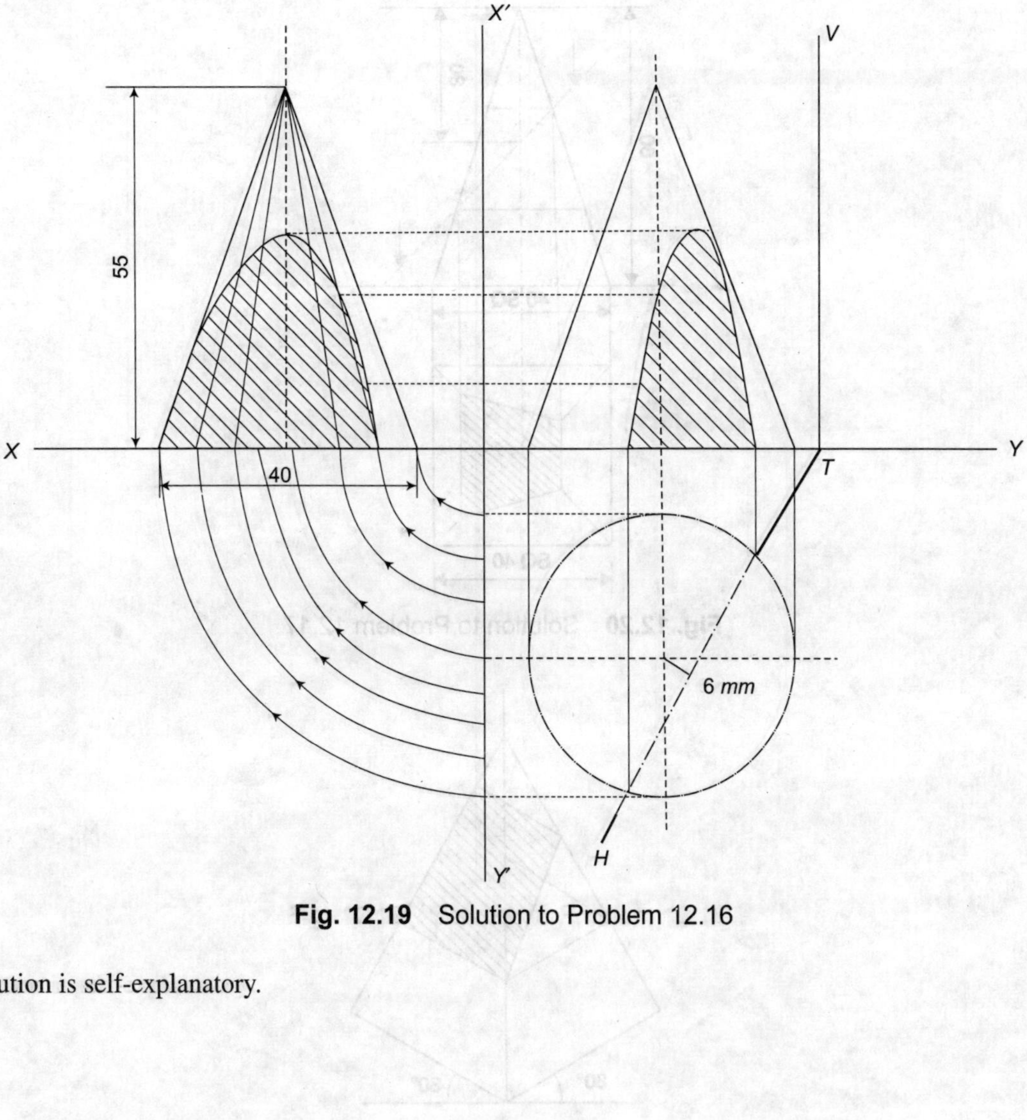

Fig. 12.19 Solution to Problem 12.16

Solution is self-explanatory.

PROBLEM 12.17 (FIG. 12.20)

A square pyramid of 40 mm base sides and 60 mm axis is cut by an inclined section plane (at 45° with respect to the base) through the midpoint of the axis. Draw isometric view of the section of the pyramid.

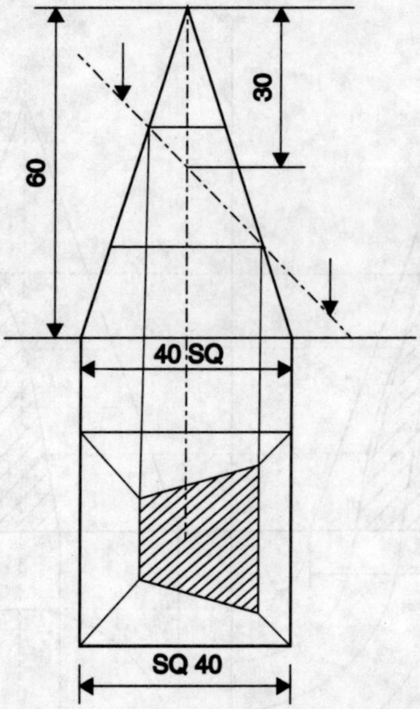

Fig. 12.20 Solution to Problem 12.17

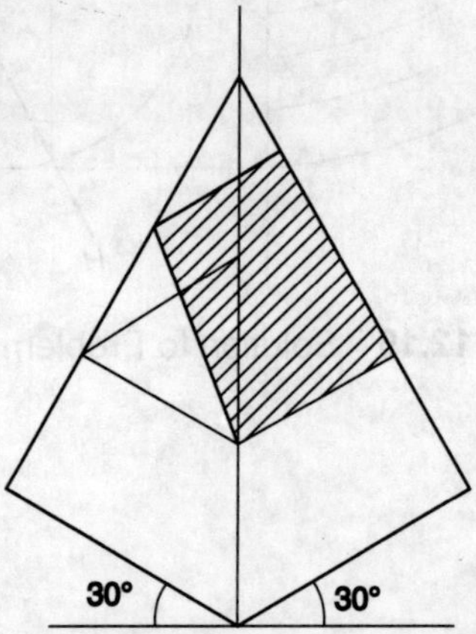

Fig. 12.21 Solution to problem isometric view of section

PROBLEM 12.18 (FIG. 12.22)

A tetrahedron of edges 45 mm long rests with one of the faces on HP and perpendicular to VP. An inclined sectional plane, at 30° to HP, cuts the tetrahedron at the middle point of the height. Draw the projection and true shape of the section.

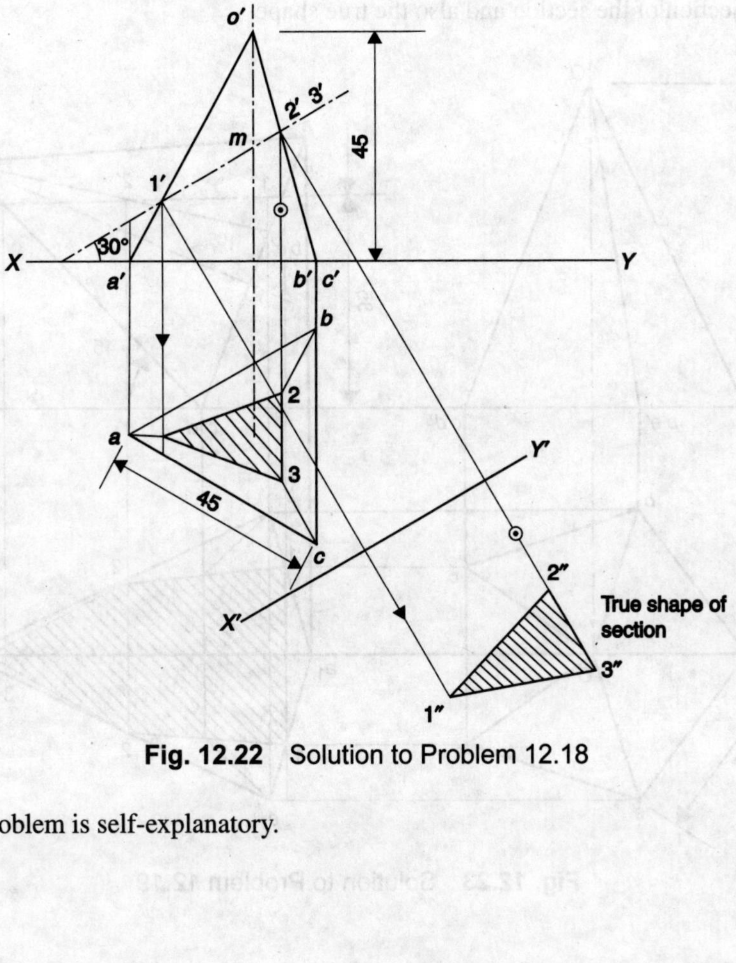

Fig. 12.22 Solution to Problem 12.18

Solution of the problem is self-explanatory.

PROBLEM 12.19 (FIG. 12.23)

A pentagonal pyramid of base edge 30 mm and height 55 mm lies on one of the base edges m HP and the triangular face makes an angle of 45° with HP. A sectional plane is parallel to HP and cuts the pyramid 35 mm above *XY* line.

Draw the projection of the section and also the true shape.

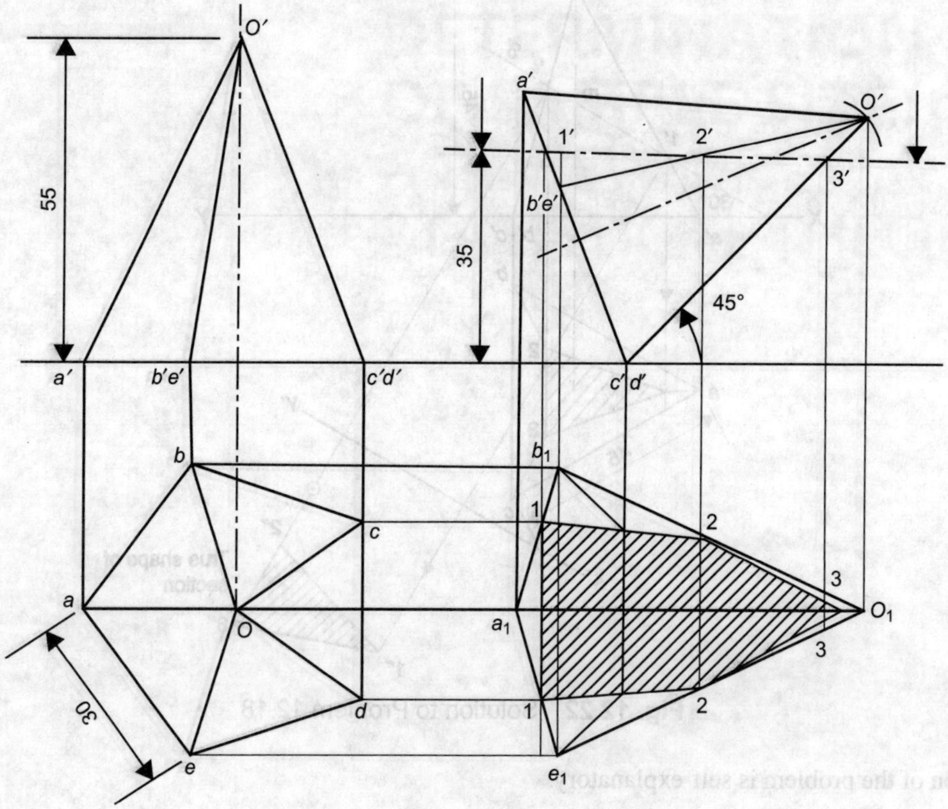

Fig. 12.23 Solution to Problem 12.19

Steps:

(1) Draw the projection of pyramid keeping *cd* base edge perpendicular to *XY*. The projection of a triangular face on VP is a line. This face makes an angle of 45° with *XY*.

(2) Draw the position of the sectional plane.

(3) The plane cuts the front view at 1′, 2′, 3′. The corresponding point in top view is as Fig. 12.23.

The sectional view on HP is also the true shape as sectional plane is parallel to HP.

PROBLEM 12.20 (FIG. 12.24)

A cone, 50 mm base diameter and 70 mm axis, is standing on its base on HP. It is cut by a sectional plane 45° inclined to HP through base end generator. Draw projection, sectional view, and true shape of section.

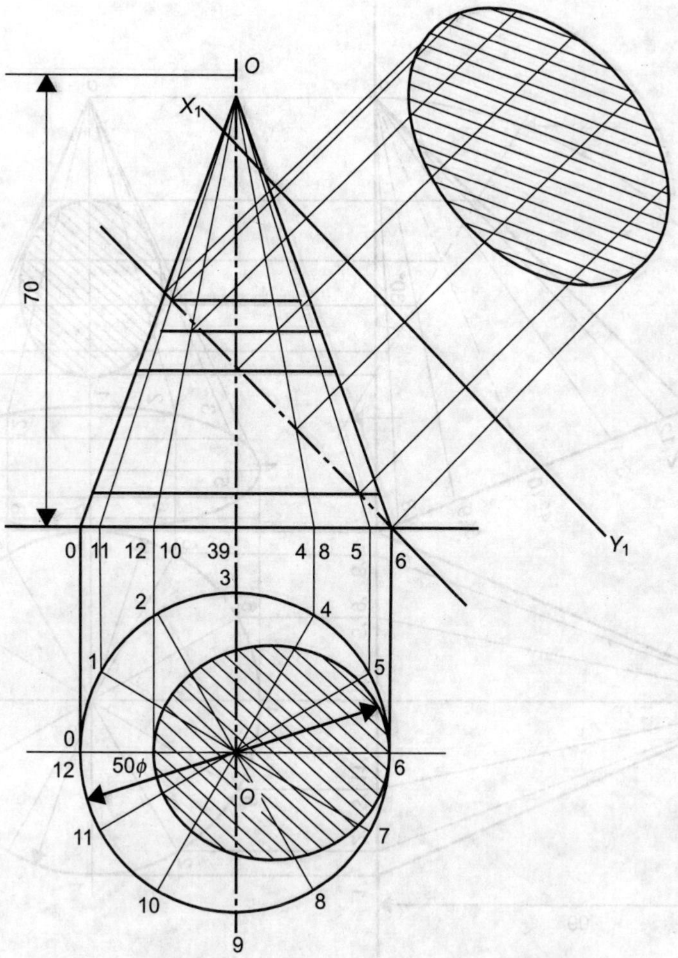

Fig. 12.24 Solution to Problem 12.20

Solution of this problem is self-explanatory.

PROBLEM 12.21 (FIG. 12.25)

A right circular cone, diameter of base circle 40 mm and height 60 mm, lies on one of the generators on HP, such that the axis is parallel to VP. A sectional plane inclined to 30° from HP meets the axis at a distance of 25 mm from the axis.

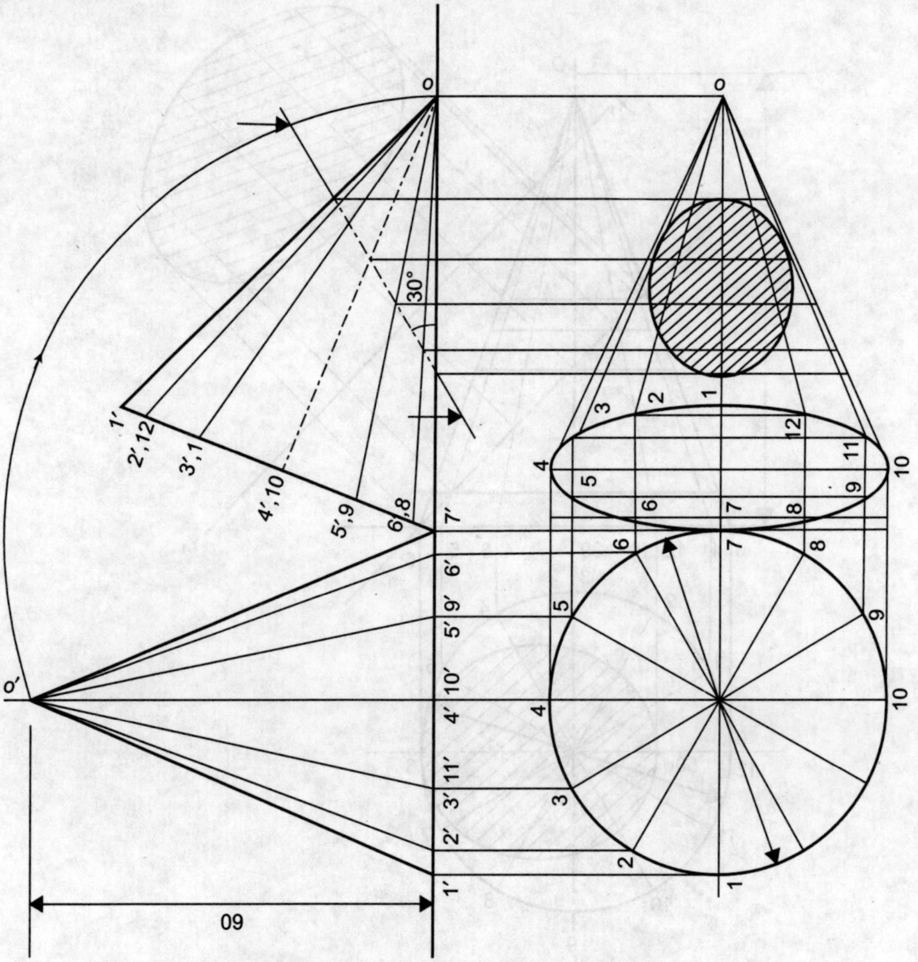

Fig. 12.25 Solution to Problem 12.21

Solution of this problem is self-explanatory.

PROBLEM 12.22 (FIG. 12.26)

A square prism of base edge 35 mm and height 60 mm has it base on HP and stands vertically. One of its vertical rectangular face makes an angle of 45° with VP. The prism is cut by a sectional plane at an angle of 45° on the axis 20 mm from top. Draw the sectional top view and the true shape. Draw the complete projection of the prism with sectional true shape.

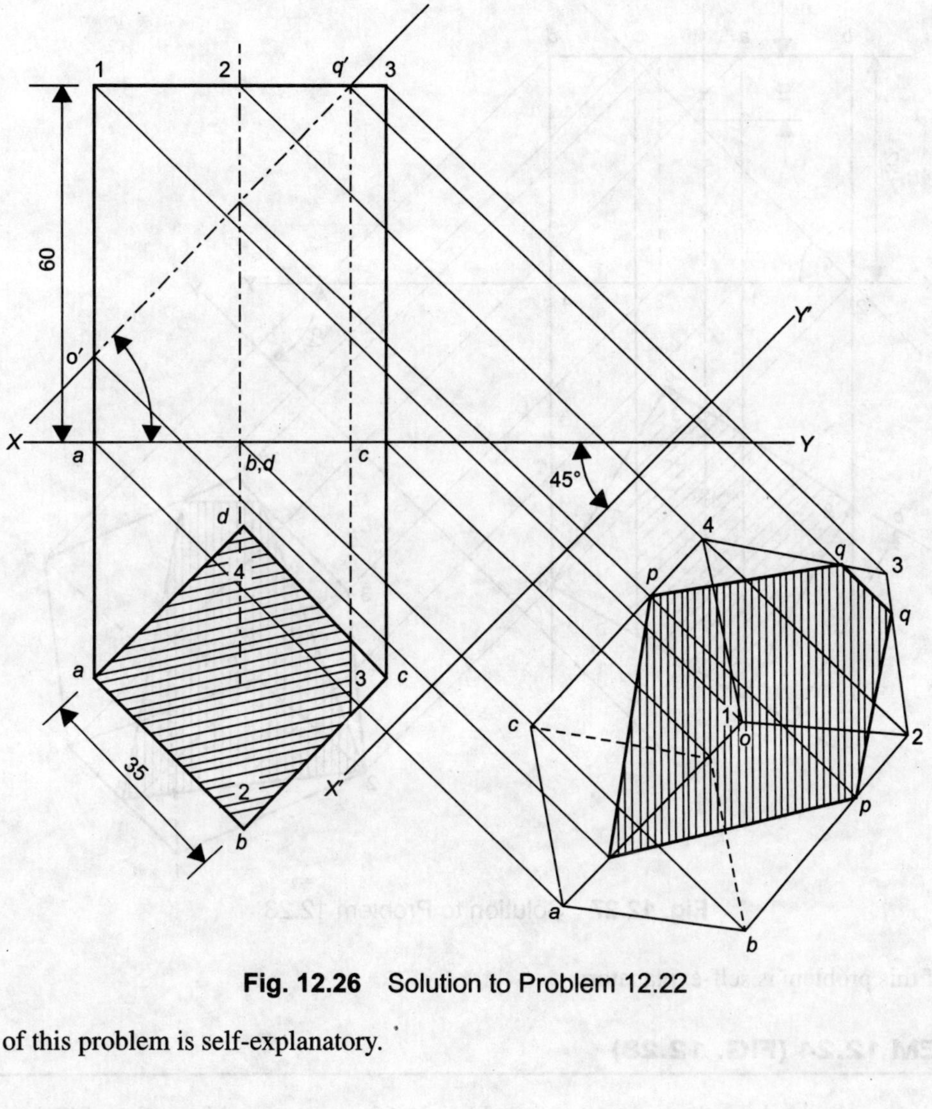

Fig. 12.26 Solution to Problem 12.22

Solution of this problem is self-explanatory.

PROBLEM 12.23 (FIG. 12.27)

A cube of edge 32 mm long rests on HP with one of the vertical face inclined at 30° to VP. It is cut by the sectional plane perpendicular to VP and inclined at 45° to HP and passing through a point 10 mm below the top of the axis. Draw the sectional top view and true shape of the section.

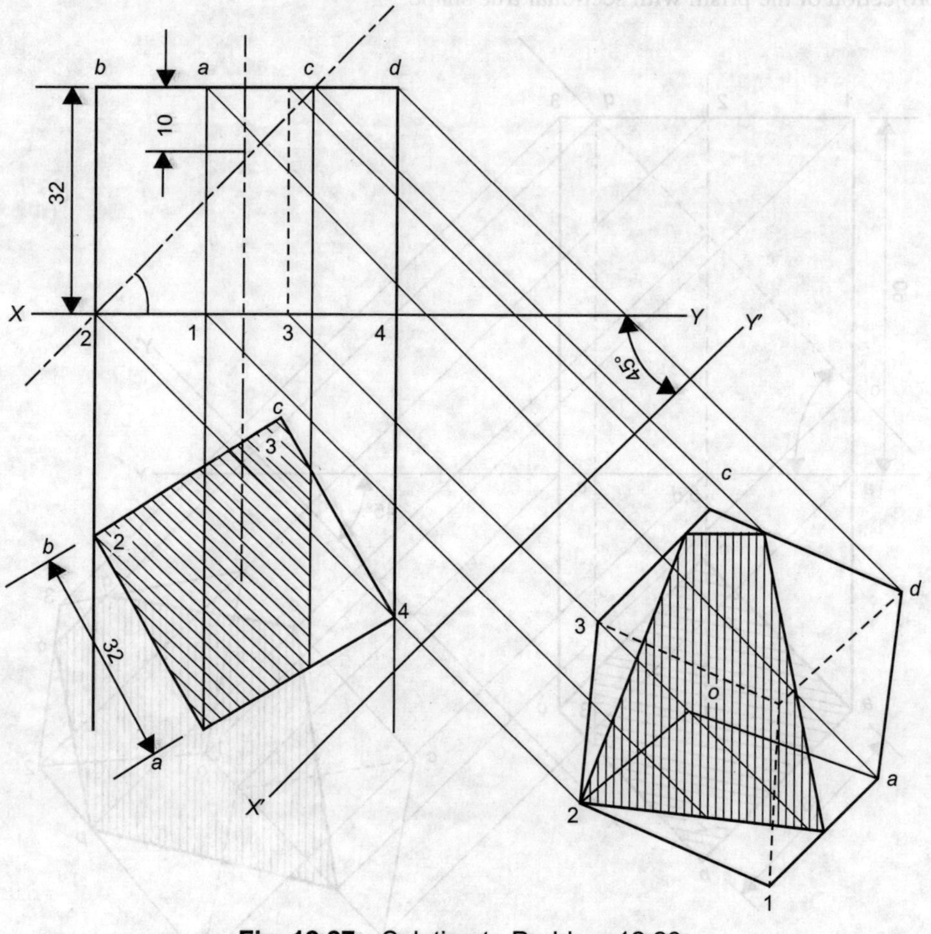

Fig. 12.27 Solution to Problem 12.23

Solution of this problem is self-explanatory.

PROBLEM 12.24 (FIG. 12.28)

A right circular cylinder, base diameter 40 mm and height 65 mm, rests with a point of its base circle on HP. Its axis is inclined at 45° with HP and is parallel to VP. A sectional plane, parallel to HP and 35 mm above HP, cuts the cylinder. Draw the sectional top view and the true shape of the section.

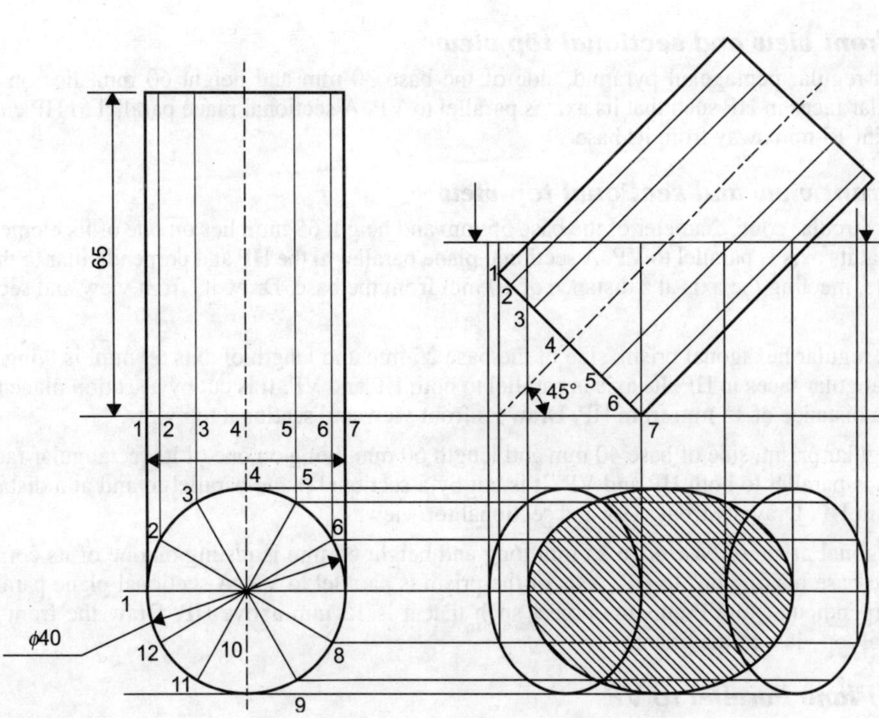

Fig. 12.28 Solution to Problem 12.24

Solution of this problem is self-explanatory.

EXERCISE

Review Questions

1. What is the difference between apparent and true shape of a section?
2. Differentiate between frustum of a solid and truncated solid?
3. Why are the sections taken?

Sectional Plane Parallel to HP

4. A pentagonal pyramid, edge of base 35 mm and height 55 mm, rests on its base on HP with one of its base edge perpendicular to VP. A sectional plane parallel to HP cuts the pyramid bisecting its axis. Draw its front view and sectional top view.
5. A right regular hexagonal pyramid, edge of the base 35 mm and height 55 mm, rests on its base on ground plane with one its base edges parallel to VP. A section plane parallel to HP cuts the pyramid bisecting its axis.

Draw its front view and sectional top view

6. A right regular pentagonal pyramid, side of the base 30 mm and height 60 mm, lies on one of its triangular faces in HP such that its axis is parallel to VP. A sectional plane parallel to HP cuts the axis at a point 15 mm away from its base.

Draw its front view and sectional top view

7. A right circular cone, diameter of the base 55 mm and height 65 mm, lies on one of its elements in HP, such that its axis is parallel to VP. A sectional plane parallel to the HP and perpendicular to the VP cuts the cone, meeting the axis at a distance of 10 mm from the base. Draw its front view and sectional top view.
8. A right regular hexagonal prism, side of the base 25 mm and length of axis 60 mm, is lying on one of its rectangular faces in HP. Its axis is parallel to both HP and VP. It is cut by a section plane parallel to and at a distance of 15 mm from HP. Draw its front view and sectional top view.
9. A triangular prism, side of base 40 mm and length 60 mm, lying on one of its rectangular faces in HP. Its axis is parallel to both HP and VP. It is cut by a sectional plane parallel to and at a distance of 25 mm from HP. Draw its front view and sectional top view.
10. A hexagonal prism of base edge 25 mm long and height 65 mm is resting on one of its corner on HP with the base making 60° to HP. Axis of the prism is parallel to VP. A sectional plane parallel to HP and perpendicular to VP cuts the object such that it is 15 mm above HP. Draw the front view and sectional top view of the prism.

Sectional Plane Parallel to VP

11. A pentagonal pyramid, edge of base 30 mm and height 60 mm, rests on its base on HP, such that one of its base edges is perpendicular to the VP. A sectional plane parallel to VP cuts the pyramid at a distance of 15 mm from the axis.

Draw its top view and sectional front view.

12. A cube 40 mm long is resting on HP on one of its faces with a vertical face inclined at 30° to VP. It is cut by a sectional plane parallel to VP and 15 mm away from the axis and further away from VP.
13. A pentagonal pyramid of base edge 35 mm and height 65 mm rests on HP on one of its corners. Its base is inclined at 45° to HP and the axis is parallel to VP.

A sectional plane parallel to the VP cuts the pyramid at a distance of 10 mm from its axis. Draw the top view and sectional front view.

14. A right circular cylinder of base diameter 40 mm and height 65 mm lying on HP with one of its generator such that its axis is inclined at 30° to VP. A sectional plane parallel to VP cuts the cylinder at a distance of 10 mm from its end face joining the axis. Draw its sectional front view and top view.
15. A right circular cone of base diameter 50 mm and height 65 mm lies on one of its generator in HP with its axis parallel to VP. A sectional plane perpendicular to HP and parallel to VP cuts the cone and is 10 mm away from its axis. Draw the top view and sectional front view.
16. A hexagonal prism of base 30 mm and height 65 mm lies on one of its rectangular faces on HP and its axis inclined at 45° to VP. A sectional plane parallel to VP cuts the prism bisecting the axis. Draw top view and sectional front view.

Sectional Plane Inclined to HP and Perpendicular to VP

17. A square pyramid of base side 35 mm and height 65 mm is resting on HP with one side of base inclined at 30° to VP. It is cut by a plane inclined at 45° to HP and perpendicular to VP and passes through the axis at a distance 25 mm from the apex. Draw its front view sectional top view and the true shape of the section.

18. A pentagonal pyramid of base 40 mm side and axis 70 mm rests on HP on its base with one of its side parallel to VP. It is cut by a plane inclined at 35° to HP and perpendicular to VP and bisects the axis. Draw its front view, sectional top view, and the true shape of the section.

19. A hexagonal prism of base side 30 mm and height 65 mm is resting on HP on one of its vertical faces perpendicular to VP. It is cut by a plane inclined at 45° to HP and perpendicular to VP and passing through a point 10 mm from the top of the axis. Draw its front view, sectional top view, and true shape of the section.

20. A right circular cylinder of diameter 40 mm and height 65 mm is resting on one of its bases on HP. It is cut by a sectional plane inclined at 60° with HP and perpendicular to VP. The sectional plane is passing through a point on the axis 15 mm from its top end. Draw its sectional top view and the true shape of the section.

21. A right circular cone, diameter of the base 45 mm and height 65 mm, is resting on its base on HP. A sectional plane cuts the cone bisecting its axis. It is perpendicular to VP and inclined to HP at 30° and cuts the cone bisecting its axis. Draw its front view, sectional top view, and true shape.

Sectional Plane Inclined to VP and Perpendicular to HP

22. A right regular hexagonal pyramid of base edge 30 mm and height 60 mm lies on one of its slant edges on HP with its axis parallel to VP. A sectional plane is perpendicular to HP and inclined to VP at 30° and it cuts the pyramid bisecting its axis. Draw its top view, sectional front view, and true shape of the section.

23. A hexagonal pyramid of base edge 25 mm and height 65 mm rests on its base on HP with one of its base edges parallel to VP. A sectional plane perpendicular to HP and inclined at 30° to VP, cuts the pyramid at 10 mm away from the axis. Draw its top view, sectional front view, and the true shape of the section.

24. A pentagonal pyramid of base edge 30 mm and height 60 mm lies on one of its triangular faces on HP with its axis parallel to VP. A sectional plane perpendicular to HP and inclined to VP at 30° cuts the pyramid bisecting its axis. Draw its top view, sectional front view and the true shape.

25. A pentagonal prism, side of base 30 mm and height 65 mm, is resting on one of its base edges on HP, such that one of its base corner lies on HP and its axis is inclined at 45° to HP and parallel to VP. A sectional plane perpendicular to HP and inclined at 45° to VP cuts the prism bisecting the axis. Draw its top view, the sectional front view, and also the true shape.

26. A right circular cone, 45 mm diameter and height 65 mm, is resting on its base on HP. It is cut by a plane which is perpendicular to HP and inclined at 45° to VP and it is passing 15 mm from the top view of the axis. Draw the sectional front view and true shape of the section.

27. A sphere of 50 mm diameter is cut by a sectional plane inclined at 60° to VP and perpendicular to HP. The sectional plane passes through the sphere at a distance of 10 mm from the centre of the sphere and in front of it. Draw the sectional front view and true shape of the section.

Objective Questions

1. The sectional views are used to see the _____ details of the object.
2. The section lines/hatching lines are usually drawn at 45° to horizontal. (True/False)
3. When a section plane is parallel to the HP, the true shape of the section is viewed in the ______.
4. The projection obtained on a VP of a cut solid is called sectional ______.
5. The true shape of a section of a cone cut by an inclined plane parallel to generator is ______.
6. The true shape of the section of a cone cut by a plane inclined to the axis is ______.
7. Sectional plane is represented by its ______ HP or VP.
8. The true shape of the section of a right circular cone when it is cut by a plane parallel to its axis and the base is ______________.
9. To obtain a sectional view of a solid, the part of the object between the sectional plane and ______ is assumed to be removed.
10. The true shape of the section obtained by cutting a cone parallel to one of its generator is ______________.
11. The true shape of a section will be seen in the front view of an object when the sectional plane is ______ to the VP.
12. Section lines/hatching lines are inclined at ______ angle to ______ line.
13. If the sectional surface is viewed in a direction other than normal, the shape of the sectional surface is ______ of the object.
14. If a right circular cylinder is cut by a plane parallel to the axis of the cylinder, the section obtained is ______.
15. The shape of the section of a cone when it is cut by a vertical plane, parallel to VP and passing through the apex of cone standing on the HP on its base, will be ______.
16. The true shape of a section is obtained by viewing the section in a direction ______ to the cutting plane.
17. A right circular cone standing on HP is cut by a vertical plane away from the axis and parallel to the axis. The sectional plane is ______.

Answers

Objective Questions

1. interior	2. True	3. top view
4. front view	5. parabola	6. ellipse
7. traces	8. hyperbola	9. observer
10. parabola	11. parallel	12. 45°, horizontal
13. apparent section	14. a rectangle	15. a triangle
16. normal	17. hyperbola	

13

CHAPTER

Development of Solid Surfaces

13.1 INTRODUCTION

The outer surface of a solid made up of a metal sheet can be unfolded and spread over a plane surface, which will result into a particular shape as shown in Fig. 13.1. The shape of spread sheet surface is called development of the surface of the object.

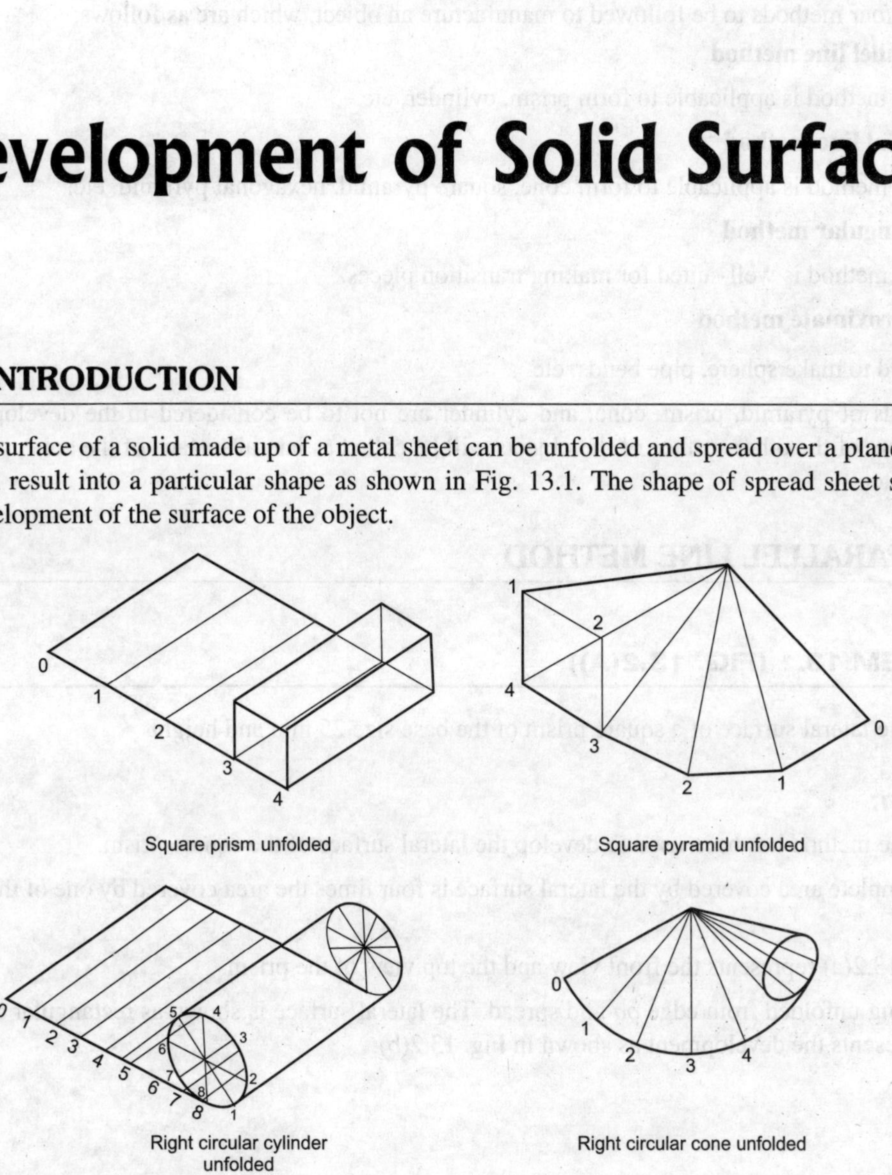

Fig. 13.1 Development of surfaces of solid

To obtain a development, an object is unfolded and spread over the plane surface.

The development of the surface will be the true shape of the object. Any line and contour on the surface will represent the true shape. The development of an object represents the correct and true surface area to manufacture an object.

Development plays an important role especially for persons engaged in sheet metal industries. It enables working engineers to cut the metal plates exactly in size to form desired products such as mug, funnel, hopper, transition pieces, bucket, ducts, etc.

There are four methods to be followed to manufacture an object, which are as follows:

1. **Parallel line method**

   This method is applicable to form prism, cylinder, etc.

2. **Radial line method**

   This method is applicable to form cone, square pyramid, hexagonal pyramid, etc.

3. **Triangular method**

   This method is well-suited for making transition pieces.

4. **Approximate method**

It is used to make sphere, pipe bends, etc.

The ends of pyramid, prism, cone, and cylinder are not to be considered in the development, so development of the other surface of the objects will be called as lateral surface of the cone, prism, and pyramid, etc.

13.2 PARALLEL LINE METHOD

PROBLEM 13.1 (FIG. 13.2(A))

Develop the lateral surface of a square prism of the base size 25 mm and height

Solution:

Parallel line method has been used to develop the lateral surface of the square prism.

The complete area covered by the lateral surface is four times the area covered by one of the vertical faces.

Figure 13.2(a) represents the front view and the top view of the prism.

It is being unfolded from edge *oa* and spread. The lateral surface is shown as rectangular area *oaa*4 and it represents the development as shown in Fig. 13.2(b).

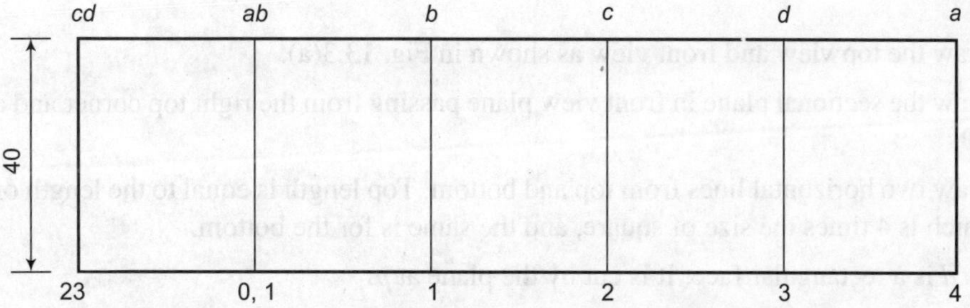

Fig. 13.2 (b) Solution to Problem 13.1

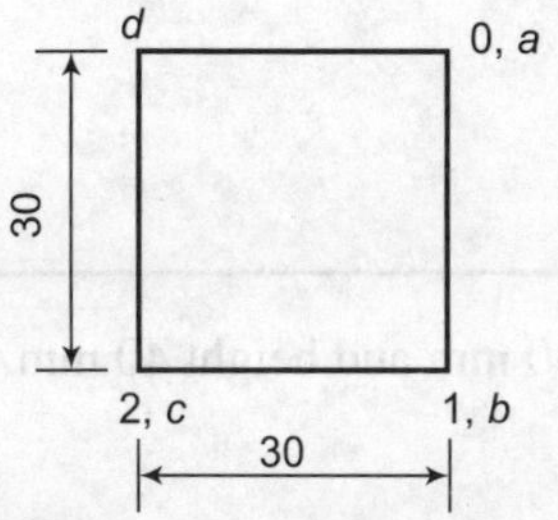

Fig. 13.2 (a) Orthographic Projection

PROBLEM 13.2 (FIG. 13.3)

The projection of a square prism is given in Fig. 13.3(a). It is cut by an AIP at 45° to HP and it passes from the right top corner. It removes the upper portion of the problem as shown in Fig. 13.3(a).

Draw the development of the lateral surface of the cut prism.

Solution:

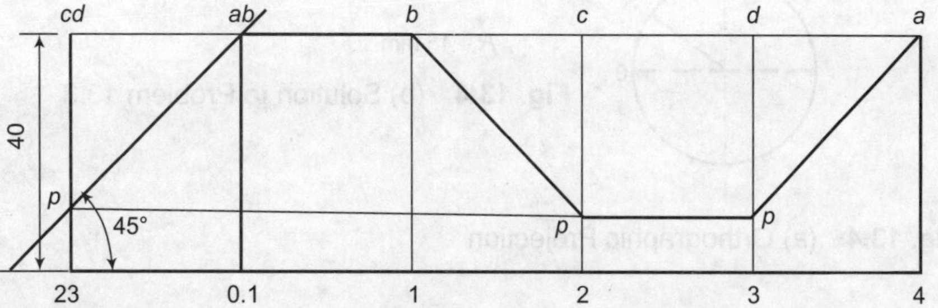

Fig. 13.3 (b) Solution to Problem 13.2

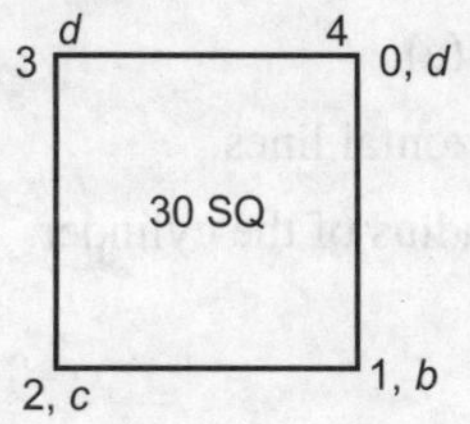

Fig. 13.3 (a) Projection

Steps:

1. Draw the top view and front view as shown in Fig. 13.3(a).
2. Draw the sectional plane in front view plane passing from the right top corner and at 45° from HP.
3. Draw two horizontal lines from top and bottom. Top length is equal to the length of perimeter which is 4 times the size of square, and the same is for the bottom.
4. 23*cd* is a rectangular face. It is cut by the plane at *p*.
5. Draw horizontal line from *p* which cuts 2*c* and 3*d*.
6. *aa*41 is the required development.

PROBLEM 13.3 (FIG. 13.4)

Draw the development of lateral surface of a cylinder of diameter 30 mm and height 40 mm.

Solution:

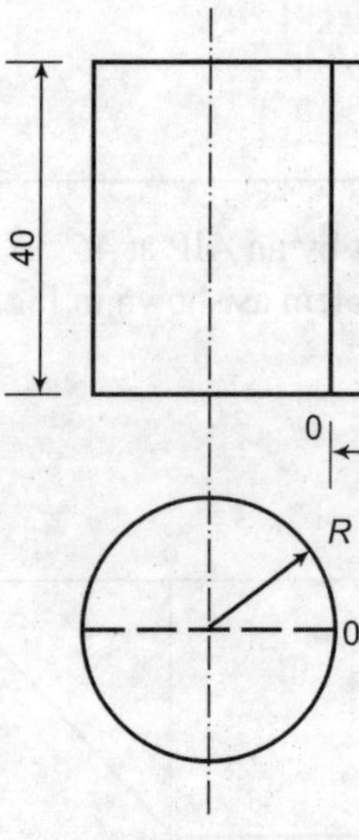

Fig. 13.4 (a) Orthographic Projection

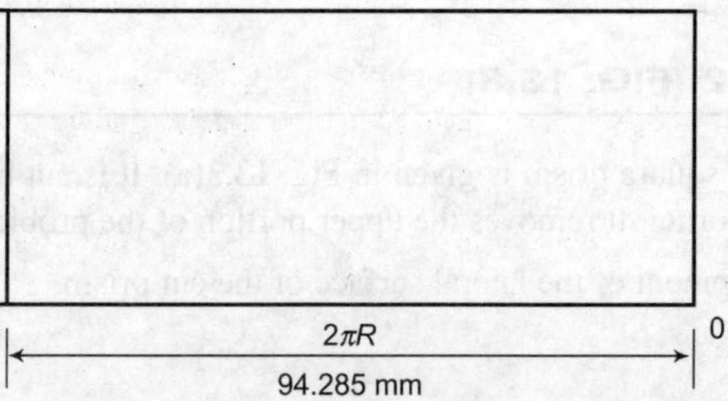

Fig. 13.4 (b) Solution to Problem 13.3

Steps:

1. Draw the top view and front view as shown in Fig. 13.4(a).
2. From the top and bottom of the cylinder, draw two horizontal lines.

   The length of the line is given by $2\pi R$, where R is the radius of the cylinder.

3. Length of the metal sheet required to make cylinder.

$$= \text{length of circumference}$$

$$= 2\pi R = 2 \times \frac{22}{7} \times 15$$

$$= 94.285 \text{ mm}$$

4. Width of the rectangular sheet is equal to the height of the cylinder (40 mm).
5. Draw the rectangle with these two lines and equal to 94.285 mm.
6. This is the required development of Fig. 13.4(b).

PROBLEM 13.4 (FIG. 13.5)

The projections of a right circular cylinder are given as shown in Fig. 13.5(a). It is cut by an AIP at an angle of 45° from HP and it passes from the middle of axis.

Draw the development of lateral surface of the cylinder. Taking diameter of cylinder 30 mm and height 40 mm.

Solution:

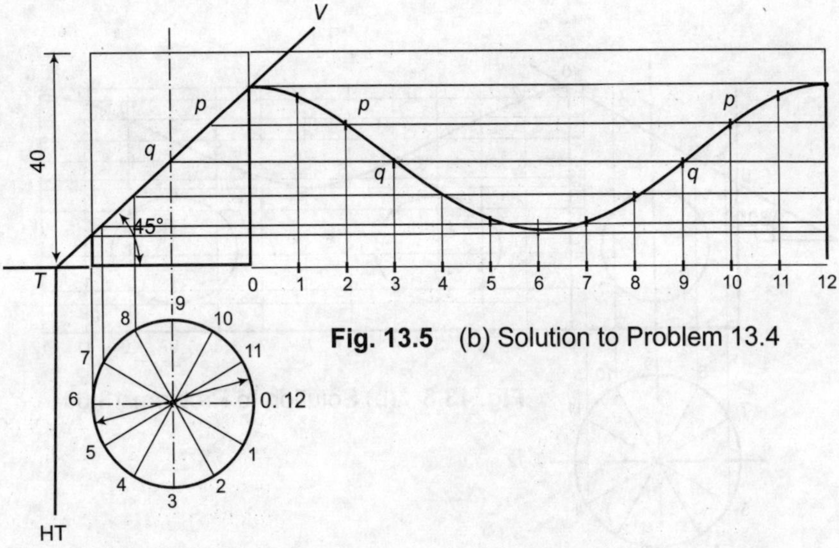

Fig. 13.5 (b) Solution to Problem 13.4

Fig. 13.5 (a) Projection

Steps:

1. Draw the top view and front view of a cylinder of diameter 30 mm and height 40 mm.
2. Draw an AIP angled at 45° to HP and passing from the middle point of the axis as shown in Fig. 13.5(a).

3. The cylinder is unfolded from generation at 0.
4. Draw two horizontal lines from the top and bottom of the cylinder.
5. Divide the circle into 12 equal parts. Also, divide the horizontal line drawn at the bottom into 12 equal parts.
6. Let p be the point which lies on generator 2 and 10. p is projected horizontally, which cuts the generator 2 and 10 on spreadsheet.
7. Similarly, 'q' which lies on sectional plane, cuts the generation 3 and 9. Draw horizontal lines form q.
8. Figure 13.5(b) represents the required development.

PROBLEM 13.5 (FIG. 13.6)

The projections of a right circular cylinder of diameter 30 mm and height 45 mm are shown in Fig. 13.6(a). It is cut by an AIP at an angle of 30° from HP and the plane cuts the cylinder at the top right corner of the cylinder. A circular hole in punched on the front surface of the cylinder through and through. In the front view, the hole looks like a circle.

Draw the development of the lateral surface.

Solution:

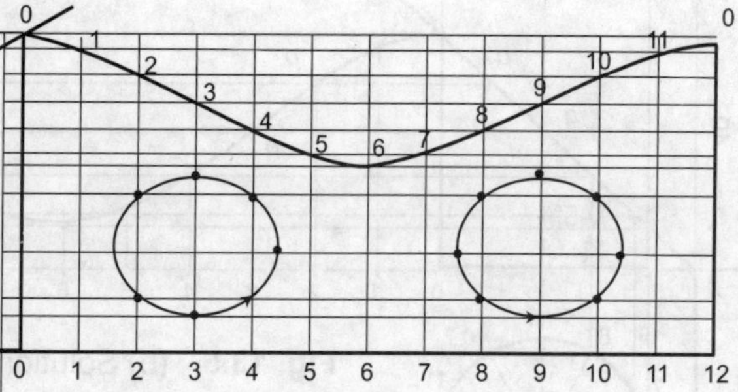

Fig. 13.6 (b) Solution to Problem 13.5

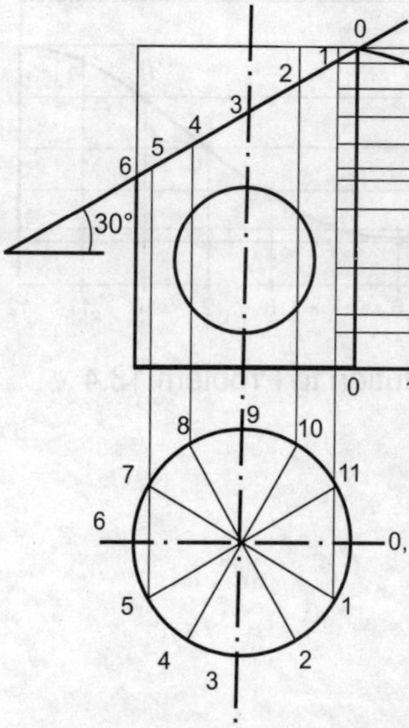

Fig. 13.6 (a) Projection

Steps:

1. Draw top view and front view as shown in Fig. 13.6(a).
2. Divide the top view into 2 equal parts.
3. Draw projections from 0, 1, 2, …, etc.
4. Mark these points on cutting plane as 0, 1, 2, …, etc.
5. Project horizontal lines from these points.
6. Take a line 0, 0 on the base line equal to the length of circumference of the base circle and divide this also into 12 equal parts as shown.
7. From all these points, draw vertical lines that will meet at 1, 2, 3, …, etc.
8. Mark these points and join them by a smooth curve. The holes position may be similarly obtained.
9. The required development is shown in Fig. 13.6(b).

PROBLEM 13.6 (FIG. 13.7)

The front view and top view of a cylinder of diameter 35 mm and height 45 mm are given. It is cut by an AIP as shown in Fig. 13.7(a). One plane cuts it, making an angle of 45° from the axis, and the other cuts it at an angle of 30° at the middle of the cylinder.

Solution:

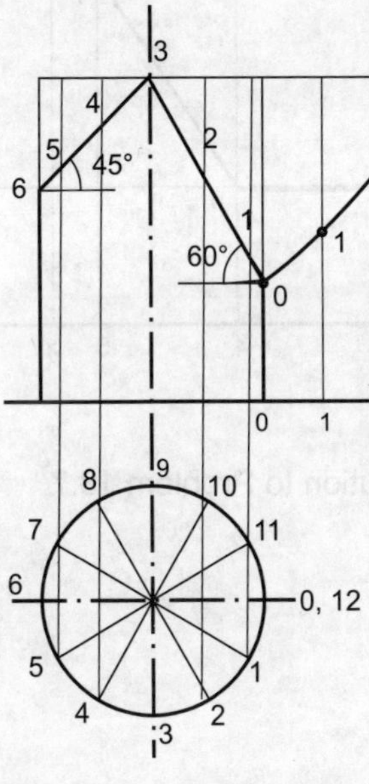

Fig. 13.7 (a) Projection

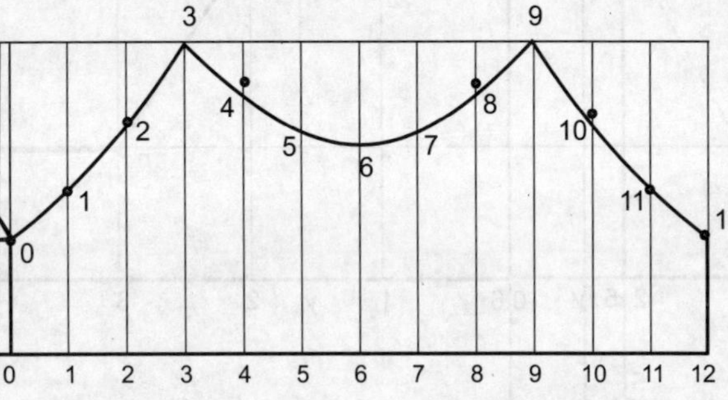

Fig. 13.7 (b) Solution to Problem 13.6

Steps:

1. Draw front view and top view as shown in Fig. 13.7(a).
2. Two cutting planes have been drawn; one makes an angle of 45° from horizontal and passing at top at the centre, and the other makes an angle of 60° from horizontal and passing at the top at the centre.
3. Divide the circle into 12 equal parts.
4. Follow the procedure as explained in Problem 13.5.

PROBLEM 13.7 (FIG. 13.8)

A hexagonal prism, with edge of the base 20 mm and height 60 mm, rests with the base on HP such that one of its rectangular faces is kept perpendicular to XY. It is cut by a sectional plane (AIP) inclined at 60° to HP and cuts the axis at 10 mm from the top. Draw the development of the lateral surface.

Solution:

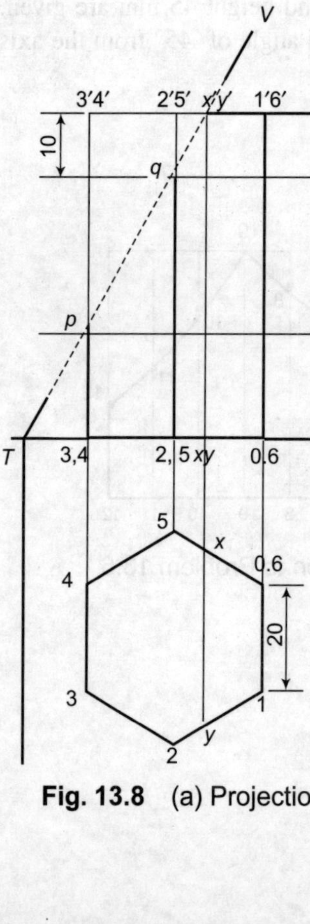

Fig. 13.8 (a) Projection

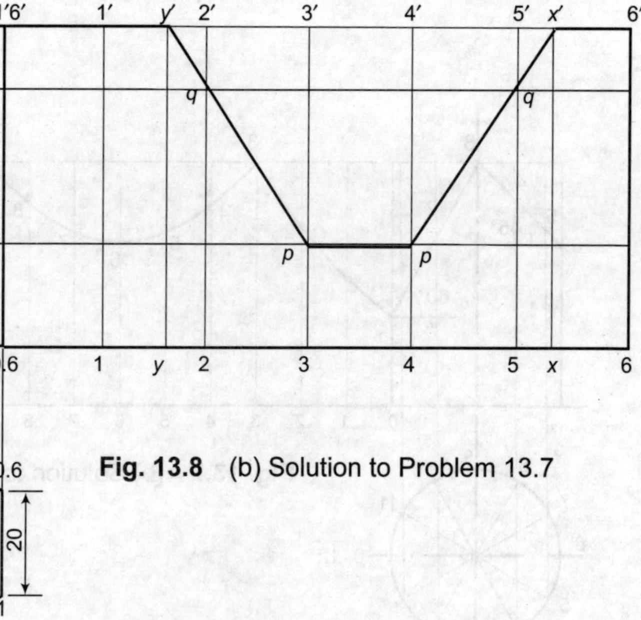

Fig. 13.8 (b) Solution to Problem 13.7

Steps:

1. Draw front view and top view of prism as shown in Fig. 13.8(a).
2. From top and bottom of the prism, draw two horizontal lines of lengths equal to the perimeter of the prism (6 × 20 = 120 mm).
3. Divide these lines into 6 equal parts and six equal rectangles as shown in Fig. 13.8(b). This represents the lateral surface.
4. From section at *q*, draw a horizontal which cuts the vertical edges 22′ and 5 at *q* on lateral surface.

Similarly, draw a horizontal line from *p*, which cuts the edges 33′ and 44′ at *p*-*p*′. Join all corresponding points as shown in Fig. 13.8(b).

PROBLEM 13.8 (FIG. 13.9)

Three cylindrical pipes, each of diameter 30 mm, are joined to form a Y-piece in front view as shown in Fig. 13.9(a). Develop the lateral surface of the cylindrical pieces.

Solution:

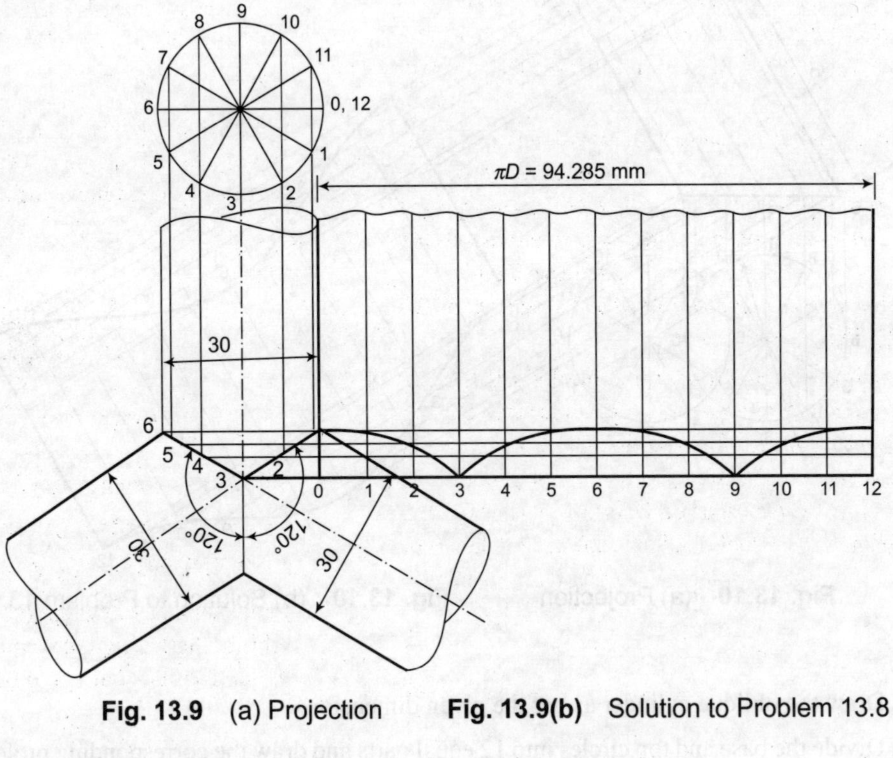

Fig. 13.9 (a) Projection **Fig. 13.9(b)** Solution to Problem 13.8

Steps:

1. Draw the front view of the Y-piece. The three pipes are of equal diameter and make 120° with each other. The development of each of them will be similar in nature and, hence, development of one pipe will be enough.
2. Draw the circle representing the view from above. Divide the circle into 12 equal parts. Draw the three lines of intersection.
3. Project from 1, 2, 3… to cut the line of intersection. Draw horizontal line from all cut points.
4. A rectangle is drawn with width equal to πD (circumference), which is to be divided into 12 equal points and corresponding projections are to be located as shown in Fig. 13.9(b).

PROBLEM 13.9 (FIG. 13.10)

Draw the development of an oblique cylinder of base diameter 30 mm and height 50 mm with its axis inclined to its base at 60° as shown in Fig. 13.10(a).

Solution:

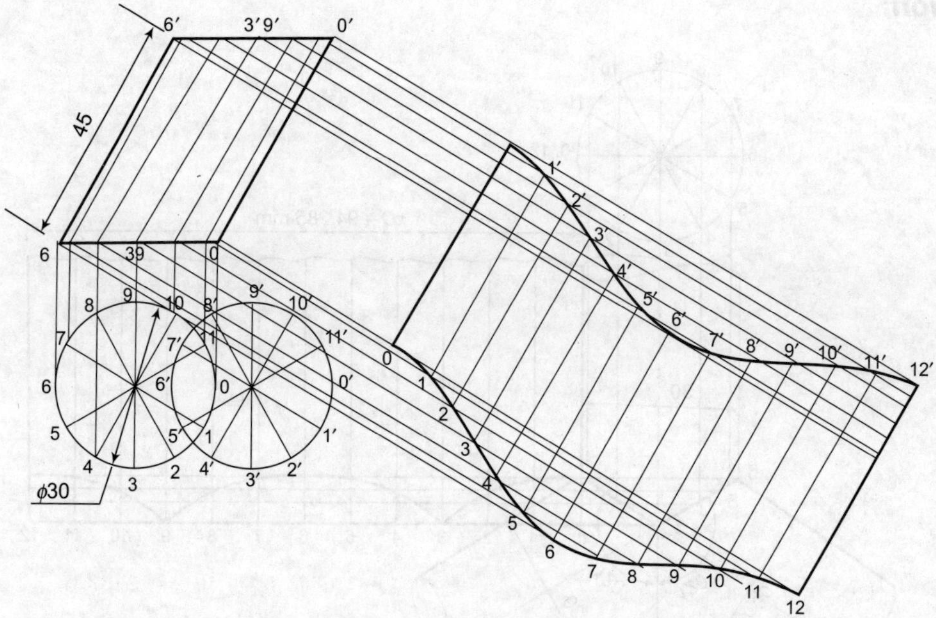

Fig. 13.10 (a) Projection **Fig. 13.10** (b) Solution to Problem 13.9

Steps:

1. Draw the oblique cylinder as per the given dimensions.
2. Divide the base and top circles into 12 equal parts and draw the corresponding projection lines in front view.

3. Draw a perpendicular line from each generator line. In this case, the stretched line of the developed pattern will not be equal to the circumference of the circle in top view.
4. At generator oo', draw perpendicular and similarly from each generator, draw a perpendicular.

   From o as centre and arc equal to 'o1', cut the projected line from '1' and so on.
5. Project the end points of the surface to the patterns as shown in Fig. 13.10(b).

13.3 RADIAL LINE METHOD

PROBLEM 13.10 (FIG. 13.11)

A square pyramid with edge of the base 30 mm and height 50 mm, lying with its base on HP such that all its base edges are equally inclined to VP. Draw the development of the pyramid.

Solution:

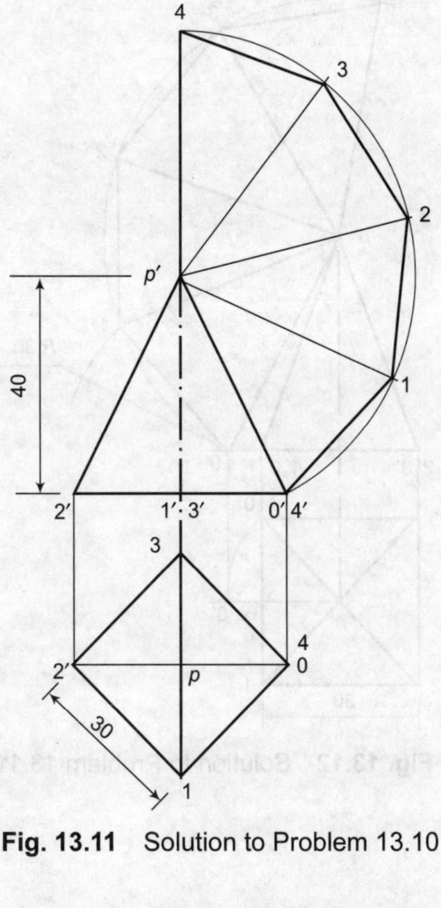

Fig. 13.11 Solution to Problem 13.10

Steps:

1. Draw the projection of a square pyramid. Top view is 0123. Keeping its base edge 23 or 34 inclined to VP at 45°, project its corresponding front view *po* parallel to VP.
2. In this case, *p′o′* is the true length because the top view *po* is parallel to VP.
3. With *p′* as centre and *p′o′* as radius, draw an arc as shown in Fig. 13.11.
4. From *o′*, cut *o′*1 on arc equal to side o1 of the base and locate '1' and from 1 to 2 and from 2 to 3 and from 3 to 4 is (four equal side) which is the required development.

PROBLEM 13.11 (FIG. 13.12)

A square pyramid with edge of the base 30 mm and height 40 mm, lying on its base on HP such that one of its base edge is parallel to VP.

Draw its projections and the development.

Solution:

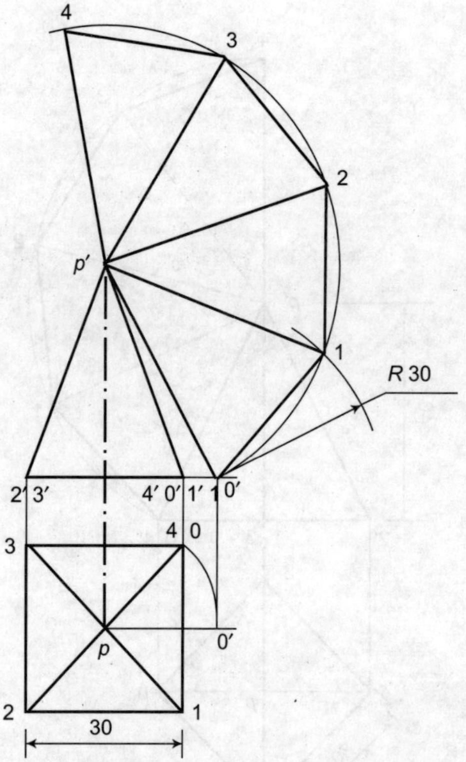

Fig. 13.12 Solution to Problem 13.11

Steps:

1. Draw the projection of square pyramid keeping its base edge 12 or 34 parallel to VP.
2. Project its corresponding front view as 0′1′2′3′4′.
3. In this case, the front view of edges does not have the true length.
4. The true length of the edge is required to be found out. *po* is to be rotated till it is made parallel to VP as *po*′.
5. Project *o*′ up to *XY*, extend it to meet on *XY*.
6. Taking *o*′*p*′ as radius and *o*′ as centre, draw an arc as shown in Fig. 13.12.
7. Select 1 on this arc and then cut off four equal divisions equal to the length of an edge from the top view.
8. Name these points as 1, 2, 3, 4 and join 01, 12, 23, and 34 which is the required development.

PROBLEM 13.12 (FIG. 13.13)

A right circular cone, with diameter of base 30 mm and height 50 mm, is lying on its base on HP. Draw the development.

Solution:

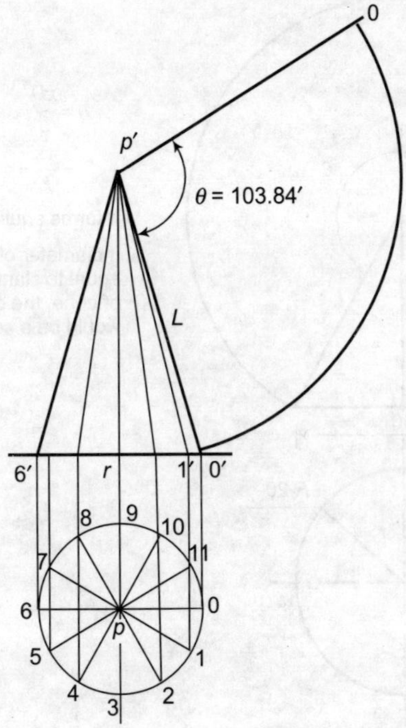

Fig. 13.13 Solution to Problem 13.12

Steps:

1. Draw the front view and top view of the cone.
2. Divide the base circle into 12 equal parts.
3. With p' as centre and radius equal to $p'o'$, draw an arc of the circle. The length of this arc should be equal to the circumference of the base circle.
4. Calculate the subtended angle 'q'.
   If L is the slant edge length and 'r' is the radius of the base circle, then
   $$\theta = 360° \times \frac{r}{L} = \frac{2\pi r}{L} = 360 \times \frac{\text{Radius of base circle}}{\text{Slant edge length of cone}} = 360° \times \frac{15}{52} = 103.84°$$
5. This can also be found out using other methods—by dividing the arc with a compass or a divider into 12 equal parts, where each division must be equal to one of the divisions of the base circle. This will give the approximate length of the circumference.
6. Join the division points to 0, thereby completing the development of the whole cone.

PROBLEM 13.13 (FIG. 13.14)

A right circular cone, with diameter of base 40 mm and the slant edge length of cone also equal to 40 mm, is lying on its base on HP. Draw the development.

Solution:

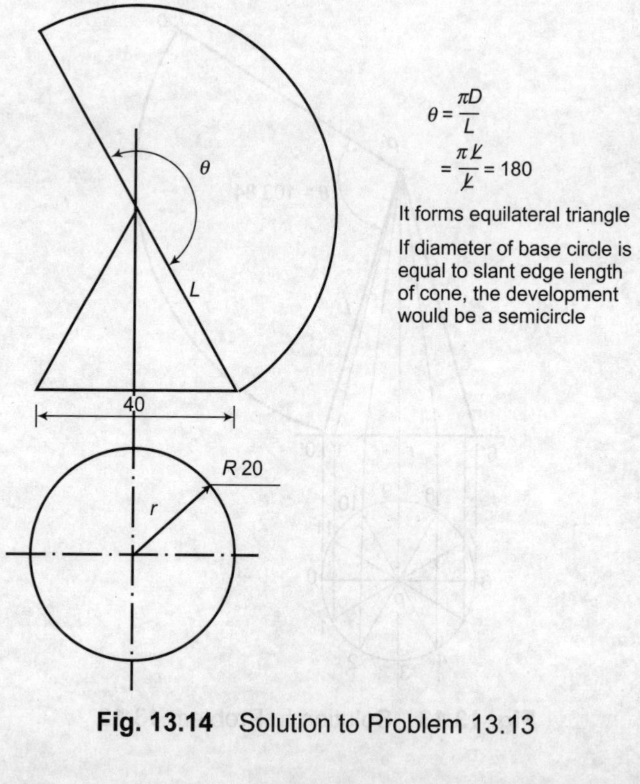

Fig. 13.14 Solution to Problem 13.13

$$\theta = \frac{\pi}{L}$$

$$= \frac{\pi \not{L}}{\not{L}} = 180°$$

It forms an equilateral triangle.

If diameter of base circle is equal to slant edge length of cone, the development would be a semicircle.

PROBLEM 13.14 (FIG. 13.15)

A right circular cone with diameter of the base 60 mm and height 30 mm, lying on its base on HP. Draw the development of cone.

***Solution*:**

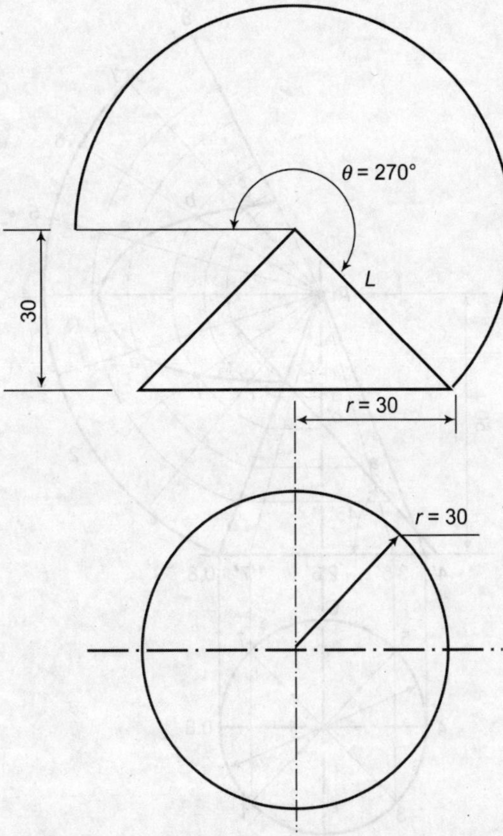

Fig. 13.15 Solution to Problem 13.14

On measurement, length of slant edge $L = 40$ mm.

Subtended angle, θ

$$\theta = 360 \times \frac{r}{L}$$

$$= 360 \times \frac{30}{40}$$

$$= 270°$$

PROBLEM 13.15 (FIG. 13.16)

A right circular cone, with diameter of the base 40 mm and height 50 mm, is lying on its base on HP. The cone is cut by a sectional plane perpendicular to VP and inclined at 45° to HP. The sectional plane cuts the cone at 25 mm from the base. Draw the development of the truncated cone.

Solution:

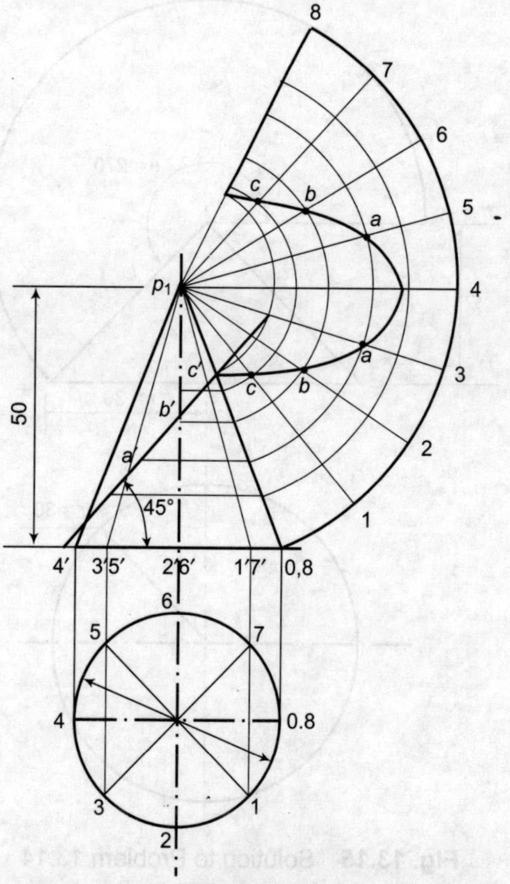

Fig. 13.16 Solution to Problem 13.15

Steps:

1. Draw the projection of the cone and locate the position of cutting plane as shown in Fig. 13.16.
2. Divide the circle into 8 equal parts. For more accuracy, it should be divided into 12 equal parts.
3. Calculate the sector angle θ.

$$\theta = 360 \times \frac{r}{L}$$

$$= 360 \times \frac{20}{45} = 160^\circ$$

4. Draw the development of the cone with the sector angle θ as explained.
5. Divide the sector angle into 8 equal parts. Each part on the arc will represent one part '01' of the base circle
6. Except $o'p_1$ and $4'p'$, no other generator gives the true length.
   The points where the sectional plane cuts the other generators may be located as a', b', c'.
7. Draw horizontal lines from a', b', c', and draw an arc taking p' as centre and radius equal to the projected length on side generator, which cuts the generator located on sector at a, b, c.
8. Join all points by a smooth curve which is the required development.

PROBLEM 13.16 (FIG. 13.17)

A right circular cone with diameter of the base 50 mm and height 65 mm rests on its base in HP. A sectional plane parallel to HP and verified to VP, cuts the cone axis at 30 mm from the top. An equilateral triangular hole is cut on the front view of the cone. Draw the lateral surface of the cone.

Solution:

Steps:

1. Draw the front view and top view of a cone.
2. Draw the development of the cone as per the method already adopted.
3. Take the number of points on triangular hole in front view as abc, 1234.
4. Transfer these points to their positions on the developed surface.
5. Join these points by a smooth curve as shown in Fig. 13.17.

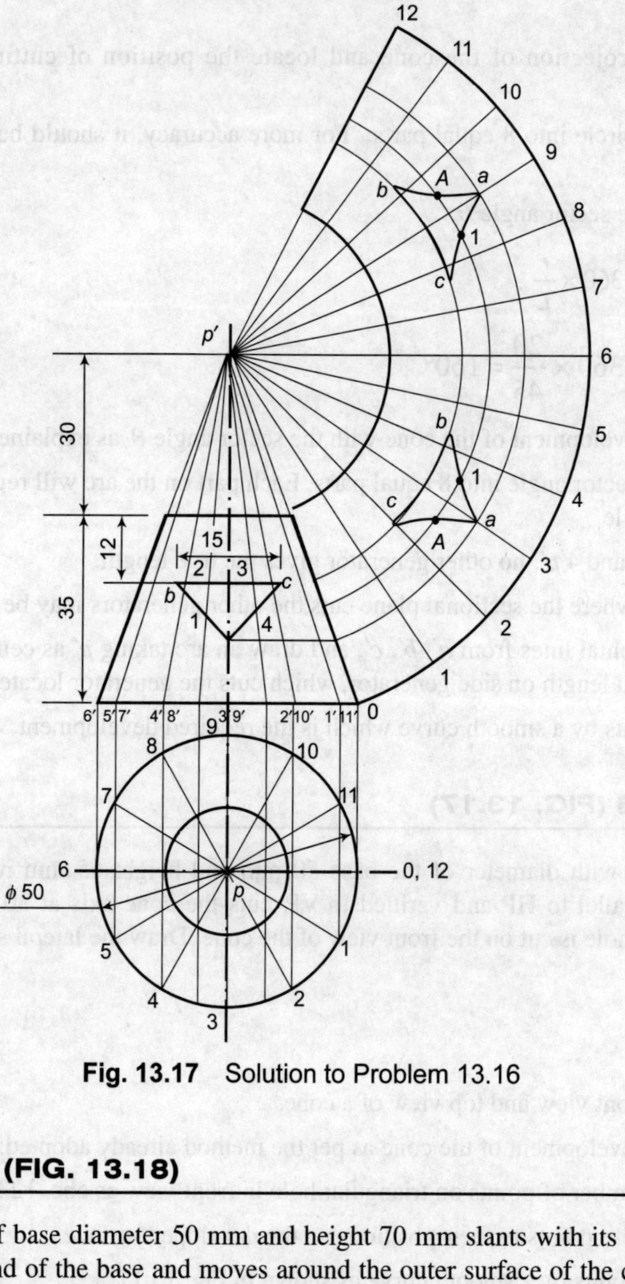

Fig. 13.17 Solution to Problem 13.16

PROBLEM 13.17 (FIG. 13.18)

A right circular cone of base diameter 50 mm and height 70 mm slants with its base on HP. A spider sits on extreme right end of the base and moves around the outer surface of the cone and comes back to the slanting point. Find the shortest path the spider can take. Show the shortest distance in front view and top view.

Solution:

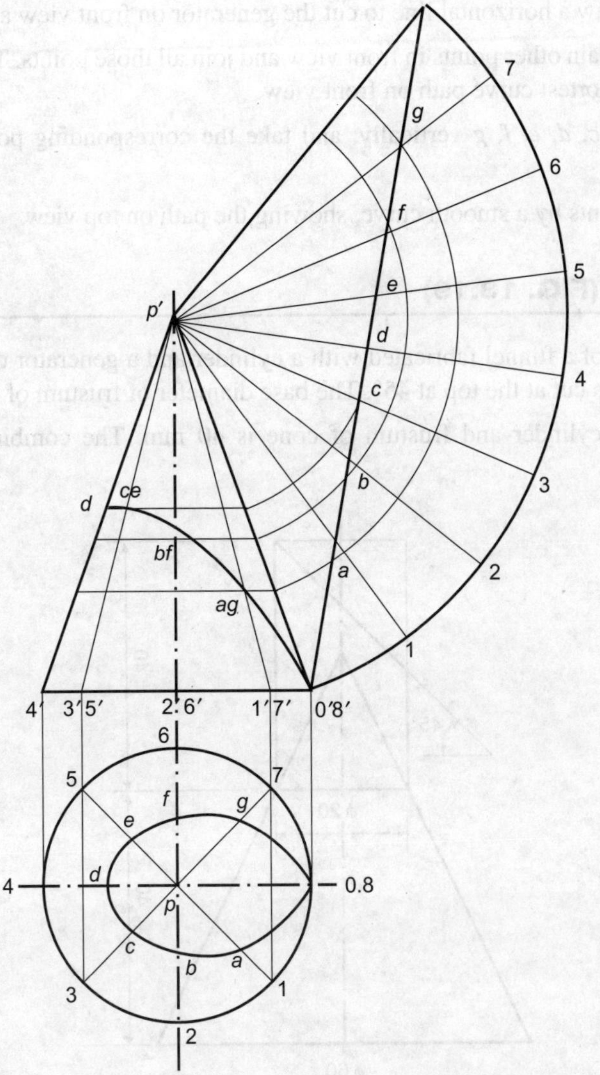

Fig. 13.18 Solution to Problem 13.17

Steps:

1. Draw the front view and top view of the cone and also the development as shown in Fig. 13.18.
2. The spider starts from o' and returns to 8.
3. On development, join 08, which represents the shortest path.

4. The shortest line cuts the generator at *a, b, c, d, e, f, g*.
5. Taking *p′* as centre and *p′a* as radius, draw an arc which cuts the extreme generator; and from that point, draw a horizontal line to cut the generator on front view at *a* and also at *g*.
6. Similarly, obtain other points in front view and join all those points. The curve drawn on front view is the shortest curve path on front view.
7. Project *a, b, c, d, e, f, g* vertically, and take the corresponding points on top view of the generator.

   Join these points by a smooth curve, showing the path on top view.

PROBLEM 13.18 (FIG. 13.19)

Draw the development of a funnel fabricated with a cylinder and a generator of cone. The diameter of cylinder is 20 mm and is cut at the top at 45°. The base diameter of frustum of cone is 60 mm.

The height of both cylinder and frustum of cone is 40 mm. The combined funnel is shown in Fig. 13.19(a).

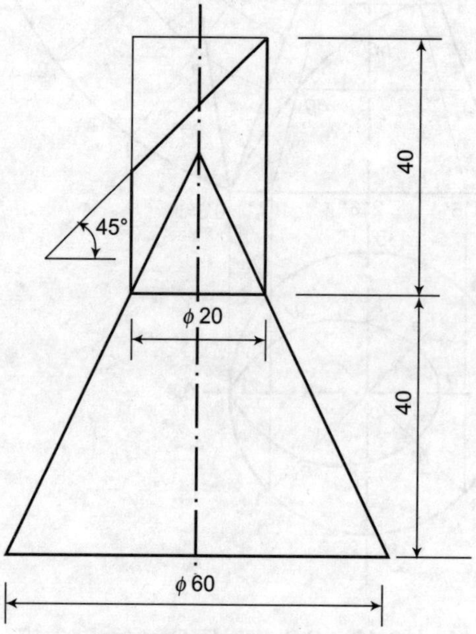

Fig. 13.19 (a) Projection

Solution:

The entire fabricated funnel is made up of a cylinder and frustum of cone. The development of the entire funnel is the development of a cylindrical portion and another development of the frustum of the cone.

1. Development of cylindrical portion

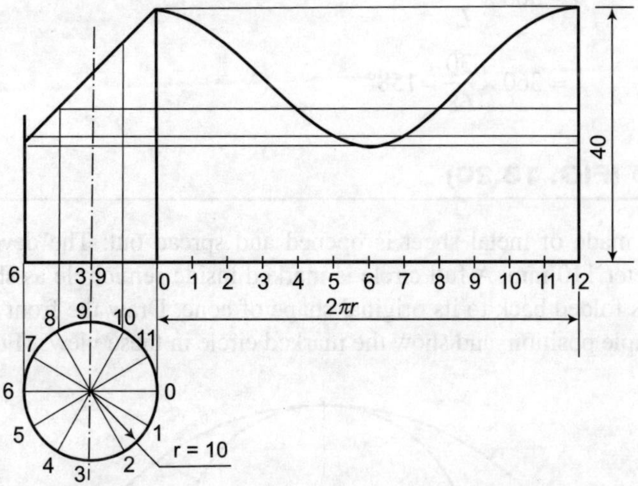

Fig. 13.19 (b) Solution to Problem 13.18

2. Development of frustum of cone

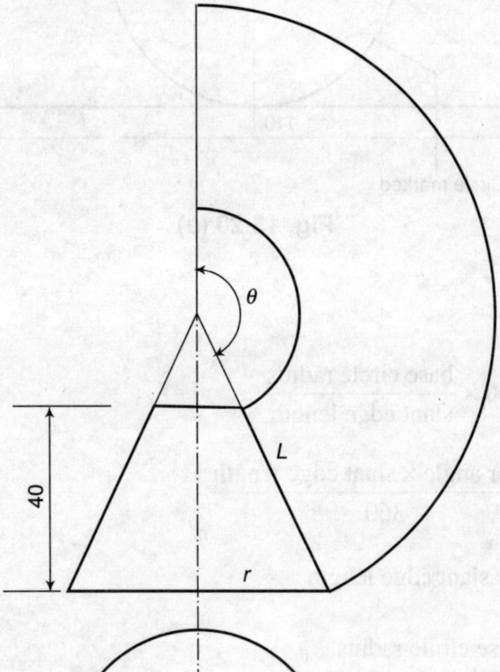

Fig. 13.19 (c) Solution to Problem 13.18

$$\theta = 360 \times \frac{r}{L}$$

$$= 360 \times \frac{30}{68} = 158°$$

PROBLEM 13.19 (FIG. 13.20)

A right circular cone made of metal sheet is opened and spread out. The development is a semi-circular cone of diameter 110 mm. A full circle is marked inside semicircle as shown in Fig. 13.20(a) and, again, the sheet is folded back to its original shape of cone. Draw the front view and top view of cone, keeping it in simple position, and show the marked circle in these views (Fig. 13.20(a)).

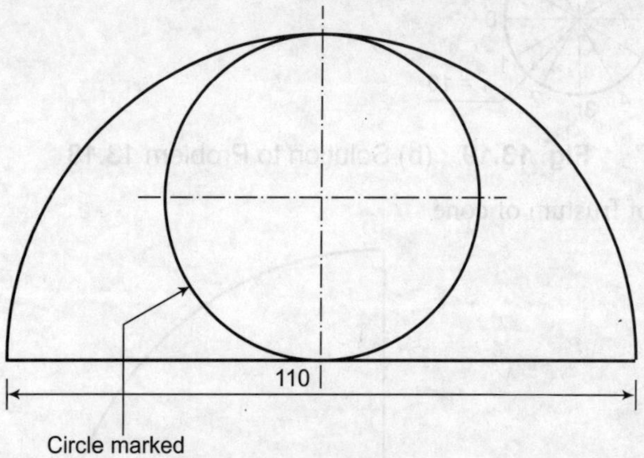

Fig. 13.20 (a)

Solution:

$$\text{Sector angle, } \theta = 360 \times \frac{\text{base circle radius}}{\text{slant edge length}}$$

$$\text{Base circle radius} = \frac{\text{Sector angle} \times \text{slant edge length}}{360}$$

$$= \frac{180}{360} \times \text{slant edge length}$$

Slant edge length = 2 × base circle radius

$$= 2 \times 55 = 110 \text{ mm}$$

This means that the front view of cone will be an equilateral triangle.

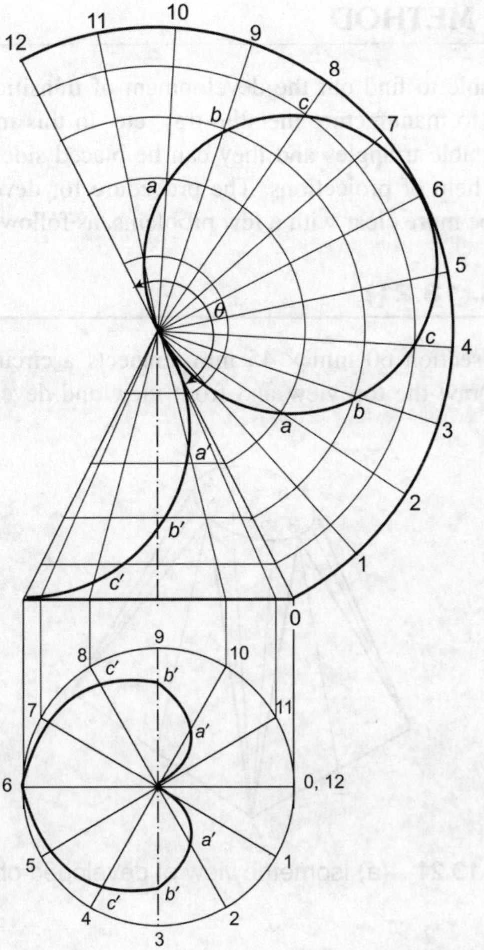

Fig. 13.20 (b) Solution to Problem 13.19

Figure 13.20(a) represents the development of the cone stated as Problem 13.19.

Steps:

1. Draw the top view, front view, and the development of a cone with a circle marked as shown in Fig. 13.20(a).
2. Divide the top view and the development in 12 equal parts as in the previous methods.
3. Draw projections as shown in Fig. 13.20(b) and obtain the usual curve in front view as well as in top view.

13.4 TRIANGULAR METHOD

Triangular method is applicable to find out the development of transition pieces, fabrication of duct in air-conditioning, and also to manufacture metallic tray, etc. In this method, the surfaces are to be divided into a number of suitable triangles and they can be placed side by side after finding out the true length of each with the help of projections. The procedure for development of transition pieces and fabrication of trays will be more clear with a few problems, as follows.

PROBLEM 13.20 (FIG. 13.21)

A duct of rectangular cross-section 60 mm × 45 mm connects a circular pipe of diameter 25 mm through a transition piece. Draw the top view and front view and develop the lateral surface of the transition pieces.

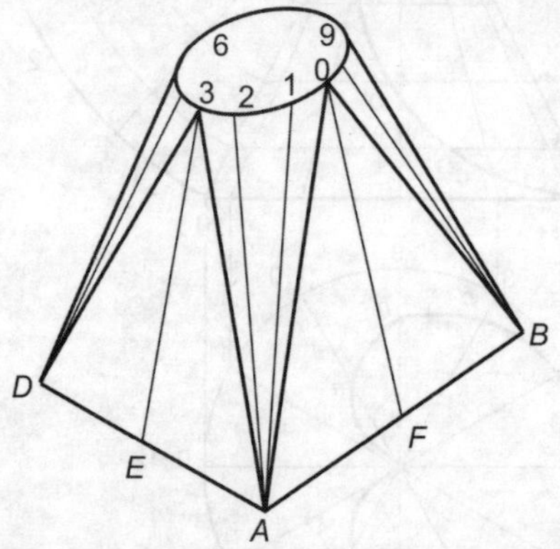

Fig. 13.21 (a) Isometric view of developed object

Solution:

In this case, there is only one possible way of making the complete transition piece. The transition piece is composed of four isosceles triangular plates and four conical surfaces. The development of conical surface may be developed by dividing it into a number of triangular segments.

Since it is symmetrical about the two axes, only one part out of four will be developed. The complete transition piece will look like as shown in Fig. 13.21(a)

Steps:

1. Draw the front view and top view of the rectangular transition piece as per the given dimensions.
2. Divide the top view circle into 12 equal parts.
3. The development of one corner will be developed.
4. Development will begin from OE. The conical surface is developed by tranquilization method as shown in Fig. 13.21(b).

   In the top view, join the divisions of the circle 0, 1, 2, 3 with the corner 'A'.

5. Project these points with front view, and then true length of each length is found out.
6. Figure 13.21(c) shows the development of its one corner. Such four parts may be required to complete development.

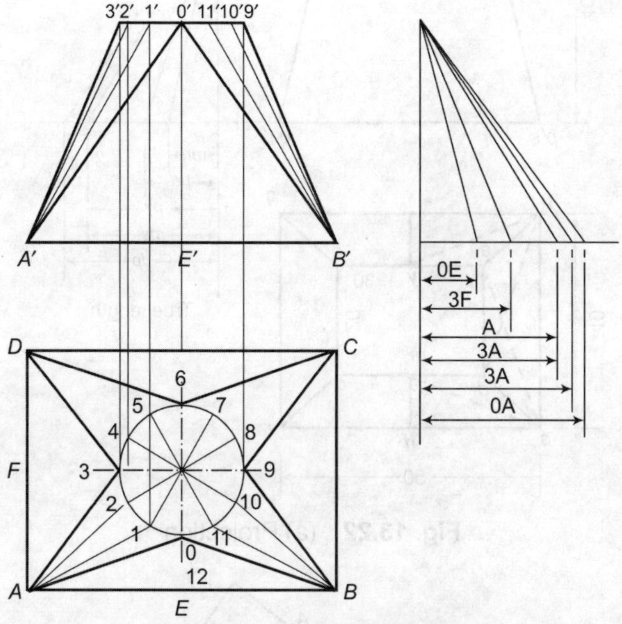

Fig. 13.21 (b) Projections

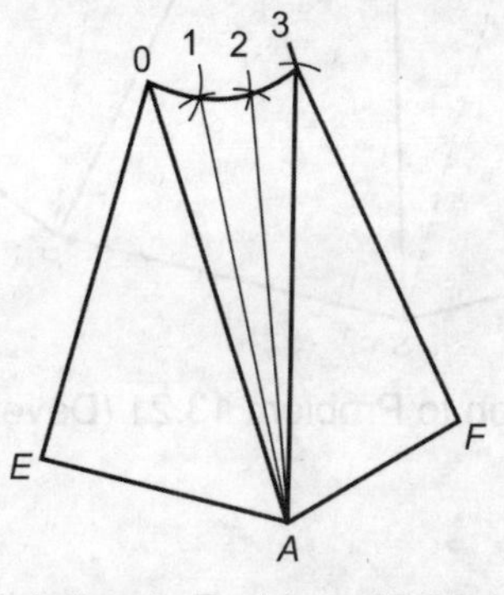

Fig. 13.21 (c) Solution to Problem 13.20 (one-fourth parts)

PROBLEM 13.21 (FIG. 13.22)

Figure 13.22(a) shows a metal tray to be fabricated. Develop the surface of the metal tray. The exact surface will be required for its fabrication.

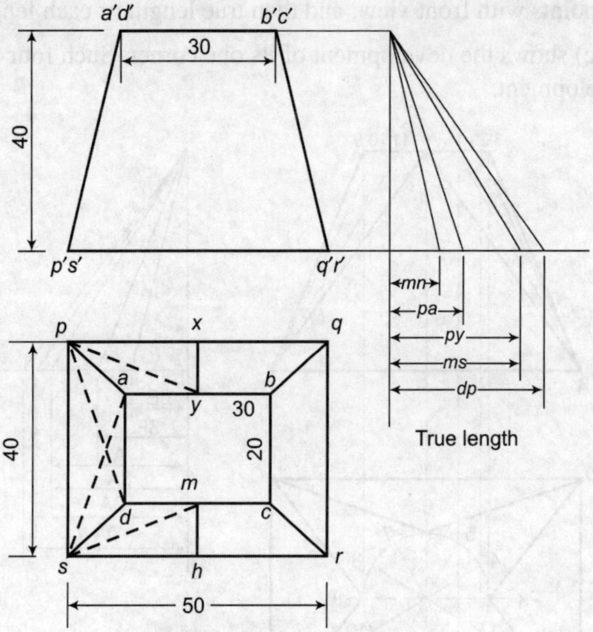

Fig. 13.22 (a) Projection

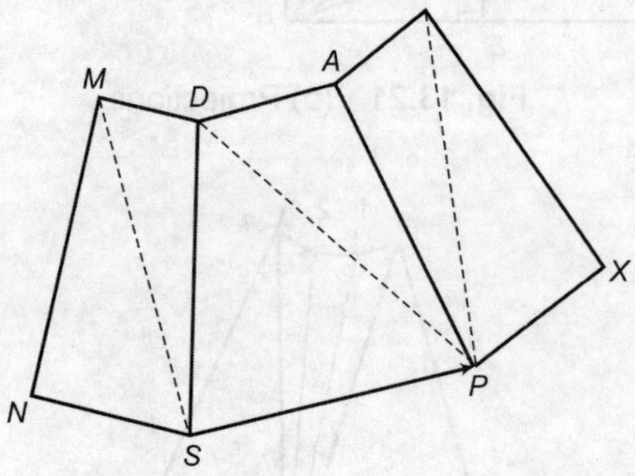

Fig. 13.22 (b) Solution to Problem 13.21 (Development of half of tray)

Solution:

Steps:

1. Draw the front view and top view as shown in Fig. 13.22(a).
2. Top view is subdivided by joining few points and corners to make it triangular. They are joined by dotted lines.
3. Begin with the development along the line 'mn'. Obtain the true length of each line.
4. Combining all the lines, the complete developments can be obtained.
5. The development has been shown in Fig. 13.22(b). It is the one half of the whole object.

PROBLEM 13.22 (FIG. 13.23)

Develop the lateral surface of an oblique cone with diameter of the base 50 mm, height 55 mm, and its axis making an angle of 50° with its base.

Solution:

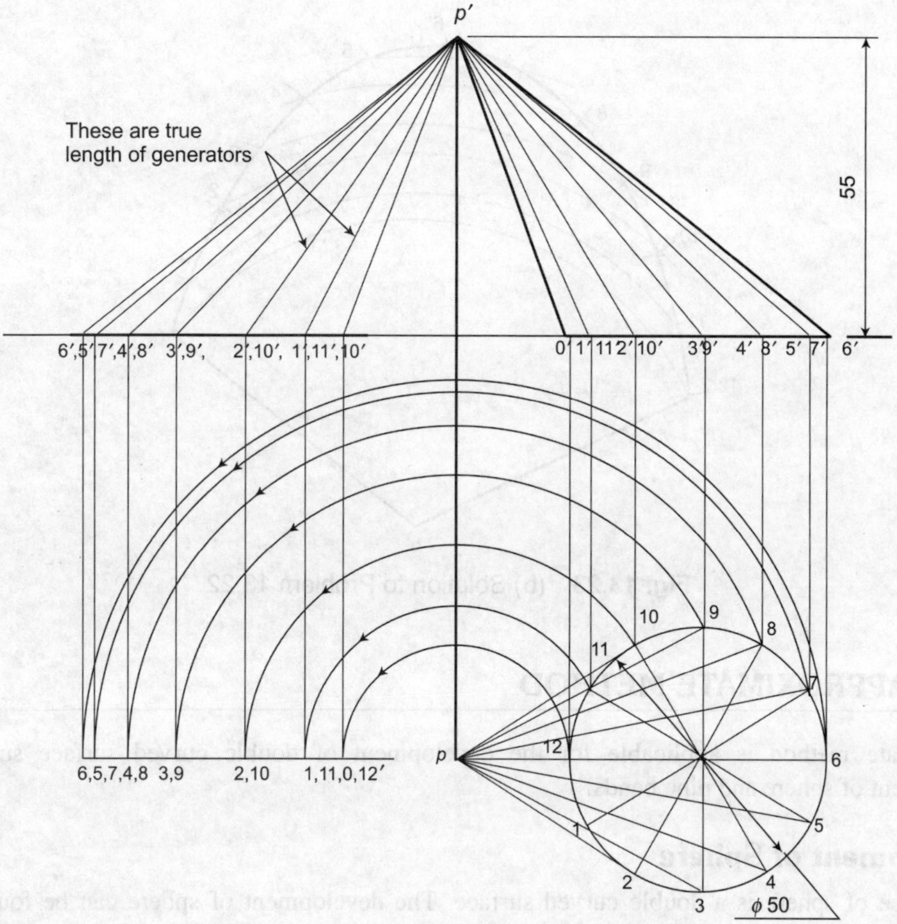

Fig. 13.23 (a)

Steps:

1. Draw the front view and top view of oblique cone as per dimensions shown in Fig. 13.23(a).
2. Divide the circle in top view into 12 equal parts. Project these points on the base line of front view.
3. Let p' be the front view of apex. Join all the points of base point to apex p'.

4. Except two generators $p'o'$ and $p'6'$, all other generators do not have true length and, hence, true length of other generators are required to be found out.
5. Taking p' as radius and p as centre, draw arc on the horizontal line meeting at 1, 11. From this point, draw vertical line as 1′, 11′. Joining the point with p'. $p'1'$, 11′ is the true length of p' and $p11$ both.
6. With all these true lengths of generators, development is drawn, as shown in Fig. 13.23(b).

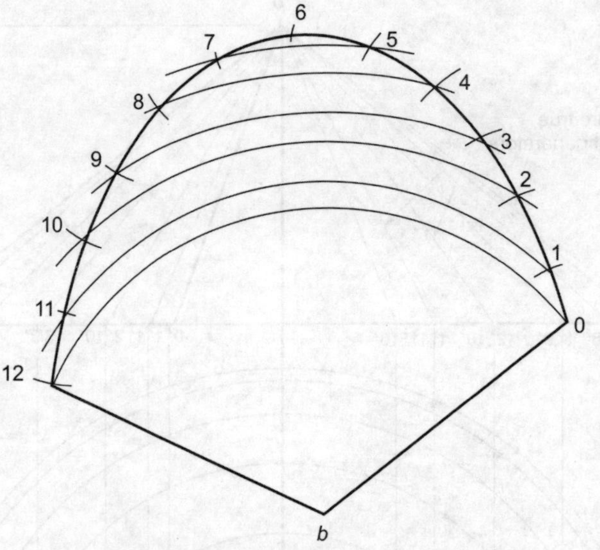

Fig. 13.23 (b) Solution to Problem 13.22

13.5 APPROXIMATE METHOD

Approximate method is applicable for the development of double curved surface such as the development of sphere and pipe bends.

Development of Sphere

The surface of sphere is a double curved surface. The development of sphere can be found out by approximate method.

There are two methods, as follows:

1. Zone method
2. Lune method or Gore method

Zone method

In this method, sphere is cut into a number of zones. Each zone is treated as the frustum of cone. The extended chords will meet at points which may be considered as the apex. Considering the number of cones, the method of development of cone may be done by radial time technique. Sphere divided into zones is shown in Fig. 13.24 (a).

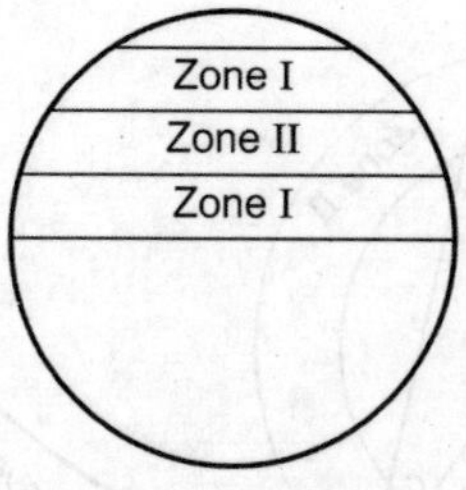

Fig. 13.24 (a)

Lune method or Gore method

In this method, the sphere is cut into a number of equal meridian sections called *lunes*. If a sphere is divided into 12 equal parts, there will be 12 lunes.

One lune will be developed and total surface area of sphere will be 12 times the surface area of one lune.

Figure 13.24(b) shows the division of the sphere by this method.

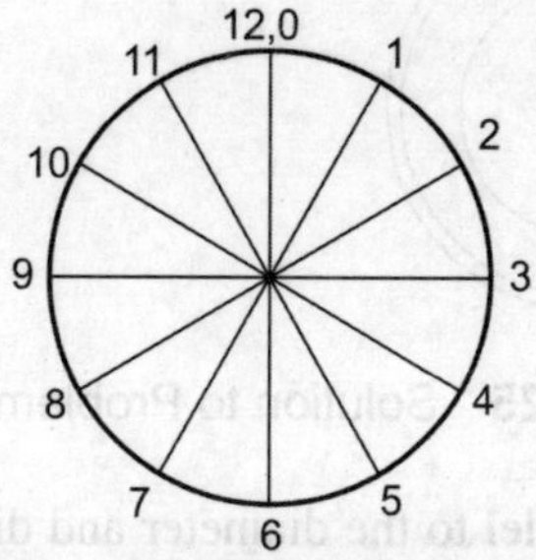

Fig. 13.24 (b)

PROBLEM 13.23 (FIG. 13.25)

Develop the lateral surface of a sphere of diameter 40 mm by zone method.

Solution:

Steps:

1. Draw the front view and top view of the sphere as shown in Fig. 13.25.

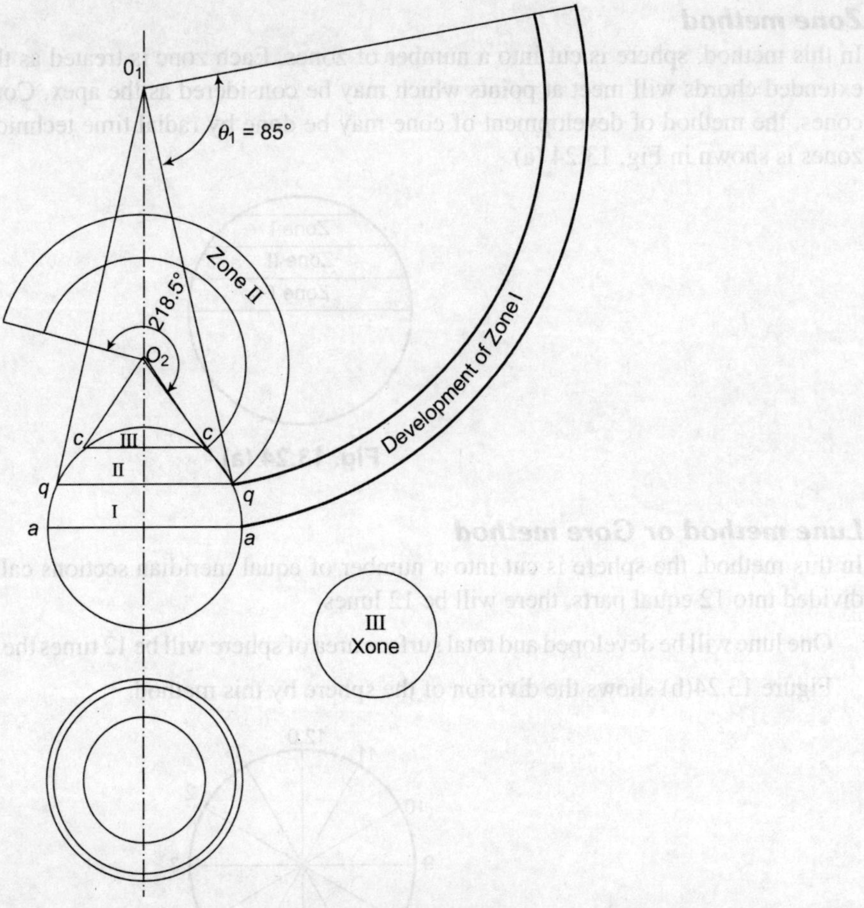

Fig. 13.25 Solution to Problem 13.23

2. Draw a number of lines parallel to the diameter and divide the half of sphere in three zones named Zone I, Zone II, and Zone III.
3. For Zone I, *ab* should be joined and extended to meet the axis at o_1.

   This makes the cone. For the cone,

$$\theta_1 = 360 \times \frac{r}{L} = 360 \times \frac{20}{85} = 84.7°$$

4. For Zone II, *bc* should be joined and extended to meet the axis at o_2.

   This also forms a cone.

   Here,

$$\theta_2 = 360 \times \frac{17}{28} == 218.57°$$

5. Draw the development of these two zones.

   In this case, each zone is assumed to be a frustum of cone. For more accuracy, the sphere may be divided into more number of zones.

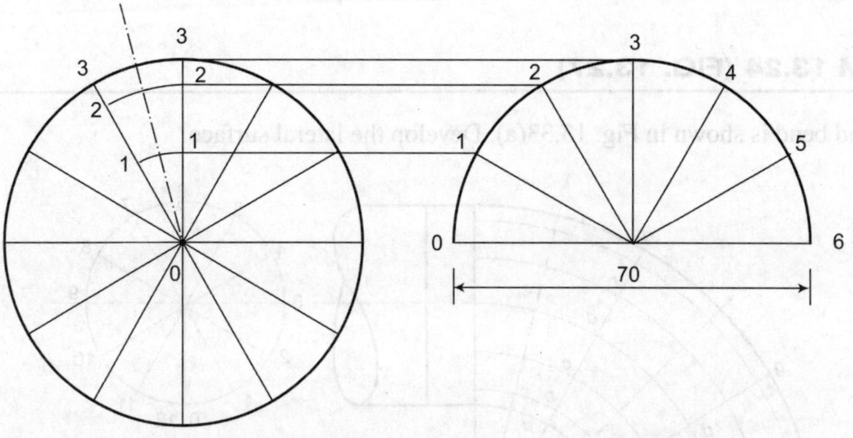

Fig. 13.26 (a) Front view and side view of sphere

Steps:

1. Draw the front view and side view of the sphere.
2. Divide the front view of the sphere into 12 equal parts, so there will be 12 lunes in all.
3. For total development of sphere, each lune is developed.

   The length of each lune is equal to one half of the circumference of the sphere ($\pi r = \pi \times 35 = 110$ mm).
4. Development of one lune is shown in Fig. 13.26(b).

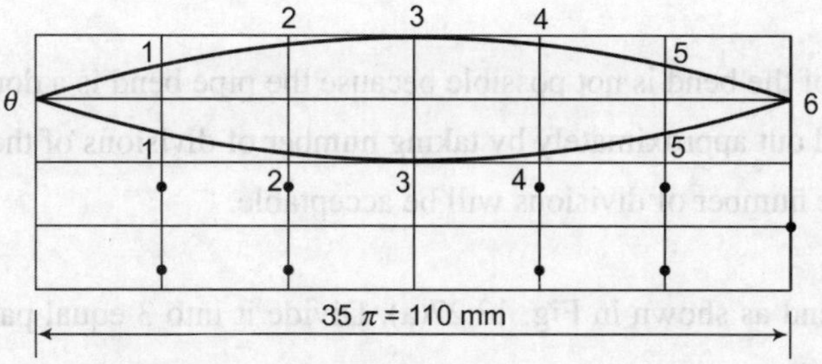

Fig. 13.26 (b) Development of one lune

5. Divide the semicircle into 6 equal parts and naming of divisions is done as 1, 2, 3, 4, …, etc.

   Project from these points to side view as shown.

   At all points, width of line si takes on measurement and is used for drawing development.

6. Draw a horizontal line from point 1, 2, 3, which will cut with their respective perpendiculars at 1, 2, 3, …, etc. Join these points to get the exact profile of the metal sheet.
7. This will approximately represent the development of one twelfth of the total surface of sphere. 12 such lunes will be required for making entire sphere.

PROBLEM 13.24 (FIG. 13.27)

A right-angled bend is shown in Fig. 13.33(a). Develop the lateral surface.

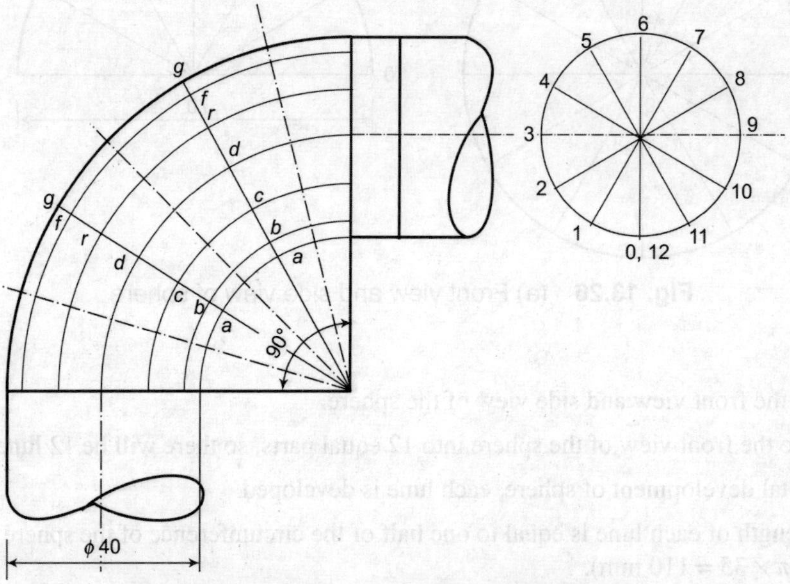

Fig. 13.27 (a) Right-angled bend

Solution:

The exact development of the bend is not possible because the pipe bend is a double curved surface.

However, it can be found out approximately by taking number of divisions of the pipe.

For more accuracy, more number of divisions will be acceptable.

Steps:

1. Draw a 90° bend as shown in Fig. 13.27(a). Divide it into 3 equal parts, each part is of 30° angle.
2. Draw side view as a circle and divide it into 12 equal parts.
3. From each point of circle, draw projection line to meet the middle segment for taking width dimensions.
4. Draw a horizontal equal to the circumference of the pipe (πD) as shown in Fig. 13.27(b).

5. Divide the line also into 12 equal parts. Each part will represent the width of the segment. The dimension of each width may be taken to locate point.
6. Join all points by a smooth curve. This will represent the development of one part of the pipe bend shown in Fig. 13.27(b).

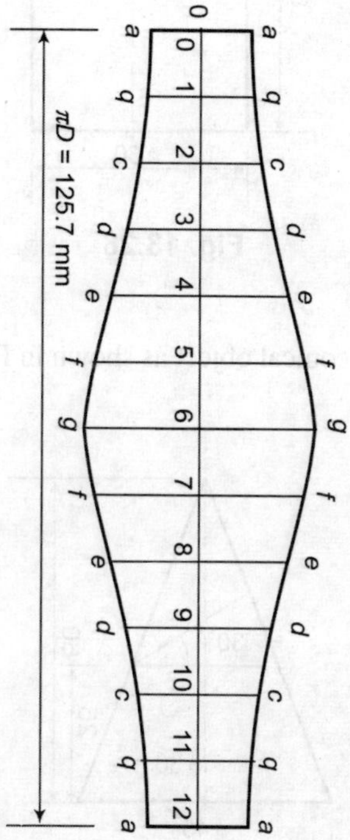

Fig. 13.27 (b) Development of one part

EXERCISE

Review Questions

1. What do you mean by development of solid surface?
2. What are the different methods of development?
3. What is the shape obtained by development of a cone?
4. What is the method used for the development of oblique cone?
5. What is the importance of development in sheet metal industries?
6. A right circular cylinder, with diameter of the base 30 mm and height 65 mm, has a cut of radius 25 mm at the top end as shown in Fig. 13.28. Develop its lateral surface.

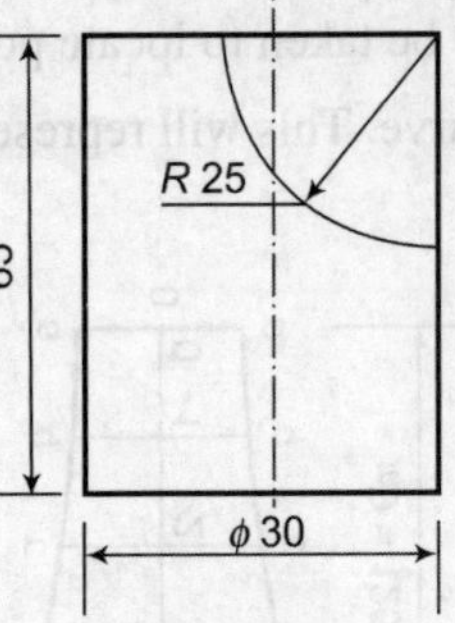

Fig. 13.28

7. Develop the lateral surface of the conical object as shown in Fig. 13.29.

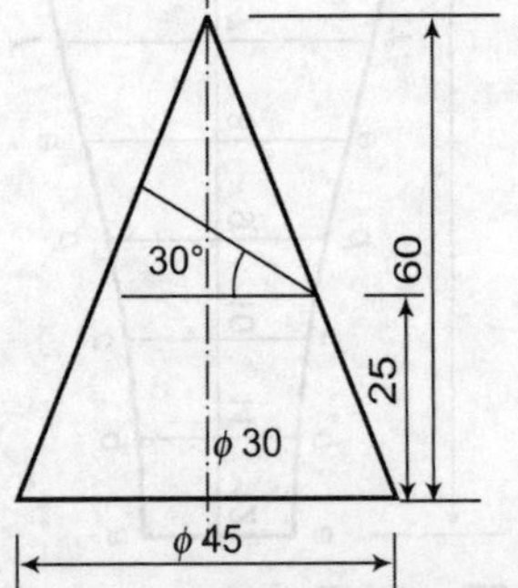

Fig. 13.29

8. Develop the lateral surface of a cone having a circular arc cut therein, as shown in Fig. 13.30.

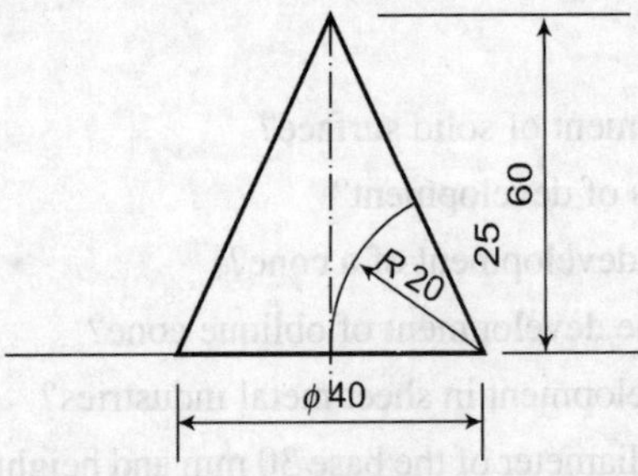

Fig. 13.30

9. Develop the lateral surface of a metal tray as shown in Fig. 13.31.

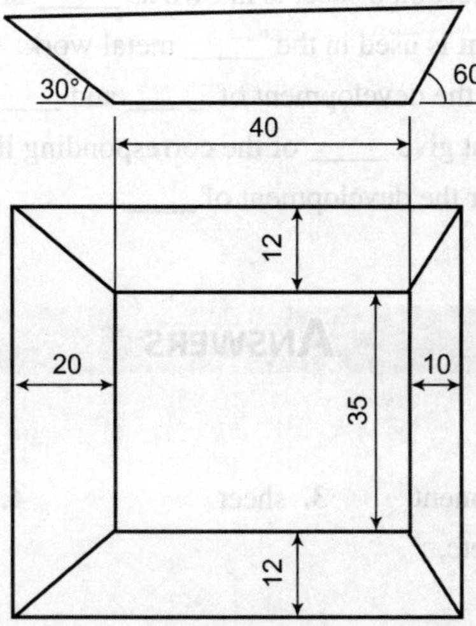

Fig. 13.31

10. Draw the development of the lateral surface of oil cans as shown in Fig 13.32. Take a suitable scale.

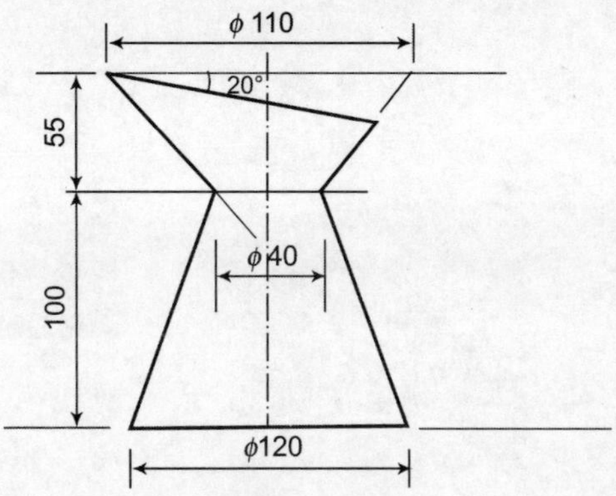

Fig. 13.32

Objective Questions

1. Approximate method is used for the development of _____.
2. The complete layout of the object on a sheet is known as _____ of surface.
3. The application of development is used in the _____ metal work.
4. Radial line method is used for the development of _____ and ____ shaped objects.
5. Each line on development must give _____ of the corresponding line.
6. Parallel line method is used for the development of ____.

ANSWERS

Objective Questions

1. sphere 2. development 3. sheet 4. cone, pyramid 5. true length
6. right circular cylinder, prism, etc.

14

CHAPTER

Intersection of Surfaces

14.1 INTRODUCTION

When the surfaces of two solids or machine components meet, they form a common line or curve of intersection. Similarly, when a solid completely penetrates another solid, the line or curve which is common to both the solids is termed as *line* or *curve of interpenetration*.

In engineering, there are many instances where two branches of pipes are joined together, forming a common curve of intersection as shown in Fig. 14.1.

The curve of intersection, to know the exact nature of the curve, becomes necessary to determine the shape of solid of the two bodies to cut exactly, to connect with each other without any differences between the two for joining.

It is a known fact that when two surfaces intersect, the line of intersection of two surfaces is a line. The line of intersection of the two planes becomes a line, which is common to both the surfaces. Its nature will depend upon the type of the object.

Figure 14.1 shows a cylinder penetrated by another cylinder, the axis of the two is at right angle to each other.

Figure 14.1(a) shows the joint, in which a vertical cylinder of small diameter is intersecting with another horizontal cylinder of large diameter. They are joined by the curve of intersection.

Figure 14.1(b) shows the joint in which two pipes of equal diameter are connected with each other. This forms a line of intersection.

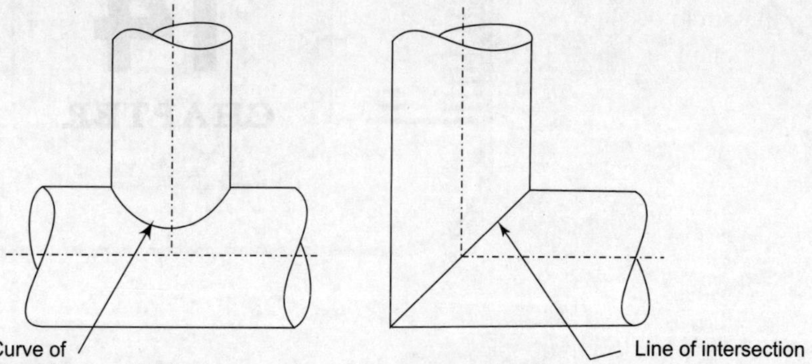

Fig. 14.1 Pipe joints

14.2 METHODS OF DETERMINING THE CURVE OF INTERSECTION

There are two methods of determining the curve of intersection, which are as follows:

(i) Line/generator method

(ii) Cutting plane method/circle method

Line/generator Method

In this method, lines or generators are drawn on the surface of the two solids' surfaces to be joined. These lines must interest at a point. Number of such points are obtained and they are connected by a smooth curve to know the line of intersection.

Cutting Plane Method

In this method, the two solid surfaces intersect each other. It is to be assumed that these are cut by a number of cutting planes, and the common lines are obtained to find the exact line of intersection.

PROBLEM 14.1 (FIG. 14.2)

A vertical cylinder of diameter 33 mm and length 73 mm is penetrated by a horizontal cylinder of some diameter and same length. The axes of the both the cylinders are perpendicular to each other. Draw the projection and the curve of intersection.

***Solution*:**

Steps:

1. Draw the front view and top view of vertical cylinder as rectangle and circle of diameter 33 mm.
2. Draw side view of the vertical cylinder as a circle of diameter 33 mm.

3. Divide the circle of side view into 12 equal parts numbered as 1″, 2″, 3″, and so on, and representation of the points on top view as 1, 2, 3, and so on.
4. Draw horizontal lines from all points in side view as 1″7″, 2″6″, 3″5″, and so on.
5. Draw vertical lines from all points in top view as 10, 9, 11, 8, 12, …, and so on.
6. These horizontal lines and vertical lines meet on front view.All meeting point can be joined
7. The curve of intersection can be obtained as shown in Fig. 14.2.

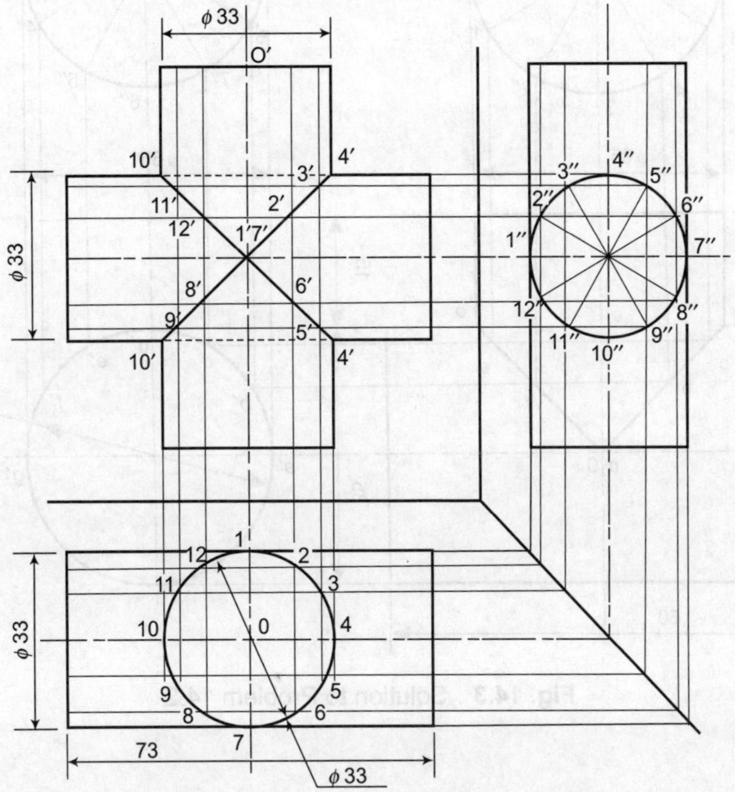

Fig. 14.2 Solution to Problem 14.1

They are meeting each other at the centre because both the cylinders have equal diameters.

PROBLEM 14.2 (FIG. 14.3)

A vertical cylinder of diameter 35 mm is penetrating a horizontal cylinder of same diameter. The axes of both the cylinders are perpendicular to each other. The vertical cylinder is enveloping the horizontal cylinder completely. Draw the projection and also the curve of intersection.

Solution:

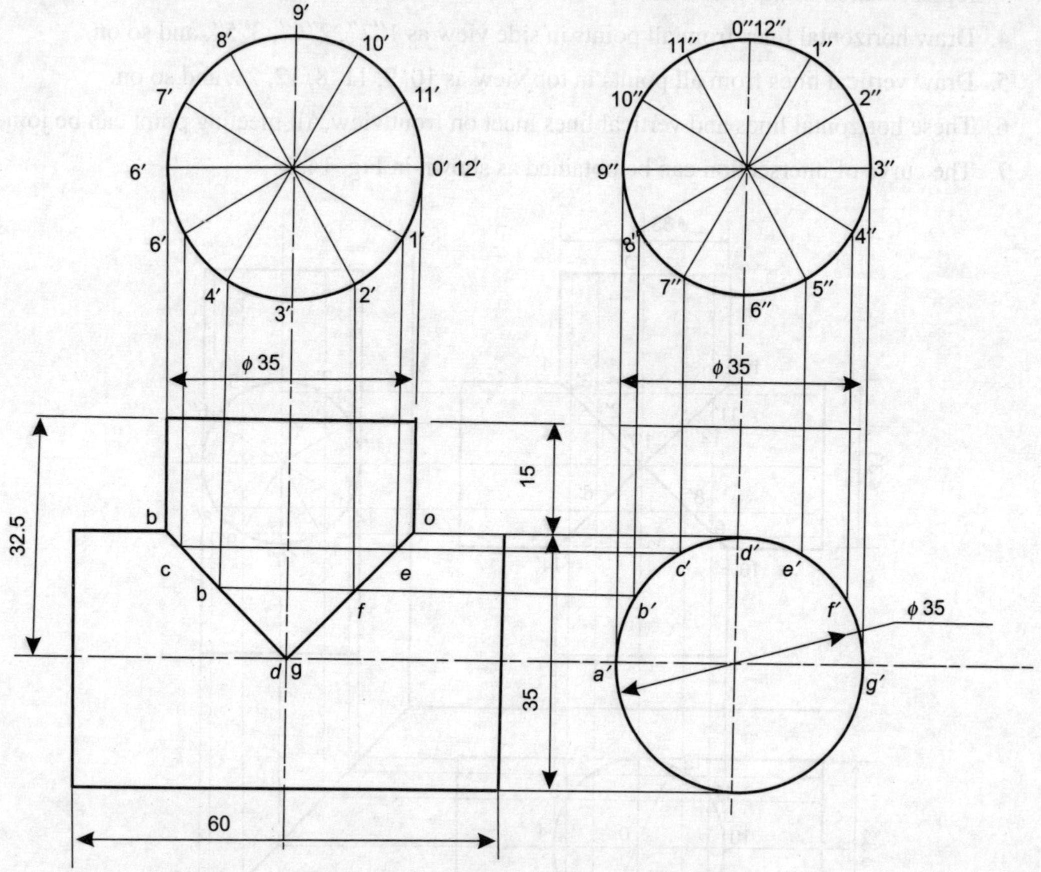

Fig. 14.3 Solution to Problem 14.2

Steps:

1. Draw front view and side view of the horizontal and the vertical cylinders. The axes of the two are perpendicular to each other.
2. Draw a circle at the top of the front view and divide the circle into 12 equal parts numbered as 0′, 1′, 2′, …, 12′.
3. Draw a circle at the top of the side view and divide the circle into 12 equal parts numbered as 0″, 1″, 2″, …, 12″.
4. Draw projections for 0″, 1″, 2″, ... in side view to meet at *a*′, *b*′, *c*′, and so on.
5. Draw projections from the front view circle.
6. From *a*′, *b*′, *c*′, … draw horizontal lines to meet there in front view. They are meeting at *a*, *b*, *c*, etc.
7. Join all the corresponding points as shown. This will represent the curve of intersection.

PROBLEM 14.3 (FIG. 14.4)

A cylinder of diameter 60 mm and length 80 mm stands vertically on its base on HP. It is penetrated by a horizontal cylinder of diameter 50 mm and length 80 mm. The axis of horizontal cylinder is parallel to VP and the axis of both the cylinders bisect to each other. Draw the projection on, showing the curve of intersection.

Solution:

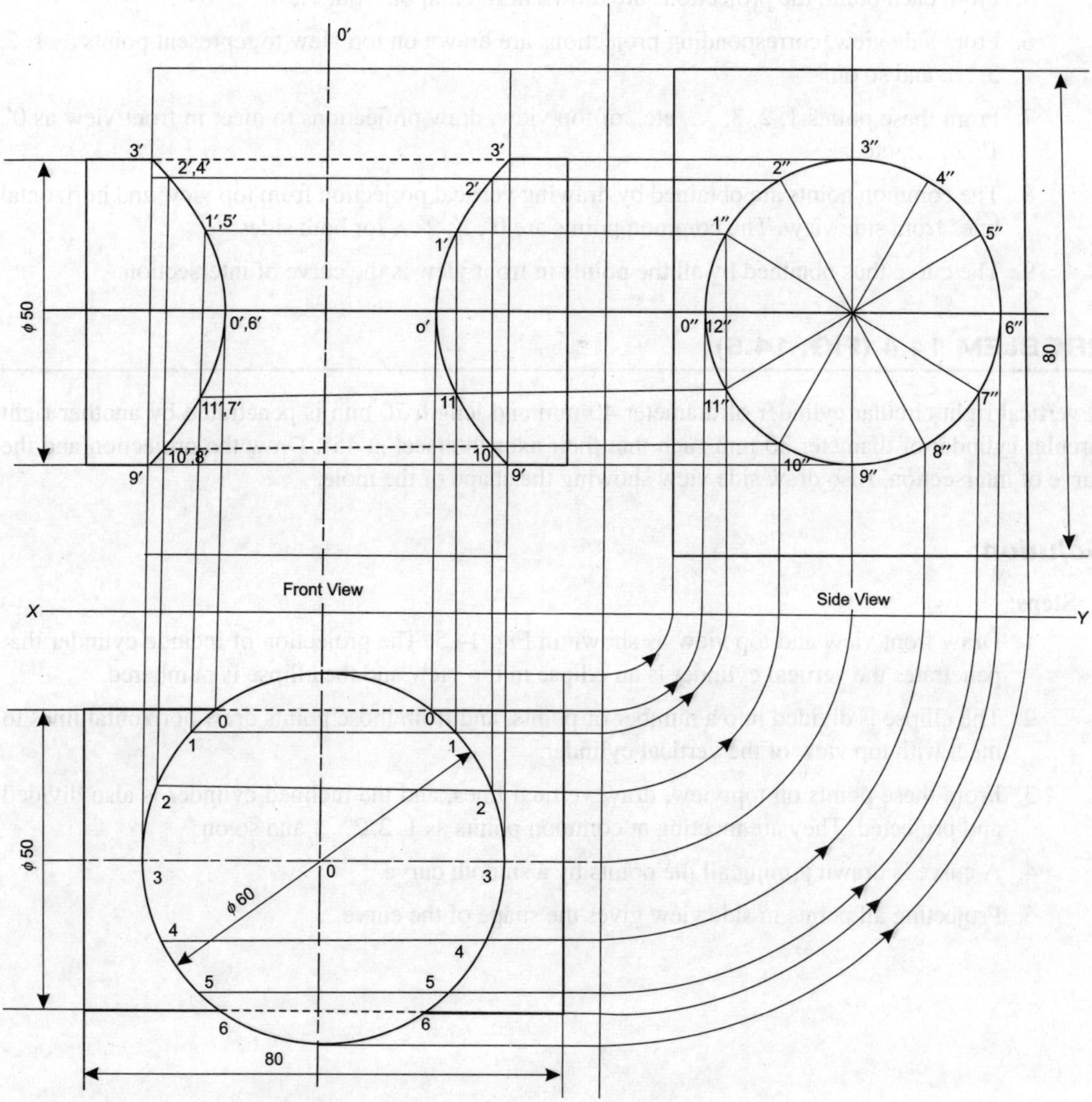

Fig. 14.4 Solution to Problem 14.3

Steps:

1. Draw the top view and front view of a vertical cylinder of base diameter 60 mm and height 80 mm.
2. The top view of the cylinder is a circle of 60 mm diameter.
3. The side view for horizontal cylinder is a circle of 50 mm diameter.
4. The solution of such a problem can be started from side view. The side view of the circle is divided into 12 equal parts numbered as 0″, 1″, 2″, …, and 12″.
5. From each point, the projections are drawn horizontal on front view.
6. From side view, corresponding projections are drawn on top view to represent points as 1, 2, 3, …, and so on.
7. From these points 1, 2, 3, …, etc., of top view, draw projections to meet in front view as 0′, 1′, 2′, …, etc.
8. The common points are obtained by drawing vertical projection from top view and horizontal lines from side view. The common points are 0′, 1′, 2′… for both sides
9. The curve thus obtained by all the points in front view is the curve of intersection.

PROBLEM 14.4 (FIG. 14.5)

A vertical right circular cylinder of diameter 40 mm and length 70 mm is penetrated by another right circular cylinder of diameter 30 mm such that their axes intersect at 45°. Draw the projection and the curve of intersection. Also draw side view showing the shape of the mole.

Solution:

Steps:

1. Draw front view and top view as shown in Fig. 14.5. The projection of include cylinder that penetrates the vertical cylinder is an ellipse in top view and the ellipse is numbered.
2. The ellipse is divided into a number of points, and from those points draw horizontal lines to meet with top view of the vertical cylinder.
3. From these points on top view, draw vertical lines, and the inclined cylinder is also divided and projected. They are meeting at common points as 1, 2, 3, … and so on.
4. A curve is drawn joining all the points by a smooth curve.
5. Projecting all points in side view gives the shape of the curve.

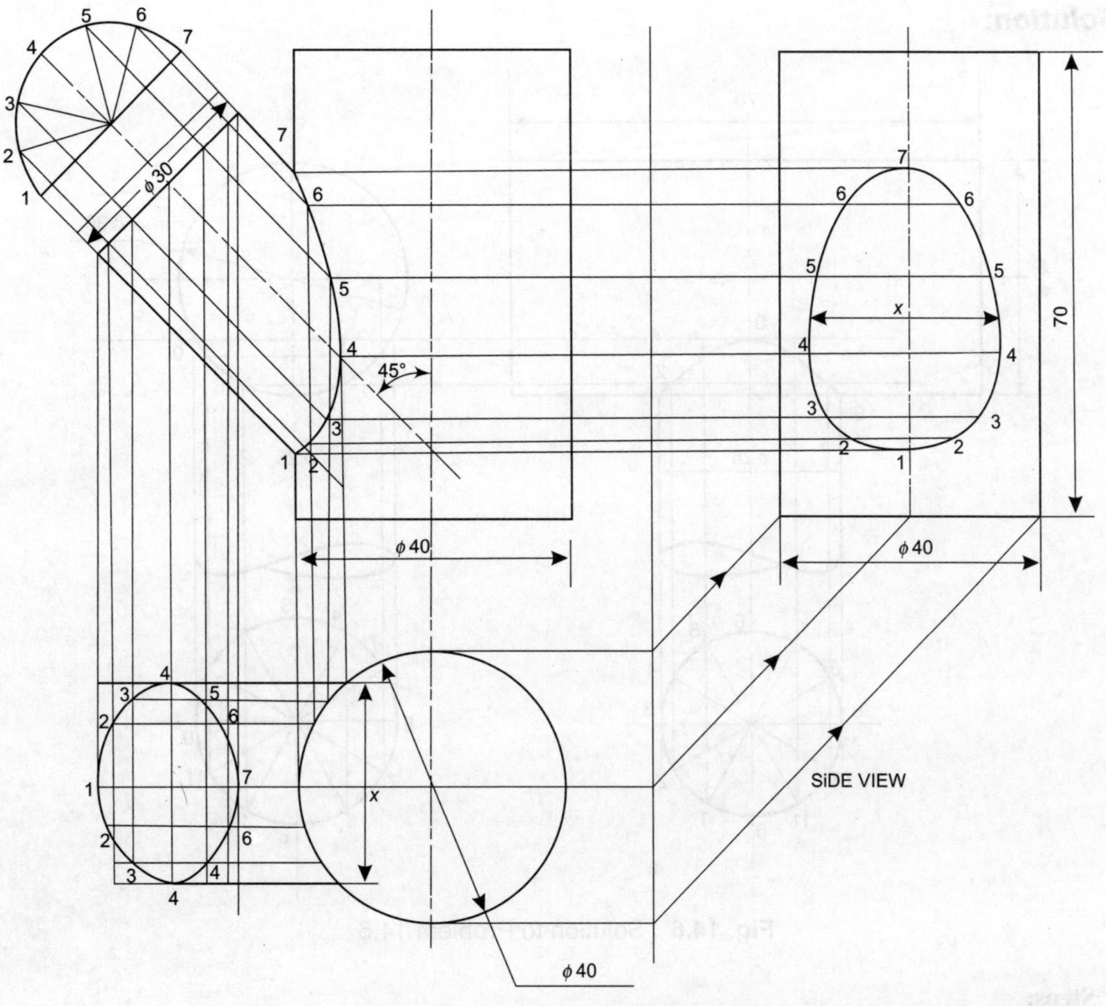

Fig 14.5 Solution to Problem 14.4

PROBLEM 14.5 (FIG. 14.6)

A horizontal pipe of diameter 30 mm and length 70 mm is connected with a pipe of small diameter, i.e., 25 mm from downward. Draw the projection and the line of intersection.

Solution:

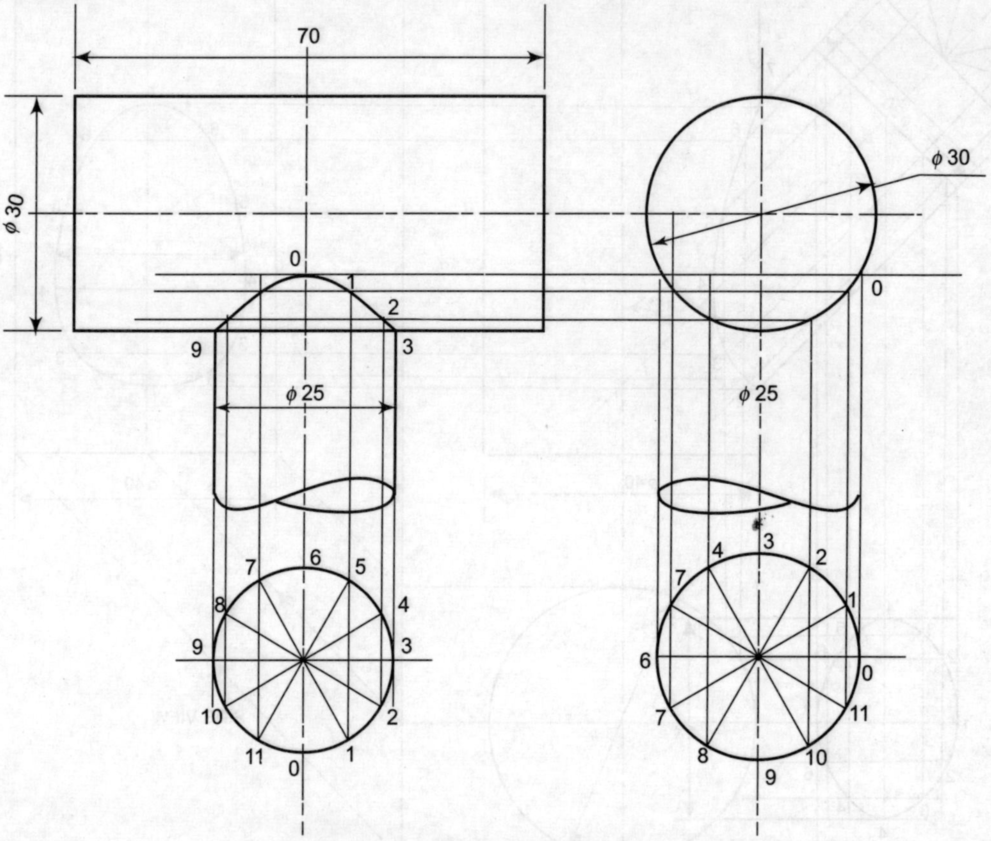

Fig. 14.6 Solution to Problem 14.5

Steps:

1. Draw the front view of a horizontal pipe of diameter 30 mm, joining it with a small diameter tube of 25 mm diameter with it downward.
2. Draw side view as shown in Fig. 14.6.
3. The projection of small diameter tube in front view and side view will be a circle, which will be divided into 12 equal parts and then numbered. The orientation of these two circles will be 90°.
4. Project upward from all these points and draw horizontal lines from 0, 1, 2, and so on, in side view.
5. Project from all points upward in front view. They are joined in front view.
6. Connect all points by smooth curve. This is the required curve of intersection.

PROBLEM 14.6 (FIG. 14.7)

Figure 14.7 shows one cylinder penetrating the other. Horizontal cylinder has the dimensions—diameter 30 mm and length 60 mm. Other vertical branch pipe has diameter 25 mm and fitted eccentrically, axes of both cylinders have the eccentricity of 3 mm. Draw the projection and also the curve of penetration.

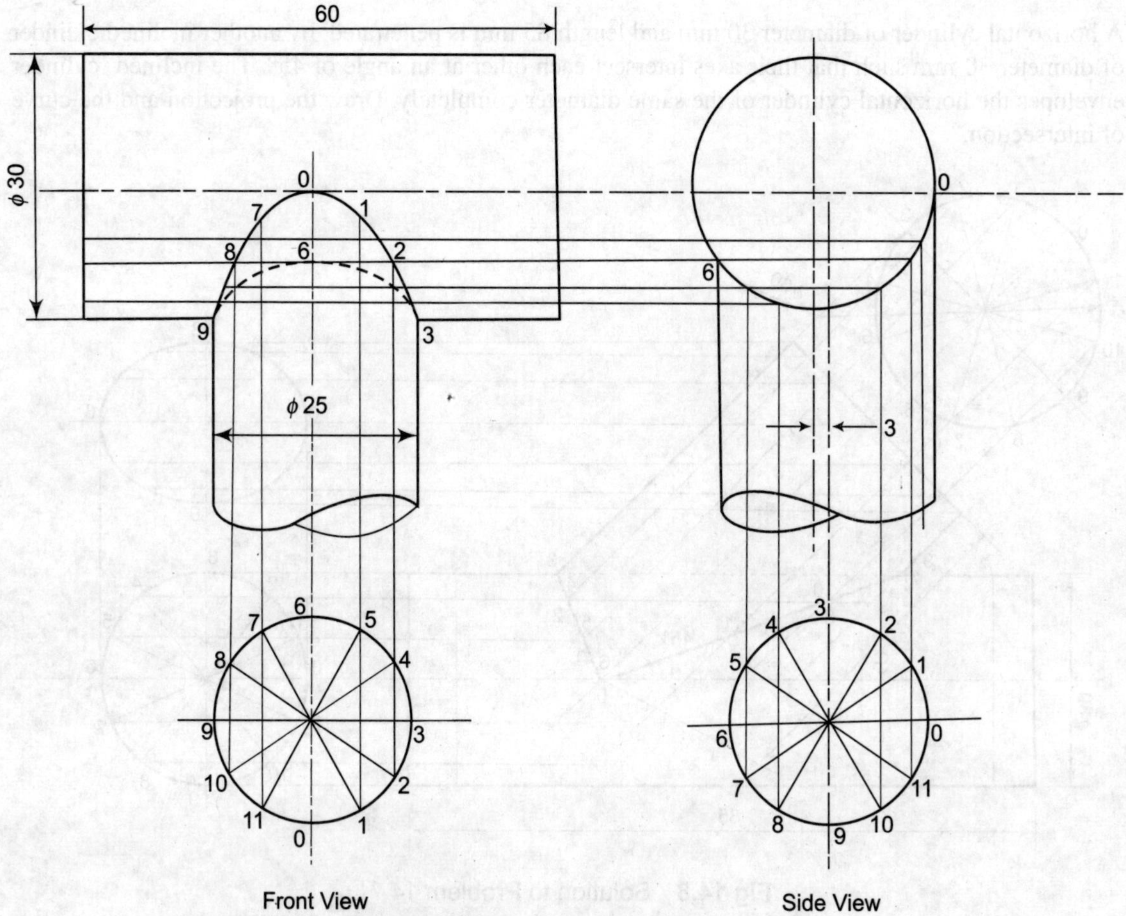

Fig. 14.7 Solution to Problem 14.6

Solution:

Steps:

Figure 14.6 which gives the solution of Problem 14.7 is self-explanatory.

PROBLEM 14.7 (FIG. 14.8)

A horizontal cylinder of diameter 30 mm and length 85 mm is penetrated by another inclined cylinder of diameter 30 mm such that their axes intersect each other at an angle of 45°. The inclined cylinder envelopes the horizontal cylinder of the same diameter completely. Draw the projection and the curve of intersection.

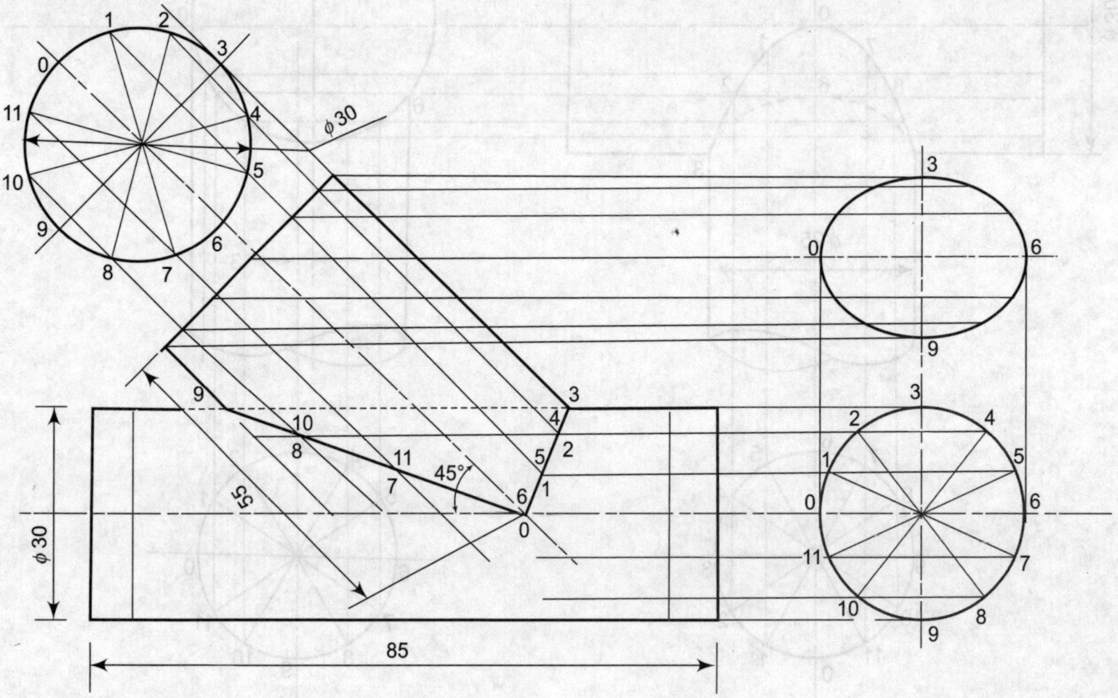

Fig 14.8 Solution to Problem 14.7

The solution of this problem is similar to Fig. 14.7.

PROBLEM 14.8 (FIG. 14.9)

A horizontal pipe of diameter 40 mm and length 80 mm is penetrated by another branch pipe of diameter 30 mm and inclined at 45° with the axis of horizontal pipe. Draw the projection and the curve of intersection.

Solution:

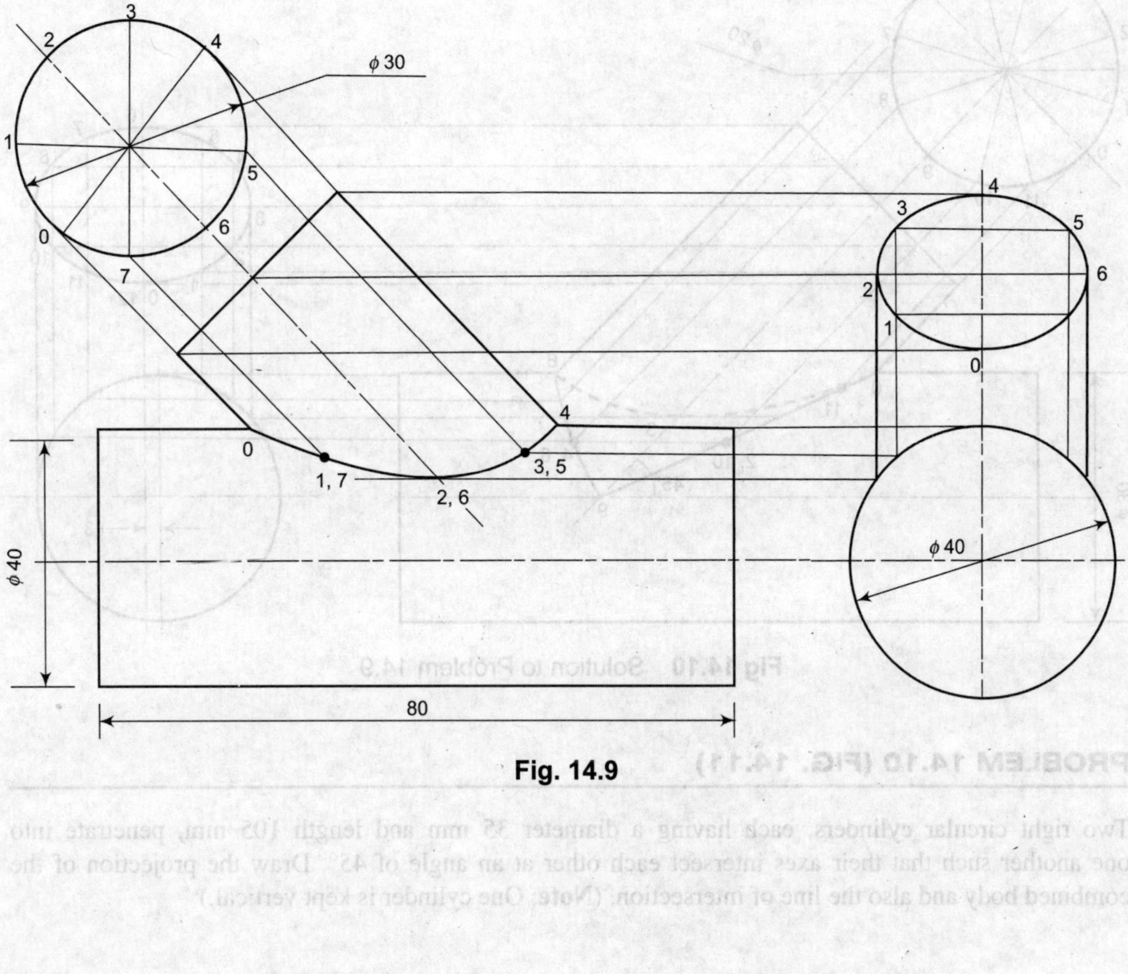

Fig. 14.9

PROBLEM 14.9 (FIG. 14.10)

A horizontal pipe of diameter 30 mm is penetrated by an inclined branch pipe of diameter 25 mm. The axis of branch pipe makes an angle of 45° with horizontal pipe axis. Draw the projection and also the curve of intersection. The branch pipe axis is offset 3 mm from the horizontal pipe axis.

***Solution*:**

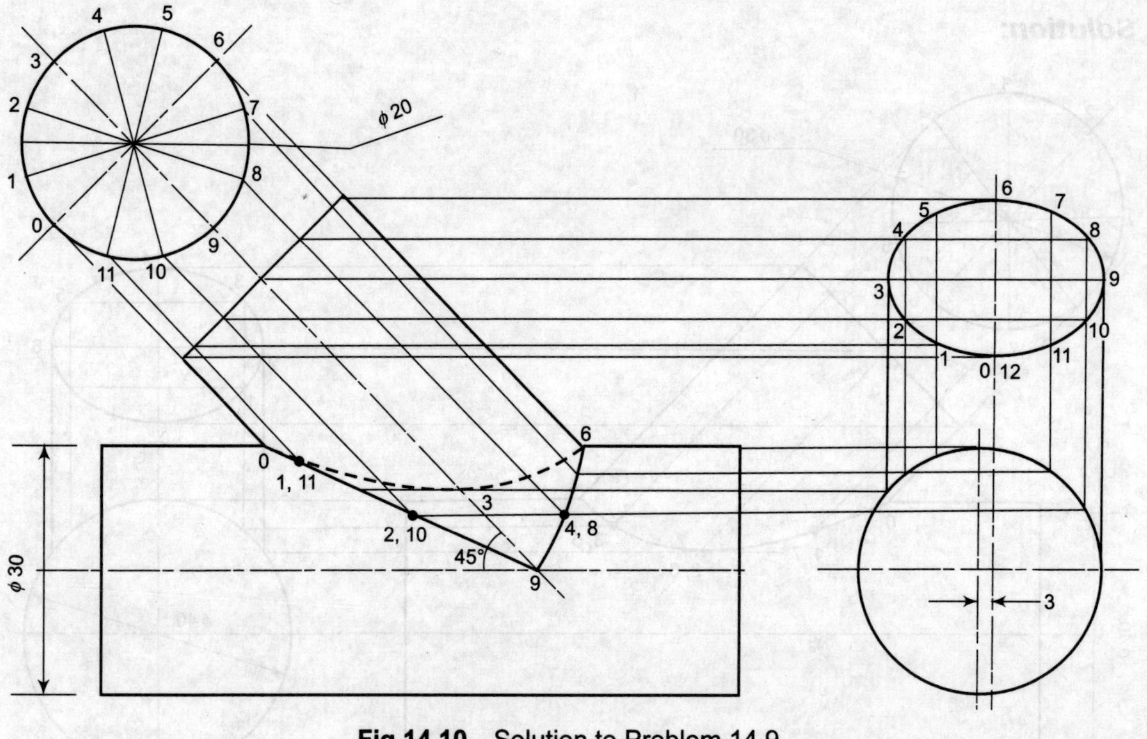

Fig 14.10 Solution to Problem 14.9

PROBLEM 14.10 (FIG. 14.11)

Two right circular cylinders, each having a diameter 35 mm and length 105 mm, penetrate into one another such that their axes intersect each other at an angle of 45°. Draw the projection of the combined body and also the line of intersection. (**Note**: One cylinder is kept vertical.)

Solution:

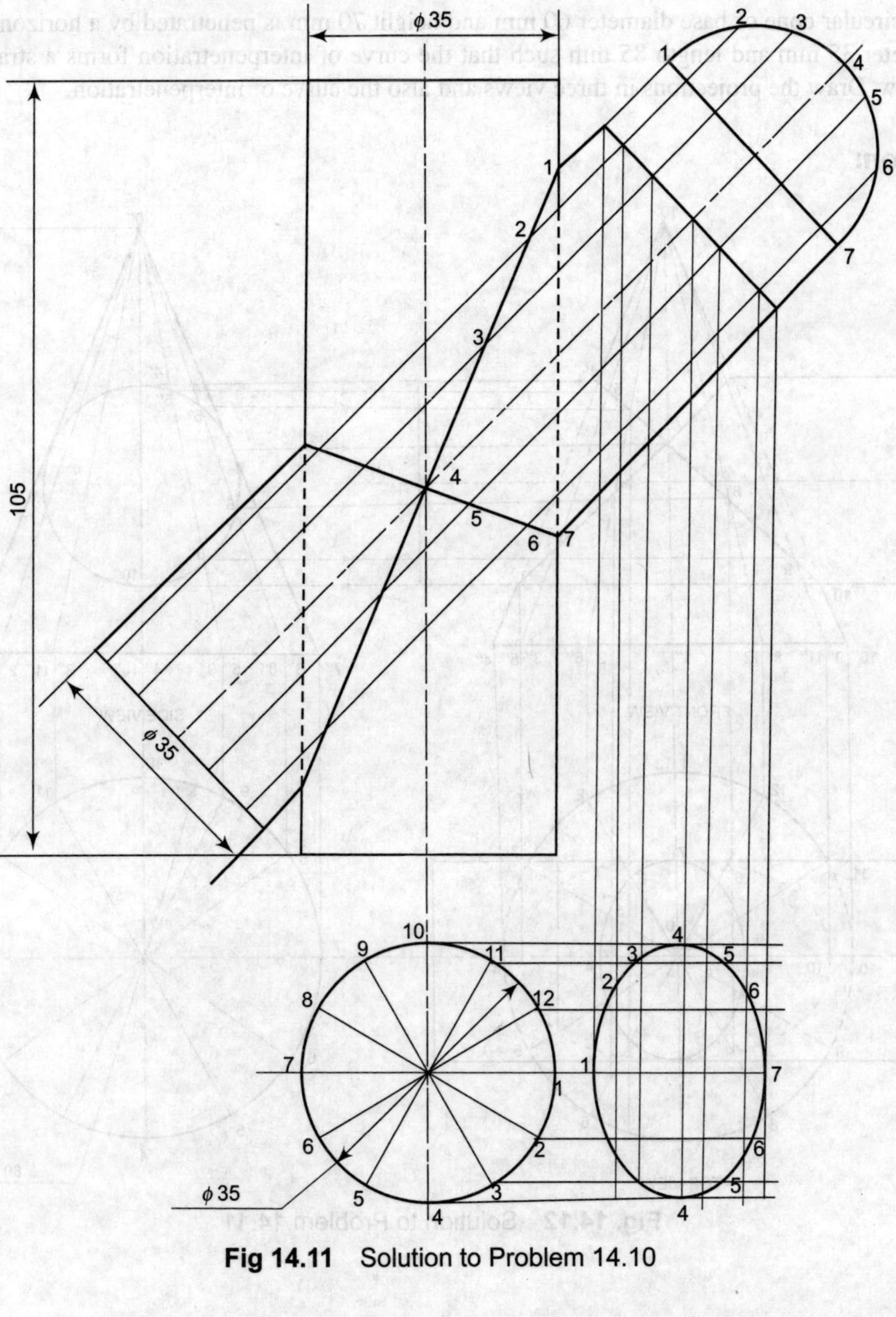

Fig 14.11 Solution to Problem 14.10

PROBLEM 14.11 (FIG. 14.12)

A right circular cone of base diameter 60 mm and height 70 mm is penetrated by a horizontal cylinder of diameter 35 mm and length 85 mm such that the curve of interpenetration forms a straight line in front view. Draw the projections in three views and also the curve of interpenetration.

Solution:

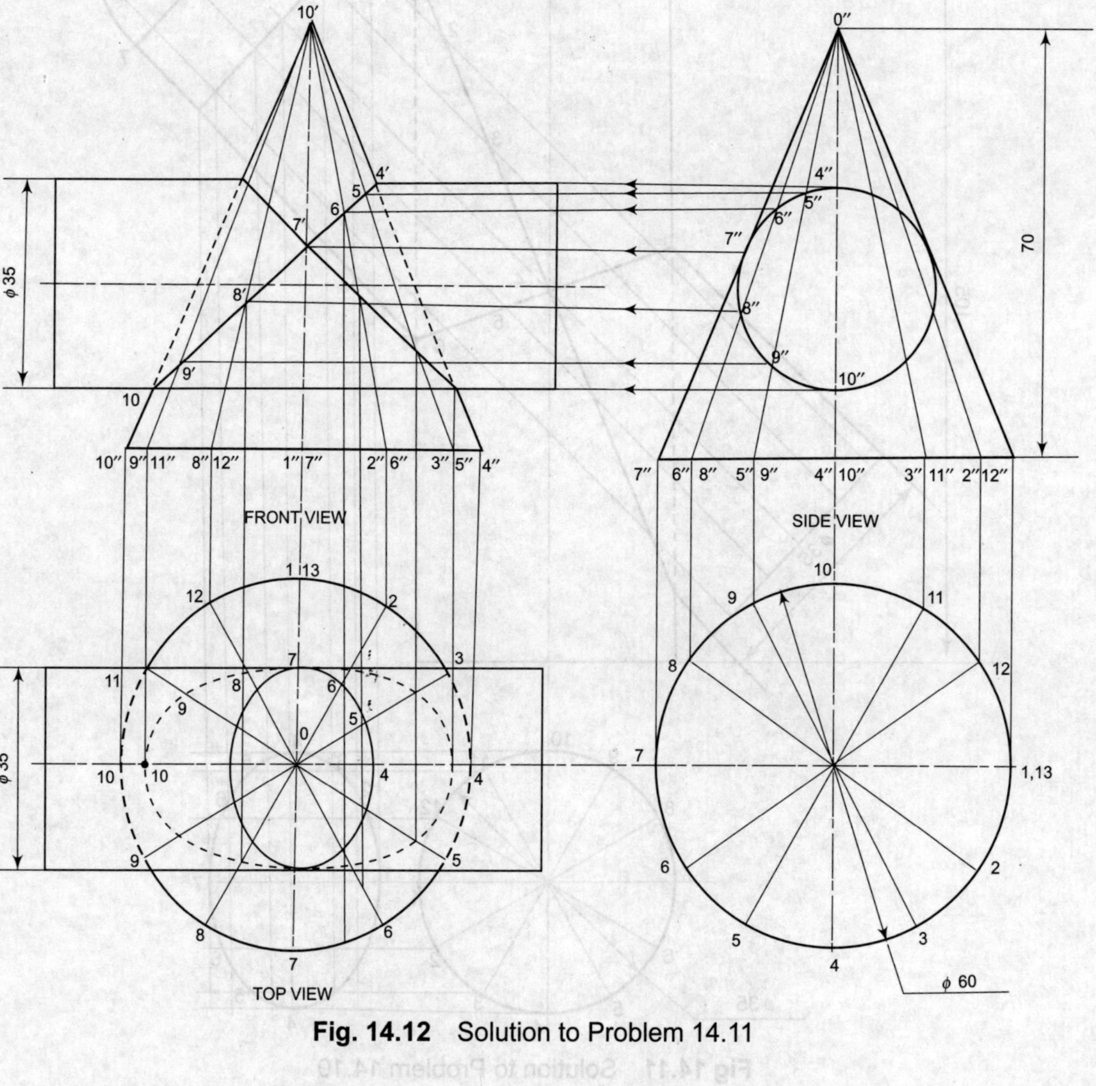

Fig. 14.12 Solution to Problem 14.11

Steps:

1. Draw the front view, top view, and end view.
2. In side view, draw a circle of diameter equal to that of horizontal cylinder, i.e., 35 mm, tangential to the two end generators.
3. In front view, the curve will be a straight line when the cylinder touches the end generators.
4. Divide the circular base of cone into 12 equal parts to represent generators 01, 02, and so on. Project the generators to front view as $0'1'$, $0'2'$, and so on.
5. Corresponding generators may also be represented as $0''1''$, $0''2''$, …, etc., in side view.
6. The circle intersects the generators in side view at $4''$, $5''$, $6''$, …, $10''$. in one side.
7. Project from these points on front view to locate $4'$, $5'$, $6'$, …, etc.
8. Project all these points on top view to locate corresponding points on generators' top view.
9. From front view, the upper portion will be visible and lower portion of the curve will not be visible.

   That is,

   $4'$, $5'$, $6'$,$7'$ will be visible.

   $8'$, $9'$, $10'$ will not be visible.
10. Similarly, the straight line for other side may also be drawn.
11. Projection of these points from front view on top view obtains the ellipse, which has been drawn on top view.

PROBLEM 14.12 (FIG. 14.13)

A right circular cone of base diameter 60 mm and height 70 mm stands vertically on HP. A right circular cylinder of diameter 35 mm intersects from vertical at the top eccentrically.

The axes are separated 10 mm away on a plane at an angle of 45° from VP. Draw the projection and the curve of intersection.

Solution:

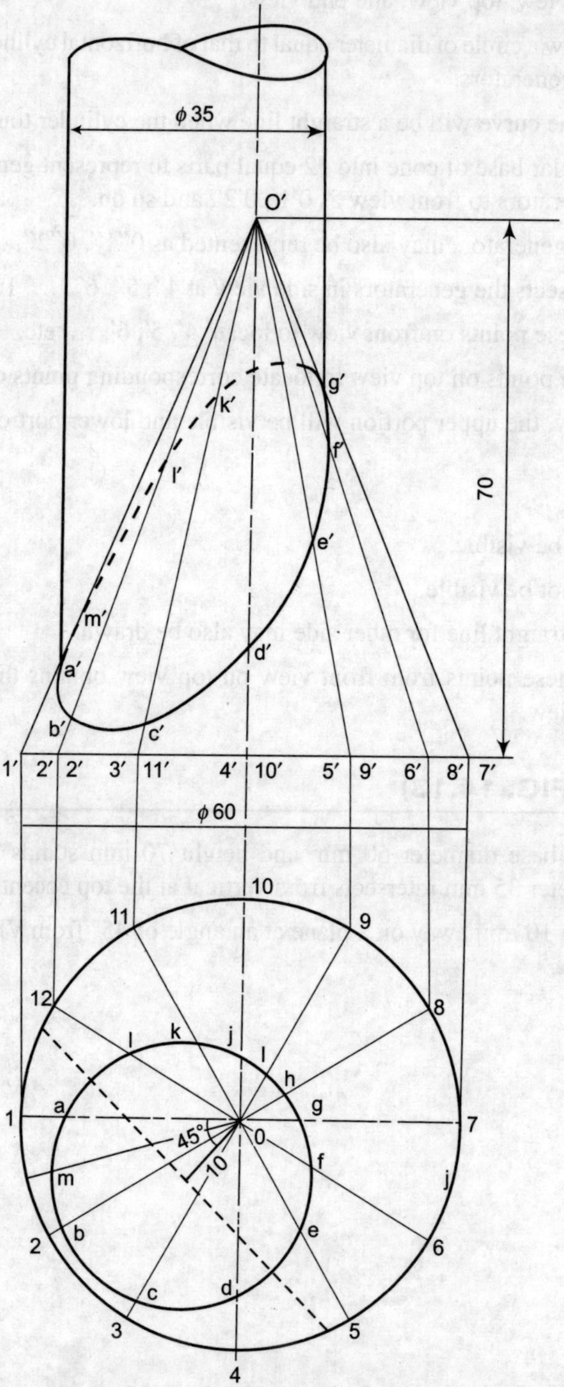

Fig. 14.13 Solution to Problem 14.12

PROBLEM 14.13 (FIG. 14.14)

A square prism of base side 35 mm and height 70 mm is lying with its base on HP. The two rectangular faces are equally inclined to VP. It is completely penetrated by a horizontal square prism of base side 20 mm and length 80 mm. The axes of the two prisms intersect each other at right angle. The two rectangular faces of horizontal prisms are equally inclined to HP and the axis is parallel to VP. Draw the intersection of the curve of the two prism and also the projection of the two.

Solution:

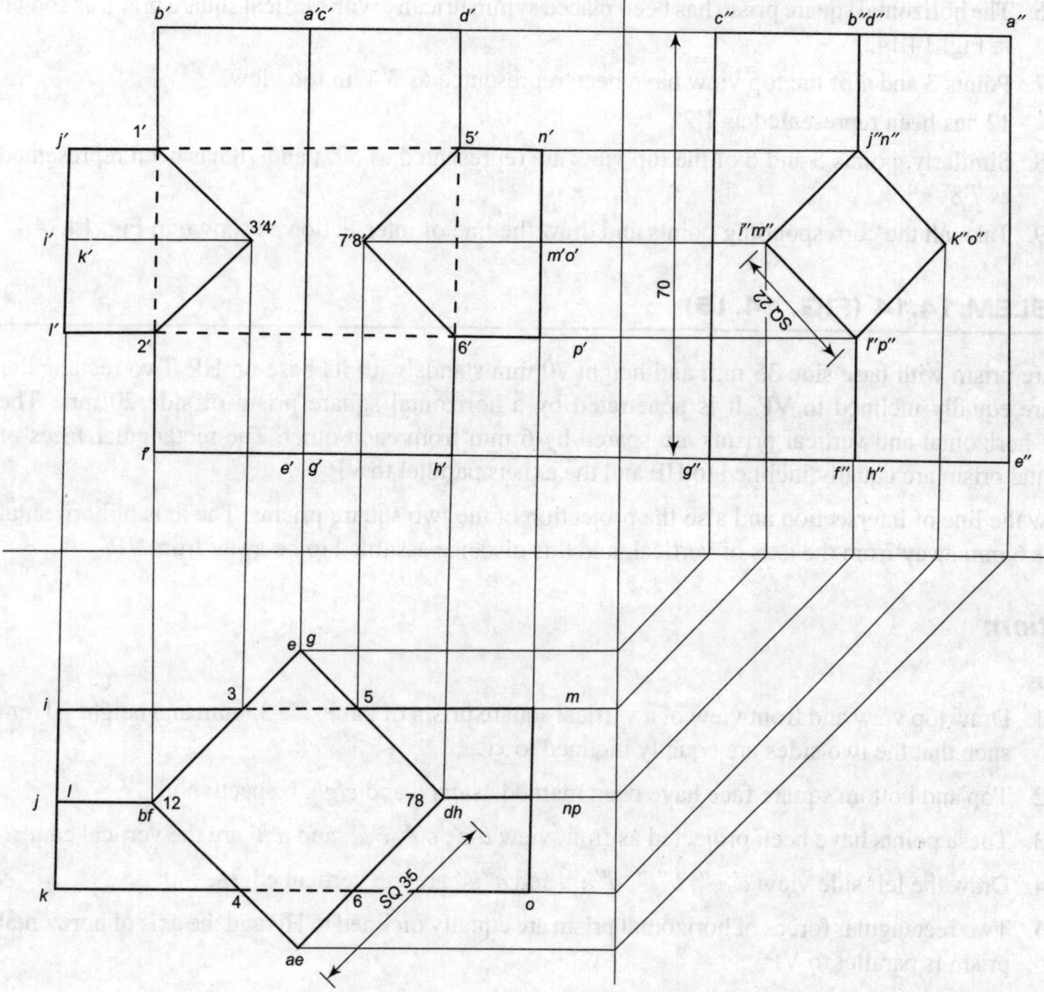

Fig. 14.14 Solution to Problem 14.13

Steps:

1. Draw top view and front view of a vertical square prism of base side 35 mm and height 70 mm such that the two sides are equally inclined to *xy*.
2. Top and bottom square faces have been marked as *abcd* and *efgh*, respectively.
3. These points have been projected as front view; *a′e′*, *b′f′*, *c′g′*, and *d′h′* are the vertical edges.
4. Draw the left side view *c″g″*, *b″f″*, *d″h″*, and *a″e″* are the vertical edges.
5. Two rectangular forces of horizontal prism are equally inclined to HP, and the axis of horizontal prism is parallel to VP.

   The end face of this will be seen as a square of 22 mm side.

   The end face has been named as *i″ j″ k″ l″* and *m″ n″ o″ p″*.
6. The horizontal square prism has been placed symmetrically with vertical square prism as shown in Fig. 14.14.
7. Points 3 and 4 of the top view have been represented as 3′4′ in top view.

   12 has been represented as 1′2′.
8. Similarly, points 5 and 6 of the top view are represented as 5′6′; and 78 has been represented as 7′8′.
9. Take all the corresponding points and draw the line of intersection as shown in Fig. 14.14.

PROBLEM 14.14 (FIG. 14.15)

A square prism with base side 35 mm and height 70 mm stands with its base on HP. Two rectangular faces are equally inclined to VP. It is penetrated by a horizontal square prism of side 20 mm. The axes of horizontal and vertical prisms are spared by 6 mm from each other. The rectangular faces of horizontal prism are equally inclined to HP and the axis is parallel to VP.

Draw the line of intersection and also the projection of the two square prisms. The axis of horizontal prism is 6 mm away from the axis of vertical, and this distance assumed to be away from VP.

Solution:

Steps:

1. Draw top view and front view of a vertical square prism of base side 35 mm and height 70 mm such that the two sides are equally inclined to *xy*.
2. Top and bottom square face have been marked as *abcd* and *efgh*, respectively.
3. These points have been projected as front view *a′e′*, *b′f′*, *c′g′*, and *d′h′* are the vertical edges.
4. Draw the left side view *c″g″*, *b″f″*, *d″h″*, and *a″e″* are the vertical edges.
5. Two rectangular forces of horizontal prism are equally inclined to HP and the axis of horizontal prism is parallel to VP.

   The end face of this will be seen as square of 20 mm side.

   The end face has been named as *i″ j″ k″ l″* and *m″ n″ o″ p″*.

6. The horizontal square prism has been placed 6 mm away from the axis of vertical prism as shown in Fig. 14.15.
7. The horizontal square prism penetrates the vertical prism completely.

   The edge of horizontal prism cutting the vertical prism in top view.

   1&5, 24, 68, 3&7

   The projection of all these points in front view as 1′,5′, 2′4′, 6′8′, and also 3′7′
8. The actual representation of line of penetration is shown in Fig 14.15.

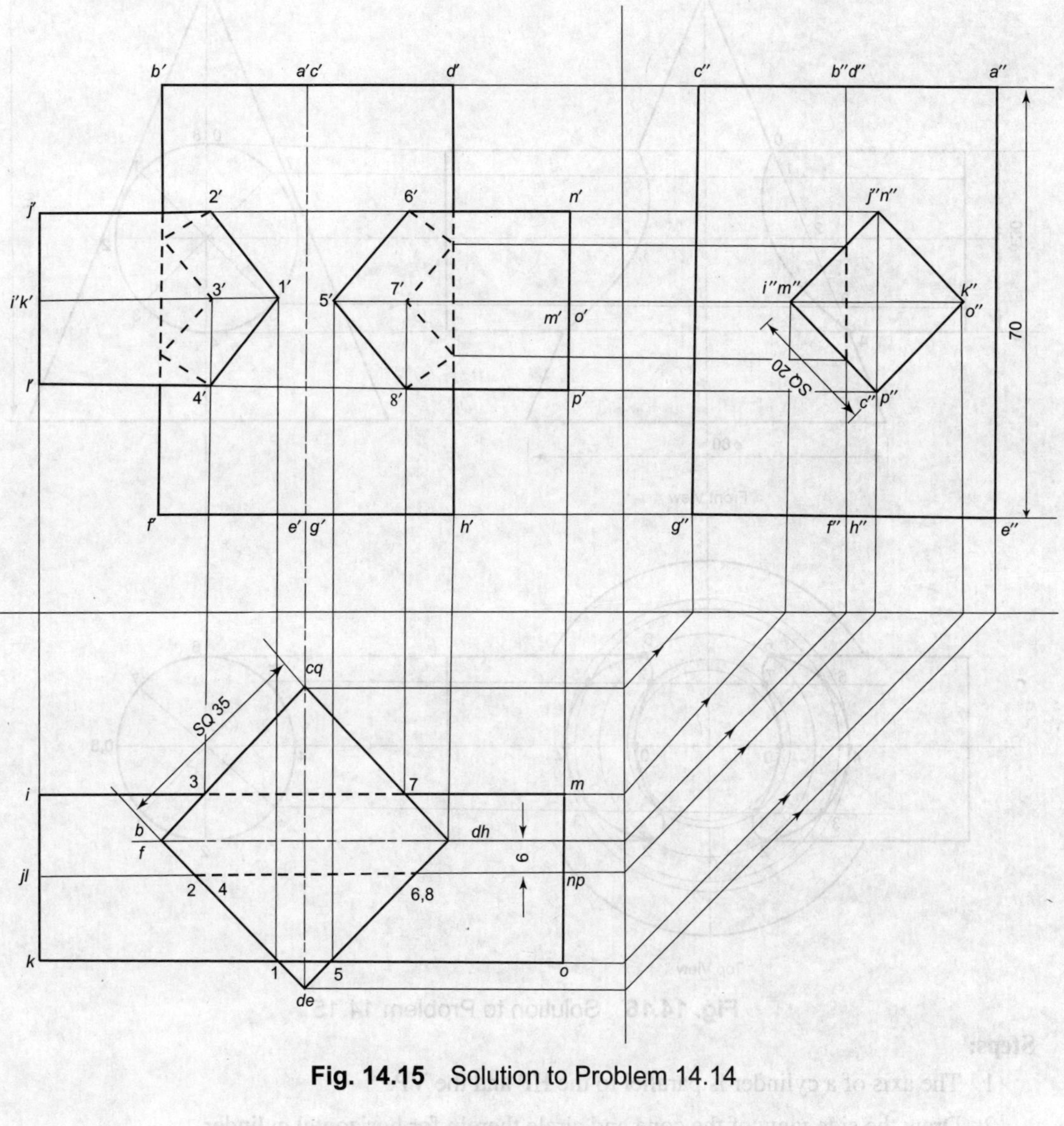

Fig. 14.15 Solution to Problem 14.14

PROBLEM 14.15 (FIG. 14.16)

A right circular cone with diameter 60 mm and height 70 mm is intersected by a cylinder of diameter 30 mm horizontally. The axis of the cylinder is 30 mm above the base of cone. Draw the projection, curve of intersection, and top view.

Solution:

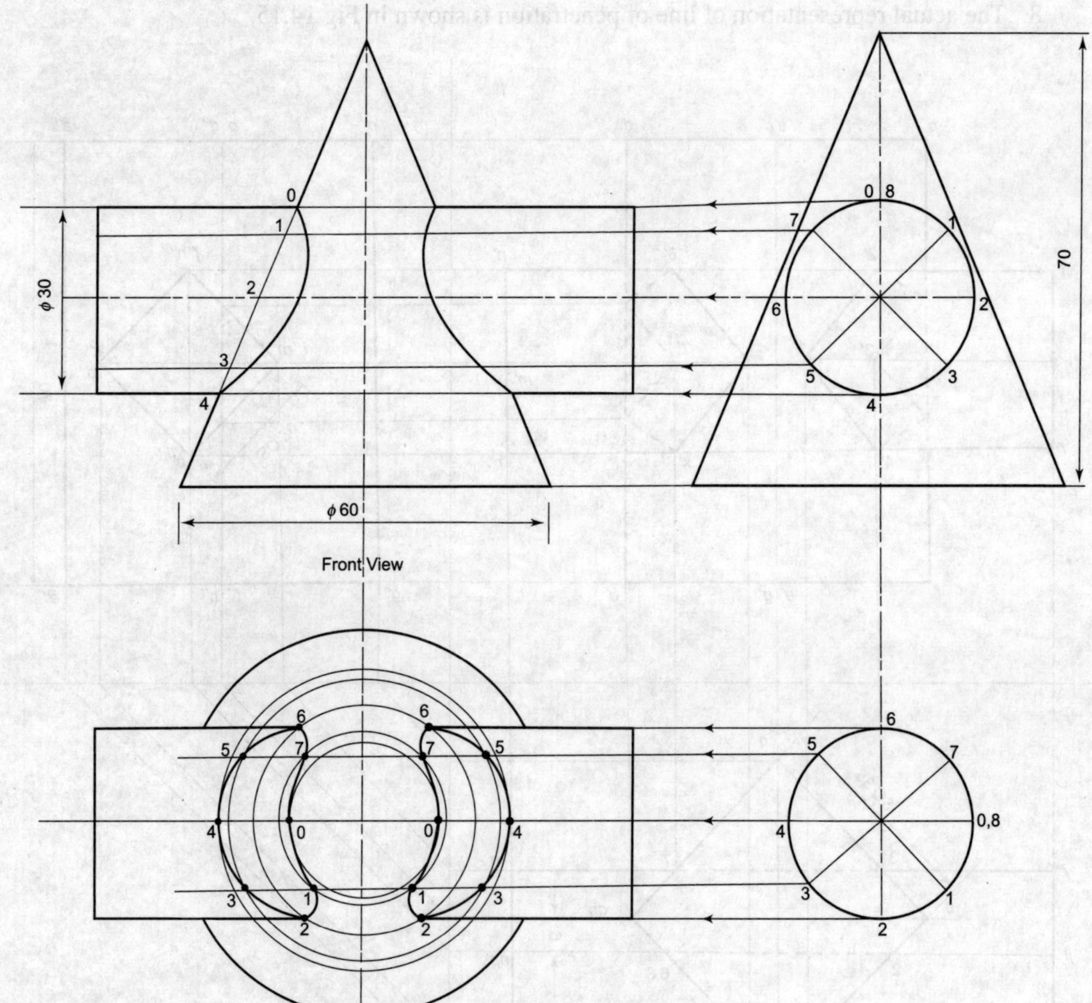

Fig. 14.16 Solution to Problem 14.15

Steps:

1. The axis of a cylinder is parallel to the HP and the VP.
2. Draw the side view of the cone and circle therein for horizontal cylinder.

3. Divide the circle into 8 equal parts. Project from these points on the front view and obtain 0, 1, 2, 3, 4.
4. Now draw projectors from these points on top view to meet the diameter of the base circle.
5. Draw another circle from the end of cylinder through top view as shown in Fig. 14.16.
6. Divide the circle into 8 equal parts and number. The orientation of this would be 90° from the circle already drawn from side view.
7. Projecting from these points, obtained curve is 01234567.
8. From these points, draw a projection to meet the projection already drawn from points on circle in side view.
9. Trace the curve on both the sides.

PROBLEM 14.16 (FIG. 14.17)

A cylinder of diameter 50 mm is intercepted by a frustum of cone, height 35 mm and base diameter 40 mm as shown in Fig. 14.17. Draw the curve of intersection and the development of cone.

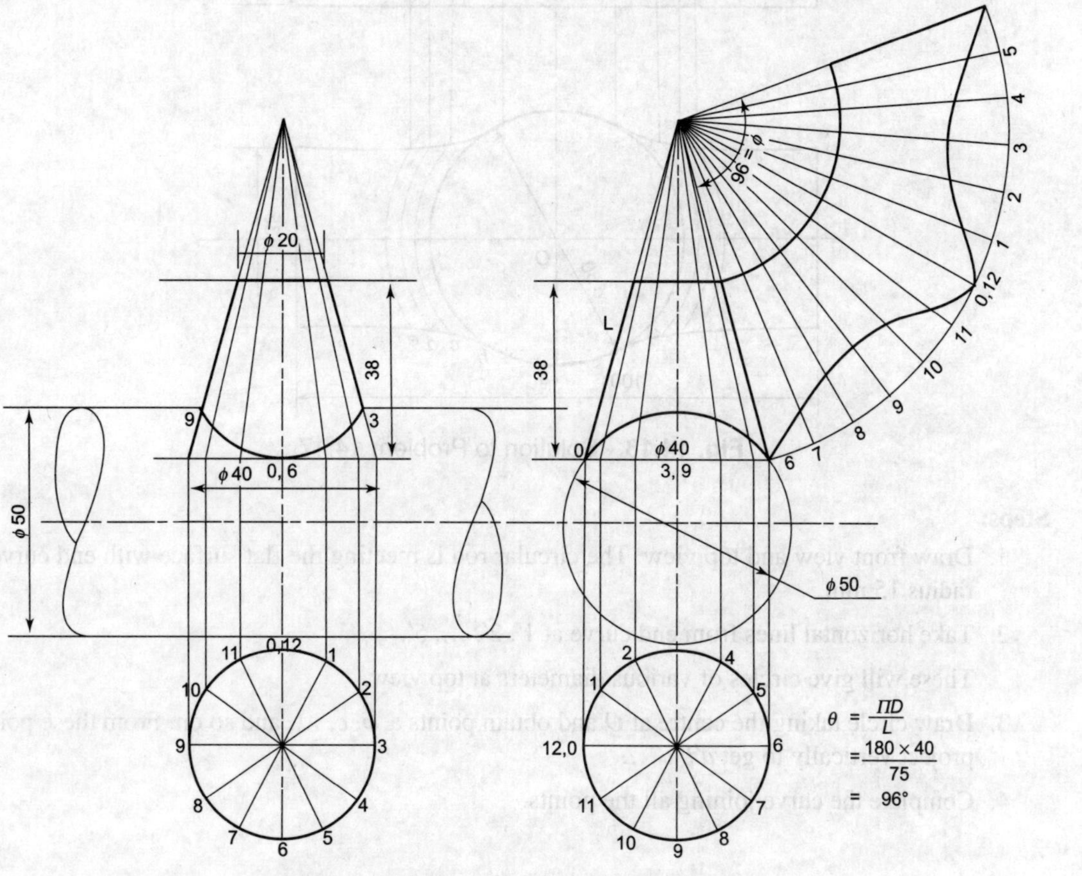

Fig. 14.17 Solution to Problem 14.16

PROBLEM 14.17 (FIG. 14.18)

A cylindrical rod of diameter 50 mm is connected vertically and symmetrically with a rectangular slab of length 100 mm, width 35 mm, and thickness 15 mm.

Draw the projection and also the curve of intersection.

Solution:

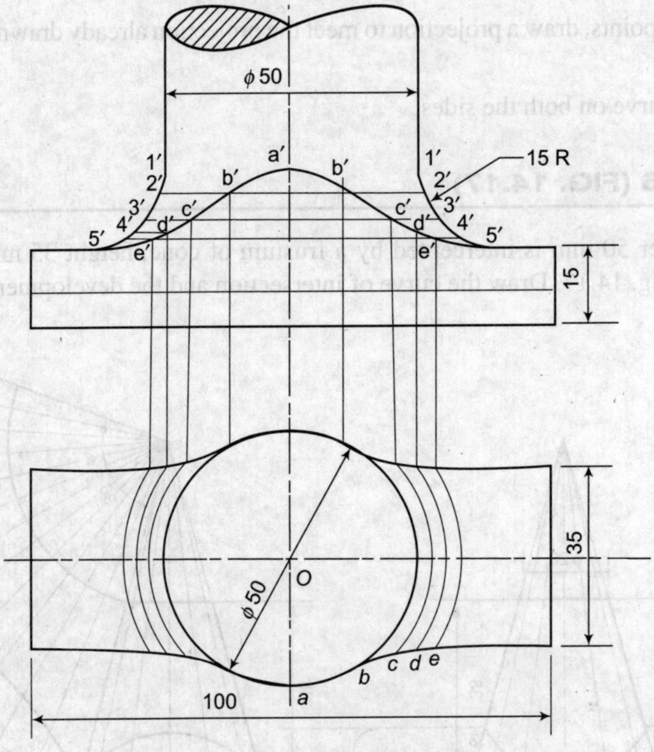

Fig. 14.18 Solution to Problem 14.17

Steps:

1. Draw front view and top view. The circular rod is meeting the flat surface with end curve of radius 15 mm.
2. Take horizontal lines from end curve at 1′, 2′, …, 5′.

   These will give circles of various diameters at top view.
3. Draw circle taking the centre at *O* and obtain points a, *b*, *c*, …, and so on. From these points, project vertically to get *a′b′c′* …
4. Complete the curve joining all the points.

PROBLEM 14.18 (FIG. 14.19)

A metallic rod of diameter 35 mm is connected with a circular slab of diameter 60 mm and thickness 15 mm. The rod is joining the slab eccentrically. Draw the projection and the curve of intersection.

Solution:

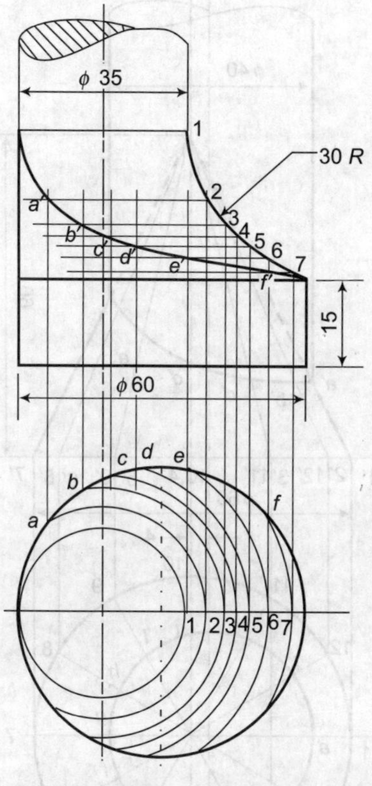

Fig. 14.19 Solution to Problem 14.18

Steps:

1. Draw the projections. The circular rod is meeting with circular slab eccentrically as shown in Fig. 14.19.
2. The circular rod is joining with end curve of radius 30 mm.
3. Draw horizontal lines in front view from 1, 2, 3, and so on.
4. These will produce circles of various diameters in top view.
5. Obtain points 1, 2, 3, … in plane by projecting from front view. Draw circles through these points and get point *a, b, c* … in top view as shown. Project vertically from these points to intersect the section at *a′*, *b′*, *c′*, and so on. Complete the curve of intersection.

PROBLEM 14.19 (FIG. 14.20)

A right circular cone of base diameter 60 mm and height 60 mm stands vertically on HP. A vertical cylinder of diameter 40 mm penetrates vertically at the top. The axes of the two are parallel to each other and are offset by 4 mm along a generator that is parallel to VP. Draw the projection and the curve of intersection.

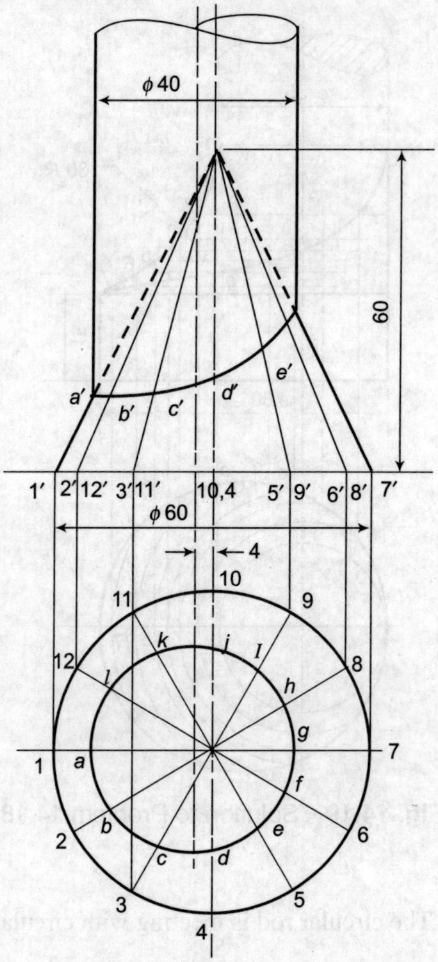

Fig. 14.20 Solution to Problem 14.19

PROBLEM 14.20 (FIG. 14.21)

A vertical right circular cylinder of diameter 40 mm and height 70 mm is penetrated by a right circular cone of base diameter 60 mm and height 70 mm. The axes of the two objects bisect each other at right angle. Draw the projections and the curve of intersection.

Solution:

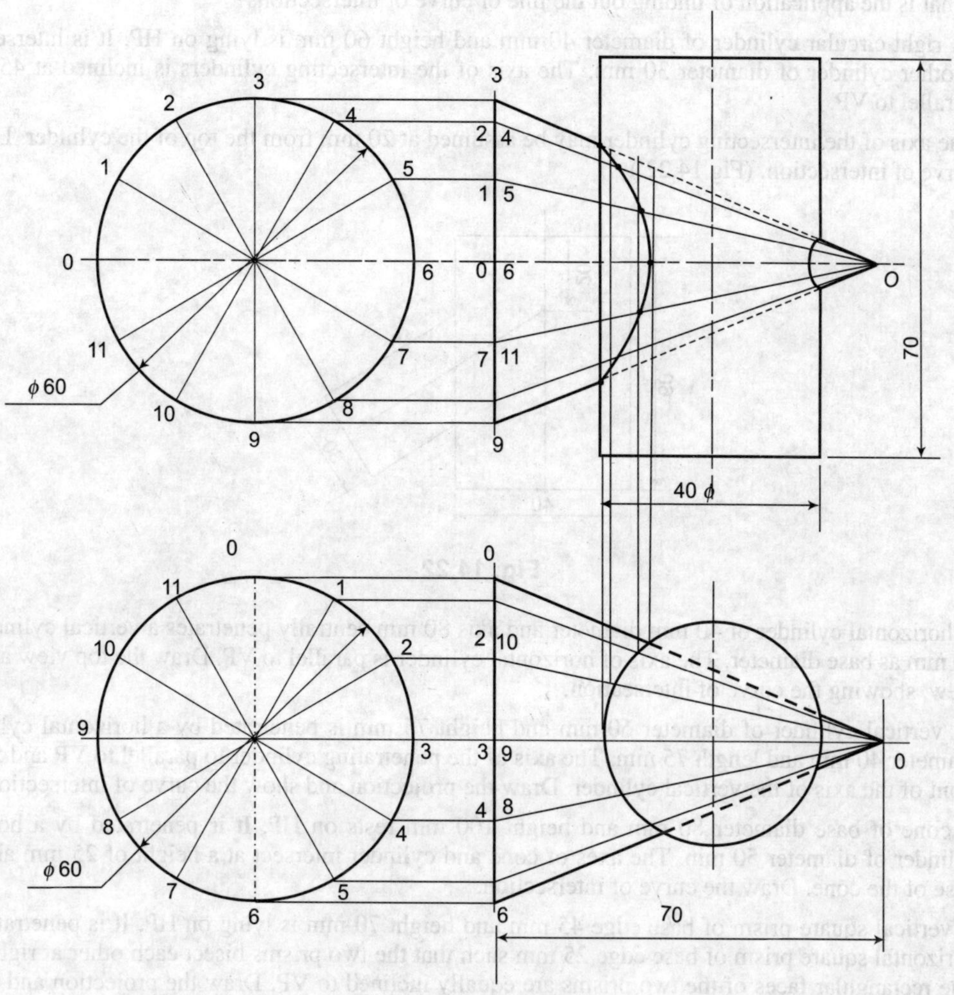

Fig. 14.21 Solution to Problem 14.20

EXERCISE

Review Questions

1. What is the difference between intersection of surface and interpenetration of solids? Explain with the help of a diagram.
2. What are the two different methods to find out the curve of intersections?
3. What is the application of finding out the line or curve of intersections?
4. A right circular cylinder of diameter 40 mm and height 60 mm is lying on HP. It is intersected by another cylinder of diameter 30 mm. The axis of the intersecting cylinders is inclined at 45° and is parallel to VP.

   The axis of the intersecting cylinder may be assumed at 20 mm from the top of the cylinder. Draw the curve of intersection. (Fig 14.22.)

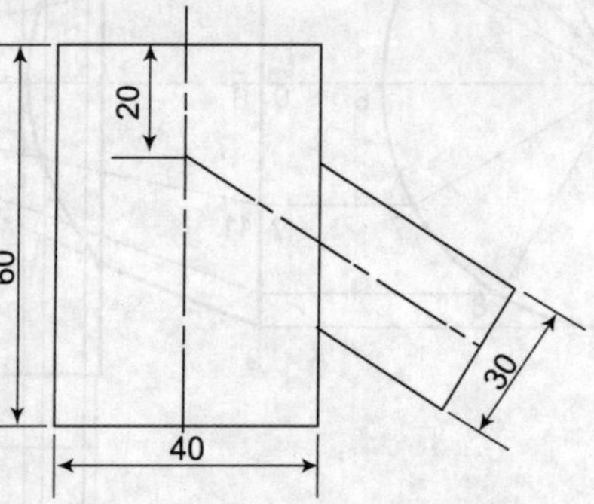

Fig. 14.22

5. A horizontal cylinder of 40 mm diameter and axis 80 mm centrally penetrates a vertical cylinder with 60 mm as base diameter. The axis of horizontal cylinder is parallel to VP. Draw the top view and front view, showing the curve of intersection.
6. A vertical cylinder of diameter 60 mm and height 75 mm is penetrated by a horizontal cylinder of diameter 40 mm and length 75 mm. The axis of the penetrating cylinder to parallel to VP and 5 mm in front of the axis of the vertical cylinder. Draw the projection and show the curve of intersection.
7. A cone of base diameter 80 mm and height 100 mm rests on HP. It is penetrated by a horizontal cylinder of diameter 50 mm. The axes of cone and cylinder intersect at a height of 25 mm about the base of the cone. Draw the curve of intersection.
8. A vertical square prism of base edge 45 mm and height 70 mm is lying on HP. It is penetrated by a horizontal square prism of base edge 25 mm such that the two prisms bisect each other at right angle. The rectangular faces of the two prisms are equally inclined to VP. Draw the projection and also the line of intersection.
9. A vertical square prism of base edge 40 mm and height 70 mm is lying on HP. With a vertical face inclined at 30° to VP. It is completely penetrated by a horizontal square prism of base edge 25 mm and 65 mm long having one of its rectangular faces inclined at 30° to VP. The axes of the two prisms bisect each other. Draw the line of intersection.

10. A vertical cylinder of diameter of base 55 mm and height 65 mm rests on its base in HP. It is penetrated by another cylinder of the same diameter. The axes of the two cylinders bisect each other at right angle. The axis of the penetrating cylinder is 10 mm in front of the axis of the vertical cylinder. Draw the projection and also the curve of intersection.
11. A right circular cone of base diameter 60 mm and height 75 mm is lying with its base on HP. It is completely penetrated by a cylinder of diameter 30 mm and length of 65 mm. The axis of penetrating cylinder is parallel to both HP and VP and intersects the axis of the cone at a distance of 25 mm from its base. Draw the projection and also the curve of intersection.
12. A right circular cylinder with diameter of base 50 mm and length 65 mm is lying on HP by its base. It is penetrated by a square prism of 25 mm base edge, such that the axes of the solids bisect each other at right angle. The faces of the prism are equally inclined to VP. Draw the projection and the curve of intersection.

Objective Questions

1. The intersection of a straight line with a solid is a _________.
2. The intersection of a cylinder and a cone is a _________.
3. The line of intersection becomes a curve when penetrating objects are _________.
4. The purpose of interpretation curve may be explained with respect to _________ applications.
5. When does curve of intersection become a line? _________
6. When two cylinders of different diameters intersect each other, what will be the nature of curve of intersection? _________

ANSWERS

Objective Questions

1. point
2. curved line
3. curved lateral surfaces
4. engineering
5. When two cylinders of equal diameters intersect each other.
6. curve

CHAPTER 15

Isometric Projection

15.1 INTRODUCTION

In engineering drawing, conventionally, it is necessary to draw the three orthographic views to visualize the true shape and size of the object. But, with all the three views, it is difficult to visualize the object unless the person is well trained to read the orthographic projection. To understand the exact shape and size of the object, one view projection of three-dimensional shape is in practice.

Only one view of the three-dimensional shape of an object is known as *pictorial drawing*.

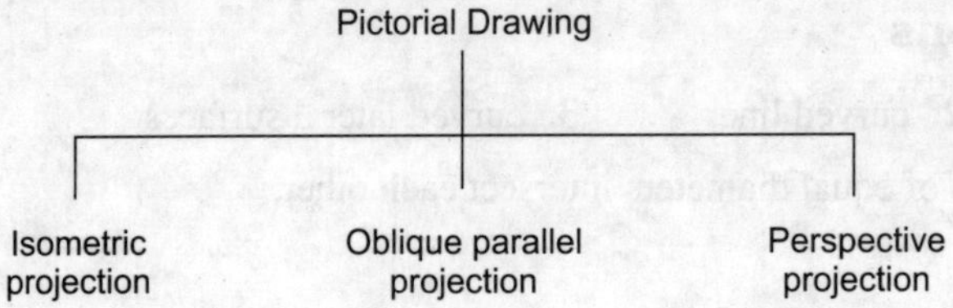

15.2 CLASSIFICATION OF PICTORIAL DRAWING

Pictorial drawing of an object shows the clear understanding because of the fact that one-view projection drawing shows all the three dimensions and true shape of the object. One-view drawing of three dimensions can be easily visualized by a person without the technical idea of the drawing. Pictorial drawings are of several forms as follows (Fig. 15.1).

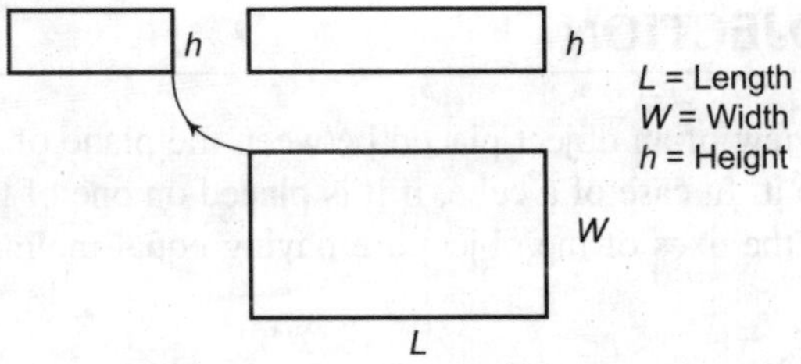

(a) Orthographic projection

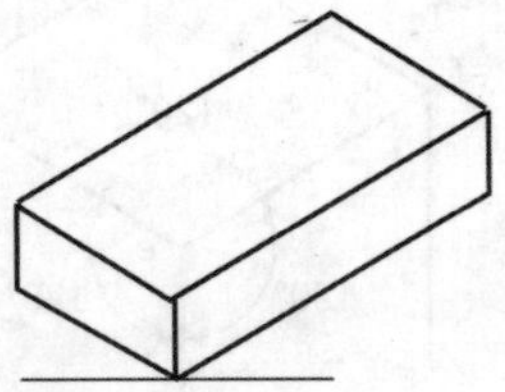

(b) Isometric projection

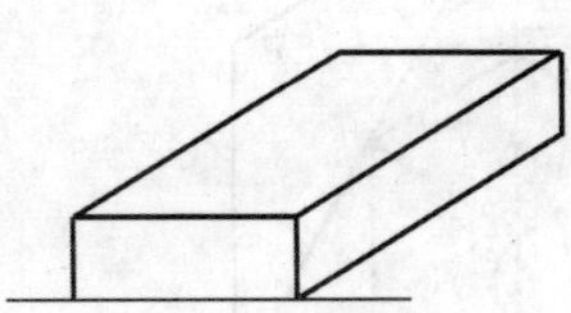

(c) Oblique parallel

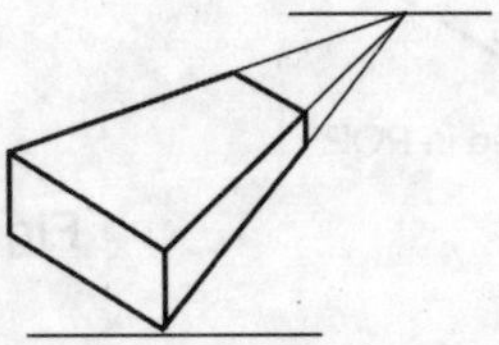

(d) Perspective View

Fig. 15.1 (b), (c), and (d) Pictorial Drawing

(a) Orthographic projection It is the conventional drawing used for comparison with pictorial drawing.

(b) Isometric projection It is a single view of the three-dimensional projection of an object as shown in Fig. 15.1(a). It is a pictorial drawing that is commonly used to make smaller objects like mechanical components, etc. It is a part of *axonometric projection*.

(c) Oblique parallel projection It is also a single view of the three-dimensional projection of an object as shown in Fig. 15.1(b). In this case, one view of the object is complete from all points parallel lines are drawn at some inclination 30°, 45°, or 60°. It is also used to prepare the pictorial drawings of smaller mechanical parts.

(d) Perspective projection It is also a single view of the three-dimensional projection of an object. It is commonly used to prepare pictorial drawing of a larger object like *architectural drawing* of a large building. Civil engineers use this perspective drawing.

From the view corner, all lines are convergent to one point in a single vanishing point.

15.3 ISOMETRIC PROJECTION

Isometric projection is a single view of an object placed between the plane of projection such that all three axes are equally inclined to it. In case of a cube, if it is placed on one of the corners between the plane of projection such that all the axes of the object are having equal inclination with the plane of projection.

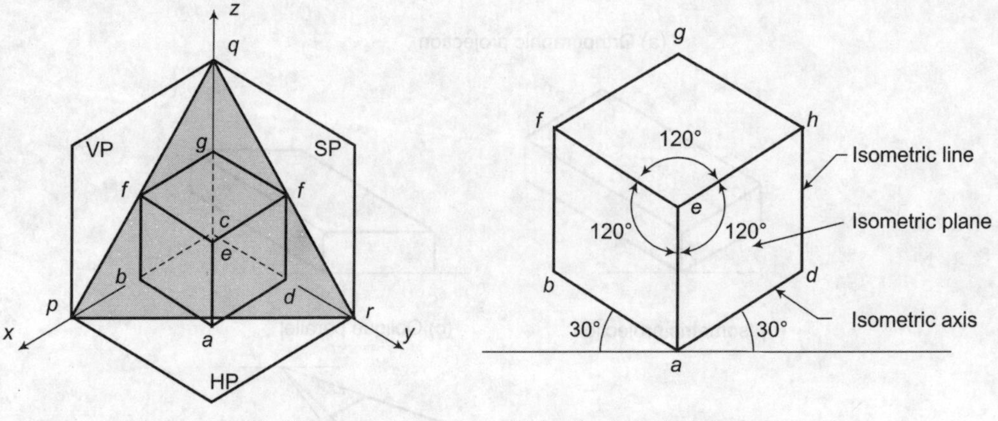

(a) Cube placed in POP

(b) Single view of a cube in isometric

Fig. 15.2

In isometric projection, every face of the cube becomes a rhombus. The isometric projection of a cube appears smaller than isometric view.

A cube, *abcdef* is resting on one of its corner '*c*' at the origin and the solid diagonal *ce* makes equal angle with the plane of projection as shown in Fig. 15.2(b). The three edges of the cube through corner *c* will lie along three axes. The projection of cube *abcdef* on the plane *pqr* is called isometric projection.

The three mutually perpendicular edges *ca*, *cb*, and *cd* are inclined at 120° to each other. Both the edges *ab* and *ad* are inclined at 30° to the horizontal line through *a*.

In this case, all edges of a cube are equally inclined to the plane of projection, they get equally shortened in isometric projection. Figure 15.2(b) shows the isometric projection of a cube.

The isometric projection can also be drawn from the orthographic projections of a cube as shown in Fig. 15.3.

If a cube is resting on one of its corners on *HP*, taking its solid diagonal perpendicular to *VP*, the front view of the cube becomes its isometric projection.

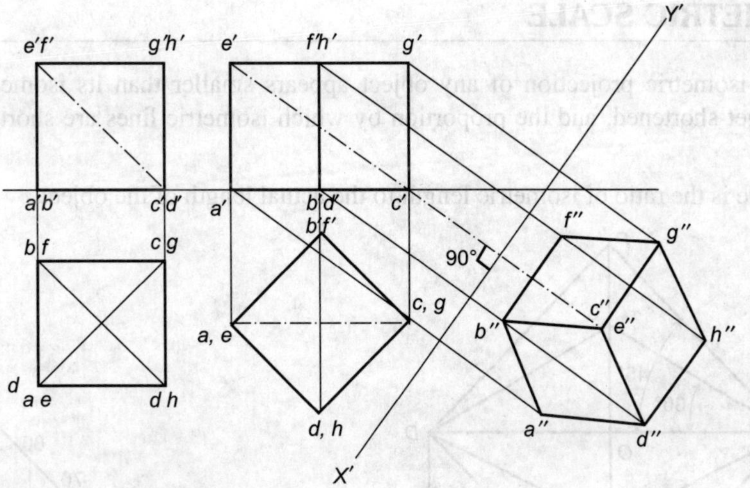

Fig. 15.3 Isometric projection of a cube

15.4 ISOMETRIC PROJECTION AND ISOMETRIC VIEW

Technically, there is a difference between the isometric projection and the isometric view. Isometric projection is drawn using isometric scale which appears smaller than its true length. Isometric view is drawn using the true length of the object and there is no reduction in size of the object and, hence, there is no need of isometric scale.

As we understand, there are a large number of dimensions of an object if the object is complex in nature.

As such, to prepare a diagonal scale and to take isometric length for making this, is always difficult and time-taking task and, hence, there is a standard practice to draw the isometric view without taking isometric length unless it is specified to draw isometric projection on reduced scale. They have been shown in Fig. 15.4.

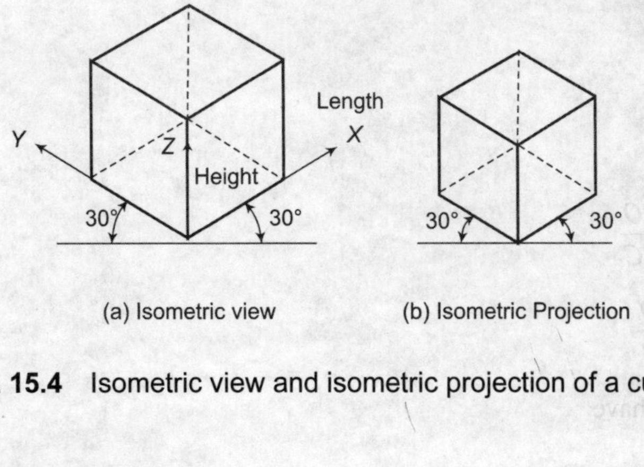

Fig. 15.4 Isometric view and isometric projection of a cube

15.5 ISOMETRIC SCALE

It is a fact that isometric projection of any object appears smaller than its isometric view. All the isometric lines get shortened, and the proportion by which isometric lines are shortened is known as *isometric scale*.

Isometric scale is the ratio of isometric length to the actual length of the object.

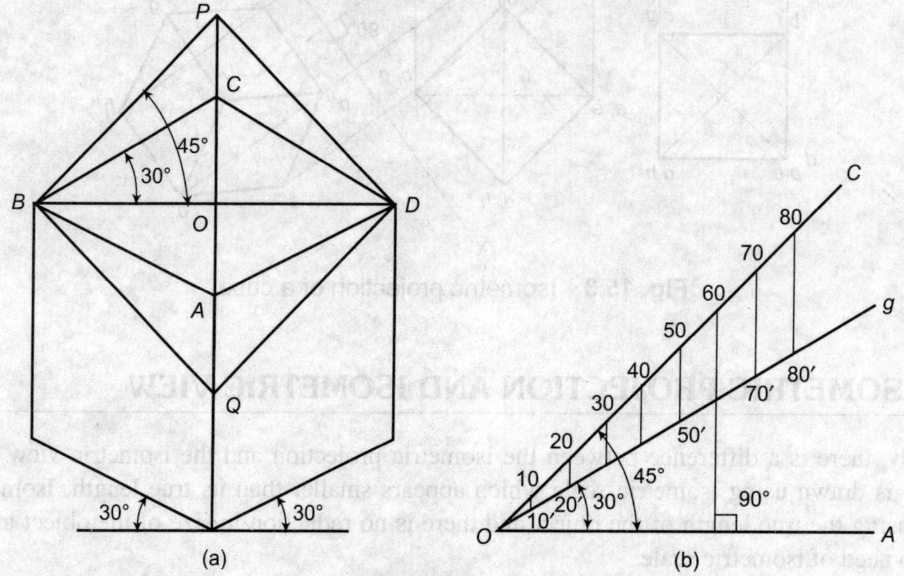

Fig. 15.5 Construction of isometric scale

As we know, all the edges of the cube are equally shortened, the square faces of the cube become rhombuses.

The rhombus *ABCD* represents the isometric projection of a top square of the cube, in which *BD* is the true length of the diagonal. Construct a square *QBPD* around *BD* as diagonal. *BC* becomes the true length of *BP*.

In ΔCBO, $\cos 30° = \dfrac{BO}{BC}$

or $$\frac{\sqrt{3}}{2} = \frac{BO}{BC} \qquad \text{(i)}$$

In ΔPBO, $\cos 45° = \dfrac{BO}{BP}$ (ii)

Dividing (ii) by (i), we have

$$\frac{1}{\sqrt{2}} \times \frac{2}{\sqrt{3}} = \frac{BO}{BP} \times \frac{BC}{BO}$$

or $$\frac{\sqrt{2}}{\sqrt{3}} = \frac{BC}{BP} \text{ or } \frac{BC}{BP} = 0.8165$$

Isometric length = 0.8165

Isometric length = 0.8165 × True length

For making an isometric projection, it is required to convert true length of the object into isometric length.

For this, an isometric scale is to be prepared first before taking up the job and all dimensions may be taken on isometric scale.

The method of constructing an isometric scale is as follows (Fig. 15.5(b)):

(i) Draw a horizontal line *OA* and another line *OB* at 30° to the horizontal line.

(ii) Draw another line *OC* at 45° to the horizontal line.

(iii) Mark 10, 20, 30, …, etc., on the line *OC* to represent the true length of the object.

(iv) Draw vertical lines from 10, 20, 30, …, on true length line on *OA*, which cut the line *OB* at 10′, 20′, 30′, …, etc.

These lengths represent the isometric lengths.

15.6 METHODS OF MAKING ISOMETRIC PROJECTION

There are two methods for making isometric projection, which are as follows:

(i) Box method

(ii) Coordinate method/Offset method

Box Method

(i) Draw the orthographic view on a suitable scale. Isometric scale is to be prepared and the isometric projection is drawn using isometric scale.

(ii) The view is to be enclosed in a rectangular box with a light impression pencil.

(iii) Construct the isometric projection of the enclosed box on the isometric axis.

(iv) Mark the corners of the object with reference to the box's sides and corners taking the distances from the orthographic projection.

(v) Draw the visible lines of the object with dark impression of the lead pencil to complete the isometric projection.

Coordinate or Offset Method

(i) When an object is constructed by a number of inclined surfaces, the coordinate method is found to be more suitable, and so this method is used. In this case, the final points of the edges are located with respect to an assumed isometric based line.

(ii) Join the visible edges to complete the isometric projection/views, as the case may be.

15.7 METHOD OF DIMENSIONING

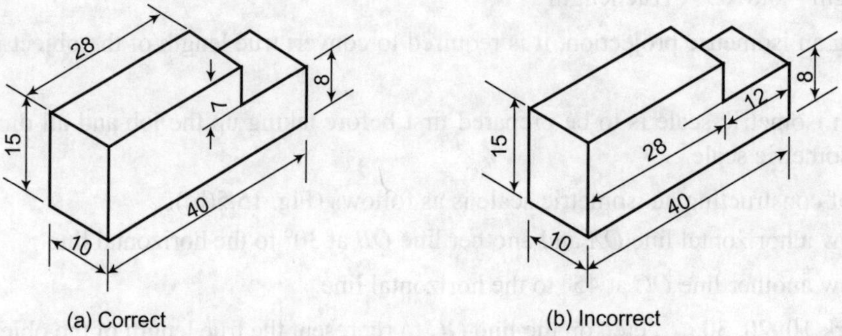

Fig. 15.6 Dimensioning method in isometric

Method of dimensioning has already been discussed in previous chapter 2 and those rules are applicable to isometric dimensioning also. The correct method as applicable to isometric projection has been presented in Fig. 15.6. As far as possible, dimensioning of invisible/hidden parts should be avoided.

15.8 ISOMETRIC VIEW / ISOMETRIC DRAWING OF PLANE SURFACE

PROBLEM 15.1

Draw an isometric view of a plane rectangular surface in three positions. The plane dimension is 35 mm × 25 mm.

Solution:

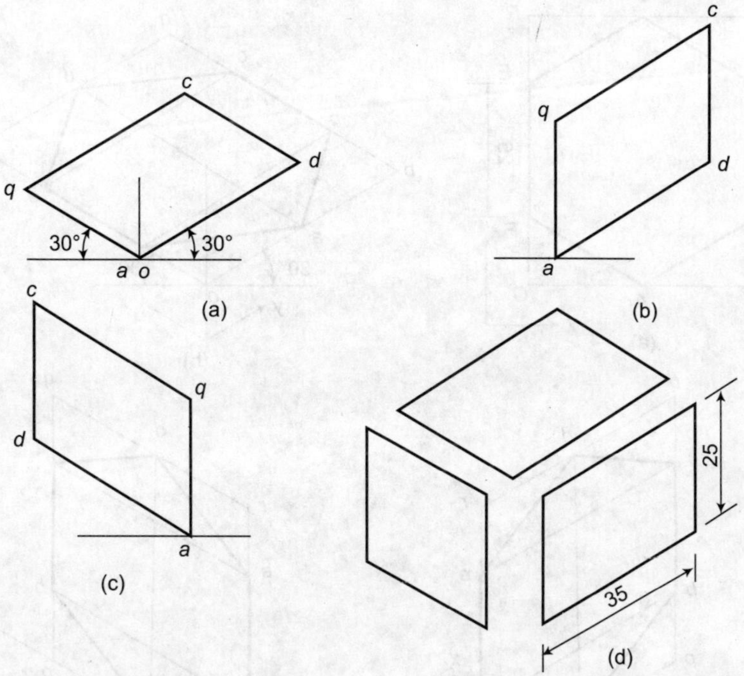

Fig. 15.7 Isometric view of a plane surface

Steps:

Considering a rectangular plane *abcd* lying horizontal as shown in Fig. 15.7(a)

1. Draw a horizontal line and mark point *O* on it.
2. Draw two lines at 30° to the horizontal and mark the distances *ad* = 35 mm and *ab* = 25 mm.
3. From *b*, draw a line parallel to *ab* which cuts at *C*.
4. From *d*, draw a line parallel to *ab* which cuts at *C*.
5. Complete the rectangle as shown in Fig. 15.7(a).
6. The same procedure can be applied with Fig. 15.7(b) and (c).
7. Figure 15.7(d) represents the isometric view of rectangular surface in all positions.

PROBLEM 15.2

Draw an isometric view of a regular hexagonal plane surface of side 25 mm in three different positions.

Solution:

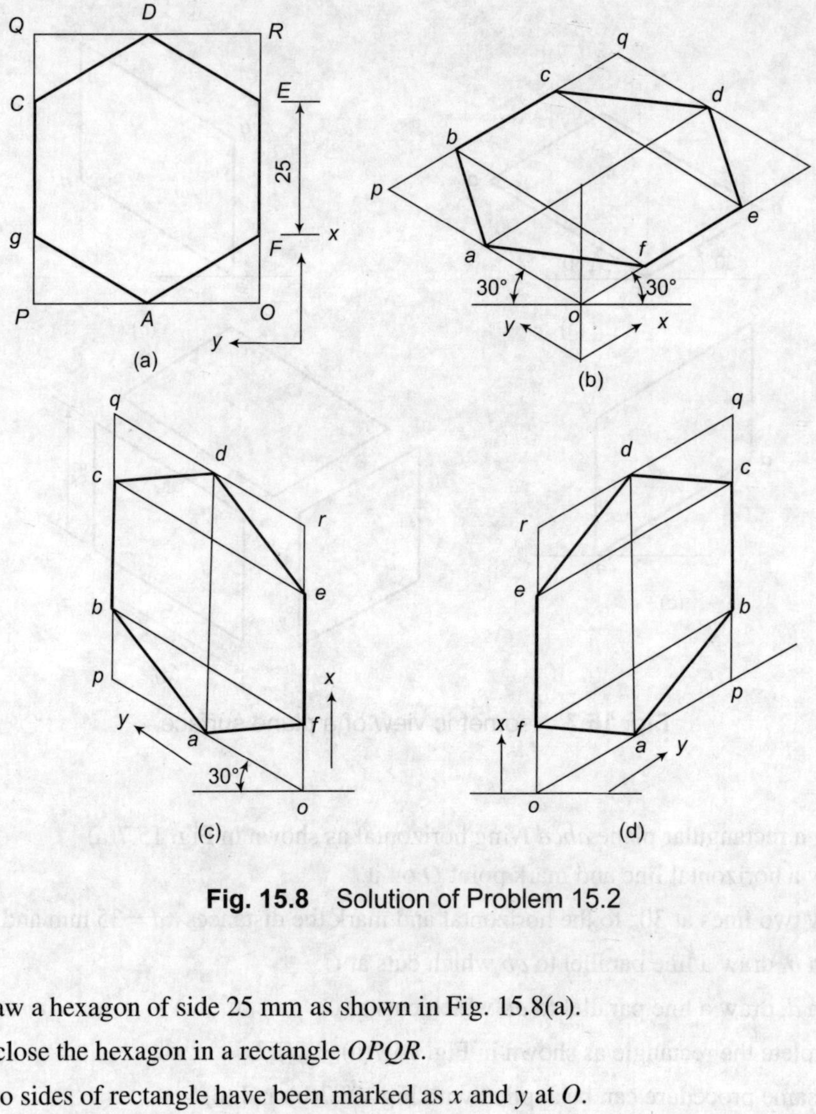

Fig. 15.8 Solution of Problem 15.2

Steps

1. Draw a hexagon of side 25 mm as shown in Fig. 15.8(a).
2. Enclose the hexagon in a rectangle *OPQR*.
3. Two sides of rectangle have been marked as *x* and *y* at *O*.
4. Draw a horizontal line and mark point *O* on it.
5. Draw two lines at 30° to the horizontal and mark the distance as *OP* and *Or*.
6. From *r*, draw parallel line *rq* parallel to *OP*.
7. From *p*, draw parallel line *pq* parallel to *Or*.
8. Rectangle *OPQR* becomes rhombus as *OPqr*.
9. Complete the isometric from the method. Mark the point.
10. *abcdef* is the required isometric view.

PROBLEM 15.3

Draw the isometric view of a circle of diameter 50 mm in three positions.

Solution:

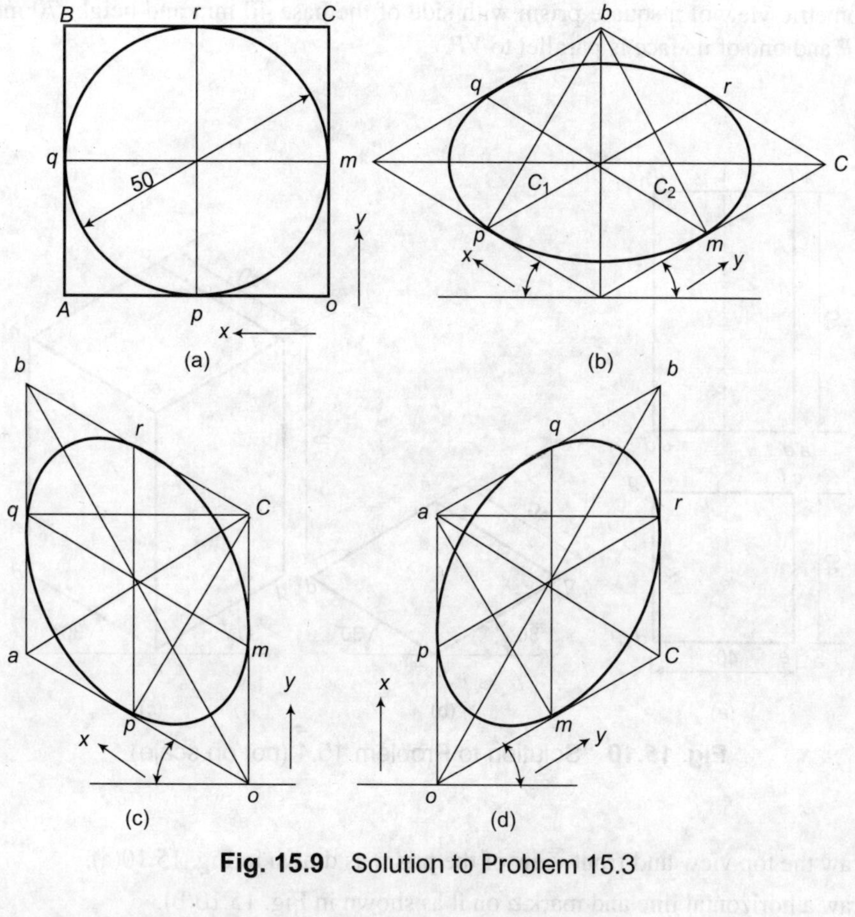

Fig. 15.9 Solution to Problem 15.3

Steps:

1. Enclose the circle in a square *OABC* as shown in Fig. 15.9(a).
2. Construct the isometric drawing of square as *Oabc* becomes a rhombus as in Fig. 15.9(b).
3. Locate middle point of square side as *pqrm* correspondingly as a rhombus side.
4. Join *pr* and *qm* and also *bp* and *bm* and also *ac*.
5. *bp* and *bm* cut *ac* at c_1 and c_2, respectively as shown in Fig. 15.9(b).
6. Taking *O* as centre, draw an arc taking *oq* as centre, which joins *qr*.
   Again, taking *b* as centre and *bp* as radius, draw a circular arc; join *p* and *m*.
7. Taking c_1 and c_2 as centres, draw circular arcs between *pq* and *mr*.
   pqrm is the required isometric view of the ellipse in Fig. 15.9(b).

15.9 ISOMETRIC VIEW OF SOLID OBJECTS

PROBLEM 15.4

Draw the isometric view of a square prism with side of the base 40 mm and height 70 mm when it is resting on *HP* and one of its face is parallel to *VP*.

Solution:

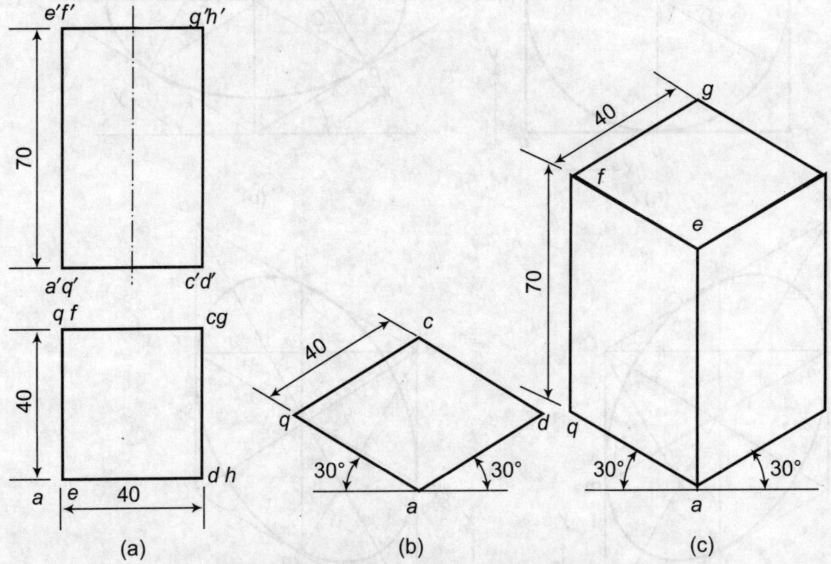

Fig. 15.10 Solution to Problem 15.4 (not on scale)

Steps:

1. Draw the top view and front view of the prism as drawn in Fig. 15.10(a).
2. Draw a horizontal line and mark *a* on it as shown in Fig. 15.10(b).
3. From *a* draw two lines at 30° with horizontal to represent isometric axes.
4. Mark *b* and *d* equal to 40 mm each.
5. From *b* and *d*, draw lines *bc* and *dc* parallel to *ab* and *ad*, respectively; both lines cut at *c*.
6. *abcd* represents the base of the prism.
7. From the points *a*, *b*, *c*, and *d*, draw vertical lines equal to 70 mm as the height.
8. From *e*, draw parallel lines *ef* and *eh* parallel to *ab* and *ad*.
9. Draw *fg* parallel to *eh*.
10. Join *efgh*, which represents the top of the prism.
11. Draw all the visible lines in isometric view.

PROBLEM 15.5

Draw the isometric view of a square prism of side 30 mm and height 50 mm. The prism is lying on horizontal with one of its rectangular face on *HP* and the axis is parallel to *VP*. The side view and front view are shown as follows:

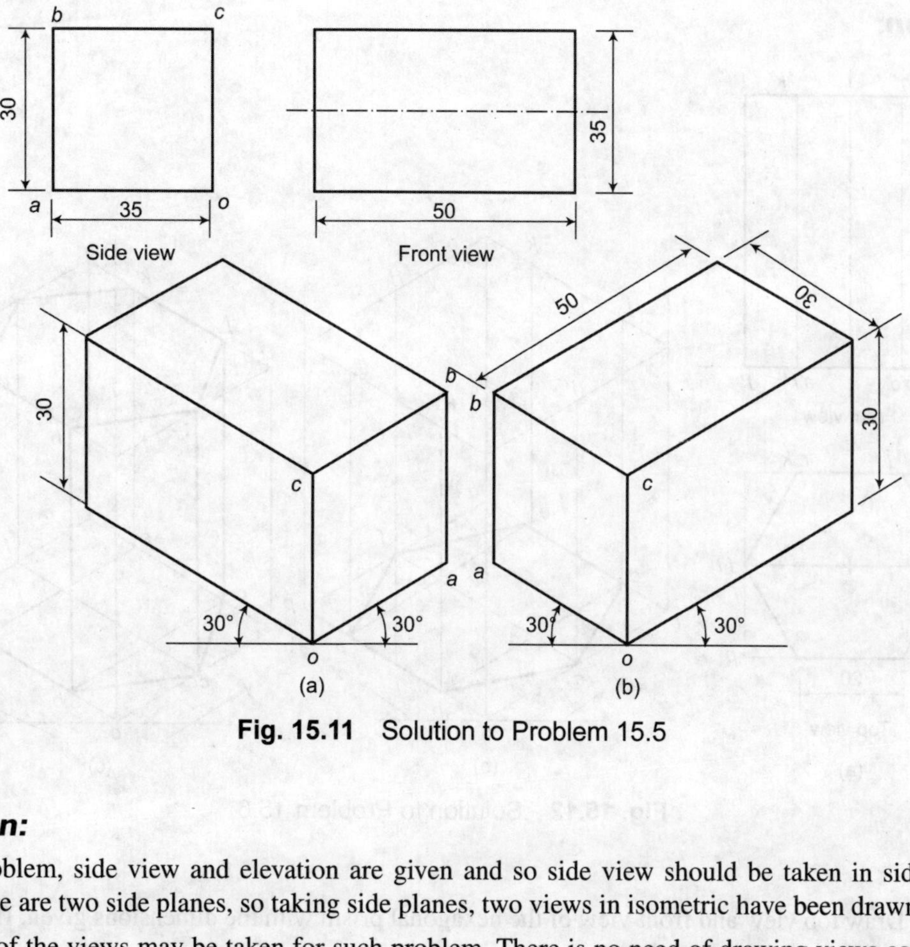

Fig. 15.11 Solution to Problem 15.5

Solution:

In the problem, side view and elevation are given and so side view should be taken in side planes. Since there are two side planes, so taking side planes, two views in isometric have been drawn.

Either of the views may be taken for such problem. There is no need of drawing views considering both the planes.

Steps:

1. Draw the orthographic view of the prism. If required, suitable scale may be taken.
2. Draw the isometric view of square on side plane as 0 *abc*, and from all the points, draw a parallel line to equal to the length of the prism.
3. Join all the corresponding points as shown in Fig. 15.11(a) and (b), considering only the visible lines.

PROBLEM 15.6

Draw the isometric view of a hexagonal prism with side of the base 20 mm and height 50 mm resting on *HP* with one of its base edge parallel to *VP* and the axis perpendicular to *HP*.

Solution:

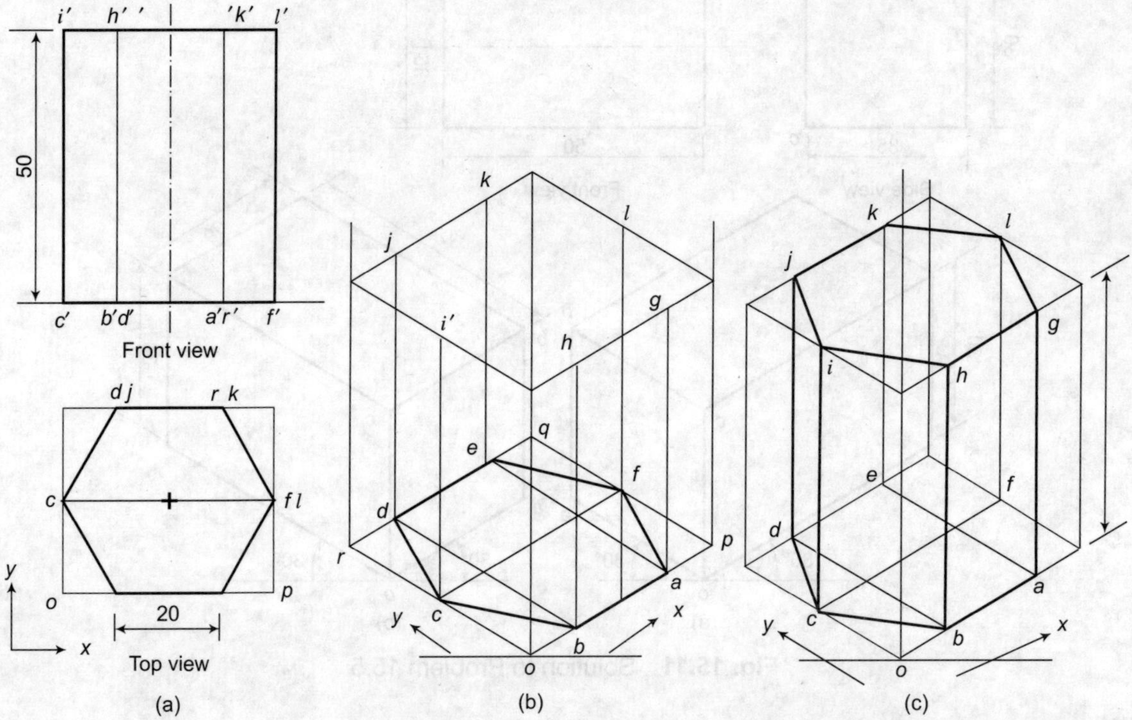

Fig. 15.12 Solution to Problem 15.6

Steps:

1. Draw top view and front view of the hexagonal prism with the dimensions given. If required, a scale may be selected.
2. Enclose the hexagon in a rectangle as *opqr*.
3. Hexagon base is drawn on isometric view as explained in previous problem.
4. From each corner, draw a vertical line taking the height of the prism.
5. Complete the top view also.
6. Ignoring the hidden line, all lines may be joined.
7. Complete view, as shown in Fig. 15.12, represents the isometric view.

PROBLEM 15.7

A hexagonal prism of base side 25 mm and height 50 mm lying on *HP*, one of its rectangular faces, and the axis of the prism is perpendicular to profile plane. Draw the isometric view of hexagon in two possible positions.

Solution:

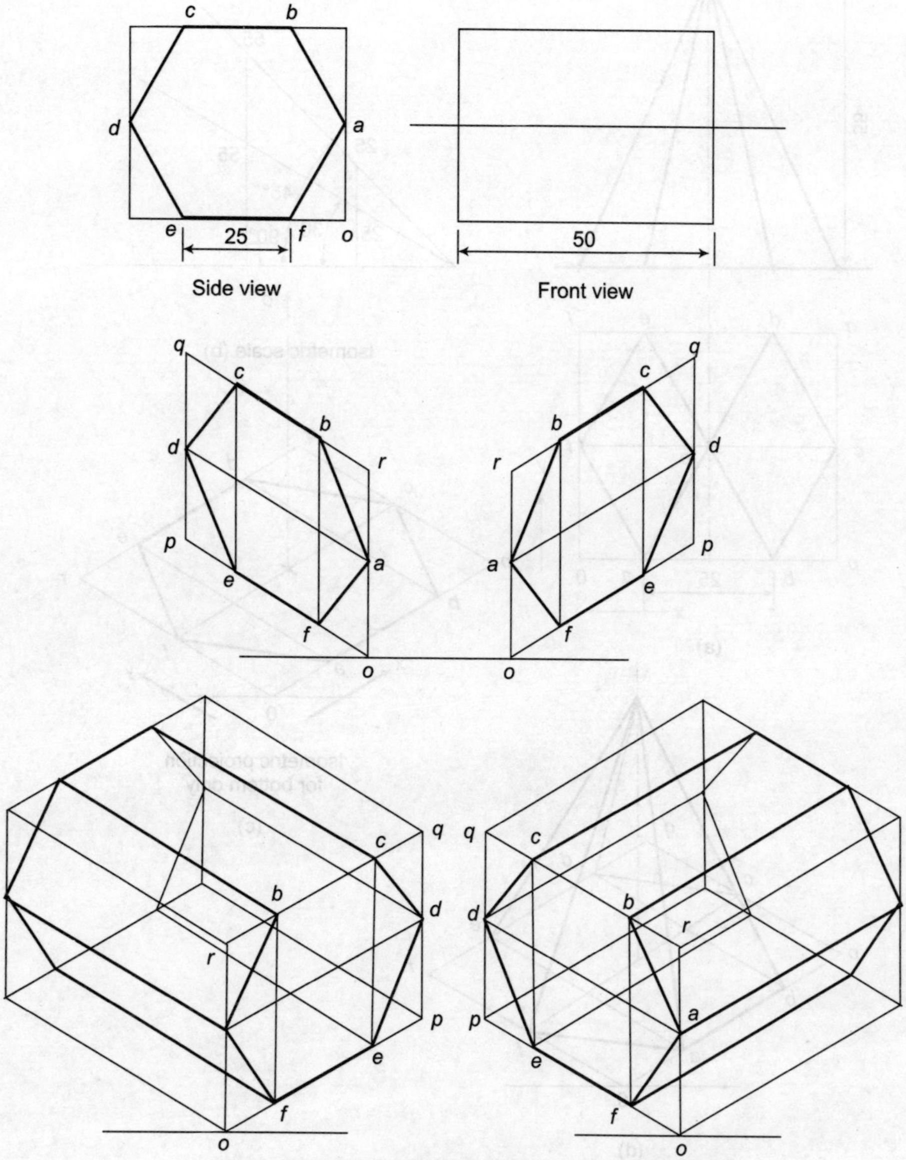

Fig. 15.13 Solution to Problem 15.7

PROBLEM 15.8

A hexagonal pyramid of side base 25 mm and height 55 mm is resting on *HP* with one of the bases parallel to *HP* and one of the base edge is parallel to *VP*. Draw its isometric projection.

Solution:

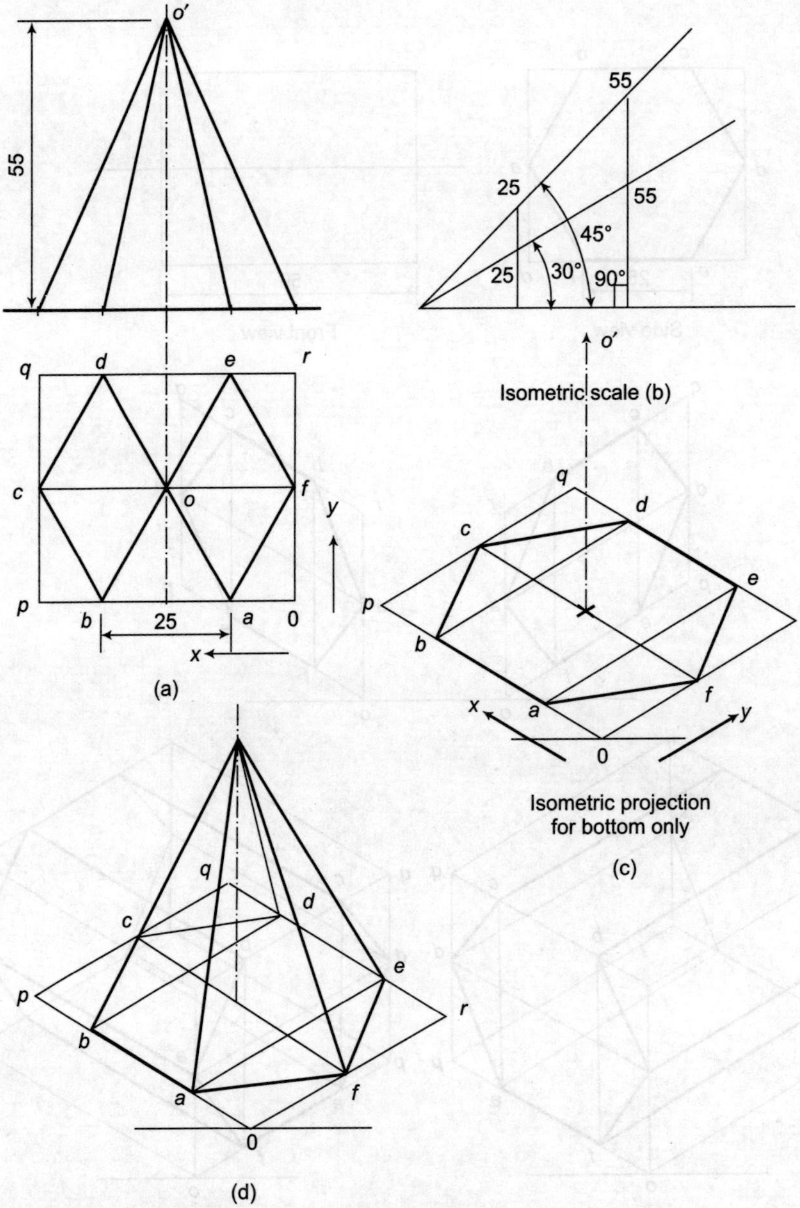

Fig. 15.14 Solution to Problem 15.8

Steps:

1. The isometric projection for the pyramid is to be drawn, so isometric scale is to be prepared first as shown in Fig. 15.14(b).
2. As per the statement, orthographic view is to be drawn as shown in Fig. 15.14(a) using isometric scale.
3. Hexagon of the base is to be enclosed in a rectangle for making isometric projection.
4. Draw the isometric projection of the base of pyramid as shown in Fig. 15.14(c) represented as *opqr*.
5. Locate the centre for the axis and draw perpendicular to it and the height of the axis may be cut on isometric scale.

   Mark point *O′* as the apex.
6. Join *O′* to all the corners.
7. Complete the isometric projection as shown in Fig. 15.14(d), ignoring the hidden lines.

PROBLEM 15.9

Draw the isometric projection of a right circular cone of base diameter 40 mm and height 50 mm when it is lying with base on *HP*.

Solution:

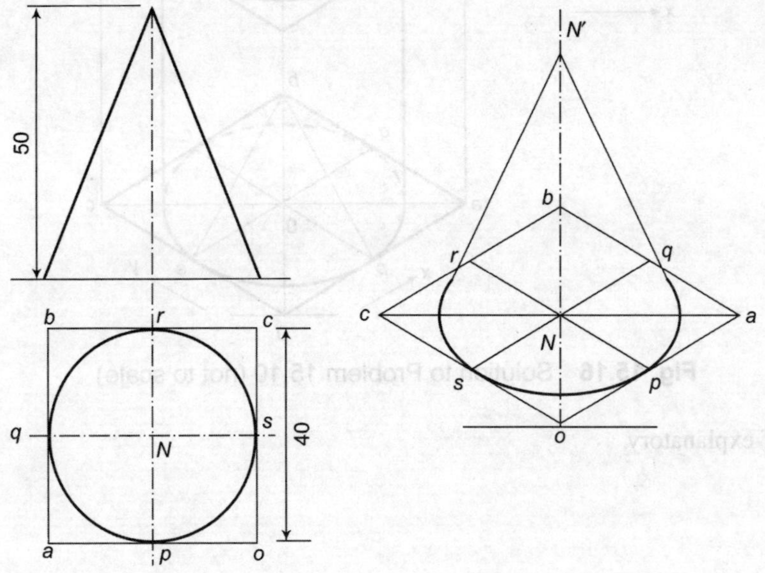

Fig. 15.15 Solution to Problem 15.9

Solution is self-explanatory.

PROBLEM 15.10

A right circular cylinder of base 40 mm diameter and height 55 mm is lying on *HP* with circular base and the axis is vertical. Draw the isometric projection.

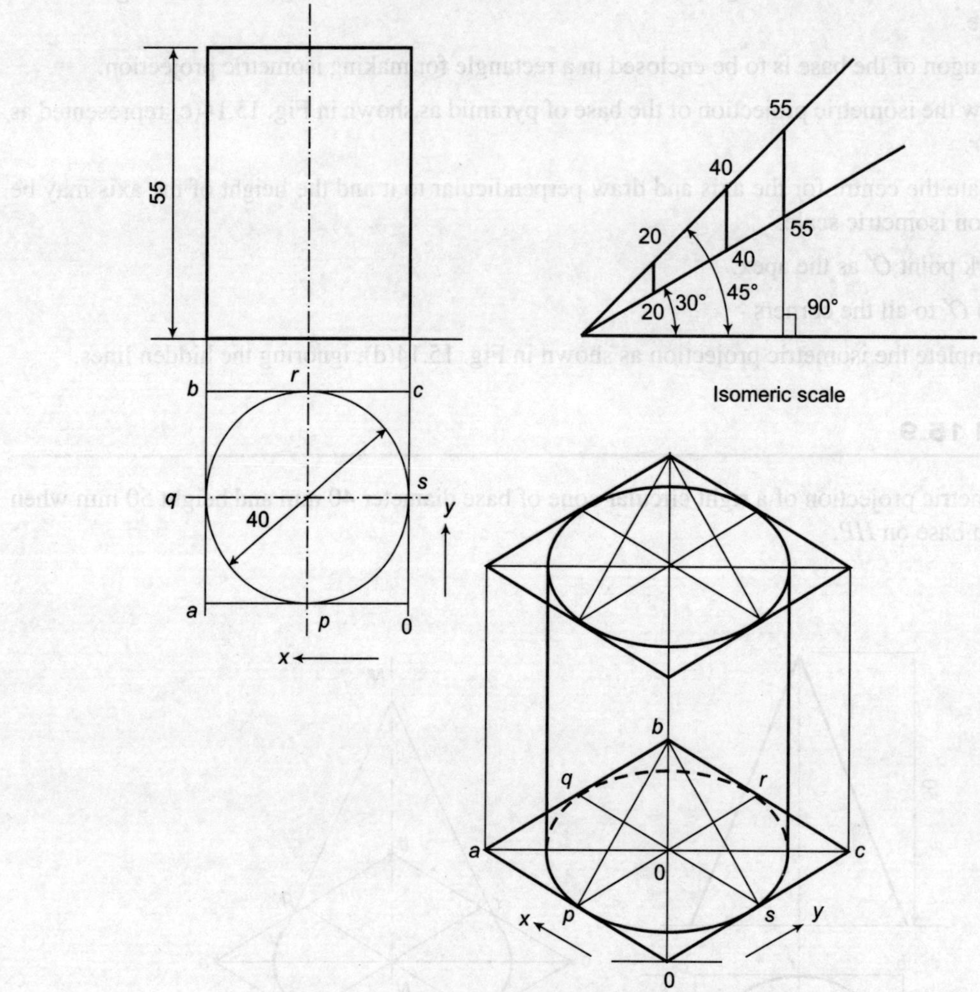

Fig. 15.16 Solution to Problem 15.10 (not to scale)

Solution is self-explanatory.

PROBLEM 15.11

A right circular cylinder of base 40 mm diameter and height 55 mm is lying on *HP*. Draw its isometric view when the axis is horizontal. In profile plane, it will be a circle.

***Solution*:**

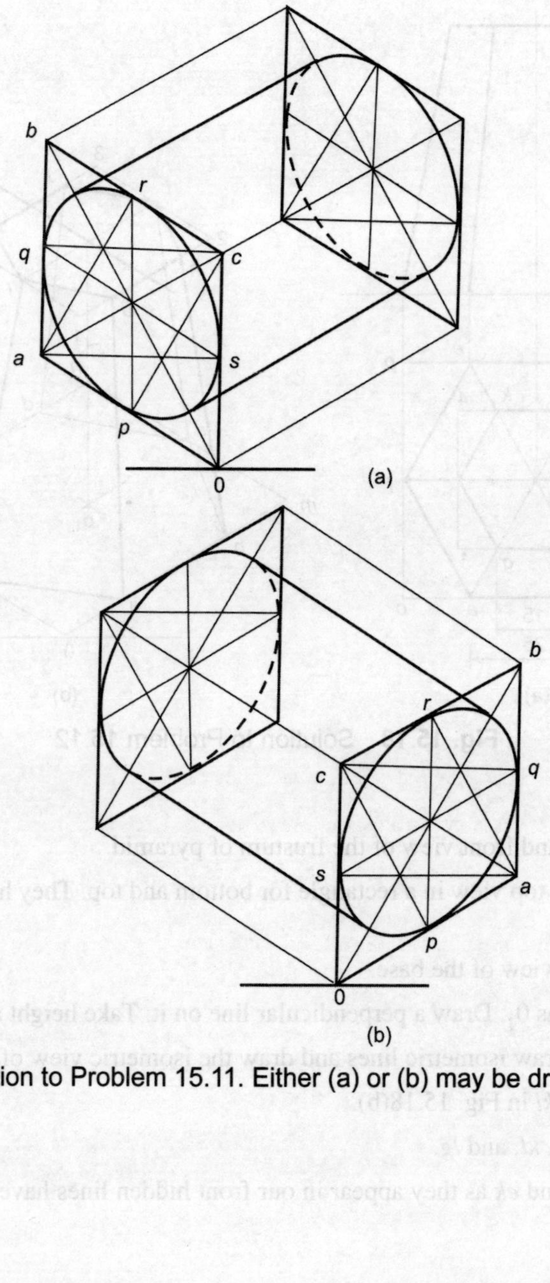

Fig. 15.17 Solution to Problem 15.11. Either (a) or (b) may be drawn (not to scale)

PROBLEM 15.12

Draw the isometric view of a frustum of right hexagonal pyramid, side of the base is 25 mm and height of the frustum is 50 mm. It is lying on *HP* from its base and one of its bases is parallel to *VP*. The side of top hexagon is 15 mm.

Solution:

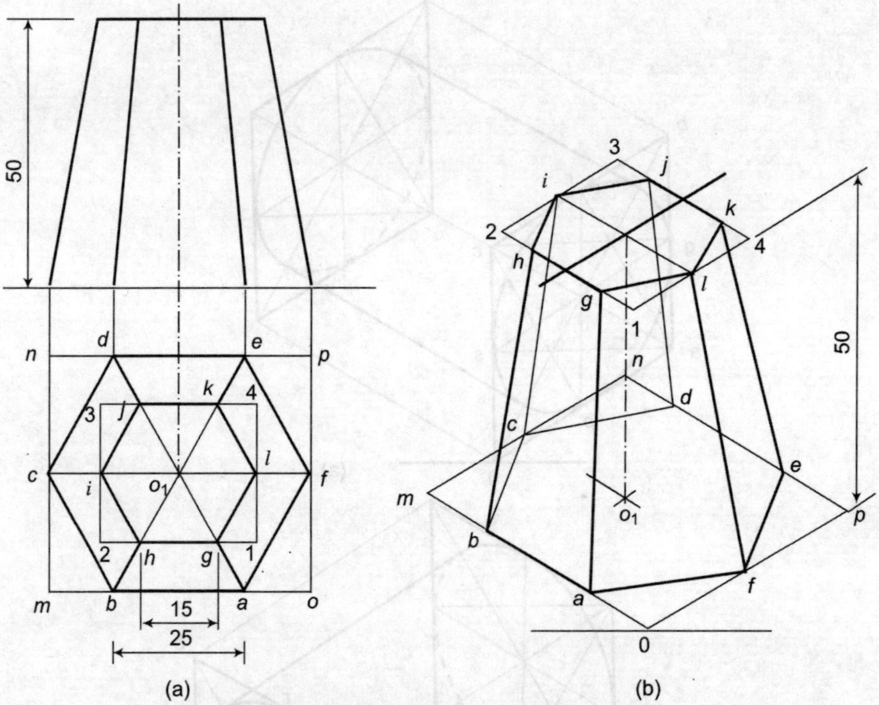

Fig. 15.18 Solution to Problem 15.12

Steps:

1. Draw top view and front view of the frustum of pyramid.
2. Enclose frustum top view in a rectangle for bottom and top. They have been named as shown in Fig. 15.18(a).
3. Draw isometric view of the base.
4. Find the centre as 0_1. Draw a perpendicular line on it. Take height as 50 mm.
5. At this height, draw isometric lines and draw the isometric view of the top hexagon. They are as *ghijkl* in Fig. 15.18(b).
6. Join *gh*, *hi*, *ij*, *jk*, *kl*, and *lg*.
7. Join *ag*, *ph*, *fl,* and *ek* as they appear in our front hidden lines have not be drawn with dotted lines.

PROBLEM 15.13

Draw the isometric projection of an object. The orthographic top view and front view are given as shown in Fig. 15.19(a).

Solution:

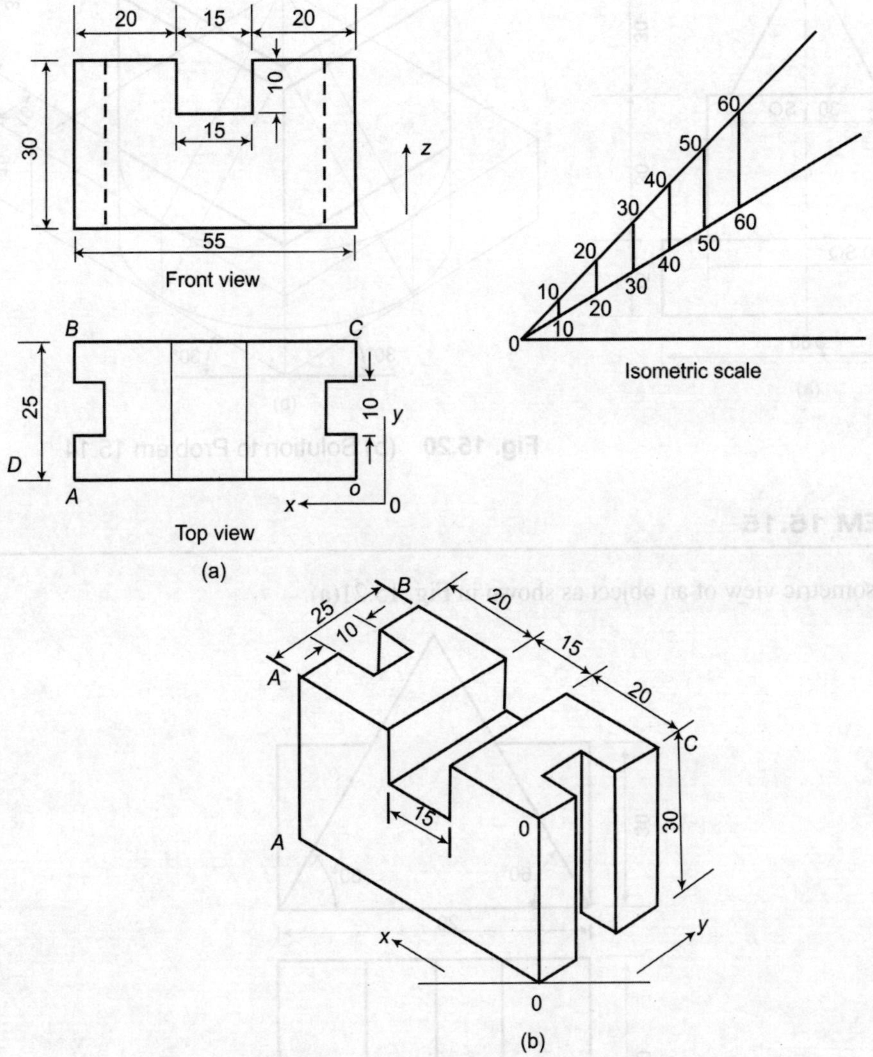

Fig. 15.19 Solution to Problem 15.13

PROBLEM 15.14

Draw the isometric view of an object as shown in Fig. 15.20(a).

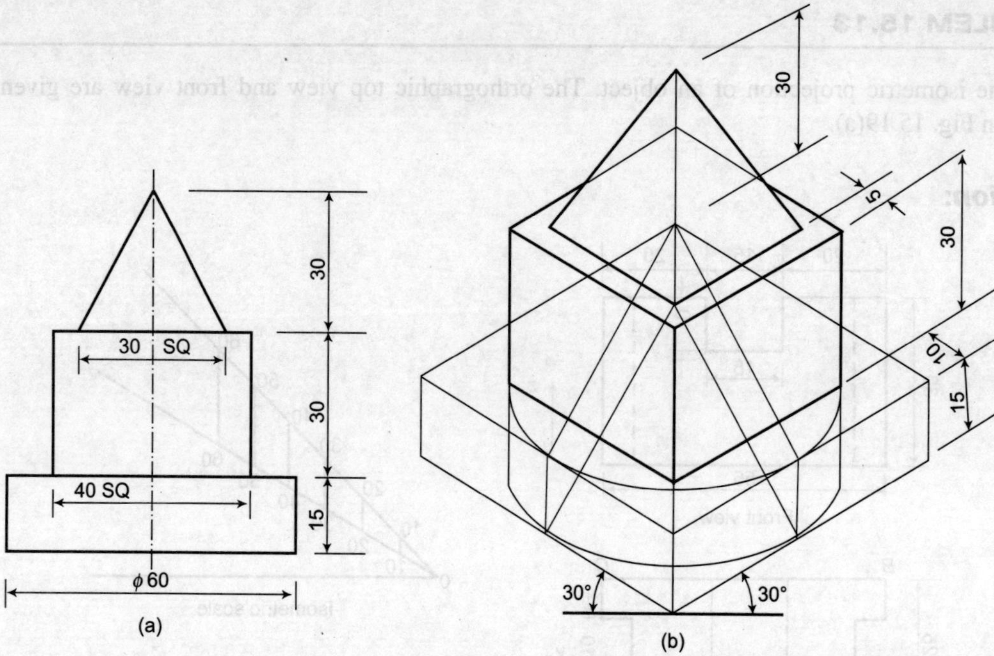

Fig. 15.20 (b) Solution to Problem 15.14

PROBLEM 15.15

Draw the isometric view of an object as shown in Fig. 15.21(a).

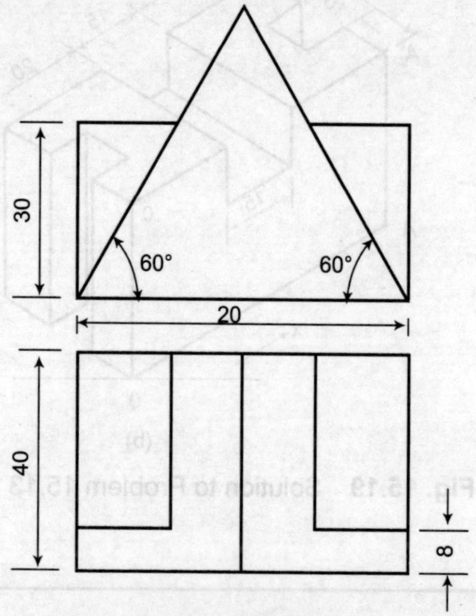

Fig. 15.21 (a)

Solution:

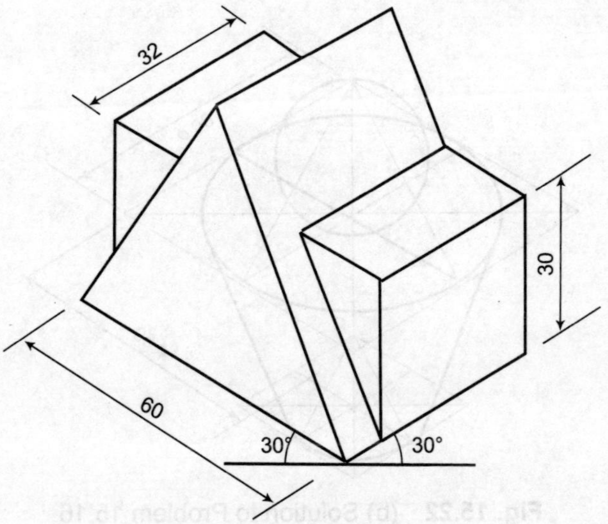

Fig. 15.21 (b) Solution to Problem 15.15

PROBLEM 15.16

Draw the isometric projection of an inverted frustum of a cone with a sphere of ϕ 30 mm resting on top of it.

Draw the isometric projection for the combined figure as shown in Fig. 15.22 (a).

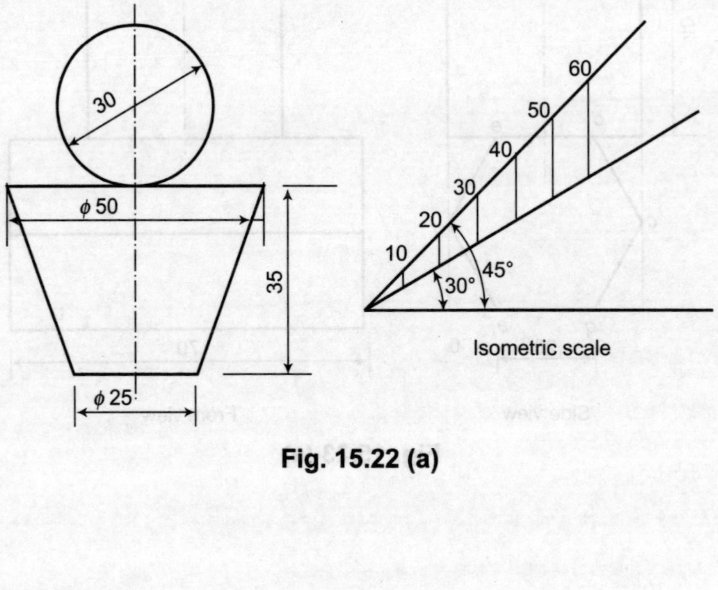

Fig. 15.22 (a)

***Solution*:**

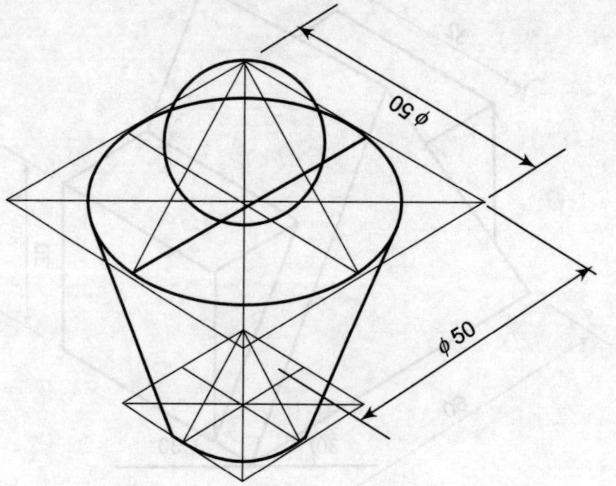

Fig. 15.22 (b) Solution to Problem 15.16

PROBLEM 15.17

Draw the isometric view of an object as shown in Fig. 15.23(a).

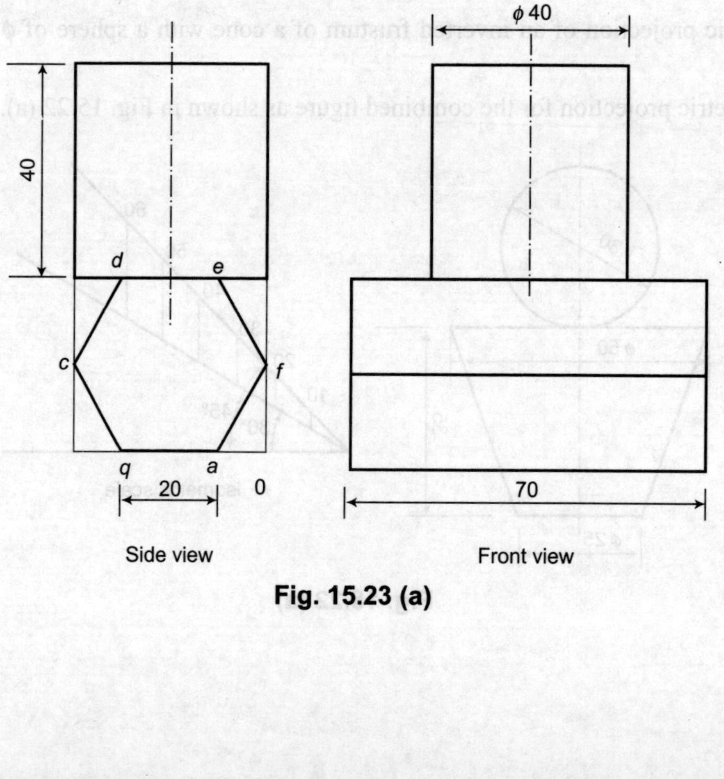

Fig. 15.23 (a)

***Solution*:**

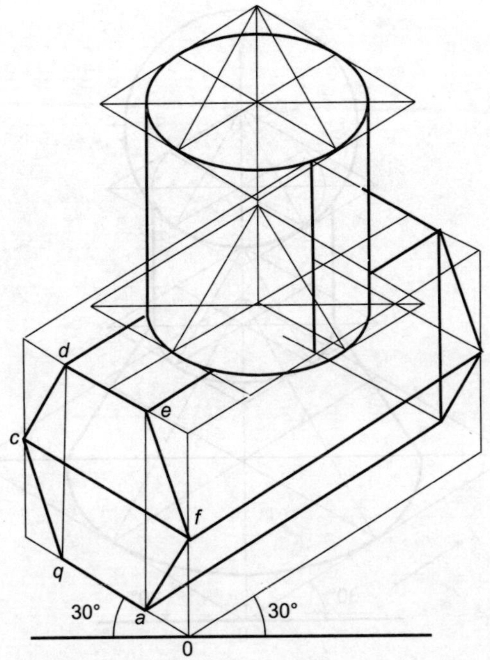

Fig. 15.23 (b) Solution to Problem 15.17

PROBLEM 15.18

Figure 15.24(a) shows the front view of an object symmetrical about its vertical axis. Draw its isometric projection.

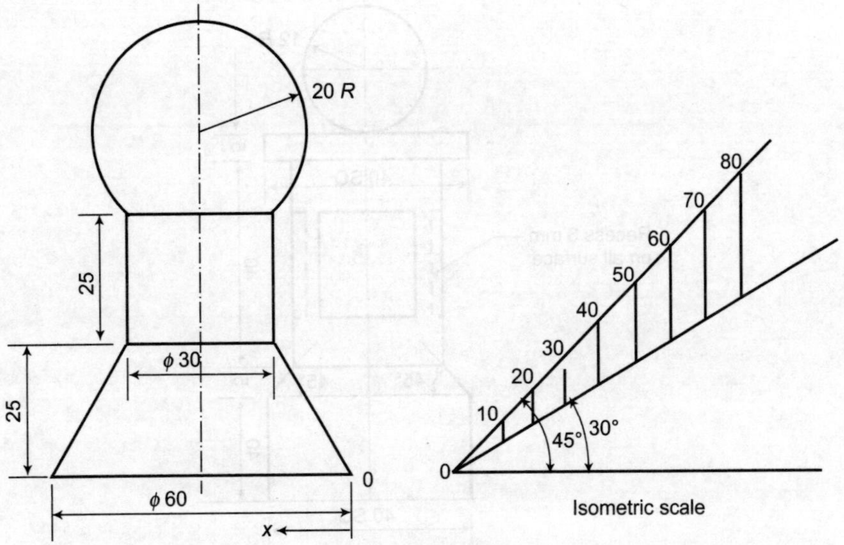

Fig. 15.24 (a)

Solution:

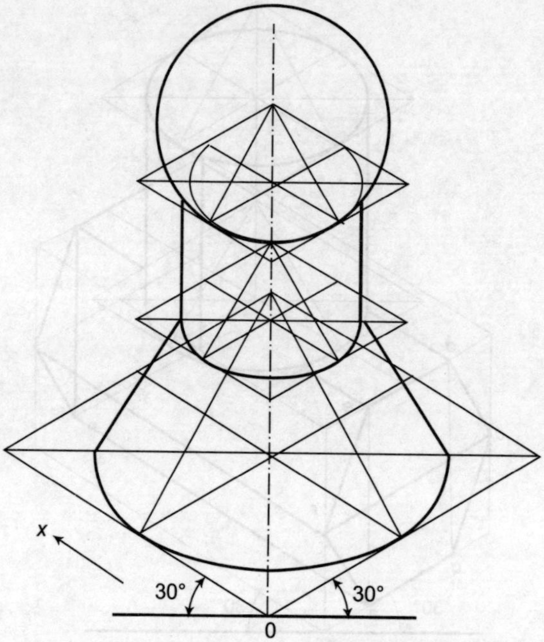

Fig. 15.24 (b) Solution to Problem 15.18

PROBLEM 15.19

Figure 15.25(a) shows the front view of an object. Draw the isometric projection.

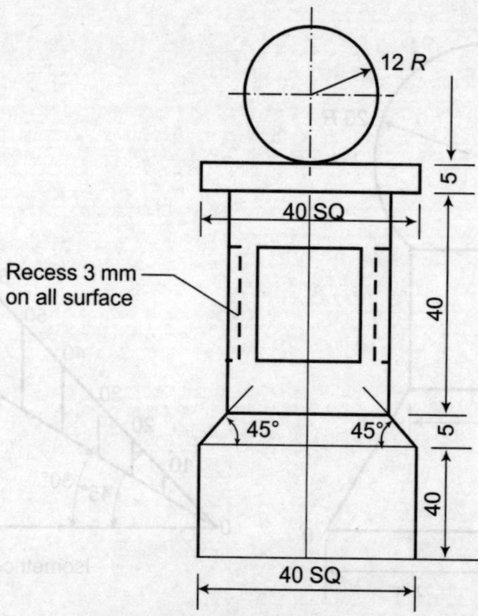

Fig. 15.25 (a) Front view

Solution:

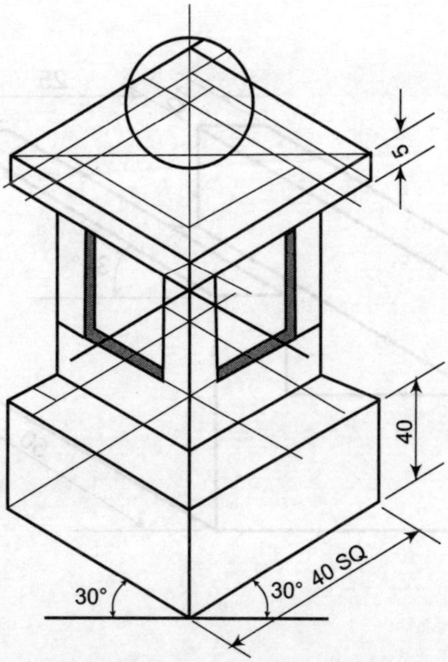

Fig. 15.25 (b) Solution to Problem 15.19

PROBLEM 15.20

Figure 15.26 (a) shows the orthographic projections of an object. Draw the oblique projection with the receding axis inclined at 30° with the horizontal. The depth of the object may be taken as per rules. (Cavalier projection)

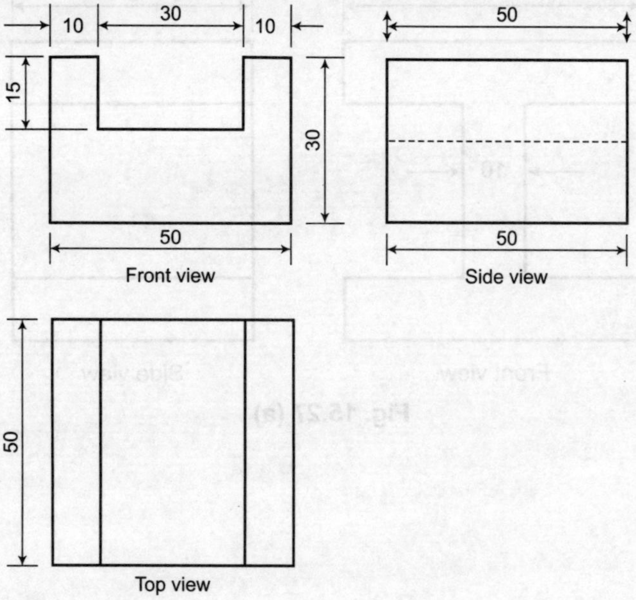

Fig. 15.26 (a) Orthographic views

Solution:

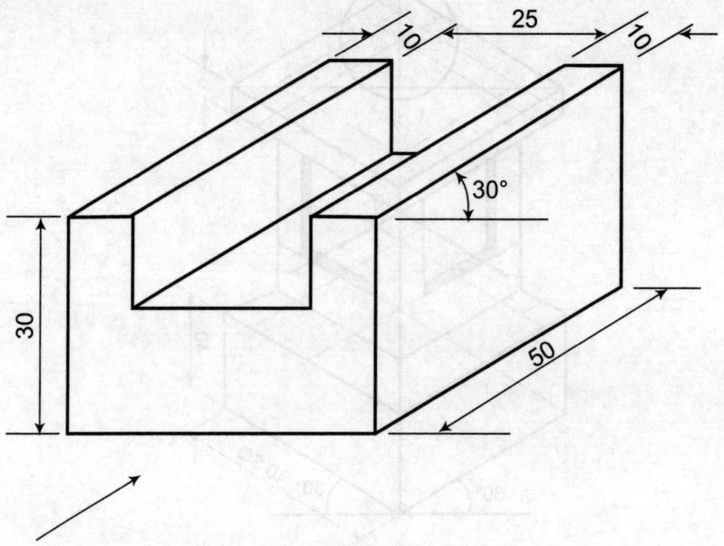

Fig. 15.26 (b) Solution to Problem 15.20 (Exact dimensions of the object are taken)

PROBLEM 15.21

Draw the oblique projection of an object shown in Fig. 15.27(a).

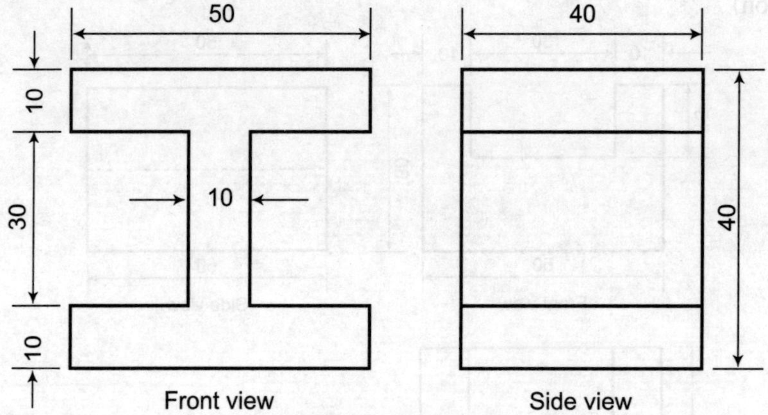

Fig. 15.27 (a)

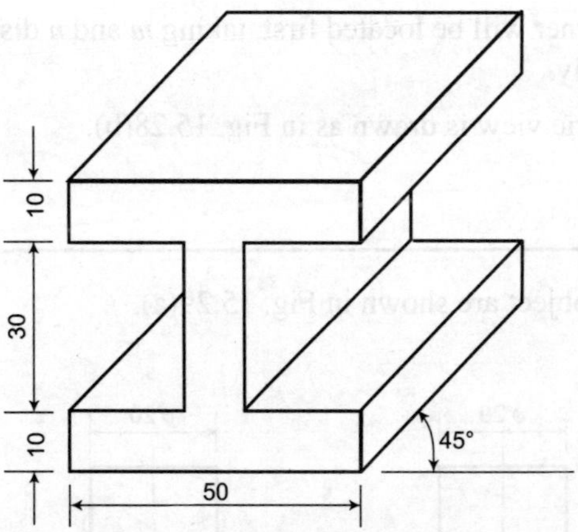

Fig. 15.27 (b) Solution to Problem 15.21

PROBLEM 15.22

Draw an isometric view of the object shown in Fig. 15.28(a).

Orthographic views of the object are shown in two views.

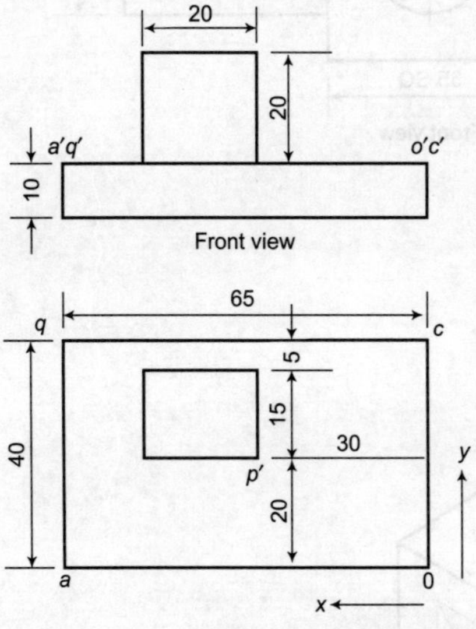

Fig. 15.28 (a) Top view and front view

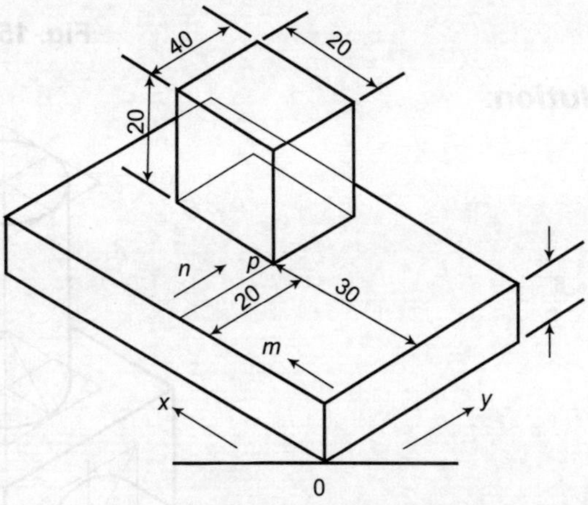

Fig. 15.28 (b) Isometric view

***Steps*:**

1. Rectangular slab is drawn on isometric view. Let *O* be the starting point.
2. The object is placed at the top of it asymmetrically.

The position of p corner will be located first, taking m and n distance in the direction of x and y from O, respectively.

The required isometric view is drawn as in Fig. 15.28(b).

PROBLEM 15.23

The orthographic views of an object are shown in Fig. 15.29(a).

Draw the isometric views.

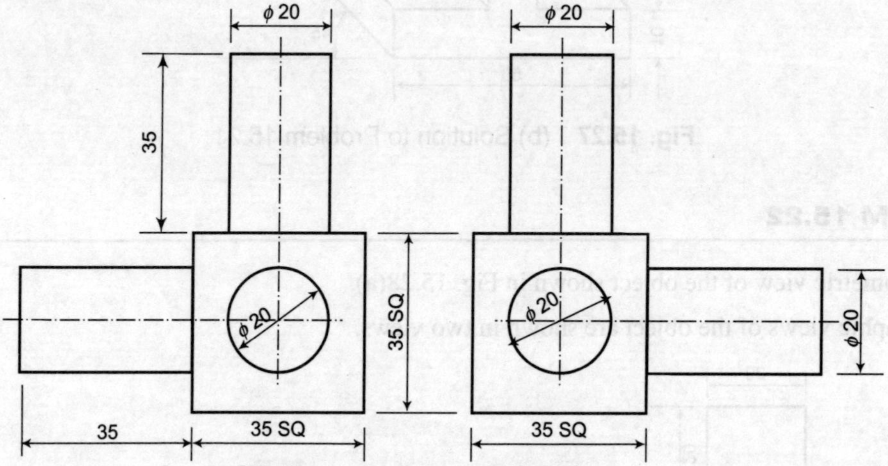

Fig. 15.29 (a)

Solution:

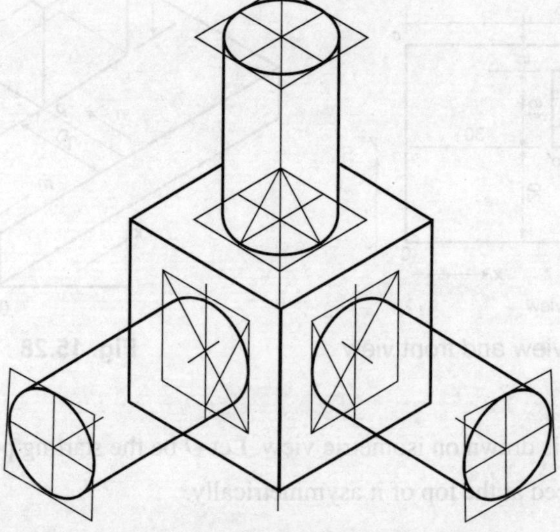

Fig. 15.29 (b) Solution to Problem 15.23

PROBLEM 15.24

Two orthographic views of an object are shown in Fig. 15.30(a). Draw the isometric views.

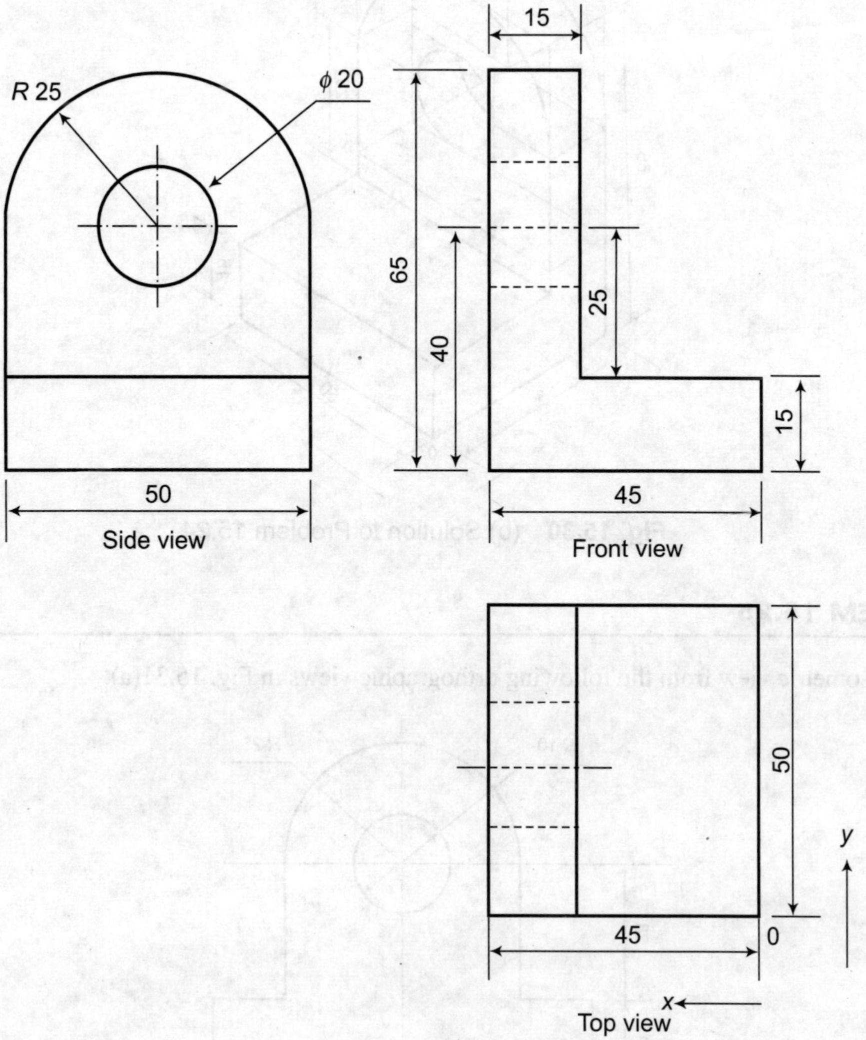

Fig. 15.30 (a)

Solution:

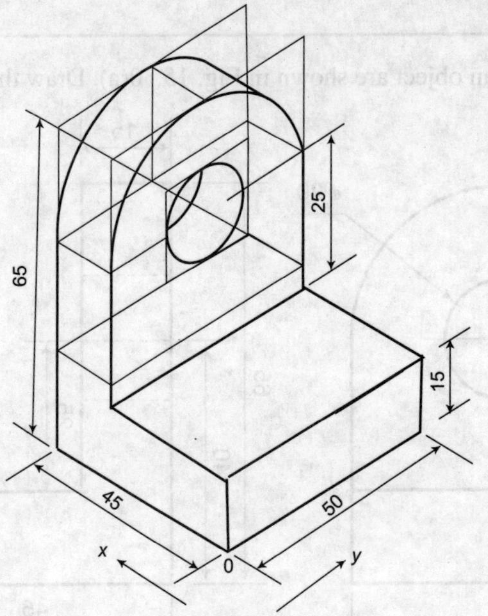

Fig. 15.30 (b) Solution to Problem 15.24

PROBLEM 15.25

Draw the isometric view from the following orthographic views in Fig. 15.31(a).

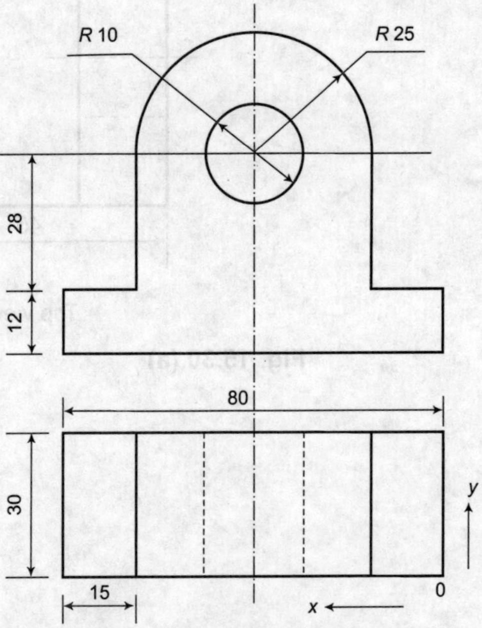

Fig. 15.31 (a) Orthographic views

***Solution*:**

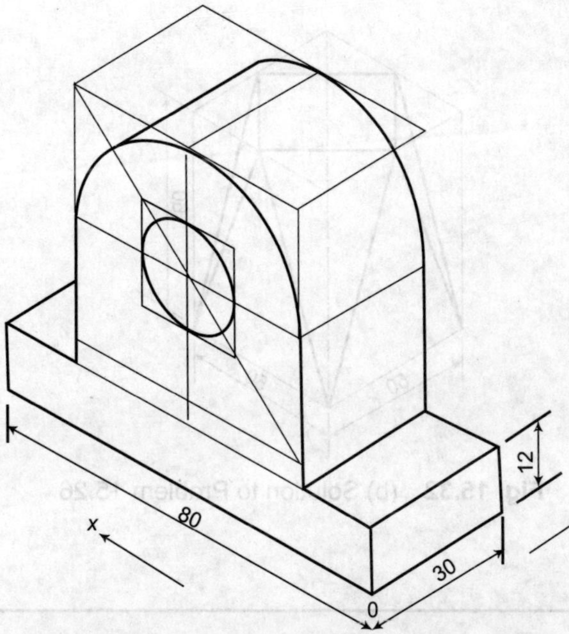

Fig. 15.31 (b) Solution to Problem 15.25

PROBLEM 15.26

Draw the isometric view from the following orthographic views in Fig. 15.32(a).

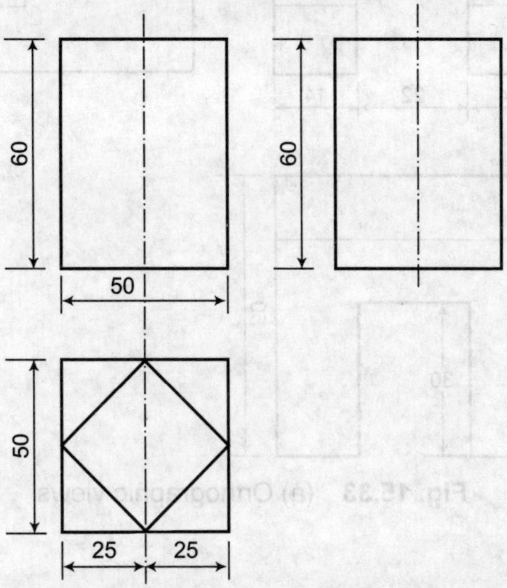

Fig. 15.32 (a) Orthographic projections

Solution:

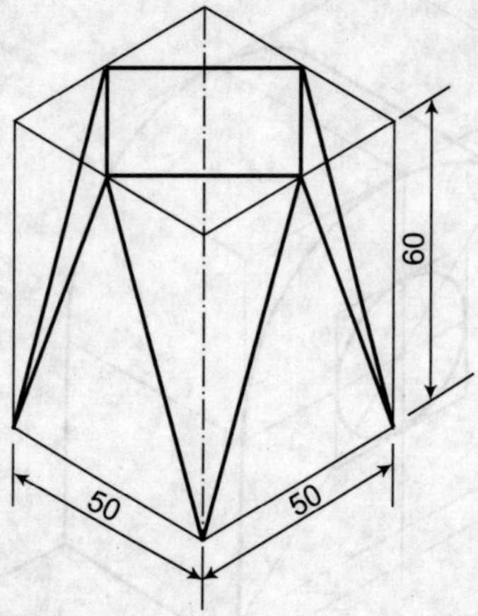

Fig. 15.32 (b) Solution to Problem 15.26

PROBLEM 15.27

Draw the isometric view from the following orthographic views in Fig. 15.33(a).

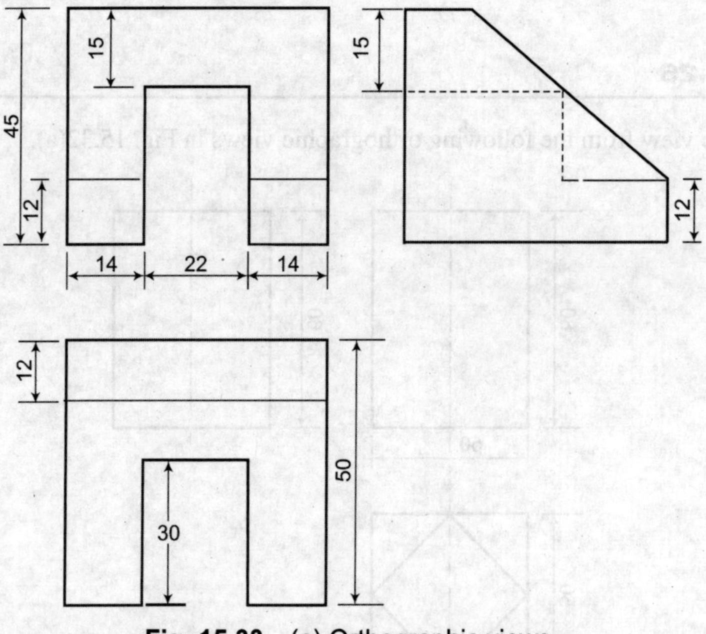

Fig. 15.33 (a) Orthographic views

Solution:

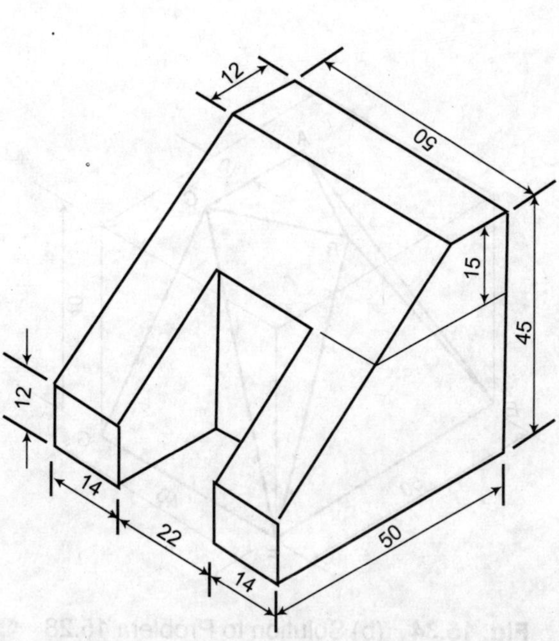

Fig. 15.33 (b) Solution to Problem 15.27

PROBLEM 15.28

Draw the isometric view from the following views in Fig. 15.34 (a).

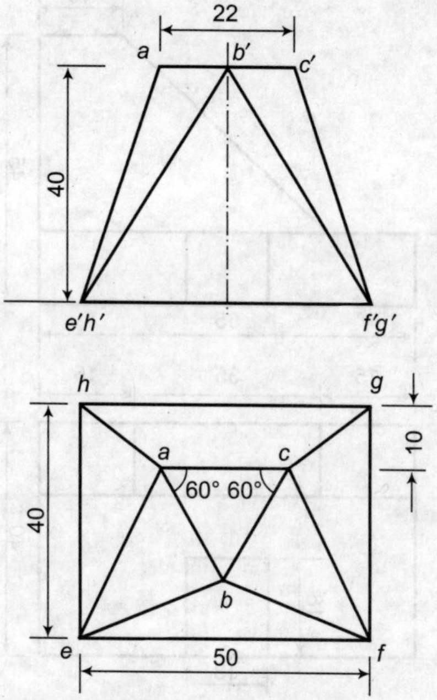

Fig. 15.34 (a) Orthographic views

***Solution*:**

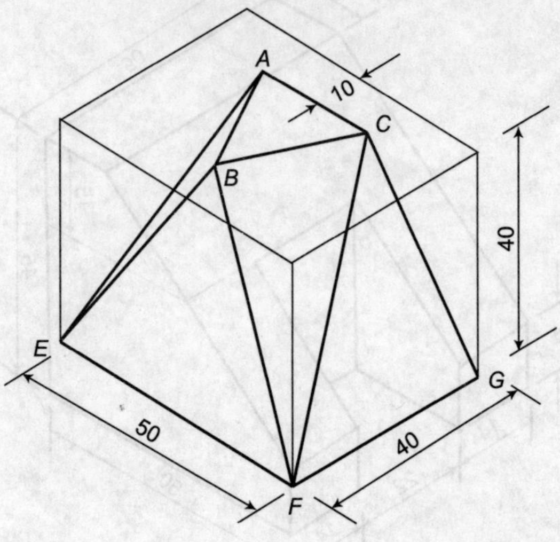

Fig. 15.34 (b) Solution to Problem 15.28

PROBLEM 15.29

Draw the isometric views from the following views in Fig. 15.35(a).

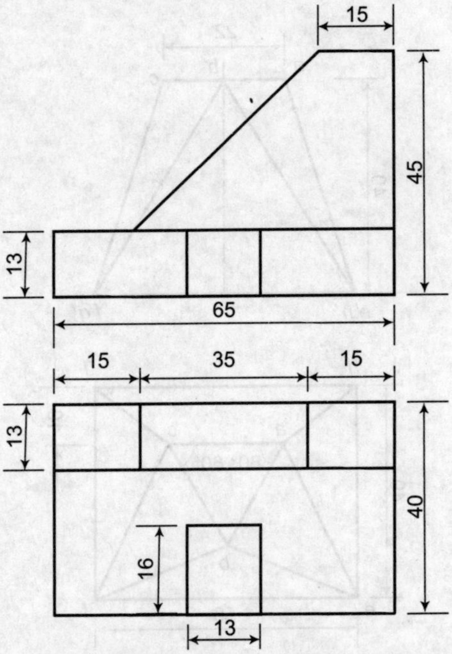

Fig. 15.35 (a) Orthogonal views

Solution:

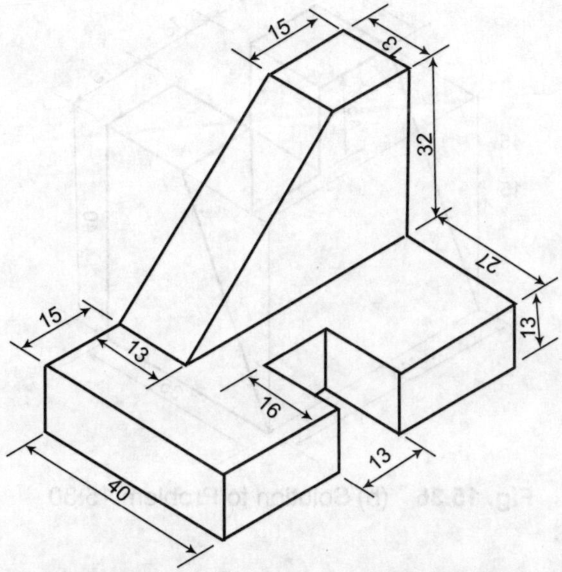

Fig. 15.35 (b) Solution to Problem 15.29

PROBLEM 15.30

Draw the isometric views form the following orthographic views in Fig. 15.36 (a).

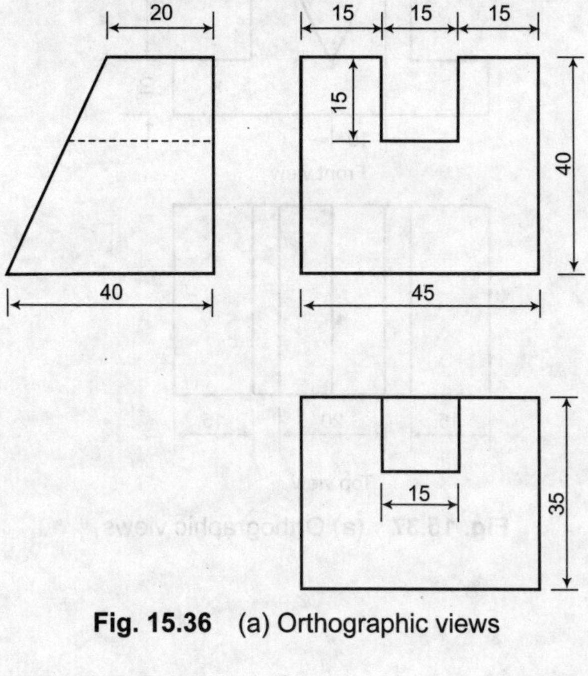

Fig. 15.36 (a) Orthographic views

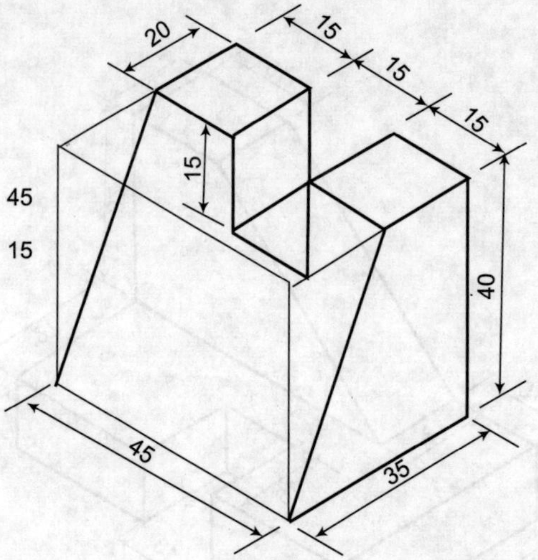

Fig. 15.36 (b) Solution to Problem 15.30

PROBLEM 15.31

Draw the isometric views from the following orthographic views in Fig. 15.37 (a).

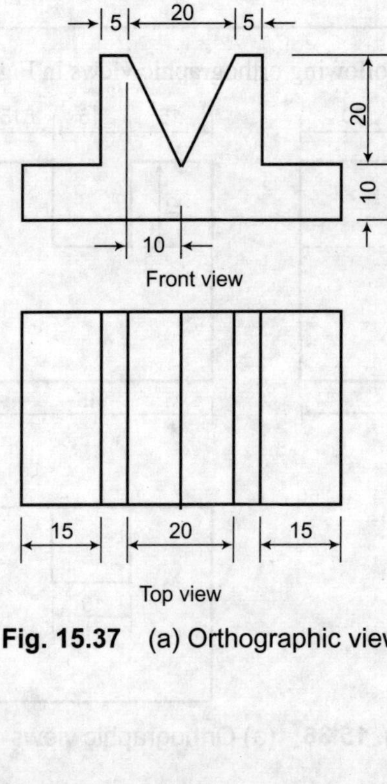

Fig. 15.37 (a) Orthographic views

Solution:

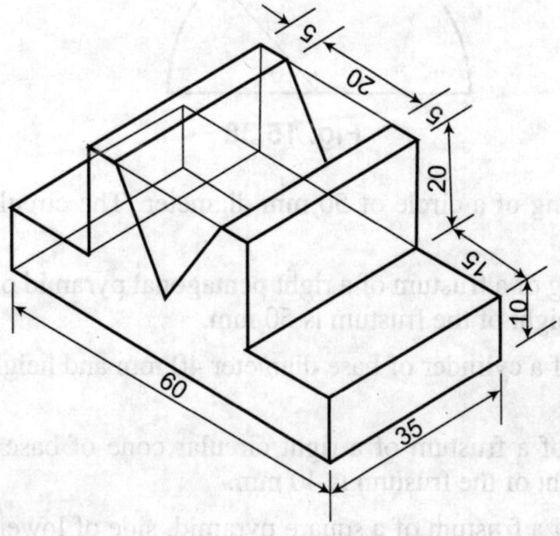

Fig. 15.37 (b) Solution to Problem 15.31

EXERCISE

Review Questions

1. Differentiate between isometric projection and isometric view.
2. Describe the simplest method of drawing an ellipse.
3. Describe the method of drawing isometric projection of a circle.
4. What is isometric scale?
5. How is isometric scale constructed?
6. What are the advantages of pictorial drawing?
7. Draw the isometric view of the following plane figures taking suitable position.
   (i) square (ii) pentagonal plane (iii) hexagonal plane
8. Draw the isometric projection of the following:
   (i) circle (ii) square (iii) rectangular plane
9. Draw an isometric projection of an equilateral triangle. The equilateral triangle front view is parallel to vertical plane. The triangle side is equal to 30 mm.
10. Draw an isometric view of a regular hexagonal plane surface of side 30 mm. The plane surface is parallel to *VP* and one of its side is parallel to *VP*.
11. Figure 15.38 shows the front view of a plane parallel to *VP*. Draw its isometric view.

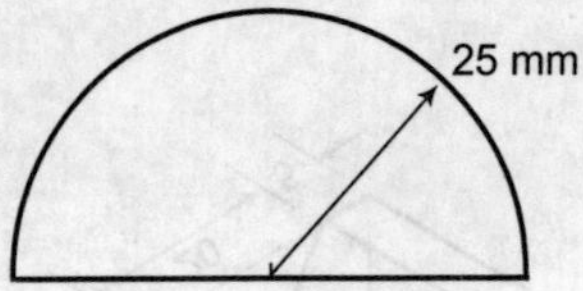

Fig. 15.38

12. Draw the isometric drawing of a circle of 50 mm diameter. The circular plane is kept on horizontal plane.
13. Draw an isometric drawing of a frustum of a right pentagonal pyramid of side base 30 mm. Side of top pentagon is 20 mm and height of the frustum is 50 mm.
14. Draw an isometric view of a cylinder of base diameter 40 mm and height 50 mm when the axis is (i) horizontal, (ii) vertical.
15. Draw an isometric view of a frustum of a right circular cone of base diameter 40 mm and the top diameter 25 mm, and height of the frustum is 40 mm.
16. Draw an isometric view of a frustum of a square pyramid, side of lower base is 45 mm, side of upper base is 20 mm, and height of the frustum is 40 mm.
17. A right circular cone of base diameter 40 mm and height 50 mm rests centrally on the top of a cube 55 mm. Draw the isometric view of the combined solids.
18. Figure 15.39 shows the orthographic projection of an object. Draw the isometric view of the object.

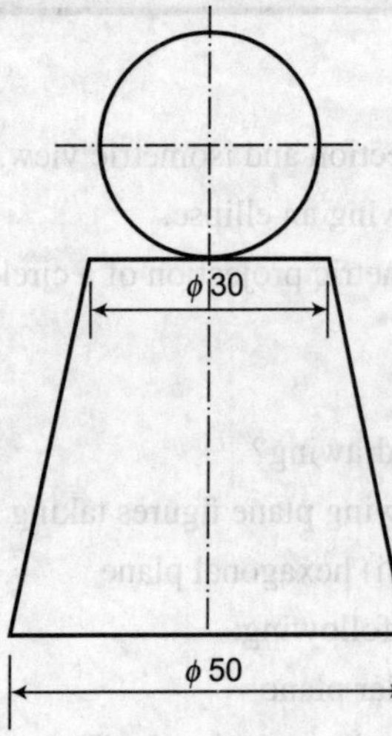

Fig. 15.39

19. Draw isometric view of a hexagonal prism with side of base 30 mm and height 50 mm surmounting a square pyramid of side 20 mm and height 45 mm, such that the axes of the two sides are collinear and at least one of the edges of the two solids is parallel.

20. A right regular pentagonal prism with edge of base 30 mm and height 55 mm has a circular hole of diameter 25 mm drilled centrally through it along its axis. Draw its isometric view.

21. Draw the isometric view of a sphere of radius 30 mm resting centrally on the top of the square prism of side 40 mm and height 60 mm.

22. A pentagonal prism is placed on a square slab 55 mm and 20 mm height. The side of prism is 25 mm and height is 50 mm. Draw the isometric view.

23. Figure 15.40 shows the orthographic view of an object. Draw the isometric projection of the object.

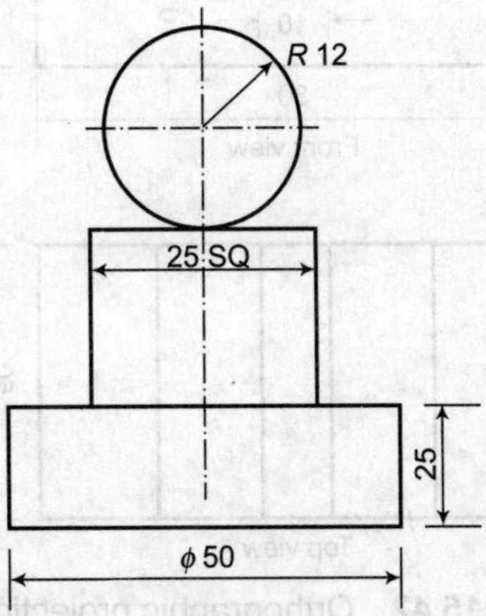

Fig. 15.40

24. Front view and the top view of an object are given in Fig. 15.41. Draw the isometric view of the object.

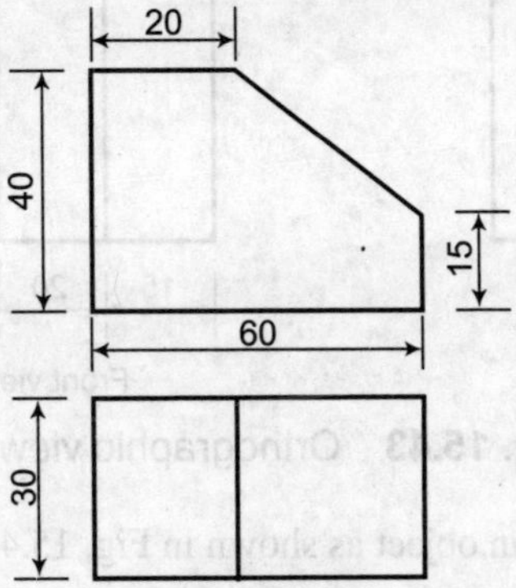

Fig. 15.41

25. Figure 15.42 shows the orthographic projections of an object. Draw the isometric view.

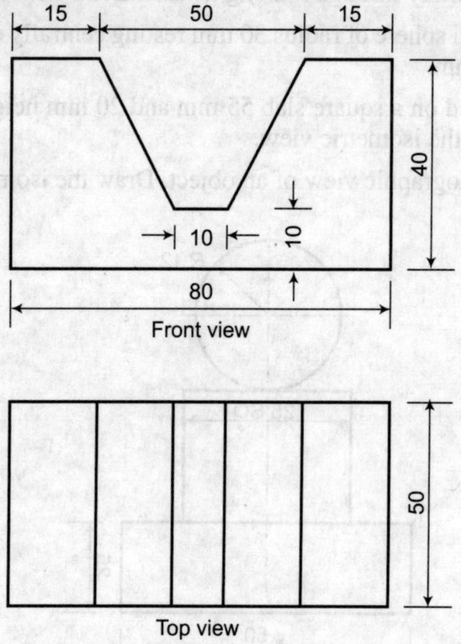

Fig. 15.42 Orthographic projections

26. Front view and side view are shown in Fig. 15.43. Draw the isometric projection.

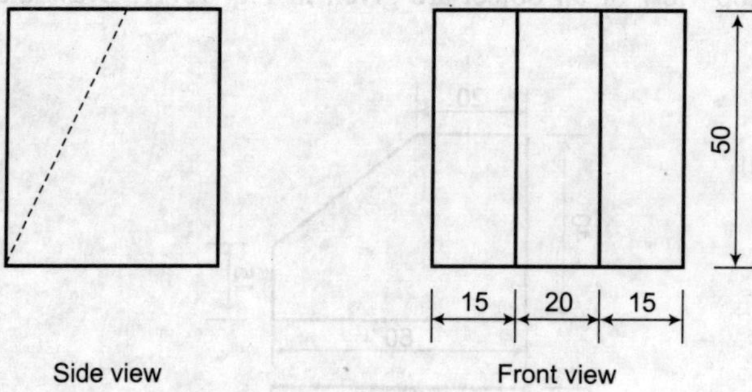

Fig. 15.43 Orthographic views

27. Draw the isometric projection of an object as shown in Fig. 15.44.

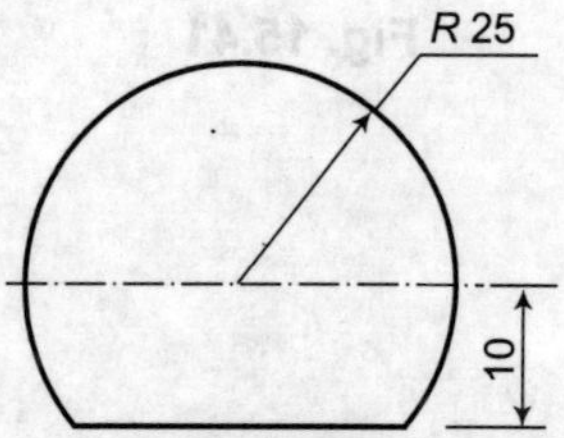

Fig. 15.44

28. Draw the isometric projection of the objects shown in Fig. 15.45(a) and (b).

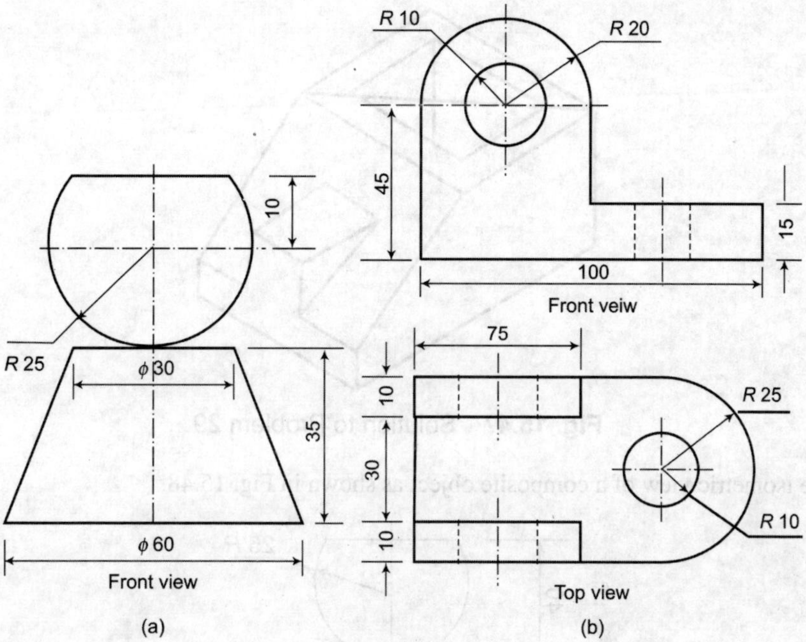

Fig. 15.45

29. Front view, top view, and side view for an object are shown in Fig. 15.46. Draw the isometric projection.

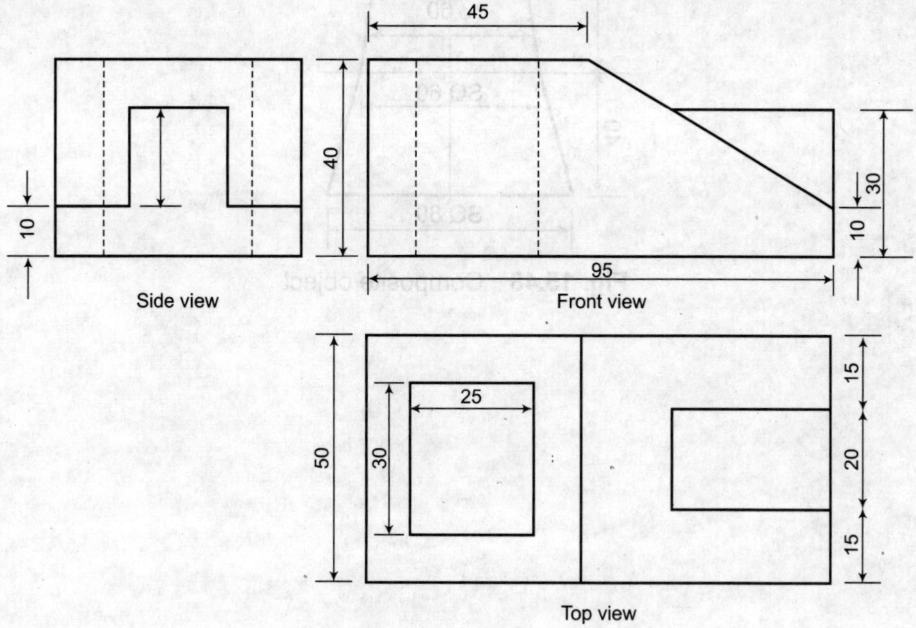

Fig. 15.46 Orthographic views

Hint:

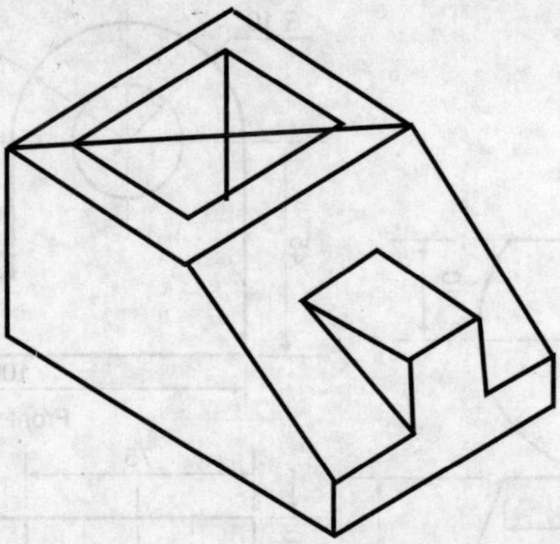

Fig. 15.47 Solution to Problem 29

30. Draw the isometric view of a composite object as shown in Fig. 15.48.

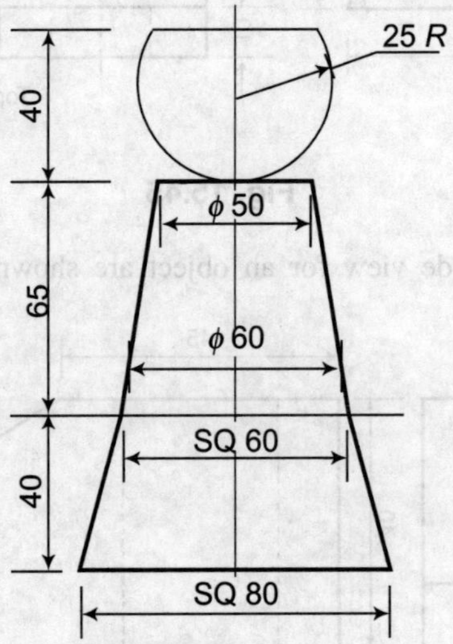

Fig. 15.48 Composite object

31. Draw the isometric projection of the object shown in Fig. 15.49.

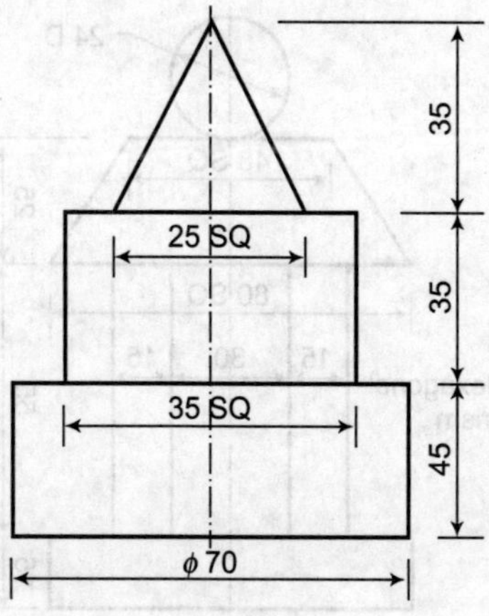

Fig. 15.49

32. Draw the isometric view of the object shown in Fig. 15.50.

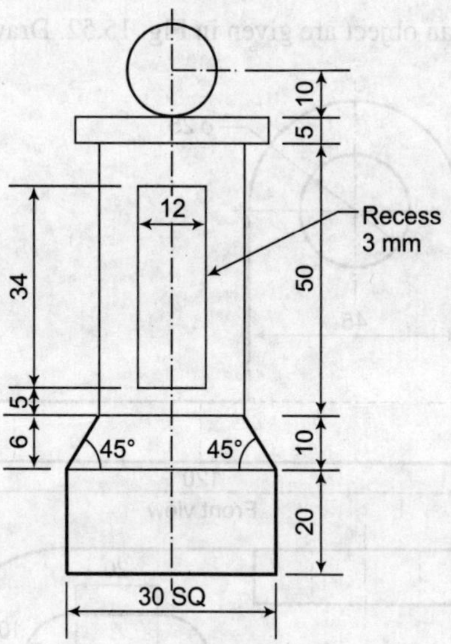

Fig. 15.50

33. Draw the isometric view of the object shown in Fig. 15.51.

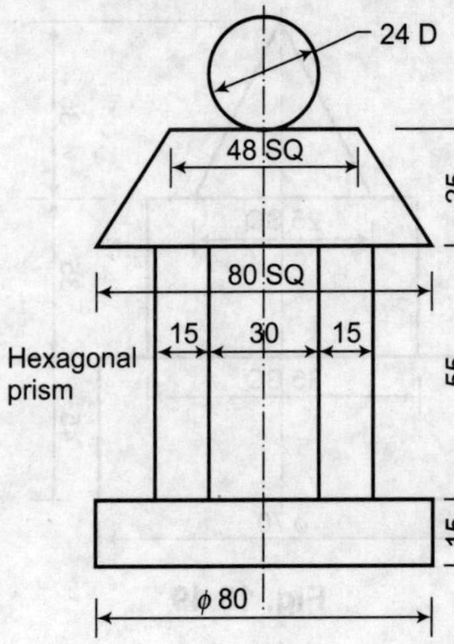

Fig 15.51

34. Top view and front view of an object are given in Fig. 15.52. Draw the isometric views.

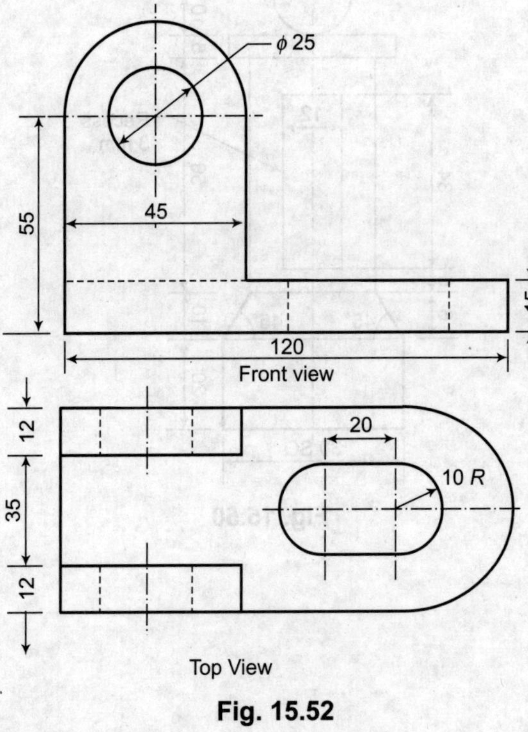

Fig. 15.52

35. Draw the oblique parallel projection of the cross given in Fig. 15.53.

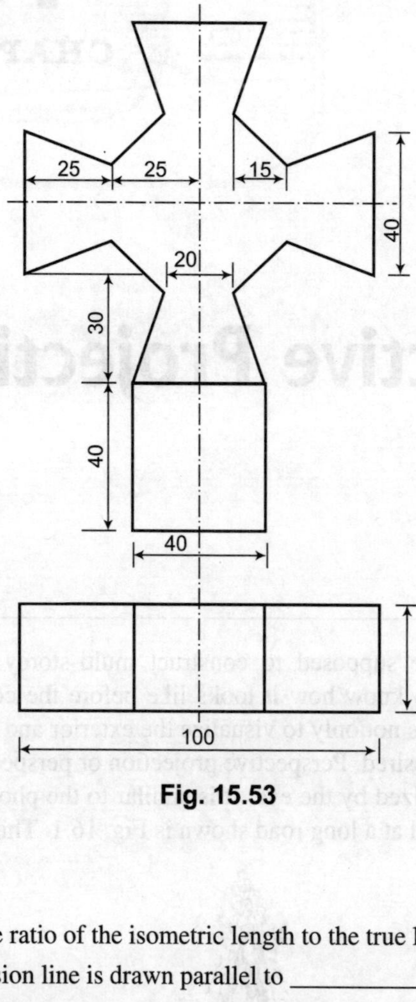

Fig. 15.53

Objective Questions

1 In isometric projection, the ratio of the isometric length to the true length is ____.

2 In isometric views, dimension line is drawn parallel to ______________.

3 A circle will appear as an ellipse in ____________.

4 The isometric projection of a sphere is a circle having radius equal to the radius of the ______________.

ANSWERS

Objective Questions

1. $\sqrt{2}:\sqrt{3}$ **2.** isometric axis **3.** isometric view

4. sphere

16

CHAPTER

Perspective Projection/View

16.1 INTRODUCTION

Civil engineers or architects are supposed to construct multi-storey buildings, bridges, etc. It is sometimes a matter of interest to know how it looks like before the construction job is taken up by them. The view of the object helps not only to visualize the exterior and interior appearance but also to modify the structural design, if desired. Perspective projection or perspective view is the pictorial view of the object which can be visualized by the eye. It is similar to the photograph of the object taken by the camera. This can be visualized at a long road shown is Fig. 16.1. This is similar to photography.

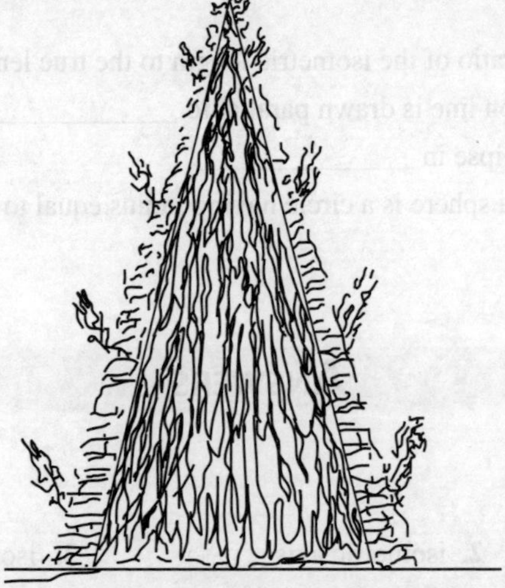

Fig. 16.1 Straight road shown in perspective

16.2 DEFINITION OF PERSPECTIVE PROJECTION

Perspective projection/view is the view of an object projected on a transparent vertical plane which is known as a picture plane from a fixed position.

The size of the perspective depends on the position of the picture plane with respect to the object. In perspective, projection of the object converges to a point which is termed as vanishing point. In this case, to visualize the object the eye is kept fixed with respect to the object.

A transparent vertical plane is kept between the object and the eye. The view obtained on the transparent plane is the required perspective view of the object. It can be seen in a figure as follows.

16.3 IMPORTANT TERMS USED IN PERSPECTIVE

The following are the important terms used in obtaining the perspective view which is also shown in Fig 16.2.

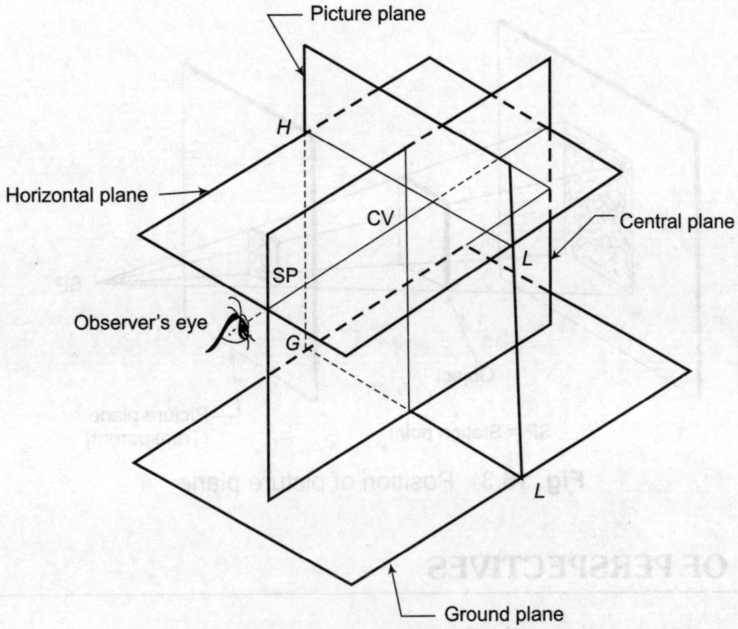

Fig. 16.2 Important terms in pictorial view

1. **Ground plane (GP):** It is the horizontal plane on which the object stands.
2. **Picture plane (PP):** A vertical transparent plane situated between a fixed point (station point) and the object. This is the plane on which perspective projection is viewed.
3. **Stations point (SP):** The point where the observer's eye is located.
4. **Horizontal plane (HP):** It is a horizontal plane at the level of station point.
5. **Central plane (CP):** A vertical plane which is passing through station point.
6. **Horizontal line (HL):** It is the line of intersection of the horizontal and picture plane.

7. **Ground line (GL):** It is the line of intersection of the picture plane and ground plane.
8. **Vanishing point (VP):** The point in space where all the parallel lines converge to meet is known as vanishing point.

GL: ground line; HL: horizontal line; SP: station point; CV: centre of vision

16.4 LOCATION OF PICTURE PLANE AND STATION POINT

The location of the picture plane with respect to an object is very important in perspective projection.

In normal case, the picture plane is either in front of the object or behind the object. If the picture plane is placed in front of the object, the perspective view will be of larger size compared to the size of the object as shown in Fig. 16.3. If the picture plane is placed behind the object, the perspective will be of reduced size as compared to the object size. When the picture plane coincides with the object, the perspective view obtained will be of equal size of the object, as shown in Fig. 16.3.

The position of station point is also very important for obtaining best perspective.

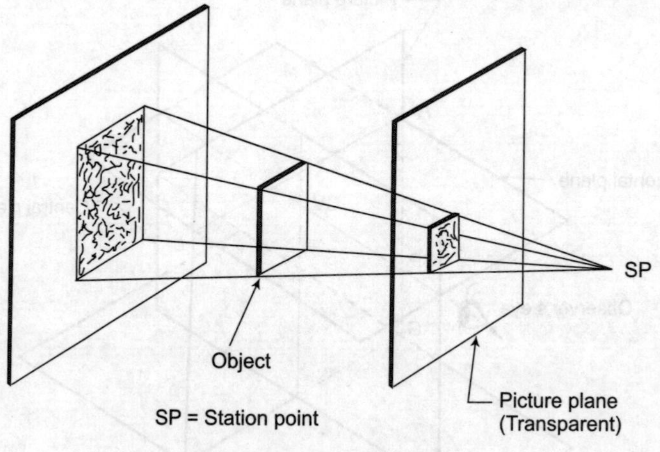

Fig. 16.3 Position of picture plane

16.5 TYPES OF PERSPECTIVES

There are three types of perspective projections:

1. Parallel or one station point perspective projection
2. Angular or two stations point perspective projection
3. Oblique or three stations point perspective projection

16.5.1 Parallel or One Station Point Perspective Projection

In parallel or one station point perspective projection, one side of the object is just parallel to the picture plane and the other side is perpendicular to it. It is a simple method to draw the perspective projection of the object. It can be best understood by Fig. 16.4.

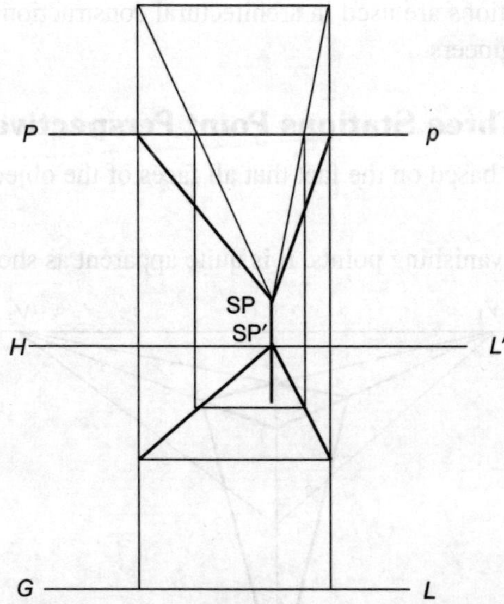

Fig. 16.4 One station point perspective

16.5.2 Angular or Two Stations Point Perspective Projection

Angular or two point perspective view is based on the fact that when two faces of the object are inclined to picture plane and parallel to it; in this projection, there shall be two points,

The method of drawing perspective is simple and can be best understood by the illustration of construction shown in Fig. 16.5.

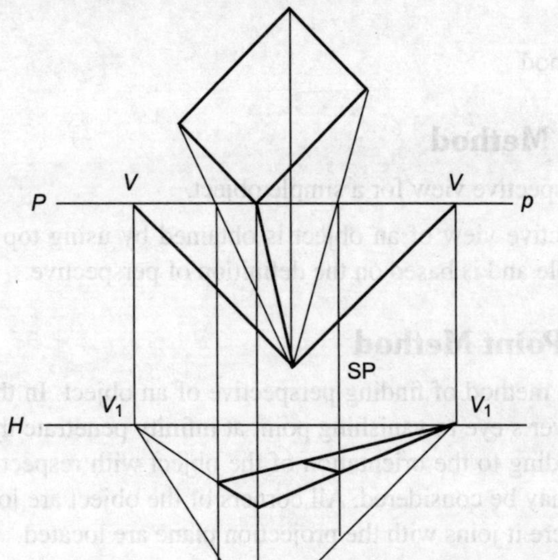

Fig. 16.5 Two point projection

Angular perspective projections are used in architectural construction of multi-storey buildings and large bridges used by civil engineers.

16.5.3 Obliques or Three Stations Point Perspective Projection

These types of projections are based on the fact that all faces of the object are oblique with the picture plane.

In this case, there are three vanishing points. It is quite apparent as shown is Fig. 16.6.

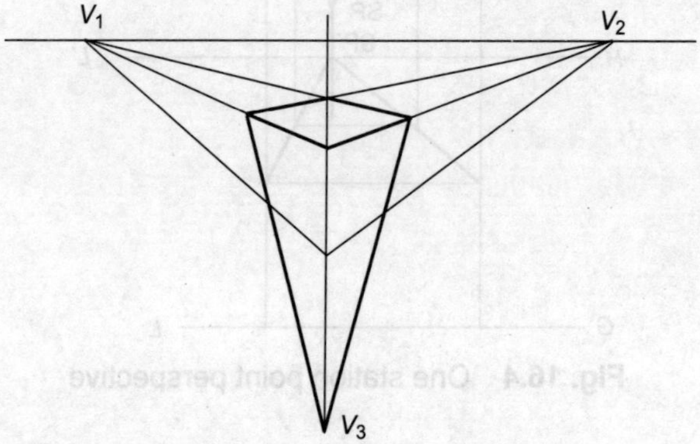

Fig. 16.6 Three point projection

16.6 METHOD FOR OBTAINING PERSPECTIVE VIEW

There are two methods which are used to determine perspective drawing:

1. Visual ray method
2. Vanishing point method

16.6.1 Visual Ray Method

It is useful for making perspective view for a simple object.

In this case, the perspective view of an object is obtained by using top and side views or top and front views. It is very simple and is based on the definition of perspective.

16.6.2 Vanishing Point Method

This is the most important method of finding perspective of an object. In this case, the point at which visual rays from the observer's eye to vanishing point at infinity penetrate the picture plane, it is called the vanishing point. According to the orientation of the object with respect to picture point, one, two, or three vanishing points may be considered. All corners of the object are joined with station points by visual rays. The points where it joins with the projection plane are located.

The joining point with projection plane gives the appropriate perspective view. Usually, we require top view, front view, or side view of the object for drawing perspective view.

As we know, the picture plane lies between an observer's eyes and the object. It is the method to use the third angle of projection. In this case, orientation of the object with respect to picture plane is important. The location of station point, ground plane, and picture plane is important.

For large objects, the station point is placed almost at the level of observer's eyes. For small object, the station point should be selected such that it must be visible from all sides of the object. The distance of station point from projection plane is almost double that of the greater dimensions of the object. Further illustration will clarify the methods for obtaining the perspective view.

PROBLEM 16.1

A straight line *PQ* 50 mm long is parallel to *GP* and it is 10 mm above *GP*. The straight line is inclined at 45° to *PP*. The end *P* is 25 mm behind *PP*. The station point is 45 mm in front of *PP* and 50 mm above *GP*, and it lies at CP passing through 10 mm right side of the mid-point of straight line (using visual ray method).

Solution:

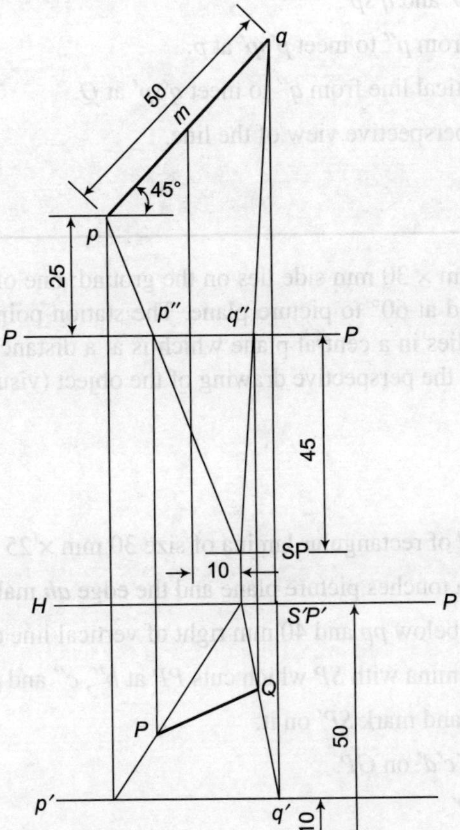

Fig. 16.7 Solution to Problem 16.1

See Fig. 16.7:

(i) Draw a horizontal line to represent picture plane (pp).

Since *PQ* line is parallel to ground plane, the top view of the line will represent the true length, and, hence, draw *pq* at 45° to *pp* equal to 50 mm length.

The end *P* is 25 mm above *PP*.

(ii) Point *m* is the middle point of the line *pq*. Draw a vertical line from *m*.

(iii) Mark *SP* (station point) 10 mm right of the vertical line which is at *m*.

(iv) Draw line from *SP* with *p* and *q* intersecting *PP* at *p″q″*.

(v) Draw a ground line *GP* = 50 mm away form *HP*, and *HP* is drawn 10 mm below *sp*. Mark *sp′*.

(vi) From *p* and *q*, draw vertical line to represent *p′q′* parallel and 10 mm above *GP*.

(vii) Draw line from *p′sp′* and *q′sp′*.

(viii) Draw vertical line from *p″* to meet *p′sp′* at *p*.

(ix) Similarly, draw vertical line from *q″* to meet *q′sp′* at *Q*.

(x) *PQ* is the required perspective view of the line.

PROBLEM 16.2

A rectangular lamina of 35 mm × 30 mm side lies on the ground: one of its corner touches the picture plane and one edge is inclined at 60° to picture plane. The station point is 35 mm in front of *pp*, 50 mm above ground plane and lies in a central plane which is at a distance of 40 mm to the right of the corner touching the *PP*. Draw the perspective drawing of the object (visual ray method).

Solution:

See Fig. 16.8:

(i) Draw top view *abcd* of rectangular lamina of size 30 mm × 25 mm.

Corner '*a*' of lamina touches picture plane and the edge *ab* makes an angle of 60° with *pp*.

(ii) Locate *sp* at 35 mm below *pp* and 40 mm right of vertical line drawn from '*a*'.

(iii) Join all corners of lamina with *SP* which cuts *PP* at *b″*, *c″* and *d″*.

(iv) Draw *HP* below *SP* and mark *SP′* on it.

(v) Draw front view *a′*b′*c′d′* on *GP*.

(vi) *Join a′*b′*c′d′* with *SP′*.

(vii) Since '*a*' touches *PP*, its perspective will be the true position.

(viii) Corner '*b*' joined from *SP* cutting *PP* at b″. Draw vertical line which cuts *b′sp′* at *B*. B is the perspective of corner *B* of lamina.

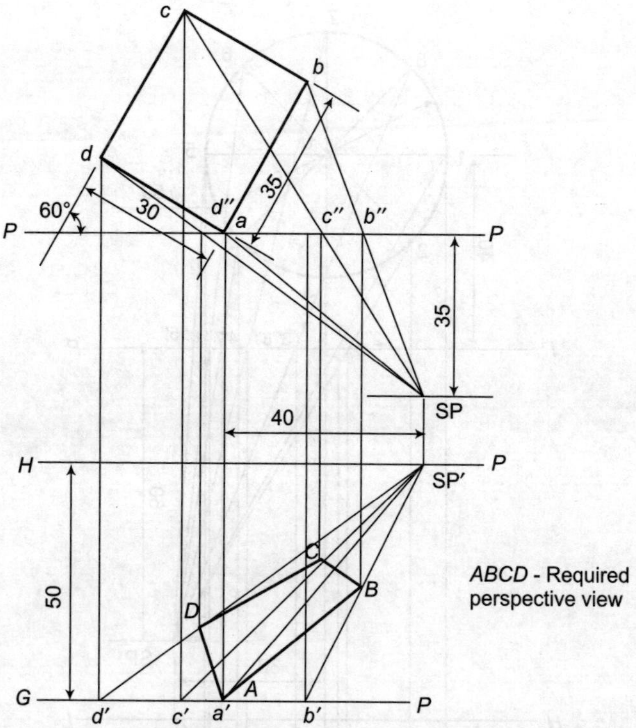

Fig. 16.8 Solution to Problem 16.2

(ix) Similarly, from c'' and d'' which gives *C* and *D*.

(x) *ABCD* is the required perspective of the lamina.

PROBLEM 16.3

A circular plate of 50 mm diameter is resting on *GP* with its centre 40 mm behind *PP*. The station point is 60 mm in front of *PP* and 55 mm above *GP*. If *CP* is 30 mm to the right of the centre of the circular plate, draw its perspective projection (visual ray method).

Solution:

See Fig. 16.9:

(i) Draw a circle of diameter 50 mm in top view and draw a line representing *PP* 40 mm below the centre of the circle.

(ii) Locate station point *SP* in top view, 60 mm below and 30 mm right of the centre of circle.

(iii) Draw *HL* line below *SP* of fix *SP* on it.

(iv) Draw *GP*, 55 mm below *HL*.

(v) Divide circle in 8 equal parts and all points are numbered as 1, 2, 3 … 8.

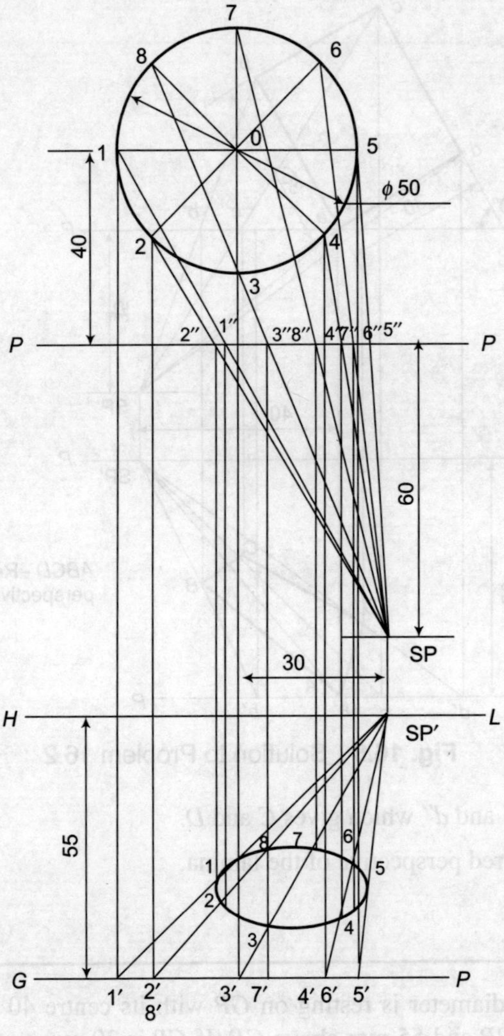

Fig. 16.9 Solution to Problem 16.3

(vi) Draw vertical line from 1, 2, 3 … 8 and project these points on *GP* to represent front view as 1′, 2′, 3′ … 8′.

(vii) Join 1, 2, 3 … 8 with *SP* to cut *PP* at 1″, 2″, 3″ … 8″.

(viii) Draw vertical line from 1″, 2″, 3″… 8″ to cut all lines which are joining from 1′, 2′, 3′ … 8′ with *SP*′.

(ix) The points are located as 1, 2, 3 … 8 and join all the points by a smooth curve.

(x) 1, 2, 3 … 8 is the required perspective of the circle in this position.

PROBLEM 16.4

A circle of diameter 50 mm is lying on G1 and touching *PP*. The station point is 60 mm in front of *PP* and 55 mm above *GP*.

If the central plane is passing through the centre of the circle, draw the perspective projection of the circle (visual ray method).

Solution:

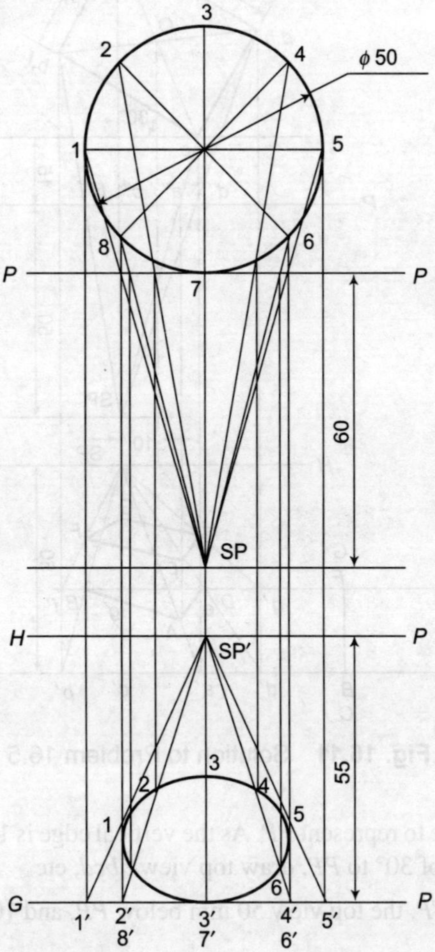

Fig. 16.10 Solution to Problem 16.4

Note: Solution of the problem is similar to Problem 16.3. The perspective of a circle will be circle when it is parallel to *PP*. In all other position, perspective will be an ellipse (Fig. 16.10).

PROBLEM 16.5

A rectangular block 40 mm × 30 mm × 20 mm is lying on *HP* with one of the longest face. A vertical edge of the block is 15 mm behind the picture plane. The longer face containing that edge makes an angle of 30° with *PP*. The station point is 50 mm above the *GP* and lying in a central plane which is 10 mm right of the centre of the block. Draw the perspective view by visual ray method.

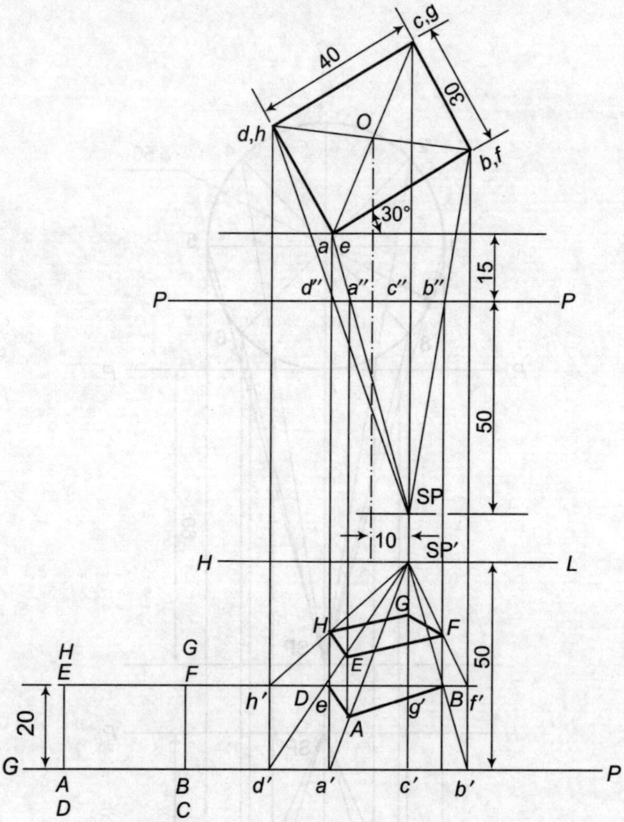

Fig. 16.11 Solution to Problem 16.5

See Fig. 16.11.

(i) Draw a horizontal line to represent *PP*. As the vertical edge is 15 mm behind *PP* and the longer face makes an angle of 30° to *PP*, draw top view *abcd*, etc.

(ii) Locate station point *SP*, the top view 50 mm below *PP*, and 10 mm right side of the centre of the block.

(iii) Draw *HP* and fix *SP′* on *HP* just below *SP*.

(iv) Join *SP* with all the corners of the block intersecting *PP* at points *a″b″c″* ..., etc.

(v) Draw a horizontal line *GP*, 50 mm below *HP*.

(vi) Draw front view of the block 20 mm above *GP*.

(vii) Join *a′b′c′*..., etc., from bottom front view with *SP′*.

(viii) Draw vertical line from $a''b''c''$ ..., etc., intersecting points at *PP*.

(ix) The lines are cutting at *ABCD*.

(x) Do similarly with the top corners of the block *EFGH*.

The figure represents the perspective view of the block.

PROBLEM 16.6

A square lamina of side 45 mm × 20 mm is lying vertical with one of its longer edges on *GP* and inclined at 45° to *PP*. The nearest edge to *PP* is 15 mm behind it. The station point is 35 mm in front of *PP* and 45 mm above *GP*, and lies 5 mm left side of the centre of the lamina. Draw the perspective projection using the vanishing point method.

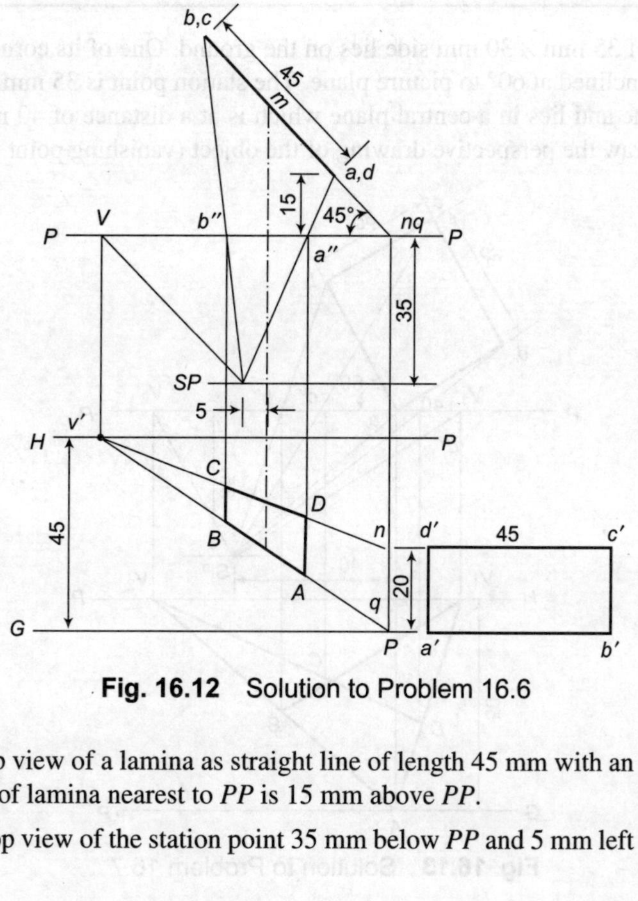

Fig. 16.12 Solution to Problem 16.6

See Fig. 16.12.

(i) Draw the top view of a lamina as straight line of length 45 mm with an angle of 45° with *PP*. The side *ad* of lamina nearest to *PP* is 15 mm above *PP*.

(ii) Locate *SP* top view of the station point 35 mm below *PP* and 5 mm left of the middle point of *adbc*.

(iii) Draw *HP* and *GP*, 45 mm below *HP*.

(iv) Join *SP* from *ad* and *bc*, which intersect *PP* at a''.

(v) Draw a line parallel to *a b* which cuts *PP* at *V*.

(vi) Draw a vertical line from *V* to cut *HP* at V'.

(vii) From $a''b''$ draw a vertical line.

(viii) Draw a front view as $a'b'c'd'$.

(ix) Extend the top view of lamina to cut *PP* at *nq*. It is means the lamina extended fill touches *PP*. Hence, *nq* is the true length in perspective.

(x) Join *n* and *q* with *V′* on *HP*.

(xi) From $a''b''$ draw vertical.

They are cutting at *ABCD*.

(xii) ABCD is the required perspective.

PROBLEM 16.7

A rectangular lamina of 35 mm × 30 mm side lies on the ground. One of its corner touches the picture plane and one edge is inclined at 60° to picture plane. The station point is 35 mm in front of *PP* and 50 mm above ground plane and lies in a central plane which is at a distance of 40 mm to the right of the corner touching *PP*. Draw the perspective drawing of the object (vanishing point method).

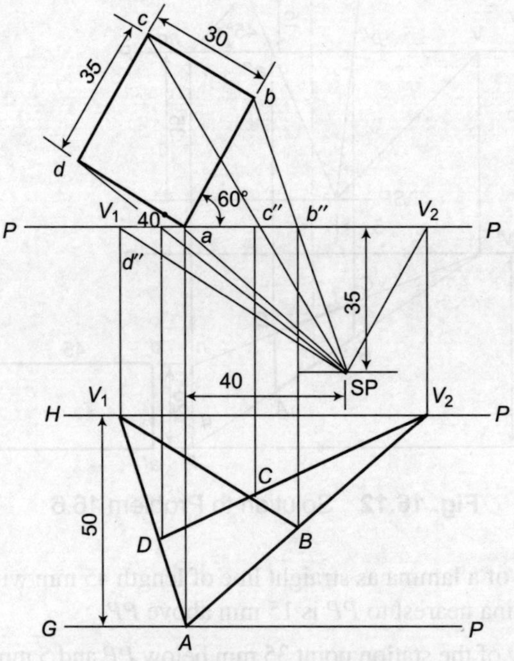

Fig. 16.13 Solution to Problem 16.7

See Fig. 16.13.

(i) Draw the top view of lamina as *abcd* 35 mm × 30 mm placing the lamina such that one of its corners '*a*' touches *PP* and the edge *ab* makes an angle of 60° to *PP*.

(ii) Locate station point SP 35 mm below PP and 40 mm right of the line vertical at corner b.

(iii) Join all the corners with SP and the lines are intersecting PP at $ab''\ c''\ d''$.

(iv) Draw two lines V_1'SP and V_2SP from SP parallel to ab and ad, respectively.

(v) From V_1 and V_2, draw vertical lines on HP.

(vi) Since 'a' touch PP, draw a vertical line from 'a' and obtain A on GP. Join B with V_1 and V_2.

(vii) Join A with V_1. Since ad is parallel to bc, the perspective view of any point on ad will lie on AV_1.

(viii) $ABCD$ is the required perspective.

PROBLEM 16.8

A rectangular prism of side of the base 40 mm × 25 mm and height 45 mm is lying with its base on the ground plane. A vertical edge coincides with PP and one of the longer edge of the base is inclined at 45° to PP and behind it.

The station point is 45 mm in front of PP and it is 60 mm above GP and lies in the central plane to be located 15 mm to the right of the axis of the prism (vanishing point method).

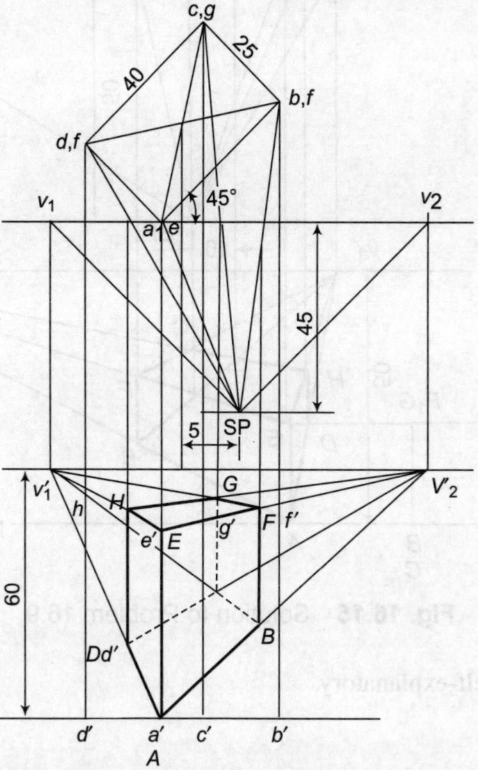

Fig. 16.14 Solution to Problem 16.8

Note: Figure 16.14 shows the perspective projection of rectangular block obtained by the top view and front view method is self-explanatory.

PROBLEM 16.9

A rectangular block 40 mm × 30 mm × 20 mm lying on *GP* with one of the longest face. A vertical edge is with *PP* and the longer face containing that edge makes an angle of 30° with *PP*. The station point is 50 mm in front of the picture plane, 50 mm above *GP*, and lies in a central plane which is 10 mm right of centre of block. Draw the perspective view (vanishing point method).

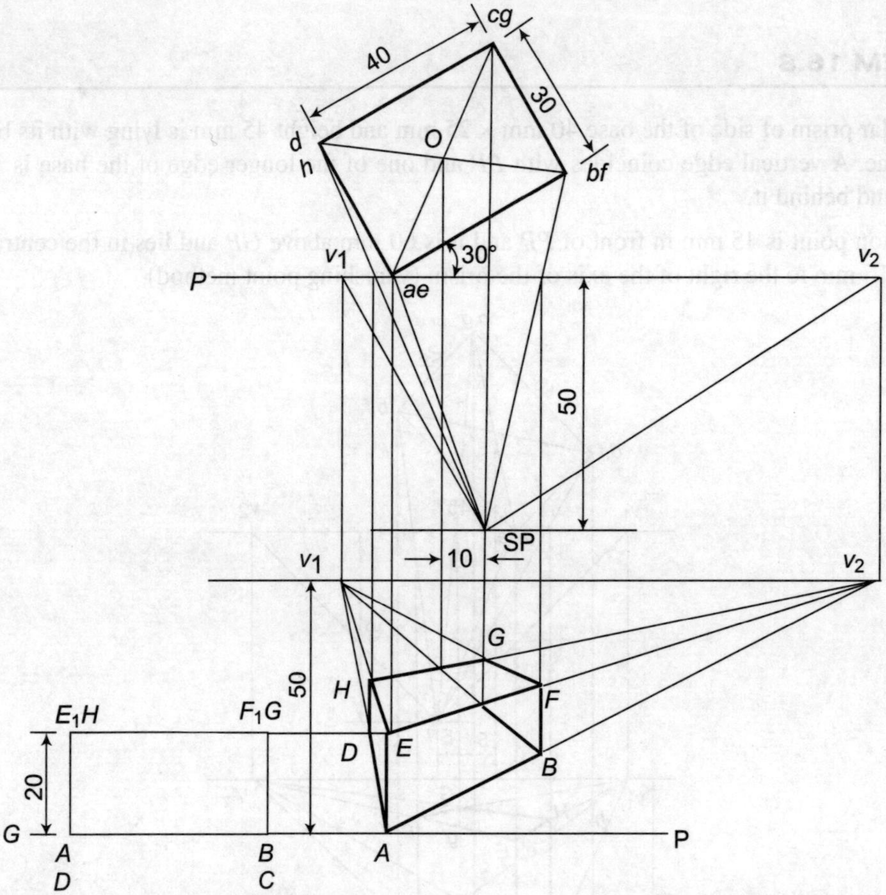

Fig. 16.15 Solution to Problem 16.9

Solution to Problem 16.9 is self-explanatory.

PROBLEM 16.10

A square pyramid of base size 40 mm and height 45 mm is placed on the ground plane with its longer base edge parallel to and 15 mm behind picture plane. The station point is 40 mm right side of the apex, 45 mm in front of *PP*, and 70 mm above *GP*. Draw the perspective projection of the pyramid using visual ray method.

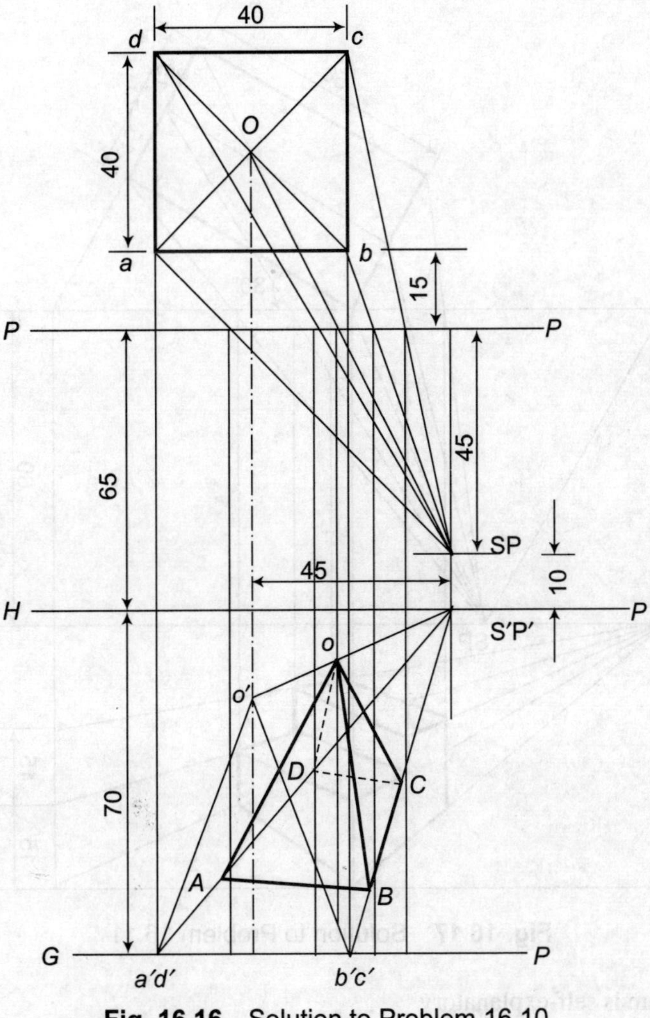

Fig. 16.16 Solution to Problem 16.10

PROBLEM 16.11

A stair has two steps of 15 mm tread and 15 mm rise. The length of steps is 50 mm. The stair is placed with the vertical edge of the first step touching *PP* and its longer edge inclined at 30° to *PP*. The station point is 60 mm in front of *PP* and 50 mm above *GP* and lies in the central plane which is at 25 mm to the left of the vertical edge touching *PP*. Draw the perspective (vanishing point method).

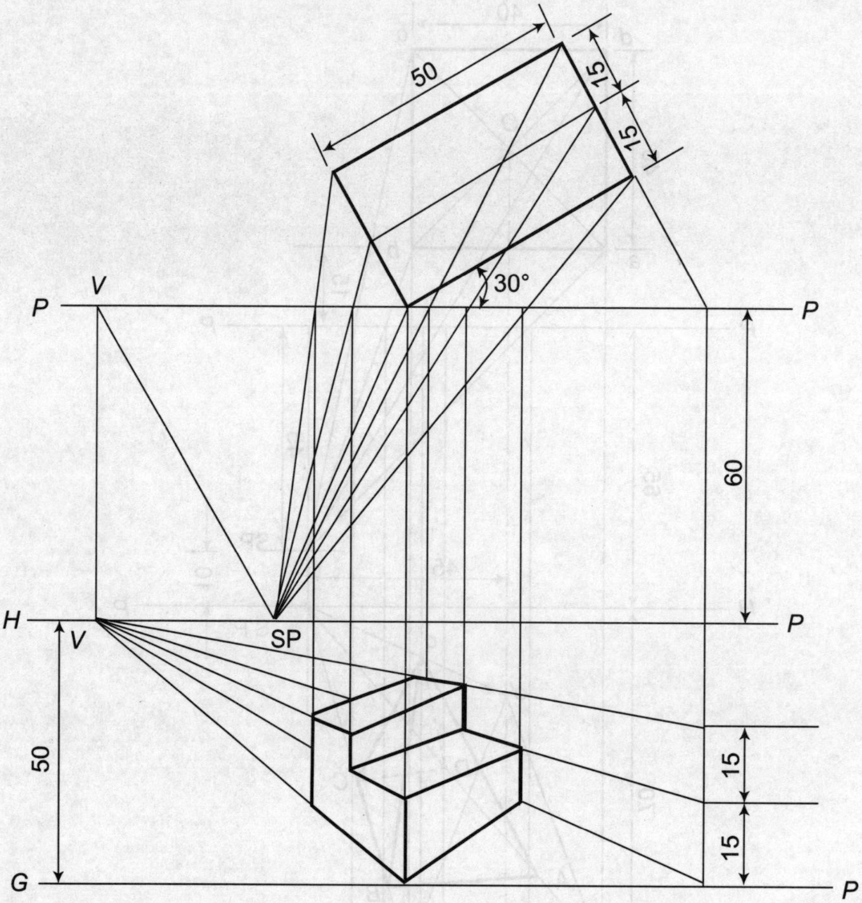

Fig. 16.17 Solution to Problem 16.11

Solution to this problem is self-explanatory.

PROBLEM 16.12

A rectangular prism of base edge 40 mm × 70 mm and height 30 mm is resting on its base on the ground with the shortest edge of the base making an angle of 45° with *PP*. The two vertical edges are in front of *PP* and the one which is the farthest is 40 mm in front of *PP*. The station point is 10 mm to the right to the farthest edge and 90 mm from *PP*. The horizon is 60 mm above the ground plane. Draw perspective view of the object (part of the object is in front of *PP*).

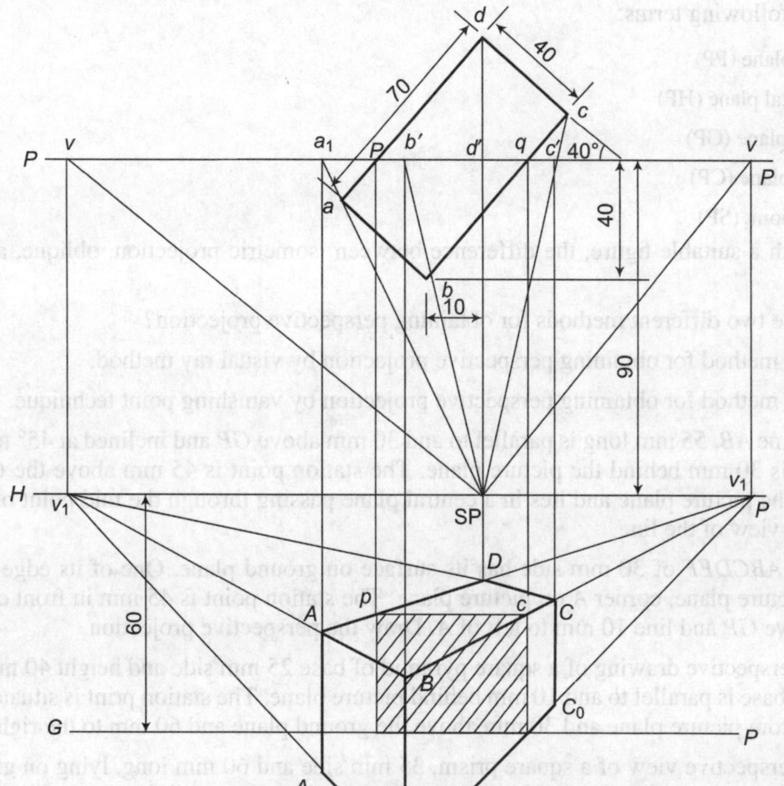

Fig. 16.18 Solution to Problem 16.12

Solution to this problem is self-explanatory.

EXERCISE

Review Questions

1. What is perspective projection?
2. What is the importance of perspective projection?
3. What are the different types of perspective projections?
4. Define the following terms:
   (i) Picture plane (PP)
   (ii) Horizontal plane (HP)
   (iii) Ground plane (GP)
   (iv) Central plane (CP)
   (v) Station point (SP)
5. Explain with a suitable figure, the difference between isometric projection, oblique, and perspective projection.
6. What are the two different methods for obtaining perspective projection?
7. Explain the method for obtaining perspective projection by visual ray method.
8. Explain the method for obtaining perspective projection by vanishing point technique.
9. A straight line *AB*, 55 mm long is parallel to and 30 mm above *GP* and inclined at 45° to picture plane. The end *A* is 30 mm behind the picture plane. The station point is 45 mm above the *GP* and 35 mm in front of the picture plane and lies in a central plane passing through the mid point of *AB*. Draw the perspective view of the line.
10. A hexagon *ABCDEF* of 30 mm side has its surface on ground plane. One of its edge *AB* is inclined at 45° to picture plane, corner *A* on picture plane. The station point is 45 mm in front of picture plane 35 mm above *GP* and line 10 mm to left of *A*. Draw the perspective projection.
11. Draw the perspective drawing of a square pyramid of base 25 mm side and height 40 mm. The nearest edge of the base is parallel to and 10 mm behind picture plane. The station print is situated at a distance of 80 mm from picture plane and 30 mm above the ground plane and 60 mm to the right of apex.
12. Draw the perspective view of a square prism, 35 mm side and 60 mm long, lying on ground plane on one of its faces. A vertical edge is 20 mm behind the picture plane and the longer face containing that edge makes an angles of 30° with picture plane. The station point, 50 mm in front of picture plane 35 mm above ground plane, lies in a central plane which passes through the centre of the prism.
13. Draw the perspective view of a circle of 60 mm diameter lying on the ground plane touching the picture plane. The station point is 70 mm in front of picture plane and 50 mm above ground plane and lies in a central plane which is 20 mm to the right of the centre of the circle.
14. A rectangular prism, side of base 40 mm × 25 mm and height 45 mm, rests with its base on the ground plane. A vertical edge is in the picture plane and one of the longer edge of its base is inclined at 45° to *PP* and behind it. The station point is 45 mm in front of *PP*, 70 mm above the *GP*, and lies in the centre plane which passes the centre of the prism. Draw the perspective view.
15. A square pyramid of side of base 40 mm and axis 45 mm long rest with its base on the ground plane such that all the edges of the base are equally inclined to the *PP*, one of the corners of the base is touching the *PP*. The station point is 60 mm in front of the *PP*, 75 mm above the ground plane, and lies in a central plane which passes through the axis of the pyramid. Draw the perspective projection.

Objective Questions

1. A photograph of an object taken by the corners is a perspective projection. (Yes/No)
2. The point in space where parallel lines are meeting is ______________. (vanishing point/station point)
3. The perspective projection of circle is a __________ (circle/line) when its plane is __________ (inclined/parallel) to the other *PP*.
4. In oblique perspective, the number of vanishing points are______.
5. A view actually appearing to the observer when viewed from fixed position is called __________.
6. In perspective projection ______________ plane is placed between the object and eye.
7. When the picture plane (PP) coincides with the object, the perspective of the object will be of its ________ size.

Answers

Objective Questions

1. Yes
2. Vanishing point
3. Circle, Parallel
4. Three
5. Perspective view
6. Picture
7. Equal

17

CHAPTER

Conversion of Pictorial View into Orthographic View

17.1 INTRODUCTION

In engineering drawing, mostly, pictorial drawings of an object or machine components are provided. Pictorial view of an object is a single-view drawing of three-directional dimensions. (length, breadth, and height). Three-dimensional view of a single drawing gives a clear understanding of the actual shape of the object.

Pictorial view helps in understanding the actual shape of the object but is not accepted in technical drawing.

In engineering, orthographic drawing is an acceptable drawing in practice with the help of pictorial drawing, it is required to make orthographic view of an object.

Figure 17.1 (a) and (b) show the pictorial and orthographic view side by side.

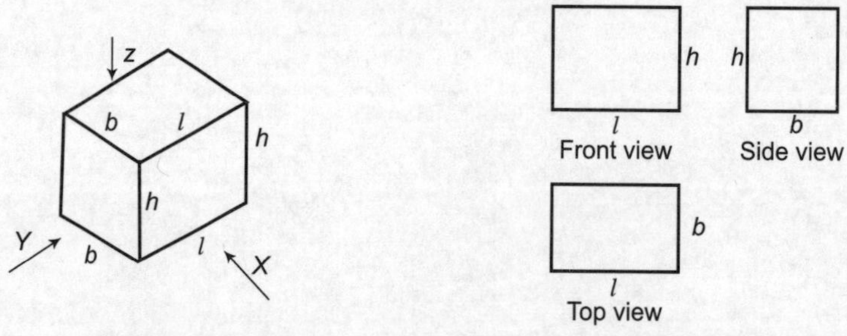

(a) (b)

Fig.17.1 (a) Pictorial view of an object; (b) I angle projection, orthographic view

17.2 ORTHOGRAPHIC VIEW

The principle of orthographic view has already been discussed in detail in Chapter 7.

In orthographic projection, three views of an object are drawn on three principal planes (HP, VP, and PP), all placed at right angle to each other. For a complete identification of the object, three views are necessary.

In this case, HP is intersecting with VP and PP both and vice versa, and they are making four quadrants.

Since there is no existence of II and IV quadrants, the views are not acceptable in II and IV quadrants and, hence, there are only two quadrants (I and III) are left for the views. For such cases, the object is placed either in first quadrant or in third quadrant. If the object is placed in the first quadrant, between HP and VP, it is called first-angle projection.

If the object is placed in III quadrant and projection is taken, it is called III-angle projection.

17.2.1 First-angle Projection Method

In this method, the object is considered to be in first quadrant between HP, VP, and PP. The projection taken on VP is called front view/elevation and projection taken on *HP* is designated as top view/plan. Projection taken on PP is called side view or the end view.

Since there are two sides of the object, the view will be different conventionally in first angle and third angle which will be clarified later. As per the convention of the rotation of HP, the front view will be at above and top view will be placed below the front view.

The front view and the top view both are aligned vertically. The front view will show the length and height of the object. The top view will show the length and breadth of the object.

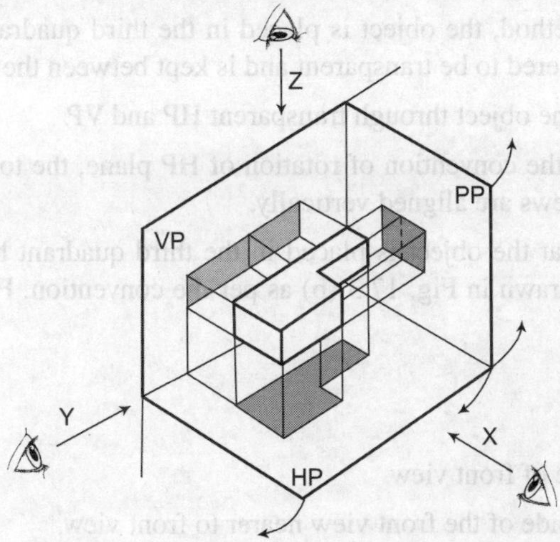

Fig. 17.2 (a) Object placed in first quadrant (first-angle projection)

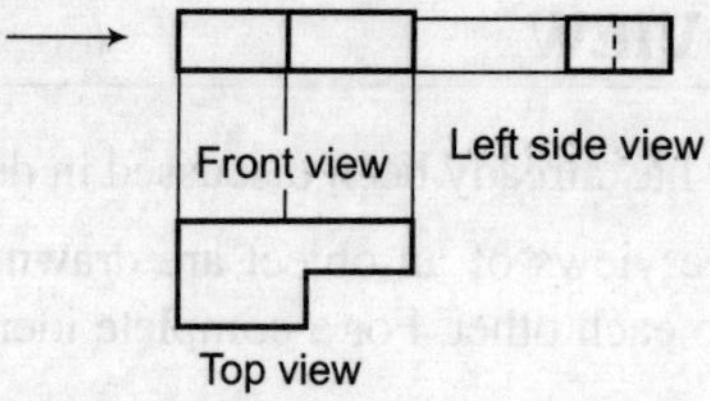

Fig. 17.2 (b) Orthographic view (first-angle projection)

Figure 17.2 (a) shows that the object is placed in the first quadrant between *HP* and *VP* and from the view already drawn in (b), it is clear as follows:

Front view above *xy*

Top view below *xy*

Left side view	Right side of front view
Right side view	Left side of front view

xy is the intersection of HP and VP.

As regards the plane of projection (HP, VP, and PP), they are simply on imagination. In fact, there is no existence of the plane of projection.

Object is placed in the first quadrant between HP, VP, and PP. By convention of rotation of HP, projection taken on HP, i.e., top view goes below the front view. Object is placed between the plane of projection and the observer.

The left side view is drawn on right side of the object in front view.

17.2.2 Third-angle Projection Method

In third-angle projection method, the object is placed in the third quadrant between HP and VP. The plane of projection is considered to be transparent and is kept between the object and the observer.

The observers visualize the object through transparent HP and VP.

After visualizing, as per the convention of rotation of HP plane, the top view will be placed above of front view, but the two views are aligned vertically.

Figure 17.3 (a) shows that the object is placed in the third quadrant between HP and VP and the orthographic view already drawn in Fig. 17.3 (b) as per the convention. From Fig. 17.3 (b), it is clear as follows:

Front view is below *xy*.

Top view is above *xy*.

Left side view on left side of front view.

Right side view on right side of the front view nearer to front view.

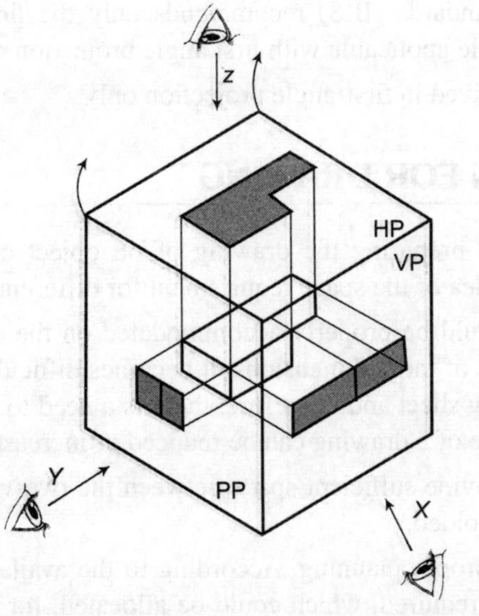

Fig. 17.3 (a) Object in third quadrant for third-angle projection

Fig. 17.3 (b) Orthographic view (third-angle projection)

Object is placed in the third quadrant between HP, VP, and PP.

By convention of rotation of plane, projection taken on *HP*, i.e., top view goes above of front view. In this care, the principal planes are considered transparent. The plane is placed in between object and observer. Front view falls below of top view. The left side view is placed in left side in front of front view.

17.2.3 Projection on Profile Plane

The projection of the object on profile plane will give the view of the object from the side. As there are two sides of the object left side and right side.

In first-angle projection, a view from left is obtained in profile plane by placing the plane in the right side of the object in front of front view. But in third-angle projection method, a view from the left is obtained by placing the plane in the left side of the object.

The projection of the object on profile plane can be easily understood by Fig. 17.2 (b) and Fig. 17.3 (b), the two methods of projection. Thus, only two systems, first-angle and third-angle projections, are in use.

The Bureau of Indian Standards (BIS) recommends only the first-angle projection method, this chapter deals with the principle applicable with first angle projection only.

Hence, all problems are solved in first-angle projection only.

17.3 PREPARATION FOR DRAWING

Before taking up the job on preparing the drawing of on object on the drawing sheet, it become necessary to get a complete idea of the space requirement for different views on the drawing sheet.

The view of an object should be properly accommodated on the drawing sheet so as to look nice and appealing. If the object is of large dimensions, it becomes difficult to accommodate it properly on the limited space on a drawing sheet and, therefore, there is a need to choose a suitable scale. With the use of a suitable scale, the size of a drawing can be reduced or increased as per need.

The draughtsman must provide sufficient space between the two views to place dimensions, notes, etc. Overcrowding must be avoided.

Thus, there is a need for proper planning. According to the available dimension of the object, we can assess how mush area is required, which could be allocated, for a particular view and for all the views separately.

PROBLEM 17.1 [FIG. 17.4 (A)]

Figure 17.1 (a) Shows the pictorial view of a cast iron. Draw the following views using I angle projection.

(a) Front view	Front view in *x* direction
(b) Side view	Side view in *y* direction, and
(c) Top view	Top view in *z* direction

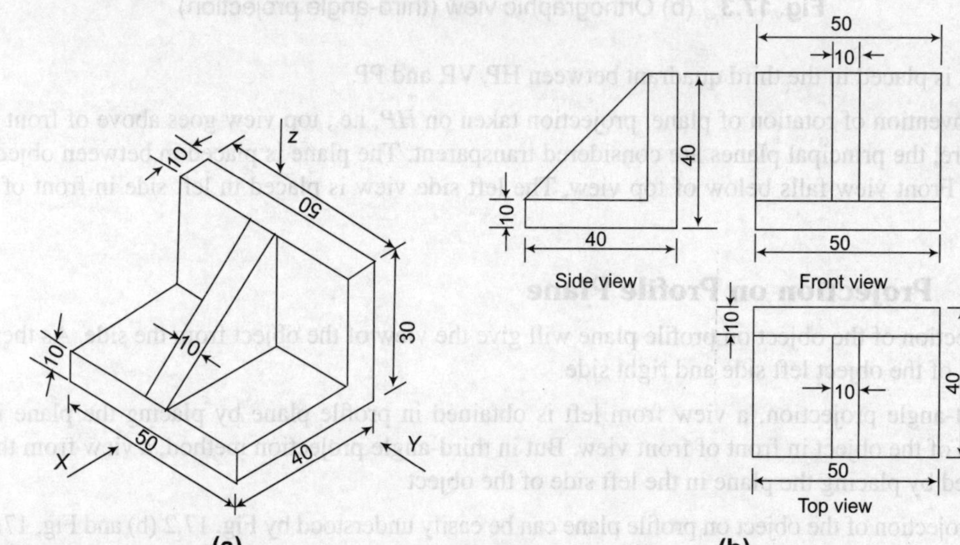

Fig. 17.4 (a) Pictorial view of angle plate; (b) Solution to Problem 17.1

PROBLEM 17.2 [FIG. 17.5(A)]

Figure 17.5 (a) shows pictorial view of a block. Draw the following views using first-angle projection front view in *x*-direction.

(a) Front view

(b) Top view

(c) Side view

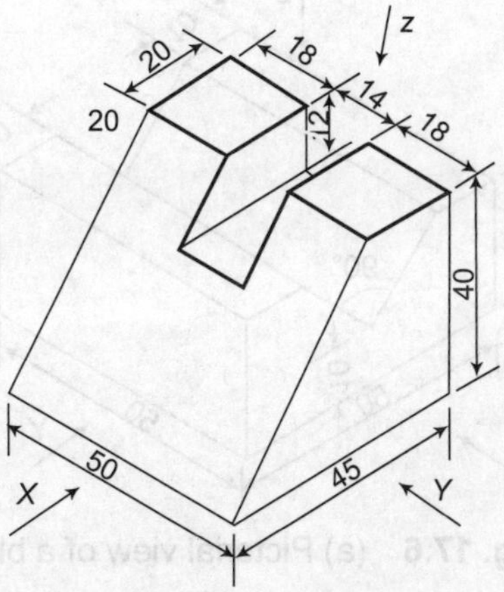

Fig. 17.5 (a) Pictorial drawing of block

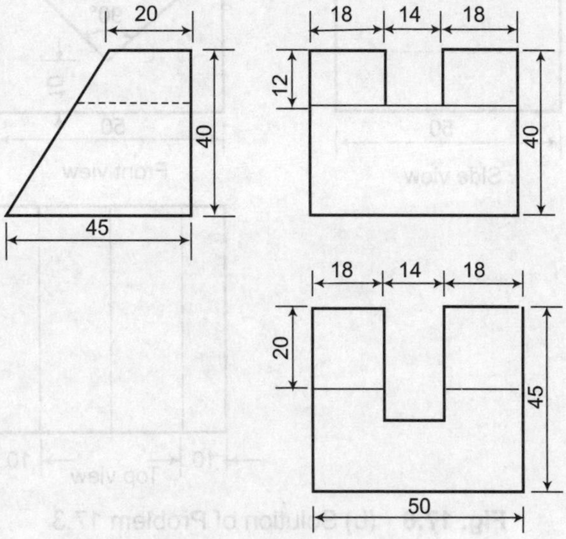

Fig. 17.5 (b) Solution to Problem 17.2

PROBLEM 17.3 [FIG 17.6 (A)]

An object is shown in Fig. 17.6 (a). Draw the following views in first-angle projection method.

(a) Front view in direction of *x*

(b) Top view

(c) Side view

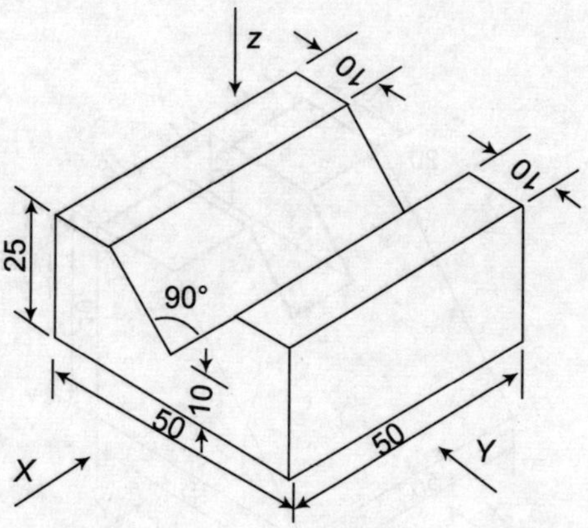

Fig. 17.6 (a) Pictorial view of a block

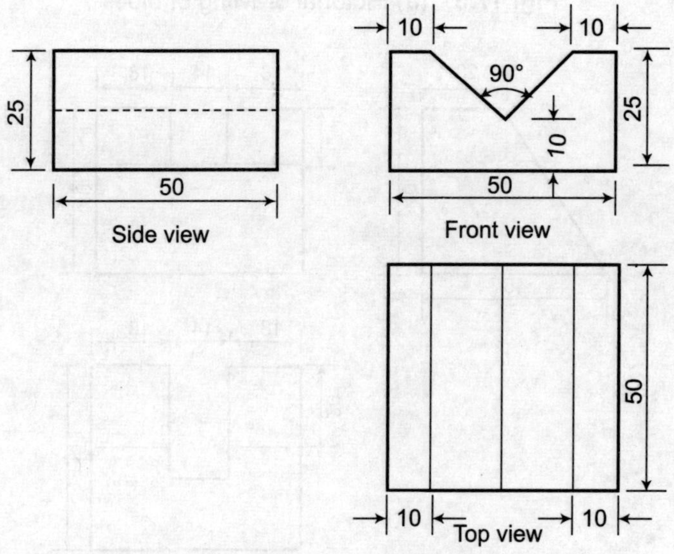

Fig. 17.6 (b) Solution of Problem 17.3

PROBLEM 17.4 [FIG. 17.7 (A)]

Draw front view, top view, and side view of an object shown in Fig. 17.7 (a) using first-angle projection.

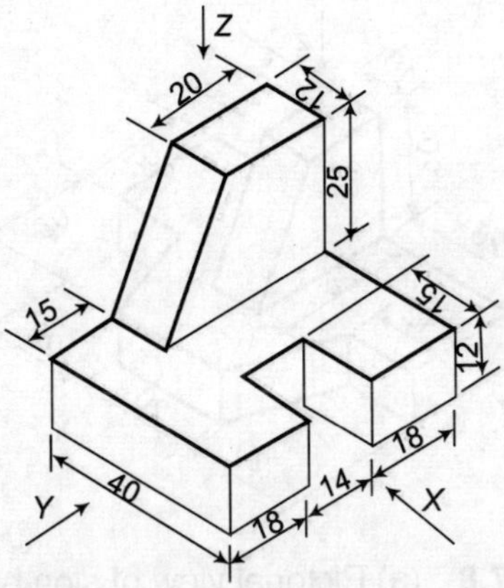

Fig. 17.7 (a) Pictorial view of an object

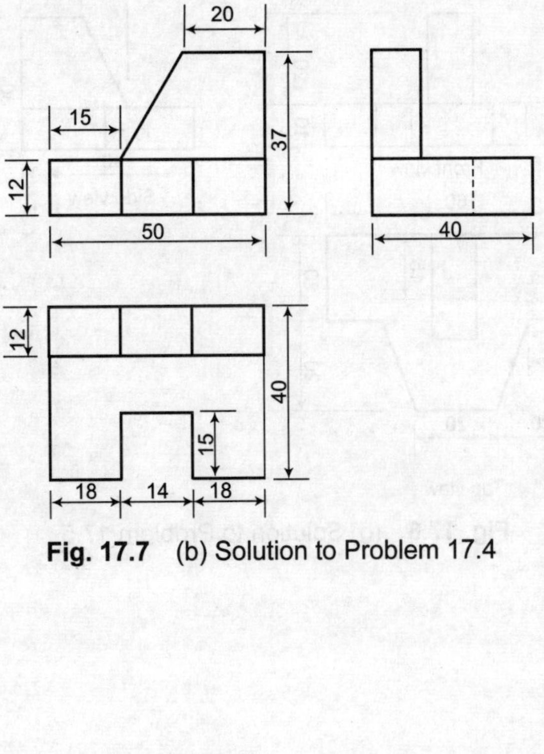

Fig. 17.7 (b) Solution to Problem 17.4

PROBLEM 17.5 [FIG. 17.8 (A)]

Draw front view, top view, and side view of the object shown in Fig. 17.8 (a) using first-angle projection. Direction 'x' is taken for front view.

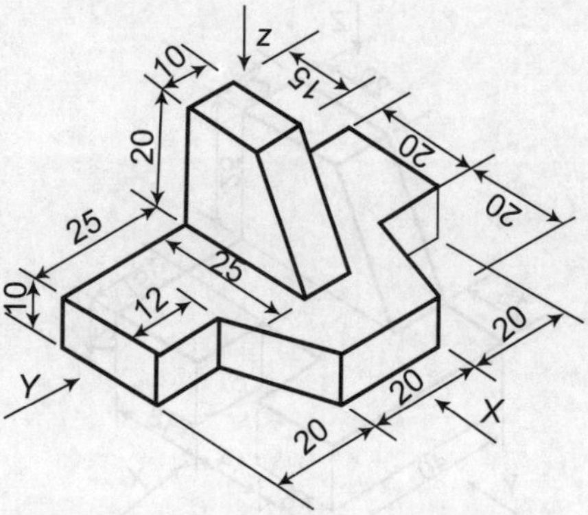

Fig. 17.8 (a) Pictorial view of slop block

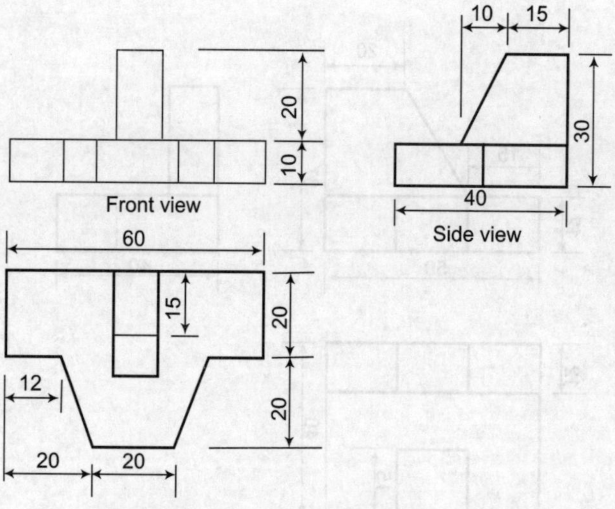

Fig. 17.8 (b) Solution to Problem 17.5

PROBLEM 17.6 [FIG. 17.9 (A)]

Draw the following views of an object using I angle. '*x*' may be taken direction for front view.

(a) Front view

(b) Side view

(c) Top view

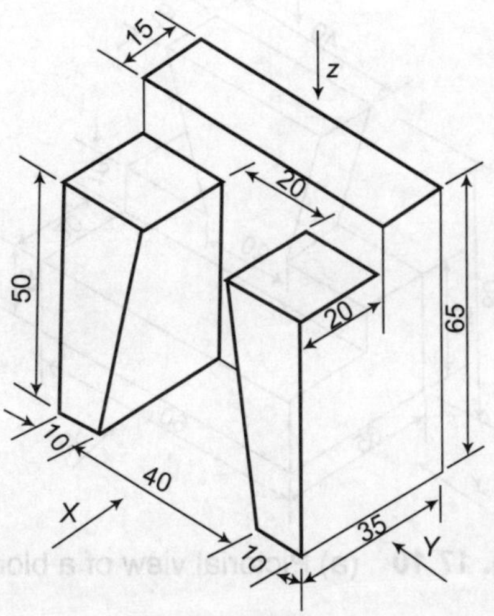

Fig. 17.9 (a) Pictorial view of an object

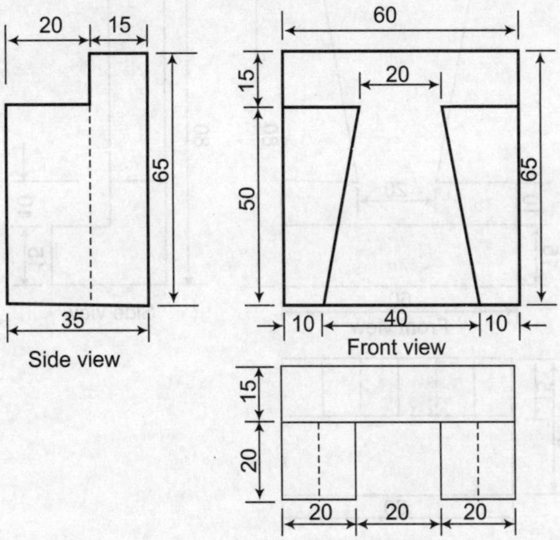

Fig. 17.9 (b) Solution to Problem 17.6

PROBLEM 17.7 [FIG. 17.10 (A)]

Draw elevation, plan, and side view in I angle projection of an object shown in Fig. 17.10 (a).

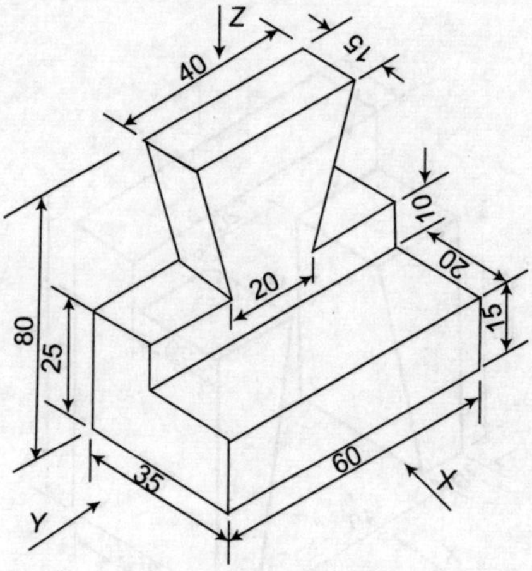

Fig. 17.10 (a) Pictorial view of a block

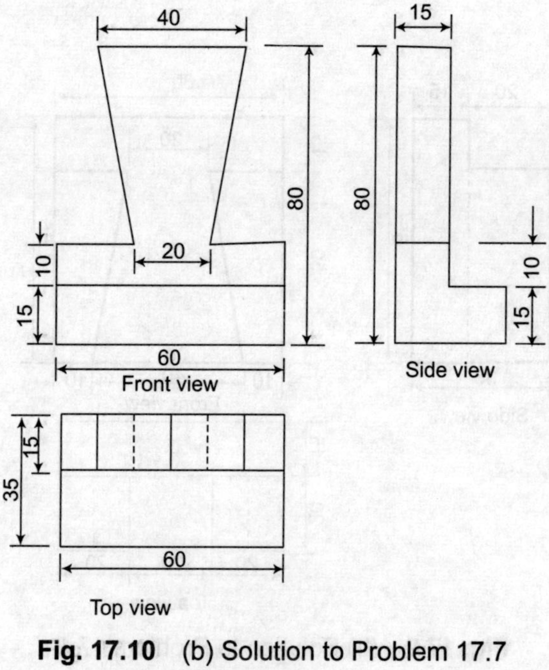

Fig. 17.10 (b) Solution to Problem 17.7

PROBLEM 17.8 [(FIG 17.11 (A)]

An object is shown in Fig. 17.11 (a). Draw the three views in I angle projection method. '*x*' direction may be taken for front view.

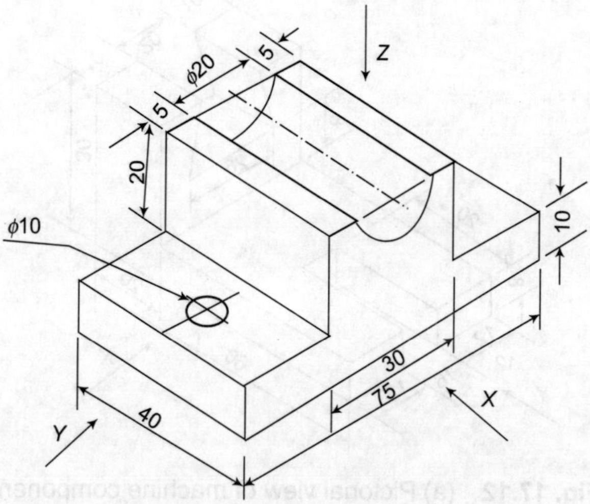

Fig. 17.11 (a) Lower bearing block

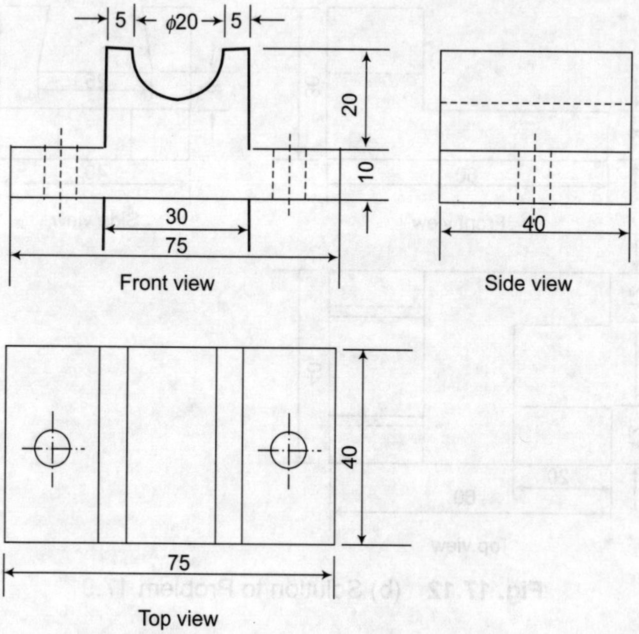

Fig. 17.11 (b) Solution to Problem 17.8

PROBLEM 17.9 [FIG. 17.12 (A)]

Draw all the three views of the object shown in Fig. 17.12 (a). Direction *x* is for front view.

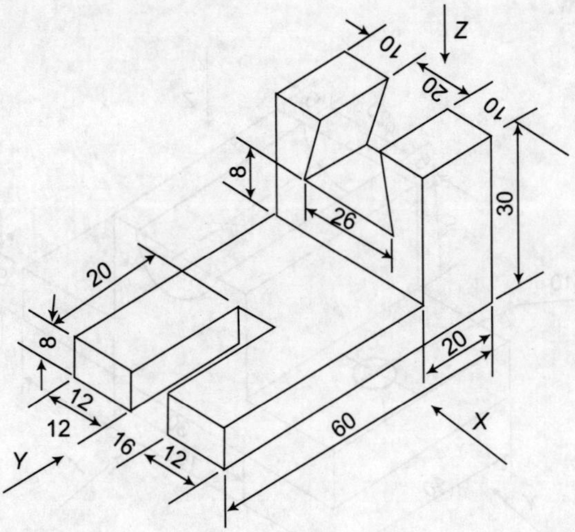

Fig. 17.12 (a) Pictorial view of machine components

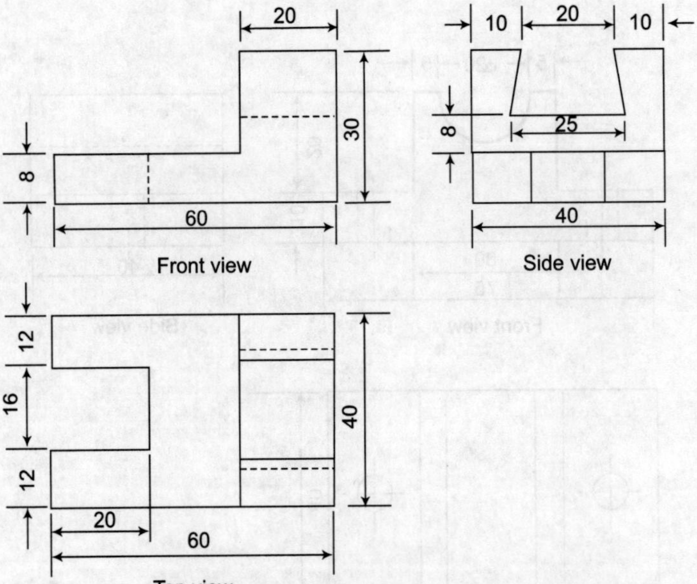

Fig. 17.12 (b) Solution to Problem 17.9

PROBLEM 17.10 [FIG. 17.13 (A)]

Draw all the three views of the object shown in Fig. 17.13 (a). Direction *x* is taken for the front view.

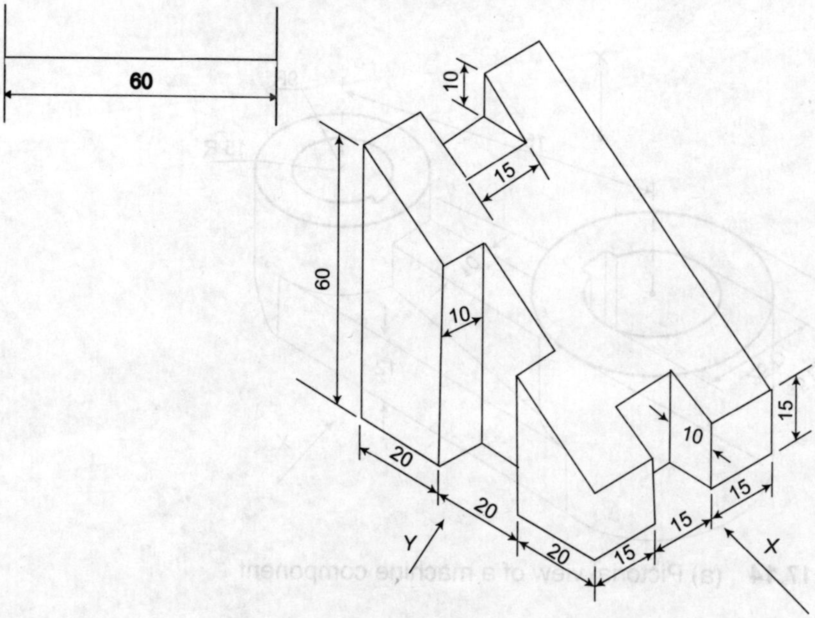

Fig. 17.13 (a) Pictorial view of block

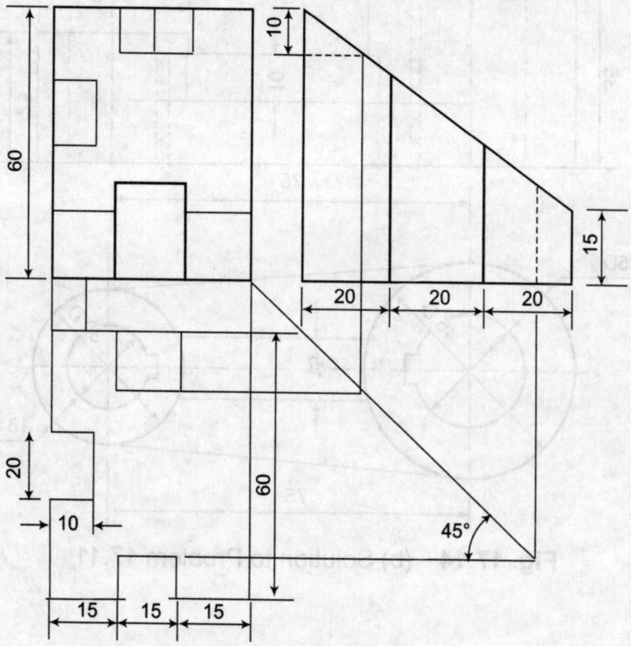

Fig. 17.13 (b) Solution of Problem 17.10

PROBLEM 17.11 [FIG 17.14 (A)]

Draw front view and top view of a machine components shown in Fig. 17.14(a). '*x*' direction is for front view.

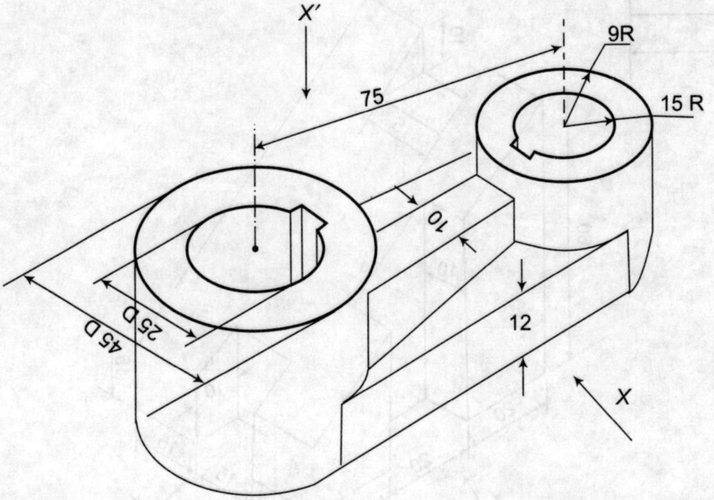

Fig. 17.14 (a) Pictorial view of a machine component

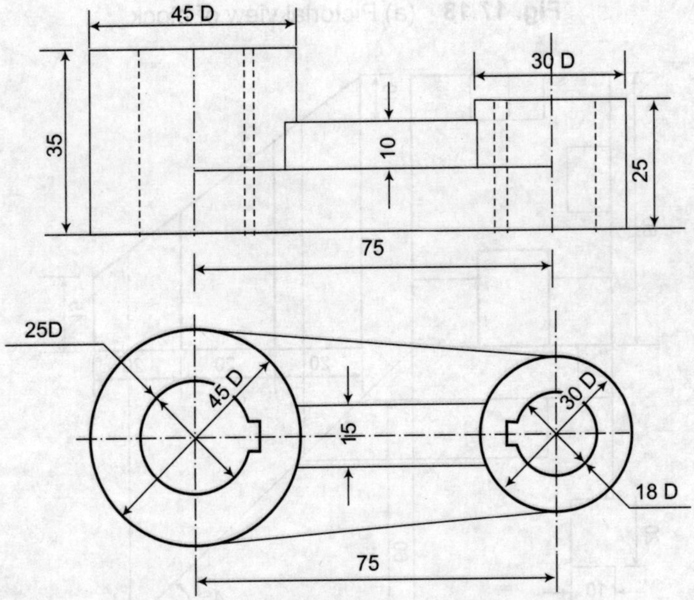

Fig. 17.14 (b) Solution to Problem 17.11

PROBLEM 17.12 [FIG. 17.15(A)]

Figure 17.15 (a) shows a machine component. Draw the following views in first-angle projection.

(1) Front view in *x* direction

(2) Top view in *z* direction

(3) Side view in *y* direction

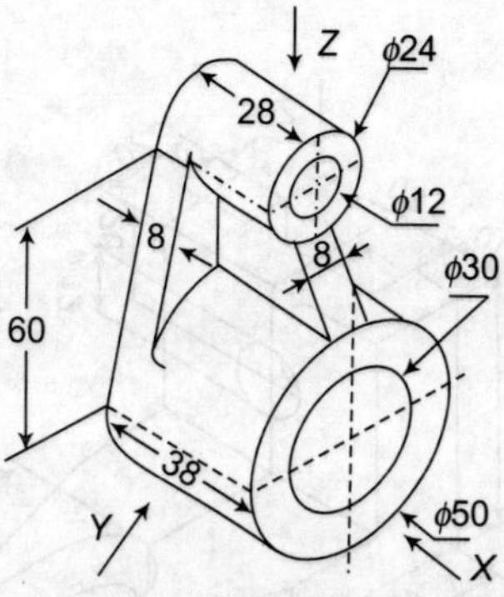

Fig. 17.15 (a)

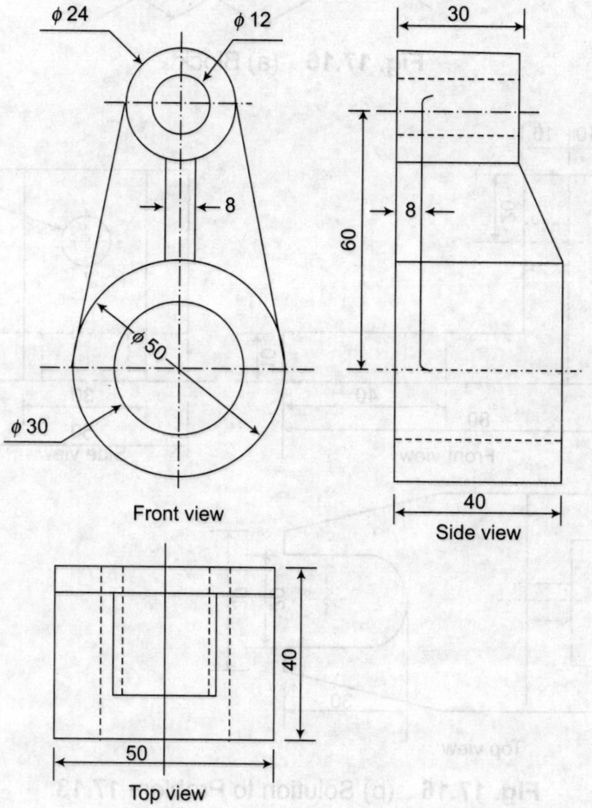

Fig. 17.15 (b) Solution to Problem 17.12

PROBLEM 17.13 [FIG. 17.16(A)]

An object is shown in Fig. 17.16 (a). Draw the following views using I angle projection method.

(1) Front view in *x* direction

(2) Top view in *z* direction

(3) Side view in *y* direction

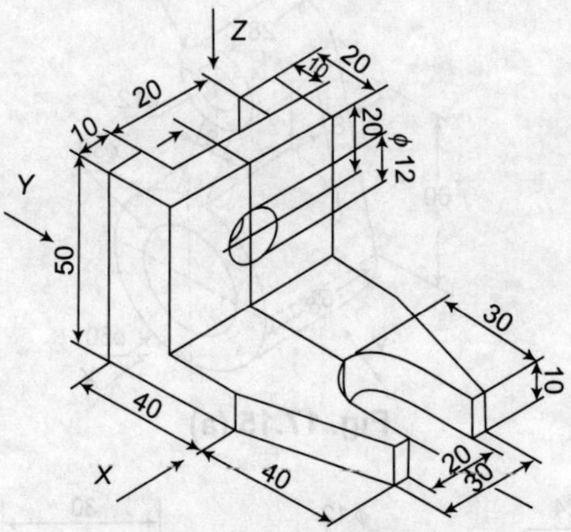

Fig. 17.16 (a) Block

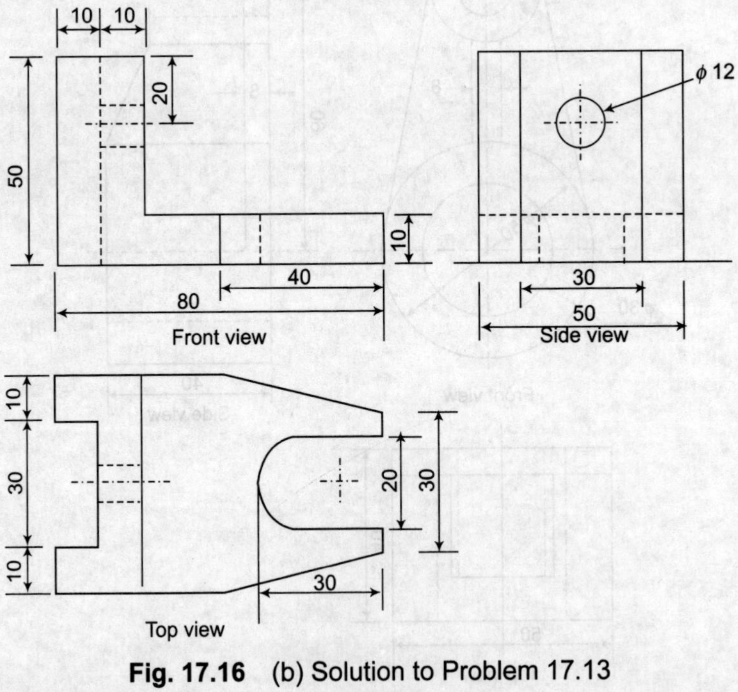

Fig. 17.16 (b) Solution to Problem 17.13

PROBLEM 17.14 [FIG. 17.17 (A)]

An object is shown in Fig. 17.17 (a). Draw the following views:

Front view, top view, and side view using I angle projection. Direction *x* is for front view.

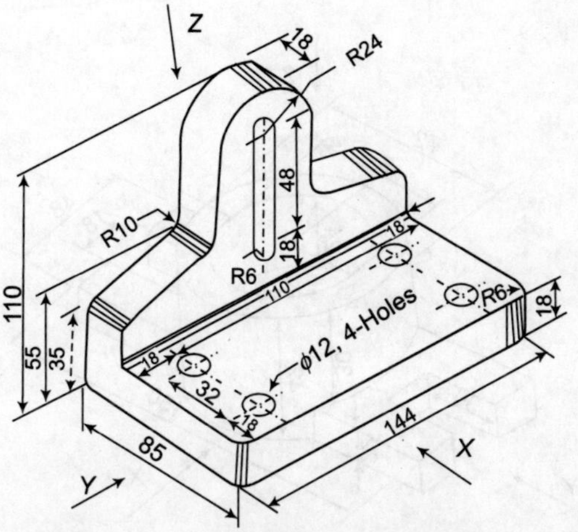

Fig. 17.17 (a) Machine component

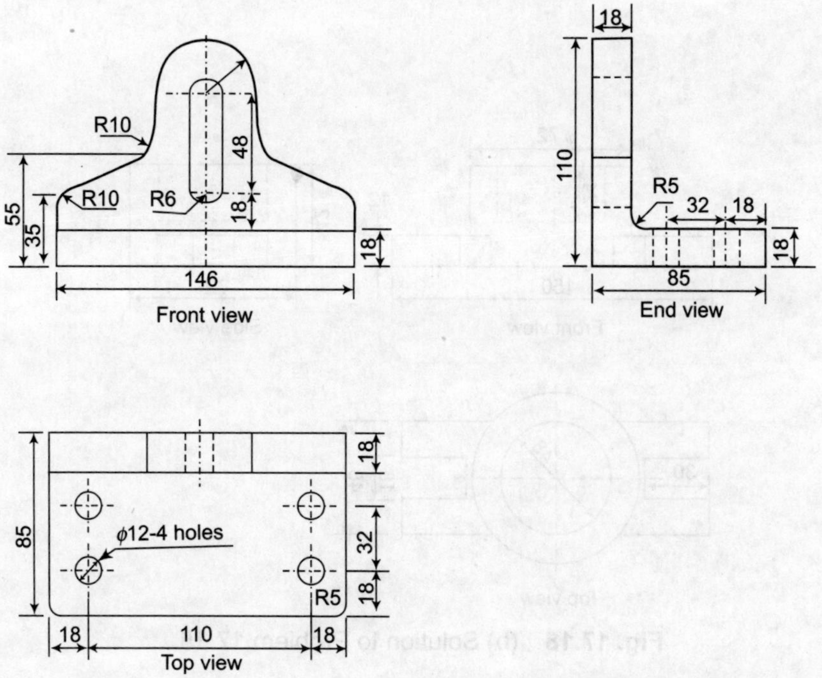

Fig. 17.17 (b) Solution to Problem 17.14

PROBLEM 17.15 [FIG. 17.18 (A)]

Draw top view, front view, and side view of an object shown in Fig. 17.15 (a). Views may be taken in the direction of arrow.

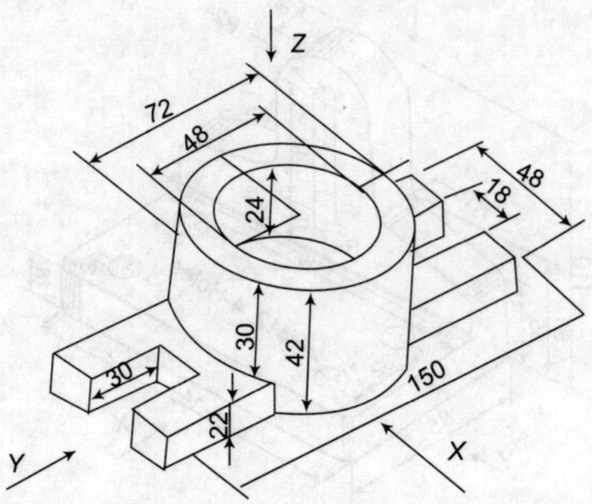

Fig. 17.18 (a) Pictorial view of an object

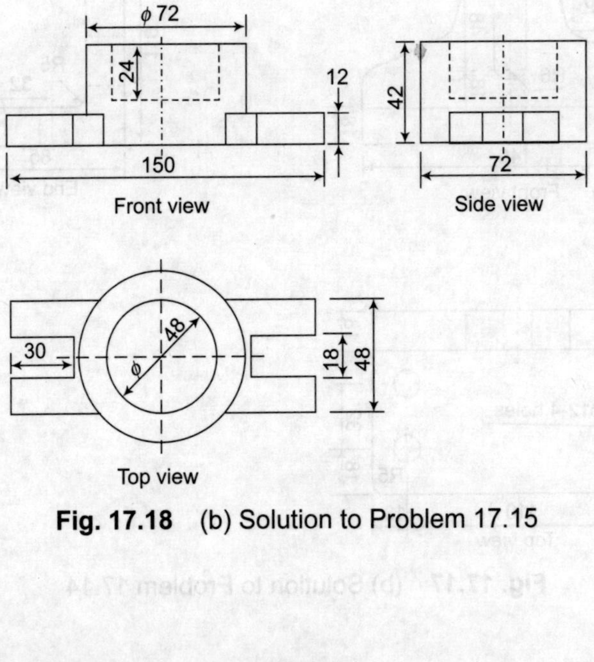

Fig. 17.18 (b) Solution to Problem 17.15

PROBLEM 17.16 [FIG. 17.19 (A)]

Draw front view, top view, and side view of an object shown in Fig. 17.19 (a).

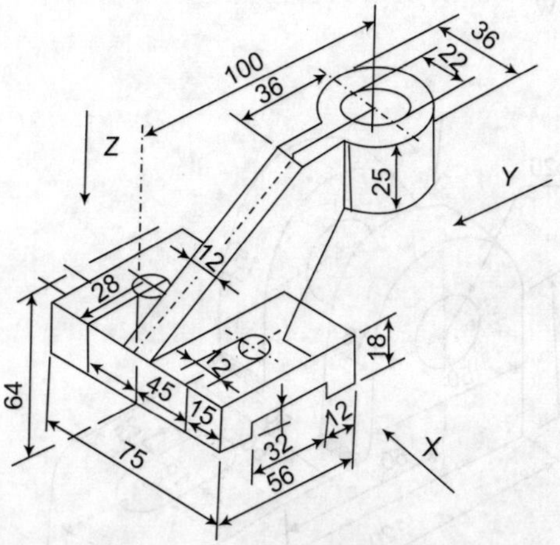

Fig. 17.19 (a) Pictorial view of bracket

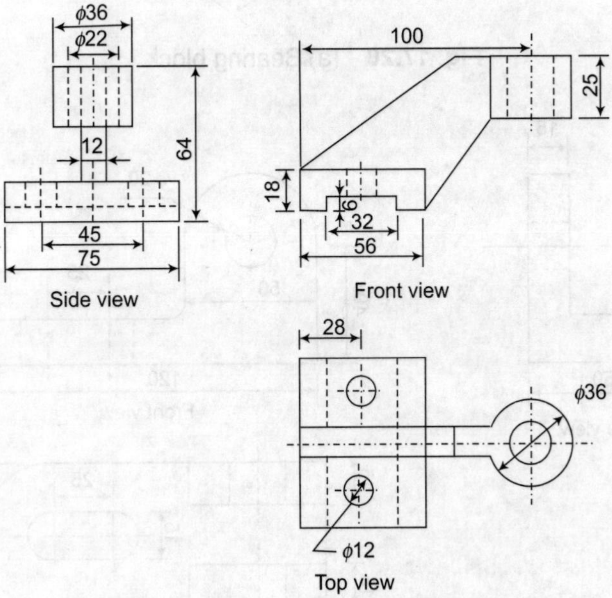

Fig. 17.19 (b) Solution to Problem 17.16

PROBLEM 17.17 [FIG. 17.20 (A)]

Figure 17.20 (a) shows a bearing block. Draw the following views:

(i) Front view in x direction

(ii) View from above/top view

(iii) Side view

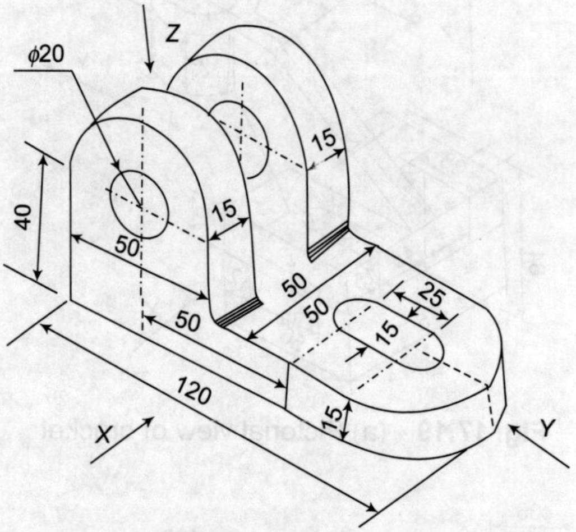

Fig. 17.20 (a) Bearing block

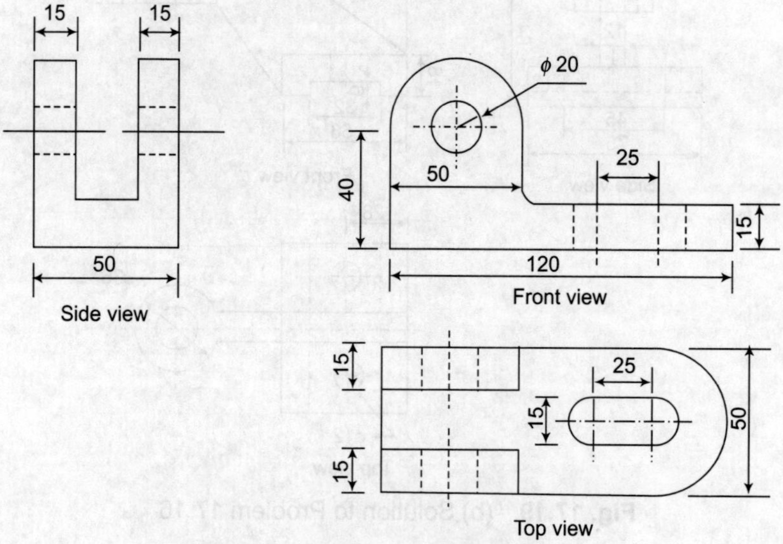

Fig. 17.20 (b) Solution to Problem 17.17

PROBLEM 17.18 [FIG. 17.21 (A)]

Figure 17.21 (a) shows the pictorial drawing of an object. Draw the following views:

(1) Front view in x direction

(2) Top view from above

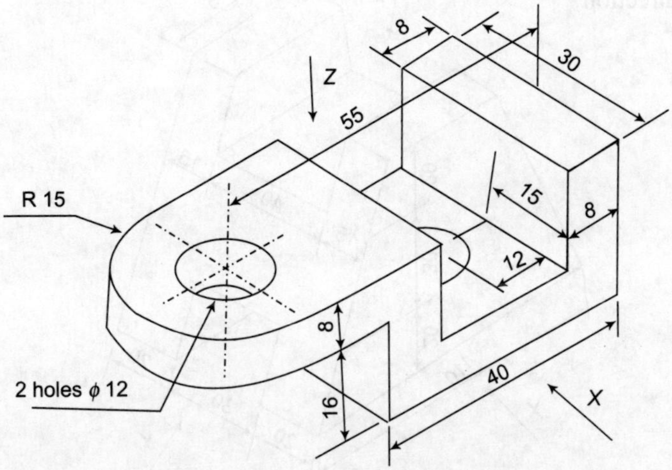

Fig. 17.21 (a) Machine component

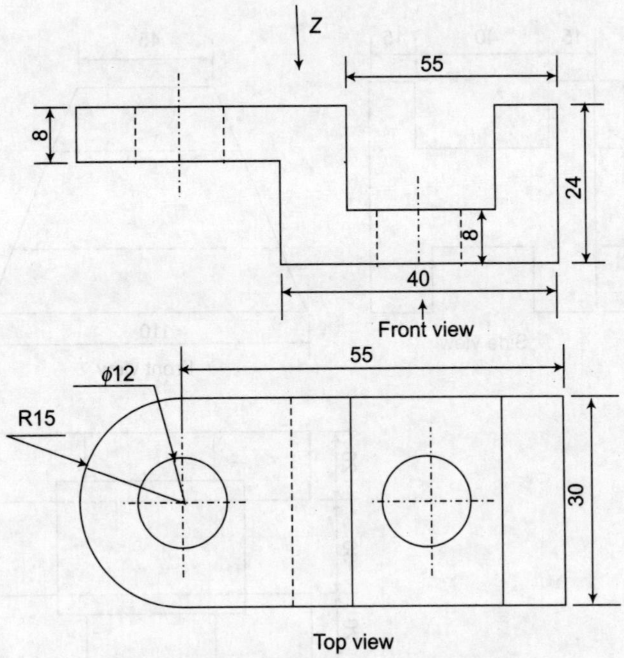

Fig. 17.21 (b) Solution to Problem 17.18

PROBLEM 17.19 [FIG. 17.22 (A)]

Figure 17.22 (a) shows the pictorial view of an object. Draw the following views:

(i) Front view in *x* direction

(ii) Top view

(iii) Side view in *y* direction

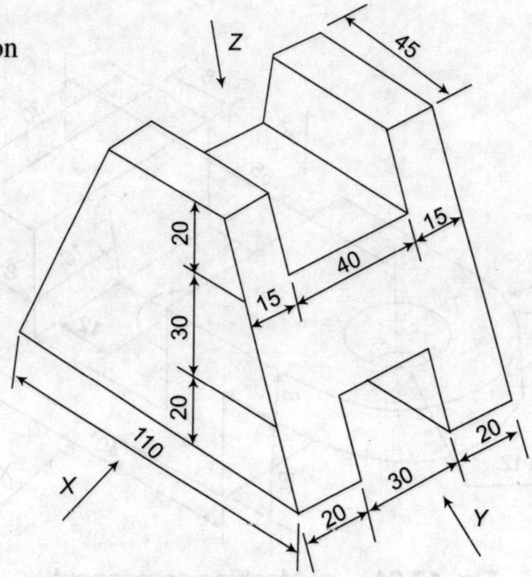

Fig. 17.22 (a) Object

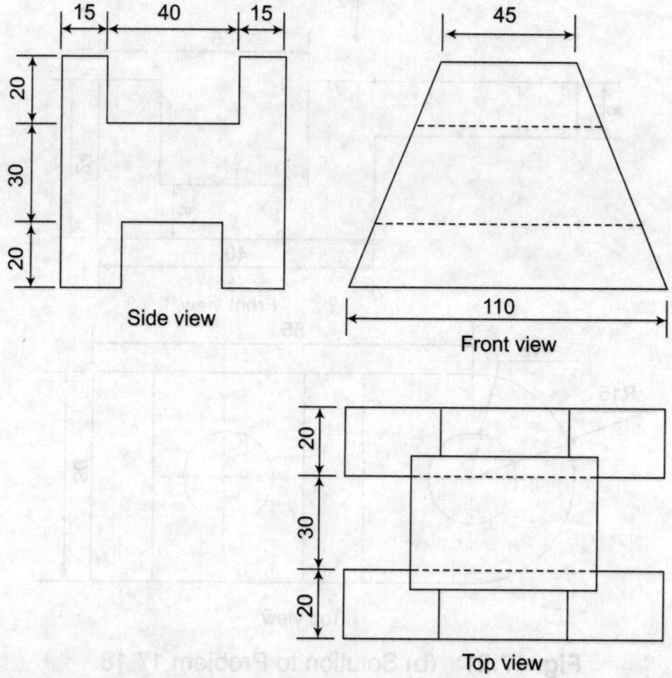

Fig. 17.22 (b) Solution to Problem 17.19

EXERCISE

Review Questions

Pictorial view of various machine components is given (Fig. 17.23–17.37). Draw the view of each stated below. Front view in each case is to be as shown in direction of '*x*'. Follow first-angle projection.

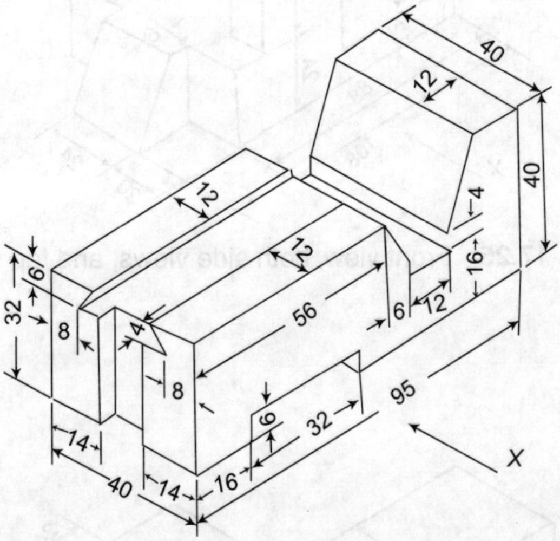

Fig. 17.23 Front view, side view from left, and top view

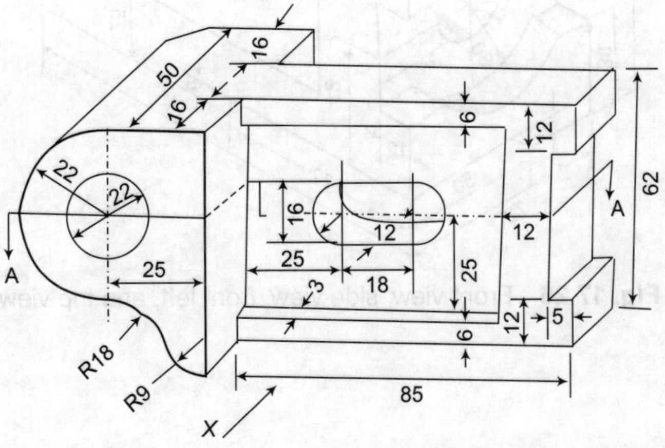

Fig. 17.24 Front view, side view from right, and top view

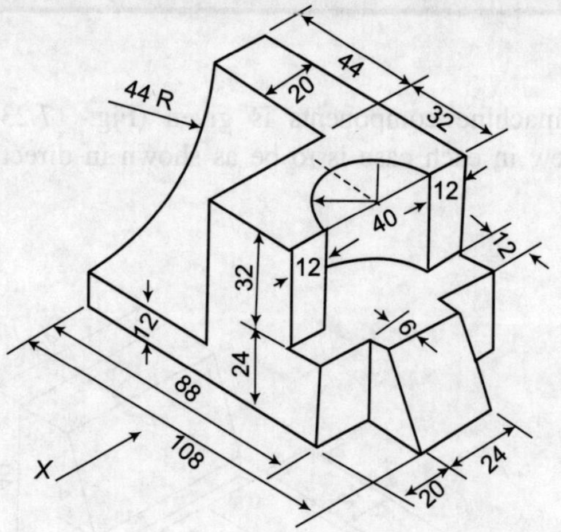

Fig. 17.25 Front view, both side views, and top view

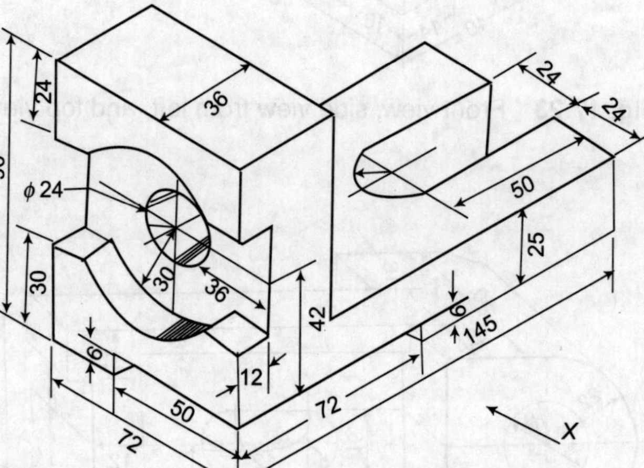

Fig. 17.26 Front view, side view, front left, and top view

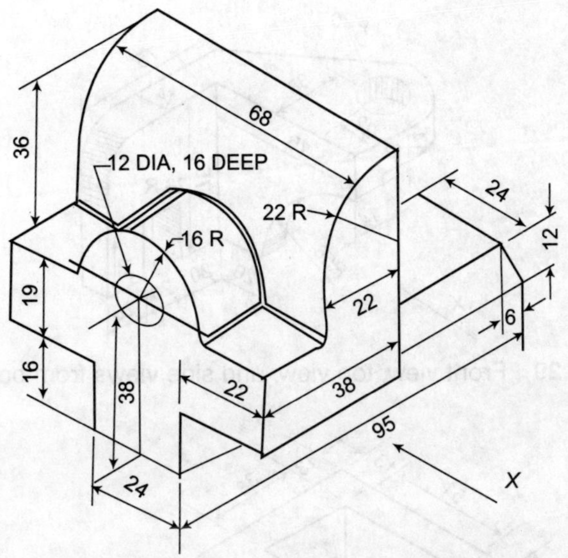

Fig. 17.27 Front view, top view, and both side views

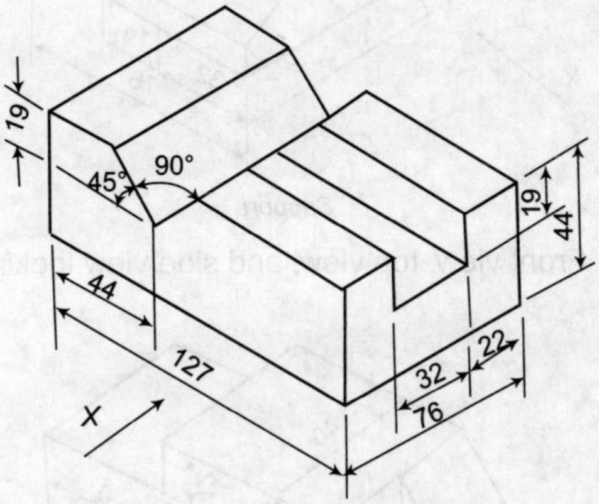

Slide

Fig. 17.28 Front view, top view, and side view from right

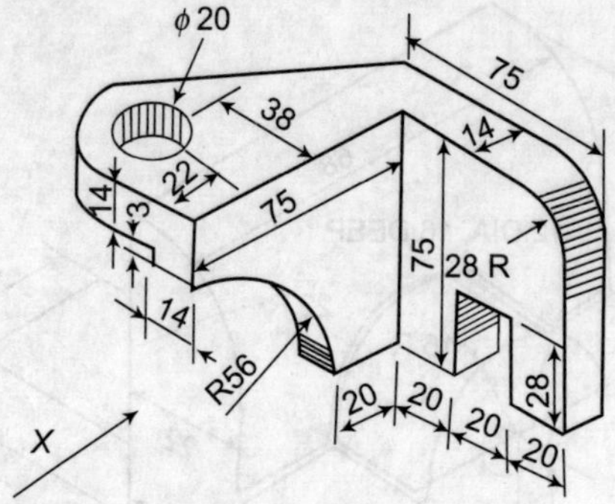

Fig. 17.29 Front view, top view, and side views from both sides

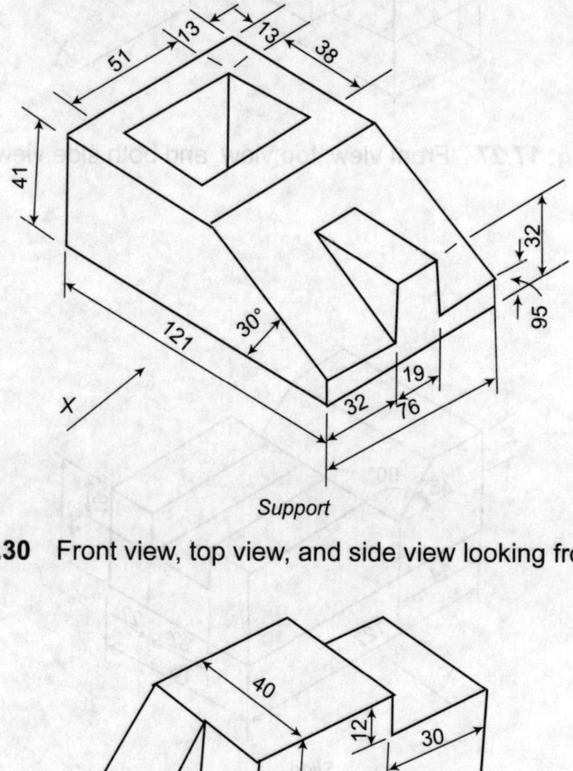

Fig. 17.30 Front view, top view, and side view looking from right

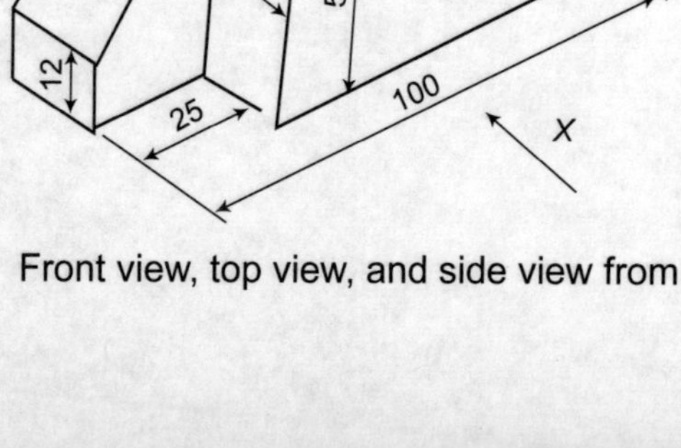

Fig. 17.31 Front view, top view, and side view from both sides

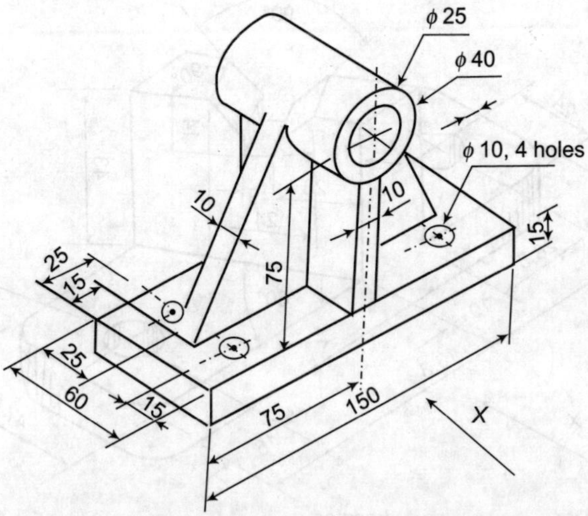

Fig. 17.32 Front view, top view, and side view from left

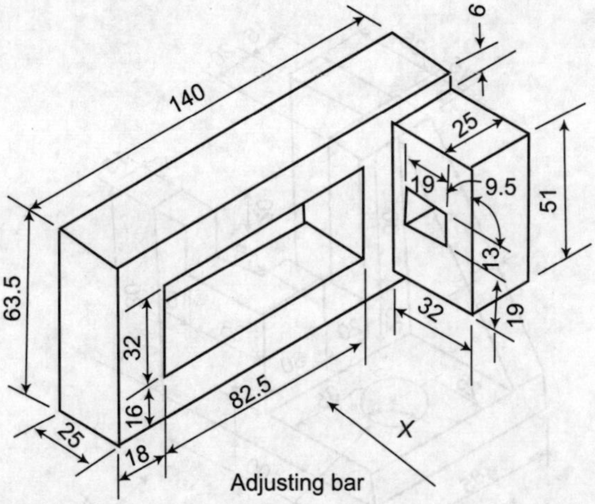

Fig. 17.33 Front view, top view, and side view from left

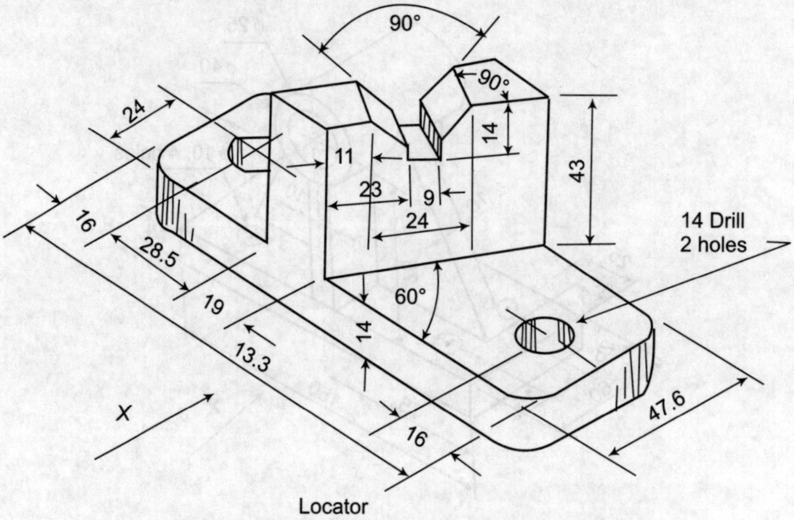

Fig. 17.34 Front view, top view, and side view from right

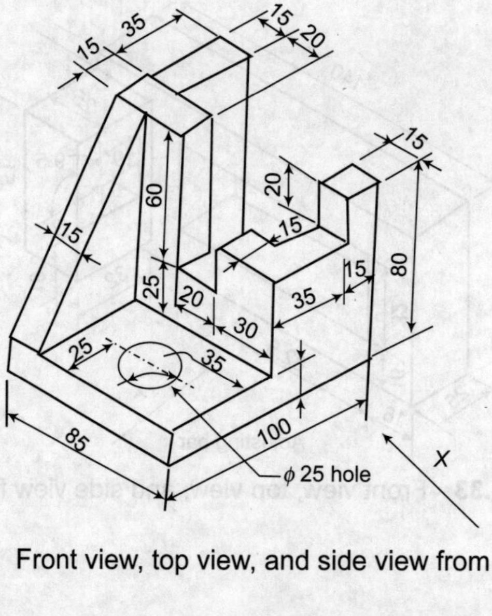

Fig. 17.35 Front view, top view, and side view from both sides

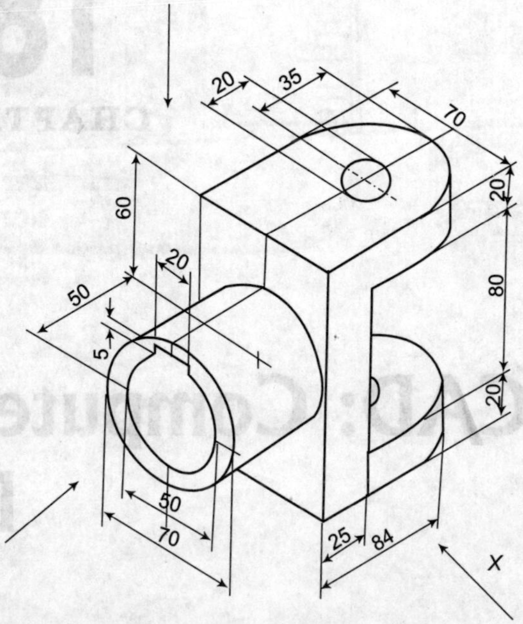

Fig. 17.36 Front view, top view, and side view from both sides

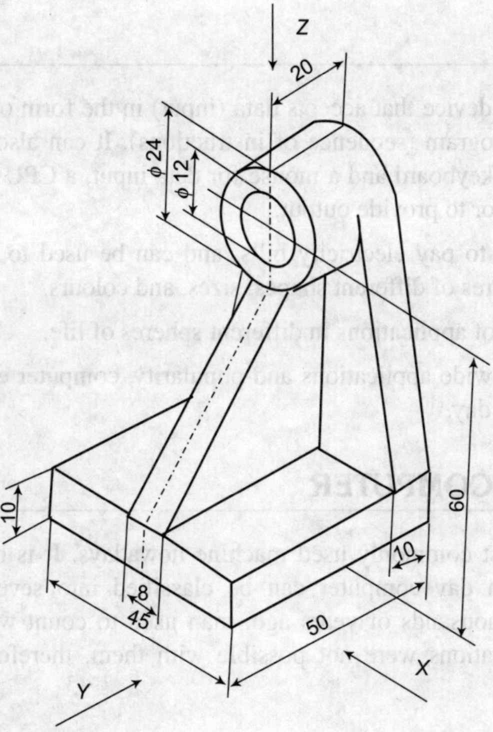

Fig. 17.37 Front view, top view, and side view

18

CHAPTER

CAD: Computer Aided Drafting

PART A

18.1 COMPUTER

A *computer* is an electronic device that accepts data (input) in the form of digits and processes it into useful results based on a program (sequence of instructions). It can also be referred as a multi-part electronic machine. It has a keyboard and a mouse for data input, a CPU (central processing unit) for processing data, and a monitor to provide output.

A computer can be used to pay electricity bills, and can be used to play exciting games. Using computer, we can draw pictures of different shapes, sizes, and colours.

A computer has a variety of applications in different spheres of life.

With an increase in their wide applications and popularity, computer education and its application have become the need of the day.

18.2 HISTORY OF COMPUTER

Computer is one of the most commonly used machine nowadays. It is being used everywhere. The development of the modern day computer can be classified into several different stages known as *computer generations*. Thousands of years ago, man used to count with fingers, stones, pebbles, or bones. But bigger calculations were not possible with them, therefore, man started developing machines for this purpose.

Table 18.1 Generations of computers

Generation	Year	Specification
First-generation Computer	1947	Weight of this computer was approximately in tonnes. It contained thousands of values.
Second-generation Computer	1959	These computers contained transistors.
Third-generation Computer	1965	These computers were having integrated circuits (ICs), which were known as *chip*.
Fourth-generation Computer	1970	These computers used micro-processor chip (chip size was smaller than a postage stamp).

18.3 COMPUTER HARDWARE AND SOFTWARE

A computer is a combination of *hardware* and *software*.

Hardware Any part of the computer that can be seen and touched from outside, such as input unit, processor unit, memory unit, speaker, etc.

Software Software is a program or a set of programs that direct the computer about what is required to be done. Some of the examples are MS Word program and the games played on computers.

All physical components of a computer is a combination of input devices such as keyboard, mouse, etc., processing unit such as CPU and Memory unit, and the output devices such as printer, plotter, monitor, etc.

Figure 18.1 shows all the elements of the hardware of a computer.

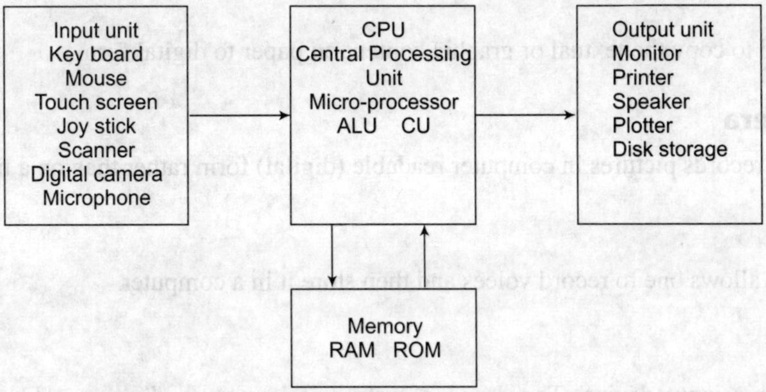

Fig. 18.1 Elements of hardware of a computer

18.4 INPUT DEVICE

To enter the input, we require input devices. There are a lot of input devices such as keyboard, mouse, touch screen, microphone, scanner, digital camera, and digitizer, etc.

Keyboard

A keyboard is used to enter data into a computer. It has alphabet keys, number keys, and functional keys, etc., arranged like an english typewriter.

Mouse

It is a graphic input device with three buttons. At the bottom of it, there is a small spherical ball which rotates with the movement of mouse on mouse pad, and thereby the cursor moves on the screen.

As the mouse is moved on the mouse pad, instructions are sent to the processor to position the cursor. By clicking on the mouse button, a command is given to the computer: pressing left button gives location, middle is just line ENTER, and right button is drop down menu. These days bottom ball mechanism of mouse is replaced by optical sensor mouse.

Touch Screen

A touchpad allows one to move his/her finger across a pressure-sensitive area and is pressed to click. It is used in laptop and tablet computers.

Joystick

A joystick consists of an upright stick and one or more click buttons. It is often used to play video games and in simulators. The joystick is moved in the direction we wish the cursor to move on the screen.

Scanner

A scanner is used to copy the textual or graphic content on paper to digital form.

Digital Camera

A digital camera records pictures in computer readable (digital) form rather than on a film.

Microphone

It is a device that allows one to record voices and then store it in a computer.

Digitizer

It is also a graphic input device. The drawing surface is known as *digitizer table*—with movable electronic pen called *stylus* and *puck*. It has single or 4 buttons. Each has fine black cross hair, which are used for giving suitable position.

Pressing the required button causes horizontal and vertical data to pass on to the computer by electrical signals. This is presented in Fig. 18.2.

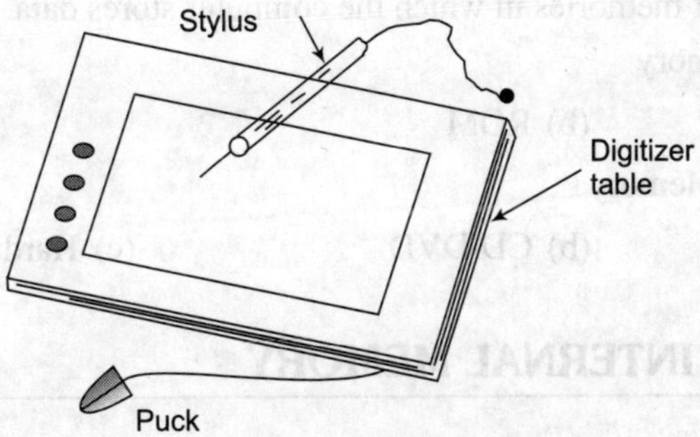

Fig. 18.2 Digitizer

18.5 PROCESSING DEVICE

The CPU is a processing device that performs all the calculations, comparisons, and decision making for a computer. It is a chip inside the CPU cabinet mounted on the mother board along with other computers.

Mother board is the main circuit board containing the CPU. All input and output devices are connected to the mother board.

The CPU further consists of the following two components:

(i) ALU (Arithmetic and Logic Unit)

The ALU does all the calculations, comparisons, and decision making for computation.

(ii) CU (Control Unit)

The CU controls the flow of information in the CPU. It extracts instructions from the memory and sends the necessary signals to the ALU to perform the operation required.

18.6 MEMORY AND STORAGE OF COMPUTER

The data and instructions that are entered into a computer though input devices are stored inside the computer. The storage media is known as *memory*. The memory of a computer is made up of chips.

A computer memory is stored in the form of *bits* and *bytes*. Bit means binary digits, i.e., 0 and 1. A bit is the smallest unit of information which a computer can process.

A byte is the basic storage unit in computer memory. One byte is one character. One byte consists of 8 bits.

8 bits = 1 byte

1024 bytes = 1 KB (Kilobyte)

1024 KB = 1 MB (Megabyte)

1024 MB = 1 GB (Gigabyte)

1024 GB = 1 TB (Terabyte)

In fact, there are two types of memories in which the computer stores data. They are as follows:

(i) Primary (Internal) Memory

(a) RAM (b) ROM

(ii) Secondary (External) Memory

(a) Floppy (b) CD/DVD (c) Hard disk

18.7 PRIMARY OR INTERNAL MEMORY

It is the built-in memory of the computer that resides inside the CPU. It stores the data instructions currently used by a computer. The size of the primary memory is 256 MB. However, this can be increased in size. It is sub-divided into *RAM* and *ROM*.

RAM (Random access memory)

This is the main working memory of a computer. It stores the data temporarily till the computer is running. It holds the data and provides the result when it is working; data disappears from RAM as soon as the power is off.

RAM is actually a volatile memory. It can contain limited amount of data at a time.

Calculator is an example of RAM. Information exists till calculation is on.

ROM (Read only memory)

This is a permanent memory. It allows the user to read but does not permit the user to store data on it. ROM is a non-volatile memory.

18.8 SECONDARY OR EXTERNAL MEMORY

The secondary memory is also called *auxiliary storage*. It is used to store information for longer period. It is required because internal storage of computer is insufficient to store large amount of data.

The data or information stored in this memory is permanent even when the computer is switched off.

Some commonly used secondary storage devices are as follows:

(a) Hard disk

A hard disk is the main storage device of a computer. It is called *hard drive*. It is fixed inside the CPU and contains all the data that is stored in computer. Data is recorded on both the sides of the disk.

Hard disks are available in different storage capacities such as 80 GB, 160 GB, and so on.

(b) Floppy disk

Floppy disk is also known as *diskette*. Floppy disks are the best and most cost-effective way to store small amount of data. They are used to transfer small amount of data from one computer to another.

Each floppy disk is made up of a thin, flexible magnet medium coated with iron oxide, and is encased in a square plastic cover.

(c) Compact disk (CD)

A CD is an optical storage device. It is a thin circular disc with a hole in centre. A CD has a reflective metal coating and can store up to 750 MB of data. CDs can hold text, graphics, sound, images, and videos.

(d) Digital versatile disk or Digital video disk (DVD)

A DVD is also an optical storage device that looks similar to a CD. It is used to store and record movies with higher video and sound qualities. It can store data upto 17 GB.

(e) Pen drive

A pen drive is also known as *flash drive*. It has replaced floppy drive. Since it is small in size, it is a state storage device with a USB (Universal Serial Bus) connector used for copying and moving data from one computer to another. A flash drive can store data upto 256 GB.

18.9 OUTPUT DEVICES

Output devices in a computer are used to display the results. Common output devices are as follows:

(i) Monitor

A monitor is the simplest and most common type of output devices. It may be of different sizes. Following types of monitors available:

(a) CRT (cathode ray tube)

(b) LCD (liquid crystal display)

(c) LED (light emitting diode)

(ii) Printer

A printer prints information and the result can be obtained on a piece of paper.

They are of different types, as follows:

(a) Dot matrix—uses black ribbon to print

(b) Inkjet—uses liquid Ink

(c) Laser—uses laser light and a dry powder called toner

18.10 SOFTWARE

As we know, computers understands only machine language. Besides machine language, scientists have developed an easier method to communicate with computers, through computer language.

Computer language is converted into machine language by computer programs, which include BASIC, FORTRAN, COBOL, C++, etc.

Software is actually the name of the program which is required on the computer through which a computer has to work on a specific problem. Without the software, the computer fails to do any work even though all hardware is available. Computer program is written in a specific sequence, which will be read by the computer to accomplish the results.

18.11 TYPES OF COMPUTERS

(i) **Mainframe computer** These are large-capacity computers with massive storage capacity to do different jobs at the same time.

(ii) **Mini computer** These computers have large capacities and are used in industries.

(iii) **Personal computer (PC)** These are the smallest-size computers. They are low-cost machines used in schools, colleges, and offices for personal work.

PART B

18.12 INTRODUCTION

Previous chapters have explained about the technique of solving problems on engineering drawing manually using various drawing kits. Conventional drawing, however, remains the base for engineering drawing. Computer aided drafting (CAD) was developed on the fundamental method of drawing. As such, CAD cannot replace and eliminate manual engineering drawing.

There are certain valid reasons to implement CAD in our course:

- Improvement in quality of drawing
- Increase in the productivity
- Improvement in communication
- Creation of a database approach manufacturing operation

18.13 DEFINITION OF CAD

Computer aided drafting is the process of making drawing on a computer screen with the help of specially developed software package, and without the use of traditional drawing kits. CAD is not a substitute for drawing fundamentals. It is simply a tool for making a drawing. It are used to solve problem, but the broad knowledge of engineering drawing is still required by the user.

The basic knowledge to solve engineering drawing problems such as orthographic projection, isometric projection, section of solids, etc., remains the same, only to here a separate technique to draw other than drawing kits.

18.14 APPLICATION OF CAD

The following are the applications of CAD.

An engineering designer prepares a drawing of machine components by a CAD software and the output is displayed on computer screen. By using the technique, the body of the components can be visualized in different positions. The designer can make necessary changes, if required.

CAD has varied applications in various fields of engineering, as follows:

Mechanical engineers use this technique for designing machine components and, hence, this can be used to manufacture components. Similarly, professionals related to almost all branches of engineering prefer to use the technique of CAD.

- It is used in circuit layout, panel design control system in electrical field.
- It is used for making schematic diagram PCS, ICS, etc., in the field of electronics.
- It is used for making communication network in the IT branch of engineering.
- It is used for designing spacecraft.
- It is used for town planning, interior decoration modelling, etc.
- It is used for mapping, contour plotting, building drawing, and structural design by civil engineers.
- It is used for making automotive parts.

18.15 ADVANTAGES OF CAD

The following are the advantages of CAD:

(1) Drawings prepared with the use of CAD software are clearer and more exact than manual drawing.

(2) The drawing can be prepared with tremendous speed by the computer, provided the man who is working with it has good knowledge of the subject.

(3) The computer has unlimited storage capacity and the work completed can be recalled quickly.

(4) The drawing prepared by CAD can be stored in 'database' at a single location which can be used in manufacturing processes.

(5) The drawing prepared by CAD can be enlarged or reduced by any scale as per the requirement.

(6) The drawing prepared by CAD can be easily edited or any modification is possible with the drawing.

(7) When CAD is used to prepare a drawing and a particular component is required to be placed at several places, the drawing is prepared for the component once and then the same drawing is inserted at several places.

(8) A simple CAD system needs a computer and a CAD software. The draftsman does not require drawing kits at all.

(9) Better visualization can be done with 'colour graphics'.

18.16 CAD SOFTWARE

A large number of softwares are available for 2D engineering drawing and 3D models. Each has a specific application. This chapter is written for AutoCAD 2000 and applicable to 2D drawings. To handle AutoCAD in 3D is beyond the scope of this book.

CAD software is just an interpreter to help the user do a specific nature of job. The following are the various types of softwares used for drafting:

(1) AutoCAD	(2) Corel DRAW	(3) Microsoft Office
(4) PageMaker	(5) Corel CAD	(6) MicroStation

All the above software are used according to the nature of job.

AutoCAD is universally used for engineering graphics.

CorelDRAW is suitable for animation. Microsoft Office can be used for simple nature of graphics.

PageMaker is very suitable for 2D drawing.

CorelCAD software is just equivalent.

18.17 AUTOCAD SOFTWARE

AutoCAD package is very suitable for accurate and neat engineering drawing. Drawing of machine components, isometric drawing, and section of solids can be successfully drawn with AutoCAD. It is a very effective software and very suitable for 2D and 3D engineering graphics.

At present, in modern age, software is available that can be easily handled by any technical user without caring to learn computer programming.

Autodesk, the developer of AutoCAD software, is world's leading supplier.

The first release of AutoCAD Version 1.0 was in 1982. After a lot of improvements, AutoCAD Release 12 was introduced in 1992. Today, AutoCAD 2017–18 is also available.

A variety of CAD software packages are available in market. The discussion on CAD is limited to 2D problems only, which is the basic requirement for first-year students; therefore, Auto CAD 2000, which can prepare accurate 2D simple drawings, has been used. AutoCAD 2000 commands have been discussed is this book.

On starting AutoCAD 2000, one can see the window as shown in Fig. 18.3.

It contains the following:

(i) Drop down menu bar
(ii) Standard toolbar
(iii) Title bar
(iv) Object properties bar
(v) Floating command line bar
(vi) Draw toolbar
(vii) Modify toolbar
(viii) Status bar
(ix) Scroll bar

Inside the screen there is an area, called as graphical window, where the user works on the drawing.

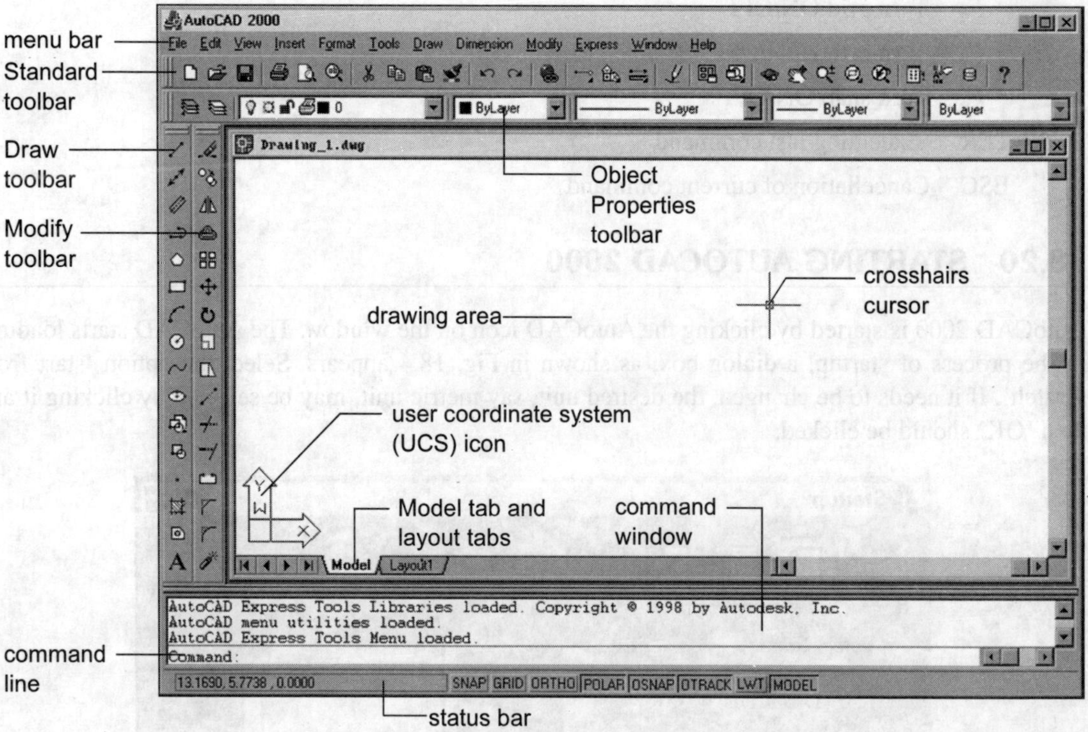

Fig.18.3 Screen of AutoCAD 2000

18.18 AUTOCAD COMMAND

The draughtsman can run AutoCAD by using the following command. Each one of them works the same.

(i) By clicking a toolbar

(ii) By choosing a menu item from a dropdown menu

(iii) By typing a command at the command line

18.19 KEYBOARD

The keyboard is used to type command text, dimensions, etc. The following are the keyboard keys:

F_1 AutoCAD help

F_3 Object snap ON/OFF

F_6 Coordinate turn ON/OFF

F_7 Turn grid ON/OFF
F_8 Turn ortho ON/OFF
F_9 Turn snap ON/OFF
ENTER Executing last command
ESC Cancellation of current command

18.20 STARTING AUTOCAD 2000

AutoCAD 2000 is started by clicking the AutoCAD icon on the window. The AutoCAD starts loading. In the process of startup, a dialog box, as shown in Fig. 18.4 appears. Select the option 'start from scratch'. If it needs to be changed, the desired unit, say metric unit, may be selected by clicking it and then 'OK' should be clicked.

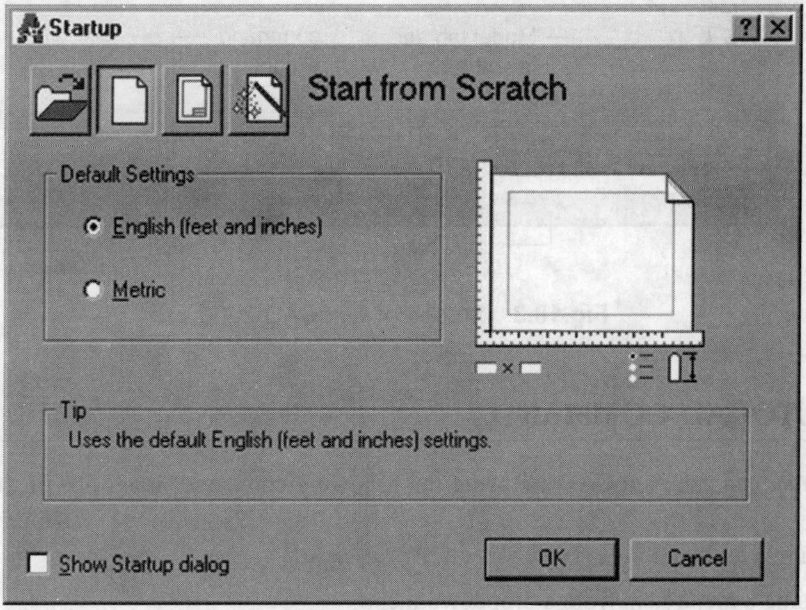

Fig. 18.4 Opening and creating AutoCAD files

18.21 COMMANDS FOR DRAWING

A drawing consists of line, arc, circle, curves, machine components, etc. When we enter a command in the command line, we need to press ENTER ↵ for its activation.

These commands are arranged in Draw dropdown menu bar or standard draw toolbar as shown in Fig. 18.5.

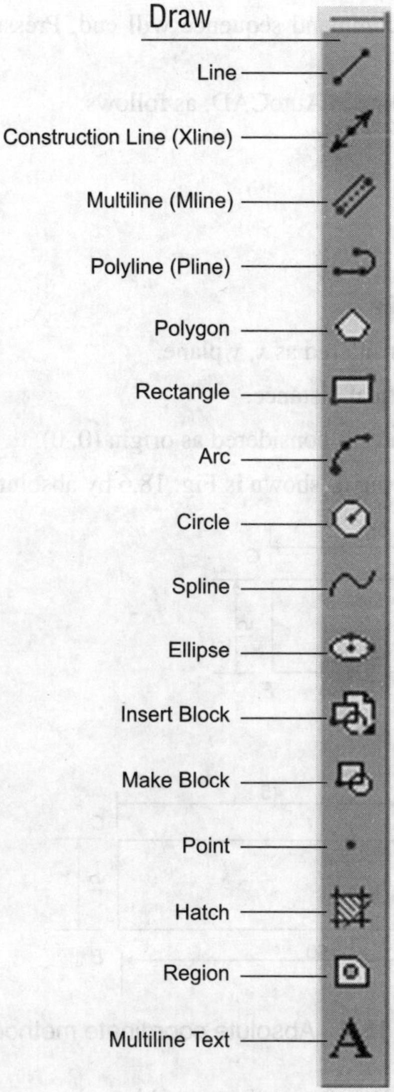

Fig. 18.5 Draw Toolbar

18.22 COMMAND FOR DRAWING A LINE

Straight line can be drawn by using command. From draw toolbar, select line icon. The line command can be obtained by typing 'line'. Command: Line; <Enter>

(i) Specify first point (*x*,*y*) by placing cursor and pressing the left button of mouse.

(ii) Specify next point or [undo] select second point using mouse.

(iii) Specify next point or [close/undo] selecting third point using mouse.

If ENTER is pressed, the line command sequence will end. Pressing ENTER a second time will start the line command.

There are three methods to draw a line in AutoCAD, as follows:

(1) by using absolute coordinate
(2) by using relative coordinate
(3) by using polar coordinate

Using Absolute Coordinate

In AutoCAD, the front screen is considered as *x*, *y* plane.

x is horizontal distance and *y* is vertical distance.

By default, the left hand button corner is considered as origin (0, 0).

Using CAD software, prepare drawing as shown is Fig. 18.6 by absolute coordinate method.

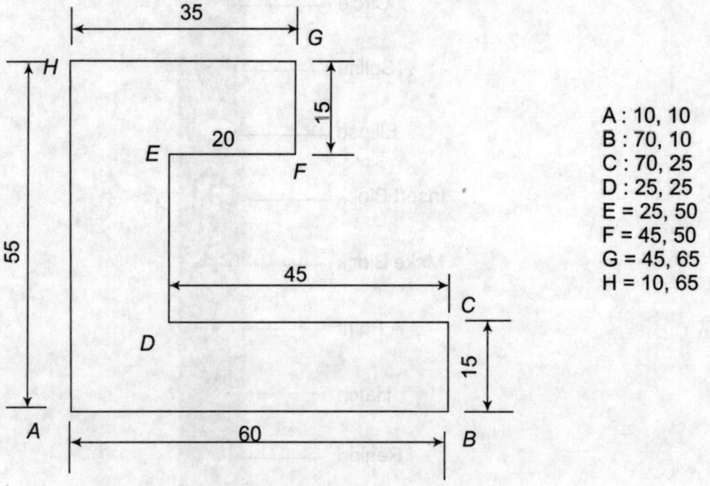

Fig. 18.6 Absolute coordinate method

To prepare drawing by AutoCAD software for the object shown, the following procedure can be followed.

Steps:

(i) Select the line tool from the draw toolbar

Command: line; ENTER

Specify first point *A*

(ii) Type 10, 10; ENTER

Specify next point or [undo], *B*

(iii) Type 70, 10; ENTER

Specify next point or [close/undo] *C*

(iv) Type 70, 25; ENTER

Specify next point or [close/undo] *D*

(v) Type 25, 25; ENTER

Specify next point or [close/undo] *E*

(vi) Type 25, 50; Enter

Specify next point or [close/undo] *F*

(vii) Type 45, 50; ENTER

Specify next point on [close/undo] *G*

(viii) Type 45, 65; ENTER

Specify next point or [close/undo] *H*

(ix) Type 10, 65; ENTER

(x) Type C, ENTER

or specify next point or [close/undo] *A*

Type 10, 10 Press

Press ESC

The drawing shown in Fig. 18.6 will be complete.

By pressing ESC is the ESCAPE command the line command is undone.

PROBLEM 18.1

Draw a line joining (3, 4) to (10, 11) and show the line with respect to XY coordinates.

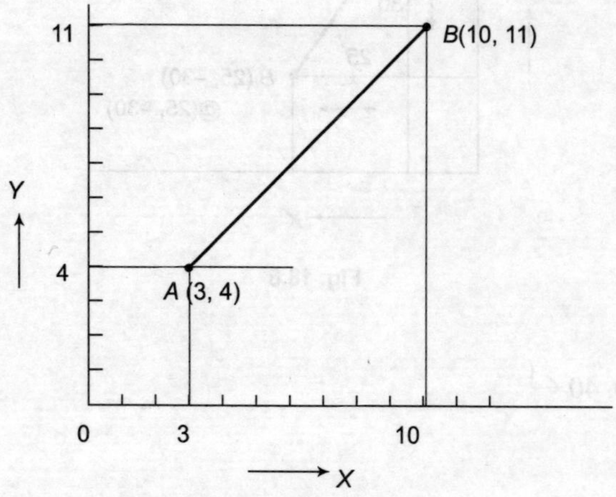

Fig. 18.7

Draw toolbar: 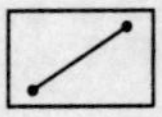 Line or

Menu bar: Draw: LINE or

Command line: *l* (for line)

Command: 1 ↵

Specify line first point: 3, 4 ↵

Specify next point or [undo]: 10, 11 ↵

Specify next point or [undo]: ↵

or

Type 3, 4 and press ENTER

Type 10, 11 and press ENTER

Press ENTER to end line command

Press ENTER to repeat line command

PROBLEM 18.2

Draw a line (10, 40) to a point 25 units on right side and 30 units below measured horizontally and vertically, respectively, from the first point.

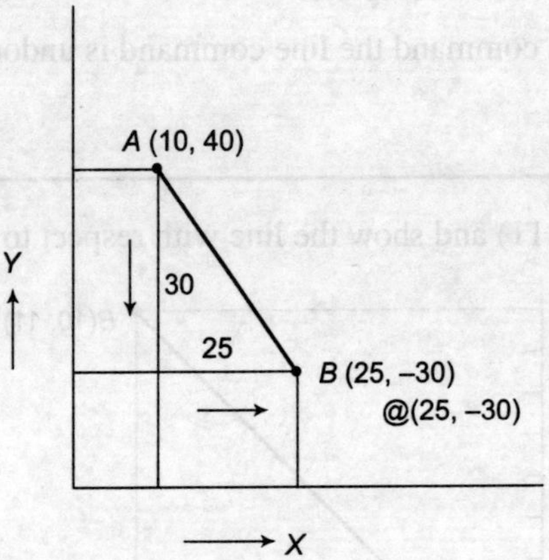

Fig. 18.8

Command: ↵

Line Specify first point: 10, 40 ↵

Specify next point or [undo]: @ 25, – 30 ↵

Specify next point or [undo}: ↵

PROBLEM 18.3

Draw a line from point (10, 12) and length 40 units and inclined at 60° to the X axis.

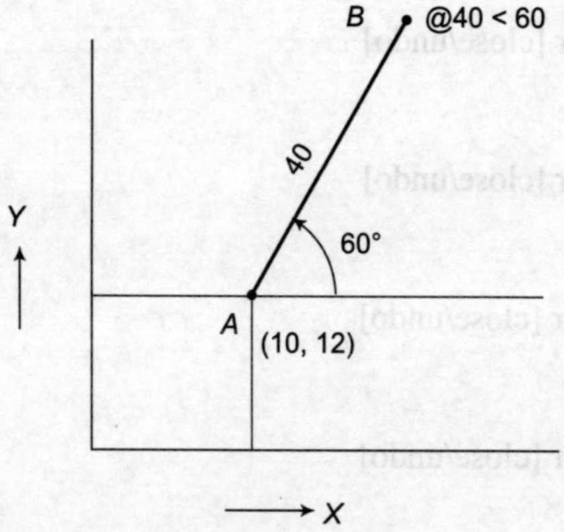

Fig. 18.9

Command: ↵

Line specify first point: 10, 12 ↵

Specify next point or [undo]: 40 < 60 ↵

Specify next point or [undo}: ↵

Using Relative Coordinate

In this method, the line is drawn with reference to previous point. Before typing relative coordinate value, the symbol @ is required to be given. The same figure as shown in Fig. 18.6 can also be drawn by this method.

Steps:

(i) Select the line tool from the draw toolbar

Command: line; ENTER

Specify first point, A

(ii) Type 10, 10; ENTER

Specify next point, *B* or [undo]

(iii) Type @ 60, 10 ↵

Specify next point, *C* or [close/undo]

(iv) Type @ 0, 15 ↵

Specify next point, *D* or [close/undo]

(v) Type @ – 45, 0 ↵

Specify next point *E* or [close/undo]

(vi) Type @ 0, 25 ↵

Specify next point *F* or [close/undo]

(vii) Type @ 20, 0 ↵

Specify next point *G* or [close/undo]

(viii) Type @ 0, 15 ↵

Specify next point H or [close/undo]

(ix) Type @ - 35, 0 ↵

Specify next point A or [close/undo]

Type @ 0, – 55 ↵

Press ESC, so that the line command is undone.

Using Polar Coordinate Method

In this method, points are located by mentioning the distance of the point from the current position and the angle made with this line; In AutoCAD, the angles measured as given in Fig. 18.10

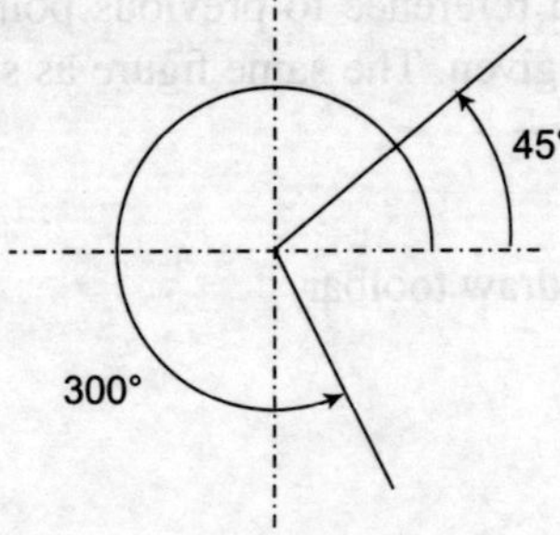

Fig. 18.10 Angle measurement

Steps:

Considering the same figure as shown in Fig. 18.6, we have as follows:

Point A : 10, 10

B : @ 60 < 0°

C : @ 15 < 90°

D : @ 45 < 180°

E : @ 25 < 90

F : @ 20 < 0

G : @ 15 < 90°

H : @ 35 < 180°

A : @ 55 < 270°

(i) Select the line tool from the draw toolbar command; line; ENTER

Specify first point, *A*

(ii) Type 10, 10; ENTER

Specify next point *B* or [undo];

(iii) Type @ 60 < 0 ↵

Specify next point C or [close/undo]

(iv) Type @ 15 < 90° ↵

Specify next point, *D* or [close/undo]

(v) Type @ 45 < 180° ↵

Specify next point, *E* or [close/undo]

(vi) Type @ 25 < 90° ↵

Specify next point, *F* or [close/undo]

(vii) Type @ 20 < 0 ↵

Specify next point, *G* or [close/undo]

(viii) Type @ 15 < 90 ↵

Specify next point, *H* or [close/undo]

(ix) Type @ 35 < 180° ↵

Specify next point, *A* or [close/undo]

(x) Type @ 55 < 270°

Press ESC to undo the line command in the drawing shown in Fig. 18.11.

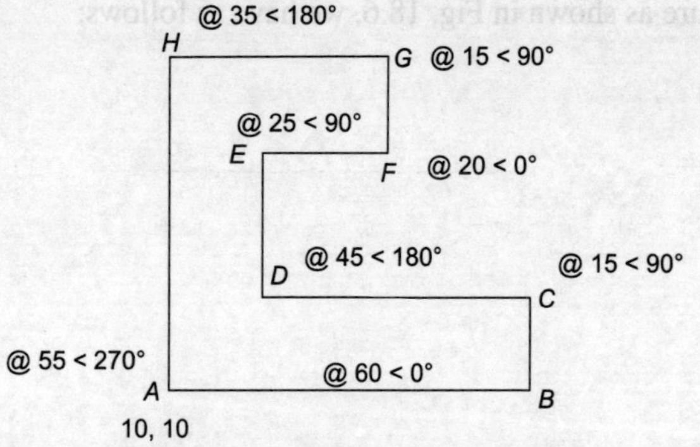

Fig. 18.11 Polar coordinates

Line command can be used to draw a line joining two points.

The points may be in Cartesian or in polar coordinates in absolute or relative mode.

Few lines have been presented taking an example.

1. Cartesian Coordinate

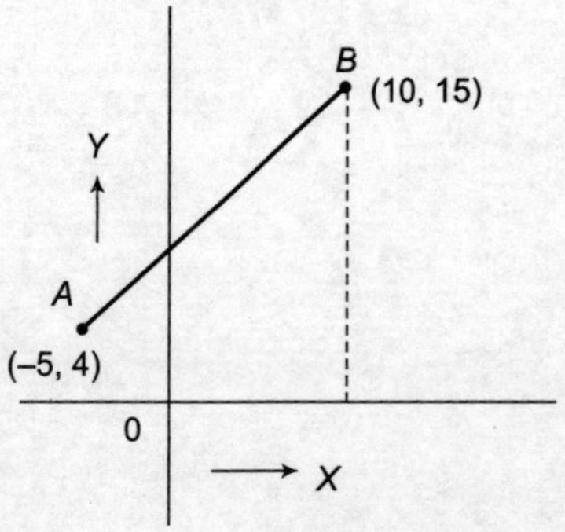

Fig. 18.12(a) Cartesian (absolute)

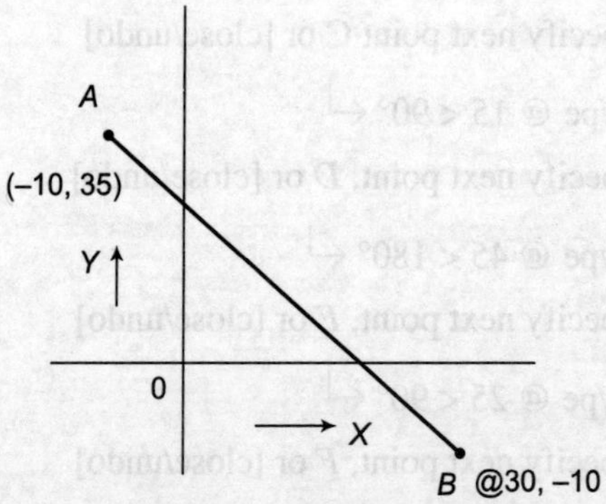

Fig. 18.12(b) Cartesian (relative)

2. Polar Coordinate

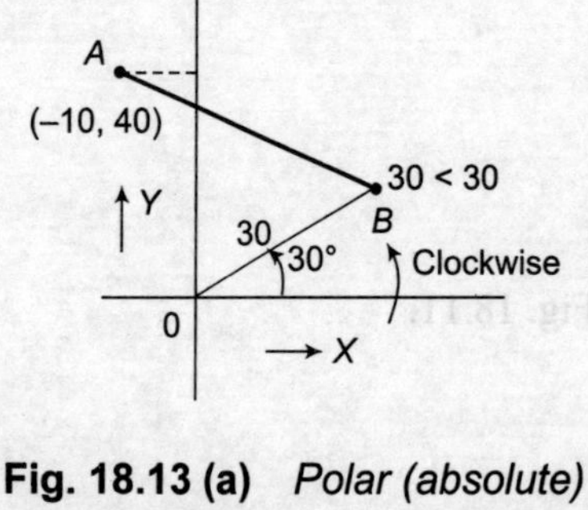

Fig. 18.13 (a) *Polar (absolute)*

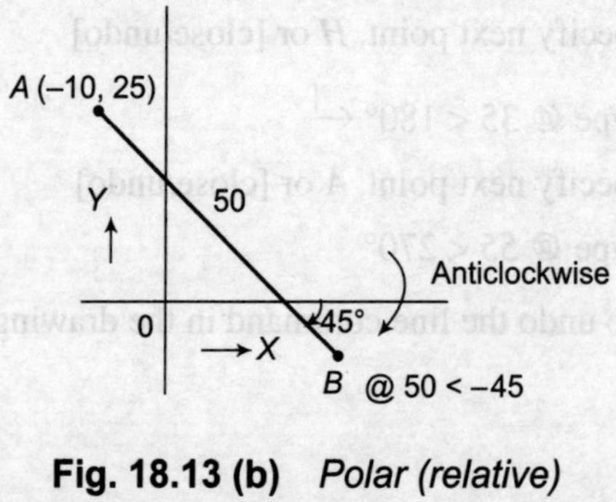

Fig. 18.13 (b) *Polar (relative)*

PROBLEM 18.4

Draw a rectangle of length 40 mm, width 20 mm, and corner at (10, 10).

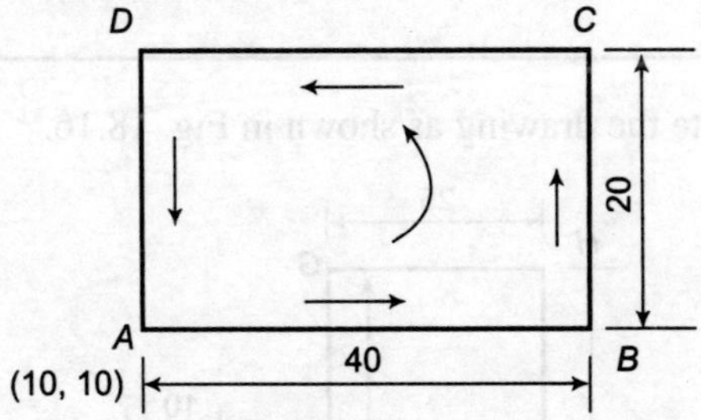

Fig. 18.14

(i) Absolute Method

Command: LINE

Specify first point: 10, 10; press ENTER

Specify second point or [undo]: 50, 10; press ENTER

Specify third point or [undo]: 50, 30; press ENTER

Specify 4th point or [close/undo]: 10, 30; press ENTER

Specify next point or [close/undo]; press ENTER to finish the drawing

(ii) Relative Method

Command: LINE

Specify the first point: 10, 10

Specify second point: @ 40, 0

Specify third point: @ 0, 20

Specify fourth point: @ – 40, 0

Specify fifth point: @ 0, –20

Specify next point or [close/undo]; press ENTER to finish the drawing

(iii) Polar Coordinate Method

Command: LINE

Specify first point: 10, 10

Specify second point: @ 40 < 0

Specify third point: @ 20 < 90

Specify fourth point: @ 40 < 180

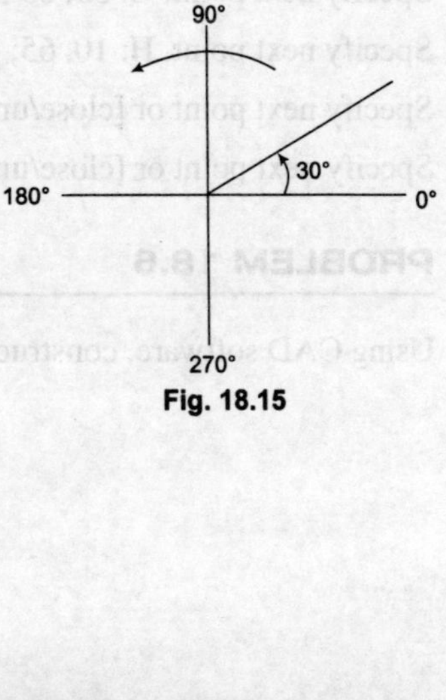

Fig. 18.15

Specify fifth point: @ 20 < 270

Specify next point or [close/ undo]; press ENTER to finish the drawing.

PROBLEM 18.5

By the use of software, complete the drawing as shown in Fig. 18.16.

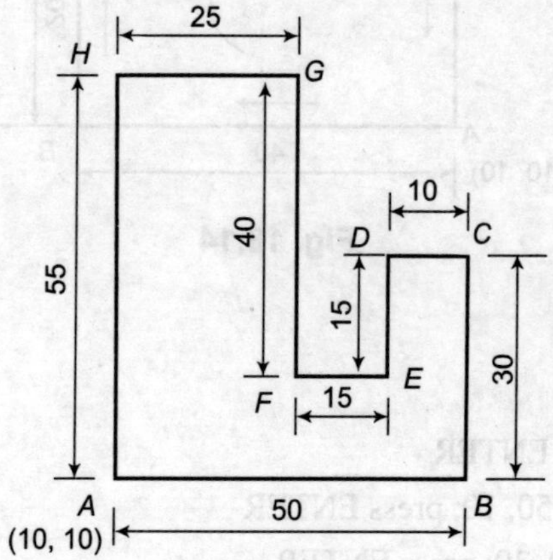

Fig. 18.16

Solving by absolute coordinate

Specify first point, A: 10, 10; press ENTER

Specify next point, B: 60, 10; press ENTER

Specify next point, C: 60, 40; press ENTER

Specify next point, D: 50, 40; press ENTER

Specify next point, E: 50, 25; press ENTER

Specify next point, F: 35, 25; press ENTER

Specify next point, G: 35, 65 Press ENTER

Specify next point, H: 10, 65; press ENTER

Specify next point or [close/undo]: 10, 10; press ENTER

Specify next point or [close/undo]; press ENTER to finish drawing

PROBLEM 18.6

Using CAD software, construct a drawing as shown in Fig. 18.17.

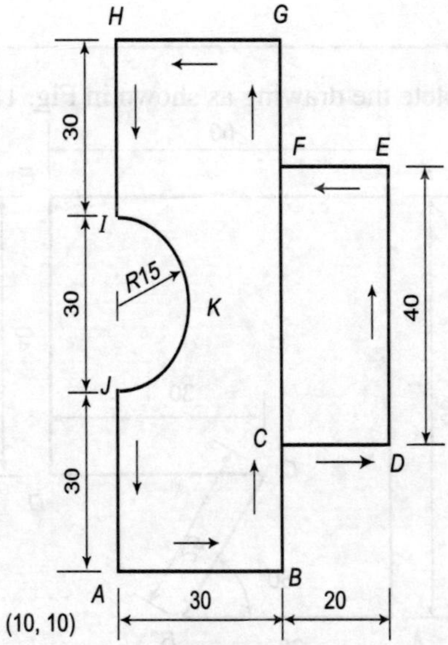

Fig. 18.17

Solution:

Command: LINE; press ENTER

Specify first point: 10, 10; ENTER

Specify next point or [undo]: 40, 10 ENTER

Specify next point, C, or [close/undo]: 40, 25; ENTER

Specify next point, D or [close/undo]: 60, 25; ENTER

Specify next point, E or [close/undo]: 60, 25; ENTER

Specify next point, F or [close/undo]: 40, 65; ENTER

Specify next point, G or [close/undo]: 40, 90; ENTER

Specify next point, H or [close/undo]: 10, 90; ENTER

Specify next point, I or [close/undo]: 10, 60; ENTER

Command: ARC; ENTER

Specify start point of arc or [center]: Select point I; ENTER

Specify second point of arc or [center/end]: Select point K; ENTER

Specify end point of arc: Select point J; ENTER

Command: LINE; ENTER specify radius of arc: R15

Specify first point J: ENTER

Specify next point or [undo]: 10, 10, or C; ENTER

PROBLEM 18.7

Using software or graphics, complete the drawing as shown in Fig. 18.18.

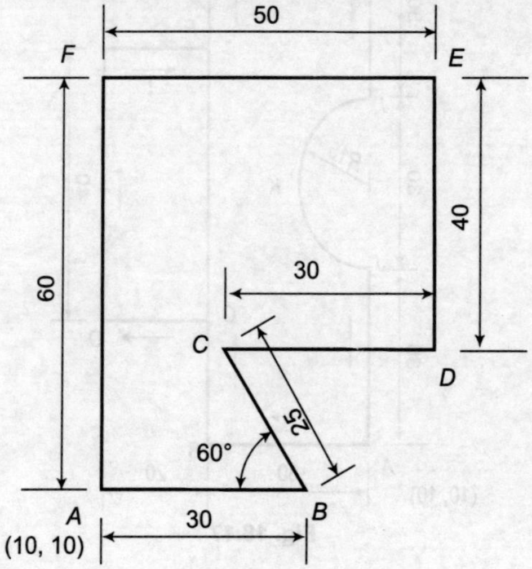

Fig. 18.18

Solution:

Command: LINE; ENTER

Specify first point: 10, 10; ENTER

Specify next point or [undo]: @ 30 < 0

Specify next point, C or [close/undo]: @ 25 < 120; ENTER

Specify next point, D or [close/undo]: @ 55 < 0; ENTER

Specify next point, E or [close/undo]: @ 55 < 90; ENTER

Specify next point, F or [close/undo]: @ 50 < 180; ENTER

Specify next point, G or [close/undo]: @ 60 < 270 or @ 60 < –90 or C): ENTER

PROBLEM 18.8

Draw the isometric view of an object shown in Fig. 18.19

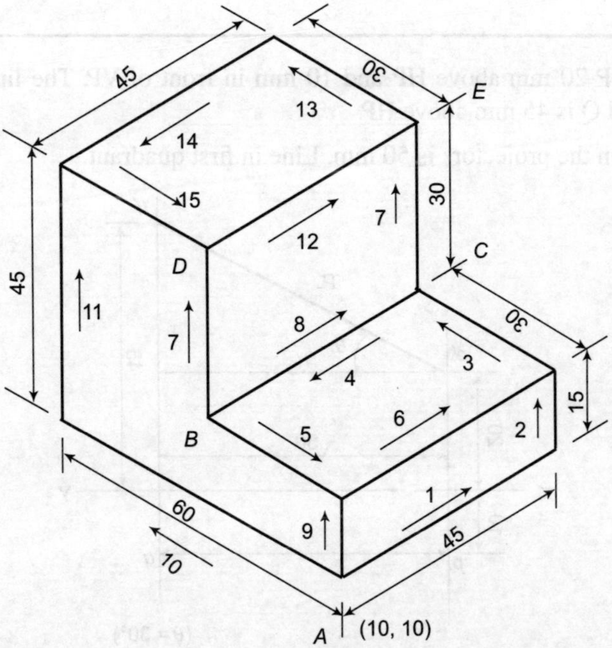

Fig. 18.19

Solution:

Command: LINE; press ENTER

Specify first point: 10, 10: ENTER

Draw a line, taking A on initial point: ENTER

Draw the following lines:

@ 45 < 30, @ 15 < 90, @ 30 < 150

@ 45 < 210, @ 30 < 330, @ 45 < 30

Again draw vertical line from B and C.

@ 30 < 90: @ 45 < 30

Again draw line from A, @ 15 < 90

From point A, draw a line @ 60 < 150, @ 45 < 90

Again from point D, draw line @ 45 < 30; @ 30 < 150; @ 45 < 210; @ 30 < 330

Mark the dimensions using DIMALINGED Command

PROBLEM 18.9

A line PQ has its end P 20 mm above HP and 10 mm in front of VP. The line is parallel to VP and inclined to HP. The end Q is 45 mm above HP.

The distance between the projectors is 50 mm. Line in first quadrant.

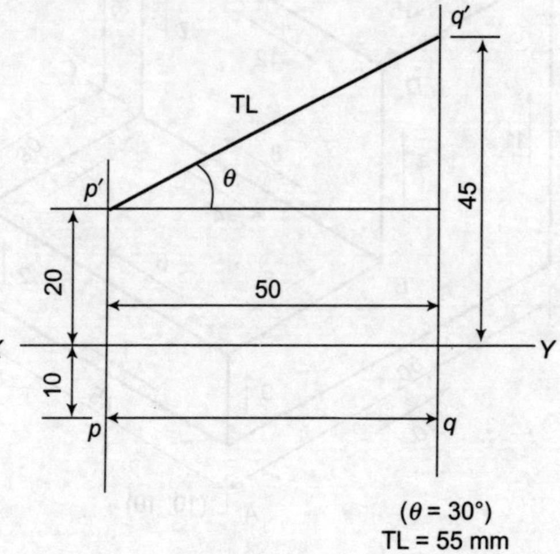

Fig. 18.20

Solution:

Draw XY line using LINE command and mark XY using TEXT command.

Choose the nearest point on XY and draw a line @ 20 < 90 and @ 10 < 270.

These two points represent front view and top view as p′ and p of the end P.

Choose another nearest point OX at 50 mm away from end P projector.

And on this projector of end Q, draw a line @ 45 < 90 and 10 < 270.

Select the point q and draw a vertical LINE.

q′ and q represent the front view and top view of end Q.

Joint p′q′ to represent front view and pq is the top view of the line.

Use DIMANG to mark and measure the inclination of line with HP.

Use DIMLIN to mark other dimensions.

18.23 POLYLINE COMMAND

A polyline is a combination of lines made from a series of individual lines. This acts as a single element

To draw a polyline, steps are as follows:

(i) Select a polyline tool from the draw toolbar.

Command: Pline; ENTER

Specify start point, *A*

(ii) Select a start point ↵

Specify next point, *B*

(iii) Select second point ↵

Specify next point C

(iv) Select third point ↵

Specify next point *D*

(v) Select fourth point↵

Specify next point E

(vi) Select fifth point ↵

(vii) Press the right button of mouse; then Enter

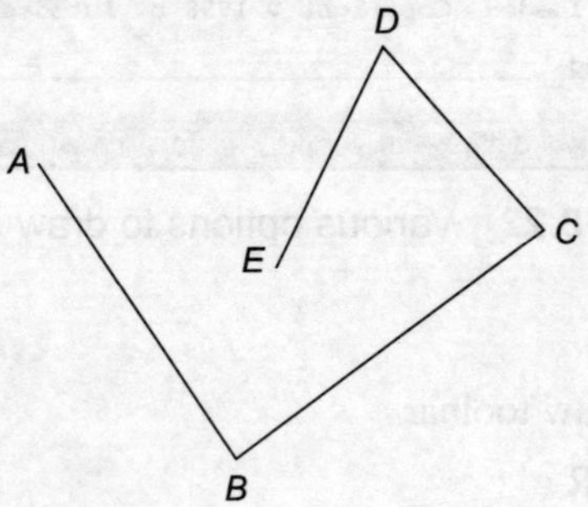

Fig. 18.21. Use of polyline command

18.24 CIRCLE COMMAND

A circle can be drawn by CIRCLE command.
A circle can be drawn based on the following:

(i) Centre point and radius or diameter given

(ii) Three points given on circumference

(iii) Two point method

(iv) Tangents, Tangent and Radius method

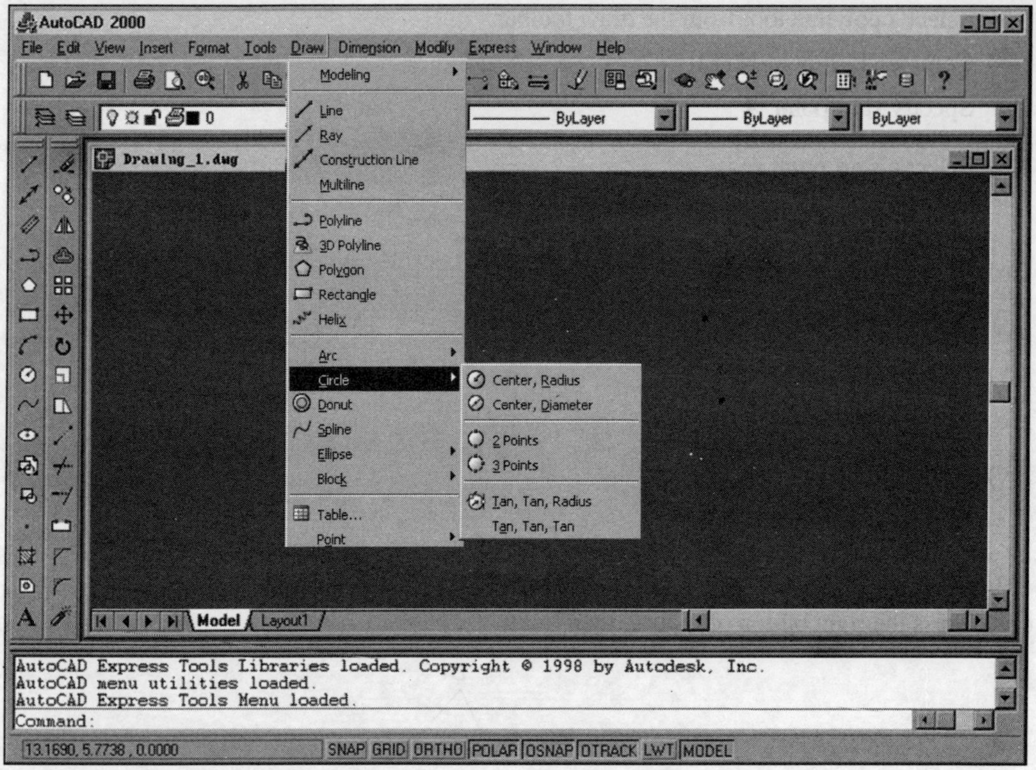

Fig. 18.22 Various options to draw circle

(i) Using centre and radius

Select circle tool from draw toolbar

Command: circle; ENTER

Specify a centre point for circle on [3*P*/2*P*/Tcr (tangent radius)]

(a) Select a centre point

Specify radius of circle or diameter

(b) Give value, then ENTER

The circle will be as shown in Fig. 18.23.

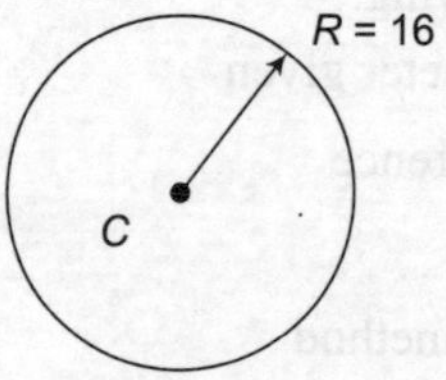

Fig. 18.23

Here, *C* = centre point value

(ii) Two point method

Draw a circle using 2*P* (two points); select a circle tool from the draw toolbar

Command: Circle; ENTER

Specify centre point for circle

Type 2*P* ↵

Specify first point of a circle, click first point *A* or type coordinate of *A*

Specify second point on circle, click second point *B* or type coordinate of *B*

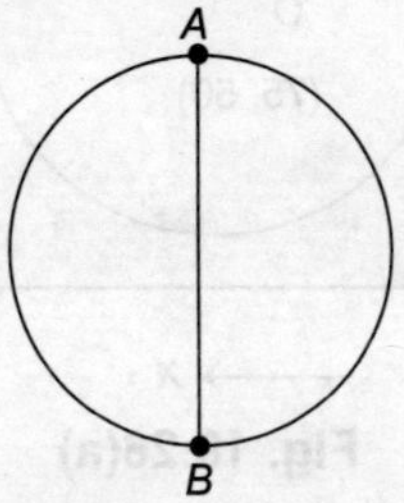

Fig. 18.24 Two point circle

(iii) Three point method

Draw circle using 3*P* $(x_1\ y_1)\ (x_2\ y_2)\ (x_3\ y_3)$

(a) Command

Type circle or select proper icon

(b) Specify centre point for circle

Type 3*P*

(c) Specify first point on circle

Click first point *A* or type coordinates of a point *A*

(d) Specify second point of circle

Click second point *B* or type coordinate of point *B*

(e) Specify third point on circle

Click third point *C*, or type coordinates of point *C*

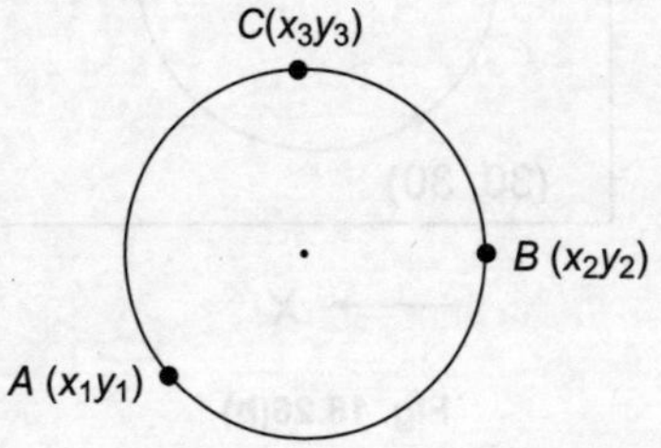

Fig. 18.25 Three points circle

PROBLEM 18.10

Draw a circle with centre (75, 50) and radius = 12 units.

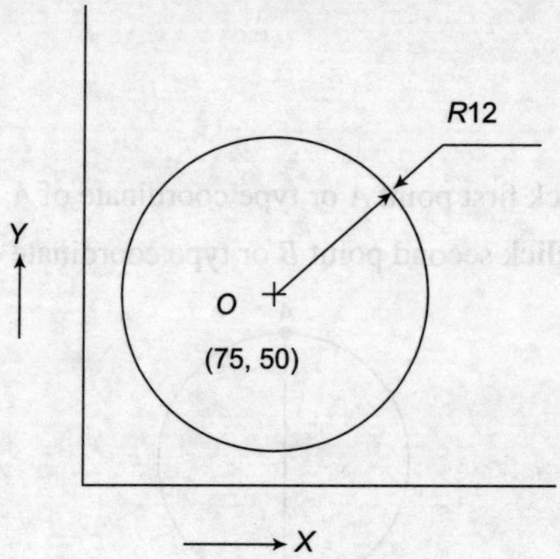

Fig. 18.26(a)

Command: C ↵

Specify centre point for circle: 75, 50 ↵

Specify radius of circle: 12 ↵

PROBLEM 18.11

Draw a circle that passes through three points (30, 30), (40, 70), and (70, 50).

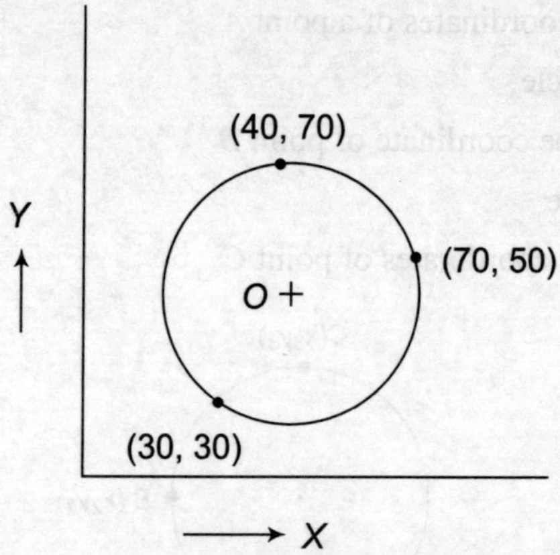

Fig. 18.26(b)

Command: C ↵

Specify centre point for circle or [3P/2P/Tr] (tan tan rad): 3P

Specify first point on circle: (30, 30)

Specify second point on circle: (40, 70)

Specify third point on circle: (70, 50)

PROBLEM 18.12

Draw a circle with a diameter (20, 40) to (60, 70).

Command: C ↵

Specify centre point for circle or [3P/2P/Tr] (tan tan radius): 2P ↵

Specify first point of circle diameter: 60, 70: ↵

Specify second point of circle diameter: 20, 40: ↵

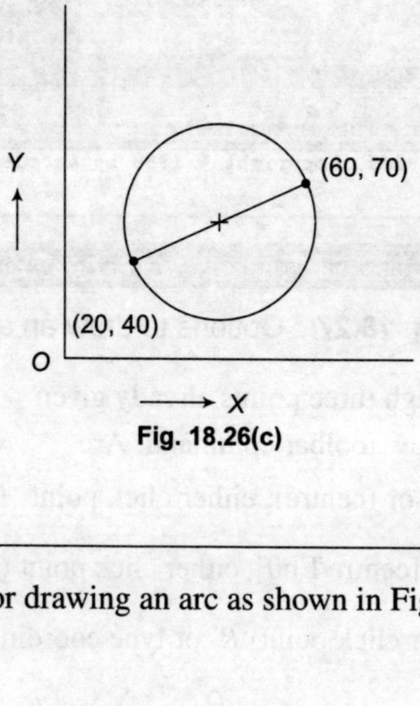

Fig. 18.26(c)

18.25 ARC COMMAND

There are many options available for drawing an arc as shown in Fig. 18.27.

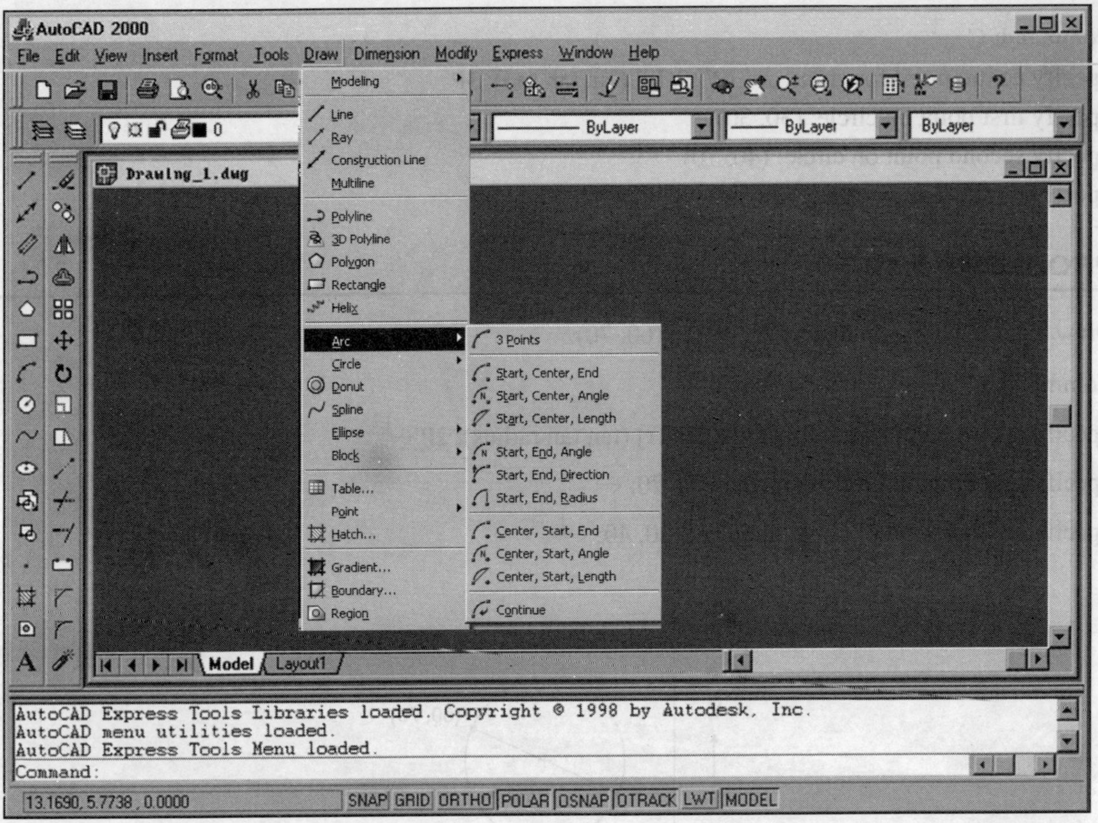

Fig. 18.27 Options to draw an arc

Draw an arc (circular) passing through three points already given

(i) Select the arc tool from the draw toolbar command: Arc

Arc; specify start point of arc or (centre), either click point '*P*' or type coordinates for point '*P*'

(ii) Specify second point of arc or [centre/End]; either click point *Q* or type coordinates of point '*Q*'↵

(iii) Specify end point of arc; either click point '*R*' or type coordinates of point '*R*'↵

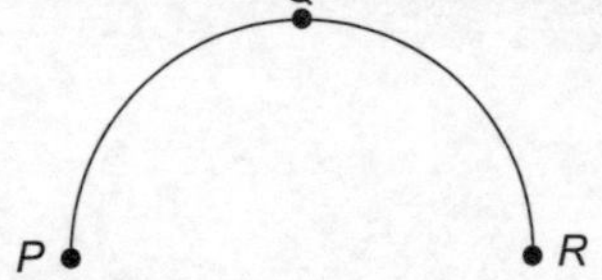

Fig. 18.28 Three point arc

An arc is a portion of a circle. There are many ways to draw an arc in ARC command. Arcs are drawn in anticlockwise direction.

PROBLEM 18.13

Draw an arc (semi-circle) with three points given as shown in Fig. 18.29.

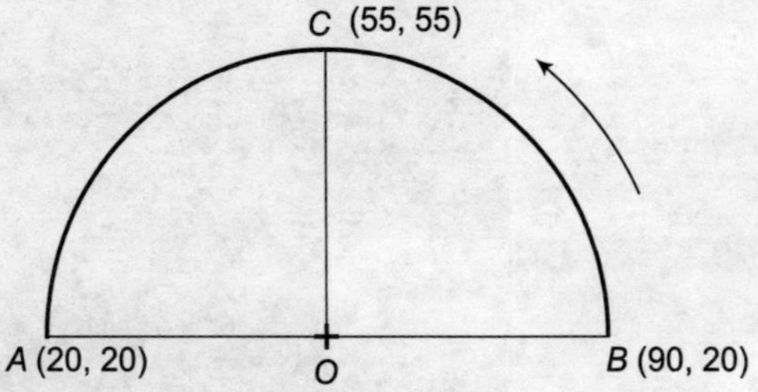

Fig 18.29

Command: a ↵

Type a and press ENTER.

Specify start point B of arc: 90, 20 ↵

Type 90, 20 and press ENTER.

Specify second point of arc B: 20, 20 ↵

Type 20, 20 and press ENTER.

18.26 ELLIPSE COMMAND

Ellipse command is used to draw ellipse.
Ellipse can be drawn by any of the options as shown in Fig. 18.30 depending on the type of the ellipse required for the drawing.

(1) Draw an ellipse when both end points of one axis along with the distance of the other axis end points are given.

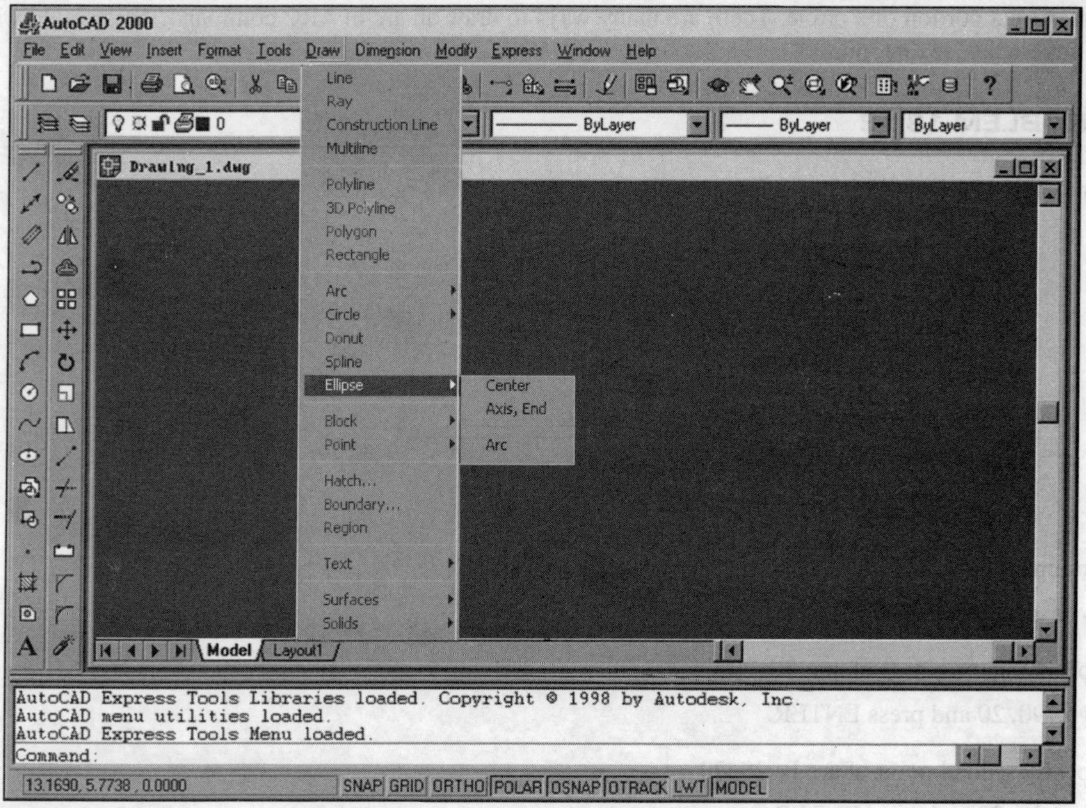

Fig. 18.30 Options to draw an ellipse

(i) Select the ellipse tool from the draw toolbar command: ellipse: ellipse ↵

Specify axis end point of ellipse or [arc/centre]

(ii) Select a start point for one of the axes

Specify other end point of axis

(iii) Select an end point which represents the length of axis

Specify distance of other axis

(iv) Select a point which represents half the length of the other axis

Point *P* and *Q* represent major axis

Point *R* and *S* represent minor axis

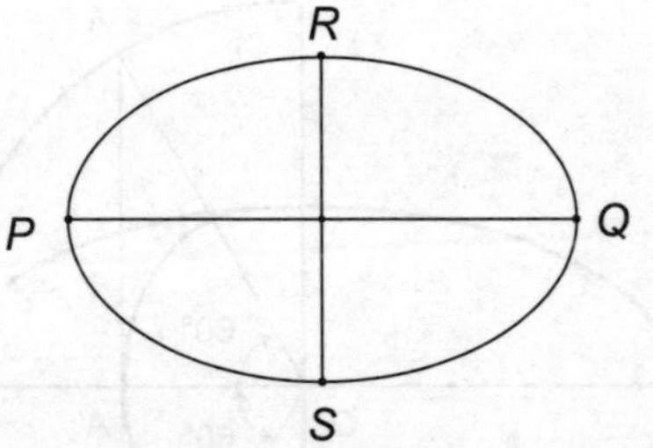

Fig. 18.31 Ellipse through axis

(2) Draw an ellipse when both end points of one axis along with distance of other axis end point from the first is known.

(i) Select the ellipse tool from the draw toolbar

Command: ellipse

Specify axis end point of ellipse or [arc/centre]

Type coordinates for end point *P* or click at *P*

Specify other end point of axis

Type coordinates for end point *Q* or click at *Q*

Specify distance to the other axis end point (say *X*)

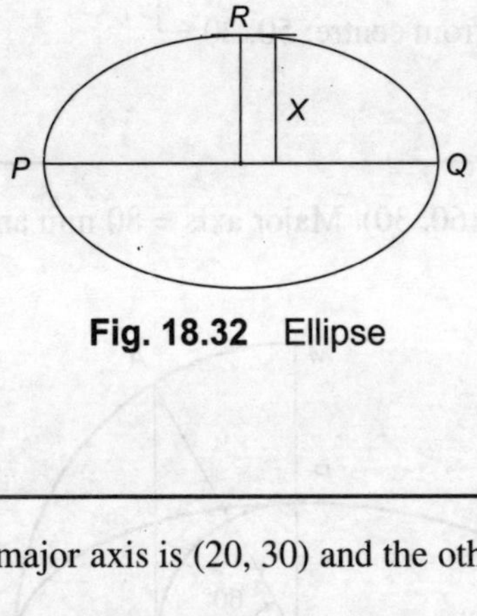

Fig. 18.32 Ellipse

PROBLEM 18.14

Draw an ellipse whose one end of major axis is (20, 30) and the other end is (80, 30). Minor axis ends at (50, 20).

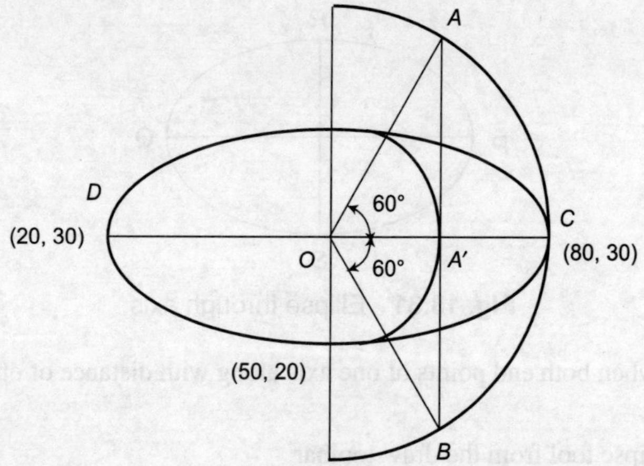

Fig. 18.33

Command: el ↵

Ellipse

Specify axis end point of ellipse: 20, 30 ↵

Specify other end point of axis: 80, 30 ↵

Specify the distance of minor axis from centre: 50, 20 ↵

PROBLEM 18.15

Draw an ellipse whose centre is at (60, 30). Major axis = 80 mm and minor axis = 20 mm (minor axis $= \frac{1}{2}$ major axis × cos 60°

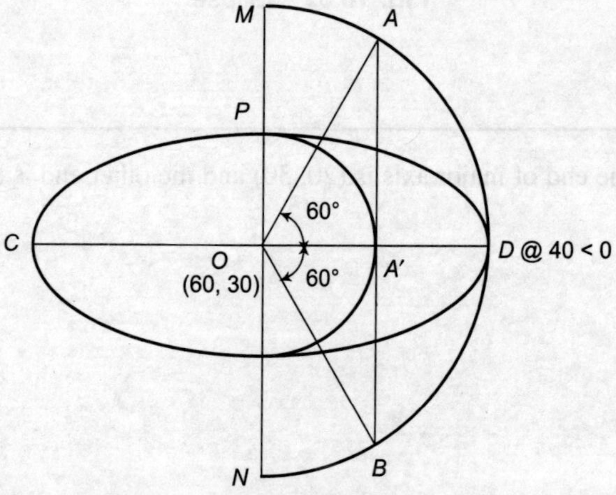

Fig. 18.34

OA = OD

$OA' = OP = OA \cos 60° = OD \cos 60° = 40 \times \frac{1}{2} = 20$

Minor axis $= \frac{1}{2} \times$ major axis $\times \cos 60° = \frac{1}{2} \times 80 \times \frac{1}{2} = 20$ mm

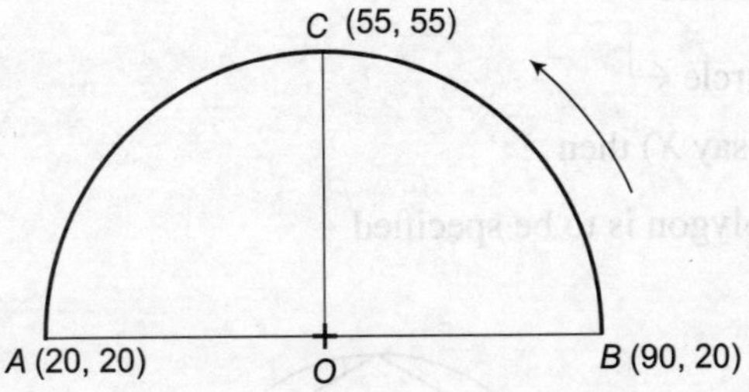

Fig. 18.35

Command: el ↵

Specify centre of ellipse: (60, 30) ↵

Specify end point of major axis: @ 40 < 0

Specify length of major axis: 80 ↵

Specify rotation around major axis: 60 ↵

18.27 POLYGON COMMAND

Polygon command is used to draw polygon. Polygon is an area bounded by equal, straight lines (regular polygon).

Let us draw a regular polygon with six sides.

The size of the polygon is identified by giving any one of the following:

(i) Polygon inscribed in circle

(ii) Polygon circumscribed about circle

(iii) Length of one edge of polygon

To draw a polygon, the following commands are given:

(i) Command: Polygon or from the toolbar select icon and press ENTER

(ii) Polygon, enter number of sides

Type number of sides of polygon to be drawn (say 6)

(iii) Specify centre of polygon or (edge)

Either specify the centre position by clicking or by typing coordinate of the point, '*O*' in Fig. 18.36

(iv) Enter an option (inscribed in a circle/circumscribed about circle)

Type *I* or *C* as per desire ↵

(v) Specify radius of circle ↵

Type radius value (say *X*) then

Note: If edge length of the polygon is to be specified

Type E and then act as above.

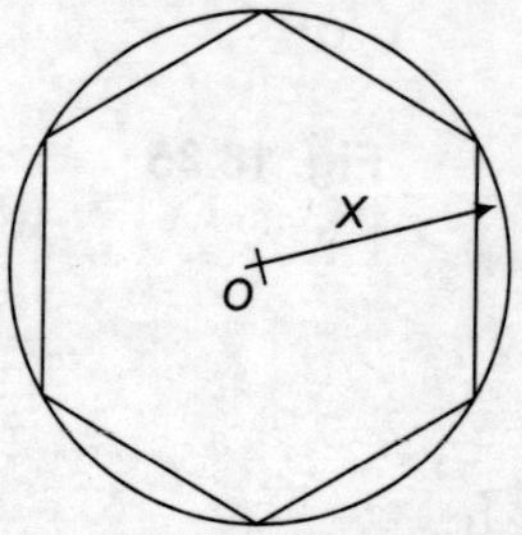

Fig. 18.36 Polygon specifying centre *O* and radius *X*

The POLYGON command is used to draw a regular polygon for a given length of edge.

PROBLEM 18.16

Draw a hexagonal polygon of end point of edge is (40, 20) and end point of edge is 25 mm.

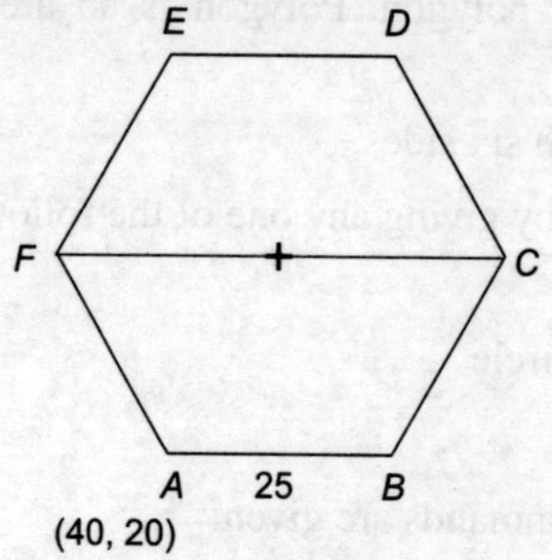

Fig. 18.37

Command: Polygon

Enter number of sides: 6 ↵

Specify centre of polygon or [edge]: 6 ↵

Specify first end point of edge: 40, 20 ↵

Specify second end point of edge: @ 25 < 0 ↵

18.28 MODIFY COMMANDS

There are many commands that are used to have specific tasks like transformation, edit, erases, trim, etc. These commands are arranged in modify command as shown in Fig. 18.38.

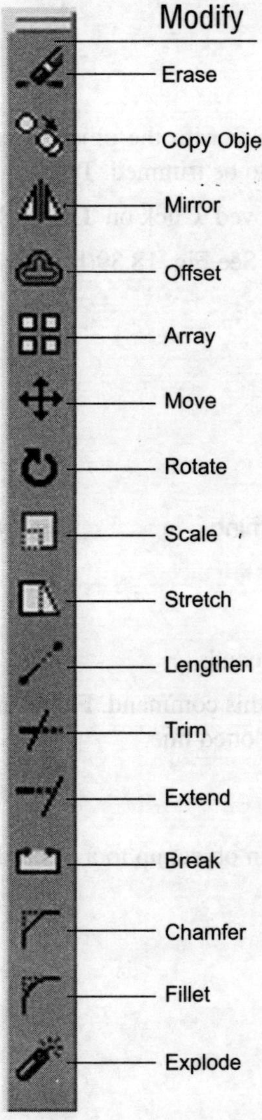

Fig. 18.38 Modify toolbar

The following is a list of editing/modifying commands:

(1) ERASE Command

It is used to delete unwanted object(s) from the main drawing.

Select the erase tool from modify toolbar command: erase ↵

Select object to be erased

(2) CHANGE Command

This command is used to alter several elements of an object. These elements may be line, scale, thickness, etc.

(3) TRIM Command

The trim command is used to cut down or trim the object to a cutting edge. First, select the cutting edge and then select a part of the object to be trimmed. Type command Trim or select proper icon.

Select cutting edge if RS is to be removed. Click on 'DC' and AB. Click on RS.

In Fig. 18.39(a), RS is to be trimmed. See Fig. 18.39(b) after trimming.

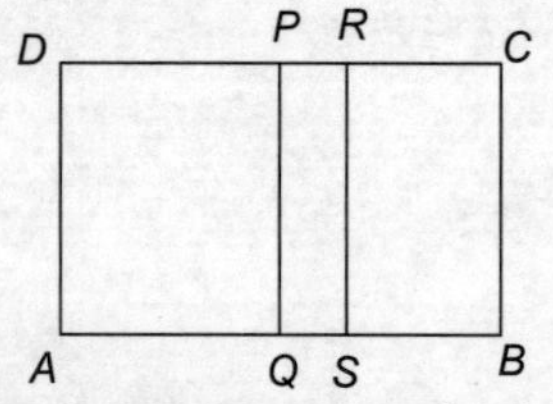

Fig. 18.39 (a) Before trimming

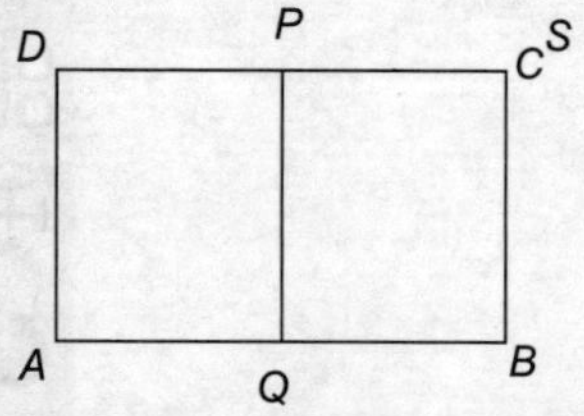

Fig. 18.39 (b) After trimming

(4) Chprop Command

This command is similar to change command.

The nature of line can be changed by this command. For example: Thin line can be changed to thick line. Continuous line can be changed to dotted line.

(5) EXTEND Command

The extend command is used to extend an object up to a desired boundary. Select the extend tool from modify toolbar

(i) Command: extend ENTER

Select boundary edge

Select object

(ii) Select a line as a boundary edge

Select object to extend

(iii) Select a line to be extended

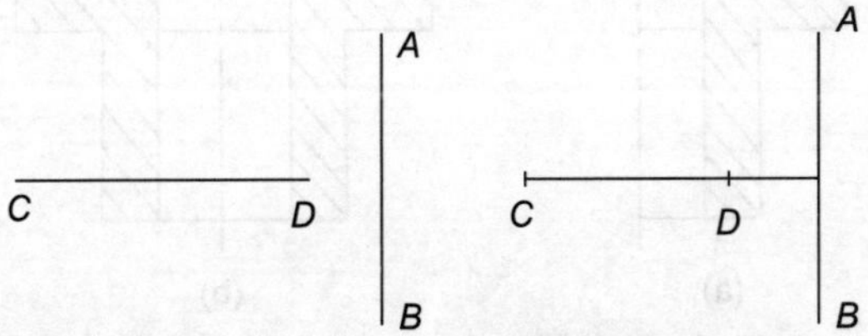

Fig. 18.40 (a) **Fig. 18.40** (b)

AB is the boundary line and CD is to be extended as shown in Fig. 18.40 (b) that shows line CD after extension.

(6) Copy Command

The copy command is used to copy an existing object. This command can also be used to copy a group of objects.

To copy an object:

(i) Select a copy tool from modify toolbar

Command: Copy ↵

(ii) Select the object 'A' to be copied, press ENTER

(iii) Specify base point, specify second point of displacement

(iv) Select a second displacement point as shown in B

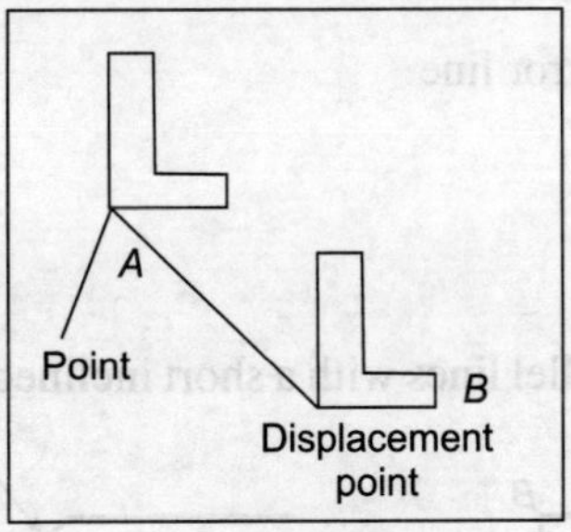

Fig. 18.41

(7) MIRROR Command

This command is used to from mirror image of an object.

If object is symmetrical about an axis, then only half of the portion of the object is to be drawn and next half can be drawn by a mirror command.

Fig. 18.42 Mirror command

As shown in Fig. 18.42(a), the object is to be taken for mirror image.

The object is symmetrical about vertical axis. After using the command, the object looks like as shown in 18.42 (b).

Method to use the command

(i) Selecting mirror tool from modify toolbar

command: mirror

Select object

(ii) Window the object

Select object

(iii) Press ↵

Specify first point of mirror line

(iv) Select a point on mirror line

Specify second point of mirror line

(v) Press ENTER

(8) CHAMFER Command

This command is to join two non-parallel lines with a short inclined line as shown in Fig. 18.43 (a) & (b).

Fig. 18.43 (a) **Fig. 18.43** (b)

AB and BC, both lines are perpendicular to each other; they are non-parallel.

(9) FILLET Command

This command is very useful to join two non-parallel lines with an arc of a certain small radius.

This command is similar to Chamfer Command.

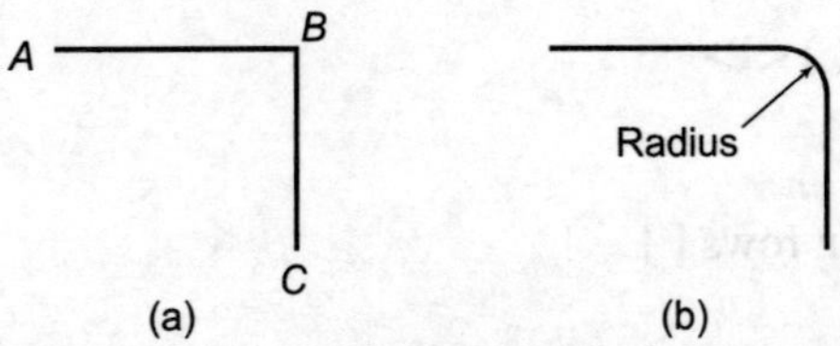

Fig. 18.44

AB and BC, both are non-parallel lines. They have been connected at the corner by a small circular arc of small radius.

(10) MOVE Command

This command is used to move an object from one place to another. The shape of the object will not change at the other position after shifting. Size of the object remains the same.

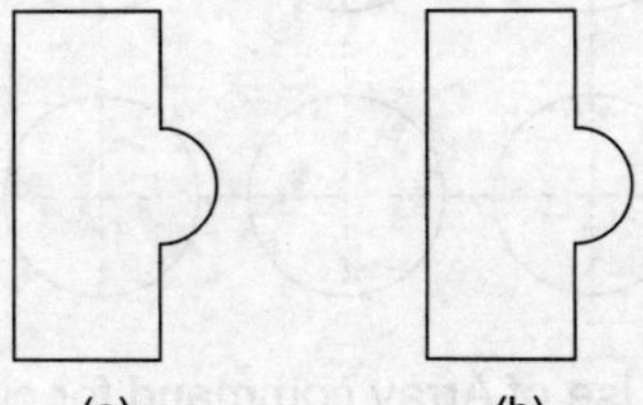

Fig. 18.45

(11) ARRAY Command

Array command is used to form multiple copies of an object. The object may be a line, rectangle, polygon, etc. A large number of polygons or any other object can be arranged in a number of rows and columns.

To array a circle: rectangular option

(i) Select the array tool from modify toolbar

Command: array; ENTER

Select object

(ii) Press ↵

Type of array [rectangular/polar] <R>:

(iii) Press ↵

Enter two number of rows (2) <1>:

(iv) Type any value ↵

Enter number of column ( ) <1>

(v) Type any value ↵

Enter the distance between rows [ ]

(vi) Type any value ↵

Specify distance between column ( )

(vii) Type any value ↵

See Fig. 18.46

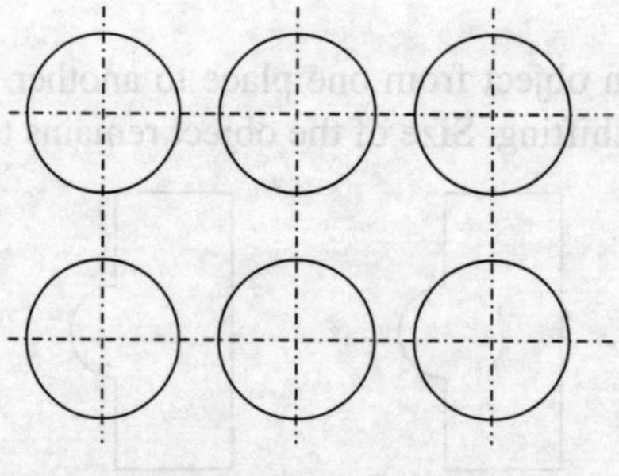

Fig. 18.46 Use of Array command for circular object

(12) OFFSET Command

This command is to construct a new element that is parallel to an existing element.

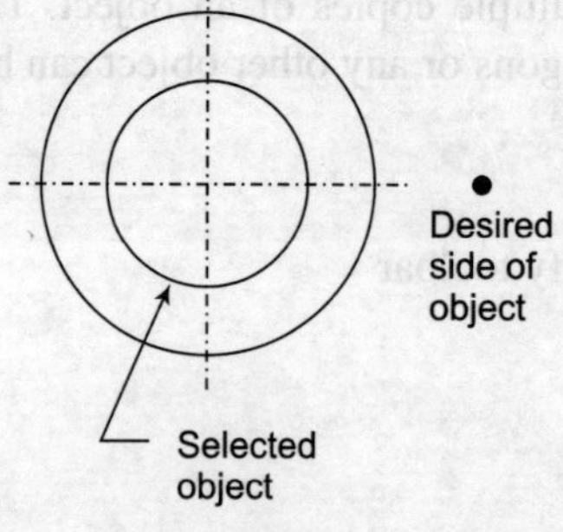

Fig. 18.47 Offset command

(i) Select offset tool from the modify toolbar.

Command: offset; Enter, specify offset distance